Western Canada

Matthew Gardner and Alison Bigg

It is wonderful to feel the
grandness of Canada in the
raw, not because she is Canada
but because she's something
sublime that you were born into,
some great rugged power that
you are a part of.

'Hundreds and Thousands:
The Journals of Emily Carr'

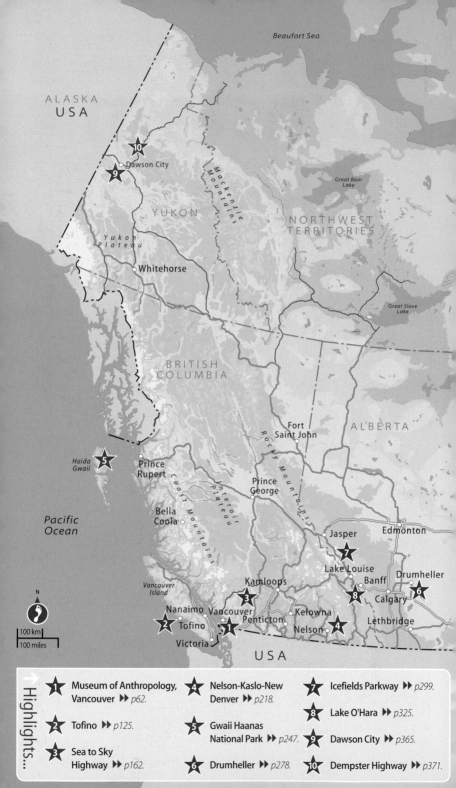

Beaufort Sea

ALASKA
USA

★10
★9 Dawson City

YUKON

Mackenzie Mountains

NORTHWEST TERRITORIES

Great Bear Lake

Yukon Plateau

Whitehorse

Great Slave Lake

BRITISH COLUMBIA

Fort Saint John

ALBERTA

Haida Gwaii ★5
Prince Rupert

Coast Mountains

Interior Plateau

Rocky Mountains

Prince George

Edmonton

Bella Coola

Jasper
★7
Lake Louise
Banff
★8
★6 Drumheller

Vancouver Island

Kamloops
★3
Nanaimo
★2 Tofino
Vancouver
★1
Victoria

Penticton
Kelowna
Nelson ★4
Calgary
Lethbridge

Pacific Ocean

N

100 km
100 miles

USA

Take an area bigger than Mexico and sprinkle with fewer people than Switzerland, fitting almost all of them into one small corner. Then cover the remaining vast wilderness with row upon row of lofty ice-capped mountains, huge lakes and mighty rivers, dense forests, broad valleys and plateaux and wide, open prairie. Throw in some bizarre Badlands moonscape, steep-sided canyons, glaciers and ice fields, Arctic tundra and even a patch of cactus-spattered desert. Now decorate the edge with a lush coastline punctuated by long, narrow fjords and fringed with islands of all sizes. Leave to simmer in the melting pot of modern history for little more than a century, and the result: Western Canada.

One of the last places on Earth to be 'discovered' by Europeans, the essence of this Brand New World is its freshness and its sheer size. This is one of the last remaining, easily accessible places in which to experience the Earth in its wildest and most pristine state; before the ancient trees were chopped down to make way for fields, roads and cities, and when numerous creatures, including many large mammals, had the space to survive. Nature still reigns supreme here and, in celebration of this fact, she flaunts her versatility as much as her overwhelming beauty.

Introduction

4

Contents

Vancouver
Vancouver Island
British Columbia
Canadian Rockies
The Yukon

USA

DAWSON CITY

WHITEHORSE

PRINCE RUPERT

PRINCE GEORGE

CALGARY

VANCOUVER

VICTORIA

USA

Essentials 9

Vancouver 47

Vancouver Island 97

Canadian Rockies 265

British Columbia 159

The Yukon 341

Real travel used to be about stretching your pesos, baht or rupees as far as possible by sleeping in filthy, airless hotel rooms, spending sleepless, back-breaking hours on bus journeys and risking food poisoning by eating at the cheapest market stalls. But things are changing. Today's travellers still have the same adventurous spirit, they just prefer to do it in a bit more style and comfort, and they're not averse to splashing out occasionally to ensure that their trip is memorable for all the right reasons.

Footprint's discover guides are designed precisely for this new breed of traveller. We've selected the best sights, sleeping options, restaurants and a range of adventure activities so that you can have the experience of a lifetime. With over 80 years' experience of writing about travel, we hope that you find this guide easy to use, enjoyable to read and good to look at.

Essentials, the first chapter, deals with practicalities: introducing the region and suggesting where and when to go, what to do and how to get around; we give the lowdown on visas, money, health and transport, and provide overviews of history, culture and wildlife. The rest of the guide is divided into area-based chapters, colour-coded for convenience. At the start of each chapter, a highlights map gives an instant overview of the area and its attractions. A star rating system also gives each area marks out of five for Landscape, Activities, Culture etc. The Costs category refers to value for money in relation to Europe and North America, where **$$$$$** is expensive and **$** is very cheap. Follow the cross references to the district that interests you to find a more detailed map, together with a snapshot of the area, showing the amount of time you will need, how to get there and move around, and what to expect in terms of weather, accommodation and restaurants. **Special features** include expert tips, inspiring travellers' tales, suggestions for busting your budget and ideas for going that little bit further.

We use a range of symbols throughout the guide to indicate the following information:
- ● Sleeping
- ● Eating
- ● Entertainment
- ● Festivals and events
- ● Shopping
- ▲ Activities and tours
- ● Transport
- ● Directory

Please note that hotel and restaurant codes, p24 and p26, should only be used as a guide to the prices and facilities offered by the establishment. It is at the discretion of the owners to vary them from time to time.

Footprint feedback We try as hard as we can to make each Footprint guide as up to date as possible but, of course, things always change. If you want to let us know about your experiences – good, bad or ugly – then don't delay, go to www.footprintbooks.com and send in your comments.

Essentials

Totem pole at the UBC Museum of Anthropology in Vancouver

Travelling

Where to go

Western Canada is vast, so be selective about what you want from your trip and don't try to squeeze in too much, or you'll end up spending too much time on the road. Whether or not you have your own vehicle may be the most significant factor in deciding where to go. Vancouver is the easiest, most convenient starting point, and it's a great year-round destination in its own right. If you want to concentrate on the Rockies, however, you would be well advised to arrive in Calgary. Combining this and the following section with the calendar of events on p27 will help you to get the most out of your trip.

One week

Those with only a week definitely have to focus on one area. For a taste of the **Gulf Islands** plus two very different but equally enticing towns, hop from Vancouver to Victoria (Vancouver Island) via Galiano and Salt Spring islands, maybe squeezing in a hike along the East Sooke or Juan de Fuca trails. For outdoor pursuits, take the Sea to Sky Highway from Vancouver to the **Coast Mountains** around Squamish, Garibaldi Park and Whistler. Drivers could return via the dramatic **Fraser Canyon**. For big trees, whale watching, hot springs, endless beaches, sea kayaking and a lively seaside scene, head straight to **Tofino** (Vancouver Island). If time allows, squeeze in a trip to Gabriola Island from Nanaimo.

Alternatively, fly into Calgary and spend the whole week in the **Rockies**. Concentrate on Banff, Lake Louise and Yoho, but try to drive as far north as the Columbia Icefield. Those drawn to the north could take an internal flight to Whitehorse, hire a vehicle, and drive a wonderfully scenic loop of the **Yukon**, including Kluane National Park, the Top of the World Highway, Dawson City, the Dempster Highway as far as the Tombstone Mountains, then back to Whitehorse on the Klondike Highway.

Two weeks

With two weeks or more, you could combine the above **Gulf Islands** and **Tofino** trips, with a brief stop in **Chemainus**. Return to Vancouver via **Nanaimo**, or continue north to Courtenay, catch a ferry to Powell River, and drive south along the **Sunshine Coast**. Alternatively, combine either of these coastal trips with a week in the **Coast Mountains**. Fast drivers could potentially see a lot of British Columbia's southern interior. From Vancouver, take the Sea to Sky Highway or Fraser Canyon routes to Salmon Arm, then spend some time in the wineries, orchards and beaches of the **Okanagan**, returning via the Crowsnest Highway. Or continue on the TransCanada Highway to Revelstoke, head south through the **West Kootenays**, and back on the Crowsnest, maybe getting a taste of the Okanagan on the way. With an open-jaw ticket flying out of Calgary, you could get a taste of the Coast Mountains, Okanagan or the West Kootenays, and the Rockies.

Consider spending all of your time in the **Rockies**. Work north from Banff to the Columbia Icefield, then on the way back down do the Lake Louise-Yoho-Kootenay Park loop. A great longer loop, for those with itchy feet, would involve driving the whole Icefields Parkway to Jasper, then heading west to Mount Robson, south to Kamloops via Wells Gray Park, then back to Calgary on the TransCanada Highway via Revelstoke and Yoho Park. The **Yukon** loop described above would make a great two- or three-week trip. If time allows, add a short canoe trip, or a diversion to Haines, Alaska or Atlin, BC.

(Top) Horses roam in the Nemiah Valley, Chilcotin. (Bottom) Sea kayaking and fishing in the Haida Gwaii.

One month

The Gulf Islands-Victoria-Tofino-Courtenay-Sunshine Coast loop could be combined with a tour of the **southern interior** including the Coast Mountains and Okanagan. Or head to the north of Vancouver Island, take the **Inside Passage** up the ruggedly beautiful West Coast to Prince Rupert; visit **Haida Gwaii** and take a kayak tour to abandoned First Nations villages; head across on the Yellowhead Highway to Mount Robson and Jasper; drive through the **Rockies** to Banff, then back to Vancouver taking in parts of southern BC. The even more ambitious could continue north from Prince Rupert to Skagway on an Alaska ferry, do a tour of the **Yukon**, then drive south on the Cassiar Highway, taking a diversion to see the glaciers on the way to Stewart.

A fantastic **inland loop** would be to drive the Crowsnest Highway to Osoyoos, then head north through the Okanagan Valley to Vernon, drive east to Nakusp, do the West Kootenays loop of New Denver-Slocan Valley-Nelson-Kaslo-New Denver, then return to Nakusp and continue north to Revelstoke; head east to the Rockies, then north up the Icefields Parkway to Jasper; return to Vancouver via Mount Robson, Wells Gray Park, Kamloops, and the Sea to Sky Highway.

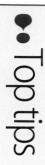

Top tips

Don't forget your toothbrush

Canada's weather is extremely changeable, so bring clothes for all occasions. For hiking and other outdoor pursuits bring plenty of layers of thin synthetic fibres, preferably long-sleeved for protection against bugs (which are less attracted to light colours); a good pair of boots and waterproof clothing are equally important. A camera is essential, and binoculars can be useful for spotting wildlife. Many situations call for a tent, sleeping bag and lightweight camp-stove. A Swiss Army knife, flashlight and compass are also key items. Visitors staying in hostels may want to bring a sleeping sheet and padlock, though such things are usually supplied. Everything you may need can be bought in Canada, often at a lower price than at home.

For an **Alberta-based loop**, drive from Calgary to Drumheller, south to the Dinosaur Park, then take in Head-Smashed-In Buffalo Jump, Cardston and Waterton Lakes Park; cross the Crowsnest Pass and head north through the West Kootenays, finally looping back to the Rockies. A month in the **Yukon** would allow you to do some hikes in Kluane National Park and the Tombstone Mountains, and take a longer canoe trip such as the two-week paddle up the Yukon River, or drive the Dempster Highway to Inuvik and visit the frozen north.

When to go

Western Canada's weather is fickle, unpredictable and highly localized. The Okanagan and Thompson valleys, for instance, are so dry as to be nearly desert, yet can get very cold in winter, while the West Coast receives copious amounts of rain year-round, but is blessed with Canada's mildest winters and earliest springs. Weather in the mountains can change from blazing sunshine to blizzards in a single day, even in July (see also p43).

With so much water to play in and around, an uninterrupted string of great festivals, outdoor pursuits galore, and (usually) as much sun as you could want, **summer** is the obvious time to visit Western Canada. Most hikes in the Rockies and other mountain regions are only snow-free between July and September, which is also the most reliable time to see those snowy peaks free of cloud. Many attractions, campgrounds and visitor centres only open from **Victoria Day** (third Monday in May) to **Labour Day** (first Monday in September). Those heading north at this time will find the summer days extremely long, with the sun barely setting at all around the summer solstice.

Many places (the Rockies in particular) are overrun with tourists during the summer. Accommodation rates are higher, and coastal ferries tend to get booked up, so reservations for both are highly recommended. The best overall time is mid-August to September: the crowds are thinning, the trails are still open, and the **autumn** colours are spectacular in the mountains and the Yukon. **Spring** is a good time for visitors concentrating on the coast, as the blossoms are out in Victoria and Vancouver, and the whales are migrating past Tofino.

Winter in Canada is a different matter entirely. Tourism is still very much alive, but attracting a different group of people: those who come to ski or snowboard. Canada offers some of the best, most affordable skiing in the world, as well as many other snow-related activities. Most sights are closed in winter, however, and transportation can be slow. Late February to March are the best months for skiing: the days are getting longer and warmer but the snow is still at its best. Vancouver, which has three ski hills, makes an excellent year-round destination.

5 best

Adventures

Rafting the Kicking Horse and Tatshenshini rivers ▸▸ *p197 and p359*
Kayaking round abandoned Haida villages on Haida Gwaii ▸▸ *p244*
Canoeing the Bowron Lakes circuit ▸▸ *p258*
A **multi-day hike** in the Rockies such as Mount Assiniboine ▸▸ *p293*,
  Skyline ▸▸ *p315*, Berg Lake ▸▸ *p316* or Rockwall ▸▸ *p332*
Driving the first 72 km of the Dempster Highway, then hiking
  in the Tombstone Mountains ▸▸ *p371*

Sport and activities

Western Canada's great tracts of near-wilderness, sensational natural beauty, extreme topographical variety, and sport-minded population combine to make this arguably the best destination in the world for outdoor pursuits. With very few exceptions, any such activity you could mention is pursued here to a world-class standard. Countless specialist tour operators are on hand to offer guidance up to any level (see p35 and in listings throughout the book). A great place to find out more about these activities is in British Columbia's extremely useful *Outdoor Adventure Guide*, available from any visitor information centre. Also very useful is www.britishcolumbia.com, which outlines what is available town by town.

Birdwatching

Western Canada is crossed by one of the most important migratory routes in the world, with thousands of geese, swans, ducks, waterfowl and other birds passing through each year. Major spots for seeing them are mentioned throughout the book.

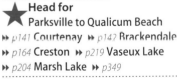
Head for
  Parksville to Qualicum Beach
▸▸ *p141* **Courtenay** ▸▸ *p142* **Brackendale**
▸▸ *p164* **Creston** ▸▸ *p219* **Vaseux Lake**
▸▸ *p204* **Marsh Lake** ▸▸ *p349*
ⓘ www.sco-soc.ca.

Canoeing

Northern BC and the Yukon are overflowing with world-class canoeing. A good guide for the latter is Ken Madsen's *Paddling in the Yukon*. Trips can be as easy or hard, remote or accessible as you wish. If going without a guide, always wear a lifejacket, and carry a bailing bucket, throw-rope and whistle. Avoid paddling in the afternoon on larger lakes because of high winds.

Head for
  Bowron Lakes ▸▸ *p236*
Tweedsmuir Park ▸▸ *p237* **Wells Gray Park** ▸▸ *p239* **Yukon River** ▸▸ *p345* **Teslin Lake** ▸▸ *p348* **Peel Wilderness** ▸▸ *p371*

ⓘ Recreational Canoeing Association of BC, T250-8474349, www.bccanoe.com.
ⓘ www.canoebc.ca.

Caving

There are many cave systems in Western Canada, especially on Vancouver Island, running from the commercial to the totally unexplored.

Head for
  Horne Lake ▸▸ *p141* **Nootka Sound** ▸▸ *p146* **Cody Caves** ▸▸ *p220*
ⓘ Caving Canada, www.cancaver.ca.

Climbing/mountaineering

Climbing is a major activity throughout the area, with thousands of routes in dozens of stunning locations.

(Left) Walking by Chilko Lake. (Right) British Columbia offers some of the best mountain biking in the world.

Mountaineers will find North America's highest peaks in the St Elias Range which runs through the Yukon and Alaska.

★ **Head for**
Squamish ▸▸ *p163* **Bugaboo Provincial Park** ▸▸ *p186* **Skaha Lake near Penticton** ▸▸ *p204* **Valhalla Provincial Park** ▸▸ *p223* **Canmore** ▸▸ *p292*

ⓘ www.alpineclubofcanada.ca.

Fishing

Freshwater

In Canada you're never far from a lake or river renowned for its fishing. A freshwater licence is required, with additional permits for national parks. Ask for the *Freshwater Fishing Regulations Synopsis*, which details possession limits, and pick up the *BCs Freshwater Fishing Guide* from visitor centres.

★ **Head for**
Fraser River ▸▸ *p172* **Kamloops** ▸▸ *p184* **Princeton** ▸▸ *p187* **Kootenay Lake** ▸▸ *p218* **Clearwater Lake** ▸▸ *p240* **Skeena River** ▸▸ *p242*

ⓘ BC Fishing Resorts and Outfitters Association, www.bcfroa.bc.ca.

Saltwater

The West Coast is famous for its year-round salmon fishing, and its giant halibut from Apr-Aug. A tidal waters sport fishing licence is required to fish in BC's waters, available at sports shops. Pick up the *BC Saltwater Fishing Planning Guide* at any visitor centre. Tour operators will take you to the best spots and supply all equipment.

★ **Head for**
Sunshine Coast ▸▸ *p67* **Clayoquot Sound** ▸▸ *p125* **Barkley Sound** ▸▸ *p126* **Campbell River** ▸▸ *p144* **Bella Coola and Stewart** ▸▸ *p238* **Prince Rupert** ▸▸ *p243* **Haida Gwaii** ▸▸ *p244*

ⓘ Fisheries and Oceans Canada, T604-6662828, sets the fishing regulations.
ⓘ Oak Bay Marine Group, T1800- 6637090, www.obmg.com, has 7 destinations in key fishing areas, and a lot of experience.
ⓘ Sport Fishing Institute, T604-2703439, www.sportfishing.bc.ca.

Golf

Golf is Canada's most popular participation sport, played by 7.4% of the population. In April 2003, the US Masters was won by Mike Weir, the first Canadian to win a golf major.

(Left) Fishermen, near Campbell River, BC. (Right) Rafting the Chilcotin River.

★ **Head for**
Vancouver ▸▸ *p88* Whistler ▸▸ *p169*
Columbia Valley ▸▸ *p197* Kelowna ▸▸ *p201*

Hiking

Western Canada has to be one of the world's best destinations for hiking and has some superlative walks. Most of these are to be found throughout the Rockies and the other mountain parks. There are also a number of one-off trails offering a chance to encounter some of the remaining old-growth rainforest on the West Coast. For details of the very best hikes, we recommend *Gotta Hike BC* by Skye and Lake Nomad (Voice in the Wilderness Press, 2001). The TransCanada Trail is an ambitious attempt to build a single trail right across the country. When completed, it will be the longest recreational trail in the world, and is destined to be a classic trek or cycle. In the meantime, whole stretches of the trail are in place, offering many hiking possibilities.

★ **Head for**
Sunscoaster Trail ▸▸ *p68* East Sooke Regional Park ▸▸ *p108* Juan de Fuca Marine Trail ▸▸ *p109* West Coast

Trail ▸▸ *p128* Cape Scott Provincial Park ▸▸ *p148* Garibaldi Provincial Park ▸▸ *p165* Banff National Park ▸▸ *p287* Jasper National Park ▸▸ *p310* Yoho National Park ▸▸ *p323* Kluane National Park ▸▸ *p359* Tombstone Mountains ▸▸ *p372*

ⓘ Outdoor Recreational Council of BC, T604-7373058, www.orcbc.ca.
ⓘ www.tctrail.ca/registry, for the latest information.

Kayaking

Exceptional kayaking is available around the West Coast. A good place to learn is Strathcona Park Lodge on Vancouver Island (see p145), but most tour operators are happy to instruct beginners.

★ **Head for**
Desolation Sound Marine Park ▸▸ *p68* Indian Arm or Bowen Island in Vancouver ▸▸ *p88* Gulf Islands ▸▸ *p107* and *p123* Clayoquot Sound ▸▸ *p125* Broken Islands Group ▸▸ *p127* Nootka Sound ▸▸ *p146* Haida Gwaii ▸▸ *p244* Tatshenshini and Alsek rivers ▸▸ *p359*

ⓘ Sea Kayak Association of BC, T604-2909653.

ⓘ Whitewater Kayaking Association of BC, T604-5156379, www.whitewater.org. ⓘ Pacific International Kayak Association, T604-5971122.

Mountain biking

BC's outdoor enthusiasts take their mountain biking very seriously and most ski hills in BC stay open in summer. See also Getting around, p21.

★**Head for**
Vancouver's North Shore ⇥ *p65* **Mt Washington Alpine Resort** ⇥ *p143* **Whistler** ⇥ *p169* **Rossland** ⇥ *p188* **Fernie** ⇥ *p189* **Kicking Horse Ski Resort** ⇥ *p197* **Nelson** ⇥ *p219* **Kaslo** ⇥ *p220* **Williams Lake** ⇥ *p236*

ⓘ Association of Canadian Mountain Guides, T250-3720118, www.acmg.ca. ⓘ Federation of Mountain Clubs of BC, www.alpineclubofcanada.ca. ⓘ www.cycling.bc.ca. ⓘ www.canadatrails.com.

Rafting

Some of the best rafting in the world is to be found in Western Canada, including anything from stomach-churning whitewater to gentle floats that are suitable for any age group or ability. In some cases rafting is the only way to access the most stunning scenery.

★**Head for**
Fraser Canyon ⇥ *p183* **Kicking Horse River** ⇥ *p197* **Columbia River** ⇥ *p197* **Chilko River** ⇥ *p237* **Tatshenshini and Alsek rivers** ⇥ *p359*

ⓘ www.raftingtherockies.com.

Sailing

With its hundreds of small islands and extensive marine life, Canada's West Coast is a mecca for sailors. Marinas and boat supply stores stock nautical charts, pilot guides and tide and current tables. The **Canadian Hydrographic Service**, www.charts.gc.ca, sells charts and tide tables. Those sailing into Canadian waters must clear customs, or could obtain an advance CANPASS permit. The BC edition of the *Guide to Federal Small Craft Harbours* can be obtained from **Fisheries and Oceans Canada**, www.dfo-mpo.gc.ca.

★**Head for**
Sunshine Coast ⇥ *p67* **Desolation Sound Marine Park** ⇥ *p68* **Gulf Islands** ⇥ *p107 and p123* **Inside Passage from Port Hardy to Prince Rupert** ⇥ *p144*

ⓘ BC Sailing Association, T604-7373126. ⓘ Canadian Coast Guard, T1800-2676687, www.ccg-gcc.gc.ca. Information on boat regulations and safety practices. ⓘ Canadian Yachting Association, www.sailing.ca.

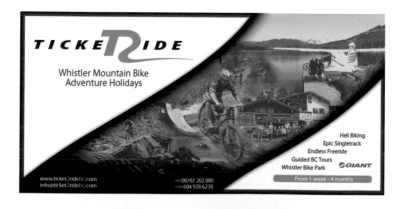

Top tips

How big is your footprint?

Responsible tourism is largely a matter of common sense, but a few points are worth underlining.

● When hiking, always stick to trails, and never pick wild flowers.

● Practise 'no trace' camping: take out everything you take in. Where no outhouses are available, bury waste and toilet paper in the ground away from paths and at least 30 m from a water source.

● Never feed or approach any wild animals. The correct disposal of litter and storage of foodstuffs is a key issue. Bears that dine well once due to a camper's laziness will keep coming back until they eventually have to be exterminated (see p271).

● Every summer, British Columbia experiences a number of forest fires that rage out of control destroying vast tracts of land. Keep an eye out for fire bans, never light a fire other than in the designated place, never leave a fire burning, and be especially careful when extinguishing cigarettes; one spark taken by the wind to the tinder-dry brush is all it takes.

● Whale-watching and bear-watching tours are major draws in Canada, and most operators are respectful towards the animals; still, there will always be the odd unscrupulous guide who oversteps the line. Don't encourage them. Visitors who come to Canada to hunt or fish should be aware of and respect the laws and limitations; they are there to protect the future of the species.

● Equally open to abuse are Canada's First Nations. Canada's native populations do not necessarily enjoy the attention of tourists. Please respect any First Nations sights such as burial grounds that are held as sacred and off-limits to outsiders, and never photograph a native American without asking their permission.

Essentials Travelling Sport & activities

Scuba diving

Thanks to its cold, clear water and abundant marine life, the Georgia Strait between the mainland and Vancouver Island's east coast has been named by the Jacques Cousteau Society as one of the top ten regions for scuba diving in the world. Visibility is best from Oct-Mar when it reaches up to 30 m.

★ **Head for**
Powell River ▸▸ *p68* Whytecliff Park and Porteau Cove near Vancouver ▸▸ *p90* Nanaimo ▸▸ *p122* Clayoquot Sound ▸▸ *p125* Barkley Sound ▸▸ *p126*

Discovery Passage around Quadra Island ▸▸ *p145* Port Hardy ▸▸ *p148*

ⓘ **Underwater Council of BC**, T604-6756964, www.ucbc.bc.ca.

Skiing

Downhill and snowboarding

Western Canada is laden with first-class ski hills that are far less busy and expensive than those in the European Alps. Many resorts are currently being expanded in anticipation of the 2010 Winter Olympics, which will be hosted by Vancouver and Whistler. A marvellous winter tour of Western Canada could be based on ski hill

Helisking and cat-skiing

Skiers and snowboarders seeking the ultimate thrill will find heli- or cat-skiing in British Columbia to be the most exciting winter experience anywhere in the world: you are taken high into the backcountry, vast tracts of terrain are available covered with abundant, powdery, untouched snow, offering spectacular landscapes and no other people. Of course, such an experience does not come cheap. Most packages start at around $750 per day, all inclusive. Some specialize in daily heli-skiing from a ski resort while others offer only week-long trips from a destination lodge. For more information, visit www.helicatcanada.com or contact **BC Heli and Snowcat Skiing Operators Association**, T250-5429020, www.bchssoa.com. In summer, heli-mountain biking is popular and can be organized through **Ticket2Ride**, www.ticket2ridebc.com.

hopping (see Where to go, p10), and indeed, many visitors come here just to ski.

⭐ **Head for**
Mt Washington ▸▸ *p143* Whistler/ Blackcomb ▸▸ *p179* Fernie ▸▸ *p189* Sun Peaks in Kamloops ▸▸ *p196* Red Mountain in Rossland ▸▸ *p197* Kicking Horse Ski Resort ▸▸ *p197* Big White in Kelowna ▸▸ *p213* Whitewater in Nelson ▸▸ *p232* Sunshine Village in Banff ▸▸ *p294* Lake Louise ▸▸ *p296*

Cross-country (or Nordic)

Most ski hills also have a cross-country area with trails that are usually groomed and track-set, but some of the best skiing is to be found in unofficial areas, where paths have been blazed by locals.

⭐ **Head for**
Cypress Mountain ▸▸ *p90* Rossland ▸▸ *p188* Manning Park ▸▸ *p191* Nelson ▸▸ *p219* Invermere ▸▸ *p* Wells Gray Park/Clearwater ▸▸ *p239* Canmore ▸▸ *p292*
ⓘ Cross-Country BC, T250-5459600, www.crosscountrybc.ca.

Backcountry

Unless you're travelling with a snow mobile, getting into the backcountry will probably entail a tour operator.

Experienced skiers can ski from the road at the Creston/ Salmo Pass on Hwy 3, and Rogers Pass on Hwy 1.

⭐ **Head for**
Revelstoke ▸▸ *p185* Golden ▸▸ *p186* Nelson ▸▸ *p219* Kaslo ▸▸ *p220*

Whale watching

In Mar and Apr, around 24,000 Pacific grey whales pass Vancouver Island's west coast. Pods of resident orca (killer whales) are easily seen from many locations, even from the shore or a ferry. Humpback whales can be seen around Feb from more northerly spots. There are plenty of reputable operators running whale-watching tours. When choosing one, bear in mind that the most important decision is whether you want to ride in an inflatable zodiac, which is a faster, wetter, more exciting trip, or a hard-shell boat, which is more sedate.

⭐ **Head for**
Victoria ▸▸ *p101* Tofino ▸▸ *p125* Ucluelet ▸▸ *p126* Johnstone Strait ▸▸ *p147* Prince Rupert ▸▸ *p243* Haida Gwaii ▸▸ *p244*

ⓘ Whale Watch Operators Association Northwest, www.nwwhalewatchers.org.

Flightseeing is not only a great way to get an unprecedented view of the mountains, but taxi planes are essential for getting out and about into areas of wilderness.

Getting there and flying around

Arriving by air

For visitors other than those from the United States, who have the option of driving (plus train and bus from Seattle), the only feasible way of getting to Canada is by air. The best-served city in the west is Vancouver, though Calgary is a much more obvious starting point for those focusing on the Rockies. One-way and return flights are available to both destinations. Enquire also about 'open jaw' tickets (flying into one and out of the other). From the UK, **Zoom**, www.flyzoom.com, offers the most options and the cheapest flights. The fact that their tickets are sold one-way also allows for more flexibility in terms of length of stay, and open-jaw possibilities.

It is advisable to start looking for your ticket early, as some of the cheapest have to be bought months in advance, and the most popular flights sell out quickly. On the other hand, those with the flexibility to leave at a moment's notice can often snap up unbelievable last-minute bargains. The best way to find a good deal is on the internet, at www.ebookers.com. Return tickets are usually a lot cheaper than buying two singles (with the exception of Zoom). The cheapest often limit your stay to two or three weeks.

From the UK

Flight time from the UK is roughly 10 hours direct. The prices below do not include tax, and are for the high season; typically, this means July and August only. The rest of the year is roughly 65% of this price, with a slight further drop in November and January.

To **Vancouver** there are daily flights from Heathrow with **Air Canada**, www.aircanada.ca, and **British Airways**, www.british-airways.com, £700 return. **Zoom**, www.flyzoom.com, flies from Gatwick three times weekly, £150 one-way, or from Cardiff, Manchester, Glasgow and Belfast for around £200 one-way. **Air Transat**, www.airtransat.com, flies twice weekly in summer from Gatwick and Glasgow, £230 one-way. To **Calgary** there are daily flights from Heathrow with **Air Canada** for £790 return. **Zoom** flies once a week from Gatwick, £180 one-way; Manchester, £200-250 one-way; and Glasgow, £320 one-way.

From the rest of Europe

To **Vancouver** there are flights from Dusseldorf with **LTU**, www.ltu.com, three times weekly in summer, €430 one-way; and from Frankfurt with **Lufthansa**, www.lufthansa.com, twice a week, €1000 return. From Amsterdam **KLM**, www.klm.nl, flies five times weekly, €760 return; and **Air Transat** flies once a week, £190 one-way. From Zurich **Belair**, www.fly belair.com, flies twice weekly in summer, CHF 2000 return. To **Calgary** there are daily flights from Frankfurt with **Air Canada**, €900 return. From Zurich **Belair**, www.flybelair.com, flies once a week, CHF 2000 return. To **Whitehorse** there are three flights weekly in summer with **Air Condor**, www.condor.com, €550 one-way from Frankfurt.

From the USA and eastern Canada

Flights from the US are numerous and frequent. To **Vancouver**, **American Airlines**, www.aa.com, and **United Airlines**, www.ual.com, fly from Chicago. **Air Canada** flies from Las Vegas, Los Angeles, Montreal, New York, San Francisco, and Toronto. **United Airlines** flies from Denver and San Francisco. **Alaska Airlines**, www.alaskaair.com, flies from Denver, San Francisco, Las Vegas and Los Angeles. **West Jet**, T1800-5385696, www.westjet.ca, flies from Montreal and Toronto. **Harmony**, www.harmonyairways.com, flies from Las Vegas and Toronto. **Philippine**, www.philippineair.com, and **America West**, www.americawest.com, fly from Las Vegas. **Cathay Pacific**, www.cathaypacific.com, flies from New York.

Flights from Australia and New Zealand

To **Vancouver** there are flights from Auckland with **Air New Zealand/Air Canada**, www.airnz.com, via Los Angeles or San Francisco, for NZ$2700 return. From Sydney **Air Canada** flights cost around AU$2130 return, and are usually via Los Angeles or Honolulu; **Qantas**, www.qantas.com, flies via Los Angeles, from AU$3000 return.

Discount travel agents

UK
STA Travel, 86 Old Brompton Rd, London SW7 3LH, T0870-1600599, www.sta travel.co.uk. Specialists in low-cost student/youth flights.

Trailfinders, 194 Kensington High St, London, W8 6FT, T020-79383939, www.trailfinders.com.

Trips Worldwide, 14 Frederick Pl, Clifton, Bristol, BS8 1JT, T0117-3114400, www.tripsworldwide.co.uk.

USA
Air Brokers International, 685 Market St, Suite 400, San Francisco, CA94105, T1800-8833273, www.airbrokers.com. Specialist and consolidator in RTW tickets.

Discount Airfares Worldwide On-line, www.etn.nl/discount.htm. A hub of consolidator and discount agent links.

STA Travel, 5900 Wiltshire Blvd, Suite 2110, Los Angeles, CA 90036, T1800-7814040, www.sta-travel.com. Discount student/youth travel company with branches in New York, San Francisco, Boston, Miami, Chicago, Seattle and Washington DC.

Travelocity, www.travelocity.com. Online consolidator.

Australia and New Zealand
Flight Centre, www.flightcentre.com.au. Throughout Australasia.

STA Travel, 702 Harris St, Ultimo, Sydney; 256 Flinders St, Melbourne, T03-96390599; and 10 High St, Auckland, T09-3666673, www.statravel.com.au. Also in major towns and university campuses.

Travel.com.au, T02-92496000/T1300-130482, Sydney, www.travel.com.au.

Trailfinders, 8 Spring St, Sydney, T1300-780212, www.trailfinders.com.au.

Top tips

Over the border

The main highways into Western Canada from the United States are Highway 5 from Seattle to Vancouver, a three-hour drive; Highway 395 from Spokane to Grand Forks; Highway 93 from Kalispell, Montana to Cranbrook; and Highway 15 from Great Falls, Montana to Lethbridge, Alberta. Traffic jams and long queues are not uncommon at the very busy Peace Arch Border Crossing on Highway 5, especially at weekends, in summer, and on Canadian or US holidays.

...and leaving again

All passengers departing from Vancouver Airport have to purchase an **Air Improvement Fee** ticket, which is $5 for BC/Yukon, $15 elsewhere. They can be bought from machines or airport booths and must be presented at security.

Regional flights

The easiest way to cover Western Canada's vast distances is with internal flights, mostly operated by **Air Canada**, www.aircanada.com, its subsidiary **Jazz**, www.flyjazz.ca, and **West Jet**, www.westjet.ca. Many mid-sized towns such as Kelowna, Kamloops, Cranbrook, Castlegar, Prince George and Prince Rupert have an airport, and some communities in the north are only linked to the outside world by air. To give an idea of prices, a one-way flight to Kelowna from Vancouver with **West Jet** costs $112. Returns are double and advance booking secures a better deal. A single from Vancouver to Calgary with **Air Canada Jazz** is $63.

Getting around by land and sea

Bicycle

Canada can be a wonderful country to explore by bicycle, but remember how vast the distances are, and try to stick to lesser-used roads. For information, ask at bike shops, or visit www.cycling.bc.ca. See also Mountain biking, p16.

Bus

Due to long distances and regular stops, travel by bus can be very slow, and seriously limits your flexibility. The network operated by **Greyhound**, T1800-6618747, www.greyhound.ca, concentrates on towns close to the TransCanada and Yellowhead highways. Getting from Greyhound depots to sights and accommodation can also be very difficult, and may mean shelling out for a taxi. If relying on public transport, it's best to keep your schedule simple, and concentrate on one area, such as the Rockies or Vancouver Island.

For those not put off by the backpacker vibe, a much better way to get around BC and the Rockies is with the **Moose/Bigfoot Travel Network**, T604-7779905, www.moosenetwork.com. At least 16 different well-planned routes, usually starting and ending in Vancouver, cover most possible itineraries. Travel is in mini-coaches seating up to 24 people, with most routes covered three or four times a week. You can get on and off where and when you want, with no time limits, allowing for maximum freedom and flexibility. They also schedule stops for sights such as hot springs, and include numerous sporting activities like hiking and kayaking.

Car

The best way to explore Western Canada properly is by car, since many of the sights cannot be reached by public transport. If hiring a vehicle seems expensive, consider offsetting this cost against accommodation by camping; in summer, a car and a tent are all you need. Older travellers tend to favour **Recreational Vehicles** (RVs), but these can be prohibitively expensive. Before hiring a vehicle, be sure to check if there is a mileage limit, and whether the insurance covers forestry roads. All-wheel, 4WD or front-wheel drive vehicles are useful if you are planning to go off the beaten track. **Hitchhiking** is a way of life in some rural areas, but even in Canada this carries a certain risk, especially for lone women.

Rules and regulations You must have a current driving licence to drive in Canada. Foreign licences are valid up to six months for visitors. If crossing the border in a vehicle, be sure to have your registration or ownership documents, and adequate insurance. Throughout Canada you drive on the right, and seat-belts are compulsory. Speed limits are 90-110 kph on the open road, usually 50 kph in built-up areas. The police advise people to drive with lights on even during the day. Compared to most countries, driving is easy and relaxed, with wildlife representing the main hazard. In many towns, traffic lights are replaced by four-way stops: vehicles proceed according to the order in which they arrived. Turning right at traffic lights is legal if the way is clear.

Fuel costs Fuel (called 'gas' here) is easy to come by anywhere but the far north. It's expensive (95 cents a litre), unless compared to British prices.

Maps We recommend investing in Rand McNally's good-value *BC and Alberta Road Atlas*, which includes the whole region covered in this book, even the Yukon, and also has larger scale maps of key areas such as the southern interior and Rockies, and most towns and cities, with additional city centre maps for the biggest. Those who really want to get off the beaten track could invest in a *Backcountry Mapbook* (2001), Mussio Ventures, $16, which shows all the secondary and forestry roads, with full details on free and forestry campsites, hot springs, and other useful features. For transport information throughout Canada, visit www.tc.gc.ca.

Vehicle hire Details of rental agencies are given in the transport sections of Vancouver, Calgary and Whitehorse. Some companies have a one-way service, meaning you can rent a car in one place and drop it off elsewhere. Prices start at about $40 per day, $200 per week, $800 per month plus tax and insurance. Another option would be to rent something you could sleep in. A mini-van works out at about $425 per week all-inclusive. RVs are the expensive but luxurious choice; prices start at about $175 per day for a small unit, $210 per day for a 24-footer, plus tax and insurance. All hire vehicles are registered with the **Canadian Automobile Association** (CAA); in case of breakdown, simply call their T1800 number and give directions to where you are, and a towing operator will take you to the nearest CAA mechanic.

Buying a car For long-term travellers, it would work out cheaper to buy a vehicle and sell it at the end of your trip. Bargains can be found in Vancouver. The classified section of the *Vancouver Sun* is a good place to start looking.

Ferry

On the west coast, ferries are a way of life. The main routes, operated by **BC Ferries**, T1888-2233779, www.bcferries.com, connect Vancouver with Victoria and Nanaimo on Vancouver Island, and with the Gulf Islands. Sailings on all these services are fairly regular (see specific locations for details, and pick up the latest timetable). You may have to wait one or two sailings in summer, however, especially during Canadian and US holidays. Vehicles can be taken on all but a few minor crossings and bikes can be taken on all.

Two very popular long-distance routes from Port Hardy on Vancouver Island – the **Inside Passage** to Prince Rupert and the **Discovery Coast Passage** to Bella Coola (see p144) – provide excellent means of accessing the north, and can be treated as cheap but beautifully

Top tips

Working in Canada

Non-Canadian residents need a permit to work legally in Canada. To get one you must first have an offer of employment. **Human Resources and Development Canada**, T1800-6226232, www.hrdc-drhc.gc.ca, must confirm this. You then have to apply to **Citizenship and Immigration Canada**, www.cic.gc.ca, for the permit. Performing artists can sometimes work legally without the permit. People without permits tend to have the best luck waiting at tables in Vancouver or picking fruit in the Okanagan. Wages for the latter can be reasonable if you work fast. Another (and legal) option is **WWOOF Canada** (Willing Workers on Organic Farms), T250-3544417, or visit www.wwoof.ca. The deal varies from place to place, but generally entails working three to five hours per day for room and board. A booklet listing 300 places costs $30.

scenic cruises in their own right. In addition, a number of free ferries provide essential links across lakes in BC's southern interior. The longest and most important of these are in the West Kootenays, crossing the Arrow Lakes near Nakusp, and Kootenay Lake near Nelson.

Two other services worth mentioning are privately run boats that provide a popular means of accessing some very remote coastal spots around Vancouver Island. The *MV Lady Rose* out of Port Alberni runs to Bamfield, Ucluelet and Barkley Sound. The *MV Uchuck III* out of Gold River runs to Nootka Sound, Tahsis and Yuquot. Both will take and launch kayaks.

Train

Only two **VIA Rail**, www.viarail.ca, services operate in this region: the *Malahat* between Victoria and Courtenay on Vancouver Island, and the Vancouver-Jasper line, which takes 16½ hours, with sleepers available.

Sleeping

Until you stray far from the beaten track, accommodation in Western Canada is plentiful and easily found across the price ranges. Mid-range, usually characterless, **hotels** and **motels** dominate the scene, especially in smaller towns. Rooms are typically clean but uninspiring, with generic decor, a TV, tub, small fridge, and coffee maker. Facilities such as saunas, hot tubs, fitness rooms and indoor pools are often small and disappointing. Many of the most impressive hotels, operated by the **Fairmont** chain, were constructed by the Canadian Pacific Railway (CPR) at the turn of the last century, and resemble French chateaux. Motel rooms are usually side by side, with an exterior door, and often a parking spot right outside.

For the same price as a mid-range motel, you can usually find an attractively furnished room in a small **B&B** or **guesthouse**, with a hearty breakfast included, representing much better value. Generally operated by friendly, helpful and knowledgeable hosts, these offer an excellent opportunity to meet Canadians on their own ground, but might deter those who value their privacy or can't shake off that feeling of staying with their auntie.

In a similar vein, many travellers have had wonderful experiences when staying in **lodges**. Often found in remote spots, sometimes associated with outdoor activities, these usually consist of a large central building containing facilities and rooms, with cabins

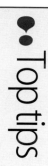

Top tips

A bed for the night

Accommodation price grades in this guide are based on the cost per night for two people sharing a double room in the high season, with breakfast, not including tax (see p32 for details). Many places offer discounts during low season or for long stays.
Prices are in Canadian dollars.

LL	Over $300	C	$90-120
L	$240-300	D	$60-90
AL	$180-240	E	$30-60
A	$150-180	F	Under $30
B	$120-150		

scattered around the extensive grounds. Some of the gorgeous log constructions, for which the west coast is famous, are exceptional, and well worth a splurge. For something more exotic, consider staying on a working **ranch** or **farm**, which abound in Alberta and the Cariboo. For more details contact the **BC Guest Ranchers' Association**, www.guest ranches.com. **Resorts**, primarily found on the coast, tend to have cabins, huts or chalets of varying standards, along with their own restaurants, beaches, and other facilities.

Almost all Canadian towns have a **hostel**, many affiliated to **Hostelling International** (HI), with a reduced fee for members. For information and reservations contact www.hihostels.ca. There is no age limit. A typical hostel has dormitories with four or more beds, usually single sex, plus a few private rooms for couples and families. Facilities include shared washrooms with showers, a common room with TV and sometimes games and a library, a kitchen/dining room, and lockers. Many organize activities or tours. Almost all are clean, friendly, a bit noisy and great for gleaning information and meeting fellow travellers. In the Rockies, a string of HI hostels enjoy locations second only to the campgrounds, making them a great budget option. A number of other low-cost options can be found at www.budgetbeds.com.

Camping is the cheapest option, and the best way to immerse yourself in Western Canada's magnificent countryside. Where the scenery is wildest, camping is often the only choice. The best campgrounds are those within provincial parks, which are not driven by profit margins and tend to have more spacious sites, with plenty of trees and privacy. The busier ones often have shower facilities and hot running water. Campsites in big towns tend to be far from the centre, expensive and ugly, making a hostel a better option. Those that cater to RVs, with pull-through sites and hook-ups, often resemble car parks, with few trees and no privacy. Almost all the campsites listed in this guide are in the **F** price category.

Seekers of calm will gravitate towards the small campgrounds that have no facilities beyond an outhouse and a water pump. Even cheaper are forestry campgrounds, which are almost always situated in remote spots on logging roads (ask at local visitor centres). 'Guerilla camping' means finding out-of-the-way spots where you can pitch your tent for free, or sleep in the back of your van, without being bothered. Much of Western Canada (but not the Rockies) is remote enough to make this possible. Logging roads are always a good place to look (and you may stumble on a forestry site). Anyone interested in this approach might want to buy K and C Copeland's *Camp Free in BC* (Voice in the Wilderness Press). Volume one covers the south, volume two the north.

Vancouver has more restaurants per capita than any other Canadian city, and West Coast cuisine is considered one of the best in North America.

Eating and drinking

Food

Western Canada, unlike the country as a whole, has developed a strong culinary identity, focused on the gastronomic playground of Vancouver. **West Coast cuisine** combines Asian, Californian and European techniques with a strong emphasis on the freshness of ingredients, a genuinely innovative, creative, eclectic philosophy and the extensive use of seafood. Elements are also taken from traditional native American cooking, such as the grilling of salmon on cedar or alder, and the use of wild game like caribou and buffalo. Many different ethnic cuisines are fused with the West Coast sensibility, which is often made healthier as a result.

Not surprisingly, **vegetarians** are well catered for in Vancouver, and in bohemian areas like the Gulf Islands and West Kootenays. The more you move into the redneck communities further north and east, however, the harder it gets to avoid the meat-and-potatoes mentality. However, if you are a meat-eater, Alberta AAA beef is as good as it gets, so if you like steak this is the place to indulge.

In Canadian cities you can find any kind of food you want, till late at night. Most towns will have an expensive 'fine-dining' establishment, which usually means old-style European, predominantly French, with the emphasis on steak and seafood. In smaller communities, however, you're often stuck with unimaginative 'family' restaurants, Chinese restaurants of dubious authenticity, pizza, and early closing. Certain ubiquitous chains like **Earl's** and **Milestone's** cover most of the comfort-food bases, and really are fine, especially if you're travelling with kids. Equally ubiquitous are the family chains like **Denny's** and **Smitty's**, which are okay for big breakfasts, but the coffee leaves a lot to be desired. All the American fast-food outlets are here, too: **Subway** is always a good bet for sandwiches.

Drink

While Vancouver has its share of sophisticated cafés, bistros and tapas bars, as well as the inevitable Irish pubs and phoney English boozers, the typical small-town Canadian pub has a pool table, a TV set screening sporting events, soft-rock or country music, a burger-dominated menu, and a handful of locals propping up the bar playing keno (a lottery game). Chances are, though, they'll be a friendly bunch.

Top tips

A bite to eat

The prices below refer to the cost of a meal for one person, with a drink. Many restaurants stay open all day, from 0800-2200, or from 1200-2200. Some just open for dinner, from 1730-2400, or may also open from roughly 1200-1500 for lunch. In smaller, more remote communities, restaurants may close as early as 2000. Prices throughout are in Canadian dollars.

♈♈♈	over $30
♈♈	$16-30
♈	under $16

Sadly, most of the **beer** sold here is tasteless, weak, watery lager, such as Molson, Kokanee, and Canadian. Yet Western Canada has pioneered the concept of **microbreweries**, which produce small-batch, carefully crafted beers using natural ingredients. All styles of beer are available, served carbonated and chilled. Breweries to look out for are Big Rock (Calgary), Nelson (West Kootenays), Yukon (Whitehorse), Tree (Kelowna), Granville Island (Vancouver) and Okanagan Spring (Kelowna). Very small but excellent breweries include Raven (Vancouver), Crannog (Shuswap), and Salt Spring (southern Gulf Islands).

While here, you should also make a point of trying some BC **wines**, the best of which are made in the Okanagan Valley. This region specializes in German-style whites, sparkling wines, pinot noir, and the sweet and sophisticated ice-wine. See p for more details and for information about taking a tour of the vineyards. It's hard to recommend specific wineries, but Tinhorn Creek and Red Rooster never disappoint.

Canadians take their **coffee** pretty seriously. Locally brewed examples to look out for include Kicking Horse (Invermere, East Kootenays), Oso Negro (West Kootenays), and Salt Spring (southern Gulf Islands).

Shopping

Canada has its share of tacky souvenirs, usually featuring moose, grizzlies or maple leaves, but a bottle of authentic maple syrup makes a nice gift, or you can buy smoked salmon (which will keep) in a hand-crafted cedar box, decorated in native Northwest Coast style. The most popular items among tourists are works by Canada's various First Nations, such as the Inuit or Haida. These include carvings in gold, silver, wood and argillite (a black slate-like rock), jewellery, masks, paintings and prints, clothing, moccasins, beadwork, dream-catchers and much more. Arts and crafts costs less in the places where they are made, such as Haida Gwaii (Queen Charlotte Islands). There is a lot of mass-produced rubbish sold to tourists, so be sure to shop around to get an idea of just how exquisite good native art can be.

Non-aboriginal arts and crafts are also exceptionally fine and often extremely good value given the workmanship involved. Regions such as the Gulf Islands and West Kootenays are overrun with artists, but Vancouver's Granville Island is the best place to see a wide range of works. Visitors to Alberta may want to buy some authentic cowboy boots, a stetson hat or a set of chaps. Music lovers will be pleased to hear that Canada is one of the cheapest places in the world for CDs. It could also be better for sports equipment than your home country.

Remember to keep your receipts so that you can claim back the tax, see p32. Most things are cheaper in Alberta where there is no provincial tax.

5 best

Places to buy arts and crafts

Granville Island, Vancouver ►► *p59*
Victoria, Vancouver Island ►► *p101*
Salt Spring Island ►► *p105*
Nelson ►► *p219*
Haida Gwaii ►► *p244*

Entertainment and festivals

While the standard and choice of entertainment and nightlife is good in Vancouver and, to a lesser degree, Calgary and Victoria, most Western Canadian towns simply don't have the populations to support a thriving cultural scene comparable to European cities. Generally you will find a cinema or two, a theatre, a museum full of pioneer artefacts, gold-rush relics and stuffed animals, maybe an art gallery, a nightclub of dubious merit frequented by teenagers, and an arena for ice hockey, Canadian football, basketball, baseball or curling. On the other hand, summer in Western Canada is a time for non-stop festivals, and even the smallest towns hosts wonderful events that might focus on music (jazz, folk, blues), street entertainment, storytelling, food, or native American culture (pow wows).

Essentials Travelling Entertainment & festivals

Calendar of events

Jan Brackendale Winter Eagles Festival, near Squamish, celebrates the world's biggest gathering of bald eagles ►► *p176*.
Feb Chinese New Year, Vancouver ►► *p83*.
All Native Basketball Tournament, Prince Rupert, a massive and popular event that celebrates its 47th year in 2006 ►► *p258*.
Mar Pacific Rim Whale Festival, held around Tofino, to celebrate the migration of up to 24,000 grey whales ►► *p135*.
Apr Telus World Ski and Snowboard Festival, Whistler. The biggest winter sports event in North America, featuring the world snowboarding championship ►► *p177*.
May Wine Festival, Okanagan ►► *p211*.
Jun Jazz festivals in Vancouver ►► *p83* Victoria ►► *p115* and Calgary ►► *p284* Mid- to

late Jun is the best time to see orca (killer whales) in the Johnstone Strait off Vancouver Island, where they stay until Oct ►► *p140*. In Whitehorse are the Yukon International Storytelling Festival and the Gathering of Traditions Potlatch, an important native celebration ►► *p353*.
Jul Celebration of Light, late-Jul to early Aug, Vancouver, a 2-week international fireworks competition ►► *p83*. Dancing on the Edge Festival, Vancouver, Canada's largest showcase of independent North American choreographers ►► *p83*. Festival of the Arts, Salt Spring Island, a month-long event ►► *p115*. Sandfest, Parksville, features the World Sandcastle Competition ►► *p154*. The annual salmon migration occurs Jul-Sep, with peaks varying in different areas ►► *p240*.

Top tips

Pow wow

Derived from the Narragansett word for shaman, pow wow traditionally refers to any gathering of native Americans. These days the word is usually used to denote a celebration, at which natives and non-natives meet in one particular area to dance, sing, socialize, and generally have a good time. Pow wows can vary in length from a single session of about five or six hours to three days with one to three sessions a day. One of the best to visit is at Head-Smashed-in-Buffalo-Jump, see p339.

Williams Lake Stampede, weekend closest to 1 Jul, is one of the biggest and oldest of its kind in BC ▸▸ *p257*. **Calgary Stampede**, a 10-day cowboy extravaganza and **Folk Music Festival**, Calgary ▸▸ *p277*. **Banff Festival of the Arts**, throughout the summer, showcases young artists in various media ▸▸ *p305*. **Buffalo Days Pow Wow**, Head-Smashed-In Buffalo Jump ▸▸ *p339*. **Great Northern Arts Festival**, Inuvik, a 10-day bonanza featuring over 100 artists from north of the Arctic Circle ▸▸ *p376*. **Dawson City Music Festival**, one of the best ▸▸ *p376*.
Aug Victoria Fringe Theatre Festival, the most important festival of its kind in BC, and Victoria's major event ▸▸ *p115*.
Filberg Festival, Comox, Vancouver Island.

A massive 4-day expo of the best arts and crafts in BC ▸▸ *p154*. **Squamish Days**, a loggers' sports festival ▸▸ *p176*. **Kamloops Pow Wow**, one of the best in the country ▸▸ *p195*. **Peach Festival**, Penticton, is a massive party ▸▸ *p211*. **Ironman Triathlon**, Penticton, a very serious event ▸▸ *p211*. **Jazzfest**, Kaslo, enjoys one of the most spectacular locations of any festival ▸▸ *p230*. **Shambhala**, a one of a kind rave in Salmo near Nelson ▸▸ *p230*.
Sep Vancouver Fringe Festival and Vancouver International Film Festival ▸▸ *p83*. **Sandcastle Festival**, Harrison Hot Springs ▸▸ *p182*. **Fall Wine Festival**, late Sep/early Oct throughout the Okanagan ▸▸ *p211*. **Oct** Vancouver Comedy Festival ▸▸ *p83*.

Essentials A-Z

Accident and emergency

Contact the emergency services on T911 and your embassy or consulate (see p95). Remember to get police/medical records for insurance claims.

Children

Canada is generally a safe country that presents few worries for people travelling with kids. There are no poisonous animals, crime levels are low, the people tend to be relaxed and tolerant, and there's plenty of space and countryside to enjoy. The only potential problem is the huge distances that often have to be covered in this vast country.

An excellent resource to explore, full of tips on kid-friendly accommodation, restaurants and attractions throughout BC is www.kidfriendly.org. A good site for resources aimed at Canadians but also useful for travellers is www.childrencanada.com.

Customs and duty free

The duty-free allowance for people over 19 (18 in Alberta) is 1.4 litres of spirits or 24 bottles of beer (355-ml), plus 200 cigarettes and 50 cigars. UK travellers can take back 1 litre of spirits, 2 litres of wine, 200 cigarettes, and £145 worth of goods, including gifts and souvenirs.

Disabled travellers

Disabled travellers should call ahead to make arrangements with hotels and restaurants, many of which will go out of their way to be helpful. Being such a young country, Canada has a relatively high proportion of modern buildings, which tend to be wheelchair friendly. Many national and provincial parks have wheelchair-accessible interpretive centres and trails. For more information, contact the **Canadian Paraplegic Association**, T604-3243611, www.canparaplegic.org. Information on accessible transport around Canada can be found at www.accesstotravel.gc.ca. **Freedom Rentals**, 4996 Westminster Av, Delta, Vancouver, T604-9524499, www.wheelchairvanrentals.com rent out wheelchair-accessible vans for about $150 per day, $900 per week. *Abilities Magazine* is a cross-disability lifestyle magazine published by the **Canadian Abilities Foundation**, www.enablelink.org.

Drugs

All the usual drugs are illegal in Canada, though this predominantly liberal country is likely to legalize cannabis in the near future. British Columbia is a large producer of high quality marijuana (BC bud), whose use is widespread. Consequently, attitudes toward the drug are pretty relaxed, but it is still advisable to be very discrete if indulging, and obviously be careful if buying.

Electricity

Canada uses 110 V, 60 cycles, with a US-style plug, usually 2 flat pins, sometimes with a third earth pin which is round. UK appliances will not work in Canada without a heavy-duty invertor to up the voltage to 220 volts, so leave them at home.

Embassies and consulates

Australia High Commission: Commonwealth Av, Canberra, ACT 2600, T02-62704000.
Ireland 65 St Stephen's Green, Dublin 2, T01-4174100.

New Zealand High Commission: 3rd floor, 61 Molesworth St, Thorndon, Wellington, T04-4739577.

South Africa High Commission: 19th floor, Reserve Bank Building, 60 St George's Mall, Cape Town 8001, T21-4235240.

UK High Commission: Macdonald House, 1 Grosvenor Sq, London, W1K 4AB, T020-72586600.

USA 501 Pennsylvania Av NW, Washington DC 20001, T202-6821740.

Gay and lesbian

Canadians are generally tolerant of homosexuality although, as everywhere, exceptions exist. Be more wary in redneck communities, especially in Northern BC, Alberta, and logging and mining towns. Places like the Gulf Islands and West Kootenays are especially tolerant, and Vancouver's West End has a flourishing gay scene .

For general information and links, check out www.gaycanada.com. An excellent site for listings of gay-friendly businesses across the country is www.purpleroofs.com. The **Gay and Lesbian Centre**, 1170 Bute St, Vancouver, T604-6845307 (programmes/services), T604-6846869 (helpline), has a library and clinic, and organizes discussion groups.

Health

Western Canada must be one of the safest places on earth: it has good medical facilities, and there are no prevalent diseases, so no vaccinations are required before entry. Tap **water** is safe to drink but drinking water from dubious sources, especially slow-moving streams, can lead to giardia, commonly known here as 'beaver fever'. The result is vomiting, diarrhoea and weakness.

Those hiking in the mountains should be aware of **altitude sickness**, which can begin at 3000 m. If you experience headaches, nausea, and shortness of breath, the best treatment is to descend. The best prevention is to ascend slowly.

To combat **hypothermia** and frostbite, which may occur when your core temperature falls below 35°C, keep warm by wearing several layers of suitable clothing (see p12). If you feel cold, move about rather than just standing still.

Sunburn also occurs easily in the mountains, so avoid extensive exposure, wear a hat and sunglasses, and use a high-protection sun cream.

The health service in Canada is maintained by provincial governments. Travellers should make sure their insurance covers all medical costs. Visitors suffering from a condition that may need immediate care, such as those with serious allergies or diabetes, are advised to carry what they need in case of an emergency. Medical services are listed in each town's directory.

Pharmacies (chemists) are plentiful and stock all the usual provisions. They are often large retail outlets that stay open late, even 24 hrs in big cities. As elsewhere, many drugs are only available with a doctor's prescription.

Insurance

Travel insurance is highly recommended and should cover theft or loss of possessions including passport and money, the cost of all medical and dental treatment, cancellation of flights, delays in travel arrangements, accidents, missed departures, personal liability and legal expenses. Keep any relevant medical bills and police reports to substantiate your claim. Note that many policies exclude 'dangerous activities' or charge a higher premium for them. This may include scuba diving, skiing, and even trekking. Some companies will not cover people over 65 years old, or may charge high premiums. **Age Concern**, T01883-346964, usually have the best deals for seniors. **Columbus Direct**, T0207-3750011, is one of the most competitive British companies.

STA Travel and other reputable student travel organizations also offer good-value travel policies. Travellers from the US should check to see if their existing policies cover travel in Canada. Otherwise, try the **International Student Insurance Service** (ISIS), available through **STA Travel**, T1800-7770112, www.sta-travel.com or **Travel Guard**, T1800-8261300; **Access America**, T1800-2848300; **Travel Insurance Services**, T1800-9371387; **Travel Assistance International**, T1800-8212828; and **Council Travel**, T1888-2686245.

Internet

All but the smallest Canadian towns will have a cyber-café, and free internet access is always available at public libraries, though you may have to register in advance to get a slot. Otherwise charges vary, averaging about $1 for every 15-20 mins, considerably cheaper in big cities. Look in each town's directory section for locations of internet access.

Language

Canada has 2 official languages: English and French, or rather Québecois, which you may hear but will never need in Western Canada. First Nations groups still speak indigenous languages in remote areas of Northern BC and the Yukon.

Media

Newspapers and magazines
There are 2 national newspapers. *The Globe and Mail* is a broadsheet that appeals to a more intellectual and liberal-minded readership. The *National Post* has a more right-of-centre and populist approach, as do BC's *Province* and the *Vancouver Sun*. The bookshop **Chapters** is a good place to browse.

Foreign newspapers and magazines, available in larger newsagents in Vancouver and Calgary, include *USA Today*,

the *International Herald Tribune* as well as weekend editions such as *The Observer*.

Radio and television
The best way to get an idea of the Canadian psyche is to tune in to *CBC Radio One*, where current issues and all manner of topics are discussed. The news is broadcast every 30 mins, with an extended national news at 1700, and world news at 1800. Shows in the morning are provincial, those in the afternoon are national. *Cross-country Check-up* (Sun, 1300-1500) and the provincial *BC Almanac* (weekdays at noon) are phone-in shows where people talk about key current issues. BC's *Sad Goat* (Mon-Fri 1400-1600), is also a phone-in show, but more light-hearted and humorous. Other shows to listen out for are: *Definitely not the Opera* (Sat 1400-1700), a pop-culture magazine usually good for new Canadian music; *Tapestries* (Sun 1500), which deals with spiritual and metaphysical matters; and *Quirks and Quarks* (Sat 1200), an intelligent magazine about science. *CBC Radio Two* is mostly dedicated to classical music.

Canadian television tells you very little about the country beyond its obvious proximity to the US. There are only 2 Canadian channels, one national (*CBC*), the other provincial (*BCTV* in BC, for example). Even these have ads and are dominated by US content.

Money

The Canadian currency is the dollar ($), divided into 100 cents (¢). Coins come in denominations of 1¢ (penny), 5¢ (nickel), 10¢ (dime), 25¢ (quarter), $1 (called a 'loonie' because it carries a picture of a loon, a common Canadian bird), and $2 (called a 'toonie'). Banknotes come in denominations of $5, $10, $20, $50 and $100. At the time of printing the exchange rate was: 1 Canadian dollar = US$0.85; €0.70; £0.49; AU$1.19.

What to take

As in most countries today, the easiest and safest way to travel in Canada is with a credit or debit card using ATMs, which are found in all but the smallest, remotest communities. The major credit cards are also accepted just about everywhere. Traveller's cheques (TCs) remain a safe way to carry money, but mean more hassle. **American Express (Amex)**, **Visa** and **Thomas Cook** cheques are the most widely accepted. You're never far from one of Canada's big banks: **Royal Bank**, **Bank of Montreal**, **CIBC**, **Scotiabank** and **TD Bank**. They all give reasonable rates for TCs and cash. Minimum opening hours are Mon-Fri 1000-1500, but they're usually open until 1630. Bureaux de change, found in most city centres, airports and major train stations have longer hours but worse rates. Avoid changing money or TCs in hotels, whose rates are usually poor. The quickest way to have money sent in an emergency is to have it wired to the nearest bank via **Western Union**, T0800-833833, or **Moneygram**, T0800-894887.

Taxes

Almost everything in Canada is subject to the federal Goods and Services Tax (GST) of 7%. A rebate can be claimed on accommodation expenditure and goods taken out of the country within 60 days; remember to keep your receipts. Rebate forms are available from visitor centres, hotels, shops, airports and Canadian embassies. Claims can also be made at the duty-free shops of certain US border crossings. For more information call T1800-6684748, or T902-4325608 outside Canada. In BC (but not Alberta, the Yukon or NWT) most goods and services carry a Provincial Sales Tax (PST) of 7%. In addition there is a hotel rooms' tax of up to 10%. None of these taxes are included in the original price, meaning everything you buy ends up costing more than you expect (up to 24% more for accommodation).

Cost of travelling

The cost of living is considerably lower in Canada than in the UK or US. Things that will cost £1 in England will often cost $1 in Canada. Notable exceptions are luxuries like beer and cigarettes which are roughly on a par with the UK and therefore more expensive than they are in the US. Petrol (gas) is cheaper than in the UK but more expensive than the US.

Canada is not a budget destination, but the weakness of the Canadian dollar makes it reasonably affordable for those coming from Britain, though less so for US travellers. Apart from accommodation, the single biggest expense is travel, due to the vast distances that need to be covered. Petrol (gas) gets considerably more expensive the further north you go. Accommodation and restaurant prices tend to be higher in popular destinations such as Whistler and Banff, and during the summer months (or winter at ski resorts).

Budget

The minimum daily budget required for those staying in hostels or camping, travelling by bus and hitching, and cooking their own meals, will be roughly $50-80 per day. If you stay in cheaper motels or B&Bs and eat out occasionally that will rise to $80-100 per day. Those staying in more upmarket places, eating out daily and visiting attractions can expect to pay at least $100-120. The best way to budget is to move around less and camp a lot. In destinations like the Rockies, this is also about the best way to experience the country. Single travellers will have to pay more than half the cost of a double room in most places, and should budget on spending around 60% of what a couple would spend.

Opening hours

Shops tend to stay open 0900-1730. Bank hours vary, but typically they are open Mon-Fri or Tue-Sat 1000-1600. Visitor centres are typically open 0900-

1700, longer in summer. Some are only operational May-Sep. All shops and businesses keep longer hours in cities, with everything shutting down earlier in smaller and more remote communities.

Post

Most towns have **Canada Post** offices, www.canadapost.ca, which are usually open Mon-Fri 0900-1700. It is often more convenient to send post from one of the major drug stores/chemists. Costs for a standard letter are 50¢ within Canada, 65¢ to the US, and $1.25 anywhere else. Prices for packages depend on exact destination and weight. Within BC this is roughly $4.95 for 1 kg then 25¢ for every additional 500 g. It is considerably cheaper to send parcels abroad as 'small packages'. To the US this includes anything up to 1 kg. To Europe, a small package can be up to 2 kg.

Note that international mail can take up to 2 weeks to arrive. In Canada, poste restante is known as general delivery. In smaller towns, regular post offices will hold general delivery. In big towns this should be addressed to the main post office, whose address will be given in the listings. Fax services are available at post offices.

Public holidays

Most services and attractions and many shops close on public holidays, or greatly reduce their opening hours. Accommodation and transport tends to be more heavily reserved, especially ferries between Vancouver and Vancouver Island.

National holidays
New Year's Day, 1 Jan; **Good Friday**; **Easter Monday**; **Victoria Day**, 3rd Mon in May; **Canada Day**, 1 Jul; **Labour Day**, 1st Mon in Sep; **Thanksgiving**, 2nd Mon in Oct; **Remembrance Day**, 11 Nov; **Christmas Day**; **Boxing Day**.

Alberta Family Day, 3rd Mon in Feb; Alberta Heritage Day, 1st Mon in Aug. **BC** British Columbia Day, 1st Mon in Aug. **Yukon** Discovery Day, 3rd Mon in Aug.

Safety

Few countries are as safe as Canada. Even here, though, common sense should prevail in cities. Avoid walking alone in remote, unlit streets or parks after dark. Elsewhere the biggest danger is from wildlife, though there are no poisonous animals to worry about. Never approach wild animals, even the ones deemed safe. More people are injured annually by elk than by bears, see p271.

Smoking

Smoking is not permitted in public places including restaurants, cafés or pubs where eating is a primary activity, or on any public transport.

Student travellers

Most sights in Canada offer a discounted price for students. **ISIC** cards are widely accepted as proof of ID. Most of Canada's hostels are affiliated to **Hostelling International** (HI), with reductions for members.

Telephone

For international calls to Canada, dial your country's IDD access code (00 from the UK) **+1**, then the local code, then the number. Local codes are: **250** for all of BC, except Vancouver, the Sunshine Coast and Sea to Sky Highway, which are **604**; most of Alberta is **403**, except the Edmonton region (including Jasper), which is **780**; the Yukon is **867**. These codes have been included throughout the guide.

Long-distance calls within North America must be preceded by **1**, then the 3-digit local code. Any long-distance numbers beginning with **1800**, **1888**,

1877, or **1777** are free in North America. For long-distance and international calls it works out much cheaper to buy one of the many cards available from newsagents and fuel stations. Those from 7-11 shops are reliable. For international calls, ask for one with no connection fee. To reach an operator, dial **0**. For all emergency services, dial **911**.

In Canada as elsewhere, the advent of the mobile phone has led to a decrease in the number of public phones, but these are still pretty numerous. Many take coins and credit cards, some take **Telus** phonecards, available at 7-11 stores, fuel stations, or larger pharmacies. Local calls are free from personal phones, with a charge of 25¢ at pay phones for an unlimited amount of time.

Time

BC and the Yukon are 8 hrs behind GMT in summer, 7 hrs behind GMT in winter. Alberta is 1 hr ahead of BC and the Yukon.

Tipping

Western Canadians take tipping very seriously. In restaurants the customary tip is 15%. Bars and pubs usually have waiter/ waitress service, and these too are tipped 10-15%. Even if you buy your drink at the bar, you are expected to leave a tip, usually change up to around 10%. Taxi drivers and hairdressers should also be tipped 10-15%. Naturally, this all depends on service.

Tourist information

Visitor information centres can be found in almost every Canadian town and are listed in the relevant sections of this book. Many are only open mid-May to mid-Sep. They tend to be well stocked with leaflets. In **British Columbia**, T1800-5345622, www.hellobc.com, literature includes a *Vacation Planner*; the indispensable *Approved Accommodation Guide*, which also includes addresses and freephone numbers for visitor centres; vacation guides for each region; the extremely informative *Outdoor Adventure Guide*; and other guides covering topics such as fishing and golf. **Alberta**, T1800-2523782, www.travelalberta.com, produces an *Accommodation Guide* and a separate *Campground Guide*, a very useful *Vacation Guide* full of attractions, and some regional brochures. The **Yukon**, T1800-661 0494, www.touryukon.com, produces a helpful *Vacation Planner*. Look out also for the excellent *Visitor Guide* put out by the **Yukon First Nations Tourism Association**, T867-6677698, yfnta@yknet.yk.ca, and the free *Guide to the Goldfields*.

Most visitor centres will provide information on local transport and attractions, and sell relevant books and souvenirs. Many also produce self-guiding walking-tour maps of their towns, and have illustrated directories of local B&Bs. **Parks Canada** operates its own offices, usually in conjunction with the local tourist board. These tend to be excellent facilities, especially in the Rockies.

Phone facts

Country code: +1 (to dial in to Canada)
Emergency number: 911
IDD access code: 011 (to dial out of Canada)
Operator: 0
Directory enquiries: 411

Tour operators

In the UK

Canada Travel Specialists, 85 Oswald St, Glasgow, G2 4PA. T0871-2260474, www.canadatravelspecialists.com. Ski packages, rail tours, motorhome holidays.
Connections Worldwide, The Old Registry, 20 Amersham Hill, High Wycombe, Bucks, HP13 6NZ, T01494-473173, www.canada-coach-tours.com. 2-week bus or train tours from Victoria to Banff, starting in London.
HF Holidays, T0208-9059558, Imperial House, The Hyde, Edgware Rd, London, NW9 5AL, www.hfholidays.co.uk. Walking tours of Western Canada.
Titan HiTours, HiTours House, Crossoak Lane, Redhill, Surrey, RH1 5EX, T01293-455345, www.coach-tours-canada.com. Bus and train tours of Vancouver and the Rockies, or Northern BC.

In North America

Adventure Link Tours, 38157 2nd Av, Squamish, BC, V0N 3G0, T604-6397036, www.adventurelinktours.com. Train tours, lodge holidays and ski vacations.
Adventures Abroad, PMB 101, 1124 Fir Avenue, Blaine, Washington, 98240, USA, www.adventures-abroad.com. 2-week bus tours from Calgary to Vancouver Island.
Midnight Sun Adventure Travel, 1845-B Fort St, Victoria, BC, V8R 1J6, T1800-2555057, www.midnightsuntravel.com. Tours of Vancouver Island, the Rockies, the Yukon, and Haida Gwaii. Also kayaking, hiking and camping tours for small groups.

In Australia and New Zealand

Costless Holidays, T1300-302891, www.costlesstravel.com. Guided tours of the Rockies.
Scenic Tours, PO Box 807, 11 Brown St, Newcastle, Australia, T1300-136001, www.scenictours.com. Tours of the Rockies.
Ski Tours Canada, T02-949909639, www.skitourscanada.com. Ski tours around resorts from Big White to Fernie.
Talpacific Holidays, 151 Victoria St West, Auckland, New Zealand, T09-914 4000, www.talpacific.com. Rail tours.

Visas and immigration

Visa regulations are subject to change, so it is essential to check with your local Canadian embassy or consulate (see p29) before leaving home. Citizens of the EU, Scandinavia and most Commonwealth countries do not need an entry visa, just a full valid passport. US citizens only need proof of citizenship and residence, such as a driving licence. All visitors have to fill out a waiver form, which you will be given on the plane or at the border. If you don't know where you'll be staying just write 'touring', though immigration officers may then ask for an idea of your schedule. They will decide the length of stay permitted, usually the maximum of 6 months. You may have to show proof of sufficient funds, such as a credit card or $300 per week of your proposed stay. If you wish to extend your stay beyond the allotted time, send a written application to the nearest Canada immigration centre well before the end of your authorized time limit.

Weights and measures

The metric system is universally used.

Women travellers

There are few if any regions in the world where women are as emancipated, and that are as safe for women travellers, as Western Canada. Naturally the usual precautions need to be taken in cities and larger towns, such as avoiding quiet unlit streets and parks at night. In more redneck logging and mining communities, or in sports-oriented places like Whistler, a surfeit of pumped-up males may result in more attention than most women would want, but even here the problem is more one of irritation than danger.
West Coast Women Adventures, www.westcoastwomen.ca, specializes in tours of BC for women over 30, featuring hiking, biking, kayaking, rafting, horse riding and wineries.

A sprint through history

c15,000 BC	The first humans cross the Bering Strait from Siberia to Alaska on a temporary land bridge created by the dramatic lowering of sea level due to ice-age glaciation. Some sites in Alaska and the Yukon, however, hint at occupation as long as 25,000 years ago.
c2500 BC	The Inuit arrive from Siberia to occupy Canada's Arctic, believed to be the very last region on earth to be inhabited by humans.
c AD1000	Following the glimpse of an unknown shore by a lost Viking ship, Eric the Red's son, Leif, stumbles over Canada's east coast. Debate is still open as to whether a group of Irish monks led by St Brendan reached the New World in AD 565.
1497	John Cabot, searching for the 'backdoor' route to China, boasts of the cod-rich water around Newfoundland, and sparks mass European interest in the region.
1534	Jacques Cartier leads the first of three expeditions looking for gold and diamonds, but only succeeds in upsetting the natives.
1608	Samuel de Champlain establishes the first European settlement on Canadian soil on the site of today's Quebec City. 'New France' is able to expand and survive thanks to the beaver and its valuable fur. The best fur came from the coldest regions, so pursuit of the beaver led directly to the colonization of the north and west.
1668	The English ship *Nonsuch* sails to the bottom of James Bay, where furs are bought directly from native trappers, cutting out the French middlemen. Two years later, the Hudson's Bay Company (HBC) is founded and given exclusive trading rights over the vast Rupert's Land. At its peak, it would control nearly three million square miles of Canadian territory, almost a 12th of the earth's land surface.
1730s	Pierre de La Vérendrye is the first explorer to push west of the Great Lakes and the Canadian Shield into the great central plains.
1763	In the Treaty of Paris, France cedes control of almost all their North American lands to the British, ending a battle for supremacy that had lasted over 150 years.
1770s	The Russians, the Spanish and the English (in the form of Captain James Cook) start trading in otter pelts with West Coast natives such as the Haida. The sea otter is consequently hunted to the brink of extinction. Captain George Vancouver starts extensively charting the coast, but makes no attempt to settle, and only stays one night on the spot that will come to bear his name.

1775	Following the American Revolution, the United States attempts to take Québec by force. They are resisted, and the attempt degenerates into a fiasco. As historian Henri Bourassa later put it: "We had to choose between the English of Boston and the English of London. The English of London were farther away and we hated them less".
1793	Working for the fur-trading North West Company, Alexander Mackenzie forges across the Rocky Mountains to the Pacific Ocean, leaving Canada's most famous bit of graffiti on a boulder near Bella Bella: "Alexander Mackenzie, from Canada, by land, 22nd July 1793".
1805-1808	Explorer Simon Fraser establishes four forts in Alberta and British Columbia, then battles his way through the Fraser Canyon ("A place where no human should venture"), eventually following his namesake river to the Pacific, believing it to be the Columbia.
1811	David Thompson finally manages to follow the Columbia River to the Pacific, only to find that the Americans have beaten him by a few weeks. He has, however, succeeded in founding a series of important trading posts along BC's winding rivers (including the one named after him).
1827	James Douglas, working for the HBC, establishes Fort Langley near today's Vancouver. He will go on to establish Fort Victoria in the 1840s on a site which he calls "a perfect Eden".
1846	Following an attempted land-grab by the USA, the Treaty of Oregon establishes the border along the 49th parallel. As a consequence, the HBC relocates its western HQ to Fort Victoria.
1858	The discovery of gold in the Fraser Valley attracts over 25,000 stampeders, precipitating the creation in 1866 of a crown colony called British Columbia.
1861	Construction of the Cariboo Wagon Road to aid gold prospectors is swiftly rewarded by a major strike at Barkerville, which soon becomes the continent's largest settlement north of San Francisco with the arrival of 100,000 hopefuls. The road also opens up the grassland valleys and rolling basins of the interior plateau to ranching.
1871	British Columbia joins the Confederation of Canada, on the condition that a wagon trail is built to link the Pacific with the prairie hub of Winnipeg. They are promised instead a transcontinental railway.
1874	Following the infamous Cypress Hills Massacre on the Alberta/Saskatchewan border, a detachment of 300 North West Mounted Police (NWMP), forerunners of today's Royal Canadian Mounted Police (RCMP) or 'Mounties', undertake a legendary 800-mile 'March West' to Alberta.
1885	The last spike of the Canadian Pacific Railway (CPR) is driven home. Crossing 5000 km of forbidding terrain to become the longest railway on earth,

Essentials About the region A sprint through history

skirting the edge of bankruptcy on several occasions, and costing thousands of lives, this "act of insane recklessness" stands as a supreme marvel of modern engineering and sheer audacity. In the words of historian Will Ferguson: "Ours was a country forged not in revolution but in a landscape traversed. Ours was a victory over sheer geography".

1889 Estimated numbers of bison on the prairies have fallen from 60 million in 1800 to 800. Ravaged by foreign diseases, half-starved through want of buffalo, and denied their traditional way of life, the remnant of the once-proud Plains Indians is coerced and cajoled into signing a series of numbered treaties that transfer their land rights to the Confederation in return for life on reservations.

1890s Following the success of Father Pandosy's apple trees, orchards are planted throughout the Okanagan Valley. Gold, silver, copper and lead are discovered around Kootenay Lake. The CPR build a line over the Crowsnest Pass to extract coal from Fernie, the Kettle Valley Railway is built eastwards from Hope, and the Dewdney Trail is blazed along much of today's Highway 3.

1896 A lucky strike on a tributary of the Klondike River leads to a stampede to the most productive goldfields of all time near today's Dawson City. Two years later the Yukon Territory is created to assert Canadian sovereignty over the region.

1907-1914 Construction of the Grand Trunk Pacific Railway from Edmonton to the Pacific Coast through the Upper Fraser, Bulkley and Skeena valleys, greatly boosts the importance of sawmill centres such as Prince George.

1917 Following the accomplishments of Canadian soldiers in the First World War, most famously at Vimy Ridge, British prime minister Robert Borden demands that the dominions be given full recognition as "autonomous nations of an Imperial commonwealth".

1920s The Indian Act following the First World War aims at complete assimilation, forcing natives to relinquish all rights and status. Racked by foreign diseases, restricted to reserves, deprived of their traditional hunting grounds, taught in schools where they are discouraged from speaking their own languages, forbidden to conduct ceremonies, and denied basic rights such as a vote, Canada's First Nations appear to be a dying breed.

1930s Canada is one of the countries hit hardest by the Great Depression. Simultaneously, the whole plains region becomes a dust bowl, afflicted with dirt storms, darkened skies and plagues of grasshoppers. As national income falls by 50% and unemployment rises to 27%, many of the homeless gravitate towards the warmer weather of Vancouver, where they set up residence on Hastings Street indefinitely.

1946 Having seen its troops used as cannon fodder by the British in the Second World War, Canada emerges as one of the richest nations on earth. While the Citizenship Act defines the people of Canada as Canadian citizens rather than British subjects, discriminatory immigration laws are set up to preserve "the fundamental character" of the country, making it very hard for blacks, Arabs, Asians and Jews to get in.

1956   At the same time as US-controlled radar lines stretch across Canadian territory – which, as one Soviet ambassador put it, is "the ham in the Soviet-American sandwich" – Canadian diplomat (and later Prime Minister) Lester Pearson earns the Nobel Peace Prize by almost single-handedly defusing the highly explosive Suez Crisis.

1957-1962   Under the leadership of Saskatchewan-born John Diefenbaker, Canada's first female cabinet minister and first native senator are appointed. Native Canadians are granted the vote, and the TransCanada Highway is completed.

1968-1984   Canadian politics is dominated by the charming, fiercely intellectual, free-spirited figure of Liberal Pierre Elliott Trudeau.

1987   Conservative Prime Minister, Albertan Brian Mulroney, proposes the Free Trade Agreement with the US, removing almost every trade barrier between the countries. One US trade representative says: "The Canadians don't understand what they have signed. In 20 years they will be sucked into the US economy".

1987   The Sechelt Inlet Band become the first native group in Canada to be granted self-government within their own reserve lands.

1993-2003   Canadian politics is dominated by Liberal Jean Chretien.

1995   The perennial issue of two warring nations reaches its apotheosis when the separatist Parti Québecois (PQ) holds a referendum in Quebec. The nation holds its breath as 50.6% of québecois vote against separation.

1999   The UN Human Rights Committee rule that Canada is in violation of international law in its treatment of aboriginal rights. The new territory of Nunavut is created. More than twice the size of BC, it covers two million sq km, about a fifth of Canada's land mass. It is the first time any single First Nations group will have a majority presence in a provincial or territorial government.

2000   In June, the UN declares Canada the best country in the world in which to live, for the seventh year running.

2003   Paul Martin replaces Jean Chretien as leader of the Liberal party, which wins a federal election (again) making him Canada's new prime minister.

2005   Federal elections are called in the wake of the 'sponsorship scandal'. Paul Martin's minority Liberal government is brought down in a vote of no confidence. Gordon Campbell is re-elected as Liberal prime minister of BC.

2006   Following federal elections in January, the Conservatives, led by right-wing Stephen Harper, form the weakest minority government in Canadian history, ending 12 years of Liberalism.

5 best

Places to see First Nations art

UBC Museum of Anthropology, Vancouver ›› *p62*
Royal BC Museum, Victoria ›› *p103*, Swans Pub ›› *p114*
   and Hill's Native Art ›› *p115*
Haida Gwaii Museum ›› *p244* and Gwaii Haanas National Park ›› *p247*
'Ksan Historical Village, Old Hazelton, Northern BC ›› *p241*
Glenbow Museum, Calgary ›› *p273*

Essentials About the region First Nations culture

First Nations culture

Before the arrival of the Europeans, the aptly named 'First Nations' occupied the whole of the North American continent and 50 different languages were spoken in Canada alone. The **Pacific Northwest** was by far the most densely populated area in Canada when the Europeans arrived, with about half of the country's inhabitants. The **West Coast** nations found their ultimate expression in the fiercest, wealthiest, most extravagant and artistically gifted nation of all: the **Haida** of Haida Gwaii in Northern BC, see p41.

West Coast society

Thanks to a mild climate and an abundant supply of food and materials, the coastal people were able to evolve into rich and complex societies. Extended families of 50 or more lived in elaborately carved cedar longhouses, divided by hanging mats, with communal fires and cooking areas. Outside stood tall cedar poles covered in rich symbolism that declared the owners' clan affiliations and flaunted their wealth. People wore weavings, furs, leather footwear and exquisite jewellery and travelled in long dugout canoes. They lived without agriculture, fashioning equipment to catch salmon, harpooning seals and porpoises, hunting deer and elk, snaring birds, gathering shellfish, fruit, berries, roots, and mushrooms.

Coastal First Nations had a complex social system that divided people into two clans: Eagle and Raven among the Haida, Crow and Wolf in many other nations. Marriage within a clan was

Pow wows are a celebration of First Nations culture, and a great opportunity to experience native dancing and traditional dress.

Traditional methods are still used to make crafts, such as baskets.

considered incestuous, so Eagles would seek Ravens and vice versa. In this way there were always ties between clans and between people from distant places. Descent was through the female line, so for a chief to keep his property within the clan, it had to be passed on to his sister's sons.

West Coast natives were (and still are) a fun-loving people who enjoy gambling, dancing, story telling, singing and drumming, games, feasts and ceremonies. They would travel long distances to gather and socialize, and today's pow wows are wonderful occasions (see p28). The most famous ceremony of the coastal people was the **potlatch**, a celebration that marked major events, from births, deaths and marriages to the raising of a totem pole.

Northwest Coast art

Objects made in the Northwest Coast traditions are so distinctive as to be instantly recognizable. The primary design element is called the formline – a continuous, flowing, curvilinear line that turns, swells and diminishes in a prescribed manner. Formlines are used for figure outlines, internal design elements and in abstract compositions. Traditionally figures were strongly coloured with primary black lines (charcoal and lignite), secondary red lines (ochres) and tertiary blue-green elements (copper minerals). Pigments were mixed with a medium derived from dried salmon eggs, and paintbrushes were made of porcupine hairs.

For at least 2500 years carvings have been created from wood, stone, horn, copper, bone, antler, leather, ivory and abalone shells. The finest are large-scale works in red cedar, including totem poles, house posts and canoes. Knives, adzes, chisels, gouges and awls were made of stone, shell and beaver teeth. Crests were usually composed of animal images (including imaginary ones like the thunderbird). Families and bands jealously guarded their crests, which were a legacy from the ancestors, acquired in mythic time from supernatural beings. To display a crest of another group is an insult to their integrity and identity.

People of the plains

The stereotypical Hollywood-style image of the painted 'Red Indian' warrior with his eagle-feather headdress, buffalo outfit, horse and rifle is based entirely on the tribes that lived on the Great Plains of central Canada. Of these, the most militant and powerful were the Blackfoot confederacy, who waged almost continual war with the Plains Cree and Assiniboine to the north and east, the Sioux and Crow to the south, and tribes such as the Kootenay and Shuswap who occupied the interior valleys of southern BC.

The whole way of life of the Plains Indians depended on the herds of buffalo that roamed the prairies, and they pioneered some ruthlessly efficient means of slaughtering them. The site of Head-Smashed-In-Buffalo Jump (see p337), for example, illustrates how whole herds of bison were tricked into stampeding off the edge of a cliff. Every part of the animal was then used; the meat was eaten fresh, dried on racks, or preserved as pemmican; and the hides were fashioned into clothes, blankets and rafts or stitched together to make and tipis – an ingenious form of dwelling that could be quickly dismantled and carried away when whole villages left to follow the buffalo's migrations. Painting on buffalo leather was the chief mode of artistic expression: tipis were lavishly decorated with naturalistic and geometric motifs, rawhide shields were symbolically painted with guardian spirits that would protect the warrior, and buffalo robes were covered in designs ranging from abstract concentric patterns to representational images.

Mythology

Spiritually the First Nations perceived the whole of nature as interconnected and alive with sacred significance, thus fostering a loving relationship with the earth, and a desire to live off the land without destroying it. Rich and complex mythologies were passed on orally from one generation to the next, providing the spiritual and social foundation of the group, imbuing existence with meaning, and helping each individual through the natural trials and rites of life.

Most of these instructive, frequently humourous, and often profound stories involve symbolic animals such as the bear or wolf. The most important character of all is the raven or crow. After the great flood, Raven the Creator, having gorged himself on shellfish left by the receding water, looked around the deserted beach to find someone to play tricks on. He discovered the remnant of the human race hiding in a clam shell on Rose Spit, Haida Gwaii, and coaxed them out using his voice. At first he amused himself with these new playthings but then he helped them to build their culture. A sculpture of the scene by Bill Reid can be seen in the Museum of Anthropology (see p63). Since then, Raven the trickster and transformer has tended to make people laugh at themselves and cry simultaneously, by revealing how human greatness is tempered with pride and vanity, and subject to the whims of fate and chance.

(Left) A young grizzly bear. (Right) A juvenile bald eagle in the Tatshenshini Valley.

(Left) Bighorn sheep grazing in the Rocky Mountains. (Right) A bison (buffalo) near Liard Hot Springs.

Land and wildlife

Landscape and climate

Canada's evolution into one of the world's most prosperous nations is largely thanks to its land and natural riches. Minerals such as gold and coal spurred Europeans to settle in BC from the mid-19th century and a number of boom towns sprung up (many of which were later deserted). Today, 70% of BC's population lives in the lower mainland area, which includes Vancouver and Vancouver Island and represents its commercial, cultural and industrial core.

Western Canada's **coast**, which stretches for more than 7000 km, is rugged and weather-beaten, lined with countless inlets and islands. Almost the entire mainland coastline is inaccessible and uninhabited, cut off from the interior by the formidable barrier of the Coast Mountains, which only three major rivers – the Fraser, Skeena and Stikine – have managed to penetrate. The Pacific Ocean keeps the coastal climate temperate, with average January temperatures of around 0° C – the mildest in Canada – and July averages of about 15-18° C. The western slopes of the Coast Mountains receive ample rainfall, particularly in autumn and winter, and support the largest remaining tracts of temperate rainforest left in the world (along with Alaska), as well as some of the planet's biggest trees, notably the giant Douglas fir, western red cedar, and Sitka spruce.

British Columbia's interior is dominated by the **Canadian cordillera**, a chain of mountains running northwest to southeast, which includes the Columbia Mountains in the south (Selkirk, Purcell, Monashee and Cariboo ranges), the Canadian Rockies to the east, and the Cassiar Mountains in the north. Vegetation of the cordillera is diverse, varying with elevation and latitude.

Sandwiched between the Coast and Cariboo ranges is an **interior plateau** which has an average elevation of about 1000 m, making it a lesser version of Bolivia's altiplano, with a Wild West appearance. The Coast Mountains prevent the ocean's moderating influence from reaching the interior, resulting in an extreme climate of cold winters and hot summers.

The **Columbia Mountains** consist of densely forested slopes and snow-laden peaks, with lakes and rivers filling the valleys, and alpine meadows covered in wild flowers. To the east of these

Background

Beavers

The humble beaver has had a greater impact on Canadian history than any other animal or plant. The reason: beaver underfur is warm, soft and waterproof, the perfect material for making the kind of material used in top hats, which were all the rage until relatively recently. Pursuit of the buck-tooth rodents was one of the leading motives of early colonizers, and led to vast explorations which eventually opened up most of the northwestern hinterland to settlement. In the process, the hapless beaver was reduced to near extinction, from an estimated 10 million at the start of the fur-trade.

mountains, basking in the rain shadows, the Okanagan and Thompson Valleys are so dry as to support desert ecosystems, eerily barren, and perfect for vineyards. The sides of these valleys have a sparse scattering of lonesome pines, interspersed with sage, antelope grass and cacti.

Separating the Columbia and Rocky mountains is the Rocky Mountain Trench, extending 1400 km from Montana to the Yukon. Many of the peaks in the **Canadian Rockies** tower more than 3000 m above sea level, the highest being Mount Robson at 3954 m. On their eastern side, the mountains drop to the Great Plains, a patchwork of flat grain fields, characterized by cold winters and short, cool summers, with predominantly clear skies and low precipitation.

The Yukon is covered by a high sub-Arctic plateau with an average elevation of 1200 m, interrupted by mountains and valleys. The steep mountain ramparts seal it off from the moderating Pacific Ocean, so winters are very cold. Canada's lowest ever temperature (-62.8° C) was recorded northwest of Kluane Lake in 1947. The short summers are hot, with little rainfall. During this time, encouraged by the short window of summer and the long hours of sunshine, the treeless expanses erupt with colourful wild flowers, such as the provincial flower, fireweed.

Wildlife

Some 22,000 grey **whales** migrate past the West Coast every year from March to May. Orca (killer whales) are year-round residents, and can often be seen from the Vancouver Island shore. The world's third largest residence of orca pods is in the Johnstone Strait close to Telegraph Cove. Humpback whales are also frequently seen in the Pacific, and further north are blue, beluga and right whales. **Dolphins** and colonies of **seals** and **sealions** are also frequently spotted along the West Coast. Of the many fish species, the most remarkable is **salmon** (see p240). **Sea otters**, once so numerous, are now only seen in Nootka Sound. Divers come to these shores to see **giant octopuses** and massive **wolf eels**.

Throughout the interior, the animal you're most likely to see is **deer**, of the white-tailed, black-tailed or mule variety. **Elk** are similar, but much larger; an adult bull elk stands about 150 cm tall at the shoulder, weighs 300-350 kg, and sports impressively large antlers, which are grown new each year in just a few months. You're most likely to see them wandering through campgrounds in the Rockies. **Caribou** are similar to the reindeer of Eurasia and both males and females carry antlers. You're most likely to see the barren-ground variety, which follow predictable migration paths seasonally across the Yukon. **Moose** are the largest members of the deer family, growing taller than horses and weighing up to 800 kg in the Yukon.

Black bears are also fairly common. Contrary to common belief, they are shy, timid vegetarians, who want nothing more than to be left alone (see p271). Bears have poor eyesight, relying heavily on well-developed senses of hearing and smell. They are excellent tree-climbers and swimmers, and can run at speeds up to 55 kph. **Grizzly** (or brown) **bears** are almost twice as heavy. They have dish-shaped (concave) profiles, large shoulder humps, and much longer front claws, which prevent them from climbing trees. Feared, misunderstood, and dependent on large territories, the grizzly's range has been steadily eroded and it has now become an endangered species. **White kermode** (spirit) bears are considerably rarer, however.

Throughout the Cordillera, but particularly in the Rockies, you stand a good chance of seeing mountain **goats**, prodigious rock-climbers with long, thin faces, and Dall or bighorn **sheep**. Among the many smaller mammals, a particular favourite is the **marmot**, a large rodent that lives on rockslides in the mountains, sometimes becoming tame and curious. There are plenty more animals out there that you won't see: cougars, lynx and bobcats, wolves and wolverines, musk oxen and polar bears in the north, narwhals and beluga whales in the ocean. The creatures you're most likely to encounter in summer are bugs: mosquitoes, black flies, deer and horse flies (both big enough to take a nasty chunk out of you) and, for a couple of weeks in spring, ticks.

The region today

Several key perennial issues continue to dominate Canadian politics. The issue of native rights, land claims and self-determination; the constant threat that the Parti Québecois will muster enough support to separate from the rest of the country; the inadequate state of the national health system; and the country's ambivalent relationship with its supersized neighbour to the south. In an address to the National Press Club of Washington, DC in March 1969, Trudeau said, "Living next to you is in some ways like sleeping with an elephant. No matter how friendly and even-tempered is the beast...one is affected by every twitch and grunt". Canada continues to be defined by the fact that it is not the US and it is unsure how long it can retain its national identity while so completely overwhelmed by the centrifugal force of US money and ideology. Some 200 million people cross the border every year, and over $1 billion of trade crosses it every day. The latest chapter involved a complete ban by the US on Alberta beef, as the result of one case of mad cow disease, costing the ranching industry millions of dollars; and a bogus (and allegedly illegal) embargo on softwood lumber, which cost BC's forestry industry millions of dollars.

Tourism is the fastest growing industry in Western Canada, as the world catches on to its unequalled expanses of unspoilt wilderness, superb recreation possibilities, and friendly, relaxed people. The process is likely to accelerate when the Winter Olympics hosted by Vancouver-Whistler in 2010 attract the global media spotlight. The challenge for the future will be protecting the wilderness from mining, oil exploration, and irresponsible logging. Having raised the moratorium on grizzly-bear hunting as one of its first acts in power, the Campbell government, clearly valuing short-term gain over long-sighted preservation of the natural beauty that is clearly BC's trump card, is in the process of opening up the province's protected parks to exploitation, the thin edge of an extremely dangerous wedge.

Essentials About the region The region today

Vancouver

Aerial view of Vancouver

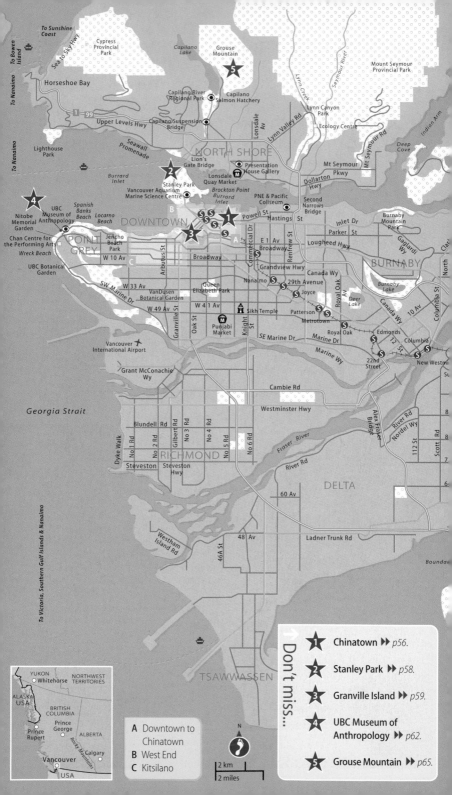

To Sunshine Coast

To Bowen Island

To Nanaimo

Cypress Provincial Park

Horseshoe Bay

Capilano Lake

Grouse Mountain

5

Lynn Creek

Seymour River

Mount Seymour Provincial Park

Capilano River Regional Park

Capilano Salmon Hatchery

Upper Levels Hwy

Capilano Suspension Bridge

Lynn Valley Rd

Lynn Canyon Park

Ecology Centre

Indian Arm

Lighthouse Park

To Nanaimo

Lonsdale Av

Deep Cove

Seawall Promenade

NORTH SHORE

Mt Seymour Rd

Dollarton Hwy

Mt Seymour

Burrard Inlet

2

Stanley Park

Lion's Gate Bridge

Presentation House Gallery

Lonsdale Quay Market

Inlet Dr

Burnaby Mountain Park

UBC Museum of Anthropology

4

Spanish Banks Beach

Locarno Beach

Vancouver Aquarium Marine Science Centre

Brockton Point

Burrard Inlet

PNE & Pacific Coliseum

Second Narrows Bridge

Gaglardi Wy

Nitobe Memorial Garden

DOWNTOWN

B

Powell St

Hastings St

Parker St

North

Columbia St

Chan Centre for the Performing Arts

POINT GREY

Jericho Beach Park

1

3

A

E 1 Av

Broadway

Renfrew St

Lougheed Hwy

BURNABY

Burnaby Lake

10 Av

Wreck Beach

UBC Botanical Garden

Arbutus St

W 10 Av

Broadway

C

Grandview Hwy

Canada Wy

Royal Oak Av

Deer Lake

Columbia St

SW Marine Dr

W 33 Av

Nanaimo

29th Avenue

Joyce

VanDusen Botanical Garden

Queen Elizabeth Park

Canada Wy

Granville St

Oak St

W 49 Av

W 41 Av

Patterson

Metrotown

12 St

Edmonds

Knight St

Sikh Temple

Royal Oak

Marine Dr

Columbia St

Punjabi Market

SE Marine Dr

Marine Wy

22nd Street

New Westmi

Vancouver International Airport

Grant McConachie Wy

Cambie Rd

Westminster Hwy

Alex Fraser Bridge

River Rd

Nordel Wy

112 St

Scott Rd

8

Georgia Strait

Blundell Rd

Dyke Walk

No 1 Rd

No 2 Rd

Gilbert Rd

No 3 Rd

No 4 Rd

No 5 Rd

Fraser River

River Rd

7

RICHMOND

Steveston

Steveston Hwy

No 6 Rd

DELTA

6

60 Av

Westham Island Rd

48 Av

46A St

Ladner Trunk Rd

Boundar

To Victoria, Southern Gulf Islands & Nanaimo

TSAWWASSEN

Don't miss...

★ Chinatown ▶▶ p56.

1

★ Stanley Park ▶▶ p58.

2

★ Granville Island ▶▶ p59.

3

★ UBC Museum of Anthropology ▶▶ p62.

4

★ Grouse Mountain ▶▶ p65.

5

YUKON

NORTHWEST TERRITORIES

Whitehorse

ALASKA USA

BRITISH COLUMBIA

Prince Rupert

Prince George

ALBERTA

Rocky Mountain

Prince George

Calgary

Vancouver

USA

A Downtown to Chinatown

B West End

C Kitsilano

N

2 km

2 miles

Vancouver

All the elements that have allowed Vancouver to top the list of the world's most liveable cities also make Western Canada's gateway a great place to visit. The beautiful Coast Mountains tower over the city, providing a breathtaking backdrop, as well as skiing, hiking, and mountain biking of the highest calibre. The ocean is equally pervasive, offering a lively beach scene, sea wall promenades, and easy access to world-class kayaking, canoeing, sailing, scuba diving and whale watching.

The population is young and vibrant and Vancouver supports more restaurants per capita than any other Canadian city. Closer to Japan than it is to Britain, with 30% of its residents of Asian origin, this is also a meeting place of east and west, affectionately nicknamed 'lotus land'.

Vancouver's distinctive neighbour-hoods, burgeoning culinary scene, delightfully eclectic architecture, and numerous parks are major selling points, as is the close proximity to many other prime destinations. Vancouver Island and the Gulf Islands are a short ferry-ride away and the sporting meccas of Squamish and Whistler are just to the north. Closer still are the outdoor pursuits and picturesque harbours of the Sunshine Coast.

Ratings
Culture
★★★★★
Landscape
★★★
Wildlife
★
Activities
★★★★
Relaxation
★★
Costs
$$$$

Vancouver

Vancouver's compact Downtown peninsula contains most of the city's sights, but none compares with the pleasure of discovering its many neighbourhoods and incredibly diverse architecture. Surrounded by water on all sides, and largely undeveloped, Stanley Park is a green oasis, containing some giant trees, and possibly the peninsula's best sight, the Aquarium. South of False Creek, Granville Island is another must, combining a Covent Garden-style market, arts and crafts studios and galleries, a marina, lots for the kids to do, and a surprisingly good museum. More museums are nearby in Vanier Park, but the most remarkable all is the anthropology museum in Point Grey. South and east Vancouver have some fascinating neighbourhoods, such as Commercial Drive and Main Street, and some beautiful parks and gardens but, if nature calls, the semi-wilderness parks that head up into the giant mountains on the North Shore are hard to resist.

⊘ **Getting there** International and domestic flights and ferries. Buses to all parts of the country, and Seattle.
⊖ **Getting around** Public buses, SkyTrain, SeaBus, taxis.
⊖ **Time required** 2-3 days.
⊚ **Weather** Moderate seasonal temperatures, with lots of rain.
⊖ **Sleeping** 5-star luxury to backpacker hostels.
⊘ **Eating** One of North America's best; West Coast cuisine a speciality.
▲▲ **Activities and tours** Hiking, skiing, biking, diving, kayaking, whale watching...you name it!
★ **Don't miss...** UBC Museum of Anthropology ›› *p62*.

Ins and outs

Getting there

All international flights land at **Vancouver International Airport** (YVR), T604-2077077, www.yvr.ca, 13 km south of Downtown. There is a **Visitor Information desk** on the arrivals floor (level 2), and an airport information desk (which operates a lost-and-found service) in the departure lounge, along with most of the shops. There are also plenty of phones and ATMs, a children's play area and a nursery. Three forms of transport head Downtown from outside the international terminal: the **Airporter Shuttle Bus**, T604-9468866, www.yvrairporter.com, leaves every 15 minutes from 0630-0010, running to Downtown hotels, Canada Place and the bus station ($12 one-way, $18 return); **taxis** operate around the clock, charging $25-30 for the 25-minute trip Downtown; a limousine from **Limojet Gold**, T1800-2788742, www.limojetgold.com, costs $40 for up to eight passengers. All the major car rental agencies are located on the ground floor of the indoor car park. The **city bus** leaves from the domestic terminal and takes 45 minutes, involving a transfer onto bus No 98B. There are also direct services to Whistler and Victoria.

All long-distance buses and trains arrive at the **VIA Rail Pacific Central Station**, 1150 Station St, T604-4828747, a short **SkyTrain** ride from Downtown. **BC Ferries** arrive from Victoria and the southern Gulf Islands at Tsawwassen, about 30 km south of Vancouver. City buses run Downtown from the ferry terminal ($4). Ferries from Nanaimo in central Vancouver Island arrive at Horseshoe Bay, 15 km northwest on Highway 99, with two direct buses Downtown ($3). ⊖ ›› *p92*.

→ **Airport art**

Vancouver International Airport is packed with some wonderful pieces of art. Before clearing the arrivals hall, have a look at the *Spindle Whorl*, a giant version of a traditional Coast Salish art form. Carved out of red cedar, it is suspended from a wall of granite shingles over which water flows to suggest the rivers that are so integral a part of Salish life. On the arrivals level of the international terminal building is a pair of 6-m high *Welcome Figures*, carved from the same red cedar log in the Salish style.

Don't even think about leaving this building without going upstairs to see Bill Reid's exquisite *Spirit of Haida Gwaii*, the *Jade Canoe* (right). This bronze casting with its distinctive green patina is considered to be the masterpiece of the man who reintroduced Northwest Coast native carving to the world (see p63). Behind it is *The Great Wave Wall*, a giant piece of glass art that changes with the light to suggest the ocean.

Getting around

Many of Vancouver's attractions are concentrated within the Downtown peninsula, which is best explored on foot. The public transport system operated by **TransLink** consists of buses, an elevated rail system called the **SkyTrain**, and a passenger ferry called the **SeaBus**. The same tickets are valid for all three. The SkyTrain is the quickest, most efficient way to get around, but its route is of limited use to visitors. Buses run everywhere, but can be slow, and information on routes is rarely displayed. If time is limited, think about taking taxis. A couple of private mini-ferries also ply the waters of False Creek. ❸ ▸▸ *p92*.

Best time to visit

As with most of Western Canada, there is little doubt that summer is the best time to visit Vancouver, unless you're looking for winter sports. Temperatures get high but not uncomfortably so (average 21.7°C), Vancouver's lively residents take to the beaches, parks and mountains, and a string of great festivals keep the party spirit flowing.

Climate

Vancouver is a rainy city, with an average of 170 days of precipitation per year. Since the local topography involves a jump from sea level to mountains within a few kilometres, plus close proximity to the Pacific Ocean, the Georgia Strait, and the mountains of Vancouver Island and Washington's Olympia Range, it's not surprising that the weather here is unpredictable. Forecasts are definitely not to be trusted. Having said that, a warm Pacific Ocean current combined with a strong airflow originating near Hawaii help make Vancouver's climate the mildest in Canada. Spring flowers start blooming in early March, and winter snowfalls are rare enough to throw the city's motorists into confusion. For these reasons Vancouver has been called the Canadian city with the best climate and the worst weather.

Vancouver Ins & outs

Downtown to Chinatown

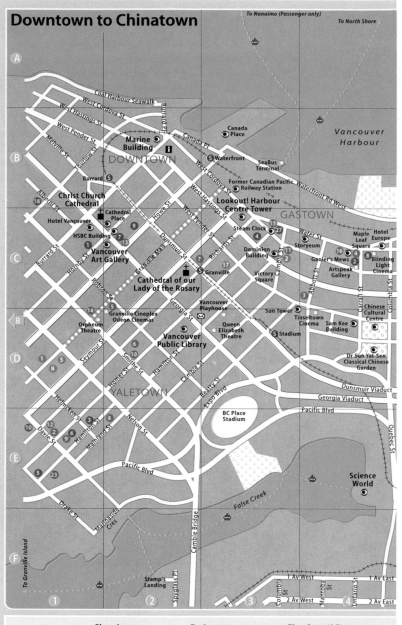

To Nanaimo (Passenger only)
To North Shore

Coal Harbour Seawalk
West Cordova St
West Hastings St
West Pender St

Canada Place

Marine Building

DOWNTOWN

Waterfront
West Cordova St
SeaBus Terminal

Burrard
Former Canadian Pacific Railway Station

Christ Church Cathedral
Cathedral Place
West Hastings St

Lookout! Harbour Centre Tower
GASTOWN

Hotel Vancouver
Steam Clock
Water St
Maple Leaf Square
Hotel Europe

HSBC Building
Storyeum

Dominion Building

Vancouver Art Gallery
Gaoler's Mews
Blinding Light Cinema

Granville
Richards St
Victory Square
Artspeak Gallery

Cathedral of our Lady of the Rosary

Vancouver Playhouse
Sun Tower
Chinese Cultural Centre

Granville Cineplex Odeon Cinemas
Georgia St
Queen Elizabeth Theatre
Tinseltown Cinema
Sam Kee Building

Orpheum Theatre
Vancouver Public Library
Stadium

Dr Sun Yat-Sen Classical Chinese Garden

YALETOWN
Dunsmuir Viaduct
Georgia Viaduct

BC Place Stadium
Pacific Blvd

Pacific Blvd

Science World

False Creek

To Granville Island
Stamp's Landing
Marinaside Cres
Cambie Bridge

Vancouver Harbour

Waterfront Rd West
Carrall St
Quebec St

1 Av West
Columbia St
Manitoba St
Ontario St
1 Av East
2 Av West
2 Av East

N

200 metres
200 yards

Sleeping
Cambie Hostel Gastown
& Cambie Pub 2 C3
Comfort Inn Downtown 5 D1
HI Vancouver Central 1 D1
Patricia 13 C6
SameSun Backpacker
Lodge 8 D1
Victorian 17 C3

Eating
Bacchus 1 C1
Blake's 2 C4
Blue Water Café & Raw Bar 3 E1
Blunt Bros 4 C3
Brix 6 E1
Café Ami 7 C2
Café Dolcino 8 C4
Coast 5 E1
DIVA at the Met 9 C2

Elbow Room 10 E1
Hon's Wun-Tun House 15 D5
Joe Forte's Seafood &
Chop House 18 B1
Rodney's Oyster House 23 E1
Water Street Café 27 C3

Bars & clubs
Alibi Room 1 C5
Cambie 11 C3

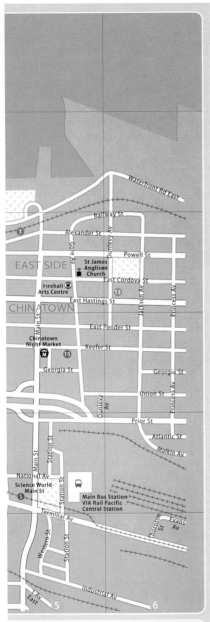

Vancouver's main tourist office is the **Visitor Information Centre** ⓘ *Plaza Level, Waterfront Centre, 200 Burrard St, T604-6832000, www.tourismvancouver.com; mid-May to Sep daily 0800-1900; Oct to mid-May Mon-Fri 0830-1700, Sat 0900-1700.* Staff are friendly and extremely efficient, and the range of facilities is excellent. A broad range of literature is available on the city and province, as well as illustrated details of hotels and B&Bs, travel information, a reservation service, currency exchange, and branches of **Ticketmaster**, through which tickets for most events are available, and **Tickets Tonight** which has half-price same-day tickets, see p81. For up-to-date listings and information, there are three magazines: *Official Visitors' Guide, Where Vancouver*, and *Visitors' Choice Vancouver*. For nightlife and entertainment listings with a more streetwise angle, pick up a free copy of the *Georgia Straight*.

Downtown 🍴🎧🍸 ⇒ *pp68-95*.

In keeping with its status as the heart of one of the world's youngest cities, Vancouver's Downtown presents the visitor with a fine example of postmodern aesthetics; a constantly evolving hotchpotch of architecture, where sleek glass-and-chrome skyscrapers rub shoulders with Gothic churches, Victorian warehouses, and a handful of curiosities. The best way to appreciate this jamboree bag is on foot, so the peninsula is presented here as a walk, starting at the visitor information centre, following an anticlockwise circle around Downtown, Yaletown, Chinatown, East Side and Gastown, then shooting north through the West End to Stanley Park.

Canada Place and around

Built to resemble an ocean liner, with five giant white masts rising from its 'deck', **Canada Place** begs comparisons with Sydney's famous opera house. The main terminus for Vancouver's thriving cruise-ship business, it also as an **IMAX theatre** ⓘ *T604-6822384, www.imax.com/vancouver, $11, $9 child*, at the

Vancouver Sights

Crush 12 *E1*
DV8 2 *E1*
Element Sound Lounge 13 *C2*
Honey Lounge, Milk &
 Lotus Sound Lounge 3 *C4*
Irish Heather 4 *C4*
Lennox 5 *C2*
Lucy Mae Brown 6 *D2*
Plaza Club 14 *D1*
Railway Club 7 *C2*

Section(3) 8 *E2*
Shine 15 *C3*
Soho 9 *E1*
Sonar 16 *C4*
Subeez Café 10 *D2*

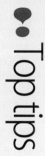

Top tips

Orientation

Unlike most North American cities, Vancouver's Downtown streets have names rather than numbers, making orientation more tricky. If in doubt, remember that the mountains are always north. Block numbering is divided into east and west by Ontario Street, which runs in a north-south direction just east of the Downtown core. So the address 39 W Broadway is in the block immediately west of Ontario, whereas 297 W 4th Av would be in the third block west. Unlike most cities built on a grid, the numbers of avenues in Vancouver do not correspond directly to block numbers. To work out the block number from a numbered avenue, add 16. So numbers between 18th and 19th Avenue will start at 3400.

back. Opposite the visitor information centre is the magnificent **Marine Building**, the British Empire's tallest building for more than a decade after its completion in 1930, and described by Sir John Betjeman as "the best art-deco office building in the world". In keeping with the architects' vision of "some great crag rising from the sea", the relief frieze around its base and the brass surroundings of its double revolving doors are dotted with marine flora and fauna. The art deco façade is decorated with panels illustrating the history of transport. Over the main entrance, Captain Vancouver's ship *Discovery* is seen on the horizon, with Canada geese flying across the stylized sunrays. The lobby is designed to resemble a Mayan temple.

Up the road at 601 West Cordova Street is the old **Canadian Pacific Railway (CPR) Station**. Built in 1914, this neoclassical beaux-arts-style building with its arches and white columned façade is now a terminus for the SeaBus and the SkyTrain. The 1978 restoration retained many features of the original interior such as the high ceilings, woodworking and tile floor. Almost opposite is the **Lookout! Harbour Centre Tower** ⓘ *555 West Hastings St, T604-6890421, www.vancouverlookout.com, daily 0900-2100, $12, $5 child, hourly guided tours included*, with its flying-saucer-shaped top level. No longer the tallest building in BC, the observation deck here still gives the best close-up 360° views of the city, particularly striking at sunset on a clear day. In 50 seconds, glass-walled elevators on the outside of the building whisk you up the 167 m. From up there it is much easier to get a feeling for the layout and architecture of the city. The ticket is expensive but allows as many visits on the same day as you wish.

Vancouver Art Gallery and around

Vancouver Art Gallery ⓘ *750 Hornby St, T604-6624700, www.vanartgallery.bc.ca; Fri-Wed 1000-1730, Thu 1000-2100, Oct-May closed Mon; $15, children under 12 free, suggested donation of $5 on Thu evenings*, occupies an imposing neoclassical marble building designed by Francis Rattenbury in 1910 as Vancouver's original courthouse, and renovated in 1983 by Arthur Erickson. Of the 7000 works in its collection, only the **Emily Carr Institute** is a permanent fixture, but this justifies a visit in itself. The world's largest collection of works by this prominent Victoria artist (see p104) are accompanied by a video about her life. The four spacious floors are dedicated to temporary exhibitions, which tend to be contemporary and hit-and-miss, but potentially involve some top names (Picasso and Rodin in 2005). One of these will provide the focus for curator's tours on Sunday at 1400, discussions in the **Philosophers' Café** on Thursday at 1900, and the Open Studio, where visitors of all ages are given material to create their own related pieces of art. There are also art courses and occasional concerts. The gallery shop is a great place for buying original crafts.

Hotel Vancouver across the road is one of the city's most distinctive landmarks. A typical
example of the grand hotels erected across Canada by the Canadian Pacific Railway, this hulking
Gothic castle sports a striking green copper roof, gargoyles, some fine relief sculpture, and an
admirably opulent interior. Dwarfed by the surrounding modern giants, **Christ Church
Cathedral** (finished in 1889) is Vancouver's oldest surviving church. Built in Gothic Revival style,
this buttressed sandstone building features a steep gabled roof, some impressive pointed-arch,
stained-glass windows, and some splendid interior timber framework. Next door is **Cathedral
Place**, a staggered glass-and-granite edifice with fine details etched into its stone, a roof that
clearly pays homage to the Hotel Vancouver opposite, and a neo-Gothic lobby full of art deco
features that leads to a lovely grassy courtyard. Opposite, the **HSBC Building** ① *Mon-Thu 0800-
1630, Fri 0800-1700*, has a towering atrium lobby containing the world's largest pendulum, and
one of Vancouver's best unofficial art galleries (free). It's also a relaxing place to stop for a coffee.

Robson Street is Vancouver's undisputed shopping focus, and Granville is the heart of
the justly named **Entertainment District**: the junction of these two busy streets is the
unofficial pivot of this bustling city.

Yaletown and the Public Library

A small triangle of land to the south, hemmed in by False Creek and Homer and Nelson streets,
Yaletown was once Vancouver's rowdy warehouse district, with more saloons per acre than
anywhere else in the world. Recently, these massive old brick buildings have been converted
into spacious apartments and trendy bars and restaurants. Many of these tread a thin line
between panache and pretentiousness, and the whole zone needs time to mellow into a
genuine sense of style, but it's still a fascinating area to explore, especially at night.

The curving walls and tiered arches of **Vancouver Public Library** bear a resemblance to
the Roman colosseum, whatever architect Moshe Safdie might say. Used to striking effect in the
Arnold Schwarzenegger film *The Sixth Day*, this postmodern masterpiece, classical and futuristic
in equal measure, contains a pleasant shop-filled atrium spanned by elegant bridges. Nearby is
the Gothic Revival **Cathedral of our Lady of the Rosary**, built in the late 1880s with
asymmetrical towers, a vaulted ceiling, and some decent stained-glass windows.

Vancouver Sights

(Left) The art deco façade of the Marine Building. (Right) The postmodern Public Library.

The Alcan Dragon Boat Festival in June involves a weekend of racing and cultural activities on False Creek.

BC Place and Science World

Just east of Yaletown is the vast air-supported dome of **BC Place Stadium**. From behind here, a ferry runs across False Creek to another of Vancouver's unusual structures, a giant silver golf ball that makes a suitably futuristic venue for **Science World** ⓘ *1455 Quebec St, T604-4437440, www.scienceworld.bc.ca; Mon-Fri 1000-1700, Sat-Sun 1000-1800; $14.50, $10 child, $19.50/$15 with Omnimax; SkyTrain, bus No 3 or 8 on Granville or Hastings, or No 19 on Pender*. Most of the interesting stuff is in the **Main Gallery**, where a wealth of interactive, mindbending and thoroughly educational exhibits will keep anyone entertained for at least a couple of hours. The **Kidspace Gallery** has lots of hands-on stuff for younger children, while the **Sara Stern Search Gallery** does a good job of making environmental lessons fun. With its 27-m diameter dome screen and 10,000-watt wraparound speakers, the **Alcan Omnimax** theatre has the edge over even the giant IMAX. Shows dealing with science, nature and adventure last 40 minutes.

Chinatown

In keeping with its east-meets-west persona, Vancouver's bustling Chinatown is the third biggest in North America after New York and San Francisco. The restaurants here are as authentic as you'll ever find outside China. The streets are lined with noisy shops selling the kind of weird and wonderful ingredients only the Chinese would know how to cook (look out for the geoducks). An experience not to be missed is the open-air **night market** ⓘ *200 Keefer St and East Pender; summer only, Fri-Sun 1830-2300*. Tours of the district are offered by the **Chinese Cultural Centre** ⓘ *555 Columbia St, T604-6588865, www.cccvan.com, Jun-Sep 1000-1400, $10, $2.50 child*, and inevitably include the disappointing **Sam Kee Building**, aka 'Slender on Pender'. The story goes that when the city appropriated most of Chang Toy's 30-ft lot for street widening, his neighbour expected to get the remaining 6 ft at a bargain price, but to frustrate him Toy constructed the world's skinniest building.

Infinitely more worthwhile is **Dr Sun Yat-Sen Classical Chinese Garden** ⓘ *578 Carrall St, T604-6623207, www.vancouverchinesegarden.com, May to mid-Jun 1000-1800, mid-Jun to Aug 0930-1900, Sep 1000-1800, Oct-May 1000-1630, $8.75, $7 child, bus No 19 or 22 east on Pender*, the first authentic Ming classical garden built since 1492, and the first ever outside China. Created by 52 experts from Suzhou, this is a carefully planned realm of symmetry, simplicity and symbolism, where buildings, rocks, water and plants recreate a microcosm of the world. There are walls within walls, courtyards within courtyards, pavilions, bridges and galleries. Hourly guided tours, included with admission, are recommended for an understanding of the Taoist principles at work. Music events and art exhibitions are hosted in summer.

East Side

Just a block north of Chinatown is Vancouver's seediest quarter, the East Side. Over a century ago, when the city's first trams connected Gastown to a newly emerging business district along Granville, Hastings Street entered a decline that has led to its current rating as Canada's lowest-income postal district. The corner with Main in particular has become notorious as a meeting place for Vancouver's homeless and drug addicts. Some of the last remaining examples of neon have survived here from an era when Vancouver had 18,000 such signs. There are also a couple of interesting buildings. In 1910, the distinctive French classical-style **Dominion Building** at 207 West Hastings was the British Empire's tallest and most modern structure. Two years later, its record height was topped by the nearby **Sun Tower** at 100 West Pender. Opposite the Dominion Building is **Victory Square**, now run-down and nicknamed 'Pigeon Park'. Just east of Main, on Cordova, is the **Firehall Arts Centre**, and **St James Anglican Church**, which combines touches of the Romanesque, Gothic, Byzantine and modern.

Gastown

Keep walking north and you arrive in **Gastown**, site of Vancouver's first industry and, maybe more importantly, the saloon of 'Gassy' Jack Deighton, after whom the district was named. One of Vancouver's favourite historic characters, he is remembered for rowing across the Burrard Inlet and offering a bunch of thirsty workers at Stamp's Mill all the whisky they could drink if they helped him build a bar. Within 24 hours the **Globe Saloon** was finished. A statue of the legendary Yorkshireman standing on a whisky barrel graces the quaint **Maple Leaf Square**. Behind him is the site of his second saloon, along with **Gaoler's Mews**, an attractive little courtyard. Opposite is the thin curved end of the wedge-shaped **Hotel Europe** (1909), the first reinforced-concrete building in Vancouver, and certainly one of its most charming constructions.

Just west of here on Gastown's main drag, Water Street, is the newly opened, ambitious and largely successful **Storyeum** ① *142 Water St, T604-6878142, www.storyeum.com; shows daily every 30 mins 1000-1700, $22, $16 child.* Here the story of British Columbia is presented on a series of seven underground stages by actors dressed as First Nations aboriginals, the first explorers, early settlers and hopeful prospectors swept along by one of the many gold rushes.

Continue along Water Street to see the much-touted **Steam Clock**, which entertains tourists every 15 minutes by tooting and erupting in a cloud of steam. The area is chock-full of tacky souvenir stores; however, some handsome old red-brick buildings and cobbled streets remain, along with some of the city's best antique stores, commercial art galleries, and nightclubs.

West End to Stanley Park ▦⦿❶ ›› *pp68-95.*

West End

The most interesting way to get to Stanley Park is via **Robson Street**, which is lined with trendy boutiques and restaurants, and perpetually thronged with trendsetters, posers and students. It marks the northeast boundary of the **West End**, Western Canada's most densely populated area, whose proximity keeps the Downtown core perpetually buzzing through the night. The rectangle is completed by Denman and Davie streets, whose numerous restaurants and cafés represent a neighbourhood vibe that gains much of its character from the district's large gay community.

Stanley Park is one of the largest urban parks in the world and includes 150-year-old forest, 10 km of sea wall, and many popular attractions.

Most of the area's traditional buildings were replaced with high rises during the 1960s. The best surviving block is **Barclay Heritage Square**, where a park-like setting contains nine historic houses built 1890-1908. One 1893 Queen Anne Revival-style home, furnished in Edwardian style, and attributed to architect Francis Rattenbury, has been converted into the **Roedde House Museum** ⓘ *1415 Barclay St, T604-6847040, www.roeddehouse.org, guided tours only, summer Tue-Fri, 1000-1600, $4, $3 child, tea and tour Sun 1400-1600, $5/4, bus No 5 to Broughton*, and provides an opportunity to see inside one of these buildings.

Stanley Park
ⓘ *T604-2578400, www.vancouverparks.ca. Stanley Park never closes. Isolated trails should be avoided after dark. Bus No 135 daytime Mon-Sat, No 23 or 25 evening or on Sun. Parking $2 hr or $5 day. A free shuttle bus runs right round the park every 15 mins mid-Jun to mid-Sep.*
The peninsula's northwestern tip is dedicated to the 1000-acre Stanley Park. Miraculously, this evergreen oasis has been allowed to remain undeveloped, most of its space filled with second-growth but still giant cedar, hemlock and fir. At the park's entrance is the extensive **Lost Lagoon**, a haven for swans, ducks, geese and the occasional blue heron. The Ecology Society based in the **Nature House** ⓘ *T604-2578544, www.stanleyparkecology.ca, Sat-Sun 0930-1630, summer Tue-Sun 1000-1800*, offers ecological information and useful maps, and organizes

two-hour Sunday discovery walks ($8), birdwatching, and other children's activities. Particularly in summer, the action is focused around the 9-km sea wall, a first-class walk, jog, rollerblade or bike ride, which follows the park's perimeter between a number of viewpoints, notably the popular **Prospect Point**. Equipment can be hired from shops at the north end of Denman Street, where cyclists and rollerbladers begin the anticlockwise circuit. A couple of decent beaches hug the west side, including **Second Beach**, whose facilities include a heated ocean-side swimming pool (T604-2578370). Nearby, the **Rhododendron Garden** shelters a collection of ornamental trees, including azaleas, camellias, and magnolia. The bulk of the park's interior is devoted to shady walking paths, which were once skid roads used by early loggers to drag mighty trees down to the water. Look for the stump of one such giant, known as the **Hollow Tree**. Between this and Third Beach is a living cedar believed to be one of the largest trees (at almost 5 m across) and oldest cedars (roughly 1000 years) in the world.

To protect this central area from overuse, most of the park's attractions are concentrated on the narrow spit that juts out north of the sheltered Coal Harbour. Next door to the Vancouver Rowing Club is an information booth, and base of the one-hour **horse-drawn tours** ⓘ *T604-6815115, www.stanleyparktours.com, mid-Mar to Oct every 20 mins, $22, $13.50 child*. To the north are a **Rose Garden** and the **Malkin Bowl**, home to the **Theatre Under the Stars** ⓘ *T604-7341917, www.tuts.bc.ca, Jul-Aug*. Nearby are the **Aquarium**, a **Water Park**, a **Miniature Railway**, and the **Children's Farmyard** ⓘ *T604-2578531, Apr-Sep daily 1100-1600, Oct-Mar weekends only; railway and farmyard $5, child $2.50*. Further round the shore of Coal Harbour, past the Royal Vancouver Yacht Club, is **Brockton Point**, which has a picturesque old lighthouse and a decent stand of Kwakiutl and Haida totem poles. At the eastern point is the 9 O'clock Gun, a cannon that has been fired at that hour every evening since a century ago, when it signalled the end of the day's legal fishing.

Vancouver Aquarium Marine Science Centre ⓘ *T604-6593474, www.vanaqua.org, daily, summer 0930-1900, winter 1000-1730, $17.50, child $9.95, bus No 19 from Georgia*, one of Vancouver's prime rainy-day activities, is even better when the sun shines, since the most exciting animals – seals, dolphins and otters – live outside. Even these are utterly upstaged by a pair of giant and graceful white beluga whales that can be watched from an underwater viewing room downstairs, where a wealth of background information includes a video of the female giving birth. It's best to save the belugas till last, though, as the other 60,000 creatures from the world's many seas tend to pale by comparison. Indoor highlights include the Treasures of the BC Coast gallery, with a giant Pacific octopus, coral, anemones, and some eerily beautiful jellyfish; a large collection of handsome frogs; and the Tropic Zone and Amazon Rainforest galleries. Outside, look out for Bill Reid's magnificent bronze sculpture of a killer whale, *The Chief of the Undersea World* (1984).

Granville Island to Point Grey ●🖊️🎒 » *pp68-95*.

Granville Island

When Vancouver was first settled, the waterfront area of False Creek was five times the size it is today. Land has been reclaimed all around the inlet, much of it for Expo '86. Nowhere has this process been more successful than at Granville Island. Originally no more than a sandbar, the area was built up into an industrial zone, then transformed into an attractive yachting, shopping and arts district, a magnet for tourists and locals, with an ambience similar to London's Covent Garden. Countless arts and crafts shops are scattered around, or clustered together in the **Net Loft** or on Railspur Alley. Although Granville Island is always open, most attractions close on Monday. Parking is a nightmare so avoid driving; the ferry ($2) from the Aquatic Centre next to Burrard Bridge is the best way to arrive, or take Bus No 50 from Granville Street and walk.

Looking out over False Creek from the Harbour Centre.

Though not strictly pedestrianized, the island is well geared to aimless strolling. Meander at will, but be sure not to miss the **Public Market** (May to September daily). As well as a mouth-watering collection of international fast food stalls, the place is packed with tempting produce from gourmet breads to seafood and sausages. The building itself is a fine lesson in the renovation of industrial structures, making great use of the natural lighting, large windows and doors, heavy timber and steel. The courtyard outside and adjacent bars are good places to watch the aquatic world float by. Nearby, **Granville Island Brewing Company** ⓘ *1441 Cartwright St, T604-6872739, www.gib.ca*, Canada's first microbrewery, runs 40-minute tours daily at 1200, 1400 and 1600, $9.75, including a decent round of tasters and a souvenir glass.

Close to the road entrance is a **Visitor Information Centre** ⓘ *T604-6665784, 0900-1800*, which provides a *Visitors' Guide* with discount vouchers and a very useful map. There's also a number of sights perfect for children, including the **Kids' Market**, the **Waterpark** – an aquatic play area with multiple slides and a playground, and the **Model Ships and Model Trains Museums** ⓘ *1502 Duranleau St, T604-6831939, www.modelshipsmuseum.ca, www.model trainsmuseum.ca; Tue-Sun 1000-1730; $7.50, child $3.50*. Tucked away in the Maritime Market, these two museums rolled into one represent one of Vancouver's most unexpected delights. Even if you have just a passing interest in models, it's well worth a visit. It includes the world's largest collection of model toy trains and a fabulous O-scale working layout that took 20,000 hours to complete. The extensive collection of model ships and submarines includes several dozen huge one-off pieces that demonstrate an obsessive attention to detail.

Vanier Park

A footpath leads west from Granville Island to Vanier Park, a small but pretty and popular summer hang-out that contains three fairly important sights. Housed in a building whose interesting shape was inspired by the hats of Haida natives, the **Vancouver Museum** ⓘ *T604-7364431, www.vanmuseum.bc.ca, Fri-Wed 1000-1700, Thu 1000-2100, closed Mon in winter, $10, $6 child, with Space Centre $17/$11, bus No 2 or 22 from Burrard then walk or take the ferry from the Aquatic Centre*, has a small collection of artefacts and recreated scenes that tell the story of the city's first explorers and settlers. Often of greater interest are the temporary exhibits that target more unusual aspects of the region's past.

Sharing the same building is the more upbeat **HR MacMillan Space Centre** ⓘ *T604-7387827, www.hrmacmillanspacecentre.com; daily 1000-1700, Sep-Jun closed Mon; $13.50, $9.50 child*. Its collection of interactive exhibits in the Cosmic Courtyard talk you through the Earth's geological composition, the nature of life in space, and the logistics of space travel. The Planetarium hosts a variety of 40-minute shows in the afternoon, and laser shows set to the music of bands like Radiohead and Pink Floyd Thursday to Saturday evenings ($10). Ground Station Canada Theatre hosts video-assisted lectures involving experiments designed to interest kids. Tickets include a 15-minute ride in the Virtual Voyages Simulator. There is also an Observatory (Friday and Saturday, 2200-2300, free).

The front section of the nearby **Maritime Museum** ⓘ *1905 Ogden Av, T604-2578300, www.vmm.bc.ca, Tue-Sat 1000-1700, Sun 1200-1700, summer daily 1000-1700, $8, $5.50 child*, has a distinctive, steep triangular shape because it was built around the RCMP vessel, *St Roch*, which has been lovingly restored to its original 1944 condition. Before exploring this hardy little ship, watch the video about all the firsts it achieved: first to travel the treacherous and long-sought Northwest Passage, a 27-month journey from Vancouver to Halifax; first to make the same trip back via the faster, more northerly route; and first to circumnavigate North America. This is the museum's highlight, but there's much more to see, with lots of artefacts and stories, a fun exhibit on pirates, a hands-on area for children, and some bigger pieces on the lawn outside. There is usually also an interesting guest exhibit.

Kitsilano

Continuing westwards, Vanier Park melds seamlessly into **Kitsilano** (or Kits) **Beach**, the most popular stretch of sand in the city, with great views of English Bay, Downtown and the Coast Mountains, and Vancouver's biggest **Outdoor Pool** ⓘ *T604-7310011, 22 May-12 Sep Mon-Fri 1200-2045, Sat-Sun 1000-2045, $4, $1 child, bus No 2 or 22 south on Burrard to Cornwall then walk*. In the 1960s, Kitsilano was the main focus of Vancouver's subculture. By the 1980s, many of the local hippies had got high-paying jobs, bought and restored their houses, and helped turn Kits into Yuppieville. Reflecting this change, many of the old wooden town houses that used to grace the area have been torn down and replaced by condos. Plenty of character remains, however, and the region's two main drags, West Fourth between Burrard and MacDonald (bus No 4 or 7), and West Broadway between MacDonald and Alma (bus No

Kits Beach has the city's largest outdoor pool and is a haven for sun worshippers in summer.

5 best

Places for kids in Vancouver

Science World ▸▸ *p56*
Vancouver Aquarium Marine Science Centre, Stanley Park ▸▸ *p59*
Model Ships and Model Trains Museums, Granville Island ▸▸ *p60*
HR MacMillan Space Centre, Vanier Park ▸▸ *p61*
Skyride Gondola, Grouse Mountain ▸▸ *p66*

10 or 16), offer some of the city's best browsing strips, with plenty of interesting speciality shops, trendy hair studios, snowboard outlets, and good restaurants. Weekend brunch here is a Vancouver institution, but parking can be a nightmare (try Fifth).

Point Grey

From Kitsilano, Fourth Avenue and the more scenic Point Grey Road lead west to the jutting nose of Point Grey, home to some of the city's best beaches, the University of British Columbia (UBC), some botanical gardens, and Vancouver's best sight, the Museum of Anthropology. On the way is Vancouver's oldest building, **Hastings Mill Store** ⓘ *1575 Alma St, T604-7341212. Mid-Jun to mid-Sep Tue-Sun 1100-1600, otherwise weekends 1300-1600; entry by donation; bus No 9 Broadway or No 4, 7 or 44 to Alma and walk.* Transported from its original Gastown site in 1930, today it houses a small museum with displays of First Nations and pioneer artefacts.

From here, a clutch of beaches and parks run almost uninterrupted around the edge of Point Grey. First of these is **Jericho Beach**, set in a large, very scenic park with a fine youth hostel (see Sleeping p70), a sailing school, and a bird sanctuary. Three unbroken kilometres lead to **Locarno Beach**, a quiet area popular with families, and **Spanish Banks**, which has a beach café and warm, shallow water that's ideal for paddling. From UBC, roughly where Marine Drive meets University Boulevard, about 100 steps lead down through the forest to the 6-km strip of **Wreck Beach**. On a hot day as many as 10,000 sun-worshippers take advantage of its clothing-optional status, while wandering peddlers supply them with cold beers, food, and the ubiquitous BC Bud.

UBC Museum of Anthropology

ⓘ *6393 NW Marine Dr, T604-8225087, www.moa.ubc.ca; summer daily 1000-1700, Tue until 2100; winter Tue-Sun 1100-1700, Tue until 2100; $9, $7 child, free Tue 1700-2100; free tours daily at 1100 and 1400, Tue 1800; bus No 4 or 10 south on Granville then walk, or change to No 42 at Alma; avoid driving as parking is the most expensive in town and is limited to 2 hrs.*

Founded in 1949, and situated on native Musqueam land, the extraordinary UBC Museum of Anthropology is the only attraction in Vancouver that absolutely must be seen. Designed by Arthur Erickson to echo the post-and-beam structures of Northwest Coast First Nations, it contains the world's finest collection of carvings by master craftsmen from many of these Nations, most notably the Haida of Haida Gwaii (Queen Charlotte Islands) and the Gitxsan and Nisga'a from the Skeena River region of Northern BC. Be sure to pick up a *Gallery Guide* at the admissions desk ($1.50). As well as providing a commentary on the exhibits, it gives a brief but excellent introduction to First Nations cultures, the stylistic differences between them, and an overview of their classic art forms.

Sculptures inside are grouped by cultural area, and informatively labelled. Most date from the early to mid-19th century, but an encouraging number are recent including several exceptional works by the late master Bill Reid, such as *Bear* (1963), *Sea Wolf with Killer Whales*

Bill Reid

Born in Vancouver to a Haida mother and Scottish-American father, Bill Reid (1920-1998) was a teenager before he was told about his native heritage. Though he only began investigating Haida arts at the age of 31, he was clearly to the manner born, quickly gaining international recognition for his carvings and castings. In the words of Barry Mowatt, President of Vancouver's Inuit Gallery: "He is the pre-eminent West Coast native artist, who is responsible for re-creation of respect for the art of Northwest Coast people. He is probably the most important and significant native artist ever to have come to the world stage". Anthropologist Edmund Carpenter wrote: "I've followed Bill Reid's career for many years and come to believe that, in some strange way, the spirit of Haida art, once the lifeblood of an entire people, now survives within him, at a depth, and with an intensity, unrelated to any 'revival' or 'preservation', but deriving from primary sources and leading to daring innovations". You can see Bill Reid's work in Vancouver at the airport, outside the aquarium and, above all, in the UBC Museum of Anthropology.

Vancouver Sights

(1962), a 7.5-m inshore cedar canoe (1985) and, housed in a natural light-filled rotunda, his most exquisite masterpiece (above), *The Raven and the First Men* (1980). Behind the Great Hall are a number of outdoor exhibits, including a large Haida family dwelling and a collection of 10 poles. The Visible Storage galleries make over 14,000 smaller carvings accessible to the public: about 40% of the museum's permanent collection. It's hard to do the museum justice in one visit, especially as a bit of energy should be reserved for the small gift shop in the lobby, which is packed with splendid books, carvings, jewellery and prints.

Nitobe and UBC Botanical Gardens

A short stroll from the museum is the **Nitobe Memorial Garden** ⓘ *T604-8229666, www.nitobe.org, daily 1000-1700, closed weekends in winter, $4, $8 with UBC gardens*, an authentic Japanese tea garden. It is a subtle experience, with every rock, tree and pool playing its part in the delicate harmony to create an ambience that encourages reflection and meditation. There are cherry blossoms in spring, Japanese irises in summer, and Japanese maples in autumn. Moving anticlockwise, the garden represents the stages of a person's life.

Commercial Drive is a cosmopolitan yet bohemian area full of cafés, bars and restaurants.

A further 3 km south on Marine Drive are the much more extensive but equally delightful **UBC Botanical Gardens** ① *6804 SW Marine Dr, T604-8223928, www.ubcbotanicalgarden.org, daily 1000-1800, $6 for botanical garden alone, $8 with Nitobe, free tours Wed and Sat 1300, bus No 4 or 10 south on Granville*, the oldest of their kind in Canada. Spread over 30 hectares are a number of expertly maintained themed gardens, such as the Physick Garden, devoted to traditional medicinal plants from 16th-century Europe. The experience is as educational as it is aesthetic, with well-labelled exhibits and regular lectures.

South and east Vancouver ⊜🚹🧍 ›› *pp68-95.*

Neighbourhoods
The broad swathe of Vancouver south of Burrard Inlet is dotted with small, interesting neighbourhoods each with its own particular atmosphere. **South Granville** abounds with antiques stores, private art galleries, boutiques, and cafés. Once known as Little Italy, **Commercial Drive** (bus No 20) still has a number of Italian coffee shops, but has become a much more cosmopolitan area, populated by artists, immigrants and bohemians. There are no 'sights' as such, but it's a fascinating place to wander, eat, drink and people-watch. Main Street south of Sixth Avenue, known as **South Main**, 'SoMa', or 'Uptown' is dominated by trendy, gritty cafés and restaurants, antique and secondhand shops. Further south on Main between 48th and 50th avenues is Vancouver's Indiatown, the **Punjabi Market**. If in the area, seek out (so to speak) the splendid **Sikh Temple** at 8000 Ross Street, another Arthur Erickson special.

Queen Elizabeth Park and VanDusen Botanical Garden
Conveniently close together near Granville, Cambie, and 33rd avenues, South Vancouver's two main pieces of green are both worth a visit. The 53-ha **Queen Elizabeth Park** ① *33rd Av/ Cambie, T604-2578570, Apr-Sep Mon-Fri 0900-2000, Sat-Sun 1000-2100, Oct-Mar 1000-1730, $4.25, $2 child, bus No 15 on Burrard or Robson*, is the former site of two basalt quarries, now converted into ornamental gardens, which make for very pleasant (and free) summer strolling. Along with an extensive rose garden, there is an arboretum said to contain a

specimen of almost every tree found in Canada. Paths lead to Vancouver's highest point (150 m), the peak of an extinct volcano, with good if rather obstructed views of the city below and the wonderfully romantic **Seasons in the Park** restaurant (see Eating p77). Nearby is the **Bloedel Floral Conservatory**, a giant triodetic dome that contains 500 varieties of exotic plants from tropical rainforest, subtropical and desert ecosystems, as well as floral displays that change with the seasons, and about 50 species of free-flying tropical birds.

The 22-ha **VanDusen Botanical Garden** ① *5251 Oak St and 37th Av, T604-8789274, www.vandusengarden.org, Jun to mid-Aug daily 1000-2100, May and mid-Aug to Sep 1000-2000, Apr and late Sep 1000-1800, Oct-Mar 1000-1600, $7.75, $4 child, bus No 17 on Burrard or Pender*, contains over 7500 different plants from around the world, including some rare species. Set around lakes, ponds and waterfalls, and dotted with sculptures, the 40-odd themed gardens are considerably more romantic and contemplative than those at UBC, and they feel bigger. A favourite with children is the Elizabethan hedge maze. In December the gardens host the **Festival of Lights** (see Festivals and events, p85).

North Shore ⊟🍴👤 ►► pp68-95.

The mountainous landscapes, tracts of semi-wilderness, and potential for outdoor pursuits offered by Vancouver's North Shore represent for many people the city's finest feature. The obvious way to get there is on the SeaBus, a lovely inexpensive chance to get out on the water. It leaves from behind the Waterfront SkyTrain in the old CPR building, and docks at **Lonsdale Quay Market**, the North Shore's only real focal point. Local buses continue from here. The glazed and galleried interior of the market, a throwback to 19th-century industrial architecture, is well worth a look.

East from Lion's Gate Bridge

The other main route to the North Shore is from Stanley Park across the **Lion's Gate Bridge**, the British Empire's longest suspension bridge when it was built in 1938, inspired by San Francisco's Golden Gate. Roughly 8 km east of from here, Lynn Valley Road leads to **Lynn Canyon Park** ① *Feb-Nov daily 1000-1700, Dec-Jan closed weekends, exit 19 from Highway 1, bus No 229 from Lonsdale Quay*, 250 ha of relatively unspoilt forest. This was home to the tallest tree ever measured on the planet, a 120-m Douglas fir. The **Ecology Centre**, by the parking zone at 3663 Peters Road, has displays, films, and information about the park, as well as a free map and guided walks. The 68-m suspension bridge that hovers 50 m above the rushing waters of Lynn Creek is free to walk across. Many hiking trails of varying length begin on the other side, including a 15-minute stroll to a wooden footbridge that crosses the creek at Twin Falls.

At the eastern end of the North Shore, Mount Seymour Road climbs steeply up 1000 vertical metres to **Mount Seymour Provincial Park**, passing two stunning viewpoints, both worth a stop. Other than the commercial ski hill, the park's semi-wilderness old-growth forest and sub-alpine wild flower meadows make for some excellent hiking (see p89). **Flower Lake Loop**, a pleasant 1.5-km stroll through bog and ponds, is a good place for spotting birds.

At the North Shore's eastern extremity is **Deep Cove** ① *SeaBus, then bus No 229 to Phibbs Exchange then bus No 211 or 212*, a picturesque spot that has retained the unspoilt feel of a seaside village, and enjoys great views across the bay to snowy hills beyond. As well as prime kayaking and biking, there's a nice green park by the water, a few good restaurants, and the best neighbourhood pub in Vancouver.

Capilano Valley and Grouse Mountain

Almost due north from the Lion's Gate Bridge, Capilano Road runs parallel to the eponymous river, valley, and regional park all the way to the dammed Capilano Lake and beyond to Grouse

Mountain. **Capilano Suspension Bridge** ⓘ *3735 Capilano Rd, T604-9857474, www.capb ridge.com, summer daily 0830-2000, otherwise varying hours from 0900, $24.95, $6.25 child, parking $3, bus No 246 from Georgia, or No 236 from Lonsdale Quay*, is Vancouver's oldest and most vaunted attraction. The current bridge is the fourth to span the 137 m across Capilano River 70 m below, making it the longest and highest suspended footbridge in the world. Beyond a small collection of totem poles, a diminutive First Nations carving shed, and a few photos and artefacts, there is little to justify the entrance fee besides the admittedly astounding natural beauty, and the short-lived excitement of walking across the bridge. The Living Forest interactive exhibition is aimed at children, with lots of displays of dead bugs.

For a free and more genuine taste of the valley's natural beauty, head up the road to the 160-ha **Capilano River Regional Park**, which protects the Capilano River as it heads south to Burrard Inlet, a journey followed by the 7.5-km one-way **Capilano Pacific Trail**, longest of 10 trails through forest of the unmanicured variety. Trail maps are available at the car park or from information centres, and outline a number of pools and other features. The park also contains the **Capilano Salmon Hatchery** (T604-6661790, free), one of the best places to see them run. Information panels tell the extraordinary story of their life.

Grouse Mountain is the most popular and easily reached ski hill on the North Shore, its lights seeming to hang from Vancouver's night-time skyline like Christmas tree decorations. Skiers and sightseers are whisked up to 1100 m above sea level in about eight minutes by the **Skyride Gondola** ⓘ *T604-9809311, www.grousemountain.com, every 15 mins year-round 0900-2200, $30, $11-17 child; SeaBus then bus No 236 from Lonsdale Quay*. At the top are year-round panoramic views, 5-m chainsaw sculptures, a 30-minute multimedia action film in the **Theatre in the Sky**, and all kinds of facilities, including a couple of fine restaurants. In summer there's hiking, mountain biking, paragliding, and horse-drawn carriage rides (the horses also come up in the gondolas); in winter there's downhill and cross-country snowboarding, ice skating, snow-shoeing, and sleigh rides (see Activities and tours, p87). All activities except access to the slopes are included with the gondola ticket.

West from Lion's Gate Bridge

The next park west is **Cypress Provincial Park** ⓘ *Snowphone T604-8789229, www.cypress mountain.com, lift passes $42, $18 child, cross country $15, $8 child, winter-only shuttle bus from*

Walking across Capilano Suspension Bridge is sure to test your head for heights.

The ski hills of Grouse Mountain look out over Vancouver.

Lonsdale Quay or Horseshoe Bay (T604-4197669), whose access road can be seen ascending the mountainous terrain in wide, drunken zigzags. This has been a popular recreation site since the 1920s, and offers the same range of summer and winter activities as Grouse Mountain, though with less extensive facilities and thinner crowds. Some of the North Shore's best hikes are here (see p89), leading to panoramic views that take in the city, Howe Sound, Mount Baker to the southeast, and the Gulf Islands, Georgia Strait and Vancouver Island to the west. There's also a lift-assisted mountain-bike park.

Still further west, the comparatively tiny **Lighthouse Park** (free, bus No 250 from Downtown), is one of the most accessible and best for strolling, and contains some of Vancouver's most rugged forest, including one of the last remaining stands of old-growth Douglas firs. A number of short trails lead to arbutus trees, cliffs and the (out of bounds) Point Atkinson Lighthouse, which has been staffed continuously since 1875.

Highway 1/99 swings north towards Squamish, passing Horseshoe Bay, terminal for ferries to Nanaimo, the Sunshine Coast, and **Bowen Island**. A mere 20 minutes away, the latter offers visitors a quick and easy taste of the Gulf Islands' laid-back atmosphere, its population of 3500 characteristically including a large number of writers and artists. Ferries leave more or less hourly from 0605-2135 with a break for lunch. Just off the ferry landing is the island's main hub, **Snug Cove**. The renovated Union Steamship Company General Store, now houses a **Visitor Information Centre** ① *T604-9479024, www.bowenisland.org*, where you can pick up a free copy of the *Bowen Island Book*, with a map, restaurant and accommodation listings, and activities (also available online). Many people come for the fine boating and kayaking in the sheltered bays that surround this 50-sq-km island. **Mount Gardner** is an excellent 16-km return day-hike that is possible almost year-round (see p89).

Sunshine Coast ⬤🅿🅷🔺🅒🅘 → pp68-95, map p98.

Beginning at Langdale, a short ferry hop from Vancouver's Horseshoe Bay, the strip of Highway 101 optimistically known as the Sunshine Coast is the only major road on the Canadian mainland's Pacific coast. The pretty harbour town of Gibsons Landing, 10 minutes' drive from Langdale, makes a worthwhile day's excursion from the city, but the area is mainly only of interest as a playground for divers, boaters and kayakers.

Gibsons Landing and the Sechelt Peninsula

Gibsons itself is nothing special, but the quarter clustered around the harbour, known as **Gibsons Landing**, is the prettiest community on the Sunshine Coast. Gathered around the **Visitor Information Centre** ⓘ *668 Sunnycrest Rd, T604-8862325, www.gibsonschamber.com*, are a number of worthwhile shops, art galleries, restaurants, an attractive boardwalk, and the **Maritime Museum**, featuring paraphernalia from the long-running TV series *The Beachcombers*, which was set here. There are also plenty of beaches and parks to explore.

The quaint little community of **Roberts Creek**, 10 km further on, has a friendly and laid-back hippy vibe that would appeal to some. Check out, for instance, the incredible Mayan mandala at the entrance to the pier. There is some good-value lodging here, plus beaches and forest.

Many hiking and biking trails criss-cross the **Sechelt Peninsula** to the west, including the 33-km **Suncoaster Trail**, whose foothills offer incredible views, and patches of old-growth forest. The shoreline has some pleasant bays and beaches, of which **Sargeant Bay** is maybe the most scenic, but few places to stay or camp.

Just before the second ferry crossing at Earl's Cove, a right turn leads to the pleasant village of **Egmont**, and **Skookumchuck Narrows Provincial Park**. Here the force of the tidal waters rushing to or from the ocean through a narrow section of the elongated inlet has resulted in a dramatic section of rapids, which kayakers and seals love to surf. The phenomenon is greatly enhanced by the beautiful 4-km trail that leads to some giant second-growth trees.

Powell River

Powell River is the Sunshine Coast's most prominent town, with the majority of its facilities and the best **Visitor Information Centre** ⓘ *4690 Marine Av, T604-4854701, www.discover powellriver.com*. Buses from Vancouver terminate here, and Westview ferry terminal has departures to Comox on Vancouver Island, opening up the possibility of a pleasant circuit back to Vancouver via Nanaimo or Victoria. This is a useful base for outdoor pursuits, and is particularly renowned for its diving. There are plenty of beaches too, three of the best being **Palm Beach**, **Willingdon Beach**, and **Mowat Bay**.

Lund and Desolation Sound Marine Park

Highway 101 ends at the village and marina of Lund, the closest inhabited point to **Desolation Sound Marine Park**. The largest water-access park in BC, with 5666 ha of high land, and 2570 ha of shoreline and water, this is a kayaker's paradise, with countless places to dock and spend the night. As well as paddling, there is ample fishing, hiking and first-class scuba diving, famous for the size of the wolf eel and giant octopus. Petroglyphs can be seen at Walsh Cove.

Savary Island, an 8-km long crescent-shaped clay ridge reached from Lund, is about as remote as the accessible islands get. The north shore is one long white- and grey-sand beach, whose calm, shallow water is the warmest in the Pacific Northwest. There is a restaurant, art galleries, campgrounds, bike rentals at the general store, and kayak rentals (T604-4833223).

⦿ Sleeping

Downtown *p53, map p52*

Many Downtown hotels have surprisingly reasonable rates. Arriving in Vancouver without a reservation is rarely a problem.
A Meridian at 910 Beach, 910 Beach Av, T604-6095100, www.meridianhotel.org. Studios, plus a attractive, open-plan, fully-equipped suites, some with patio/balcony.

Floor-to-ceiling windows take advantage of the great location on False Creek, with views of the water and Granville Market or the city. Continental breakfast.
B Comfort Inn Downtown, 654 Nelson St, T604-6054333, www.comfortinn downtown.com. Long-standing hotel in the heart of Downtown, with attractive and very clean rooms. Continental breakfast and fitness pass included.

C Victorian Hotel, 514 Homer, T604-6816369, www.victorianhotel.ca. One of Vancouver's only standout deals. A renovated 1898 house whose rooms are mostly pretty small, but comfortable, and tastefully decorated in pastel shades with hardwood floors, good art, and nice bathrooms. Continental breakfast.

D Patricia Hotel, 403 E Hastings, T604-2554301, www.budgetpathotel.bc.ca. Housed in a nicely renovated 1914 building enlivened with many plants, the Patricia is surprisingly classy given the seedy area, and certainly the best non-hostel budget option in town. Rooms are simple, clean and comfy, with en suite baths. Some have fine views. Off-season weekly rates available. Staff on duty 24 hrs.

E Cambie Hostel Gastown, 300 Cambie St, T604-6846466, www.cambiehostels.com. Well run and handily situated, the atmosphere of this busy backpacker hostel is somewhat influenced by the popular down-to-earth pub downstairs. Beds are mostly in dorms, plus a few private rooms, all with shared bath. The common room (with TV) is a good place to meet travellers and pick up information. There's a small kitchen, and free coffee and muffin from the excellent bakery next door.

E HI Vancouver Central, 1025 Granville St, T604-6855335. Another great, centrally located, and fairly new hostel offering dorms and private rooms, as well as many facilities: common room, express kitchen (microwaves, no stove) and lockers. They also organize daily activities.

E SameSun Backpacker Lodge, 1018 Granville St, T604-6828226, www.samesun.com. This centrally located, colourful hostel has everything you need: lots of dorms, double rooms with en suite bath, a newly renovated kitchen, 2 large common rooms with sofas, a pool table, a TV room, a licensed bar serving meals, an outdoor patio, internet, laundry, lockers/ storage room and a **Moose** travel desk. Also organizes activities around town.

p57, map p72

A Blue Horizon Hotel, 1225 Robson, T604-6884461, www.bluehorizonhotel.com. Best of a cluster of mid-range hotels on Robson. Rooms are large and plain but well appointed, with balconies and good views. Those with 2 beds ($10 more) sleep 4 and are much bigger. There's a small pool, hot tub, sauna and gym.

E HI Vancouver Downtown, 1114 Burnaby St, T604-6844565, www.hi hostels.ca. Clean and professional hostel on a central but quiet street. 4-bed dorms, and simple private rooms with shared bath. Top-notch facilities include a large kitchen, TV room, library, games room with pool table, laundry, lockers, and dining room. Many cheap activities are arranged. Free shuttle from bus/train station.

Kitsilano *p61, map p70*

A-B Penny Farthing Inn, 2855 6th Av, T604-7399002, www.pennyfarthing inn.com. 2 comfortable, very attractively decorated rooms, and 2 suites, all well equipped, with TV and CD player, en suite or private bath. Guests have their own living room, 3 patios, a garden, and enjoy a large gourmet breakfast.

B-C Mickey's Kits Beach Chalet, 2146 1st Av, T604-7393342, www.mickeys bandb.com. 3 bright and pleasant rooms in a quiet spot close to Kits Beach, with a friendly and helpful host. Breakfast included.

C Graeme's House B&B, 2735 Waterloo St, T604-7321488, www.graemewebster.com. 3 rooms in a pretty heritage house with lots of interesting features plus a deck and a beautiful flower garden. Close to the most interesting section of Broadway.

C-D Between Friends B&B, 1916 Arbutus, T604-7345082, www.betweenfriends-vancouver.com. 3 small but very nice rooms in a classic Kitsilano home close to 4th Av. 1 room has en suite bath, another has a balcony and skylight. Guests share a pleasant sitting room, and the friendly hostess serves up a big breakfast.

E HI Jericho Beach Hostel, 1515 Discovery St, T604-2243208, www.hihostels.ca. Built in the 1930s as barracks for Jericho Air Station, this vast and interesting building is the largest hostel in Canada, with 288 dorm beds and 10 private rooms, all with shared bath. All the usual top-notch facilities are here: a massive kitchen and dining room, TV room, games room, library, laundry, lockers, bike rental. Free or cheap tours, hikes, and activities like sailing. The main factor here, however, is the location: a beautiful and quiet spot right on the beach, but a long way from town. A free shuttle runs frequently to and from the HI Vancouver Central hostel (see p69) and bus station. Take bus No 4 (UBC).

South and east Vancouver *p64*

B Delta Vancouver Airport, 3500 Cessna Dr, T604-2781241, www.deltavancouver airport.com. The nicest place to stay close to the airport, thanks to a riverside location by dozens of scenic little boats, with a pub housed in a small pagoda, and lovely gardens. There's also an outdoor pool, exercise room and restaurant.

B Douglas Guest House, 456 W 13th Av, T604-8723060, www.dougwin.com. 8 fairly large rooms/suites, with elegant decor, and en suite bath in all but 2. Guests share a small common room. Breakfast served in a sun room with patio. One of many B&Bs in an area called Mt Pleasant.

Kitsilano

200 metres
200 yards

Sleeping ◉
Between Friends B&B **1** *B5*
Graeme's House B&B **3** *D2*
HI Jericho Beach Hostel **4** *C1*
Mickey's Kits Beach Chalet **6** *B4*
Penny Farthing Inn **7** *C3*

Eating ◑
Benny's **3** *C3*
Bin 942 **1** *C6*
Bishop's **2** *B3*
Calhoun's **7** *C2*
Eatery **5** *C2*
Feenie's **8** *C3*

Greens & Gourmet **6** *C3*
Lumière **8** *C3*
Naam **10** *B3*
Pastis **13** *B4*
Sophie's Cosmic Café **15** *B5*
Tangerine **16** *B4*

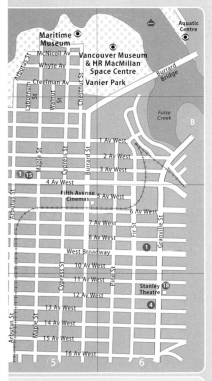

North Shore *p65*

AL Thistledown House B&B, 3910 Capilano Rd, T604-9867173, www.thistle-down.com. This tastefully restored and decorated 1920s heritage home set in lovely gardens has 5 well-equipped en suite rooms, plus a guest lounge and a patio. A full gourmet breakfast is included.

Camping

Capilano RV Park, 295 Tomahawk Av, near Lion's Gate Bridge, T604-9874722. Unattractive but the best located. Facilities include full hook-ups, pool, jacuzzi, playground and games room.

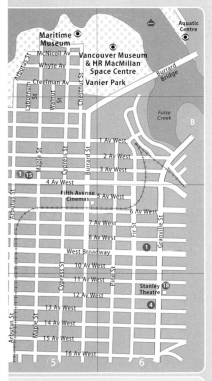

Terra Breads **12** *B4*
Vij's **18** *D6*
West **4** *D6*

Bars & clubs 🎵

Fringe Café **1** *C2*
Lou's Grill & Bistro **2** *C2*

Gibsons Landing and the Sechelt Peninsula *p68*

There are lots of very nice B&Bs in the picturesque harbour of Gibsons Landing, all good value compared to Vancouver prices, many with only 1 or 2 rooms. The information centre has listings, or visit www.bbsunshinecoast.com. Roberts Creek also has plenty of options, and is better value still.

AL-B Lord Jim's Resort Hotel , about 16 km beyond Sechelt on Secret Cove, T604-8857038, www.lordjims.com. There are plenty of resorts dotted along the beaches of the peninsula. This is one of the best: self contained with a fine strip of private beach, cabins with kitchens, kayak and bike rentals, a licensed restaurant, playground and pool. Good for families.

A A Woodland Garden Inn, 1214 Lysander Rd, Roberts Creek, T604-7400322, www.awoodlandgardeninn.com. Perhaps the most romantic of all. 3 gorgeous suites, with private hot tubs, in-room massage, a bottle of champagne, TV/DVD player, chocolates and flowers included in the price. The West Coast-style house is also magnificent, with common areas such as an atrium with pool table, a living room, and a sunroom.

A Bonniebrook Lodge B&B, 1532 Ocean Beach Esplanade, Gibsons Landing, T604-8862887, www.bonniebrook.com. 7 gorgeous suites in an immaculate ocean-front home offering a romantic treat close to Vancouver. Suites are exquisitely furnished, with their own jacuzzi tubs, fireplace and sundecks, and either right on the beach, or with views. A gourmet breakfast in their expensive, highly-praised restaurant is included.

B OceanLook B&B, 1371 Gower Point Rd, Gibsons Landing, T604-8863777, www.oceanlookbandb.com. This new custom-built West Coast-style wooden home is lovely, set within beautiful landscaped grounds, and full of stylish touches such as a river rock fireplace, and locally produced art. 2 plush suites offer

Vancouver Listings

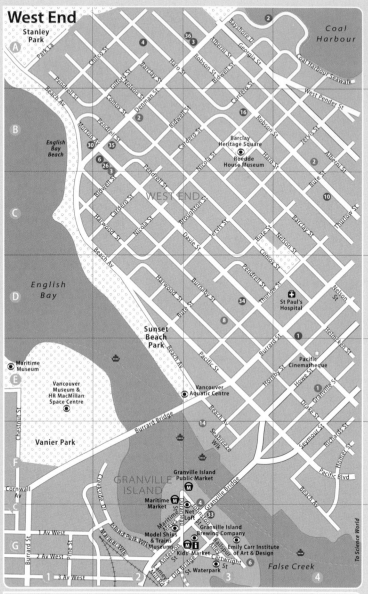

West End

Stanley Park

Coal Harbour

English Bay Beach

WEST END

Barclay Heritage Square
Roedde House Museum

English Bay

Sunset Beach Park

St Paul's Hospital

Maritime Museum

Vancouver Museum & HR MacMillan Space Centre

Vancouver Aquatic Centre

Pacific Cinematheque

Vanier Park

Burrard Bridge

Granville Island Public Market

GRANVILLE ISLAND

Maritime Market

Net Loft

Granville Island Brewing Company

Model Ships & Trains Museum

Kids' Market

Emily Carr Institute of Art & Design

Waterpark

False Creek

To Science World

200 metres
200 yards
N

Sleeping 🛏

Blue Horizon **2** *B4*
HI Vancouver Downtown **8** *D3*
Meridian at 910 Beach **14** *F3*

Eating 🍴

Benny's Bagels **6** *B2*
Bin 941 **1** *D4*
Bojangles Café **3** *A3*
CinCin **10** *C4*

Granville Island Coffee House **33** *G3*
Gyoza King **16** *B3*
Lift Bar Grill View **2** *A3*
Liliget Feast House **26** *B2*
Parkside **4** *A2*
Raincity Grill **30** *B1*
Sand Bar **33** *G3*
Stepho's Souvlaki **34** *D3*
Tanpopo **35** *B2*
Tapastree **36** *A3*

Bars & clubs 🍸

Backstage Lounge **4** *F3*
Balthazar **3** *B2*
Delilah's **2** *B2*
Dockside Brewing Co **6** *G3*
Morrissey Pub **1** *E4*

private decks and sitting areas, TV/DVD, soaker tubs. Outdoor hot tub and a deck with ocean views. Great value.

C Ritz Inn, 505 Gower Pt Rd, Gibsons Landing, T604-8863343, www.ritzinn.com. Situated close to the harbour, this is the most appealing motel in town. Some rooms have ocean views and kitchenettes.

C Secret Garden Cottages B&B, 925 Byng Rd, Roberts Creek, T604-8865999, www.thesecretgardnebnb.com. 2 very nice suites with private bathroom, TV, wood stove, kitchen, private garden and deck with BBQ and patio, surrounded by 1 ha of gardens with trees, vines, and a large duck pond.

E Up the Creek Backpackers B&B, 1261 Roberts Creek Rd, Roberts Creek, T604-8850384. The best budget option around, with mostly dorms, kitchen, large sun deck with hammocks and BBQ, friendly social areas, a hot tub and a book swap. 10-min walk to the village, beach and forest.

Camping

Porpoise Bay Provincial Park, 4 km north of Sechelt up Sechelt Inlet Rd, T604-8983678. A large and very popular campsite, featuring 84 private leafy sites, showers, and a large sandy beach.

Roberts Creek Provincial Park, on the highway in Roberts Creek. 25 primitive campsites in a beautiful old-growth forest with some walking trails. The day use area of the park, 1.5 km south, also has a beach.

Powell River *p68*

B Ocean Point B&B, 3344 Cortez Av, T604-9975999, www.oceanpointbb.com. 2 large and luxurious suites in an impossibly grandiose mansion with features like a spiral staircase and antique furnishings, near the beach and Westview ferry.

C Adventure B&B, 7439 Nootka St, 2 km south of Westview ferry, T604-4857097, www.adventureb-b.com. 2 comfortable rooms with lofts, and 1 suite, in a grand, cottage-style wooden house surrounded by 2 ha of gardens. Sun room, deck and sauna. Good value.

C-D Beach Gardens Resort and Marina, 7074 Westminster Av, on the ocean, T604-4856267, www.beachgardens.com. A large, attractive wooden building, hotel-like with 2 storeys of pleasant rooms side by side featuring big windows, balconies and views. Lots of activities available.

D The Old Courthouse Inn, 6243 Walnut St, T604-4834000, www.oldcourthouse inn.ca. Situated by the water in the heart of the historic townsite, this Tudor-style building, formerly a hostel, has been reopened as a boutique hotel. The rooms have plenty of character and charm. There's also TV and a bistro.

E Harbour Guesthouse, 4454 Willingdon Av, T604-4859803, www.powellriver hostel.com. Dorms and private rooms in a central location, plus a full kitchen, 2 common rooms with views, internet, storage, laundry, parking, a café and an activity booking centre.

Camping

Haywire Bay Regional Park, 5776 Marine Av, 7 km N on Powell Lake via Manson Av, T604-4831097. 42 sites, some with lake access, plus a playground, beaches, showers and hiking trails.

Saltery Bay Provincial Park, Mermaid Cove, just north of ferry. Attractive and private sites in a beautiful forest 200 m from the beach.

Lund and Desolation Sound Marine Park *p68*

B Lund Hotel, on the marina, T604-4140474, www.lundhotel.com. A pretty hotel, built in 1889 and totally renovated in 2000. The rooms are pleasant with interesting murals. Views can be enjoyed from the balcony and from the extensive deck of the pub/restaurant downstairs.

Camping

Okeover Arm Provincial Park, end of Malaspina Rd, T604-8983678. 28 very pleasant but basic sites close to a rocky beach with oysters, mussels, and clams. Open year round.

⊘ Eating

One of the best things to do in Vancouver is eat. International food critics have started to notice that Vancouver's culinary scene is now as dynamic as anywhere in North America, and set to steal some of the accolades usually reserved for San Francisco. Vancouver's chefs have all but pioneered a style of cooking known as West Coast cuisine (see p26), and embrace an innovative, pan-global fusion mentality. Given the cosmopolitan population, it's no surprise that you can find whatever international cuisine you crave, but we've mostly ignored ethnic restaurants, concentrating instead on purveyors of original West Coast and fusion cuisines. When in Rome...

Downtown *p53, map p52*

Bacchus, 845 Hornby St, in the **Wedgewood Hotel**, T604-6085319. This plush, romantic venue offers modern, eclectic French cuisine, and has built up quite a following for its weekend brunch, afternoon tea; and cocktail hour. The bar is worthy of attention in its own right.

Blue Water Café and Raw Bar, 1095 Hamilton St, Yaletown, T604-6888078. Impossibly chic and upmarket, this spacious venue features brick walls, big wooden columns, leather chairs and couches, soft lighting and jazzy music. The open kitchen is renowned as serving some of the best, freshest seafood in town, raw and cooked, plus great steaks. Also a large selection of wines and beers.

Coast Restaurant, 1257 Hamilton St, T604-6855010. Dominated by pale wood furnishings, high ceilings, waterfall, and a large 'community' table, this is a tranquil and elegant location to enjoy all manner of seafood creations, including multi-course tasting menus.

C Restaurant, 1600 Howe St, False Creek, T604-6811164. The prototype for many of Vancouver's finest new West Coast venues, famous for its broad range of fresh local seafood, prepared in exciting and innovative new ways. The large, open, airy interior offers appropriate ocean views that are even better from the more intimate balcony upstairs. There's also a great wine list that includes many sakes.

DIVA at the Met, 645 Howe St, T604-6027788. A contender for the best in town, the food here is classic nouveau French, prepared with flair, creativity, and a West Coast sensibility. Decor is bright and elegant, sophisticated but not stuffy. Main courses feature 1 of every type of fish and meat. The taster menu is a choice of 3 downsized main courses (entrées), or try the cheese taster menu. An extensive wine list includes many offered by the glass.

Joe Forte's Seafood and Chop House, 777 Thurlow St, T604-6691940. This beautifully opulent room is fitted out with brass banisters and trimmings, wrought iron, marble columns, high ceilings, and huge mirrors, and dominated by a large horseshoe bar. Seafood is the speciality, with a broad choice of oysters. The selection of beers is great, and the wine list has been winning prizes for years. There's a roof garden with smoking lounge and fireplace, and live piano music nightly.

Water Street Café, 300 Water St, Gastown, T604-6892832. The menu is unimaginative – mainly pasta, with some steak and seafood – but the elegant, classy ambience, massive windows and outdoor seating, make this the most enticing option in Gastown.

West, 2881 Granville, T604-7388938. Large and idiosyncratic, dominated by a library of wine bottles, here is yet another superlative purveyor of imaginative, fresh and tasty West Coast cuisine. Has been voted the city's best restaurant and chef.

Bin 941, 943 Davie St, T604-6831246. This small and intimate bistro combines quirky decor, a lively atmosphere, inspirational tapas plates, and a well-stocked bar.

Brix, 1138 Homer St, Yaletown, T604-9159463. Progressive Pacific Northwest cuisine and fondues, served in a classic, stylish brick room.

66 99 I've never seen so much coffee in all my life. The whole town is on a caffeine jag, and still nothing gets done any faster...

Bette Midler

The Elbow Room, 560 Davie St, T604-6853628. A popular breakfast spot that has become famous for its large portions and the abuse regularly dished out to those who fail to polish off their plateful.
Rodney's Oyster House, 1228 Hamilton St, Yaletown, T604-6090080. Classic converted warehouse space with brick walls and huge wooden beams. Downstairs is casual with stools at the bar, upstairs a little smarter. Clientele is slightly older but the ambience is lively and crowded. Focusing on oysters, mussels and chowder, the food is excellent, and there's a good selection of wine and beer.
Hon's Wun-Tun House, 268 Keefer St, T604-6880871. There are countless options in Chinatown, and it's hard to go wrong, but this is the obvious choice, having for some time scooped up most awards for best Chinese, best restaurant under $10, and so on. The decor is cafeteria-style, the menu huge.

For a snack try one of the numerous local bakeries for a curry beef, BBQ pork or honey bun; they quickly become addictive.

Cafés

During one Vancouver performance, Bette Midler remarked: "I've never seen so much coffee in all my life. The whole town is on a caffeine jag, and still nothing gets done any faster". People here do take their coffee pretty seriously, so you never have very far to go to get a decent cup.
Blake's, 221 Carrall St, Gastown, T604-8993354. Exceptional downbeat, tasteful coffee house with good music, brick walls, beer on tap, and a modest menu.
The Blunt Bros, 317 W Hastings St, East Side, T604-6825868. Calling itself

"a respectable joint", this is the main bastion of attempts to sell Vancouver as the new Amsterdam. Toking is permitted, and large amounts of pot paraphernalia sold, but there's no booze. The interior is spacious, with lots of couches for vegging out. Live music, mainly acoustic, Wed-Sat.
Café Ami, 885 W Georgia St, in the HSBC building, Downtown, T604-6880103. Easily the area's most pleasant spot for coffee.
Café Dolcino, 12 Powell St, Gastown, T604-8015118. Perfectly situated on picturesque Maple Leaf Sq, with a couple of tables outside to take in the scene.
Gastown Café, 101 W Cordova St. Cosy little spot with armchairs and antiques.

West End to Stanley Park
p57, map p72
The West End's large and lively population breathes constant life into the city's most competitive culinary district, with Robson, Denman and Davie representing the finest streets for restaurant window-shopping.
CinCin, upstairs at 1154 Robson St, T604-6887338. Often rated as the best Italian food in town, with lots of awards, many for its wine list. The Mediterranean decor is warm and romantic, sophisticated and comfortable, with balcony seating for those hot summer evenings.
Lift Bar Grill View, 333 Menchion's Mews, off Bayshore Dr, T604-6895438. A new seafood venue whose modern, sophisticated interior has floor-to-ceiling windows with views of Stanley Park. Try their signature 'whet' plates.
Liliget Feast House, 1724 Davie St, T604-6817044. First Nations specialities are served in a beautiful cellar space featuring cedar columns and tables, West

Coast art, and seating designed by Arthur Erickson. Authentic regional dishes are cooked on an alderwood grill. The platter for 2 with salmon, caribou, and fiddleheads is an obvious choice.

Raincity Grill, 1193 Denman St, T604-6857337. One of the original exponents of West Coast cuisine. Ingredients are fresh, locally produced, organic when possible, and used with subtlety and panache. The decor is modern and elegant, while the award-winning wine list focuses on BC's finest, with many by the glass.

Sequoia Grill at the Teahouse, Stanley Park at Ferguson Point, T604- 6693281. The nicer of the park's 2 restaurants, set in a bright and breezy summerhouse with lots of plants, and big windows that offer fabulous views of English Bay. The menu has eclectic West Coast inclinations.

Gyoza King, 1508 Robson St, T604-6698278. Dark, atmospheric and very popular spot for small, tapas-style, Japanese dishes and sake.

Parkside, 1906 Haro St, T604-6836912. Elegant Art Deco room with a courtyard garden patio. The menu is eclectic, with a West Coast sensibility.

Tanpopo, 1122 Denman St, T604-6817777. One of many sushi houses near the Robson/Denman junction. Probably the best choice for all-you-can-eat.

Tapastree, 1829 Robson St, T604-6064680. A large, casual but elegant space filled out with tasteful art, an open kitchen and bar, and with a patio at the front for people-watching. About the largest selection of tasty tapas in town, at around $10 each.

Stepho's Souvlaki, 1124 Davie St, T604-6832555. Don't be put off by the generic exterior: the food here is top-notch Greek, with generous portions and very low prices. The long queues pay testament to its legendary status.

Cafés

Benny's Bagels, 1780 Davie St, West End, T604-6857600. Good coffee and a patio with unbeatable views of English Bay.

Bojangles Café, 785 Denman St, West End, T604-6873622. One of the best coffee houses in town, a West End neighbourhood institution.

Granville Island to Point Grey
p59, map72

The Sand Bar, 1535 Johnston St, Granville Island, T604-6699030. A beautiful renovated warehouse with high ceilings, industrial metal trimmings, vast windows overlooking False Creek, and a heated roof patio. West Coast food, including tapas and seafood, wood-grilled burgers and pizza, washed down with a fine selection of ales and wines.

Granville Island Public Market. Countless excellent, cheap fast-food stalls selling all kinds of international cuisine, with seating outside by the water.

Cafés

Granville Island Coffee House, on the boardwalk behind the **Sand Bar**, T604-6810177. Cosy little spot away from the hustle and bustle.

Kitsilano *p61, map p70*

Kitsilano contains many of the city's most celebrated restaurants, and also the best selection for vegetarians.

Bishop's, 2549 W 4th Av, T604-7382025. The quintessential West Coast eatery. Owner John Bishop is famous for his impeccable hospitality, and for changing his menu frequently to highlight the best locally grown organic ingredients available. The extensive wine list favours BC's best.

Feenie's, 2563 W Broadway, T604-7397115. Casual and affordable, offering high-class versions of more homely Canadian fare. Expect queues.

Lumière, 2551 W Broadway, T604-7398185. The fame of owner Rob Feenie has grown considerably in recent years. Vaunted as one of the city's (if not country's) finest, his restaurant has no à la carte, just tasting menus from $80-120 without wine, apparently worth every penny. The modern interior is stylish to the point of being intimidating.

Pastis, 2153 W 4th Av, T604-7315020. This is another of Vancouver's key high-class venues, whose small, ever-changing menu uses the freshest fish and meats to give a West Coast twist to classic French nouvelle cuisine. The seriousness of the food contrasts with the relaxed decor.

Vij's, 1480 11th Av, T604-7366664. The only Indian restaurant that is regularly cited as one of the city's finest overall eateries, with skilful, innovative variations on old favourites. Reservations are not accepted, so queues are common. **Rangoli**, next door, T604-7365711, is a more casual and inexpensive version.

Bin 942, 1521 W Broadway, T604-7349421, 1700-0200. Thin room stuffed with weird and wonderful pieces of art. Trendy and lively, with modern but mellow dance music. Reasonable beer selection, and an incredible menu of involved, delicious tapas.

The Eatery, 3431 W Broadway, T604-7385298. Trendy, very popular spot for Japanese-Western fusion food, with a dark, atmospheric interior, a small patio at the front, and a good range of beers on tap.

Greens and Gourmet, 2681 W Broadway. T604-7377373. An oasis for vegetarians, with a calming plant-filled interior, and a broad variety of delicious salads and hot dishes sold by the 100 g.

The Naam, 2724 W 4th Av, T604-7387151. The city's oldest vegetarian restaurant, and something of an institution. Portions are generous, with lots of desserts, beers on tap, and wine at very reasonable prices. The decor is simple, with a heated atrium-style patio. Open 24 hrs, with live jazz/folk/world music every night from 1900-2200.

Sophie's Cosmic Café, 2095 4th Av, T604-7326810. An eccentric, diner-style Kitsilano institution that is legendary for its weekend brunches (hence the queues) and large portions. Almost too popular for its own good, but a great spot to observe Vancouverites in their natural habitat.

Tangerine, 1685 Yew St, T604-7394677. Small and trendy neighbourhood favourite close to Kits Beach, with an eclectic West Coast menu at moderate prices.

Cafés
Benny's, 2505 W Broadway, Kitsilano. A wonderful arty, trendy and quirky atmosphere with great music. Good for coffee, bagels and melts.

Calhoun's, 3035 W Broadway, Kitsilano, T604-7377062, open 24 hrs. A huge and lively coffee shop with a slightly rustic feel, serving great coffee, juices, breakfasts and baking.

Terra Breads, 2380 W 4th Av, Kitsilano, T604-7361838. Baking to die for: breads, croissants, muffins, cakes and sandwiches to eat in or take away, and good coffee too.

South and east Vancouver *p64*
Seasons in the Park, Queen Elizabeth Park, T604-8748008. One of the most romantic, high-class choices in town, with a sumptuous interior and exquisite views. Fresh seafood and steak, good appetizers and brunch.

Tojo's, 777 W Broadway, T604-8728050. The undisputed best (and most expensive) sushi restaurant in western Canada, with the freshest fish, best sake and most beautiful presentation.

Banana Leaf Malaysian Cuisine, 820 W Broadway, T604-7316333; also 1096 Denman, West End, T604-6833333. Gloriously tasty Malaysian cuisine served in a beautiful plant-laden interior whose bright yellow walls are adorned with traditional works of art. The broad and reasonably-priced menu features lots of vegetarian and seafood options.

Bukowski's Bistro, 1447 Commercial, T604-2534770. Great atmosphere and large portions of food that is fairly standard but never disappoints. There's a lively bar at the back, with live jazz on Mon, Thu and Sat, along with other events. Stays open later than most.

Latin Quarter, 1305 Commercial St, T604-2511144. Tapas, paella and sangría

in a crowded, party atmosphere with
frequent live music.

♥♥ **Monsoon**, 2526 Main St, T604-8794001.
Full of colour and character, this trendy
favourite specializes in gourmet Asian
fusion cuisine at reasonable prices.

♥♥ **Slickity Jim's Chat 'n' Chew**, 2513
Main St, T604-8736760, 0800-1700.
Small and quirky, overflowing with
weird and wonderful artefacts, this is
the breakfast place of choice for a mixed,
predominantly arty or bohemian crowd.
Variations on the eggs bennie theme
abound, with very silly names. Portions
tend to be on the small side.

♥ **Thai Away Home**, 1736 Commercial Dr.
Also at 1206 Davie St (West End), and
3315 Cambie St. Cheap but great Thai
food in a very casual atmosphere.

Cafés

La Casa Gelato, Venables/Glen Sts, near
Commercial Dr. Tucked away in an
unlikely spot is Vancouver's finest ice-
cream emporium, with 198 flavours to
choose from and servers who are pleased
to let you taste and try before you buy.

Lugz Coffee House, 2525 Main St, T604-
8736766. Comfy, downbeat atmosphere
with couches and outdoor seating. Some
food and smoothies.

Soma Coffee House, 2528 Main St, T604-
8731750. Minimalist, arty interior attracting
a more trendy clientele. Magazines to
browse or buy, and some tasty snacks.

Turk's Coffee Exchange, 1276
Commercial Dr. Probably the best coffee
in town, in a small but elegant interior.
Great people-watching from
the outdoor seating area.

North Shore *p65*

♥♥ **Beach Side Café**, 1362 Marine Dr,
West Vancouver, T604-9251945.
Wonderful West Coast cuisine, with the
emphasis on seafood, and one of the best
decks in town, with views across Burrard
Inlet to Stanley Park and Point Grey.

♥♥ **Hiwus Feasthouse**, Blue Grouse Lake,
Grouse Mountain, T604-9840661. May-

Oct, evenings only. A traditional cedar
longhouse on an attractive lake. Nightly
show costs $65 per person and includes
native storytelling and legends, dancing,
singing and a full dinner of Pacific
Northwest Native cuisine. Reservations
essential by 1630 the previous day.

♥♥ **The Observatory**, Main Building,
Grouse Mountain, T604-9840661. Fancy
restaurant serving fine West Coast cuisine
with magnificent views (reservations
necessary and free gondola ride included).

♥♥ **Moustache Café**, 1265 Marine Dr,
T604-9878461. An ever-changing menu
of taste- heavy international food prepared
with a West Coast sensibility, and served
in an attractive, colourful 1920's house
with an open kitchen. With its friendly
staff and fine wine list, this is possibly
the best all-round dining experience
on the North Shore.

♥ **The Raven**, 1052 Deep Cove Rd.
Superb neighbourhood pub with
enormous portions of superior
pub-style food.

**Gibsons Landing and the
Sechelt Peninsula** *p68*

♥♥ **Chez Philippe** at the Bonniebrook
Lodge (see Sleeping, p71). The finest
restaurant on the Sunshine Coast,
with an excellent reputation for French
fine dining in impeccable romantic
surroundings, with a great wine list
and attentive service.

♥♥ **Leo's Tapas and Grill**, 274 Gower
Point Rd, T604-8869414. Fine Greek
dishes and ouzo specials.

♥ **Backeddy Marine Pub**, 16660
Backeddy Rd, Egmont, T604-8832298.
Good food and great views.

♥ **Molly's Reach**, on the boardwalk,
T604-8869710. Good plentiful pub food,
including a very cheap dinner special. The
deck out front is the town's most obvious
spot for enjoying wonderful ocean views.

Powell River *p68*

♥♥ **Chiang Mai**, 4463 Marine Av, T604-
4850883. Good Thai food, poor ambience.

La Casita, 4578 Marine Av, T604-4857720. Funky blue adobe joint with authentic, reasonably priced Mexican food.
Le Sextant, 4623 Marine Av, T604-4859414. Tapas and Mediterranean dishes.
Shinglemill Pub and Bistro, on Powell Lake, north of town at 6233 Powell Place, T604-4832001. Well-located pub rated for its restaurant, which specializes in seafood.
Flying Yellow Bread Bowl, 4722 Marine Av. A delightful spot with an arty, eccentric ambience, and good wholesome food.

Lund p68

Laughing Oyster, just beyond Okeover Arm Park, T604-4839775. Exquisite West Coast cuisine and seafood, served on a romantic patio with striking views. Almost obligatory, having come this far.

Bars and clubs

Like most big cities, Vancouver offers something for everyone and has developed a reputation for excellent microbrewed beers and a panoply of funky, atmospheric little bistros and tapas bars. See also under Eating.

For the short-term visitor there are more than enough nightclubs to check out. Those listed here tend to host DJs spinning different music every night. Most charge a cover of $5-10, and drinks can be on the pricey side. Look out for the quarterly magazine *Nitelife*. For more specific night-to-night details consult the indispensable *Georgia Straight* or the useful site www.clubvibes.com. For gay bars see p82.

Downtown p53, map p52

Alibi Room, 157 Alexander St, Gastown, T604-6233383. Owned and frequented by movie people, this is a seductively hip and happening hot spot. On top of the atmosphere and well-chosen, modern music, their small menu is exciting, innovative, and reasonably priced.
The Cambie, 300 Cambie St, Gastown, T604-6846466. Gritty, down-to-earth and

friendly, this huge and smoky boozer is understandably popular for its wide selection of cheap beer and food, pool tables, and crowded summer patio.
Crush, 1180 Granville St, Downtown, T604-6840355. Calling itself a 'champagne lounge', this plush spot aims for an older, wealthier clientele. Music is lounge, R&B, jazz and soul. Queues are common, and it tends to close earlier than most.
DV8, 515 Davie St, Downtown, T604-6824388. Dark, funky bar, with interesting art and music. Popular with a trendy, alternative crowd. DJs play some very modern sounds till 0300, 0400 Fri-Sat.
Element Sound Lounge, 801 Georgia St, T604-6690806. Fancy club aimed at the upmarket Martini set. Top DJs play funk, techno and house.
Honey Lounge, 455 Abbott St, Gastown, T604-6857777. Dark, capacious and open-plan, this hip and happening bar sucks you in with impossibly comfortable couches smothered in huge velvet cushions, and a good Martini list. Loud, upbeat, conversation-killing music makes for a club-like atmosphere without the dancing. Open late. **Milk**, next door, is a trendy gay bar, and **Lotus Sound Lounge** downstairs is one of the city's best clubs.
The Irish Heather, 217 Carrall St, Gastown, T604-6889779. An upmarket version of the kind of genuine Irish pub that has spawned so many clones of late.
The Lennox, 800 Granville/Robson Sts, Downtown, T604-4080881. Standard pub with some outstanding but overpriced beers. Located right on Downtown's busiest corner, the small patio is an ideal spot for watching the city rush by.
Lucy Mae Brown, 862 Richards St, Downtown, T604-8999199. Genuinely stylish favourite with the young and trendy crowd. Downstairs is a hip and modern Martini bar playing trip hop-style music. Upstairs is an expensive, reservation-only restaurant with a Pacific Rim menu whose strongest point is its starters.
Morrissey Pub, 1227 Granville S. Big, dark and stylish with a river-stone fireplace

and lots of dark wood and leather. Many beers on tap, and some decent cheap food.

Plaza Club, 881 Granville St, T604-6460064. One of the classiest of the DJ-led party atmosphere dance hot-spots, with one of the best sound and lighting systems. Very popular on Sat.

The Railway Club, 579 Dunsmuir St, Downtown, T604-6811625. Long-standing, down-to-earth upstairs bar, cosy and atmospheric with lots of wood, knick-knacks and intimate corners. Varied live music every night, sometimes with cover.

Section (3), 1039 Mainland St, Yaletown, T604-6842777. The decor here is arty, interesting and very modern: high silver booths, hardwood floor, weird art, wrought-iron stools at a curved bar. This and the funky music attract a more hip and savvy crowd than the usual Yaletown yuppies. The food covers many bases, and can be enjoyed on a heated patio.

Shine, 364 Water St, Gastown, T604-4084321. Smart, colourful and intimate club with varied DJ-led music, attracting a 20s-30s crowd that's a bit more well-heeled than usual. One to dress up for.

Soho, 1144 Homer St, Yaletown, T604-6881180. Stylish but unpretentious Yaletown pub kitted out in brick and wood, with simple, rustic tables. Beer, billiards, food, tea and coffee.

Sonar, 66 Water St, Gastown, T604-6836695. Nice basement space with brick walls and wood floors. One area for bands/dancing and another for lounging. Music varies from house to hip-hop and reggae. Possibly the number one choice in town.

Subeez Café, 891 Homer St, Yaletown, T604-6876107. A vast, open warehouse-style space with very high ceilings and huge concrete pillars. Add dim lighting, weird art, odd music, big screens showing silent black and white films, and you have a strange and compelling atmosphere. There's a large selection of good draught beers and non-alcoholic drinks, and some overpriced food, including breakfast.

West End to Stanley Park
p57, map p72

Balthazar, 1215 Bidwell St, West End, T604-6898822. Spacious restaurant/lounge that stays open and busy till late with 2 rooms where DJs spin progressive house and more mainstream sounds.

Delilah's, 1789 Comox St, T604-6873424. With its red walls and soft lighting this bar has a wonderfully louche atmosphere and is one of the best spots for a Martini.

Granville Island to Point Grey
p59, map p72

Backstage Lounge, 1585 Johnston St, T604-6871354, in the **Arts Club**. Great airy and down-to-earth spot with a lively patio, decent food, and live music most nights.

Dockside Brewing Co, 1253 Johnston St in the **Granville Island Hotel**, T604-6857070. Tucked away from the hordes, with comfy leather armchairs and fine in-house beers. The menu is mid-range with wood-oven pizza and seafood.

Kitsilano *p61, map p70*
The Fringe Café, 3124 W Broadway, T604-7386977. Tiny downbeat bar with a bohemian attitude.

Lou's Grill and Bistro, 3357 W Broadway, T604-7369872. Largish trendy bar/restaurant with terracotta walls, interesting art and a patio. Dim lighting, jazzy music, and a great selection of beer on tap, with some of the cheapest Guinness around.

South and east Vancouver *p64*
WaaZuBee Café, 1622 Commercial Dr, T604-2535299. Large, comfortable space, dark, atmospheric and arty, playing loud upbeat music. Good selection of beers and good food served in large portions. Best place for a drink on 'the Drive'.

North Shore *p65*
The Raven, 1052 Deep Cove Rd, T604-9293834. Spacious, English-style pub with the best selection of draught beers in town, including 19 microbrews

and 6 imports. Lots of malt whiskies, too. And the food comes in mammoth portions. Live music once or twice a week. Understandably popular.
The Rusty Gull, 175 E 1st St, T604-9885585. Lively neighbourhood pub with good ales on tap, food, and frequent live music. Magical views from the patio of the city with shipyards and derelict warehouses in the foreground.

⦿ Entertainment

The first place to look for weekly listings is the *Georgia Straight*, available free on most major streets. The visitor centre has a branch of **Ticketmaster**, T604-2804444; and **Tickets Tonight**, www.ticketstonight.ca, which has half-price same-day tickets for many events.

Art galleries
The Arts Hotline, T604-6842787, www.allianceforarts.com, has a weekly events calendar and pages of information on the arts in Vancouver. Apart from the major galleries mentioned in the Sights section, Vancouver has a wealth of smaller spaces, usually highlighting the work of contemporary, local artists. See also Shopping p85 for commercial galleries, which are usually just as interesting.

Granville Island is good for commercial galleries, and has the **Charles H Scott Gallery** in the Emily Carr Institute (see p54), which always has interesting, sometimes controversial displays, with entrance by donation. The adjacent **Concourse Gallery** has frequent displays of student work.

There are a few worthwhile artist-run galleries in **Gastown**, such as **Artspeak Gallery**, at 233 Carrall St, and **Vancouver Access Artist Run Centre**, 206 Carrall St.

Elsewhere, the **Grunt Gallery**, 116-350 E 2nd Av, and **Or Gallery**, 208 Smithe St, usually have interesting displays. **Western Front**, 303 E 8th Av, tends to exhibit video and performance art.

On the **North Shore** there is an active art scene: **Presentation House Gallery**, 333 Chesterfield Av, is one of Vancouver's oldest, with a good reputation for its photography and media arts exhibitions.

Cinemas
The 2 best cinemas in town are:
Hollywood, 3123 W Broadway, T604-7383211, www.hollywoodtheatre.ca; and **Ridge**, 3131 Arbutus St/16th Av, T604-7386311, www.ridgetheatre.com. Both tend to screen well chosen films just off the first-run circuit, or less well known but worthwhile choices. Built in 1950, the Ridge is a delightful building, and the last to still offer a glassed-in 'crying room' for parents with babies or noisy children.
Blinding Light, 36 Powell St, T604-8783366. A micro-theatre in the back of a café, showing serious alternative films and documentaries.
Fifth Avenue Cinemas, 2110 Burrard St, T604-2222991, gets most of the more mainstream international films, and has a good screen on which to see them.
Granville Cineplex Odeon Cinemas, 855 Granville St, T604-6844000. The most convenient Downtown location, but small screens.
Pacific Cinematheque, 1131 Howe St, T604-6883456, www.cinematheque.bc.ca, is the main venue for rep, independent, art-house, foreign or just plain off-the-wall films. Shows change nightly.
Tinseltown, 88 W Pender St, T604-8060799. One of the best and most reasonably priced.

Comedy
The Gastown Comedy Store, 19 Water St, T604-6821727. Stand-up and improvisation.
New Revue Stage, 1601 Johnston St, Granville Island, T604-7387013. Wed-Thu 1930, Fri-Sat 2000, 2200 and 2345. Host of Vancouver Theatre Sports League, 6 times world champions of comedy improvisation.
Yuk Yuk's, 750 Pacific Blvd, Downtown, T604-6875233. The city's premier venue for stand-up comedy.

Gay and lesbian

The **West End**, and **Davie Street** in particular, is the most gay-friendly part of a very gay-friendly city, and host of the summer Gay Pride Celebration (see Festivals and events, p84). To find out what's going on pick up a copy of *XtraWest*. **Little Sister's Book and Art Emporium**, 1238 Davie St, is a gay and lesbian bookstore where you can get a free copy of the *Gay and Lesbian Business Association Directory*, www.glba.org.

Celebrities, 1022 Davie St, www.celebrities nightclub.com. A newly reopened club with state-of-the-art light and sound system, a big dance floor, top DJs, theme nights and speciality performers.

The Fountainhead Pub, 1025 Davie St, T604-6872222. Gay-friendly neighbourhood pub, with a heated and covered patio, and weekend brunch.

Milk Bar, 455 Abbott, T604-685777. Stylish gay bar, with the gay-friendly **Lotus** club below.

Numbers, 1042 Davie St, T604-6854077, www.numbers.ca. Vancouver's longest-running gay bar, whose recent renovation includes new lights and sound system. Karaoke and a heaving dance floor entertain a very cruisy, older denim/leather-type crowd.

The Oasis Pub, 1240 Thurlow St, T604-6861724. A gay-friendly upmarket piano bar, with a heated outdoor patio, decent food, and 200 Martinis.

Odyssey, 1251 Howe St, T604-6895256. The main surviving gay club, with high-energy dance music and nightly entertainment attracting a young, multicultural crowd.

Pumpjack Pub, 1167 Davie St, T604-6853417. A pub with DJs in the evening, and varied theme nights.

Live music

Several restaurants offer regular live jazz, including: **Bukowski's Bistro**, 1447 Commercial Dr, T604-2534770; **Ouisi Bistro**, 3014 Granville, T604-7327550; **O'Doul's**, 1300 Robson, T604-6611400;

Rossini's, 162 Water St, Gastown, T604-4081300, and 1525 Yew St, Kitsilano, T604-7378080. Live jazz nightly for diners. Call the **Jazz Hotline**, T604-8725200, www.vancouverjazz.com.

Other popular places include:

Backstage Lounge, Arts Club, Granville Island. A small but atmospheric venue for local and/or progressive acts.

Cellar Jazz, 3611 W Broadway, T604-7381959. The principal jazz venue in town, with local or visiting musicians most nights.

Chan Centre for the Performing Arts, 6265 Crescent Rd, T604-8222697. Mostly dedicated to classical performances, this UBC venue has 3 stages in one complex; the main hall is one of the city's finest.

Commodore Ballroom, 868 Granville St, T604-7394550. A wonderful old venue with a 1000-seat capacity and a massive dance floor built on rubber tyres. One of the best and most popular venues for international touring acts.

Orpheum Theatre, 884 Granville St, T604-6653050. Probably the best venue in town for highbrow acts of all types (but no dancing allowed). When it was built as a part of the vaudeville circuit in 1927, this 2800-seat venue was the largest theatre in Canada. The elegant Spanish baroque-style interior with its arches, tiered columns and marble mouldings was almost converted into a cinematic multiplex before the city intervened. Home to the Vancouver Symphony Orchestra, it hosts most major classical events.

Queen Elizabeth Theatre, Hamilton/Georgia Sts, T604-2999000. This 1960s modernist building with almost 3000 seats is one of the main venues for classical music but also hosts ballet, musicals, and major rock and pop acts.

Richard's on Richards, 1036 Richards, T604-6876794. A great venue attracting some of the best local and visiting acts: small and atmospheric with a brick wall as a backdrop behind the band, a balcony above for views, and arguably the best sound, lighting and sightlines in town.

Rime, 1130 Commercial Dr, T604-2151130. Brand-new venue for varied mid-range acts, from jazz to flamenco.
The Yale Hotel, 1300 Granville, T604-6819253. A rough-looking bar that's the city's premier blues venue.

Spectator sports
Nat Bailey Stadium, Queen Elizabeth Park. Home to the Canadians baseball team, www.canadiansbaseball.com, Jun-Sep, Tickets $7.47.
Pacific Coliseum, 100 Renfrew N/Hastings St E, at the PNE, T604-4442687, is home to the Vancouver Giants junior hockey team, www.vancouvergiants.com. Tickets $16-18, T604-2804400.
Hastings Park Raceway, Renfrew N/Hastings St E, at the PNE, T604-2541631, www.hastingspark.com, has been hosting thoroughbred horse racing since 1889.

Theatre and performing arts
The main season for concerts, opera and ballet is Oct-Apr, but a number of festivals run continual shows through the summer (see Festivals and events, below). As well as an active theatre world, Vancouver has achieved recognition for its dance scene. The 2 main areas for theatre are Granville Island (see p59) and the Entertainment District of Downtown (see p55).
Arts Club Granville Island Stage, 1585 Johnston St, T604-6871644. Small venue for casual theatre such as musical comedies.
Centre in Vancouver for the Performing Arts, 777 Homer St, T604-6020616. Opposite the main library, and designed by the same architect, this state-of-the-art theatre, formerly the Ford Centre, is Vancouver's main Broadway-type venue for large-scale and popular theatre, dance and musicals.
Firehall Arts Centre, 280 E Cordova, T604-6890926, www.firehallartscentre.ca. An operating firehall from 1906-1975, the building now provides a small, intimate setting for quality dance and theatre.
Patricia Theatre, 5845 Ash Av, historic townsite, Powell River,

T604-4839345. Built in 1928, this architectural gem, resembling a classic Hollywood fantasy movie palace, has just been restored, and is once again showing well-chosen first-run and independent films on a daily basis, as well as more occasional concerts and live theatre. There's also a tea room and bistro, with tours by arrangement.
Performance Works, 1218 Cartwright St, Granville Island, T604-6890926. Small-scale contemporary works of a generally high standard.
Stanley Theatre, 2750 Granville/12th Av, T604-6871644. An elegantly restored 1931 cinema, now an arts club venue for drama, comedy or musicals.
Vancouver East Cultural Centre, 1895 Venables, near Commercial Dr, T604-2519578. Affectionately known as 'The Cultch', this converted Methodist church is one of the best performance spaces in the city, thanks to great acoustics and sightlines, and an intimate 350-seat capacity. It hosts a range of events, including theatre, music and dance, with an emphasis on the modern and sometimes controversial.
Vancouver Playhouse, Hamilton/Georgia St, T604-2999000 for info, T604-6653050 for tickets. Fairly intimate venue for serious theatre, including many modern Canadian works.
Vogue Theatre, 918 Granville St, T604- 2804444. A 1941 art deco-style building that has remained much the same, right down to the neon sign. Light-hearted pieces such as comedies and musicals.

⊛ Festivals and events

Jan The **Polar Bear Swim**, T604-6653424, has taken place since 1819. Every year on 1 Jan, lunatic locals prove themselves by starting the new year with an icy dip at English Bay Beach.
Feb The **Chinese New Year Festival**, T604-6811923, www.vancouver-china town.com, involves a parade in Chinatown,

and numerous activities at the Dr Sun Yat-Sen Classical Chinese Garden.

Mar The **Vancouver Storytelling Festival** www.vancouverstorytelling.org, is the main event. In mid-Mar is the long-running **International Wine Festival**, T604-8733311, www.playhousewine fest.com, 40 events focused on the Vancouver Playhouse involving 500 wines from around the world. At the same time is the **Vancouver Celtic Festival**, T604-6838331, www.celticfestvancouver.com, centred around St Patrick's Day and the Entertainment District.

May In late May the **International Children's Festival**, T604-7085655, www.youngarts.ca, involves a host of events to delight the youngsters in Vanier Park. **Cloverdale Rodeo**, T604-5769461, www.cloverdalerodeo.com, at about the same time, is the 2nd biggest of its kind in the west after the Calgary Stampede (see p277), attracting cowboys from all over the continent.

Jun In mid-Jun is the **Alcan Dragon Boat Festival**, T604-6882382, www.adbf.com, a weekend of racing and cultural activities on False Creek. At the month's end is the major **International Jazz Festival**, T604-8725200, www.coastaljazz.ca, 10 days of big and small acts on 40 stages around town, plus a free 2-day New Orleans-style street festival in Gastown.

Jun-Aug **Bard on the Beach Skakespeare Festival**, T604-7390559, www.bardonthe beach.org, outside theatre for 3 months.

Jul The month kicks off with the 10-day **Dancing on the Edge Festival**, Firehall Arts Centre, T604- 6890926, www.dancingon theedge.org, Canada's largest showcase of independent choreographers. Starting mid-Jul are the **Vancouver Folk Music Festival**, T604-6029798, www.the festival.bc.ca, 3 days of music and storytelling at Jericho Beach and other venues; and **Theatre Under the Stars**, T604-6870714, www.tuts.bc.ca, a month of classical musical theatre in Stanley Park's Malkin Bowl. At the end of Jul is the **Vancouver Chamber Music Festival**, T604-6020363, www.vanrecital.com, 12 days of musical talent in Vanier Park's Crofton Schoolhouse and elsewhere.

Jul-Aug **Celebration of Light**, T604-7384304, is an international fireworks competition held over 2 weeks from late Jul. The most popular places for watching are the West End beaches, and Vanier Park. Straddling Jul and Aug is the week-long **Pride Week Celebration**, T604-6870955, www.vanpride.bc.ca, the year's major gay and lesbian event, and a massive party for all who want to join in the spirit. The Gay Pride parade moves down Denman to Beach Av and on to the main party zone, Sunset Beach on English Bay. A little later is the **Vancouver Queer Film and Video Festival**, T604-8441615, www.outonscreen.com, featuring over 200 films, mostly at Cinemark Tinseltown.

Aug **Festival Vancouver**, T604-6881152, www.festivalvancouver.bc.ca, fills the first fortnight of Aug with over 80 classical and jazz concerts around town. The 2-day **Vancouver Chinatown Festival**, T604-6323808, www.vancouver-chinatown.com, features all manner of entertainment. **Abbotsford International Air Show**, T604-8528511, held on the month's 2nd weekend is the 2nd-largest air show in North America. State-of-the-art aircraft from around the world compete and perform. **Richmond Tall Ships Festival**, T1877-2470777, www.richmondtallships.ca, is held every 3 years (next in 2008).

Aug-Sep From late Aug-early Sep, the **PNE Fair** at the Pacific National Exhibition, T604-2532311, www.pne.bc.ca, includes live entertainment, exhibits, livestock and the Playland Amusement Park. Take Bus No 4, 10 or 16 north from Granville.

Sep Things wind down in Sep, but for 10 days the **Vancouver Fringe Festival**, T604-2570350, www.vancouverfringe.com, involves performances by 100 international companies in indoor and outdoor venues. And at the end of the month the 17-day **Vancouver International Film Festival**, T604-6850260, www.viff.org, kicks off with about 300 films from 50 countries.

Oct The main event in Oct is the Vancouver International Comedy Festival, T604-6830883, www.comedy fest.com, featuring over 100 acts.
Dec For most of Dec the VanDusen Gardens are illuminated with 20,000 lights and seasonal displays during the Festival of Lights, T604-7366754, www.vandusengarden.org.

Sunshine Coast
Mar For over 30 years the Sunshine Coast Festival of the Performing Arts, Sechelt, T604-8857637, www.coast festival.com, has run throughout Mar.
Jun The mostly outdoor Jazz Festival, Gibsons, occupies 3 days in early Jun, www.coastjazz.com.
Aug The Festival of the Written Arts, T604-8859631, www.writersfestival.ca, at the Rockwood Centre, Sechelt, is apparently the largest of its kind in the country. Blackberry Festival, Powell River, T604-4852511, is a week of various events at the end of Aug.
Sep The 2-day Sunshine (Folk) Music Festival, T604-4871906, www.sunshine musicfest.com, held in early Sep on Palm Beach, is a great event, celebrating its 25th year in 2006.

○ Shopping

Antiques
Many antique, junk and consignment shops are clustered on stretches of South Main and South Granville. Most are seriously overpriced. There are also many on Richards between Hastings and Pender.

Arts and crafts
The best place for art-seeking is Granville Island. Cartwright St contains some of the key galleries, including Federation Gallery at No 1241, operated by members of the Federation of Canadian Artists; Gallery of BC Ceramics at No 1359, T604-6695645, run by members of the Potters' Guild of BC, with a large selection of top-notch pottery that changes

monthly; and **Crafthouse Gallery** at No 1386, T604-6877270, whose collection of quality work includes pottery, textiles and jewellery. The **Net Loft** opposite the public market also houses many fine stores. **Railspur Alley** is a nucleus for small and unique artists' studios.

Gastown has some interesting galleries, including **Industrial Artifacts** at 49 Powell St. A stunning collection of furniture and art, ingeniously fashioned from reclaimed pieces of old industrial machinery. South Granville is the best place to pick up works by established artists: **Art Emporium** at No 2928, T604-7383510, has been open since 1897, selling big-name domestic and international artists from the famous Group of Seven to Picasso; **Monte Clark Gallery** at No 2339, T604-7305000 specializes in avant-garde paintings, prints and photography.

Books
The best selections of new books are found at **Chapters**, and the more likeable **Duthie Books**, 2239 W 4th Av, T604-7325344. **Granville Book Co**, 850 Granville St, has a large selection of interesting books and magazines, great for browsing and open till midnight. For used books, huge selections can be found at **Macleod's Books**, 455 W Pender, T604- 6817654; **Pulp Fiction Books**, 2418 Main; and **Tanglewood Books**, 2709 Granville St and 2932 W Broadway, the latter specializing in non-fiction. For travel books and accessories, head for **The Travel Bug**, 2667 W Broadway; or **Wanderlust**, 1929 W 4th Av. For the best selections of magazines and newspapers, including some of international provenance, head for **Does Your Mother Know?**, 2139 W 4th Av, or **The Great Canadian News Co**, 1092 Robson, T604-6880609.

Clothes and accessories
Most major fashion and shoe chains are found on Robson St between Burrard and Jervis, or nearby in the **Pacific Centre Mall**

at Georgia and Howe. Granville St is good for off-the-wall new and used clothing and footwear shops. **The Bay**, nearby, is forever having sales where bargains can often be found. More exclusive designer labels are found on **W Hastings**. For clothes that are less expensive but maybe more original, **4th Av** west of Burrard in Kitsilano is a good bet. **Pharsyde** at 2100 4th Av, T604- 7396630, stocks hip, casual clothing and shoes for men and women. **Lulu Lemon**, 2113 4th Av, T604-7326111, sells unique items designed for sports and yoga, but phenomenally popular for fashion. The best area for funky used and retro clothing is Gastown around **W Cordova St**, including **Deluxe Junk Co**, at No 310.

First Nations arts and crafts

The best place to start looking for native art is on **Water St** in Gastown. Galleries here include **First Nations Creative Gallery and Artist Co-operative** at No 20, T604-6029464, owned and operated by aboriginal artists, with contemporary experimental works as well as the usual more traditional stuff. Prices can be more reasonable than elsewhere. **Hill's Native Art**, No 165, T604-6854249. 3 floors of Northwest Coast arts and crafts, including some spectacular pieces. **Inuit Gallery**, No 345, T604-6887323, www.inuit.com. North America's leading Inuit art gallery, with very beautiful modern and traditional sculpture and prints. **Spirit Wrestler Gallery**, No 8, T604-6698813. Works by major artists of various First Nations, with some very high-class pieces of sculpture.

Gifts

For touristy souvenirs head to Water St in Gastown. For more unusual ideas check out the speciality shops on 4th Av in Kitsilano. **Obsessions**, at 595 Howe or 1124 Denman, has a wide range of gift ideas, while the **Vancouver Art Gallery Shop** has lots of inspiringly beautiful items. For something more off the wall, **Salmagundi West**, 321 W Cordova,

T604-6814648, is a really fun shop, packed with eccentric oddities, toys and tit-bits. **The Postcard Place** in the Net Loft, Granville Island, has the city's best selection. See also Arts and crafts, p85.

Kids

Kid's Market, 1496 Cartwright St, Granville Island, T604-6898447, contains 25 shops just for children: many of the toys and clothes here are one-offs, educational and handmade locally. Other shops include: **The Games People**, 157 Water St; **It's all Fun and Games**, 1308 Commercial; **Kidsbooks**, 3038 W Broadway; **Lil 'Putian's fashions for kids**, 2029 W 4th Av; and **The Toybox**, 3002 W Broadway, T604-7384322.

Markets

The best place for food shopping is the **Granville Island Public Market**, T604-6666477, a mouth-watering high-end food hall and produce market open daily in summer 0900-1800. **Lonsdale Quay Market**, T9856261, where the SeaBus arrives at the North Shore, is a good second choice, open 0900-1830, Fri till 2100. **Chinatown** is a great place to browse, especially the open-air **night market** at 200 Keefer St and E Pender, Jun-Sep, Fri-Sun 1830-2300. The best venue for bargain-hunting is the weekend **Flea Market** on Main St in the block south of Terminal Av.

Music

A&B Sound, 556 Seymour St, T604-6875837. Best deals on new music; large selection, listen before you buy. **Zulu**, 1972 W 4th Av, T604-7383232. Big selection of new and used music of all kinds, with an emphasis on modern or alternative sounds.

Photography

ABC Photocolour, 1618 W 4th Av, are good for professional developing. **Dunne & Rundle** 891 Granville, and **Lens & Shutter**, 2912 W Broadway, are also recommended for developing, and carry a good variety of film and equipment (including used). For quick, cheap developing try **London Drugs**, which has branches at 70 Granville, 1187 Robson and 1650 Davie.

Sports equipment

The biggest sports equipment stores are grouped together around W Broadway and Cambie. **Mountain Equipment Co-op**, 130 W Broadway, T604-8727858, has the widest and best selection, and often the best deals, though you have to buy a $5 membership first. **3 Vets**, nearby at 2200 Yukon/6th Av, is also huge and all-inclusive. **Coast Mountain Sports** at 2201 W 4th is the other biggest and best all-round supplier. This is also the area for ski and snowboard shops, such as **Pacific Boarder** at 1793 W 4th Av, T604-7347245. For general supplies Downtown there's **Sport Mart** at 735 Thurlow, T604-6832433. For a great selection of used equipment head for **Sports Junkies** at 600 W 6th Av, or **Cheapskates** at 3644 W 16th, 3228 Dunbar or 3496 Dunbar.

▲▲ Activities and tours

Adventure tours

For information on hiking, kayaking and skiing in BC visit www.trailpeak.com. **Lotus Land Tours**, T604-6844922, www.lotuslandtours.com. Offers a broad range of activity-based tours including eagle watching, snowshoeing, whale watching, rafting, sea kayaking and hikes.
Moose Travel Network, T604-7779905, www.moosenetwork.com. Runs a wide selection of 2- to 25-day tours around BC departing from hostels, aimed at young, independent travellers. The Whistler 'Sea to Sky Pass' is $62, while trips around BC and Rockies cost $420-700.
Outblaze Tours, 1829 Venables St, T604-7101948, www.outblazetours.com. Runs hiking, biking, camping, surfing and ski tours for small groups (4-10).

George C Reifel Migratory Bird Sanctuary, Westham Island, Richmond, T604-9466980, is a 360-ha sanctuary in the Fraser River for thousands of birds on their way from Mexico to Alaska. There's a good viewing tower close to the car park. Shore birds start arriving in mid-Aug, followed by mallard and pintail ducks. Numbers rise during Sep-Oct, and peak in early Nov, when about 20,000 snow geese noisily arrive. Many birds remain all winter. Nesting occurs Apr-May.

Boating/fishing

Granville Island has plenty of operators. Check the **Charter Information Centre** by the Maritime Market for information and **Granville Island Boat Rentals**, behind Bridges Restaurant, T604-6826287. **Bites-on Salmon Charters**, 200-1128 Hornby, T1877-6882483, www.bites-on.com. 5- to 8-hr fishing tours from $450. **Coal Harbour Boat Rentals**, 1525 Coal Harbour Quay, T604-6826257, rents speedboats.

Boat tours

Accent Cruises, T604-6886625, www.champagnecruises.com. Sunset cruise ($25); dinner cruise 1730-2030 ($60). **False Creek Ferries**, (see Getting around, p22), runs tours for $10, $7child, which can be joined at any stop along the route. **Harbour Cruises**, north tip of Denman St, T604-6887246, www.boatcruises.com. Tours include sunset dinner cruises, Indian Arm luncheon cruise, and Vancouver harbour tour ($25 for 1 hr 15 mins).

Bus tours

Grayline, T604-8793363, www.grayline.com. Bus tours anywhere, any size. Tour Vancouver in a double-decker bus ($35), overnight packages from $135. **Vancouver Trolley**, T604-8015515, www.vancouvertrolley.com. 2-hr trolleybus tours with 23 stops, and on-off privileges, starting in Gastown, 0900-1430. $30/15 concessions day ticket.

Vancouver Listings

Cliffhanger Indoor Rock Climbing Centre, T604-8742400. 750 sq m to climb over with views of the North Shore Mountains. For the best climbing nearby, head to Squamish.

Golf

There are some excellent golf courses around Vancouver, the best being situated outside the city. These include: **Meadow Gardens**, in Pitt Meadows to the east, T604-4655474. Constructed by Les Furber and aimed at experienced players. **Morgan Creek**, T604-5314653, the par-73 home to BC's CPGA, set in a naturally attractive landscape; course designed by Arnold Palmer that includes a 14-ha wildlife refuge. **Westwood Plateau**, in Coquitlam, T604-9454007. Famed for its spectacular natural features and mountain setting. Closer to town are: **McCleery**, T604- 2578191, and **Fraserview**, T604-2801818, both on Southwest Marine Dr and open year round; and the **University Club**, T604-2241818 at UBC.

Hiking

Hiking in the Coast Mountains on the North Shore is prime (see p89), but even better trails are found further north around Squamish, Whistler and Garibaldi. **Eco Trail Escapes**, T604-9295751, www.ecotrailescapes.com. Offers hikes in and around Vancouver, lunch, water and transport included.

Kayaking

The best local kayaking is up **Indian Arm**, reached from Deep Cove. This 30-km fjord reaches deep into the Coast Mountains, passing old-growth forest and waterfalls, with ample chance to view wildlife. The second-best local starting point is **Bowen Island**, from where the 8 Paisley Islands can be visited as a day trip. **English Bay** and **False Creek** offer mellow paddling in the heart of the city. For rapids, head for the **Capilano** and **Seymour** rivers.

Takaya Tours, 3093 Ghum-Lye Dr, North Vancouver, T604-9047410, www.takayatours.com, runs trips up Indian Arm from Deep Cove with First Nations guides. The following companies offer rentals, and 3-hr lessons or tours for around $65:
Bowen Island Sea Kayaking, T604-9479266, www.bowenisland kayaking.com.
Deep Cove Canoe and Kayak, 2156 Banbury Rd, North Vancouver, T604-9292268, www.deepcovekayak.com.
Ecomarine Ocean Kayak Centre, Granville Island, T604-6897575, www.ecomarine.com.
Ocean West Expeditions, 1750 Beach Av, T604- 6885770, www.ocean-west.com.

Mountain biking

There are a lot of first-class, hard-core mountain bike trails around Vancouver, not for the inexperienced. The 3 main areas are **Cypress**, **Seymour** and **Fromme Mountains**. Trail maps of these areas ($6 each), along with some much-needed advice, are available at bike shops. See also *Mountain Biking BC* by Steve Dunn. Seymour is probably the least difficult of these, but **Burnaby Mountain** and **Fisherman Trail** are more appropriate rides for intermediates/beginners. Note that by law you must wear a helmet.

For detailed professional information or tours contact Johnny Smoke at **Bush Pilot Biking**, T604-9857886, www.bush pilotbiking.com. For rentals, there's **Simon's Bike Shop**, Downtown at 608 Robson, T604-6021181; **Deep Cove Bikes**, 4310 Gallant Av, T604-9291918; **John Henry** on the North Shore at 400 Brooksbank Av, T604-9865534; **Spokes Bicycle Rentals**, near Stanley Park at 1798 W Georgia St, T604-6885141, with road bikes, tandems, child trailers, baby joggers; **Bayshore**, 745 Denman, T604-6882453, rents rollerblades and pushchairs.

Best hikes

Hiking around Vancouver (west to east)

▲▲ **The Lions** ⓘ *15 km round trip, 1525 m elevation gain. Trailhead: at Lions Bay on Hwy 99, turn east onto Oceanview Rd then left onto Cross Creek Rd, right onto Centre Rd, left onto Bayview Rd, left onto Mountain Drive, left onto Sunset Drive and park at the gate.* This is a steep hike, but the views are great from the base of the Lions, especially if you can scramble down to the gap between them.

▲▲ **Mount Gardner** ⓘ *16 km round trip, 750 m elevation gain. Trailhead: take the ferry from Horseshoe bay to Bowen Island.* Directions are complicated so ask at the information centre or consult *Don't Waste Your Time in the BC Coast Mountains*. This is a fairly demanding but highly rewarding hike that is possible almost year-round. Catch an early ferry to allow plenty of time. Panoramic views from the top are spectacular.

▲▲ **Hollyburn Mountain** ⓘ *8 km round trip, 405 m elevation gain. Trailhead: by the ski area map next to the car park in Cypress Provincial Park.* This is one of the finest and easiest trails on the North Shore with panoramic views from the top. You also walk through what is probably the finest stand of ancient giant cedar, fir and hemlock within reach of the city. Snow-free from mid-June to mid-November.

▲▲ **Mount Strachan** ⓘ *10 km round trip, 534 m elevation gain. Trailhead: as above.* A first-rate hike, this route follows the Howe Sound Crest Trail for a while before heading through Strachan Meadows then steeply up the edge of a gorge, alongside precipitous cliffs and through a beautiful stretch of old-growth forest. The north summit offers the best views. This trail is rarely free of snow before mid-July.

▲▲ **Brothers and Lawson Creeks** ⓘ *10 km loop, 437 m elevation gain. Trailhead: From Highway 1 or Marine Drive take Taylor Way north. Turn left onto Highland Drive and continue until you can turn left onto Eyremount Drive. Park where this road intersects Millstream Rd.* Walk west on gated road and look for signs for Brothers Creek Forest Heritage Walk. This short, undemanding hike takes in a gorge and some cascades, but is best recommended for the ease with which you can see some really big cedars in their natural environment.

▲▲ **Mount Seymour** ⓘ *9 km round trip, 440 m elevation gain. Trailhead: Mount Seymour Provincial Park car park.* Providing one of the easiest routes to astonishing summit panoramas, this trail is understandably very popular. But it is certainly no pushover. The route can be confusing, and is dangerously exposed to bad weather. Views from the top are some of the most extensive around. The route is rarely snow-free before August.

Sailing

The *Yellow Pages* is full of luxury yacht cruises. For something more authentic, go for **Cooper's Boating Centre**, 1620 Duranleau St, T604-6874110, www.cooperboating.com, or just shop around in this part of Granville Island. **Jericho Sailing Centre**, Jericho Beach, T604-2244177, www.jsca.bc.ca, arranges trips, lessons, and rentals. **Simplicity Sailing Charters**, North end of Denman, T604-7650074, www.simplicitysailingcharters.com, offers sailing tours from $320 for 3 hrs.

Scuba diving

Whytecliffe Park at the western tip of the North Shore, **Cates Park** in Deep Cove, and **Porteau Cove** on Hwy 99, are all renowned underwater reserves, and the waters around **Vancouver Island** have been named the second-best place in the world to dive by the Jacques Cousteau Society.

Diving Locker, 2745 W 4th Av, T604-7362681, www.kochersdiving.com. PADI diving instructors for 30 years. Beginners' course $299 all inclusive. A wide range of advanced courses available, as well as 2- and 3-day dive trips. Sun Safari day trips for $100 including all the gear, and equipment rental ($50 per day for the works). **BC Dive and Kayak Adventures**, 1695 W 4th Av, T604-7321344, www.bcdive.com; and **Rowand's Reef Dive Team**, 1512 Duranleau St, Granville Island, T604-6693483, www.rowandsreef.com, also come recommended for courses, trips and rentals.

Skiing

Cypress Mountain, T604-9265612, www.cypressmountain.com, is geared towards more advanced skiers, with the largest vertical drop, and terrain that divides up as 23% beginner, 37% intermediate, 40% expert. 5 chair lifts lead to 34 runs on 2 mountains, with night skiing on all runs. There is also a snowboard park with half-pipe, and 10 km of snowshoeing trails. A SnowPlay area has tubing and tobogganing. All rentals are available, and lessons are given for skiing and boarding. There is a café and a lounge. A ski pass is $42. The hill is open daily 0900-2230. Also in the park at Hollyburn Ridge are 19 km of track-set cross-country trails including 7 km lit up at night, $17, T604-9220825.

Grouse Mountain, T604-9809311, www.grousemountain.com, has easy access, tremendous views, night skiing, and the best facilities. Day pass is $42, $18 children; less for night skiing (1600-2200); 5-day pass is $165/75. A high-speed gondola takes you to the base, from where other lifts fan out. Also ice skating, snowshoeing, and 5.3 km of cross-country trails, lit at night.

Mount Seymour, T604-9862261, www.mountseymour.com, is good for beginners and snowboarders, with 3 snowboard parks. Open 0930-2200 weekdays, 0830-2200 weekends. Day pass $33, $14 child, with reduced rates from 1300 and 1600. Book of 5 tickets $119, $59 children. Ski and snowboard rentals, plus lesson/ticket/ rental packages. Snowshoeing: $17-20 including rentals. For the Snow Tube Park schedule call T604-7187771. Shuttle bus from Lonsdale Quay $7 return, $4 one-way.

See Shopping, p87, for equipment sales. **Sigge's Sport Villa**, 2077 W 4th Av, T604-7318818, has the biggest selection of cross-country equipment, plus lessons and rentals. They run shuttles to Manning Park on Sun ($54 return with trail pass).

Swimming

The 2 best swimming spots in town are the large open-air pool at **Kits Beach** (see p61) and the professional-sized heated saltwater pool in the **Vancouver Aquatic Centre**, 1050 Beach Av, T604-6653424. The latter also contains a fitness centre.

Walking tours

Architecture Institute of BC, 100-440 Cambie St, T604-6638588 ext 333, www.aibc.ca. 6 different guided

architectural tours, Jun-Aug, Tue-Sat: Gastown, Chinatown, Downtown, West End, False Creek North/Yaletown. Tours start at 1300, $5 per person.
Walkabout Historic Vancouver, 6038 Imperial St, T604-7200006. Walking tour with costumed guides recounting stories and folklore. **The X-tour**, T604-6092770, www.x-tour.com, visits sites used in filming the X-Files. Prices from $30-$150, with a maximum of 7 people.

Sunshine Coast *p67*
For information see www.roughlife.com. Windsurfing is popular at **Douglas Bay** to the south of Powell River.

Boat tours
Sunshine Coast Tours, T1800-8709055, www.sunshinecoasttours.bc.ca. Tours to Chatterbox Falls on Princess Louisa Inlet, a beautiful spot.

Canoeing and kayaking
Powell Forest Canoe Route. An excellent 5- to 7-day trip travelling through 12 lakes, as well as rivers and creeks, with a choice of 20 forestry campgrounds and a few B&Bs along the way. Open Apr-Nov, the route includes 80 km of canoeing, with 10 km of portage along good trails. Start at Lois Lake, 7 km down logging roads from a clearly marked turning 10 km past Saltery Bay.
Pedals and Paddles, Tillicum Bay Marina, Sechelt, T604-8856440, www.pedals paddles.com. Wonderful trips up the inlet.
Porpoise Bay Charters, 5718 Anchor Rd, Sechelt, T604-8855950. Tours and kayaking at the Skookumchuck Narrows.
Powell River Sea Kayak, T604-4832160, www.prcn.org/kayak. Rentals, equipment, drop-off/pick-up, and all manner of tours around Malaspina Peninsula, Desolation Sound and beyond, ranging from a $39 sampler to 7 days for $1999.
Rockfish Kayaking, Lund Harbour. Rental.
Sunshine Kayaking, Molly's Lane, Gibsons Landing, T604-8869760, www.sunshine kayaking.com. Rentals and tours.

Diving
This area has some of the best diving in the world, with at least 20 sites, many right from the shore. Expect to see octopuses, lots of wrecks, and, at **Saltery Bay**, a 9-ft mermaid.
Alpha Dive Services, 6789 Wharf St, Powell River, T604-4856969, www.dive powellriver.com. Equipment rentals, charters, instruction and information.
Pristine Charters, Lund Harbour, T604-4831131, www.pristine charters.com. As above.

Fishing
Seaborne Adventure Charters, Pender Harbour, T604-8839120, www.sunshine coastcharters.com. A highly recommended operator for charters and tours.

Hiking and biking
The **Sunshine Coast Trail** stretches from Saltery Bay to the tip of the Malaspina Peninsula north of Lund, a total of 178 km. Pioneered by volunteer enthusiasts as a means of connecting the region's remaining sections of old-growth forest, this hike is still young and quite unknown, but destined to become a classic. Incorporating shorelines, lakes and views , it's accessed from several points along the highway, skirting close to campsites, B&Bs and hotels, and connecting with a canoe route. Look out for a number of interesting wooden bridges crossing creeks. The trail can also be used by mountain bikers, starting at Lund (take a water taxi). For details contact Powell River Information Centre or www.sunshinecoast-trail.com. There are dozens of other hikes inland. A good but easy hike, with wheelchair access, is around **Inland Lake**.
Taw's Cycle and Sports, 4597 Marine Av, Powell River, T604-4852555. Bike rentals.

Rock climbing
The **Eldred River Valley** has a number of challenging climbs of varying difficulty. Pick up the *Climbers Guide to Powell River* at the visitor centre.

⊖ Transport

TransLink, T604-5210400, www.trans link.bc.ca, operates an inadequate network of city buses, a fast and generally efficient elevated rail system called the SkyTrain, and a passenger ferry between Waterfront SkyTrain Station and North Vancouver's Lonsdale Quay called the SeaBus. Tickets bought on any of these are valid for any number of journeys in any direction on all 3 within a 90-min period. The system is divided into 3 fare zones, with Zone 1 covering almost everything of interest. Fares are $2.25 for 1 zone, $3.25 for 2 and $4.50 for 3. Concession fares are $1.50 for 1 zone, $2 for 2 and $3 for 3. Zone 2 and 3 tickets are $2 after 1830, at weekends and on holidays. A day pass is $8 ($6 seniors).

There is also a transit service for the disabled called HandyDART (see Directory, p95, for details). Information on all services, including maps and timetables for individual lines, is available at the visitor centre, public libraries, and SkyTrain ticket booths.

Air

For information and flight arrivals/ departures, T604-2077077, www.yvr.ca, see also Ins and outs p50. For international flights see Essentials p19. One-way fares in summer from Vancouver are: $105 to Kelowna with WestJet; $175 to Castlegar (for Nelson) with Air Canada Tango; $132 to Calgary with Air Canada Tango; $195 to Whitehorse with Air North. Air Canada, West Coast Air and Pacific Coastal have several flights daily to Victoria (Vancouver Island), $110. Pacific Coastal, T604-4822107, www.pacific-coastal.com, flies up to 6 times daily in summer to Powell River (Sunshine Coast), $129 return, $99 one-way, less with 10 days' notice.

Airline offices Air Canada, 1030 W Georgia, T1888-2472262; American, T1800-4337300; British Airways, T1800-2479297; Continental, T1800-2310856; KLM, T1800-2252525; Lufthansa, T1800- 5635954; Qantas, T1800-2274500; WestJet, T1800-5385696. In Canada, it is sometimes cheaper to book flights with a travel agent. Flight Centre, www.flightcentre.ca, is cheap and helpful, with many branches, including 903 Denman St, T604-6640365. Travel Cuts, 1114 Burnaby St, HI Hostel, T604-6592845, is also useful.

Floatplanes West Coast Air, T604-6066888; and Harbour Air, T250-3859131, flies to Victoria's Inner Harbour from Downtown (by Canada Place) or from the airport. The cost is about $120, saving an hour of bus time.

Bus

Local Vancouver's bus system is rather slow and not geared towards visitors. The exact fare is dropped into a machine, which doesn't give change. If you have bought a ticket in the last 90 mins (time of purchase is on the ticket), feed it into the machine, which will give it back. The service, which is split between diesel buses and electric trollies, is being consistently cut back with fewer buses on all but the busiest routes and none at all after about 0300. Very few bus stops, and no vehicles, carry any information. Thankfully most routes run through Granville St, Downtown.

Long distance Buses (and trains) all leave from the VIA Rail Pacific Central Station, 1150 Station St, in a grim but handy part of town near the Main St/Terminal Av intersection and the Science World SkyTrain Station. Greyhound, T604-4828747, www.grey hound.ca, has connections to most Canadian towns and to Seattle. The following prices are one-way for adult/concession/child and times are approximate. There are 5 daily buses to Banff (11 hrs, $106/$95/$53); 5 to Calgary (15-17 hrs, $125/$113/$63); 2 to Jasper (11 hrs, $106/$95/$53); 5 to Kamloops (5 hrs, $51/$46/$26); 6 to Kelowna (6 hrs, $56/$51/$28); 3 to

Prince George (12½ hrs, $104/$94/$52); 4 to **Toronto** (70 hrs, $332/$299/$166); 7 to **Whistler** (2½ hrs, $21/$19/$10); and 8 to **Nanaimo** (2¾ hrs, $12.25/$11/$6 including the ferry, no need to catch a city bus to Horseshoe Bay). Look out for special deals such as the 'Go Anywhere' fares, as little as $119 one-way or $189 return to anywhere in Canada if booked 14 days in advance.

Pacific Coach Lines, T604-6628074, www.pacificcoach.com, runs every 2 hrs to **Victoria** from the bus station or airport. $35, $17.50 child, one-way including ferry. There are a few choices to **Whistler**: the **Snow Shuttle**, T604-7779905, leaves 3 times daily from all Vancouver hostels. $35 one-way/$65 return, cheaper with hostel membership or student card. The **Snowbus**, T604-6857669, www.snow bus.ca, costs $36 return, sometimes as low as $29 return. **Perimeter Whistler Express**, T604-2665386, picks up at the airport and major hotels and charges $65 one-way. **Malaspina Coach Line**, T1877- 2278287, runs 2 buses daily to **Powell River** on the Sunshine Coast (6 hrs).

Moose Travel Network, T604-7779905, www.moosenetwork.com, is the simplest way to get around BC and the Rockies. At least 16 different routes, mostly starting and ending in Vancouver, cover most possible itineraries. You can get on and off at whatever stops you want, with no time limits. Travel is in 11-24 seat mini-coaches, with lots of activities on the way. See Essentials p21, and Adventure Tours, p87.

To/from USA Greyhound, T1800-2312222, runs 6 daily buses between **Seattle** and Vancouver (4 hrs, $27 one-way). The **Quickshuttle**, T604-9404428, www.quickshuttle.com, also connects Vancouver with Downtown **Seattle**: 8 services daily from the Holiday Inn at 1110 Howe St, Downtown, stopping at the airport, with an express service from Canada Place Fri-Mon (4 hrs, $41, $23 child one-way).

Car

For advice on travelling by car, including the cost of rental, see Essentials p22. All the major car hire agencies have offices Downtown and at the airport. **Avis**, T604-6062869; **Budget**, T604-6687000; **Hertz**, T604- 6064711; and **Thrifty**, T604-6061666, offer a one-way service. **Rent-a-wreck**, T604-6880001, rents minivans which you can sleep in. The following offer one-way RV rentals, often just to Calgary: **Candan**, T604-5303645, www.candan.com; **Cruise Canada**, T604-9465775, www.cruisecanada.com; **Go West**, T604-5283900, www.go-west.com.

Ferry

Local SeaBus ferries leave every 15 mins and take 12 mins to make the gorgeous journey across **Burrard Inlet** from Waterfront Station to Lonsdale Market. They are wheelchair accessible and can carry bikes. On **False Creek**, the Aquabus runs from the south end of Hornby St to Science World, stopping at the Arts Club on Granville Island, the end of Davie St in Yaletown, and behind Monk McQueens at Stamp's Landing. Each stop is $2-3 depending on length. False Creek Ferries run from the Maritime Museum in Vanier Park to Science World, stopping at the Aquatic Centre on Beach Av, Granville Island Public Market, Stamp's Landing, and BC Place. From $3-5 one-way. 40-min tours are $8, $5 concessions.

Long distance BC Ferries run from Tsawwassen, about 30 km south of Vancouver, to **Victoria**, the **southern Gulf Islands** and **Nanaimo**. To get Downtown from here take bus No 404 and transfer to No 98 at Airport Junction ($4.50). The crossing to Victoria takes 95 mins and runs roughly 0700-2100. Horseshoe Bay, some 15 km northwest of the city on Hwy 99, is a far nicer terminal, and much more convenient for **Nanaimo**, as well as **Bowen Island** and the **Sunshine Coast**. To get Downtown take bus No 250 or No 257 ($3.25). The crossing to Nanaimo takes 95 mins and runs every 2 hrs or so from 0630-2100, more frequently in summer. A new, passenger-only, high-speed ferry operated by **Harbour Lynx**, T604-7534443, will take you from the waterfront SeaBus terminal to **Nanaimo** in 75 mins. From there **Tofino Bus Lines**, T604-7252871, run minibuses to **Tofino**.

Train

Local The SkyTrain is a much better and faster service than the bus, but with only a few really useful stops: Waterfront in the old Canadian Pacific Station next to Canada Place; Burrard at Burrard/Dunsmuir; Granville, beneath the Bay on Granville St; Science World-Main St; and Broadway at the Broadway/Commercial junction. The SkyTrain route out to the airport is scheduled to be finished in time for the 2010 Winter Olympics. Ticket machines give change.

Long distance Like buses, trains leave from the **VIA Rail Pacific Central Station**, 1150 Station St. **VIA Rail's** *The Canadian*, T1888-8427245, www.via rail.ca, connects Vancouver and **Toronto** via **Kamloops** and **Jasper**. It runs 3 times per week each way, leaving Vancouver on Fri, Sun and Tue. The journey takes 3 days and costs from $780 one-way to a rather steep $1660 per adult in a double room. **Amtrak**, T1800-8727245, www.am trak.com, runs daily trains to **Seattle**.

Taxis

Taxis are well regulated and compare favourably with public transport prices. After 2400 they are about the only way to get around. The main companies are **Black Top/Checker Cabs**, T604-7311111, and **Yellow Cab Co**, T604-6811111.

Sunshine Coast *p67*
Air

Pacific Coastal, T604-4822107, www.pacific-coastal.com, flies up to 6 times daily in summer between **Vancouver** and Powell River, $129 return, $99 one-way, less with 10 days' notice.

Bus

Local Powell River is the only town too large to get around on foot. **Powell River Transit System**, T604-4854287, runs the local service, including connections between the airport and Downtown. Bus No 1 runs every hour on the hour from the Mall, inland on Alberni, to the historic townsite and Powell Lake.

Long Distance Malaspina Coach Lines, 4675 Ontario St, T1877-2278287, www.malaspinacoach.com, runs 1 daily bus between Powell River and **Vancouver** (6 hrs), with all stops along the way, leaving Vancouver at 1515, with an extra bus Fri-Sun at 0715, returning 0645 (and 1630). Buses terminate at the Coast Hotel, also stopping at the Westview ferry.

Car/Ferry

Driving from Vancouver to the Sunshine Coast involves 2 ferries. The first, from Horseshoe Bay to Langdale leaves every 2 hrs or so, 0720-2115 (0620-2020 on the way back). The second, from Earls Cove to Saltery Bay, also runs every 2 hrs, 0630-2210 (0540-2115 on the return). $9 per person, $27.75 per vehicle for a return from Horseshoe Bay to Langdale or a one-way to Saltery Bay.

Ferry/water taxi

BC Ferries, www.bcferries.bc.ca, runs 4 times daily between Powell River and Comox/Courtenay on **Vancouver Island**, $7.50, $32.50 with vehicle (80 mins). 0800, 1200, 1715, 2045 from Powell River; 0620, 1000, 1515, 1915 from Comox. **Lund Water Taxi**, T604-4839749, runs to **Savary Island**, $7.50 one-way (subject to change).

☉ Directory

Banks

Finding an ATM in Vancouver is never a problem. The main Canadian banks are clustered in a few blocks around Burrard and Georgia. **Currency exchange**: **Thomas Cook**, 777 Dunsmuir St in the

Pacific Centre Mall. **Custom House**, 999 West Hastings St or 355 Burrard St.

Canada Post
The main post office with General Delivery (Poste Restante) is at 395 W Georgia. Others are at 595 Burrard St, 418 Main, 732 Davie. Letters can be posted at major pharmacies.

Consulates
Australia, 1225-888 Dunsmuir, T604-6841177; **Germany**, 704-999 Canada Place, T604-6848377; **Italy**, 1100-510 W Hastings, T604-6847288; **Japan**, 900-1177 W Hastings, T604-6845868; **Netherlands**, 595 Burrard St, T604-6846448; **New Zealand**, 1200-888 Dunsmuir, T604-6847388; **Norway**, 200 Burrard, T604-6827977; **Sweden**, 1100-1188 W Georgia, T604-6835838; **Switzerland**, 790-999 Canada Place, T604-6842231; **UK**, 800-1111 Melville, T604-6834421; **United States**, 1075-1095 W Pender, T604-6854311, 24-hr visa information for US citizens, T1900-4512778.

Disabled access and facilities
For more information, see Essentials p95. With more than 14,000 sidewalk ramps, Vancouver claims to be one of the most wheelchair-accessible cities in the world. Half of the buses and all but the Granville St SkyTrain station are wheelchair accessible, and the HandyDART is a bus service designed for wheelchair users. It mainly runs 0630-1900 weekdays, for more information and booking call T604-4302692. Vancouver Airport was designed to be friendly to those with hearing, visual and mobility difficulties. For accessible taxis call **Vancouver Taxi** at T604-2555111. **Greyhound** has lift-equipped services to **Kelowna**, **Calgary** (via **Banff**) and **Prince George**, and the Pacific service to **Victoria** is also accessible.

Emergencies
Fire and Rescue T604-6656000. **Police** 2120 Cambie St, T604-7173321, www.city.vancouver.bc.ca: **24-hr Crisis Centre** T604-8723311. **Women's Shelter**, T604- 8728212; **BC Women's Hospital and Health Centre** , T604-8752424. **Rape Crisis Centre**, T604-2556344.

Internet
Free in public libraries. **Cyber Space**, 1741 Robson, $1 per 30 mins; **Virtual Coffee Bean**, 1595 W Broadway; **Websters Internet Café**, 340 Robson.

Laundry
Davie Laundromat, 1061 Davie; **Kitsilano Laundromat**, 2208 W 4th Av; **Swan's**, 1352 Burrard.

Medical services
Dentists Acute Dental Centre, 6325 Fraser St, T604-3274406. **Hospitals** Vancouver General, 855 W 12th St, T604-8754111. St Paul's, 1081 Burrard, T604-6822344. **Pharmacies** London Drugs has branches at 70 Granville, 1187 Robson and 1650 Davie (24-hr); **Shoppers Drug Mart** has branches at the Pacific Centre at 700 Georgia, and 1020 Denman. **Travel clinics** 1030 W Georgia, T604-6815656; 601 W Broadway, T604- 7369244. **Walk-in Clinics** Care-Point Medical Centres, T604-8781000, www.carepoint.bc.ca, 0900-2100, till 1800 weekends: 1123 Davie and 1175 Denman.

Powell River *p68*
Bank Royal Bank, 7035 Barnet St, T604-4855968. **Internet** Visitor Centre and Public Library, 4411 Michigan Av. **Laundry** Harbour Guest House, 4454 Willingdon Av. **Medical services** Powell River General Hospital, 5000 Joyce Av, T604-4853211. **Post Office** 4812 Joyce Av, T604-4855552.

Vancouver Island

Flores Island, Clayoquot Sound

Don't miss...

1 Victoria's Inner Harbour ▶▶ *p102.*

2 Salt Spring Island ▶▶ *p106.*

3 Tofino ▶▶ *p125.*

4 Cortes Island ▶▶ *p145.*

5 Strathcona Provincial Park ▶▶ *p145.*

To Prince Rupert

Klemtu

YUKON
Whitehorse
NORTHWEST
TERRITORIES

ALASKA
USA

BRITISH
COLUMBIA

Prince
Rupert

Prince
George

ALBERTA

Vancouver

Vancouver
Island

USA

Rocky Mountains

Calgary

Firvale

Stuie

Cambell
Island

Ocean Falls

Waglisla
Bella Bella
Shearwater

Hunter Island

Namu

Calvert Island

Rivers Inlet

Dawsons
Landing

Good Hope

Queen
Charlotte
Sound

Margaret Bay

Allison Harbour

Seymour Inlet

BRITISH COLUMBIA

Kleena Kleena

Chilcotin Hwy

Chilanko
Forks

Redst

Tatla
Lake

Tatlayoko
Lake

Coast Mountains
Pacific ranges

Mt
Waddington

Ts'ylos
Provincial Park

Chilcotin Ran

Cape Scott
Provincial Park

Holberg

Coal Harbour

Winter
Harbour

Quatsino

Port Alice

Port Hardy

Port McNeill

Telegraph
Cove

Malcolm
Island
Sointula

Alert Bay

Sullivan Bay

Kingcome
Inlet

Simoom
Sound

Knight Inlet

Queen Charlotte Strait

Kyuquot

Zeballos

Tahsis

Nootka
Island

Nootka
Sound

Gold River

Vancouver Island Ranges

19

28

Port Neville

Kelsey Bay

Sayward

Rock Bay

Granite Bay

Bloedel
Heriot Bay

Quinsam

Jackson Bay

Roy

Thurlow

Stuart Island

Redonda Bay

Read
Island
Quadra
Island

Cortes
Island

Cortes Bay

4

Strathcona
Provincial Park

5

Mount
Washington
Ski Area

Merville

Comox

Courtenay

Vancouver Island

Union Bay

Cumberland

Campbell
River

Landing
Lund

Blubber
Bay
Westview

Vananda

Denman
Island

Hornby
Island

Bowser

Powell River

Stillwater

Irvines
Landing

Sunshine Coast

Garibaldi

Brackendale

Squamish

Britannia Beach

Port Mellon

Sechelt
Peninsula

Sechelt

Gibsons Landing

Horseshoe
Bay

West V

Clayoquot
Sound

Ahousat
Kakawis

Tofino

Long Beach

3

Pacific Rim
Provincial Park

Ucluelet

Sproat Lake

Port Alberni

Coombe

Kildonan

Barkley
Sound
Broken Islands
Group

Bamfield

Qualicum
Beach

Lasqueti

Halfmoon Bay

Parksville

Nanaimo

Extension

Cassidy

Gabriola
Island

Georgia Strait

Vancouver

Richmond

Delta

Tsawwassen

91

99

West

White
Rock

Pacific Ocean

p139

p120

West Coast Trail

Pacific Rim
Provincial Park

Youbou
Lake
Cowichan

Ladysmith

Chemainus

Crofton

Duncan

Galiano
Island

Salt
Spring
Island

Fulford
Harbour

2

18

Cobble Hill

Sidney

San Juan
Island

Anacortes

Port Renfrew

Juan de Fuca
Provincial Park

Malahat

Colwood

Sooke Esquimalt

17

14

Saanich

Victoria

p100

USA

N

30 km
30 miles

To Seattle

Dissected lengthwise by a central mountain range, Vancouver Island has two distinct faces. Most inhabitants live on the sheltered east coast, which enjoys Canada's mildest climate. Located on a picturesque natural harbour and known as the City of Gardens, Victoria is the province's capital and its most attractive town. Nearby in the Georgia Strait, the Gulf Islands are friendly and laid-back with plenty of walks, viewpoints and beaches. Halfway up the coast, the town of Courtenay offers skiing at Mount Washington and hiking in Strathcona Provincial Park, while further north there is increasing wilderness, outdoor pursuits, and the chance to see orca whales. The scenic Inside Passage from Port Hardy to Prince Rupert, and the remote Cape Scott Trail also lie beyond the island's salmon capital, Campbell River.

Wild and weather-beaten, the west coast has some of the world's biggest and oldest trees. Pacific Rim National Park contains the ever-popular West Coast Trail, the kayaker's paradise of Barkley Sound, and the endless surf-beaten sands of Long Beach. The seaside village of Tofino is a fun base for numerous great excursions while, further up the coast, Gold River is the gateway to wild and pristine Nootka Sound, another magnet for kayakers and cavers.

Introduction

Vancouver Island

Ratings
Culture
★★★
Landscape
★★★★
Wildlife
★★
Activities
★★★★
Relaxation
★★★★★
Costs
$$$

Victoria and the southern Gulf Islands

British Columbia's capital is arguably the most charming town in Western Canada. Surrounded by water on three sides, Victoria huddles around a picturesque harbour, and seduces visitors with its pleasant ocean walks, fresh air and whale-watching trips. There's also a first-class museum, and a fine selection of restaurants, pubs and bars. A liberal scattering of gardens, parks and flowers complements the grandiose architecture, adding to the natural beauty of the location, though the pervasive Englishness might make this an unwise first stop for visitors from the UK.

⊘ **Getting there** Ferry, bus, car or plane.
⊖ **Getting around** Bus or car.
⊕ **Time required** 4-7 days minimum.
⊜ **Weather** Mild but windy.
⊜ **Sleeping** 5-star boutique hotels to camping.
⊕ **Eating** Excellent quality and range, lots of seafood.
▲▲ **Activities and tours** Whale watching, kayaking, cycling and hiking.
★ **Don't miss...** Salt Spring Island's Saturday market ›› p116.

A short ferry ride away are Salt Spring and Galiano islands, the two most enticing southern Gulf Islands, where bucolic landscapes and a laid-back lifestyle are combined with a thriving arts and crafts scene, and plenty of hiking, cycling and kayaking opportunities. To the west of Victoria, the rugged coast leads to the attractive community of Sooke, with some decent beaches, and a couple of great hikes, ending at Port Renfrew, southern terminus of the famous West Coast Trail.

Ins and outs

Getting there and around

Victoria International Airport (YYJ), www.victoriaairport.com, is 20 km north of town on Highway 17. The **Airport Shuttle Bus**, T250-3862525, $15, leaves from

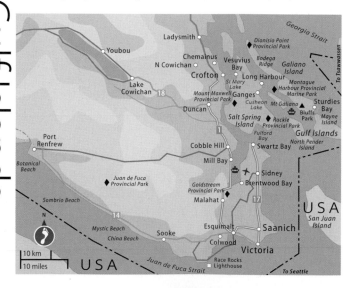

arrivals every 30 minutes 0700-2100, and takes one hour, stopping at the major Downtown hotels; taxis charge around $45. It's also possible to take a floatplane from Downtown Vancouver, which lands directly in Victoria's Inner Harbour, saving an hour of bus time. Ferries from Vancouver's Tsawwassen terminal arrive at Swartz Bay, 40 km north of Victoria, from where bus No 70 runs to Douglas Street in Downtown Victoria ($2.75); taxis are $55. Drivers are advised to book their ferry tickets well ahead, especially in summer. There are also ferries to the southern Gulf Islands (see p106), which can be conveniently visited en route. The **bus terminal** is Downtown at 700 Douglas Street. The **VIA Rail station** ⓘ *450 Pandora, T1888-8427245, www.viarail.ca*, is on the waterfront and connects with points north.

The majority of Victoria's sights can be easily reached on foot. Most buses run from the corner of Douglas and Yates, and there are numerous bicycle lanes. Driving in Victoria can be confusing, with many one-way streets, and parking can be tricky. ● ▸▸ *p118*.

Best time to visit

Protected from the harsh winds of the Pacific by Washington's Olympic Peninsula, Victoria boasts the mildest climate in Canada, which means it can be enjoyed any time of year. January is the coldest month, with an average temperature of 6.5°C. Spring can begin as early as the end of February, and is arguably the most beautiful season, when the cherry trees are in bloom. A holiday atmosphere reigns throughout the summer, when Victoria's many gardens erupt into colour, hanging baskets adorn the lamp posts, thousands of tourists mill around the Inner Harbour, and some kind of festival is usually underway. Autumn begins in late September, when the gardens take on a fresh set of colours and many of the tourists disappear.

Tourist information

Victoria has a very useful **Travel Information Centre** ⓘ *812 Wharf St, Inner Harbour, T250-9532033, www.tourismvictoria.com, summer 0830-1830, winter 0900-1700*. For more general enquiries try the **Tourism Association of Vancouver Island** ⓘ *T250-7543500, www.islands.bc.ca*. Also useful are www.vancouverisland.com and www.ecoisland.ca. Note that accommodation can be heavily booked throughout the summer.

Victoria ●❼❶♪❀❍▲❶❶ ▸▸ *pp109-119*.

Downtown

Concentrated around Fisgard Street and the 'Gate of Harmonious Interest' is the oldest **Chinatown** in Canada. Eating is the main event here, but Fan Tan Alley, former red-light district and apparently the narrowest street in Canada, has some interesting little shops to explore. **Market Square**, to the south, is worth a quick look, and the streets around Yates are the best for food and drink. You'll be drawn to Wharf Street just to be by the water, but many of Victoria's oldest and finest brick and stone buildings are on **Government Street**, disguised by the tacky ground-floor façades. Check out the art nouveau-style tobacconist at No 1116.

Bastion Square, site of the original Fort Victoria, is pleasant enough, but there's little to see except the handsome former provincial courthouse, which today houses the **Maritime Museum** ⓘ *28 Bastion Sq, T250-3854222, www.mmbc.bc.ca, 0930-1630, $8, $3 child*. Exhibitions contain many artefacts from the Pacific Northwest's maritime history, the highlight of which is the *Tillikum*, a dugout canoe in which Captain John Voss made his three-year attempt to circumnavigate the globe in 1901. One block north of the Empress Hotel is **Victoria Bug Zoo** ⓘ *631 Courtney St, T250-3842847, www.bugzoo.bc.ca, mid-Jun to Sep daily 0930-1900, otherwise Mon-Sat 1000-1730, Sun 1100-1730, $7, $4.50 child*, an off-beat but strangely compelling collection of weird and wonderful insects from around the world.

Victoria's focal point is the picturesque Inner Harbour. A multitude of craft, from kayaks and ferries to yachts and floatplanes, ply these waters where passenger steamships once unloaded their genteel cargo. The wide-open space and undeniable grandeur of the surrounding architecture create a magical atmosphere, especially at night, or in summer

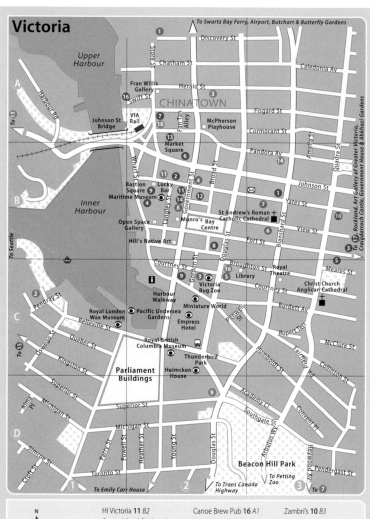

200 metres
200 yards

Sleeping 🛏
Admiral Inn **2** *C1*
Agra House **3** *A2*
Dashwood Manor **7** *D3*
Helm's Inn **9** *D2*

Eating 🍴
Blue Crab Bar & Grill **15** *C1*
Blue Fox Café **5** *B3*
Café Brio **3** *B3*
Camille's **4** *B2*

HI Victoria **11** *B2*
Ocean Island Backpackers Inn **14** *B3*
Spinnakers **15** *A1*
Strathcona **16** *C2*
Swans Suite & Pub **18** *A2*

Canoe Brew Pub **16** *A1*
Demitasse Café *B3* **1**
Ferris' Oyster Bar & Grill **2** *B2*
Green Cuisine **6** *B2*
Kaz Japanese **7** *A2*
Med Grill **17** *B3*
Pagliacci's **8** *B2*
Re-bar **9** *B2*
Reef **11** *B2*
Solstice Café **13** *A2*
Tapa Bar **12** *B2*
Torrefazione Italia **14** *B2*

Zambri's **10** *B3*

Bars & clubs 🍸
Evolution **1** *A2*
Hugo's Grill & Brewhouse **3** *C2*
Hush **4** *B2*
Irish Times **8** *B2*
Legends **5** *C2*
Red Jacket & Hermann's Jazz Bar & Grill **6** *B3*
SYN Bar & Grill **7** *B3*

With its attractive setting and a host of pubs and restaurants overlooking the water, Victoria's Inner Harbour is an ideal place to soak up some colonial charm.

when the harbour walkway is thronged with art peddlers, buskers and tourists. The view landwards is dominated by Victoria's two grandest constructions: the Empress Hotel, and the lavishly illuminated Parliament Buildings, both designed by architect Francis Rattenbury.

Built in 1908, the **Empress Hotel** retains the opulence of the Victorian era quite splendidly. While you may not want to splurge on a room, a self-guided tour is recommended to explore the many lounges, lobbies and dining halls, all dripping with colonial excess. Have a drink in the Crystal Lounge, or partake in the popular (but expensive) ritual of high tea in the Tea Lounge. Next door, **Miniature World** ⓘ *649 Humboldt St, T250-3859731, www.miniatureworld.com, summer 0900-2100, autumn and spring 0900-1900, winter 0900-1700, $9, $8 child*, features tiny reconstructions of various themes such as the World of Charles Dickens, Space 2201 or Fantasyland. The highlight is the scale model of the coast-to-coast Canadian Pacific Railway.

Royal British Columbia Museum
ⓘ *675 Belleville St, corner of Government St, T250-3567226, www.royalbcmuseum.bc.ca, daily 0900-1700, $12.50, $8.70 child.*
Housed in a modest building to the south of the Empress, this highly informative museum ranks as one of Canada's finest, and provides an excellent introduction to the fauna, landscapes and culture of this province. There are three permanent exhibitions and always an excellent temporary exhibition. In the **Natural History Gallery**, a series of realistic dioramas evoke BC's extraordinary landscapes; particularly popular is a life-sized example of the woolly mammoths that roamed these lands until 13,000 years ago. The **First Peoples Gallery** uses wooden masks, carvings, artefacts and audiovisual displays to recount the tragic history of BC's aboriginal population. The journey through time continues with an exploration of the white man's world in the **Modern History Gallery**, which contains displays on the gold rush and early pioneers, plus a recreation of turn-of-the-20th-century Victoria, complete with cobbled streets, buildings, and a cinema showing silent films. Located inside the museum is the **National Geographic Imax Theatre** ⓘ *T250-4804887, www.imaxvictoria.com, 0900-2000, $10.50, $5 child. Show and museum, $21, $15 child.*

Background

Emily Carr

Born and raised in a Victorian household, Emily Carr (1871-1945) made many tours of native Canadian sites, capturing on canvas hundreds of ancient villages, longhouses and totem poles that would soon fall into complete neglect. It wasn't until 1928 that she slowly began to receive the kind of national exposure and critical recognition that she deserved, though financial success remained elusive. Following a heart attack in 1937, she began devoting more of her time to writing, an art form at which she was equally proficient. She was awarded the prestigious Governor General's Award for *Klee Wyck* in 1941, followed by the equally fine *The Book of Small* (1942), and *The House of All Sorts* (1944). Her very readable journals *Growing Pains*, *The Heart of a Peacock*, *Pause*, and *Hundreds and Thousands* were published posthumously. Large collections of her work are held at both the Vancouver and Victoria art galleries, and her Victoria house can also be visited, see below.

Behind the museum on Elliot Street is **Thunderbird Park** ⓘ *May-Oct 0900-1700, by donation*, where a small collection of modern totem poles complements the First Nations Gallery within. A carving-shed offers the chance to see native masters at work. Next door, at 10 Elliot Street, is **Helmcken House**, the oldest surviving house in BC. Built in 1852 for a pioneer physician, it contains an intact set of frightening 19th-century medical implements.

Parliament Buildings and around

Built in 1897, the very British-looking **Parliament Buildings** ⓘ *501 Belleville St, T250-3873046, daily 0830-1700,* set the tone for the whole town, especially at night when they are atmospherically illuminated by 3333 tiny lightbulbs. The interior can be visited on a free guided tour but, despite the anecdotes and efforts of the guides, and a few historical artefacts (such as the dagger that killed Captain Cook), it's really not as impressive as the outside.

In front of the Parliament Buildings are a number of attractions suitable for children. The **Royal London Wax Museum** ⓘ *470 Belleville St, T250-3884461, www.waxmuseum.bc.ca, daily 1000-1900, winter till 16.30, $10, $5 child,* also designed by the prolific Rattenbury, is in the same vein as London's Madame Tussaud's, and just as inexplicably popular. Children inevitably favour the gory Chamber of Horrors. Jutting out into the harbour, the **Pacific Undersea Gardens** ⓘ *490 Belleville St, T250-3825717, www.pacificunderseagardens.com, daily 0900-2000, winter 1000-1700, $8.50, $4.50 child,* is a giant underwater aquarium full of octopuses, eels and various kinds of fish.

Emily Carr House

ⓘ *207 Government St, T250-3835843, www.emilycarr.com, Jun-Oct daily 1100-1600, Sep and May Tue-Sat 1100-1600, $5.35, $4.28 child.*

Four blocks behind the Parliament Buildings is the house where this much-loved Canadian painter and writer was born, and lived most of her twilight years, surrounded by animals. Built in 1864, the house features some of her paintings, which are important historically as well as artistically (see box above). There is a small art gallery showing the work of other local artists.

Beacon Hill Park and the coast

Douglas Street leads south to the ocean, and to beautiful **Beacon Hill Park**, where the bounty of Victoria's warm climate can be appreciated. Winding paths lead between all manner of different trees, from mighty old-growth giants to ornamental deciduous species, past duck ponds, swans and roaming peacocks, and through gardens where tens of thousands of flowers are lovingly tended. There are free tennis courts, lawn bowling, a soccer field and a cricket pitch, as well as a children's **Petting Zoo** ⓘ *mid-Mar to mid-Oct, $2 donation.*

The park leads down to a cliff-front promenade, popular with dog owners, paragliders, and winter storm-watchers. Occasionally, pods of orca can be seen from here. It's a lovely stroll along the shore, with access down to rock pools and the long breakwater. Those with a vehicle or bike could follow the coast east along Dallas Road, taking the scenic routes and admiring the grand houses, or take bus No 5 or 11, maybe as far as the genteel community of **Oak Bay**.

Art Gallery and Craigdarroch Castle

A few sights are clustered together in an area called **Rockland**, east of Downtown along Fort Street. None necessarily justifies the distance on its own, but together they make for a decent morning's diversion. The **Art Gallery of Greater Victoria** ⓘ *1040 Moss St, T250-3844101, www.aggv.bc.ca, Fri-Wed 1000-1700, Thu 1000-2100, $8, $2 child, bus No 11, 22 or 14 from Downtown*, has an extensive and varied permanent collection, including a massive store of Japanese art, and quite a few less-distinguished works by Emily Carr. A short walk away is **Craigdarroch Castle** ⓘ *1050 Joan Cres, off Fort St, T250-5925323, www.craigdarrochcastle.com, summer 0900-1900, winter 1000-1630, $10, $3.50 child, bus No 11 or 14*, built 1887-1889 by Robert Dunsmuir, a Scottish mining expert. He was drafted in to help exploit the black seams, and ended up discovering the most productive coal mine in North America (see p122), becoming BC's first millionaire in the process. Thanks to a shrewd business sense and utter lack of scruples, his net worth when he died – a mere six months before the castle's completion – was $20 million. The rooms are exquisitely decorated, with magnificent stained glass, immaculate Victorian furnishings, and a few oddities like a 3D picture made of human hair. The first few rooms are the best.

Victoria has a lively, cosmopolitan restaurant scene with everything from cheap eats to the finest West Coast cuisine. Fish is delivered fresh from the harbour on a daily basis.

Vancouver Island Victoria & the southern Gulf Islands

While in the area you might also want to take a stroll around the 6 ha of ornamental gardens at **Government House** ⓘ *1401 Rockland Av, T250-3872080, dawn till dusk, free, bus No 1*, where the British royal family stays when visiting.

Butchart Gardens and Butterfly Gardens

If Beacon Hill has whetted your appetite, Victoria has plenty of other magnificent gardens to admire. The hype and price of the **Butchart Gardens** ⓘ *20 km north of Victoria, T250- 6525256, www.butchartgardens.com, summer daily 0900-2230, $23, $11.50 child, follow red signs west onto Keating Rd from Hwy 17, or take Central Saanich bus No 75 from Douglas St*, are equally excessive, but its 20 ha of gardens – including Japanese, rose, Italian, and sunken varieties – are beautifully executed, exceptional in any season, and magical when illuminated at night. Firework displays set to music take place on Saturday evenings in July and August, and live music or puppet shows are frequent. There's a gift shop, restaurant, coffee shop, and a dining room serving the inevitable high tea. Having come this far, visit the nearby **Butterfly Gardens** ⓘ *1461 Benvenuto Rd, 3 mins' drive before Butchart Gardens, T250-6523822, www.butterflygardens.com, Mar-Sep 0900-1700, $10, $5.50 child*, an indoor conservatory packed with the colourful critters.

An alternative to the above is the **Abkhazi Gardens** ⓘ *1964 Fairfield Rd, T250-5988096, www.conservancy.bc.ca, Mar-Oct daily 1100-1700, $10, $7.50 child, bus No 7 from town*, a gorgeous property created by Prince and Princess Abkhazi in the 1940s, and recently saved from housing developers through a purchase by the Land Conservancy. The upper garden affords great views of Victoria and the Juan de Fuca Strait.

Southern Gulf Islands ⬛🖋🍴❄🅾▲🅾🅾 ›› *pp109-119.*

Ins and outs

Salt Spring Island and Galiano Island are reached by ferry from Vancouver's Tsawwassen terminal and Victoria's Swartz Bay. **Seair**, T1800-4473247, operates scheduled flights from Vancouver to Salt Spring ($77 one-way). Salt Spring and Galiano have limited transportation, though there are ferries between the islands. Cycling, driving and kayaking are great ways to get around, and hitchhiking is a way of life. Both islands have small visitor information centres. Pick up a copy of the *Gulf Islander* (available on the islands or ferry), which has good hotel listings; or check www.gulfislands.net and www.gulfislands-bc.com. ⊖ ›› *p119.*

Salt Spring Island

The southern Gulf Islands are an archipelago of odd-shaped landmasses huddling together in the Georgia Strait, famous for their laid-back atmosphere and artist communities. Salt Spring is the biggest, busiest, and most populated, and the only island with any kind of urban focus, the oddly named **Ganges**. There are plenty of eating and drinking options here, with the best chance of finding walk-in accommodation in summer, and an unmissable **Saturday Market** (see Shopping, p116). The trade-off is a lesser degree of tranquillity and quaintness, though these are easily found elsewhere on this sheep-dotted island. There is a small but eager-to-please **Visitor Information Centre** ⓘ *by the shopping centre car park, 121 Lower Ganges Rd, T250- 5375252, summer 0900-1600, winter 1100-1500*. The websites www.salt springtoday.com and www.saltspringmarket.com are useful sources of information. Be sure to pick up a self-guided tour map of 42 nearby **artist studios**.

At the southern end of the island, 9 km east of Fulford Harbour at the end of Beaver Point Road, is **Ruckle Provincial Park**, the largest and one of the nicest on the Gulf Islands. Trails here incorporate forest, 7 km of shoreline, farmland, and historic buildings. There's a good chance of spotting marine life and birds, but the park's outstanding feature is its

Known as the 'Garden City', Victoria's mild climate supports a wonderful array of year-round flowering trees and shrubs. The impeccable Butchart Gardens is the epitome of English gentility.

campground (see Sleeping, p110). For some truly awe-inspiring views of the island-dotted Georgia Strait, head to the top of **Mount Maxwell Provincial Park** ⓘ *just south of Ganges take Cranberry Rd west to Mt Maxwell Rd, then climb steeply for 8 km.* There are some trails through big old trees, but the temptation is just to sit and gawp. It's also a good place to experience the full power of the winds whistling down the strait. West of Fulford Bay, some longer hikes lead up Mount Tuam and Mount Bruce. Swimming is good at **Vesuvius Bay**, or at **St Mary Lake** (north of Ganges) and **Cusheon Lake** (south) for fresh water. There's cheese tasting at **Salt Spring Island Cheese**, 285 Reynold Road, T250-6532300, and **Moonstruck Organic Cheese**, 1306 Beddis Road.

Galiano Island

Despite its rising and understandable popularity, Galiano Island strikes a good balance between adequate infrastructure (unlike many Gulf Islands) and scant development. The closest thing to a village is the ferry terminal of **Sturdies Bay**, which has a small **Visitor Information Booth** ⓘ *2590 Sturdies Bay Rd, T250-5392233.* Pick up the all-important map here, on the ferry, or at www.galianoisland.com. The main activity is hiking through old-growth forest, much of which has been protected by the determined efforts of locals. The longest hike covers the entire eastern coast (about 25 km).

The long, skinny finger of Galiano sits in the Georgia Strait pointing westwards away from Sturdies Bay in the east. Just after the ferry terminal, a left turn down Burrill takes you along Bluff Road and through **Bluffs Park**, a beautiful chunk of old-growth forest. Shortly after, a left fork leads to Active Pass Drive, and the trailhead for ascending **Mount Galiano**, a satisfying hike leading to views of the Olympic Mountains, Navy Channel and, on a clear day, all of the southern Gulf Islands.

Take the right fork instead, then left down Montague Road, to connect back with Porlier Pass Road, and reach **Montague Harbour Provincial Marine Park**. There are three white shell beaches here, a café and store, cracking sunsets, a great campground, and a 3-km shoreline trail around Gray Peninsula. Two-thirds of the way along the island, Cottage Way gives access to **Bodega Ridge**, a 3-km walk with views all the way. **Dionisio Point Provincial Park** at the west end has camping but marine access only, with many rare flowers, fine views, and diving.

The Race Rocks lighthouse on the Juan de Fuca Strait was built on granite imported from Scotland. Three days before it was lit in 1860 a 385-ton tall ship crashed into the rocks and sank.

West to Port Renfrew 🍴🛏️⛰️🏨 ▸▸ *pp109-119.*

Hatley Castle and Fort Rodd

West of Esquimalt Harbour is a brace of sights of a historical bent. **Hatley Castle** ⓘ *8 km west of Victoria off the Sooke Rd (Highway 14), bus No 50 to Western Exchange then Nos 39, 52 or 61, or Galloping Goose Trail by bike*, was built in 1909 for James Dunsmuir, son of Robert, and would appeal to those who enjoyed Craigdarroch Castle. It's situated on the campus of Royal Roads University and is surrounded by a pretty park containing 65 ha of gardens.

Nearby is **Fort Rodd National Historic Park** ⓘ *Fort Rodd Hill Rd, T250-4785849, 1000-1730, bus No 50 to Western Exchange then No 39*, a tranquil 45-ha park that contains some historic military installations and the attractive **Fisgard Lighthouse**. Overlooking the harbour from the end of a causeway made out of scrap cars, this is the oldest lighthouse on the Pacific, having been in continuous operation since 1860.

Sooke

A short 30-km hop west from Victoria, easily reached by bus No 61 or the Galloping Goose bicycle trail, Sooke has a great collection of B&Bs, a couple of excellent restaurants, and a thriving artist community. For a full list of artists' studios, pick up the *Art Map* from the **Visitor Information Centre** ⓘ *2070 Phillips Rd, T250-6426351, www.sooke.org, daily 0900-1700, closed Mon in winter.*

On a warm summer day, you'd be mad not to pay a visit to **Sooke Potholes Park**, north of town at the end of Sooke River Road. It's a magical spot with natural swimming pools carved out of rock, and mellow waterfalls that have caves hidden behind them.

East of Sooke, Gillespie Road leads south from Highway 14 to a peninsula that contains the wonderful and surprisingly underused **East Sooke Regional Park**, a little pocket of wilderness full of hiking trails and viewpoints. The **Coast Trail** is an excellent one-day hike that stretches 10 km between trailheads at Pike Road and Aylard Farm. With jagged cliffs, windswept bluffs and beautiful, unspoilt rainforest, this trail is in good condition and compares favourably with the Juan de Fuca Marine Trail (see p109). Allow at least six hours. Beechey Head is a favourite spot for spotting turkey vultures or watching the annual hawk migration at the end of September.

Juan de Fuca Provincial Park

Between Sooke and Port Renfrew the highway never strays far from the coast, which is dotted with a string of deserted, surf-beaten beaches looking out over the Juan de Fuca Strait. Just west of sleepy Jordan River, the trail and sand of **China Beach** mark the beginning of Juan de Fuca Provincial Park, which protects several long sandy beaches and a strip of coastal rainforest, all of it connected by the **Juan de Fuca Marine Trail**. This 47-km wilderness route opened in 1995 to provide an alternative to the over-burdened West Coast Trail. A guidebook is available from the **Sooke Information Centre** ($18). There are no fees or registration. Four trailheads along the highway provide access: from east to west, China Beach, Sombrio Beach, Parkinson Creek and Botanical Beach. **Mystic Beach**, just west of China Beach, has a 45-minute hike through rainforest and over a suspension bridge to good sand, a waterfall and some shallow caves. **Sombrio Beach** is the best point for surfing while **Botanical Beach** is a great place for exploring tidal pools.

Port Renfrew

There's little reason to visit this logging and fishing village other than to start or finish the Juan de Fuca Trail at Botanical Beach 6 km to the south, or the West Coast Trail (see p128). The latter starts across a narrow inlet at **Gordon River**, which also has an **Information Centre**. Services are few, so hikers are advised to stock up on supplies in Victoria. Forestry recreation sites and a few campgrounds are dotted along the logging roads to the north; ask at the Gordon River Information Centre.

Sleeping

Victoria p101, map p102

L-AL Dashwood Manor, 1 Cook St, T250-3855517, www.dashwoodmanor.com. A broad range of elegant Victorian rooms, with en suite bath, kitchen, and balcony, jacuzzi, or sea views. The location is hard to beat, right on the ocean near Beacon Hill Park. Breakfast included.

AL Admiral Inn, 257 Belleville St, T250-3886267, www.admiral.bc.ca. The most reasonably priced of many expensive choices on the Inner Harbour, with decent rooms and kitchenettes, a nice guest lounge, and breakfast included.

A Spinnakers, 308 Catherine St, T250-3842739, www.spinnakers.com. Tastefully furnished and spacious heritage rooms, or gorgeous garden suites (**L**) adjacent to the first-class pub-restaurant. All have en suite baths, private entrances, and decks or patios onto the lovely garden. Breakfast included. The location on Victoria Harbour is attractive, but a fair walk from Downtown.

A Swans Suite Hotel, 506 Pandora Av, T250-3613310, www.swanshotel.com. Exceptionally stylish rooms and huge suites (**L**) built of brick and wood, with high ceilings and lots of great art. Downstairs is a pub-restaurant with a wonderful collection of native art. Excellent value, and a great location.

B Helm's Inn, 600 Douglas St, T250-3855767, www.helmsinn.com. Given its location between the Inner Harbour and Beacon Hill Park, this is a great deal. There's a variety of recently refurbished rooms and suites, with continental breakfast included, parking and laundry.

C Agra House, 679 Herald St, T250-3801099, www.agrahouse.com. Plain but pleasant, good-value rooms in a handy, central location. Parking and breakfast included.

C Strathcona Hotel, 919 Douglas St, T250-3837137, www.strathconahotel.com. Nicely decorated, good-value rooms in a very central location.

E HI Victoria, 516 Yates St, T250-3854511, www.hihostels.ca. This quiet, professionally-run hostel is conveniently located in the heart of Downtown. The spacious building has nice high ceilings. Facilities include a large kitchen, common room, laundry, lockers, and private rooms for $4 extra.

E Ocean Island Backpackers Inn, 791 Pandora Av, T250-3851788, www.ocean island.com. In a historic building Downtown, this is a very social hostel with plenty of facilities including TV room, licensed bar/lounge hosting regular music events, atmospheric dining room, kitchen, patio, laundry, internet access, storage and bike lock-up. Dorms or private rooms, some with bath and or/TV. They also arrange various tours and activities.

Camping

Thetis Lake, 1938 W Park Lane, T250-4783845. The closest campground to town (10 km away), with showers and laundry. The location is great, with good swimming, a beach, and some nice walks.

Salt Spring Island *p106*

Apart from a couple of standard motels, Salt Spring's beds are mostly in B&Bs, of which there are over 100. The visitor centre has a picture book to help you choose, and will take reservations. Particularly in summer, booking ahead is recommended, using www.saltspringtoday.com or www.saltspringmarket.com.

A Anchor Point B&B, 150 Beddis Rd, 1 km south of Ganges, T250-5380110, www.anchorpointbb.com. 2 lovely, well-appointed en suite rooms, with lounge, library, balcony, hot tub, and ocean views. Breakfast included. Will pick up at ferry.

A Salt Spring Lodge, 641 Fulford-Ganges Rd, T250-5379522, www.saltspring lodge.com. This beautiful property close to Ganges has 2 very attractive and spacious suites that could sleep 6, with kitchenettes and ocean views, plus 1 smaller double.

A-B Quarrystone House, 1340 Sunset Dr, 6 km from Vesuvius Bay, T250- 5375980, www.quarrystone.com. 4 gorgeous en suite rooms with balconies, fireplaces, jacuzzis, and private entrance, in a beautiful ridge location with ocean views. Breakfast provided by the hospitable hosts.

B-C Wisteria Guest House, 268 Park Dr, 10 mins' walk from Ganges, T250-5375899, www.wisteriaguesthouse.com. 7 large, newly renovated rooms, some with private bath, some with kitchen. There's a guest lounge, and breakfast is included.

D-E Salt Spring Island Forest Retreat, 640 Cusheon Lake Rd, T250-5374149, www.saltspringforestretreat.com. May-Oct only. Situated in 4 ha of forest, within walking distance of beaches and the lake, this friendly and very popular lodge has en suite rooms with shared kitchen and living room, 2 small but delightful (and heavily booked) treehouses, and a cosy, brightly coloured gypsy caravan. Access by shuttle bus and taxis. Bikes for hire.

E Valhalla Sleeping Units, 601 Upper Ganges Rd, T250-5381992, www.valhalla sleepingunits.com. Situated halfway between the 2 ferries, 4 cute little cabins with shared outhouse.

Camping

Ruckle Provincial Park, 9 km east of Fulford Harbour at the end of Beaver Point Rd, T250-3912300. The 8 spots for RVs are nothing special, but those with a tent can walk in and claim one of the 70 sites dotted along the shore with exquisite views of Swanson Channel. One of the best camping experiences in Western Canada.

Galiano Island *p107*

AL Galiano Inn, 134 Madrona Dr, T250-5393388, www.galianoinn.com. One of the best lodges on the islands, set in gorgeous grounds overlooking the ocean. The spacious rooms have sumptuous decor, fireplaces, and balconies. Breakfast in the lovely restaurant is included. There's a full spa on site, ask about packages.

A Bellhouse Inn, 29 Farmhouse Rd, T1800- 9707464, www.bellhouseinn.com. A historic farmhouse on the ocean near the ferry. 3 romantic en suite rooms have balconies with wonderful views. Ask them to arrange the bus for you ($3).

B Serenity by the Sea Retreat, 225 Serenity Lane, T250-5392655, www.serenity

bythesea.com. 3 gorgeous en suite rooms high above the ocean, with cosy homely decor, vaulted ceilings, and a private deck. Breakfast and morning yoga included; bodywork and counselling available.

C **Bodega Resort**, 120 Monastee Rd, at west end of island, T250-5392677, www.bodegaresort.com. Spacious and comfortable log cottages that sleep up to 6, situated in beautiful, expansive grounds full of fruit trees and stone carvings, with great views. Horseback riding available.

C **Driftwood Village Resort**, 205 Bluff Rd E, T250-5395457, www.driftwood cottages.com. In a pleasant setting near the ocean, the cottages are a bit old fashioned, but good value. Ask about ferry pick-up.

C **Moonshadows Guest House**, 771 Georgeson Bay Rd, T250-5395544, www.moonshadowsbb.com. 3 colourful, spacious en suite rooms (1 with private deck) in a wood house with lots of light, on a 40-ha farm between Sturdies Bay and Montague Harbour. Free shuttle bus.

C **Rocky Ridge Bed and Breakfast**, 55-90 Serenity Lane, 15 km north of ferry, T250-5393387, www.cedarplace.com/rocky ridge/galianoisland. 3 lovely big rooms (2 with shared bath) in a gorgeous open-plan wooden house on a rocky bluff, with extensive ocean views.

Camping

Montague Harbour Provincial Park, T250-5392115. Wonderful walk-in sites overlooking the ocean, and some nice vehicle sites too. Trails and beaches. Reservation crucial in summer.

Sooke p108

Sooke is famous for its West Coast-style B&Bs, characterized by their wood-dominated decor, vaulted ceilings, and very large windows with ocean views. Below is the cream, but many more can be found at www.sookenet.com, www.sookebnb.com and the visitor centre. Reservations are recommended.

AL **Point No Point**, 10829 West Coast Rd (23 km west), T250-6462020, www.point nopoint.com. Attractive cabins and suites situated on a long private beach. Their highly renowned restaurant serves lunch, English tea and dinner.

B **Arbutus Cove Guesthouse**, 3018 Manzer Rd (6 km east), T250-6426310, www.arbutuscoveguesthouse.com. Large, West Coast style rooms with en suite bath, gorgeous views of the ocean, hot tubs on guest deck right outside the rooms. Breakfast included. A fantastic deal.

B **Coopers Cove Guesthouse**, 5301 Sooke Rd, T250-6425727, www.coopers cove.com. 4 lovely big en suite rooms overlooking the ocean, with fireplaces, decks, and homemade truffles. Connected to a prestigious cooking school (inclusive packages available).

Camping

French Beach Provincial Park, 20 km west, T250-6899025, www.discovercamping.ca. Nice campground with wooded sites and a mile-long sand and gravel beach. Grey and orca whales can be spotted May-Oct.

Sooke River Flats Campsite, T250-6426076, by visitor centre. Basic but handy.

Juan de Fuca Provincial Park p109
Camping

Wilderness camping is allowed at **Mystic**, **Bear**, **China** and **Sombrio** beaches, or in the forest at **Little Kuitche Creek** and **Payzant Creek**. A fee of $5 per person per night is payable at trailheads. Vehicle camping ($14) is available at all trailheads except Botanical Beach. Be aware that wood ticks exist in this region, most prevalent Mar-Jun. Yurts are available at China Beach ($50), T250-6899025. Must have own bedding.

Port Renfrew p109
A-C **Soule Creek Lodge**, off Powder Main Rd, T250-2776853, www.soulecreek lodge.com. The only nice place to stay in Port Renfrew, so book ahead. The lovely, homely lodge rooms have leather couches and en suite or shared baths. Or stay in a surprisingly luxurious yurt. The

112

food is exceptional, so stay for dinner. Can arrange shuttles from trailheads or town. **C West Coast Trail Motel**, Parkinson Rd, T250-6475565. Standard but cheap motel rooms for tired and undemanding hikers.

Camping
Pacheedaht First Nation Campground and RV. No reservations. On a 2-km long beach at the start of the West Coast Trail.

⊘ Eating

Victoria *p101, map p102*
Victoria has a very active culinary scene for a town its size, with a fairly rapid turnover. For the latest developments, check out www.eatmagazine.ca. For cheaper food, walk a block east of Douglas to Blanshard, or check out the many Chinese restaurants around Fisgard Street.

Blue Crab Bar and Grill, 146 Kingston St, T250-4801999. On the harbour behind the Parliament Buildings, with great views onto the ocean. A good choice for fresh seafood, prepared West Coast style from local ingredients. There's also a less expensive menu in the lounge.

Café Brio, 944 Fort St, T250-3830009. European-style fine dining with a West Coast sensibility, using the freshest of local ingredients. The decor and ambience are perfectly pitched: colourful and lively, a fusion of modern and traditional.

Camille's, 45 Bastion Sq, T250-3813433. Fine dining in a classy but casual environment. The diverse menu couples international flavours with West Coast leanings, concentrating on fresh local seasonal produce. The well-chosen wine list features many of BC's finest.

The Blue Fox Café, 919 Fort St, T250-3801683. A breakfast/brunch institution. Small and atmospheric, always crowded with queues out the door. Friendly service, great food, and prime people-watching.

Canoe Brew Pub, 450 Swift St, T250-3611940. A wonderful reclaimed industrial warehouse with big wooden beams, and a huge summer patio overlooking the ocean. There's live music at weekends, and a decent mid-range menu.

Ferris' Oyster Bar and Grill, 536 Yates St, T250-3601824. A personal favourite: small, perennially crowded venue with a lively atmosphere, excellent menu that concentrates on seafood, and reasonable prices. Try their baked oyster platter.

Green Cuisine, Market Square, 560 Johnston St, T250-3851809. A casual and comfortable spot with a wide range of vegan dishes, salad bar, hot buffet, baked goods, and fresh juices and smoothies.

Kaz Japanese, 100-1619 Store St, T250-3869121. A small, unpretentious, family-run venue, serving the best sushi in town.

Med Grill, 1063 Fort St, T250-3813417. In a building covered with a striking mosaic, this modern and attractive eatery has an enticing menu that mixes Mediterranean bistro fare and tapas with a West Coast sensibility.

Pagliacci's, 1011 Broad St, T250-3861662. A great place to encounter locals letting their hair down. The interior is dark, full of theatrical detail, usually packed and noisy with nightly live music. The food is mainly Italian, with a good range of wines and Martinis at reasonable prices. Some people just drop in for drinks and dessert; their cheesecake is legendary.

Re-bar, 50 Bastion Sq, T250-3602401. Another locals' favourite, owned by 2 gifted, very creative cooks. Food is vegetarian, international and varied: curries, enchiladas, perogies, salads, and a great brunch. The lively, colourful interior also features a fresh juice bar.

The Tapa Bar, 620 Trounce Alley, T250-3830013. A lively venue with colourful, Mediterranean interior with lots of art, or seating outside in the alley. Broad selection of mouth-watering tapas.

Zambri's, 911 Yates St, T250-3601171. The menu in this Italian favourite changes daily, incorporating fresh local produce, and homemade sausages and salami.

¶ **The Reef**, 533 Yates St, T250-3885375. A vibrant, increasingly popular spot for good-value Caribbean favourites such as jerk chicken, fish tacos and spiced ribs.

Cafés

Demitasse Café, 1320 Blanshard St. Possibly the best coffee in town, and a good inexpensive lunch menu, too.
Solstice Café, 529 Pandora Av. Coffee and baking in comfortable surroundings with a more youthful, alternative vibe.
Torrefazione Italia, 1234 Government St. Great coffee, and a nice place to hang out, with magazines and papers to browse.

Salt Spring Island *p106*

¶¶¶ **Hastings House**, 160 Upper Ganges Rd, T250-5372362, www.hastingshouse.com. Featuring locally raised lamb, fresh seafood, and herbs from their own garden, this highly renowned restaurant, with an intimate household ambience, is well worth a little extra expense.
¶¶¶ **House Piccolo Restaurant**, 108 Hereford Av, Ganges, T250-5381844, www.housepiccolo.com. Highly regarded gourmet European cuisine in casual but smart surroundings with outdoor seating, and a great wine list.
¶¶ **Moby's Marine Pub**, 124 Upper Ganges Rd, T250-5375559. As well as being perhaps the only place to experience locally brewed Gulf Island beers on tap (the Porter is excellent), this popular locals' hangout also serves up some decent food. Try the teriyaki salmon burger.
¶¶ **Oystercatcher Bar & Grill**, Harbour Building, Ganges, T250-5375041. A casual seafood restaurant with a nice deck overlooking Ganges Harbour.
¶¶ **Tree House Café**, 106 Purvis Lane, Ganges, T250-5375379. This tiny outdoor venue is invariably packed, with quality live music every night May-Sep, making for a quintessential Salt Spring experience. The menu covers several bases, or there's baking and coffee in the morning.

Cafés

¶ **Barb's Buns**, off McPhillips Av, Ganges. A popular bakery serving pizza, pastries, and all sorts of delicious baking.
¶ **Salt Spring Roasting Co**, 109 McPhillips Av, Ganges, T250-6532385. Renowned for their roasted java beans, this café is also the meeting place of choice for locals, with some decent baking and snacks, and good art on the walls.

Galiano Island *p107*

¶¶¶ **Atrevida**, Galiano Inn, 134 Madrona Dr, T250-5393388. Delicious West Coast style food. Gorgeous location, ocean views.
¶¶¶ **La Bérengerie Restaurant**, Montague Rd, close to the park, T250-5395392. 4-course menu of French cuisine only, with reservations required, plus an attractive open-air café in summer (mid-range). Also 3 rooms to rent (**C**).
¶¶ **Hummingbird Pub**, 47 Sturdies Bay Rd. This cosy pub is the best place to meet locals, and also serves some decent food. Their pub bus makes runs to and from the marina hourly 1800-2300.
¶ **Max & Moritz Spicy Island Food House**, T250-5395888, by the ferry landing. Take-out German and Indonesian food.

Sooke *p108*

¶¶¶ **Sooke Harbour House**, 1528 Whiffen Spit Rd, T250-6423421, www.sooke harbourhouse.com. A popular outing for Victorians, and frequently voted one of the best restaurants in BC. Casually classy with ocean views, a sophisticated West Coast menu that changes daily, and a great wine list. The emphasis is on fresh seafood, with herbs and vegetables from their own garden. They also have some excessively opulent and expensive rooms.
¶¶ **17 Mile Pub**, 9 km east, on the highway. English-style pub in a historic building, with a good selection of beer and food.
¶¶ **Mom's**, unmissable in the very centre of town. The epitome of a diner with grouchy waitresses, booths, cheap breakfast, the whole bit. A local institution.

Vancouver Island Victoria & the southern Gulf Islands Listings

¶¶ **Stone Pipe Landing Restaurant**, 5449 Sooke Rd (6 km south), T250-6420566. Seafood with an international flair, including upscale burgers, and fish and chips. Eat on a patio right on the water.

¶ **The Crab Shack**, 6947 West Coast Rd. If you're camping, this is a good place to pick up some fresh seafood.

¶ **The Fish Trap**, on the highway in town, beside the **PetroCan**. The choice in town for fish and chips.

⊕ Bars and clubs

Victoria *p101, map p102*
For a full run-down of clubs, visit www.club vibes.com or pick up the free *Monday Magazine*. Victoria has an active but discreet gay scene, www.gayvictoria.ca.
Evolution, 502 Discovery St, T250-3883000. No cover before 2200. This small, energetic, unpretentious club has different nightly music themes, and is well known for its cheap drinks.
Hugo's Grill and Brewhouse, Magnolia Hotel, 625 Courtney St, T250-9204844. Open till 0200. With its dark, industrial-style interior, and well-chosen music, this is one of Victoria's hippest, most popular venues. There's a restaurant and Martini-bar vibe in the evening, and progressive DJs every night. More relaxed than most clubs. Their beers, brewed on the premises, are also excellent.
Hush, 1325 Government St, T250-3850566. Loud techno, house, and drum'n'bass, with an atmosphere dominated by dramatic red lights. Rated by many as Victoria's best club, and certainly gets some top DJs.
Irish Times, 1200 Government St, T250-3837775. A superior Irish-style pub, with 20 different beers on draught, live Celtic music every night, and a great location that makes its patio the best people-watching spot in town.
Legends, 919 Douglas, T250-3837137. One of the friendlier, more casual clubs, with music that ranges from Top 40 to

hip-hop, house, alternative and retro. Also receives some top live acts.
The Red Jacket, 751 View St, T250-3842582. The best of both worlds, with a dance floor on one side and a lounge on the other. Especially popular Fri-Sat.
Spinnakers Brewpub, 308 Catherine St (cross Johnston St Bridge or take the harbour ferry), T250-3862739. With its exceptional house-brewed beers, and superb food prepared from scratch using local ingredients, this is a superior pub in every way, and a Victoria institution.
Swans Pub, Swans Suite Hotel (see p109), 506 Pandora Av, T250 3613310. A superlative brewpub, with a great selection of quality ales, a roomy yet cosy atmosphere, and most notably one of the best collections of West Coast aboriginal art you'll see anywhere.
SYN Bar and Grill, 759 Yates St. Upmarket but casual chic ambience, one of the best spots for a Martini.

♫ Entertainment

Victoria *p101, map p102*
Galleries
Fran Willis Gallery, 200-1619 Store St, www.franwillis.com. Some wonderful, whimsical local art.
Open Space, 510 Fort St. Artist-run gallery.
Starfish Glassworks, 630 Yates St, T250-3887827. Locally crafted glasswork.

Live Music
Victoria has no shortage of small venues for live music. Pick up the free *Monday Magazine*, or check out www.monday mag.com for listings.
Hermann's Jazz Bar and Grill, 753 View, T250-3889166. The premier jazz venue.
Lucky Bar, 517 Yates, T250-3825825. A trendy, wacky, colourful little bar with live music almost every night, plus house DJs on Saturdays. The sound system is great, and the atmosphere is always high energy.
McPherson Playhouse, 3 Centennial Sq, Government/Victoria, T250-3866121.

Open since 1914, this is a delightful venue for films, dance and music, and features a gallery showing local visual art.
Royal Theatre, 805 Broughton St, T250-3866121. With over 1400 seats, this attractive 1913 heritage building is the major music venue, hosting the Symphony Orchestra, Pacific Opera, major plays, dance, and visiting names of all genres.

Theatre
Belfry Theatre, 1291 Gladstone, T250-3856815, www.belfry.bc.ca. In a beautiful former church, this venue is host to the island's largest professional theatre group, staging high-quality, serious drama.

Salt Spring Island *p106*
There is plenty of art to be seen around Salt Spring, see also Shopping, p116.
Art Spring, 100 Jackson Av, T250-5372102, www.artspring.ca. Vast timber space usually hosting some art exhibitions or events, contains a 265-seat theatre.

⊛ Festivals and events

Victoria *p101, map p102*
Jun JazzFest International, T250-3884233, www.vicjazz.bc.ca is a 10-day event, with jazz, blues and world beat occupying free and ticketed stages around town.
Jul FolkFest in early Jul, www.icafolkfest.com, T250-3884728, $5/day, occupies the Inner Harbour and Market Sq with 10 days of performing arts, wonderful food, arts and crafts, fireworks, and a world feast stage featuring local chefs.
Jul-Aug Victoria Shakespeare Festival, at the Heritage Theatre, St Ann's Academy, 835 Humboldt St, T250-3600234. $13/11 for performances at 2000, less for matinees or late shows.
Aug The annual Chinese Dragon Boat Festival, T250-4722628, www.victoriadragonboat.com, involves 90 boats in the Inner Harbour, with 24-crew paddlers, full dragon regalia, drums, food and crafts.
Victoria Fringe Theatre Festival, T250-3832663, www.victoriafringe.com, in late Aug, is the event for which Victoria is most famous, with countless venues staging all manner of shows from 1200-2400 for 11 days. $8 for indoor shows.

Salt Spring Island *p106*
Jun-Sep Art Craft, Ganges' Mahon Hall, 114 Rainbow Rd, T250-5370899, provides a great opportunity to see (and buy) the work of some 200 or so Gulf Island artists.
Jul Festival of the Arts, T250-5374167. A month-long orgy of Gulf Islands' art.
Jul-Aug Art Spring (see Entertainment) hosts 'Sizzling Summer Nights', featuring performers of all genres.
Sep Salt Spring Fall Fair, during the 3rd weekend, is the biggest event of the year. Held at the fairgrounds, with frequent free shuttles from Ganges.

○ Shopping

Victoria *p101, map p102*
Arts, crafts and gifts
Fort St between Douglas and Linden is known as 'Antique Row'. For gift ideas, try the shop at the museum, or in and around **Market Square** between Johnston and Pandora; the attractive brick building and courtyard is a lovely place to stroll.
Hill's Native Art, 1008 Government St, T250-3853911. The place for genuine First Nations art and crafts, with a wide selection of masks, carvings and jewellery.

Books
Munro's, 1108 Government St, T250-3822464. Arguably Canada's most gorgeous book store. The 7.5-m coffered ceiling, stained-glass windows, wall hangings and well-chosen art create an environment perfect for browsing.

Clothes
Downtown is the place for shopping, with most of the key chain and fashion stores found in the **Bay Centre**, a whole block between Government and Douglas, Fort

and View, and surprisingly tasteful as malls go. **Johnston St** is the place for trendy clothing stores, while **Pandora Av** is your best bet for more off-beat and funky clothes.

Food and drink

The Wine Barrel, 644 Broughton St. Carries only BC wines, as well as a wealth of information on them.

Sports equipment

Sports Traders, 508 Discovery St. A huge selection of used sporting equipment.

Salt Spring Island *p106*

Residents are very proud of their local currency, the Salt Spring Dollar. You can exchange Canadian dollars for Salt Spring Dollars and spend them in local shops. Any interest is spent on community projects.

Arts and crafts

Art galleries and studios are all over Ganges and most offer the chance to meet the artist. Ask at the visitor centre for a full list.
Coastal Currents Gallery, Hereford Av. A very tasteful selection of arts, crafts and gifts, well arranged in a big house.
Saturday Market, Centennial Park, Ganges, www.saltspringmarket.com. Apr-Oct 0830-1530. Excellent for local crafts and organic produce, cheeses and conserves, music and food.
Vortex Gallery, Grace Point Sq, www.vortex gallery.com. Displays works by local artists who have made a name for themselves internationally. Browsing welcome.

⛰ Activities and tours

Victoria *p101, map p102*
Cycling
Victoria is famous for its biking, with plenty of trails and several off-road areas. Buses are bike equipped, and a very good map can be bought at any bike shop for $6.50. The 60-km **Galloping Goose Trail** starts in View Royal, stretching to Sooke and beyond. For trail information, call T250-5924753, www.outpostbc.ca. For rentals try **Cycle Victoria Rentals**, 950 Wharf St, T250-3852453; **Cycle BC Rentals**, 747 Douglas St, T250-3802453; or **Chain Chain Chain**, 1410 Broad St, T250-3851739. **Cycle Treks**, 450 Swift St, T250-3862277. Tours of Victoria, the Gulf Islands and Vancouver Island.
Switch Bridge Tours, 800 Tyee Rd, T250-3831466. Tours of the Galloping Goose, Victoria and wineries.

Golf
Close to town and highly scenic are:
Cordova Bay , T250-6584444. 18 holes overlooking the ocean and Gulf Islands.
Olympic View, 643 Latoria Rd, T250-4743673. 18 holes, 12 lakes, 2 waterfalls.

Hiking
Mt Douglas, 9 km north of Victoria at Cordova Bay, is a 10-ha park overlooking the Haro Strait and Washington's San Juan Islands. There are hiking trails leading up to a viewpoint, and a decent beach. To get there take bus No 28 from Downtown. **Elk Lake**, north off Patricia Bay Hwy, and **Thetis Lake**, 15 mins' west off the Island Hwy, have mellow hikes around the lakes.

Tour operators
For general information, check out www.ecotoursvictoria.com. *South and Central Vancouver Island Recreation Map*, $5, published by Carmanah Forestry Society, is well worth picking up. It covers biking, hiking, kayaking and camping for south/central Vancouver Island.
Adam's Fishing Charters, 19 Lotus St, T250-3702326, www.adamsfishing charters.com. Fishing tours.
Architectural Institute of BC, T1800-6670753, www.aibc.ca. Guided walking tours of Victoria with an architectural slant. There are 5 tours, 2 of which are available on any given day. Jul-Aug, Tue-Sat leaving at 1130 and 1430 from

the Community Arts Council Office, G6, 1001 Douglas St. They last 1½-2 hrs, $5.
Black Beauty Carriage Tours, 225 Belleville St, T250-3611220. Horse and carriage tours.
Ghostly Walks, 634 Battery St, T250-3846698, www.discoverthepast.com. Tours depart nightly from the visitor centre.
Gray Line, 700 Douglas, T250-3886539. English double-decker, narrated bus tours.
Ho Horse-drawn Tours, Menzies/Belleview, T250-3835067. Or pick one up outside the Parliament Building.
Island Adventure Tours, 1032 Oliphant St, T250-8127103, www.islandadventure tours.com. Hiking, kayaking and cultural tours with a First Nations perspective.
Royal Blue Line, Belleville St, in front of the Coho ferry terminal, T250-3602249, www.royalbluelinetours.com. Uses double-deckers imported from England for its narrated tours of town.
Travel with Taste Tours, 356 Simcoe St, T250-3856052, www.travelwithtaste.com. 1-day or 1-week tours of local wineries, farms and restaurants.
Vancouver Island Paragliding, 1594 Fairfield Rd, T250-8864165, www.vipara gliding.com.
Victoria Harbour Ferry, 4530 Markham St, T250-7080201. Regular 45-min narrated harbour tours or 50-min narrated gorge tours for $16, $8 child.
Victorian Garden Tours, 2-145 Niagara St, T250-3802797, www.victoriagarden tours.com. Narrated tours of private and public gardens in a 6-person van.
Victoria's Best Walking Tours, 715 Eastridge Pl, T250-4797610.

Watersports
Crystal Pool, 2275 Quadra St, T250-3610732. Swimming pool.
Harbour Rentals, 450 Swift St, below the Harbour Canoe Club. Rents kayaks, canoes or rowing boats for exploring the Inner Harbour and Gorge Harbour.
Ocean River Sports, 1824 Store St, T250-3814233, www.oceanriver.com. Rents paddling equipment.

Ogden Point Dive Centre, 199 Dallas Rd, T250-3809119, www.divevictoria.com.
Pacifica Paddle Sports, 575 Pembroke, T250-3619365, www.pacificapaddle.com. Canoe and kayak tours.
Sports Rent, 1950 Government St, T250-3857368. Rents sports equipment such as skis, bikes, tents, kayaks and surfboards.

Whale watching
There are at least 10 whale-watching operators on the Inner Harbour alone. They all offer similar deals and trips last for 3 hrs, the real decision being whether you want to go in a zodiac, hard-shell, sail boat or cruise ship.
Great Pacific Adventures, T250-3862277, 811 Wharf St, www.great pacificadventures.com.
Naturally Salty Excursions, T250-3829599, 950 Wharf, www.naturallysalty.com.

Salt Spring Island *p106*
Bike hire
From **Saltspring Kayaking**, see below; or try **Silver Shadow Taxi**, T250-5373030.

Kayaking
There are destinations for all levels, but the inexperienced should go with a guide.
Saltspring Kayaking, 2923 Fulford-Ganges Rd, T250-6534222, www.saltspring kayaking.com. Rents kayaks and bikes, offers tours and lessons. Will deliver your bike/kayak from any ferry for $15.
Sea Otter Kayaking, 149 Lower Ganges Rd, on the dock, T250-5375678, www.sea otterkayaking.com. Rentals and tours.

Tour operators
Island Escapades, 163 Fulford-Ganges Rd, T250-5372553, www.islandescapades.com. Highly respected company for sailing, kayaking, hiking and climbing; rentals, lessons and tours.
Island Gourmet Safaris, T250-5374118, www.islandgourmetsafaris.com. Culinary tours around the island stopping to taste local cheese, wine, coffee and seafood. $89/person. Also art studio tours.

Lorenda Sailing, Moby's Pub, T250-5380084. Currently charges $49 for 4 hrs. **Salt Spring Air**, T250-5379880. Air tours. **Salt Spring Guided Rides**, 121 Wright Rd, T250-5375761. Horse riding.

Galiano Island *p107*

Galiano Adventure Company, 300 Sticks Allison Rd, T250-5390233. Rents mopeds and boats.
Galiano Bicycle, 36 Burrill, T250-5399906. Rents bicycles and does repairs.
Galiano Boat Rentals, Montague Harbour, T250-5399828.
Gulf Islands Kayaking, Montague Harbour, T250-5392442, www.seakayak.ca, offers kayak rental and tours.
Sporades Tours Inc, T250-5393506. Sightseeing tours on a fishing vessel. The Captain has 40 years' experience.

Sooke *p108*

Sooke Cycle, 6707 West Coast Rd, T250-6423123. Bicycle rental.

⊖ Transport

Victoria *p101, map p102*
Air

Airline offices Air Canada, T1888-2472262, www.aircanada.com, **West Coast Air**, T250-3884521, www.westcoastair.com, and **Pacific Coastal**, T250-6556411, www.pacific-coastal.com, have several daily flights to **Vancouver** for $110 one-way.

Float planes Harbour Air Seaplanes, T250-3859131, www.harbour-air.com, has regular flights daily between Canada Place in **Vancouver** and Victoria's Inner Harbour, $121 one-way.

Bus

Local BC Transit, T250-3826161, www.bctransit.com, operates a comprehensive and efficient bus service throughout the city. Single-fare tickets cost $2 ($1.25 child) or $2.75 ($2 child) for 2 zones. If taking more than 1 bus in the same direction, ask for a transfer at no extra charge. A sheet of 10 tickets costs $17.50 ($11 child). A day pass is $6 ($4 child). The low-floor buses are wheelchair accessible, but only from designated stops.

Long distance All buses leave from 700 Douglas St, behind the Empress Hotel. Greyhound, T250-3854411, runs 6 daily buses north to **Nanaimo**, from where 1 service runs to **Tofino** and 5 run to **Campbell River**. Pacific Coach Lines, T250-3854411, operates a service to and from **Vancouver**, leaving Victoria bus station daily every 2 hrs 0600-1800, leaving Vancouver bus station and airport every 2 hrs 0545-1945, $35 one-way.

Ferry

BC Ferries, T250-3863431, www.bcferries.com, run to **Tsawwassen** (for Vancouver) and the **southern Gulf Islands**. Ferries between Swartz Bay and Tsawwassen leave every 2 hrs, 0700-2100 or hourly at peak times, $10.30, $5.15 child, $35 for a vehicle. Several daily ferries run from Brentwood Bay on the Saanich Peninsula to **Mill Bay** across the inlet, $5.25, $13.05 for a vehicle.

To the US Victoria Clipper, T250-3828100, runs from the Inner Harbour to **Seattle**, US$75; Washington State Ferries, T250-4646400, Sidney to **Anacortes**, US$15, $50 with vehicle.

Taxi

AAA Airport Taxi, T250-7278366, or Empress Taxi, T250-3812222.

Train

The **Malahat** service leaves daily at 0815, more often in summer, running as far north as **Courtenay** with several stops on the way including **Chemainus** and **Nanaimo**. $51 one-way, cheaper if you book in advance or buy a return ticket.

Vehicle hire

Budget, 757 Douglas, T250-9535300, car hire; Airport, T250-6572277, discount car and truck rentals; Cycle BC Rentals, 747 Douglas St, T250-8852453, scooter hire.

Salt Spring Island *p106*

Air
Harbour Air Seaplanes, T250-5375525, www.harbourair.com. Regular daily flights to/from Downtown **Vancouver** and from the international airport, $83 one-way, **Salt Spring Air**, T250-5379880, www.salt springair.com, operates scheduled and chartered flights to/from **Vancouver**.

Ferry
Ferries arrive at 3 different harbours on Salt Spring. Fulford Bay receives ferries from **Swartz Bay** (Victoria), $7.05, $3.55 child return ($23 for car); Long Harbour receives ferries from **Tsawwassen** (Vancouver), $11.80, $6.20 child one-way ($43.50 for car). Curiously, Long Harbour to Tsawwassen fares are almost half the price, $5.80, $3.20 child ($23.45 per car) one-way. Vesuvius Bay receives several sailings daily from **Crofton** in the Cowichan Valley, $7.35, $3.85 child return ($23.80 for car). **Gulf Island Water Taxi**, T250-5372510, runs to **Galiano Island** Wed and Sat, Jul and Aug, $25 return. They will transport your kayak for $5.

Shuttle
Ganges is at the northern end of the island, some 15 km along the main Fulford-Ganges Rd from Fulford Bay, about 6 km from the other harbours. **Ganges Ferry Mini Shuttle**, T250-5376758, runs shuttles between all ferry landings and Ganges, Ruckle Park, and Fernwood, and will drop off anywhere between. Best to book ahead. Rates are $7.50-12.50.

Galiano Island *p107*
See Activities and tours, p118 for rental of bicycles and boats.

Ferry
Several daily sailings from **Swartz Bay** (Vancouver Island), return fare $7.65, $4 child, $26.15 car. 2 sailings daily to **Tsawwassen** (Vancouver). $11.60, $6

child, $42.85 car one-way to the island from Schwartz Bay; $5.60, $3 child, $22.80 car from Tsawwassen. 2 sailings daily to **Long Harbour** (Salt Spring Island) via Pender and Mayne Islands, $4.10, $2.15 child, $8.50 car one-way.

Shuttle
Go Galiano Island Shuttle, T250-5390202, is a taxi and bus service, which meets every ferry Jun-Sep ($6 to Sturdies Bay).

Water taxi
Gulf Islands Water Taxi, T250-5372510, connects with **Salt Spring** (see above).

West to Port Renfrew *p108*
The Juan de Fuca Trail Shuttle Bus, T250-4778700, runs from the bus station on Douglas St, **Victoria**, daily at 0640, stopping at **Sooke** and every trailhead. Return leaves Port Renfrew at 1630. $40 one-way. Shuttles between trail -heads charge $20, flag them. Reservations are advised.

🛈 Directory

Victoria *p101, map p102*
Canada Post 714 Yates, T250-9531352. **Emergencies** Ambulance, T911, T250-7272400. **Police**, T911 emergency, T250-9957654 otherwise. **Internet** Peacock Billiards/Cyber Café, 834 Johnston St, open till late; or any library. **Laundry** The Laundry, 1769 Fort St. Maytag Homestyle Laundry, 1309 Cook St. **Library** Greater Victoria Public Library, 735 Broughton St. **Medical services** Royal Jubilee Hospital, 1900 Fort St, T250-3708000; Mayfair Walk-In Clinic, 3147 Douglas St, T250-3839898.

Salt Spring Island *p106*
Laundry Mrs Clean, Gasoline Alley, behind the Petrocan in Ganges. **Medical services** Lady Minto Gulf Islands Hospitals, 135 Crofton Rd, T250-5385545.

Tofino and the west coast

Fringed with rocky bays, countless islands, and dense rainforest that contains some of the world's biggest trees, Vancouver Island's ruggedly beautiful and relatively unspoilt West Coast is surely its most outstanding feature. The busy but still picturesque little resort town of Tofino makes a perfect base, with great facilities and several outstanding excursions. Whale watching is particularly prime, especially in spring, when some 22,000 grey whales are migrating through. Nearby Ucluelet is a more down-to-earth base, offering easy access to the Broken Islands Group, an archipelago of tiny islands in Barkley Sound that's a paradise for kayakers. Between Tofino and

⦿ Getting there Ferry or plane to Nanaimo; then bus or car.
⦿ Getting around Bus or car, then by bike or on foot.
⦿ Time required 3-5 days. (more for West Coast Trail).
⦿ Weather Often rough: rain, wind, storms.
⦿ Sleeping All kinds: many B&Bs and resorts.
⦿ Eating Fair range in Tofino
⦿ Activities and tours Whale watching, kayaking, hiking, surfing, hot springs.
★ Don't miss... Whale watching/Hot Springs Cove combo from Tofino ⟩⟩ *p137*.

Ucluelet is Long Beach, a 20-km series of rain- and wind-lashed beaches ideal for surfing, storm watching, and beachcombing, and lined with short trails through lush rainforest. Heading south from the boardwalk village of Bamfield, the West Coast Trail is one of the most challenging, rewarding and popular hikes in North America. The region's main gateway, Nanaimo, has an interesting, gritty downtown core, with Gabriola Island, well worth exploring, a short ferry ride away.

Ins and outs

Getting there and around

Nanaimo Airport (YCD), T250-2454191, www.nanaimoairport.com, 15 km south of the city on Highway 19, receives daily flights from Vancouver. The **Nanaimo Airporter shuttle bus**, T250-7582133, runs frequently to town. Nanaimo is also reached by ferry directly from Downtown Vancouver or

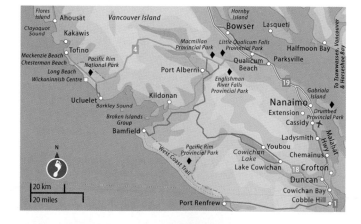

Tsawwassen, or more regularly from Horseshoe Bay (on the Sunshine Coast). The 0900 Harbour Lynx ferry from Vancouver's Waterfront SeaBus terminal connects with the **Tofino Bus** to the West Coast, a total journey of 5½ hours. The bus station is at 1 Terminal Avenue, T250-7534371, walking distance from Downtown. Nanaimo is served by several daily buses (one continuing to Tofino), or one train, from Victoria. The train station is on Selby Street, walking distance from Downtown. Getting around Tofino is possible on foot or bike, with a **Beach Bus** shuttling to Long Beach and Ucluelet. The *MV Lady Rose* from Port Alberni is a delightful way to reach Ucluelet, Bamfield and the Broken Islands. ➊ ➻ *p137*.

Best time to visit

For most West Coast activities, summer is the obvious time. However, the great grey whale migration takes place mid-March to early April, beginning with the annual Pacific Rim Whale Festival. Winter would only really appeal to those interested in storm watching.

Tourist information

Tofino's **Visitor Information Centre** ⓘ *1426 Pacific Rim Hwy, T250-7253414, www.tourism tofino.com, Feb-Dec*, is busy but helpful. Close to the Tofino-Ucluelet junction on Highway 4 as you approach Long Beach is the **Parks Information Centre** ⓘ *T250-7264600, mid-March to mid-Oct*. It provides all sorts of information including an indispensable map of Long Beach which gives details of the hiking trails, and includes smaller maps of Tofino and Ucluelet, as well as listings. A parking fee of $10 per day per vehicle ($45 season pass) is payable here and applies throughout the park. Recommended books include the *Official Guidebook to Pacific Rim National Park Reserve* (MacFarlane et al, 1996), *The Pacific Rim Explorer* by Bruce Obee, and *Island Paddling* by MA Snowden. Nanaimo's **Visitor Information Centre** ⓘ *2290 Bowen Rd, from Hwy 1, turn west onto Comox Rd then follow signs, T250-7560106, www.tourism nanaimo.com, summer daily 0700-1900, winter Mon-Fri 0900-1700, Sat 1000-1600*, is well stocked but inconveniently situated far from Downtown.

Victoria to Nanaimo ➊➋➌✲ ➻ *pp129-138*.

Those travelling up from Victoria will find few reasons to stop along the busy Malahat Highway. **Goldstream Provincial Park** has some nice walks, including the Prospectors' Trail (details from the Freeman King Visitor Centre by the picnic area), and up to the viewpoint atop Mount Finlayson. From mid-October to December, salmon can be seen in the Goldstream River.

Those with their own vehicle and lots of time may wish to explore the broad **Cowichan Valley**, whose winding country roads weave through fertile landscapes to pretty little villages such as Cowichan Bay, whose waterfront buildings are all on stilts. A number of wineries clustered around Cobble Hill, and a few local cheese producers, are usually open for tasting. It's easy to get lost, so pick up a *Cowichan Tourism Association* map in Mill Bay or Victoria, or visit the helpful **Visitor Information Centre** ⓘ *381A Hwy 1, T250-7464636, www.duncancc. bc.ca*, in Duncan, the region's main town. While there, be sure to pick up a map of the 80-odd totem poles scattered around town and along the highway, which constitute the town's main draw. Enthusiasts could also buy a copy of *The Totem Walk of Duncan* ($5).

Chemainus

Despite its excessive hype and popularity, Chemainus is the best stop on the road north, thanks to a famous collection of 37 high-quality **murals** that depict the history of the town and area. The first was commissioned in 1982 as a brave attempt to attract tourism after the local sawmill went into decline and threatened to sink the town with it. The ploy worked, with tourists, murals and artisans continuing to arrive long after the mill ironically reopened.

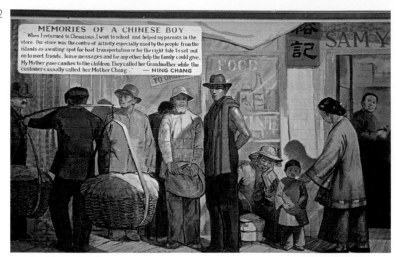

MEMORIES OF A CHINESE BOY

When I returned to Chemainus, I went to school and helped my parents in the store. Our store was the centre of activity especially used by the people from the islands as a waiting spot for boat transportation or for the right tide to set out on to meet friends. leave messages and for any other help the family could give. My Mother gave candies to the children. They called her Grandmother while the customers usually called her Mother Chang'. — NING CHANG

The murals at Chemainus are a visual record of the village's history.

Such success owes much to the fact that Chemainus is a charming little village in its own right. You can pick up a useful mural map for $1 at the friendly **Visitor Information Centre** ⓘ *9796 Willow St, T250-2463944, www.chemainus.bc.ca, daily 0900-1700, closed Sun in winter*. Just outside, you can take a 45-minute horse-drawn carriage tour of town ($7).

Nanaimo and around ⊜⊘⊕⊕⊛⊡▲⊟⊕ ►► *pp129-138, map p131.*

The urban sprawl lining the highway into and around Vancouver Island's second city is so repellent that travellers en route from Victoria to Tofino will be tempted to keep driving. However, Nanaimo's Downtown comes as a pleasant surprise, with a real sense of history, and a genuine, if somewhat seedy, character. The warren of twisty streets around Church and Commercial streets is conveniently close to the ferry and train, and packed with decent pubs, authentic diners, book and music shops, and art galleries. It's also adjacent to the scenic harbour. There are some nice beaches and sea walks, as well as the usual watersports.

In 1852 the local Salish natives made the mistake of showing samples of the 'black rock' that existed locally in staggering proportions to agents from Hudson's Bay Company (HBC). The white men came in droves to exploit one of the greatest coal mines of all time, and a few of them became millionaires, notably Robert Dunsmuir. The following year, in order to keep the natives under control while their land got plundered, the HBC constructed the **Bastion**, a squat, wood-plank building that's the oldest of its kind in the west. In summer, a small **Museum of HBC memorabilia** ⓘ *63 Front St, Jun-Aug 1000-1700, donation*, is open, and a ceremonial cannon fires at noon Monday to Saturday to the accompaniment of Scottish bagpipes and Highland dancing.

The nearby **Nanaimo District Museum** ⓘ *100 Cameron Rd, T250-7531821, www.nanaimo museum.ca, daily 0900-1700, closed Sun-Mon in winter, $2, $1.75 child*, has predictable reproductions of native dioramas. Displays on the old Chinatown and a coal mine are not as impressive as the ones in the Royal BC Museum in Victoria, but the collection of petroglyph copies on the lawn at the back (which can be seen for free) are well worth a look. Close by, and more worthwhile, is **Nanaimo Art Gallery** ⓘ *150 Commercial St, T250-7541750, www.nanaimogallery.ca, Tue-Sat 1030-1730, donation*, which showcases work by over 40 West Coast artists.

The unusual rock formations of the Malaspina Gallery on Gabriola Island.

Gabriola Island

Gabriola is one of the quickest Gulf Islands to get to, and one of the most worthwhile. Straight ahead from the ferry on North Road, Village Centre is the hub of local activity, with decent cafés, many of the island's galleries, and the summer-only **Visitor Information Centre** ⓘ *T250-2479332, www.gabriolaisland.org*. A farmers' market is held on Saturdays and Wednesdays.

Wonderful rock formations can be seen from the approaching ferry, and in various parks throughout the island, but the best is the highly photogenic **Malaspina Gallery** (from the ferry, turn left onto Taylor Bay Road and left again onto Malaspina Drive), a collection of beautiful wave-shaped stone sculptures carved by the sea. **Drumbed Provincial Park** at the island's southeast corner has good swimming and an easy, pleasant walk leading to the island's best views, with a chance to see otters and eagles. A number of **petroglyphs** are scattered around the island. Many are inaccessible but you can see some on South Road (behind the United Church). *Gabriola: Petroglyph Island*, by M and T Bentley, is a valuable resource for those keen to seek them out. A collection of decent reproductions decorates the garden of the small **Gabriola Museum**. ⓘ *winter Sat-Sun 1300-1600, summer Wed-Sun 1030-1600, $2*.

West to Pacific Rim National Park 🏨🚲⛰ ›› *pp129-138*.

Travellers bound for Tofino might do best to bypass Nanaimo and dreary Parksville altogether, but for those with their own wheels, there are a few places along Highway 4 to stop and enjoy a rare taste of Vancouver Island's forested interior. Before long, signs appear for **Englishman River Falls Provincial Park** to the south, where there's hiking, biking, fishing and a pleasant campground, as well as a waterfall. **Little Qualicum Falls Provincial Park**, at Km 19, has a more impressive waterfall, plus enticing swimming holes and a large, scenic campground. In summer the adjacent **Cameron Lake** with its splendid beach, is always popular.

Macmillan Park, opened by the eponymous logging giants, features Cathedral Grove, a tiny patch of old-growth spruce and cedar left behind almost as a sick joke to show tourists how the whole island once looked. A few points still exist around the island where the real thing can be seen, notably in Clayoquot Sound close to Tofino, but this spot is always worth a leg-stretch: the giant trees are magnificent.

Facing the Pacific Ocean, Long Beach has become a popular spot for surfing and storm watching.

Port Alberni is worth mentioning mainly as the place to catch the *MV Lady Rose* (see p126), a fantastic way to access the Broken Islands or Bamfield. Boats leave from Harbour Quay, which is the nicest part of town. If you have time to kill, the best local diversion is the **McLean Mill National Historic Site** ① *west of town, 5633 Smith Rd, T250-7231376, www.alberni heritage.com, 1000-1800, $6.50, $4.50 child*, Canada's only steam-operated mill and an interesting building in its own right. The mill can be reached by hiking or biking the 20-km **Log Train Trail**, which starts at the **Visitor Information Centre** ① *2533 Redford St, T250-7246535, www.avcoc.com.* Staggeringly popular when first operated in 2001, an old **steam train** ① *Thu-Mon, last train leaves Port Alberni 1300, $20 return, $15 child including mill*, runs from Harbour Quay, a half-hour ride along the water with staged horse-back robberies along the way.

Long Beach

Frequent views of wild, rocky landscapes during the 130-km roller-coaster ride from Port Alberni provide a fitting introduction to the West Coast and Pacific Rim National Park. Unless you're heading to Ucluelet, the Pacific Rim Highway soon enters Long Beach, the collective name for a 20-km stretch of forest-fringed bays and beaches. Generally too rough for swimming and sunbathing, this is becoming a world-famous location for surfing. Storm watching is an increasingly popular winter activity, and the very ruggedness has a romantic quality conducive to long walks, with plenty of rockpools to explore. Almost immediately on the right is the **Parks Information Centre.** Pick up the free *Long Beach Map*, which describes nine well-tended trails, mostly short and sweet explorations of rainforest ecosystems, with explanatory panels. The **Spruce Fringe Trail** is recommended. The highway runs parallel with the ocean, offering access to these trails and a number of beaches.

At the eastern end of Long Beach itself, the **Wickaninnish Centre**, T250-7267706, has films and exhibits on the natural and cultural history of the Pacific Rim, and is a useful place for information. There's a restaurant and a whale-watching telescope, and it's a popular, safe spot for storm watching. Note that the rip-tides here are particularly dangerous. Wickaninnish (meaning 'having no one in front of him in the canoe') is named after a powerful native chief, who gained much respect for his mediation between the White Man and native fur trapper.

Shortly before **Cox Bay**, and **Chesterman** and **Mackenzie beaches**, a short drive and walk lead up to **Radar Hill**, with panoramic views of Clayoquot Sound.

Tofino ⬛🌙🎏❄️💠🔺🚌🛥️🏠 ›› *pp129-138, map p125.*

The overwhelming popularity of this whaling-station-turned-surf-town is partly due to its idyllic location. Sitting at the end of a narrow peninsula in the middle of beautiful **Clayoquot Sound**, surrounded on all sides by ocean and islands, it is also the closest base for exploring the vast shoreline of Long Beach and visiting some of the destinations nearby (see below). Other local activities include whale watching, world-class sea kayaking, the country's best surfing, hiking, bear watching, beachcombing and storm watching.

Despite being packed to the gills in summer, Tofino itself just about manages to remain a scenic seaside village, but with a fine selection of restaurants, cafés, shops and accommodation. For most people the happy holiday atmosphere only adds to the experience. However, if you want to avoid other tourists, think about going to Ucluelet instead. The **Eagle Aerie Gallery** ⓘ *350 Campbell St, summer 0900-2100, winter 0930-1730*, housed in a splendid replica longhouse with some beautiful carvings and a dugout canoe, highlights the work of the highly respected native artist, Roy Henry Vickers. The **Rainforest Interpretive Centre** ⓘ *451 Main St, T250-7252560, by donation*, is a good place to find out about the remarkable ecosystems of temperate rainforests. For a more visual learning experience, head to the 5 ha of old-growth forest at the **Botanical Gardens** ⓘ *just out of town towards Long Beach, 0900-dark, $10, $6 child, valid for 3 days*, which also contains an acclaimed restaurant, see Eating p134.

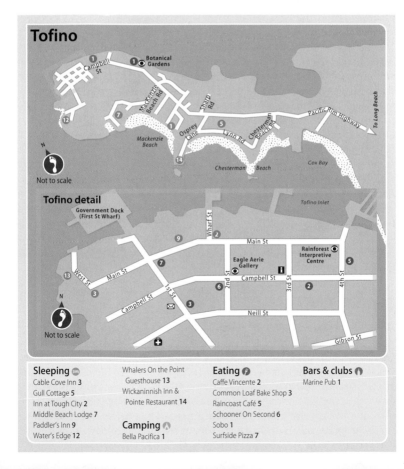

Vancouver Island Tofino & the west coast

Sleeping 🛏️		Eating 🍴	Bars & clubs 🍸
Cable Cove Inn 3	Whalers On the Point	Caffe Vincente 2	Marine Pub 1
Gull Cottage 5	Guesthouse 13	Common Loaf Bake Shop 3	
Inn at Tough City 2	Wickaninnish Inn &	Raincoast Café 5	
Middle Beach Lodge 7	Pointe Restaurant 14	Schooner On Second 6	
Paddler's Inn 9		Sobo 1	
Water's Edge 12	**Camping 🏕️**	Surfside Pizza 7	
	Bella Pacifica 1		

Background

The *MV Lady Rose*

Originally the sole function of this Scottish freighter was to transport mail and supplies from Port Alberni to isolated communities around Barkley Sound. However, passengers bound for difficult-to-access locations such as Bamfield and the Broken Islands Group began using the vessel as transportation, making the most of the meandering route to savour the dramatic scenery and spot wildlife. The journey became so popular that a second boat had to be added, the Norwegian *MV Frances Barkley*. Though the pioneering spirit has now been diluted by popularity, this is still a fantastic way to travel, though the boats were not built for comfort, and still make frequent stops. Reservations are essential, and should be made in Port Alberni on Argyle Street, T250-7238313, www.ladyrosemarine.com. There are three sailings a week from Harbour Quay to Bamfield, Ucluelet and Broken Islands (Sechart), $50 return. Additional sailings in the summer.

Excursions from Tofino

There are plenty of things to do around Tofino. For more details see Activities and tours, p136. The most popular excursion is the 37-km boat trip to **Hot Springs Cove**. From the cove jetty, a 2-km boardwalk leads through rainforest to the gloriously romantic springs, where waters emerge at 43°C (108°F) before cascading down to the sea through a series of ever-cooler pools. Many operators combine this trip with whale watching but, if you want to avoid the summer crowds, it is also possible to travel independently and sleep at the springs.

The lush rainforest of **Meares Island**, closest of the local big islands, is just 15 minutes away from Tofino by water-taxi. This is one of the best places in Canada to go for a walk through giant ancient trees. On the 3-km loop of the **Big Cedar Trail** you'll gasp at trees that are more than 6 m across, and wonder why the logging companies are still intent on cutting them down. A shorter boardwalk stroll leads to the 2000-year-old **Hanging Garden Cedar**, the biggest tree in Clayoquot Sound at 18.3 m in circumference.

Vargas Island, 5 km north of Tofino, is a beautiful, relaxing place with fine sand beaches, and little else. **Flores Island**, 20 km from Tofino by **Cougar Island Water Taxi**, T1888-7268427, $45 return, is home to **Ahousat** village, one of the best places to encounter First Nations people and culture. Their Ahousat Wildside Heritage Trail is a marvellous 11-km hike through rainforest and beaches to Mount Flores viewpoint.

Ucluelet ⬤⬤⬤⬤⬤⬤ ▸▸ pp129-138.

Meaning 'people of the sheltered bay', Ucluelet is a major fishing port that has retained the feel of an ordinary village. This is the place from which to get to **Barkley Sound** and the Broken Islands Group, and there's just as good a chance of seeing whales here as in Tofino. The very helpful **Visitor Information Centre** ⓘ *100 Main St, T250-7264600, www.ucluelet info.com, Mon-Fri 0900-1700*, can tell you more about B&Bs and the many operators for whale watching, fishing and kayaking. At the south end of town, the **Wild Pacific Trail** is a very pleasant 2.7-km loop that passes a lighthouse, with views of Barkley Sound and (sometimes) whales. Amphitrite Point on this trail is one of the best locations for storm watching.

Kayaking at Clayoquot Sound is one of the best ways to experience the natural beauty of the area.

Broken Islands Group

Pacific Rim National Park's central section consists of an archipelago of over 100 islands scattered throughout Barkley Sound, a dream location for sea-kayakers who come here in droves despite the difficult access. Coastal wilderness doesn't get much more remote than this, so the scenery is spectacular, with plenty of undisturbed temperate rainforest, lagoons, sandbars, blowholes, and a good chance of seeing marine wildlife, including major colonies of sea lions. Archaeological digs have shown that native peoples also favoured the spot, with evidence of habitation on the islands dating back thousands of years, including ancient middens, village fortifications, and stone fishtraps.

These days the Broken Islands are known internationally among kayaking and scuba diving circles, and can be shockingly overrun, especially in July and August, with campsites regularly full. The waters are also notoriously treacherous, thanks to submerged rocks, reefs, sea caves, exposed channels, extreme and unpredictable weather, and freezing water. Only the highly experienced should even think about paddling here without a guide, of which there are many in Tofino, Ucluelet and Bamfield.

Bamfield

ⓘ *Tourist information: T250-7283006 www.bamfieldcommunity.com, summer only.*

Bamfield is a tiny town on the edge of Barkley Sound, at the mouth of the Alberni Inlet. Unless arriving on the oft-vaunted *MV Lady Rose*, access is on a horrible 100-km logging road from Port Alberni. Nobody would bother, but this (or Pachena Bay, 5 km away) is the northern end of the formidable West Coast Trail (see p128). Having come so far, however, it's worth having a look round. The main part of town is a somewhat drab, no-nonsense service centre for the forestry industry, but on the other side of a narrow inlet, accessible only by water taxi (**Bamfield Express Water Taxi**, T250-7283001), is a boardwalk village the very unlikelihood of whose location has kept it much more unspoilt than certain others further north. Here a community of artists has taken root. Wandering along boardwalks from studio to studio is a delightful way to spend an afternoon, and there's a café with a lovely deck where the ferry docks. **Brady's Beach**, a 20-minute walk away, is a fine and popular place to catch some rays: long, sandy, and a little bit wild.

West Coast Trail

At least 66 ships at the bottom of the ocean bear witness to the treacherous nature of a strip of coast known as the 'graveyard of the Pacific'. Following the sinking of the *SS Valencia* in 1906, the decision was taken to convert an old 1890 telegraph trail between Port Renfrew and Bamfield into an escape route for survivors of shipwrecks, since this stretch of coast is practically uninhabited, covered in the densest forest, and subject to appallingly heavy rainfall. From the 1960s, BC's trailblazing hiker community began to take the opportunity to experience some of the most pristine and spectacular wilderness imaginable. Today it is recognized as one of North America's greatest hikes, and quotas are in operation to limit numbers.

The trail runs 75 km from **Pachena Bay**, 5 km south of Bamfield, to **Gordon River**, a ferry ride from Port Renfrew. It takes an average of six or seven days, and is a commitment not to be entered into lightly. Over 60 hikers have to be evacuated each year, usually with strained knees and ankles. As the official blurb puts it: "You must be self-sufficient, prepared for foul weather, slippery terrain, creek fording, long days and heavy packs. You must be prepared to wait out storms and high water on creek crossings". If in doubt, it is possible to hike half of the trail, beginning at **Nitinat Lake**. Full camping equipment, plenty of food, good rain gear and boots, and a proper map and tide table are essential. Camping on the beach above the tideline is recommended. Driftwood campfires are allowed on the beach only, but take a small stove and fuel for cooking. Avoid shellfish, which could be poisonous.

Trail logistics

The trail is open 1 May to 30 September, and gets heavily booked. Quotas limit the number of starters per day with five standby places at each; go on the waiting list at the trailhead, and be prepared to wait for a few days. There is no hiker quota in the shoulder season (1 May to 14 June and 16 to 30 September) from Monday to Friday. Reservations, T250-381642/T1800-4355622, cost $25 and are taken up to three months in advance. Register at the trailhead by 1300 on your allotted day, or your spot may be taken. Mandatory 1½-hour orientation sessions are held at the trailhead information centres, Pachena Bay, T250-7283234, and Gordon River, T250-6475434, both open daily 0900- 1700. For year-round information, contact the **Park Administration office** ⓘ *Ucluelet, T250-7267721, www.parkscanada.ca*. The trail user fee is $110. There are two ferries during the hike, at Gordon River and Nitinat Narrows, $14 each, payable when registering. In addition, those starting at Nitinat Lake have to take a water taxi costing $25. There is no bank or ATM at either Bamfield or Port Renfrew. The **West Coast Trail Shuttle Bus**, T250-4778700, runs daily from Victoria, Nanaimo and Port Alberni and between trailheads; there is also a service to Nitinat from Port Renfrew; advance booking recommended, see Port Renfrew and Bamfield for more details. If all this seems too complicated, crowded or expensive, or if you just plain can't get a place, consider doing the **Juan de Fuca** (see p109) or the **Sunshine Coast Trail** instead (see p91).

The West Coast Trail passes through pristine wilderness and otherwise inaccessible terrain.

⊖ Sleeping

Victoria to Nanaimo *p121*

A Fairburn Farm Country Manor, 3310 Jackson Rd, Duncan, T250-7464637, www.fairburnfarm.bc.ca. A Lovely 19th-century manor house set in 52 ha, with lots of trails and animals. There are 4 tasteful and comfy en suite rooms and a cottage, plus a library, lounge and patio. Cooking lessons and dinner available.

D-E Iguana Ranch, 5070 Culverton Rd, Duncan, T250-7099010, www.iguana ranch.com. 7km out of town off Lake Cowichan Rd, take local transit No 7. B&B-style hostel, $35 for dorm room with breakfast. Also has some private rooms. Hot tub, sauna, bike rentals and tours.

Nanaimo *p122, map p131*

A Coast Bastion Inn, 11 Bastion St, T250-7536601. It's a chain hotel, so the rooms are clean and comfortable, if somewhat lacking in character, but the central location and harbour views are hard to beat. Facilities include a sauna, exercise room, restaurant and lounge.

B Long Lake B&B, 240 Ferntree Pl, T250-7585010, www.lodgingnanaimo.com. 3 en suite rooms with private entrances, situated on a private beach on the lake close to town. Canoes for guests to use.

C Best Western Dorchester, 70 Church St, T250-7546835, www.dorchester nanaimo.com. The rooms and suites here are fairly plain and predictable but, again, the central location and harbour views make this a great option and good value.

D-F Painted Turtle Guesthouse, 121 Bastion St, T1866-3094432, www.painted turtle.ca. Located near the harbour, with small but stylish en suite rooms, family rooms, and hostel-style bunks. Guests share a kitchen, dining room and lounge.

E The Cambie, 63 Victoria Cres, T250-7545323. A more rough and ready backpacker hostel, with single-sex dorms, and some en suite rooms. There's a small kitchen and common room, and a great café and pub downstairs. Breakfast and admission to weekend gigs included.

E Nicol St Hostel, 65 Nicol St, T250-7531188, www.nanaimohostel.com. A first-class hostel with private rooms or dorms, and some tent sites. Out of the centre, but facilities include a common room, kitchen, laundry, free internet.

Camping

Newcastle Island Provincial Park, T250-7547893. 10 min ferry ride (see Transport, p137). Ideal for those with time who value their tranquillity. 18 beautiful walk-in sites, first-come first-served, May-Sep only. Showers and flush toilets.

Gabriola Island *p123*

AL The Melville Grant Inn, 2310 Windecker Dr, T250-2479687, www.melvillegrantinn.com. Set on an oceanfront rocky bluff, surrounded by woods, beaches and gardens, this gorgeous home is opulently furnished. The 4 romantic en suite rooms each have jacuzzis; a couple have private verandas. Gourmet West Coast breakfast included.

B Hummingbird Lodge B&B, 1597 Starbuck Lane, T250-2479300, www.hummingbirdlodgebb.com. A giant, delightful West Coast lodge with high ceilings, lots of decks and windows, gardens, art, and wood everywhere. The 3 en suite rooms have bags of character.

C Haven By the Sea, 240 Davis Rd, T250-2479211, www.haven.ca. This centre for personal development courses is also open to casual guests, who can enjoy the oceanfront location and the facilities, which include gym, sauna, outdoor hot tub and swimming pools. The rooms and cabins (some with kitchen) are a bit faded but the restaurant serves wholesome buffet-style meals at reasonable prices.

C Surf Lodge & Sunset Lounge, 885 Berry Point Rd, T250-2479231, www.surf lodge.com. 7 rooms in an attractive wood lodge, and 8 cabins (**A**) in ample treed grounds with ocean views. There's also a pub and restaurant.

Vancouver Island Tofino & the west coast Listings

Descanso Bay Regional Park, 595 Taylor Bay Rd, near ferry terminal, T250-2478255. 28 sites in a nice forest setting close to the water. Open year round.

Chemainus *p121*

Chemainus is overflowing with 'quaint' B&Bs. Ask at the visitor centre. As it leaves town, however, Chemainus Rd passes a string of old renovated mill houses, and a couple of good-value places to stay.

B-C Olde Mill House, 9712 Chemainus Rd, T250-4160049, www.oldemillhouse.ca. 3 very nice, cosy rooms with great beds and en suite baths. Ask for the one with TV and its own private garden and deck.

D Horseshoe Bay Inn, 9567 Chemainus Rd, T250-4160411. The best place for a drink, this pub also has some surprisingly nice (and cheap) rooms, some with clawfoot bath and king-size bed.

Camping

Bald Eagle Campground, T250-2469457. A decent campground on a river 5 km south of town.

West to Pacific Rim National Park *p123*

B Cedar Wood Lodge, 5895 River Rd, Port Alberni, T250-7246800. Away from the centre but not too far. 8 very nice rooms with down duvets and fireplaces. Breakfast is included.

E Fat Salmon Backpackers, 3250 3rd Av, Port Alberni, T250-7236924, www.fat salmonbackpackers.com. A brand new hostel, cosy and friendly, with 6 dorms, a kitchen and communal area.

Camping

Sproat Lake Provincial Park, 13 km northwest of Port Alberni, off Hwy 4. This is a huge and attractive lake, good for warm swimming, watersports and fishing, and very popular in summer. All the lakeside sites are RV pull-through types, the nicest being on the north side.

Stamp River Provincial Park, off Beaver Creek Rd, just north of Port Alberni on Hwy 4. A small, forested, attractive campground set on a river renowned for its fishing. From late Aug-Dec, half a million salmon travel up the falls via ladders, an incredible sight.

Tofino *p125, map p125*

Tofino's B&Bs represent a better deal than the motels, which are overpriced. For those with a vehicle, Mackenzie and Chesterman beaches, 7 km away, are ideal: quiet, waterside locations, with copious resorts and lodges offering anything from ugly old cabins to luxurious suites. Prices drop considerably after Labour Day in Sep. In summer, reservations are essential.

A Cable Cove Inn, 201 Main St, T250-7254236, www.cablecoveinn.com. 7 beautifully decorated, romantic rooms with fireplaces, huge beds, and private hot tubs. There are decks with ocean views. Direct beach access. Breakfast included.

A The Inn At Tough City, 350 Main St, in town, T250-7252021, www.tough city.com. 8 vibrant and modern en suite rooms with balconies and big windows in an attractive brick building, with a sushi bar and lounge downstairs.

B Gull Cottage, 254 Lynn Rd, Chesterman Beach, T250-7253177, www.gullcottage tofino.com. 3 lovely bright en suite rooms in a Victorian home set among the trees. Guest lounge and hot tub.

B Middle Beach Lodge, 400 Mackenzie Beach, 3 km south, T250-7252900, www.middlebeach.com. The best of many lodges on the beaches near Tofino. The beautiful, spacious timber lodge features hardwood floors, pine furnishings and stone fireplaces, and the grounds enjoy their own strip of beach. Cosy lodge rooms with decks with views, and some more luxurious suites (**LL**) and oceanfront cabins. Continental breakfast included, West Coast dinners available. Adults only.

C Water's Edge, 331 Tonquin Park Rd, T250-7251218, www.watersedgeinn.ca. The rooms and suites in this West Coast home are not as luxurious as some, but the views from the common room are about as good as it gets. There's a hot tub, a private staircase down to the tide pools, and breakfast is included.

D Paddler's Inn, 320 Main St, T250-7254222. If you favour motels, this is almost the only choice. Simple but pleasant rooms with views, shared baths and kitchen. Breakfast included.

D-F Whalers On the Point Guesthouse, 81 West St, T250-7253443, www.tofino hostel.com. This very spacious, HI-affiliated

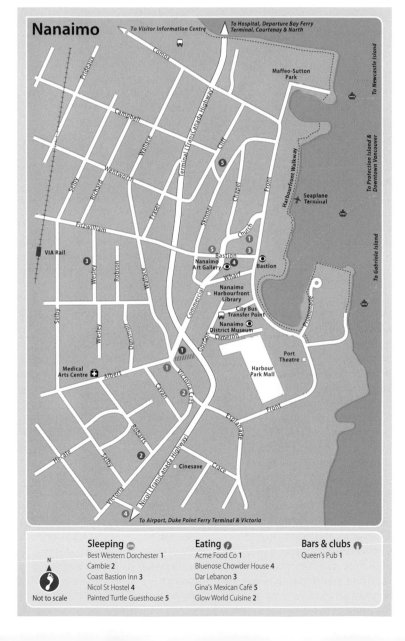

Sleeping
Best Western Dorchester **1**
Cambie **2**
Coast Bastion Inn **3**
Nicol St Hostel **4**
Painted Turtle Guesthouse **5**

Eating
Acme Food Co **1**
Bluenose Chowder House **4**
Dar Lebanon **3**
Gina's Mexican Café **5**
Glow World Cuisine **2**

Bars & clubs
Queen's Pub **1**

N
Not to scale

Budget buster

LL **Wickaninnish Inn**, Osprey Lane, Chesterman Beach, Tofino, T250-7253100, www.wickinn.com. One of the most stylish places to stay in Western Canada, its rooms tastefully decorated in West Coast style, with handmade driftwood furniture. There are fireplaces, CD players, shelves of books, binoculars, oversized tubs, huge TVs. Balconies and floor-to-ceiling windows make the most of the spectacular ocean views. There's a full spa (not included, but ask about packages), and the Pointe Restaurant is highly renowned.

LL-L **Tauca Lea By the Sea**, 1971 Harbour Cres, Ucluelet, T250-7264625, www.taucalearesort.com. This beautiful West Coast lodge is situated on a point out in the water. Luxurious, fully equipped waterfront suites come with kitchen, fireplace and jacuzzi. Full spa available. The expensive Boat Basin restaurant serves gourmet cuisine in elegant surroundings with fantastic views.

hostel is one of the best in the West, with first-class facilities that include a solarium sitting-room with harbour views, a kitchen, laundry, sauna, and discounts on tours. Mostly dorms, with some private rooms. Reservation essential.

Camping
Bella Pacifica Campground, 3 km south, T250-7253400, www.bellapacifica.com. The best of a few places offering camping possibilities with access to Mackenzie Beach. Sites are small, but some are right on the beach. Coin showers and laundry.
Greenpoint Campground, T1800-6899025, 19 km south of Tofino. The only campground on Long Beach, and easily the best in the area, this heavily over-subscribed, park-run site operates on a first-come first-served basis, so arrive early, get on the waiting list, and pray. The sites are small but densely treed and private, with some overlooking the beach.

Excursions from Tofino *p126*
B **Innchanter**, Hot Springs Cove, T250-6701149, www.innchanter.com. This 1920s arts and crafts-style coastal freighter, moored just off the dock, offers the cove's most intimate and stylish lodging. The 5 rooms are small but full of character,

with shared bath. The living room has a fireplace, sofas and a splendid library. The price includes breakfast and dinner, excellent food, lots of local seafood.
C **Hot Springs Lodge**, T1888-7819977. A motel-style set-up with kitchenettes in the en suite rooms. Situated across the water from the springs, free use of boats. Guests are advised to bring groceries. They also have a campground.
E **Hummingbird Hostel**, Ahousat, T250-6709679, www.hummingbird-hostel.com. Basic dorm beds and shared kitchen facilities. The **General Store Café** opposite has good fish and chips.

Ucluelet *p126*
A **Reef Point Cottages**, 1012 Peninsula Rd, T250-7264419, www.reefpoint cottages.com. Small and simple, but comfortable and fairly attractive new 1- and 2-bedroom cottages with hardwood floors, close to the beach.
C **Thornton Motel**, 1861 Peninsula Rd, T250-7267725. One of a few unexciting but cheap motels on this road.

Broken Islands Group *p127*
Camping is in designated areas only, for which there is a charge of $9 per person per night. There is very little drinking

water available on the islands so take all you will need with you.

A Sechart Lodge, T250-7238313, www.ladyrosemarine.com. Operated by **Alberni Marine Transport** who run the *MV Lady Rose*, which will deliver you here. Otherwise, take a water taxi from Toquart Bay ($30). This gloriously remote 1905 whaling station makes a great base from which to explore the region. Kayaks and canoes are rented for $35 per day, and for $30-45 the owners will provide transfers for you and your boat. Rooms are simple with shared bath. Price includes meals.

Bamfield *p127*

AL-B Woods End Landing Cottages, 380 Lombard St, T250-7283383, www.woodsend.travel.bc.ca. Fully equipped, 2-bedroom cottages with private decks. Situated on the water amidst secluded gardens. Use of rowing boat, and kayak rentals.

C Bamfield Lodge, on the boardwalk side, will pick up, T250-7283419, www.bamfieldlodge.com. Rustic but pleasant cabins with kitchen, adjacent to a wood lodge with common room. They also have a boardwalk bistro.

Camping

Pachena Bay Campground, T250-7281287. Right on a very fine beach, at the end of the West Coast Trail, this wonderful, native-run campground is a perfect place to relax before or after the hike. Reservations essential.

⦿ Eating

Victoria to Nanaimo *p121*

⫪⫪ Vigneti Zanatta, 5039 Marshall Rd, Glenora, T250-7482338. One of the best wineries in this area with a beautiful, very popular (but expensive) restaurant, with a lovely garden patio, offering excellent lunches and dinners, Wed-Sun, Mar-Dec. Definitely worth the drive for those with wheels, but phone ahead.

Nanaimo *p122, map p131*

⫪⫪ Glow World Cuisine, 7 Victoria Rd, T250-7418858. With its lounge atmosphere and delectable menu of tapas, this attractive venue attracts the hip and savvy. Dinner from 1700, and Sun brunch 1030-1400.

⫪⫪ Mahle House, Cedar/Hemer Rd, T250-7223621. Gourmet cuisine in a house setting, whose ever-changing menu features venison, crab and lamb, with an emphasis on the sauces.

⫪ Acme Food Co, 14 Commercial St, T250-7530042. Stylishly fitted out with antique wood tables, brick walls and high ceilings, this trendy eatery boasts an international menu with a West Coast accent, and a sushi bar in the back. There's also often live music.

⫪ Bluenose Chowder House, 1340 Stewart Av, T250-7546611. This is a great option for quality seafood, with a nice patio for those long summer evenings.

⫪ Dar Lebanon, 347 Wesley St, T250-7559150. Delicious Middle-Eastern food served in an elegant Victorian house a short walk from the centre, or on a pleasant outdoor patio with a fountain.

⫪ Gina's Mexican Café, 47 Skinner St, T250-7535411. Authentic Mexican food in suitably bright and colourful surroundings.

⫪ The Cambie, 63 Victoria Cres. There are a couple of authentically seedy diners on Church/Commercial Sts, but this bakery/café is a better choice for a cheap breakfast, as well as excellent cakes and pastries, and cheap pints.

Gabriola Island *p123*

⫪ Raspberry's Jazz Café, in the village centre, T250-2479959, is a hip little licensed café with very good coffee and occasional live jazz.

⫪ Silva Bay Pub, T250-2478662, is the nicest place for a drink, and also has very good food, a patio and a pool table.

⫪ Suzy's Restaurant, in the village centre, is a cosy little spot with some good daily specials.

♟ **White Hart Pub**, directly off the ferry, is a decent pub with a patio.

Chemainus *p121*

♟ **Hummingbird Tea House**, 9893 Maple St, T250-2462290. One of a few quaint little restaurants in the Old Town offering small but sophisticated menus with European leanings.

♟ **Willow Street Café**, 9749 Willow St. This beautiful big house with a nice patio is the best spot for coffee and snacks in the New Town.

West to Pacific Rim National Park *p123*

♟ **The Clam Bucket**, 4479 Victoria Quay, Port Alberni. Not the most central location, but this is the restaurant most consistently recommended by locals, with large portions of good seafood.

♟ **Swale Rock Café**, 5328 Argyle St, Port Alberni. A central and reliable choice for varied dishes including seafood, curry and burgers. The atmosphere is down-to-earth, the portions large.

♟ **Blue Door Café**, 5415 Argyle St, Port Alberni. Conveniently close to Harbour Quay, this is the place for cheap breakfasts and lunches. For coffee shops, head down to the quay.

Tofino *p125, map p125*

Fresh crab is widely available year round for about $10-15 each (look for signs).

♟ **Pointe Restaurant**, Wickaninnish Inn, T250-7253100. As well as offering spectacular panoramic ocean views and sumptuous surroundings, this place has an excellent reputation for gourmet dining with a West Coast accent. For a real splurge, there's a 9-course meal with wine for $165. A drink in the lounge is more affordable and almost as gratifying.

♟ **Raincoast Café**, 4th/Campbell St, T250-7252215. Thanks to its exquisite Asian-West Coast fusion cuisine, and minimalist decor that focuses on an open kitchen, this chic eatery has a firm reputation as the place to eat in Tofino.

♟ **Schooner On Second**, 331 Campbell St, T250-7253444. This long-standing favourite has a conservative but romantic atmosphere, and is still rated as the best place for traditional gourmet seafood. The menu also features some fine salads.

♟ **Sobo**, T250-7252341. Operating from a parked truck at the gates of the botanical gardens, this funky venue has a good menu of fresh seafood prepared with exotic flare, including excellent fish tacos and buckwheat soba noodles.

♟ **Surfside Pizza**, 120 1st St, T250-7252882. For something central, down-to-earth, tasty and inexpensive, this is a good choice, serving the best pizza in town, plus traditional Italian dishes.

♟ **Caffe Vincente**, 441 Campbell St, T250-7252599. An upscale café with fancy sandwiches and cakes at moderate prices. Also internet ($7/hr).

♟ **The Common Loaf Bake Shop**, 180 1st St, T250-7253915. A warm, friendly place for good coffee, fresh baking and light meals. Popular as a meeting-place, with a very useful bulletin board.

Ucluelet *p126*

♟ **Blueberries Café**, 1627 Peninsula Rd. A down-to-earth and licensed spot for home-cooked food, with the bonus of views from the patio.

♟ **Matterson House**, 1682 Peninsula Rd. The local's choice for big servings of home-cooked food in a relaxed environment.

♟ **Smileys**, further west on Peninsula Rd. A popular diner, good for fish and chips and cheap breakfasts.

🌙 Bars and clubs

Nanaimo *p122, map p131*

The Cambie, 63 Victoria Cres. A cheap, spit- and-sawdust style boozer with live music on weekends.

Queen's Pub, 34 Victoria Cres. A dark and slightly dingy venue that's ideal for the nightly live music.

On the Rocks Lounge, T250-7253100, at the **Wickaninnish Inn** (see Sleeping, above). Has the best views.
The Marine Pub at the **Weigh West Resort**, 634 Campbell St, T250-7253277. The best choice in town, with good views and a few beers on tap.

🔊 Entertainment

Nanaimo *p122, map p131*
Gallery 223, 223 Commercial St, T250-7411188. A large space in a renovated heritage house with regularly changing exhibits by local artists.
Port Theatre, 125 Front St, T250-7544555, www.porttheatre.com. Outside Victoria, this is the best venue for plays and the performing arts on the island.

🎉 Festivals and events

Victoria to Nanaimo *p121*
Jun The visually delightful **Cowichan Bay Boat Festival** has run for over 20 years.

Nanaimo *p122, map p131*
Jun The Cadillac Van Isle 360° Yacht Race, is a 2-week, 580-nautical mile race that begins and ends in Nanaimo. It happens every 2 years, next in 2007.
Jul On the 3rd weekend, the 4-day **Marine Festival** features music, fireworks on the harbour, and the famed **World Championship Bathtub Race**, when hopefuls compete for the coveted silver plunger trophy.

Gabriola Island *p123*
Aug The island's major event is the **Salmon BBQ**, which has taken place annually for over 50 years.
Oct On thanksgiving weekend the island's many artist studios open their doors to the public for 3 days during the **Gallery Tour**.

Mar The **Pacific Rim Whale Festival** is a 2-week celebration throughout the Pacific Rim National Park, with various whale-related events, to mark the beginning of the annual grey whale migration.

⊙ Shopping

Nanaimo *p122, map p131*
Arts and crafts
Artisans' Studio, 70 Bastion St, T250-7536151. A co-operative with a broad range of arts and crafts from Island artisans.
Hill's Native Art, 76 Bastion St, T250-7557873. One of the largest selections of glorious First Nations artwork on the West Coast, including jewellery, sculptures, masks, clothes, totem poles and paintings.
Nanaimo Art Gallery. A decent giftshop showcasing local artisans.

Books and maps
Bygone Books, 99 Commercial St. The best of many used-book stores on this street, with a great selection including lots of Canadian fiction and non-fiction.
Nanaimo Maps & Charts, 8 Church St. A giant collection of nautical and topographical maps.

Music
Fascinating Rhythm, 174 Commercial St. One of the best new and used CD stores in the West, with a huge selection.

Gabriola Island *p123*
Gabriola Artworks, 575 North Rd. Representing many of the 50-plus resident artists. Also a café.
The Yew Tree Gallery, 535 North Rd, T250-2477555. An art gallery with jazz or classical concerts.

Tofino *p125, map p125*
Storm Light Outfitters, 390 Main St. The place for camping and sports gear.

Wildside Booksellers and Espresso Bar, 320 Main St. A well-chosen selection of new fiction and books about the area.
The Village Gallery, 321 Main St. There is a lot of fake and tacky First Nations 'art' around, but this gallery has a good, authentic selection including wooden masks and paintings.

▲▲ Activities and tours

Nanaimo *p122, map p131*
Bikes can be hired from **Chain Reaction**, 21 Lois Lane. **Nanaimo Leisure and Aquatic Centre**, 741 3rd St, has a good pool, plus sauna, hot tub and exercise room.

Diving
Several places around Nanaimo are recommended for diving, such as the sunken *HMCS Saskatchewan*, an artificial reef teeming with marine life. Contact the **Nanaimo Diving Association**, 2290 Bowen Rd, T250-7531246, for information. **Ocean Explorers Diving**, 1690 Stewart Av, T250-7532055, www.oceanexplorers diving.com. Lessons, charters and dives.

Kayaking and sailing
The many little islands off the coast, with resident sea-life such as octopus, seals and otters, also help make this a prime location for sailing and kayaking.
The Kayak Shack, T250-7533234, just off the ferry, arranges tours and lessons.
Seadog Kayaking & Sailing, T250-4685778, www.seadog.bc.ca. Lessons, tours and rentals. A skippered sailing charter is $70 per 2 hrs, $320 overnight.

Gabriola Island *p123*
Cycle and Kayak, T250-2478277, for bike and kayak rental.
High Test Dive Charters, T250-2479753, www.hightestdive.com $150 per person per dive. Gear rental extra.
Sundog Gulf Island Adventures, T250-2470114, www.sundogadventures.com. for kayaking, hiking and biking tours.

West to Pacific Rim National Park *p123*

Rendezvous Dive Adventures, Port Alberni, T250-7355050, www.rendez vousdiving.com. Accommodation and diving in Barkley Sound. $180/day for lodging, meals and diving, but you must be certified and bring your own gear.

Tofino *p125, map p125*
Fibre Options, Campbell/4th, T250-7252192. For bike hire.
Jay's Clayoquot Ventures, 564 Campbell St. T250-7252700. Fishing trips.

Float Plane
Tofino Air Adventures, T250-7254454, www.tofinoair.ca. Flights to Hot Springs Cove, wildlife tours, glacier tours, and guided fishing by float plane.

Kayaking
Clayoquot Sound may well be the coast's best overall location for kayaking. It's less crowded than the Broken Islands Group but more so than Nootka Sound, and the beauty of the scenery is almost unparalleled. Be careful though: the currents and waves here are dangerous, causing a few deaths every year. If in doubt, go with a professional.
Rainforest Kayak, T250-7253117, www.rainforestkayak.com. Eco-friendly lessons and tours.
Remote Passages Sea Kayaking, T250-7253330, www.remotepassages.com. Day and evening paddles and instruction.
Tofino Sea Kayaking Co, T250-7254222, www.tofino-kayaking.com. Offers tours and will rent to experienced kayakers.

Surfing
Tofino has become an internationally recognized surf destination. The following are recommended for gear, rentals, lessons (around $80 including board) and advice:
Live To Surf, 1180 Pacific Rim Hwy, T250-7254464; **Pacific Surf School**, 440 Campbell St, T250-7252155; **Surf Sister**

Surf School, 625 Campbell St, T250-7254456, is an all-girl surf school.

Whale watching

The number one activity hereabouts. For excellent value, combine it with a trip to Hot Springs Cove. There are many decent operators in town. To narrow them down decide if you want to go in an inflatable zodiac or a rigid-hull cruiser. The former tend to get thrown around a bit, making for an exciting and wet ride, the latter are a little calmer. **Ocean Outfitters**, T250-7254412, www.seatrektours.bc.ca, and **Adventures Pacific**, T250-7252811, both offer one-way transportation to or from Hot Springs Cove for $55. The companies below are widely recommended and have a long-standing good reputation. **Remote Passages**, T250-7253330, www.remotepassages.com. Zodiacs only, with an emphasis on educational trips. $70/2½ hrs, whales and hot springs, $110/6½ hrs. Also sea kayaking, $69 for 4 hrs, including a walk on Meares Island. **Sea Trek Tours**, T250-7254412, www.sea trektours.bc.ca. Whale watching in a glass-bottomed boat, $65 per 2 hrs; Hot Springs Cove/whale watching, $95 for 6½ hrs; one-way to Hot Springs Cove $50 on stand by. Also bear watching, $75 per 2 hrs. Times vary according to tides, but the website is updated daily.

Bamfield *p127*
Broken Island Adventures, T250-7283500. Whale watching, diving and kayaking.

⊖ Transport

Nanaimo *p122, map p131*
Air
Air Canada, T250-2457123, www.air canada.com, has several flights daily to **Vancouver** ($80 one-way). **Harbour Air Seaplanes**, T250-5375525, operates regular flights from the Seaplane Terminal behind the Bastion to **Vancouver Harbour** (15 mins).

Ferry
There are 5 separate terminals in Nanaimo. **Harbour Lynx**, T1866-2065969, www.harbourlynx.ca, runs 3 daily high-speed catamaran ferries to/from **Downtown Vancouver**'s Waterfront SeaBus terminal, $30/$17 one way, 80 mins. **BC Ferries**, T1888-2233779, www.bcferries.com, operates the following services: Departure Bay, 2 km north of Downtown (Bus No 2) to Vancouver's **Horseshoe Bay**. Every 2 hrs 0630-2100, $10.65, $5.50 child, $33.50 vehicle one-way (95 mins); Nanaimo's inconvenient Duke Point (12 km south, with only taxis into town) to Vancouver's inconvenient **Tsawwassen**, every 2½ hrs 0515-2245 (2 hrs); Gabriola Island to **Nanaimo Harbour** behind the Harbour Park Mall Downtown. Roughly hourly 0615-2255, $6.60, $3.45 child, $16.75 vehicle (20 mins). Smaller ferries leave from behind the Bastion for **Protection Island**, and from Maffeo-Sutton Park to the north for **Newcastle Island**.

Bus
Local City buses, T250-3904531, www.rdn.bc.ca, all meet Downtown at Harbour Park Mall and go as far north as Qualicum Beach.

   Long distance Pacific Coach Lines, T1800-6611725, www.pacificcoach.com run 6 buses daily to **Victoria** ($20), 2 west to **Port Alberni** and **Tofino** (0830 and 1230), 5 north to **Campbell River**, of which the 0830 continues to **Port Hardy** and 4 to **Departure Bay**. Greyhound, www.greyhound.ca, runs 8 daily buses to **Vancouver**, 2½ hrs. Tofino Bus operates services to **Tofino**, **Vancouver** and **Victoria** (see Tofino, below).

Train
VIA Rail runs one train daily each way between **Victoria** and **Courtenay**.

Taxis
AC Taxi, T250-7531231. **Budget Car Rentals**, 17 Terminal Av, T250-7547368.

Gabriola Island *p123*

The easiest way to get around the island is by bike or kayak (see Activities and tours, p136). Hitching works well too, or you can use **Island Taxi**, T250-2470049.

Air

Tofino Air, T250-2479992, runs a floatplane from Silva Bay at Gabriola's eastern tip to **Vancouver**'s Air Seaplane Terminal in Richmond, $70 one-way for the 15-min flight.

Ferry

BC Ferries, T1888-2233779, www.bc ferries.com, run hourly 0615-2255 from **Nanaimo Harbour**. See Nanaimo, above.

Tofino *p125, map p125*

Everything in Tofino is close, clustered around Campbell St and Main St. Bikes are recommended for getting to the beaches, see Activities and Tours, p136. **Beach Bus**, T250-7252871, www.tofinobus.com, runs shuttles between Tofino, **Long Beach**, and **Ucluelet**. Meares Island Big Tree Taxi, T250-7267848, charges about $25 return to **Meares Island**.

Air

Orca Air, T1888-3596722, www.flyorca air.com. Daily flights to and from **Vancouver**, $135 one-way.

Bus

Tofino Bus, T1866-9863466, www.tofino bus.com, runs 1 daily service to/from **Downtown Vancouver**'s Waterfront Station at 0900 using the Harbour Lynx ferry ($55 one-way, 5½ hrs); 1 daily service from HI in **Victoria** at 0815 ($50, 5 hrs). Also services to **Nanaimo** and **Port Alberni**. Pacific Coach Lines, T1800-6611725, www.pacificcoach.com, operates 1 morning service to **Victoria** and **Nanaimo**.

Bamfield *p127*

Travellers to Bamfield or the Broken Islands Group should consider getting off the bus in Port Alberni, and completing the trip aboard the *MV Lady Rose* (see p126). Drivers taking the abominable 100-km logging road from Port Alberni to Bamfield should be very careful, and carry at least one good spare tyre.

Bus

The **West Coast Trail Shuttle Bus**, T250-7233341, www.trailbus.com, leaves daily from 700 Douglas St, **Victoria** at 0640 stopping in **Nanaimo** and **Port Alberni** ($60 one-way). Another leaves **Gordon River** and **Port Renfrew** at 0900 ($55), for hikers who need to get back to their vehicles. Both go to town and **Pachena Bay**, leaving again at 1300.

Water taxi

Juan de Fuca Express Water Taxi, T250-7556578, operates between **Port Renfrew**, **Nitinat Narrows**, and Bamfield. Nitinat Lake Water Taxi, T250-7453509, crosses **Nitinat Narrows** to the village daily at 1700.

● Directory

Nanaimo *p122, map p131*
Canada Post In the Shoppers Drug Mart, 530 5th St. **Internet** At the library. **Laundry** Boat Basin Laundry, 650 Terminal Av. **Library** Nanaimo Harbour-front Library, 90 Commercial St. **Medical services** Nanaimo General Hospital, 1200 Dufferin Cres, T250- 2482332. **Medical Arts Centre**, 350 Albert St, T250-7533431. **Police** 303 Prideaux St, T250-7542345.

Tofino *p125, map p125*
Canada Post 1st/Campbell. **Internet** Whalers On the Point Guesthouse or Caffe Vincente, 441 Campbell St. **Medical services** Hospital 261 Neill St, T250-7253212. Medical Clinic, T250-7253282.

Central and north Vancouver Island

The further north you go on Vancouver Island, the more remote and unexplored it becomes. Courtenay, a pleasant town in its own right, is handy for Mount Washington Ski Hill and the western section of Strathcona Provincial Park, with some great hiking among the island's highest peaks. The bulk of the park is reached from the salmon-fishing mecca of Campbell River via Highway 28. The road continues to the largely undiscovered West Coast wilderness of Nootka Sound, a paradise for kayakers and cavers. A visit to at least one of the Gulf Islands is highly recommended,

⚑ **Getting there** Car, bus, ferry or plane.
⊜ **Getting around** Car or bus.
⊖ **Time required** 2-7 days.
⊚ **Weather** Can be wet and windy.
⬤ **Sleeping** Fairly limited.
⚐ **Eating** Limited outside Courtenay and Campbell River.
▲▲ **Activities and tours** Whale watching, hiking, skiing, kayaking, caving, diving.
★ **Don't miss...** Kayaking around the hundreds of small islands in Nootka Sound ▶ p146.

particularly Hornby or Cortes which, two steps removed from the main island, are even more relaxed, yet brimming with character.

There's little infrastructure beyond Campbell River, except the interesting native community of Alert Bay, the tiny village of Sointula, with its fascinating history, and the phoney boardwalk village of Telegraph Cove, one of the world's top spots for seeing orcas. Most travellers are heading to Port Hardy, to catch the Inside Passage ferry to Prince Rupert or the Discovery Coast Passage ferry to Bella Coola, two stunning journeys, or to hike in Cape Scott Provincial Park, as rugged, remote, and notoriously wet a place as anyone could desire.

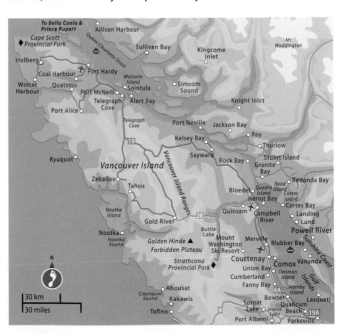

Ins and outs

Getting there and around

Greyhound runs four buses daily as far as Campbell River; one continues north to Port Hardy. **VIA Rail** runs one train daily between Victoria and Courtenay. **BC Ferries** has four daily sailings from Powell River to just north of Comox/Courtenay, plus services to all the Gulf Islands, Alert Bay and Sointula, and to Port Hardy from Prince Rupert and Bella Coola. There are many sailings from Vancouver to Nanaimo, just to the south. There are flights from Vancouver to Courtenay, Nanaimo, Campbell River, and Port Hardy. There is no public transport to Gold River and Nootka Sound. Getting around can be difficult without a car, especially as you go further north. ➲ ▸▸ *p156.*

Best time to visit

Mid- to late June is the best time to see orca whales in the Johnstone Strait, though many whales remain until mid-October. The salmon migration, so significant for Campbell River, peaks between July and September. Except for skiers, summer is best.

Courtenay and around ⊜⊘⊙⊙⊛▲⊜⊙ ▸▸ *pp149-157.*

North to Courtenay

A major parting of roads occurs north of Nanaimo. With its dearth of scenic interest, the Inland Island Highway (Highway 19) is only for those in a hurry, or wanting to branch west towards Pacific Rim National Park on Highway 4. The older and more scenic Coast Highway (Highway 19A), winds its way through Parksville, a drab town whose only attraction is **Rathtrevor Beach Provincial Park**, containing one of the coast's finest and busiest beaches. In July, the park attracts thousands of visitors for **Sandfest**, featuring the World Sandcastle Competition.

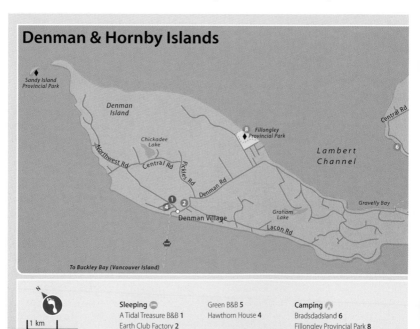

Denman & Hornby Islands

Sandy Island Provincial Park

Denman Island

Chickadee Lake

Fillongley Provincial Park

Northwest Rd

Central Rd

Pickles Rd

Denman Rd

Central Rd

Lambert Channel

Graham Lake

Gravelly Bay

Lacon Rd

Denman Village

To Buckley Bay (Vancouver Island)

N

1 km
1 miles

Sleeping ⬭
A Tidal Treasure B&B **1**
Earth Club Factory **2**
Good Morning B&B **3**

Green B&B **5**
Hawthorn House **4**

Camping ⬭
Bradsdadsland **6**
Fillongley Provincial Park **8**
Tribune Bay **7**

The stretch of coast to the north is a great birdwatching zone. The Coast Highway offers increasingly striking views of the island-dotted coastline and mainland Coast Mountains as it passes through a series of sleepy seaside villages and bays, of which **Qualicum Beach** is the most promising prospect for a bite to eat on the waterfront, also offering a few unusual sleeping options, see p149. About 15 km further on, a gravel road leads 12 km to **Horne Lake** ⓘ *T250-2487829, www.hornelake.com*, where a set of caves can be explored either alone or on one of several tours lasting from 1½ to 7 hours ($15-130). There's also a campground, and some first-class rock-climbing, including the Horne Lake Amphitheatre, one of the toughest climbs of its kind in the country. Further north, huge piles of oyster shells define **Fanny Bay** as one of the world's most prolific suppliers of the fabled aphrodisiac.

Denman Island

From Buckley Bay, ferries cross to super-mellow Denman Island, another magnet for all kinds of artists, whose work can be seen on display at the annual **Festival of the Arts** in early August. There are no information points on Denman or Hornby, so pick up a copy of the very useful *Denman & Hornby Islands Visitor's Guide* from information centres elsewhere, and visit www.denmanisland.com, or www.hornbyisland.com. Both have useful maps.

Denman Village, walking distance from the ferry, is the island's focal point, with bikes and scooters for rent at the local store, but no ATMs. **Fillongley Provincial Park**, 4 km away on the opposite (east) side, has a long pebble shoreline with great beachcombing, plus large stands of old-growth cedars and Douglas firs, views of the Coast Range, and a number of trails, one of which is wheelchair-accessible. **Boyle Point Provincial Park** at the south end also offers trails through giant trees, great views, and a good chance of seeing eagles and sea lions. Off the northwestern tip, only accessible by water, is **Sandy Island Provincial Park**, where camping is allowed. **Denman Island Canoes and Kayaks** (see Activities and tours, p154) will help you get there.

Hornby Island

From Gravelly Bay in the southeast of Denman, several daily ferries make the 10-minute journey to **Hornby Island**. From the dock at Shingle Spit, a single road (Central Road), leads most of the way round the island. One small hub of activity is near a bakery roughly 4 km away, but the island's main centre is on the east side, clustered around the **Ringside Market** and the **Co-op**, a health-conscious grocery store that doubles as post office and liquor outlet. Close by is an ATM machine and bike rentals. Within walking distance is **Tribune Bay Provincial Park**, with a beautiful long sandy beach, bike rentals and camping. St John's Road, north of the Co-op, leads down the island's south-eastern spit to **Helliwell Bay Provincial Park**, where a gorgeous 5-km circular walk takes in some amazing bluffs with great views and nesting eagles. Apart from the **Performing Arts Festival** (see p154), another summer draw is scuba diving and the rare

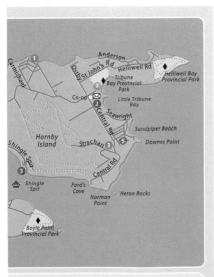

Eating ⓕ
Cardboard House **2**
Denman Bakery
& Pizzeria **1**
Denman Café &
General Store **1**
Jan's Café **2**
Thatch **3**

Vancouver Island Central & north Vancouver Island

Hiking in Helliwell Park, Hornby Island.

chance to see six-gilled sharks. There's a diving base, marina and accommodation at **Ford's Cove**, though equipment has to be rented on Vancouver Island.

Courtenay

Back on the mainland, **Courtenay** is the most prominent of three sister towns clustered within the farming landscape of the Comox Valley and, unpromising as its outskirts may be, must rank as Vancouver Island's most attractive settlement after Victoria and Tofino. A clutch of decent shops, restaurants, cafés and galleries make this a more alluring base than Campbell River to the north, and it's well placed for hiking the **Forbidden Plateau** section of Strathcona Park, skiing or mountain biking at **Mount Washington**, or visiting Denman and Hornby islands. Since many of Vancouver Island's places of interest are either close to Courtenay or further south, it's worth taking the ferry from Courtenay to Powell River on the Sunshine Coast as part of a nice loop back to Vancouver (see Transport, p156).

Highly significant for over-wintering waterfowl, this area is popular for birdwatching, and from October to March trumpeter swans can be seen from the **Air Park Walkway**, which makes for a pleasant stroll at any time. It's conveniently close to the helpful **Visitor Information Centre** ⓘ *2040 Cliffe Av, T250-3343234, www.tourism-comox-valley.bc.ca*, which can provide a bird checklist, a book of nature viewing sites, and information about the many local outdoor pursuits. Fossils from an 80-million-year-old sea bed at nearby Puntledge River are on display at the **Courtenay and District Museum and Palaeontology Centre** ⓘ *207 4th St, T250-3340686, www.courtenaymuseum.ca, summer daily, winter Tue-Sat 1000- 1700, by donation, tours $20, $17.50 child, book in advance*, along with dinosaur replicas and the usual local-history fare. Fossil tours, twice daily in July and August (less in spring and autumn), include a lecture and tour of the museum and a drive to the site to find fossils.

The outskirts of town merge seamlessly with the more genteel **Comox**, pleasantly situated on Comox Harbour, and home to a significant airport and Canadian naval base, a marina, a few decent pubs, and **Filberg Lodge and Park** ⓘ *61 Filberg Rd, Comox, T250-3392715, park year round 0800-dusk, lodge Jun-Aug daily 0800-dusk, May and Sep Sat-Sun only, $3, tours daily at 1100 and 1400, $10, $15 with tea and scone*, whose 3.6 ha of meticulously landscaped grounds are open to the public.

ⓘ *Day-pass $51, $42 youth and senior, $28 child, for alpine; $18.75, $14 youth and senior, $9.50 child, for cross-country. Some trails are lit up for night skiing, Fri and Sat 1630-2100.*

Situated 25 km northwest of Comox (reached most easily on the Inland Island Highway), this medium-sized hill receives a lot of powder, an average of almost 9 m annually. Canada's first six-person chairlift was recently added as part of an expansion programme that has considerably raised the hill's profile. Small, unintimidating, and with superb ocean views, it's great for beginners and intermediates. Eight lifts lead to 50 alpine runs (25% beginner, 40% intermediate, 35% expert). There are also 55 km of track-set cross-country trails, and 20 km of snowshoeing trails. You could also try snow-tubing.

In September and October the gondola opens from 1100 to 1600 for biking and hiking, with views of Comox Glacier, the Coast Mountains, and the Georgia Strait ($11 for hiking, $28 biking). Bikes can be rented here, but it's cheaper in town, see p154. Favourite downhills include the steep and scary Monster Mile, and Discovery Road. There's also a nine-hole golf course ($5.75 including frisbee rental) and horse riding for $30 per hour. Open in the summer is a pub/restaurant, a coffee bar and on Sundays the arts and crafts Mountain Market.

Strathcona Provincial Park: Forbidden Plateau

Established in 1911, this is BC's oldest park and it contains the lion's share of Vancouver Island's most elevated peaks, including its highest point, **Golden Hinde** (2200 m). It also provides one of the few chances to sample the beauty of the island's gloriously undeveloped interior. Hiking is the main activity, with most trails clustered in two areas: the Forbidden Plateau region, and Buttle Lake (see p145). The more remote southern section of the park, including the famous **Della Falls**, is accessed, with difficulty, from Port Alberni, and not recommended. Seek trail information from the visitor information centres in Courtenay or Campbell River. Serious hikers might invest in the *National Topographic Series* maps, scale *1:50,000: -92 F/11 Forbidden Plateau*, and *-92 F/12 Buttle Lake.*

Jutting out from the park's eastern flank, the high altitude of the Forbidden Plateau means that hikers barely have to climb to reach alpine scenery and views. **Paradise Meadows** trailhead, 1.5 km from Mount Washington Road down Nordic Lodge Road, 35 km from Courtenay, gives the easiest access to this formidable zone. A 4-km hike, with minimal

An aerial view of Hornby Island.

Vancouver Island Central & north Vancouver Island

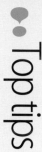

Top tips

The Inside Passage

Most visitors to Port Hardy are there to embark on one of two spectacular ferry journeys up the coast: the **Inside Passage** to Prince Rupert, or the **Discovery Coast Passage** to wild and remote Bella Coola. Both routes lead through rugged and pristine stretches of wilderness coast, dissected by long fjords, dotted with tiny islands and lined with steep mountains, waterfalls and rainforest. There's a good chance of seeing whales, dolphins, sea lions and eagles.

These two popular northbound services are run by **BC Ferries**, T250-3863779/T1888-2233779, www.bcferries.com. The ferry dock is at **Bear Cove**, 10 km east, on the other side of Hardy Bay. The Inside Passage ferry to Prince Rupert runs every other day in summer (leaving at 0730, arriving at 2230, $116 one-way, $61 child, plus $274 for a car). Check the website for times and prices in the low season.

elevation gain, leads to **Kwai Lake**, an excellent base with a backcountry campground and a network of trails radiating out like spokes in all directions. The **Wood Mountain** trailhead, 19 km from Courtenay, is lower and less convenient, and its trails are not maintained. Kwai Lake is 15 km away via the **Plateau Trail**. The **Mount Becher Trail** is a 9-km round-trip with 580-m elevation gain, leading to excellent views.

Campbell River and around ⬛🚻🏊❄🏔🚌🍴 » pp149-157.

Campbell River

The strip of seafront houses and hotels emanating from Campbell River stretches so far south down the Coast Highway that the town itself, nicely placed around the water, comes as a pleasant relief, though Courtenay, Strathcona Park Lodge, and the nearby Discovery Islands are all more enticing places to stay. There is some justification for Campbell River's claim to be the salmon capital of the world, and in winter there's halibut a-plenty to keep the angling industry going. Open 24 hours, 182 m long (46 m of it jutting out over the ocean), and illuminated at night, **Discovery Pier** is a popular and easy place to fish. Rods can be rented, but remember that you'll need a Sport Fishing Licence ($108 for non-residents). Alternatively, you can go snorkelling to see the aquatic superstars up close (see Activities and tours, p155), or visit **Quinsam Salmon Hatchery** ① *5 km west on Hwy 28, 0800-1600, free*, to see them and learn all you want to know about their life adventure. The salmon spawning run peaks between July and September.

Campbell River Museum ① *470 Island Hwy, T250-2873103, www.crmuseum.ca, summer Mon-Sat 1000-1700, Sun 1200-1700, winter Tue-Sun 1200-1700, $5, $4 child*, has exhibits on pioneers, salmon fishing, and First Nations' history, plus an unusual multimedia presentation of a mystical journey beneath the sea from a native perspective. **Wei Wai Kum House of Treasures**, also on the highway, at the Discovery Harbour Centre, sells and exhibits First Nations' arts and crafts. Inside is **Gilda's Box of Treasures Theatre** ① *T250-2877310, shows summer only Tue-Fri 1600, Sat 1300 and 1600, $20, $10 child*, a venue for performances by aboriginal dancers, drummers and singers, and for salmon feasts, modelled on a West Coast 'Big House'. The **Visitor Information Centre** ① *1235 Shoppers Row (Ocean Hwy), T250-2874636, www.campbellrivertourism.com, summer Mon-Sat 0900-1700, winter Mon-Fri 0900-1700, Sat 1000-1600*, is next to the **Art Gallery** ① *Tue-Sat 1200-1700, free*.

At the northern end of the Georgia Strait is a complex cluster of large and tiny islands, known collectively as the Discovery Islands, through which are threaded numerous narrow channels and inlets. One can only imagine the difficulty with which Captain George Vancouver would have negotiated, let alone charted, this maze. The landscapes here are even more dramatic, best enjoyed from the only easily accessed islands, Quadra and Cortes. All these closely huddled, virtually uninhabited islands, along with the proximity of Desolation Sound Marine Park (see p67) on the other side of the strait, make this an exciting playground for sailors and kayakers. A good source of information is www.discoveryislands.ca.

Quadra is the biggest of the Northern Gulf Islands, and one of the most populated. The main hub is **Quathiaski Cove**, which hosts most stores and a popular Saturday Farmers' Market. A short drive or hitch across the island is the nicer village of **Heriot Bay**, which has a summer-only **Visitor Information Booth** ① *T250-2852724, www.quadraisland.ca*, an adjacent Credit Union, and bike/kayak rentals. Neither village is as good a place for soaking up the Gulf Island vibe as similar centres on Cortes, Hornby or Gabriola, though the usual plethora of galleries and studios is easily found.

The island's main attraction for visitors is the native village of **Cape Mudge** at its southern tip. The **Carving and Artist Centre**, adjacent to the outstanding but currently closed Kwagiulth Museum, exhibits a number of old totem poles, and craftsmen can be seen creating new works. A walk from here leads to a 100-year-old lighthouse, and a beach with over 50 petroglyphs.

The vast bulk of the island is north of the two main communities, barely inhabited, and criss-crossed with some very fine hiking and biking trails. The most popular hike is up **Chinese Mountains**, with splendid panoramas at the top. Nearby **Morte Lake** is also a worthwhile destination. The trail to **Nugedzi Lake** is a steady climb through old-growth forest also leading to excellent views. For mountain biking, Mount Seymour has most of the best descents, with some 400-m drops. For swimming and mainly rocky beaches head for **Village Bay Park** or Rebecca Spit Provincial Park; the latter also makes a nice stroll.

Cortes Island

Cortes, www.cortesisland.com, is in many respects the quintessential Gulf Island. As with Hornby, being two steps removed from Vancouver Island has ensured the laid-back and friendly spirit of the people. **Manson's Landing**, 15 km from the Whaletown ferry landing, is the best place to meet them, and has a café, ATM, post office, and launderette. The **Arts Festival** in mid-July is the best time to visit.

Manson's Landing Provincial Park has one of the better sand beaches around, and a warm freshwater lagoon for swimming, with the chance to legally pick some of the clams and oysters that are all around the island. The adjacent **Hague Lake Provincial Park** is good for hiking. **Smelt Bay Provincial Park**, 25 km south of the ferry, has camping and a nice beach walk to **Sutil Point**. At Cortes Bay is the bizarre folly of **Wolf Bluff Castle**, an eccentric, five-storey structure, including a dungeon and three turrets. The island's most famous feature, worth the trip on its own, is the popular **Hollyhock Retreat Centre**, where you can follow courses on yoga and meditation, or simply enjoy the relaxing grounds, great vegetarian food, and decent accommodation.

Strathcona Provincial Park: Buttle Lake

This second key section of the wonderful park begins 48 km from Campbell River on Highway 28. Just outside the park boundary is the superlative **Strathcona Park Lodge**, hands down the best base from which to explore the region, and an excellent outdoor pursuits centre, especially for novices. All manner of rentals, lessons and tours are available, and the staff tend to be friendly, young and enthusiastic. All-inclusive holiday packages, including meals and unlimited use of kayaks and canoes, run from $129 per person. Transport from Campbell River can be arranged through the lodge ($50, then $10 for each additional person).

From the nearby junction, Buttle Lake Road heads south along the edge of this long, skinny strip of water into the very heart of the park. It's a fantastic drive, lined with hiking trails of all lengths. **Lupin Falls**, near the north end, **Karst Creek**, two-thirds down, **Myra Falls** at the bottom, and **Lady Falls**, off Highway 28, are all short and easy walks leading to gorgeous waterfalls, usually through lush rainforest.

Most of the longer hikes start at the lake's south end. **Flower Ridge**, at Km 29.6, is a steep and rough 14-km round trip (extendable to 24 km), gaining 1250 m elevation as it climbs to an open alpine ridge. **Bedwell Lake** (with complicated access, see BC Parks map) is a 12-km hike with 600-m gain, also leading to good mountain views and a campground on the lake. Accessible only by boat from the Auger Point day-use area is the **Marble Meadows Trail**, 13 km return, 1250 m gain. Many different peaks can be reached from here, and the Golden Hinde is visible. From Highway 28 at the western edge of the park, the **Crest Mountain Trail**, 10 km return with 1250-m gain, gives quick access to the alpine scenery and views. South-facing, it's a good choice early in the season.

Nootka Sound and Gold River

Nootka Sound is touted as the birthplace of BC, for it was here at Yuquot in 1778 that Captain James Cook made his first West Coast landing. When he asked the Mowachaht people (whose ancestors arrived at least 6000 years ago) the name of their land, they thought he wanted directions around a smaller island, and replied 'Nutka, itchme' ('Go around that way'). Mistaking it for a place name, Cook dubbed the region Nootka, a name that was eventually extended to the people themselves. So warm was the welcome he received from Chief Maquinna, that he nicknamed the place 'Friendly Cove', and quickly entered into a burgeoning trade in sea otter fur that made Yuquot the busiest port north of Mexico for several years, and almost wiped out Canada's sea otter population. Ironically, the last remaining survivors are found here in Zeballos.

Today this wild and undeveloped portion of Vancouver Island's Northwest Coast is attracting a new breed of adventurer. It is quickly being discovered by BC's in-the-know

A kayaker pulls up onto Sand Beach at Benson Point, Nootka Island.

The sheltered islands around Nootka Island are becoming a popular place for kayakers to get away from it all and explore.

outdoor community, who come to kayak around its hundreds of small islands, surf the Pacific breakers, dive the reefs and walls where gill shark roam, fish, explore the numerous local cave systems, rock climb, or hike a section of the West Coast that is guaranteed to be crowd-free. If all that sounds too hard-core, another option for seeing this rugged strip of coast is aboard the *MV Uchuck III* which has become a popular way to take a cheap cruise (see Transport, p157).

Many drivers and cyclists agree that the beautiful 91-km ride on Highway 28 from Campbell River to **Gold River** is one of the most gratifying in the province. Utterly dominated by logging until the pulp-mill closed in 1998, the inhabitants of this remote little town have increasingly looked towards tourism for their survival, though there's still very little infrastructure to encourage interest in the region beyond the summer-only **Visitor Information Centre** ⓘ *Hwy 28/Scout Lake Rd, T250-2832418, www.village.goldriver.bc.ca*. **Tahsis**, an even smaller, more remote community at the end of a long inlet leading from Nootka Sound, has some of Canada's best caving, particularly at the 100-plus **Upana Caves**, 17 km west. There is a summer-only visitor information booth at Rugged Mountain Road, T250-9346667. Still more remote, **Zeballos** (with a summer-only visitor information booth at 122 Maquinna Avenue, T250-7614070) and **Kyuquot** are even tinier communities, accessible only with the *MV Uchuck III*, but perfectly placed for adventurous and experienced kayakers to push further into pristine territory.

North to Port Hardy and beyond ⊟𝟬▲⊟ » pp149-157.

North of Campbell River, the solitary highway heads inland through increasingly wild, uninhabited scenery, with no real reason to stop until the coast is regained. **Robson Bight Ecological Reserve** in Johnstone Strait is one of the most reliable places in the world to see pods of orca, who like to rub their bellies on the gravel beaches. The best time is mid- to late June, though they stay until mid-October. Most people take tours from the picturesque boardwalk village of **Telegraph Cove**, 11 km down a windy logging road, 8 km south of **Port McNeill**. A short ferry ride from the latter, **Alert Bay** on Cormorant Island is a more interesting base for tours, and one of the best places in BC to learn about First Nations' culture.

Everything in Alert Bay is close and easy to find, including the **Visitor Information Centre** ⓘ *116 Fir St, T250-9745024, www.alertbay.ca*. To the left when disembarking from the ferry is the **U'mista Cultural Centre** ⓘ *T250-9745403, www.umista.org, daily 0900-1700, $5.35*, which contains a large selection of wooden masks and other Potlatch items confiscated and dispersed by the government, and now slowly being returned. The **World's Tallest Totem Pole** (at 52.7 m) is just up the road, as are the **'Namgis Burial Grounds**, which contain many more poles, though respect demands that these be viewed from the road. Ask for the totem poles brochure at the visitor centre. Though rebuilt in 1999, the **Traditional Big House** is still an impressive building. The inside can only be seen during traditional dance performances of the **Tsasala Cultural Group** ⓘ *T250-9745475, Jul-Aug Thu-Sat at 1315; $15, $6 child, 1 hr*.

Meaning 'harmony' in Finnish, the most compelling thing about nearby **Sointula** on Malcolm Island is its history. Much of the population today is descended from a group of Finnish coal miners from Nanaimo who attempted to establish their own Utopia here in 1900. Orcas can be seen from the 10 km of ocean trails at **Bere Point Regional Park**, which also has camping. A speciality of the island is sea-foam green rugs made of fishing nets.

Port Hardy

Vancouver Island's northernmost community, 230 km from Campbell River, is a long way to go for what is essentially just another fishing village. Apart from the lure of the Inside Passage and Cape Scott Provincial Park, however, this is a fantastic location for scuba diving, with excellent visibility and a good chance of seeing dolphins and wolf eels. Whale watching and kayaking are also prime, and the area possesses a great rugged beauty.

Most of the town is on Market Street, including the **Visitor Information Centre** ⓘ *No 7250, T250-9497622, www.ph-chamber.bc.ca*. Otherwise, there is little reason to venture Downtown. Hardy Bay Road, which shoots off to the right on the way in from the south, is a far nicer place to stay, with the two best hotel-restaurants-bars around, both nicely situated on a marina. **Fort Rupert**, 10 minutes south of the ferry terminal, contains the **First Nations Copper Maker Gallery** ⓘ *114 Copper Way, T250-9498491, www.calvinhunt.com, Mon-Sat 0900-1700*, a good place to see traditional artisans at work. Nearby is the long **Stories Beach**, and the trailhead for the **Tex Lyon Trail**, which goes to **Dillon Point** along the shoreline (nine hours return). **Coal Harbour** to the southwest is a historic whaling station.

Cape Scott Provincial Park

Situated at the island's northwestern tip, Cape Scott Provincial Park brings new meaning to words like rugged, wet and wild. Due to the remoteness and consistently appalling weather, a long hike here is a serious undertaking, and the mosquitos can be brutal. However, the forest is incredibly lush and beautiful and there are 23 km of deserted white-sand beaches from which grey whales, orcas, seals and otters are frequently seen.

All trails start at the San Josef Bay trailhead, at the southeast corner of the park. a 67-km drive from Port Hardy on gravel logging roads past the small town of **Holberg**. The biggest hiking challenge is the tough 48-km return trip to **Cape Scott**, located at the end of a narrow spit that does a very convincing impression of the end of the world. Before embarking on this, get thoroughly briefed at the Port Hardy visitor information centre. Maps can usually also be found at various information shelters. There are also some fine shorter trails. The **San Josef Bay Trail** is the most accessible, a 5-km return hike to some sandy beaches. The best beach is **Nels Bight**, a six-hour hike one-way. On a clear day climb to the top of **Mount St Patrick** for fantastic views. The trail then continues to **Sea Otter Cove**, a 10-km, five-hour hike one-way.

● Sleeping

North to Courtenay *p140*

C **Qualicum College Inn**, 427 College Rd, Qualicum Beach, just off the highway, T250-7529262, www.qualicumheritage inn.com. The most interesting of several options, this Tudor-style ex-college has an authentic historic interior, and an extensive garden. Rooms have a fireplace and/or balcony; there's a restaurant and lounge.

Denman Island *p141, map p140*

Accommodation on Denman is particularly scarce. There are a few B&Bs scattered around, but many require bookings for 2 nights or more. The best place to find details is at www.gulfislands-bc.com.
C **Hawthorn House**, 3375 Kirk Rd, just off Northwest Rd, T250-3350905, www.hawthornhouse.ca. One of the few B&Bs in or near the village and ferry, this 1904 heritage home offers a hot tub, garden, hearty breakfasts, and good views, with 3 attractive en suite rooms.
E-F **Earth Club Factory**, 3806 Denman Rd, T250-3352688. This lovely wooden home has 5 reasonable private rooms with shared bath, dorm beds, and a bistro.

Camping

Fillongley Provincial Park, T1800-6899025. 10 drive-in campsites right on the beach. Be sure to reserve a spot.

Hornby Island *p141, map p140*

Hornby also has a shortage of beds, with many places only renting rooms for 2 nights or more. Book as early as possible at www.hornbyisland.com.
A-B **A Tidal Treasure**, 3495 Harwood, T250-3353006, www.hornbyisland.net/a tidaltreasure. An elegant oceanfront home, whose 3 lovely, light-filled rooms have private entrances, en suite baths, beach access, and views of the Inside Passage from the deck or private balcony. Full breakfast included.

D **Good Morning B&B**, 7845 Central Rd, T250-3351094. A charming West Coast home (though owned by hospitable Europeans) in gorgeous forested surroundings. The 3 rooms have shared bath. A large breakfast is included
D **Green B&B**, 5075 Kirk, T250-3350920. A Tudor-style Hornby house with 3 large elegantly decorated rooms, a garden patio, gourmet breakfast, and a large guest living room with hardwood floors and vaulted ceilings.

Camping

Bradsdadsland Campsite, 3 km from the ferry on Central Rd, T250-3350757. Situated on the bluffs, with a friendly, family ambience, and good sunsets.
Tribune Bay Campsite, T250-3352359. 120 drive-in sites, some with hook-ups.

Courtenay *p142*

In addition to those listed below, there's a good selection of B&Bs close to town.
L-A **Kingfisher Oceanside Resort**, 4330 Island Hwy S, 7 km south, T250-3381323, www.kingfisherspa.com. A number of resorts line the highway to the south. This is one of the best, with luxurious beach-front suites with balconies, fireplaces, and ocean-view rooms. Extensive facilities include a hot tub, pool, sauna, fitness room, spa, restaurant, and lounge.
B-D **Copes' Islander B&B**, 1484 Wilkinson Rd, T250-3391038. Not as central as some but convenient for those taking the ferry to Powell River. Nice rooms with private entrance, views, and easy access to the beach.
C **Greystone Manor**, 4014 Haas Rd, 2 km south, T250-3381422, www.greystone manorbb.com. This waterfront heritage home is surrounded by beautiful flower gardens, and has 3 nice rooms with private bath.
D **Estuary House B&B**, 2810 Comox Rd, T250-8900130. About the best of the B&Bs in this price range, with good value en suite rooms. They also run sailing trips and weaving lessons.

D Sleepy Hollow Inn, at 1190 Cliffe Av, T250-3344476. If you're after an inexpensive motel, there are many strung along Cliffe Av heading south from Downtown. This is one of the better options, though rooms are predictable and standard; kitchen available.

E Courtenay Riverside Hostel, 1380 Cliffe Av, T250-3341938. A friendly and helpful hostel handily situated Downtown in a lovely big old house. All the usual facilities are on offer, including a kitchen, lockers, laundry, and internet.

E Shantz Hause Hostel, 520 5th St, T250-7032060, www.shantzhostel.com. Also conveniently located in the centre of Downtown. Dorms and private rooms with shared bath.

Camping

Miracle Beach Provincial Park, 22 km north at 1812 Miracle Beach Dr, exit Hwy 19 at Hamm Rd, T250-3372400. 200 sites close to a large sandy beach. Showers. Very popular in summer.

Mount Washington Ski Resort *p143*
Accommodation at the resort is generally expensive, with package deals sometimes offering the best value. Try **Central Reservations**, T250-3381386, www.mtwashington.bc.ca, or **Peak Accommodations**, T250-8973851, www.peakaccom.com.

Campbell River *p144*
C Haig-Brown House, 2250 Campbell River Rd, T250-2866646. About the nicest of the few B&Bs, this heritage house/museum has a very large garden on the river, and 3 rooms with shared bath.
C Hotel Bachmair, 492 S Island Hwy, T250-9232848, www.hotelbachmair.com. Not too central, but best value of many hotels stretching away to the south. Rooms have balconies, with kitchens available in the nicer ones.
C Rustic Motel, 2140 N Island Hwy, T250-2866295, www.rusticmotel.com. Our pick of the many mid-range motels in

this area. The recently renovated rooms are better than most, with kitchens for $10 extra. Amenities such as laundry, sauna, hot tub and dry room are included, as well as breakfast.
D Town Centre Inn, 1500 Dogwood St, T250-2878866. One of many cheaper options Downtown. Breakfast included.

Camping

Elk Falls Provincial Park, 2 km west on Hwy 28, T250-6899025, www.discovercamping.ca. 122 very nice sites on the Quinsam River, with trails leading to the dramatic 24-m falls. It's also a very popular fishing spot. The smaller **Loveland Bay Provincial Park**, T250-9564600, is further away, but very quiet and private as a result. Follow signs from Hwy 28, then 15 km on a gravel road.
Morton Lake Provincial Park, T250-6899025, www.discovercamping.ca, is even smaller and more remote and has sites on the lake. Head north on the Island Hwy to Menzies Bay, then take a logging road west for 20 km.

Quadra Island *p145*
B Tsa-Kwa-Luten Lodge, 1 Lighthouse Rd, Cape Mudge, T250-2852042, www.capemudgeresort.bc.ca. This beautiful wooden-beam building, based on a traditional West Coast 'Big House', is owned and operated by the local Kwagiulth First Nation, and full of traditional and contemporary native art. The location is very peaceful – on bluffs right by the ocean surrounded by 450 ha of forest. There are very nice lodge rooms, and 2- to 4-bedroom cabins with kitchen. Sauna and jacuzzi are included, plus they offer spa facilities, guided tours and activities, and native cultural events. They also have sites for RV camping.
C Heriot Bay Inn, T250-2853322, www.heriotbayinn.com. A good mid-range option, offering rooms with private bath, cottages, plus 60 tent sites with showers. Kayak, bike and canoe rentals

are available, and there's a pub and restaurant. Price includes breakfast.
E Coast Mountains Kayak Lodge, at the end of Surge Narrows Rd, T250-2852823, www.seakayaking-be.com. Dorms in a beautiful wood lodge on stilts, particularly suited to those wanting to try their hand at kayaking, with lessons, tours and hire.
E Travellers' Rural Retreat, 10-15 mins' drive from Heriot Bay ferry on a logging road, T250-2852477 for directions. A small and extremely remote guesthouse right on the water, favoured by artists or those seeking silence and solitude.

Cortes Island *p145*
AL-B Hollyhock, T250-9356576, www.hollyhock.bc.ca. Essentially a retreat offering meditation, yoga, and mind and body workshops, this well-known institution can also be treated as a surprisingly affordable treat. The surroundings are peaceful and beautiful, and good-value packages are offered that include all meals – the menu is gourmet vegetarian with an excellent reputation – plus the activities mentioned above, hot tub, and kayak or sailing trips. Reservations are recommended.
C Cortes Island Motel, close to Manson's Landing, T250-9356363. A standard motel in a very convenient location.
C Picard's B&B, Gorge Harbour, T250-9356683. Surrounded on 3 sides by water, this splendid house has 3 en suite rooms with patios and ocean views, and the use of a rowing boat.
D Gorge Harbour Marina Resort, 5 km from ferry on Hunt Rd, T250-9356433. Reasonable rooms, also a 46-site campground with hook-ups for RVs, plus scooter, boat and kayak rentals.

Camping
Smelt Bay Provincial Park, 25 km south of the ferry. Definitely the best choice for tent camping, with attractive, private sites, and a nice beach walk to Sutil Point.

Strathcona Provincial Park: Buttle Lake *p145*

LL-D Strathcona Park Lodge, just before the Buttle Lake junction, on Hwy 28, T250-2863122, www.strathcona.bc.ca. See p145 for more details. Many options including basic but pleasant rooms in the lodge, cabins of all sizes and comfort-levels, and all-inclusive holiday packages. You don't have to be a guest to partake of the healthy all-you-can-eat buffet meals.

Camping
Buttle Lake at the north end and **Ralph River** at the south end are both vehicle- accessible campgrounds on Buttle Lake Rd, with spacious and private sites on the lake, and outhouses but no showers. They're free after 30 Sep. Backcountry camping, including use of designated areas such as Kwai Lake, is $5 per person per night, self-registration, cash only. Many are accessible by boat only. For **Forbidden Plateau** day-hikers, lodging is available at Mt Washington Ski Area or Courtenay.

Nootka Sound and Gold River *p146*
C Mason's Lodge, 203 Pandora Av, Zeballos, T250-7614044, www.masons lodge.zeballos.bc.ca Fairly nice rooms, some with kitchenettes, views, and decks. Tours arranged.
C Ridgeview Motor Inn, 395 Donner Court, Gold River, T250-2832277. Reasonable rooms and nice views over the village.
C Zeballos Inlet Lodge, 167 Maquinna Av, Zeballos, T250-7614294, www.masons lodge.zeballos.bc.ca. 5 fairly large rooms with private baths and TVs. There's a covered patio with BBQ, laundry facilities, and continental breakfast is included.
D Peppercorn Trail Motel,100 Muchalat Dr, Gold River, T250-2832443. Cheaper, more basic rooms, plus 75 tent sites.
D Tahsis Motel, Head Bay Rd, Tahsis, T250-9346318. Basic rooms, plus a pub and restaurant.

D-F Yuquot Cabins and Campground, Kyuquot, T250-2832054. Fairly basic accommodation on a native reserve.

Alert Bay *p148*

D Orca Inn, 291 Fir St, T250-9745322. Basic hotel rooms with ocean views, pub and restaurant. Walking distance from ferry. **E Sunspirit Guest House**, 549 Fir St, 2 km from the ferry, T250-9742026. A very nice, cosy hostel.

Camping

Alert Bay Campground, 101 Alder Rd, T250-9745024. Fairly basic, but quiet and private.

Sointula *p148*

C Ocean Bliss B&B and Cottage, 1st/ Rupert, T250-9736121, www.ocean bliss.com. 1 room with private bath and balcony, and a rustic cedar cottage that could sleep 4, with kitchen and shower. **D Sea 4 Miles Cottages**, 145 Kaleva Rd, 2 km from ferry, T250-9736486. 2 fully equipped 2-bedroom cottages right next to the ocean.

Port Hardy *p148*

Due to the popular ferry journeys, Port Hardy is a busy place in summer, so it's best to have a reservation, especially if catching the day ferry from Prince Rupert, which arrives at 2230. Some of the best places are out of town on Hardy Bay Rd. **B Glen Lyon Inn**, 6435 Hardy Bay Rd, T250-9497115, www.glenlyoninn.com. Decent rooms with balconies and views, and a mid-range restaurant/pub that is probably the best around for food, and very popular with locals. **B Quarterdeck Inn**, 6555 Hardy Bay Rd, T250-9020455, www.quarterdeck resort.net. The best option for beds, with luxurious, spacious rooms, and use of a hot tub. Breakfast included. The restaurant/pub here is also good: more attractive than the Glen Lyon next door, but less popular. **C-D Seagate Hotel**, 8600 Granville St, T250-9496348. This is certainly the best

Downtown option. The decent rooms have big windows, and are priced according to views. Some have balconies, or kitchenettes for a few dollars more. **D The Green House**, 9470 Scott St. T250-9492364. There are plenty of B&Bs in town, but none are great, all resembling ordinary houses with the kids' old bedrooms rented out. This one has 2 rooms and a hot tub.

Camping

Quatse River Regional Park and Campground, 8400 Byng Rd, T250-9492395. Very nice, quiet sites set among trees, with showers and laundry. All proceeds go to the salmon enhancement programme. Vehicle parking. **Wildwoods Campsite**, signed from road 2 km from ferry, T250-9496753. Closest to harbour, and consequently a bit crowded, but fairly private, with showers and laundry. Vehicle parking.

Cape Scott Provincial Park *p148*

There is only wilderness walk-in camping in the park, in designated sites or where you please. Locals recommend the beach, which is best for drainage, but check tidal charts at the information shelters first. $5 per person. Pay at the trailhead or someone will come around to collect.

🍴 Eating

North to Courtenay *p140*

🍴 **The Beach House**, 2775 W Island Hwy. Qualicum Beach is an ideal spot to stop for lunch and enjoy the ocean views. Of several good restaurants concentrating on seafood, this is our favourite. The menu is eclectic and of a high calibre, the interior stylish, and the patio as popular in summer as it is inviting. 🍴 **Fish Tales Café**, 3336 W Island Hwy. Good fish and chips in a Tudor-style house.

Denman Island *p141, map p140*

Choices on Denman are limited. In the village, **Denman Café and General Store** is good for vegetarian food, burgers, and coffee; while **Denman Bakery and Pizzeria** has fresh baking daily, and pizza. For more interesting fare, the bistro at **Earth Club Factory**, see Sleeping p149, T250-3352688, is the best bet.

Hornby Island *p141, map p140*
Hornby is similarly limited. **Jan's Café**, beside the Co-op, is the clear choice for breakfast and coffee. For a pint and food, head for **The Thatch** by the ferry dock, which has a lovely deck and Fri night jazz. **The Cardboard House** by the Co-op has fresh baking, pizza and coffee.

Courtenay *p142*
♥♥♥ Fitzgerald's Bistro, 932 Fitz Av. Sophisticated fine dining in a cosy, intimate setting.
♥♥♥ The Old House,1760 Riverside Lane, T250-3385406. Set in a gorgeous, atmospheric wooden house full of romantic nooks and crannies, fireplaces, gables, and a nice patio, this is the clear choice for something special, and a long-standing favourite with locals and visitors alike. The menu is seafood and steak with an international touch. If you're not hungry, at least go for a drink.
♥♥ Atlas Café, 250 6th St, T250-3389838. A popular choice with locals. Vegetarian global food, great breakfasts, salads, curries, wraps and coffee in pleasant, friendly surroundings right Downtown.
♥♥ Thai Village, 2104 Cliffe Av, T250-3343812. Authentic Thai food in quaint surroundings.
♥♥ Tita's Mexican Restaurant, 536 6th St, T250-3348033. Authentic Mexican dishes in suitably colourful, upbeat surroundings.
♥ Bar None Café, 244 4th St. Excellent coffee and fresh baking, vegetarian food, and good breakfasts.

Campbell River *p144*
♥♥♥ Harbour Grill, 1334 Island Hwy, T250-2874143. The town's best fine dining, focusing on seafood and French cuisine.

♥♥ Baan Thai Restaurant, 1090B Shoppers Row, T250-2864853. An extensive Thai menu, with the bonus of a rooftop patio.
♥♥ The Lookout! Bar and Grill, 2158 Salmon Point Rd, T250-9237272. A down-to-earth and satisfying experience: buckets of scallops or mussels, oysters a-plenty, beer on tap, and great views from the patio.
♥ Dick's Fish and Chips, 151 Dogwood St. Fresh fish and homemade burgers.

Quadra Island *p145*
♥♥♥ April Point Resort, on the marina. If you're looking for a fancy restaurant offering upmarket cuisine with a West Coast bias, or a sushi bar, this is the place.
♥♥ Gateway Café, Quathiaski Cove. Organic fair-trade coffee, brunch and baked goods.
♥♥ Heriot Bay Inn, see Sleeping p150. Pub and restaurant food. Try the red snapper burger.

Cortes Island *p145*
♥♥ Cortes Café, Manson's Landing. The place of choice for most locals, with good food using local ingredients, coffee, smoothies, and a popular summer deck.
♥♥ Old Floathouse, Gorge Harbour. Recommended if you fancy something slightly more upmarket.

Port Hardy *p148*
There are a few other cheap eating options Downtown, but none is particularly enticing. Better are the 2 inns on Hardy Bay Rd, listed under Sleeping, p152.
♥ Captain Hardy's, 7145 Market St, T250-9497133. Has character, along with cheap breakfasts, fish and chips, and burgers.

♥ Bars and clubs

Courtenay and around *p142*
The nicest pubs around are in Comox, particularly the **Edge Marine Pub** at 1805 Beaufort Av, which has a deck onto the ocean, and a bistro with good food.

ⓔ Entertainment

Courtenay *p142*
Sid Williams Theatre, 442 Cliffe Av, T250-3382420, www.sidwilliamstheatre.com. Music, dance and live theatre.

Campbell River *p144*
Capri Cineplex, 100-489 Dogwood St S, T250-2873233; **Galaxy**, 250 10th Av, T250-2861744. **Tidemark Theatre**, 1220 Shoppers Row, T250-2877415. Distinctive peppermint-pink venue for live theatre and music, with art displays in the lobby.

ⓕ Festivals and events

North to Courtenay *p140*
Jul Rathtrevor Beach Provincial Park in Parksville attracts thousands of visitors for **Sandfest**, the highlight of which is the **World Sandcastle Competition**, with spectacular creations guaranteed.

Hornby Island *p141, map p140*
Aug Though smaller than Denman, and more remote, there is always lots going on here, especially in summer. A perfect time to visit is during the week-long **Hornby Island Performing Arts Festival**, T250-3352734, www.hornbyfestival.bc.ca.

Courtenay *p142*
Jul Vancouver Island Music Festival, www.islandmusicfest.com. 3 days of Canadian and world music.
Aug On the 1st weekend, the massive **Filberg Festival**, T250-3349242, www.filberg.com, ($10), takes over Filberg Lodge and Park at 61 Filberg Rd in Comox. 4 days of the best arts and crafts in BC, plus some great food and music.

Nootka Sound and Gold River *p146*
Jun Gold River hosts the **Burning Boot Festival**, culminating in the **Great Walk**, a 70-km trek to Tahsis on gravel roads, allegedly the toughest in North America.

ⓐ Activities and tours

Denman Island *p141, map p140*
Bikes and scooters can be rented at the **Earth Club Factory** or **General Store**. **Denman Island Canoes and Kayaks**, 4005 East Rd, T250-3350079, www.denmanpaddling.ca. Tours, lessons and rentals.

Hornby Island *p141, map p140*
Hornby Island Outdoor Sports, 5875 Central Rd, T250-3350448, www.hornbyoutdoors.com. Bike rentals. Their website describes all the trails.
Hornby Ocean Kayaks, T250-3352726, www.hornbyisland.com/kayaking. For kayak lessons, rentals and tours.

Courtenay *p142*
Comox District Mountaineering Club, T250-3362101. Group hikes and climbing.
Comox Valley Kayaks, T250-3342628, www.comoxvalleykayaks.com. Lessons and rentals.
Mountain Meadows, 368 5th St, T250-3388999, www.mountainmeadowssports.com. General sports equipment and rentals. Also runs eco-tours.
Pacific Pro Dive and Surf, T250-3386829, www.scubashark.com. Rentals and tours.
Tree Island Kayaking, T250-3390580. Ditto, plus day trips.

Mountain biking
Mountain biking is huge in the **Comox Valley**, with 50 km of trails around **Cumberland**, and more at **Mt Washington**. Try **Seal Bay Park** for an easy scenic ride. Several races and mountain bike festivals are held each year.
For rentals and trail information go to **Dodge City Cycles**, 2705 Dunsmuir Av, Cumberland; or **Simon's Cycles Ltd**, 1841 Comox Av, Comox.

Campbell River *p144*
Aboriginal Journeys, T250-8501101, www.aboriginaljourneys.com. Whale-

and bear-watching tours with some native history and culture thrown in.
Campbell River Kayaks, 1620 Petersen Rd, T250-287228. Rentals and tours.
Eagle Eye Adventures, T250-2860809, www.eagleeyeadventures.com. With an emphasis on a conscientious approach.
Paradise Found Adventure Tour Co, 165-1160 Shellbourne Dr, T250- 9230848, www.paradisefound.bc.ca. Snorkel beside the migrating and spawning salmon, early Jul-late Oct. Also arranges climbing, hiking, whale watching, caving, snowshoeing, or snorkelling with colonies of sea-lions at Mitlenach Island.

Quadra Island *p145*
Maps can be found online at www.discoveryislands.ca.
Abyssal Diving Charters, T250-2852427, www.abyssal.com. Diving here is excellent, with great visibility, a very knowledgeable guide, and lots to see and photograph. The all-inclusive package ($150 per person per day) includes 2 dives, air, tanks, weights, meals, and accommodation at their lodge (also open to non-divers, $95 for a room).
Discovery Charters, T250-2853146. Whale watching tours and hiking trips.
Island Cycle, Heriot Bay, T250-2853627. Trail maps, tours, information and rentals.

Kayaking
Coastal Spirits Sea Kayaking, T250-2852895, www.kayakbritishcolumbia.com.
Coast Mountain Expeditions, T250-2870635, www.coastmountain expeditions.com. Kayaking tours and rentals. They also have a lodge/hostel, which makes a great base.
Island Dreams Adventures, T250-2852751. Kayaking tours.
Spirit of the West Kayak Adventures, T250-2852121, www.kayakingtours.com.

Cortes Island *p145*
Gorge Harbour Marina Resort, T250-9356433, rents scooters and kayaks.

Caving
With over 1000 known caves, **Nootka Sound** is one of Canada's top caving destinations. **Tahsis** is the epicentre, with networks like the **Thanksgiving Cave System**, **Wyameer Park Caves**, and many others appropriate for professionals only. **Quatsino Cave** is the deepest in North America. **Upana Caves Recreation Area**, 17 km northwest of Gold River on the road to Tahsis, has a group of caves with 15 entries and 450 m of passages, which can be self-guided. Details can be found at www.village.goldriver.bc.ca. **Little Huson Cave Regional Park** near Zeballos also contains several easily accessed caves.
BC Speleological Federation, T250-2832283. For information.
Vancouver Island Nature Exploration, T250-9022662, www.nature-exploration.com. Runs cave tours.

Climbing and hiking
Climbing is excellent at **Crest Creek Crags** on Hwy 28, 15 km east of Gold River, with 100 or more routes. A 35-km 3-day hike runs along the rocky shorelines of **Nootka Island**, passing old First Nations sites. Access is by floatplane or the *MV Uchuck III* (see Transport, p157).

Kayaking
Nootka Sound cannot compare to Clayoquot Sound for scenery, but is just as outstanding for kayaking, and far less crowded. The best spots are **Nuchatlitz Inlet** and **Marine Provincial Park** to the west of Tahsis, and **Catala Island Provincial Marine Park**, still further west. The former offers the best chance of spotting sea otters. **Gold River** has 3 different stretches popular with experienced whitewater kayakers, including a famous section known as the **Big Drop**. The *MV Uchuck III* offers canoe and kayak trips.

Vancouver Island Central & north Vancouver Island Listings

There is great surfing at **Beano Creek**. **Tatchu Adventures**, Tahsis, T1888-8952011, www.tatchuadventures.com. Surfing, kayaking and hiking trips. Lodging is in treehouses, with an emphasis on healthy living, organic foods.

Alert Bay *p148*

Seasmoke Whale Watching, T250-9745225, www.seaorca.com. Tours in a whale-friendly yacht, $89/5 hrs, $170/8 hrs (including lunch); and 4-hr cruises in a motorboat, $75.

Waas Eco-Cultural Adventures, T250-9748400. Cultural tours in a giant canoe, with traditional food and storytelling.

Port Hardy *p148*

There are excellent opportunities for outdoor pursuits such as scuba diving, whale watching, kayaking, fishing or hiking **Catala Charters**, 6170 Hardy Bay Rd, T250-9497560, www.catalacharters.net. A reliable operation, offering diving trips and water taxis to Cape Scott. **Odyssey Kayaking Ltd**, T250-9020565, www.odysseykayaking.com. Rentals and tours.

⊖ Transport

Denman Island *p141, map p140*

Several daily ferries, roughly hourly till 2300, to/from **Buckley Bay** just north of Fanny Bay, $6 return, $14.65 return for a car, 10-12 min crossing.

Hornby Island *p141, map p140*

Several daily ferries, at sporadic times till 1835, to/from **Gravelly Bay** in the southeast of Denman Island, $6 return, $14.65 car, 10-min crossing.

Courtenay *p142*

Courtenay is small enough to get around on foot. Local buses are operated by **Comox Valley Transit System**, T250-3346000, www.busonline.ca. Bus No 11 runs to the ferry and airport, stopping at 4th Av/Cliffe, where many other routes converge, $1.25. No service on Sun. For a taxi try **United Cabs**, T250-3397955.

Air

Comox Valley Airport receives daily flights from **Vancouver** with **Pacific Coastal**, T250-8900699 and **Central Mountain Air**, T1888-8658585; and from **Calgary** with **West Jet**, T1888-9378538, www.westjet.com. Book these flights with **Uniglobe**, T250-3389877.

Bus

The station is Downtown at 9-2663 Kilpatrick Av. **Greyhound**, www.greyhound.ca, has 4 daily buses to/from **Victoria**.

Ferry

BC Ferries, T1888-2233779, www.bcferries.com, runs 4 daily sailings from **Powell River** on the Sunshine Coast to Little River, 13 km north of Comox. $9, $4.75 child, $31 vehicle, 1½ hrs.

Train

The station is on McPhee Av, a short walk from Downtown. **VIA Rail**, T1800-5618630, www.viarail.ca, currently runs 1 train daily to/from **Victoria**, $51 one-way, 0815 from Victoria, 1330 from Courtenay.

Campbell River *p144*

Air

Daily flights arrive at Campbell River and District Regional Airport (YBL) from **Vancouver**, with **Helijet**, www.helijet.com, T1800-6654354, and **Pacific Coastal Airlines**, T1800-6632872, www.pacific-coastal.com.

Bus

Greyhound, T250-3854411, www.greyhound.ca, run 4 buses per day to and from **Nanaimo**, $24, and **Victoria**, $45. 1 daily bus continues north as far as **Port Hardy**.

Quadra Island *p145*

BC Ferries, T1888-2233779, www.bc
ferries.com, leave **Campbell River**
every hour on the half hour, arriving at
Quathiaski Cove on Quadra, $6.10 return,
$14.90 car, 45 mins. There is no public
transport here, but hitching is easy.

Cortes Island *p145*

6 ferries daily leave from **Heriot Bay** on
the east side of Quadra Island, arriving at
Whaletown, $7.10 ($18.15/car), 45 mins.
Cortes Connection, T250-9356911,
www.cortesconnection.com, runs to/from
the Greyhound depot in **Campbell River**,
$14, $12 child, plus $7.10 for the ferry. It
also covers scheduled routes on the island:
one end to the other is $8, $4 child.

Strathcona Provincial Park:
Buttle Lake *p145*

Campbell River Airporter, T250-2863000,
run a service to/from **Campbell River** on
request, $50 for 2. **Strathcona Lodge** will
also transport guests, $50, then $10 for
each additional person.

Gold River *p146*

There is no public transport to Gold River,
or Tahsis, another 70 km northwest on a
rough but scenic logging road. Once
here, the 100-passenger *MV Uchuck III*,
T250-2832325, www.mvuchuck.com, a
1942 US minesweeper, is the ultimate
way to get around. One-way to **Tahsis**
$28, to **Zeballos** $40. Meals available on
board. There's also Maxi's Water Taxi,
T250-2832282. **Air Nootka**, T250-2832255,
www.airnootka.com, runs chartered and
flightseeing trips, and scheduled trips to
Kyuquot, but they don't fly to Gold River
from anywhere useful.

Alert Bay and Sointula *p148*

Alternate ferries from **Port McNeill** run
to Alert Bay on Cormorant Island, and
Sointula on Malcolm Island. There are
several daily sailings to each, but no direct
transport between the islands. Both are
$7.10 return, $18.05 vehicle. There is no
transport on the islands, but bikes
can be rented in Alert Bay at **Adam's
Cycles**, Fir St.

Port Hardy *p148*

Air

Flights from **Vancouver** ($200 one-way)
and **Bella Coola** with Pacific Coastal
Airlines, T250-2738666, www.pacific-
coastal.com.

Bus

Greyhound, T250-3854411, www.grey
hound.ca, operates 1 daily bus to/from
Nanaimo (0830) and **Campbell River**
(1215), leaving Port Hardy at 0900 (0945
Sat), and stopping at the ferry.

Water taxi

Catala Charters, T250-9497560,
www.catalacharters.new, runs a water
taxi service to Cape Scott Park and
numerous remote fishing and diving
lodges that are otherwise inaccessible.

ⓘ Directory

Courtenay *p142*
Canada Post 1812 Comox Av, Comox.
Internet At the library, or **Cardero
Coffee & Tea Co**, 208 5th St. **Laundry**
King Koin Launderette, 467 4th St.
Medical services St Joseph's General
Hospital, 2137 Comox Av, T250-3392242.

Campbell River *p144*
Canada Post 1251 Shoppers Row.
Laundry Campbell River Laundry,
1231 Shoppers Row. **Medical services**
Campbell River Hospital, 375 2nd Av,
T250-2877111.

Vancouver Island Central & north Vancouver Island Listings

British Columbia →

Kokanee Glacier Provincial Park

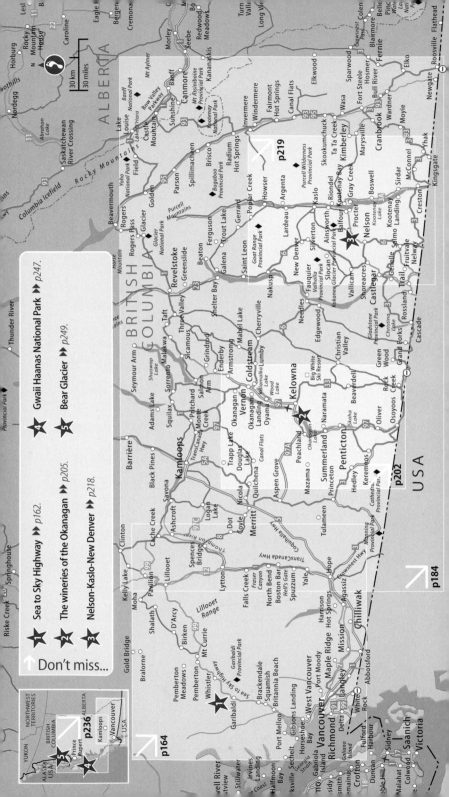

Don't miss...

1 ★ Sea to Sky Highway ▶▶ *p162.*

2 ★ The wineries of the Okanagan ▶▶ *p205.*

3 ★ Nelson-Kaslo-New Denver ▶▶ *p218.*

4 ★ Gwaii Haanas National Park ▶▶ *p247.*

5 ★ Bear Glacier ▶▶ *p249.*

p164

p236

p219

p202

p184

Introduction

British Columbia's southern interior is criss-crossed with towering mountain ranges, broad river valleys and long skinny lakes. In two days you can drive through snowy peaks and glaciers in the Coast Mountains; arid, semi-desert hills covered with orchards and vineyards in the Okanagan; the forested slopes, pristine lakes and glaciers of the Columbia Mountains in the West Kootenays; moonscapes of muted colours in the Thompson Valley; and the sheer cliff walls of the Fraser Canyon.

All the outdoor pursuits you could want are here, too. The Sea to Sky Highway provides access to some of Canada's best skiing, climbing and biking. If you want to lie on a beach or tour a few wineries, head for the sun-baked Okanagan. The West Kootenays have charming former mining communities, a laidback vibe and first-class hiking, biking and skiing.

North of the TransCanada Highway lies a vast under-populated hinterland of unimaginable proportions, where big animals and First Nations culture still thrive. Highlights include tours of abandoned ancient villages on Haida Gwaii, the Wild West ranching landscapes and gold-rush history of the Cariboo and Chilcotin, and a region of sublime scenery on the Cassiar Highway around Stewart.

Ratings
Culture
★★★
Landscape
★★★★★
Wildlife
★★★
Activities
★★★★
Relaxation
★★★
Costs
$$-$$$

Sea to Sky Highway

The Sea to Sky Highway (Highway 99) heads north from Vancouver to a treasure trove of activities. After Howe Sound, the road leaves the coast towards Canada's climbing, windsurfing and bald eagle capital, Squamish, before heading upwards through the gloriously scenic Coast Mountains to Garibaldi Provincial Park, and the world famous ski resort of Whistler – venue for the 2010 Winter Olympics. Almost every outdoor pursuit is available along this road, including hiking trails that rival the best in the Rockies. Beyond Whistler, the road gets rougher, passing the small villages of Lillooet and Pemberton, before emerging close to the TransCanada Highway.

🚌 **Getting there** Bus or car.
🚌 **Getting around** Bus or car.
🕑 **Time required** 3 days or more.
🌦 **Weather** Varied across the region.
🛏 **Sleeping** 5-star hotels to camping; expensive in Whistler.
🍴 **Eating** Limited outside Whistler.
⛰ **Activities and tours** Rock climbing, scuba diving, cross-country skiing, backcountry skiing, heli-skiing, dog sledding, horse-drawn sleigh rides, snow-mobiling, windsurfing, hiking.
★ **Don't miss...** Hiking, mountain biking or skiing on Whistler/Blackcomb mountains ›› *p179*.

Ins and outs

Getting there and around

Buses from Vancouver run as far as Whistler, with **Greyhound** continuing to Pemberton. All towns, with the possible exception of Whistler, are small enough to get around on foot, and Whistler has an efficient local bus network. 🚌 ›› *p180*.

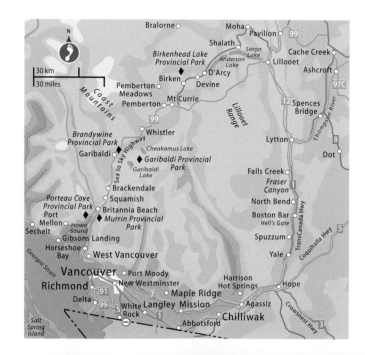

Summer is prime for most of the region's activities, while Whistler is at its busiest during the ski season (December to April). Roads are kept open throughout the winter as far as Whistler. Beyond Pemberton, snow chains are often required and road closures are common.

Tourist information

There are visitor information centres in all towns, but the most useful are in Whistler and Squamish. *99 North*, a free and widely distributed magazine, is an extremely useful source of information about the Sea to Sky Highway. For details on hiking, refer to Kathy and Craig Copeland's *Don't waste your time in the BC Coast Mountains* (Voice in the Wilderness Press).

North to Squamish ⊜𝟀✿⏣◐⚠⊖❶ »» *pp172-181.*

The opening stretch of Highway 99 is dramatic indeed, as the twisting road clings tenaciously to sheer cliffs, with views of Howe Sound and mountains on both sides swinging abruptly into view. It also contains no less than 10 important scuba-diving sites renowned for oversized sea life such as wolf eels and giant octopuses. **Whytecliff Park** at Horseshoe Bay is a famous marine reserve, and **Porteau Cove Provincial Park**, at Km 37, is the Lower Mainland's most popular diving destination, with warm, shallow water and a series of artificial reefs created by sunken shipwrecks, including a Second World War minesweeper. There's a rocky beach here and a rather unattractive campground.

The first clear destination is the **Mining Museum** ① *Britannia Beach, T604-6888735, www.bcmuseumofmining.org, May to mid-Oct 0900-1630, $9.50, $7.50 child*, 11 km south of Squamish. This was once the largest copper mine in the British Empire, with a population of 60,000, an output of £1.3 billion of copper in 70 years, and a reputation for polluting the surrounding waters. Housed in the run-down but striking 'Concentrator' building, the museum is full of relics, photos and working machinery. Demonstrations such as gold panning are part of the tour, but the highlight is the train ride through an old mine tunnel.

Murrin Provincial Park, 2 km north, marks the beginning of hiking and climbing country. A hike to the Giuseppe Garibaldi Lookout gives a taste of the amazing views to come. **Shannon Falls** is the next obvious stop, an impressive 335-m waterfall visible from the road but worth the five-minute leg-stretch to see up close. From here, or from the campground 1 km down the road, you can watch climbers grappling with the granite walls of the sublime Stawamus Chief (see below).

Squamish and around

Thanks to the 2010 Winter Olympics, Whistler's exorbitant real estate prices and its own fairly justifiable claim to be 'the outdoor recreation capital of Canada', Squamish has entered a period of mass expansion and its hitherto poor infrastructure is improving all the time. This includes a new hostel and a very useful **Visitor Information Centre** ① *T604-8154994, www.squamishchamber.bc.ca, www.squamish.ca, Jun-Sep daily 0900-1800, Dec-Feb daily 0900-1700, otherwise Mon-Fri 0900-1700, weekends 1000-1400*, unmissable right on the highway. Despite its extraordinary mountain-ringed location, however, the town is not much to look at and offers little distraction for those not of a sporty persuasion.

Approaching from the south, you can't miss the 95-million-year-old **Stawamus Chief**, the second biggest granite monolith on Earth. The Chief is the centrepiece of Squamish's world-famous rock-climbing, attracting some 200,000 hopefuls per year. These massive rock walls that funnel the Howe Sound's perpetually strong ocean winds straight into Squamish, are also responsible for the town's name, 'Mother of the Wind' in Coast Salish, and its recognition as the country's windsurfing capital.

Taking a tea break on a hike near Squamish.

A third local claim to fame is held by **Brackendale**, 10 km to the north, where more bald eagles have been counted than anywhere else in the world. Attracted by the spawning salmon, an estimated 10,000 of these magnificent birds stop by every winter and are now protected by the 550-ha **Brackendale Eagles Provincial Park**. The best places to see them and get more information are the **Brackendale Art Gallery** ⓘ *Government Rd, north of Depot Rd, T604-8983333, www.brackendaleartgallery.com*, and the **Sunwolf Outdoor Centre** ⓘ *70002 Squamish Valley Rd, 4 km off Hwy 99, T604-8981537, www.sunwolf.net*.

Those with an interest in trains or locomotion will enjoy a visit to the **West Coast Railway Heritage Park** ⓘ *39645 Government Rd, T604-8989336, www.wcra.org, daily 1000-1700, $6, $5 child*. It's packed full of vintage railway paraphernalia, including carriages, 50 locomotives, a restored executive business car and the celebrated *Royal Hudson*. A 3-km miniature steam train ride takes visitors around the park.

Hikes around Squamish (north to south)

▲▲ **Stawamus Chief** ⓘ *6- to 11-km round trip, 612 m elevation gain. Trailhead: Shannon Falls Provincial Park or 1.2 km further north*. The mighty chief makes an excellent not too difficult hike and is snow-free as early as March and as late as November. With fantastic views and close proximity to Vancouver, this is one of the busiest hikes around. Most people make for the first (south) of the three summits, so try heading for the second or third, or even hike to them all. Descending is more fun via the second summit than on the east trail.

▲▲ **Lake Lovely Water** ⓘ *10 km round trip, 1128 m elevation gain. Trailhead: 10.6 km north of town, turn west onto Squamish Valley Rd. Turn left onto a dirt road at Km 6 and park by the BC Hydro right of way at Km 2*. You need to canoe across the river or arrange a ferry (roughly $20 per person) with **Kodiak Adventures**, T604-8983356. This is a very tough, demanding hike on a steep and narrow trail. However, the aptly named destination is possibly the most spectacular lake in the Coast Mountains. Consider packing a tent and spending an extra day or two exploring, or book a place in the **Alpine Club of Canada** hut, T604-6872711.

▲▲ **High Falls Creek** ⓘ *12 km round trip, 640 m elevation gain. Trailhead: Take Squamish Valley Rd as above. At Km 24.2 stay right on Squamish River Rd. Park at Km 3.1 and look for sign 100 m further on the right*. As well as falls and gorges, this sometimes steep route offers views of the Tantalus Range. Continue up to the logging road and descend it in a loop.

Whose name is it anyway?

Before the arrival of the Europeans, Squohomish Natives came to the Squamish Valley to hunt and fish; the area became known as Squamish, meaning "Mother of the Wind" in Coast Salish. Their first glimpse of white men was in 1792, when Captain Vancouver arrived and began trading. The settlers that eventually followed made a living from cattle raising and agriculture. Around 1912 some real-estate promoters decided a more 'civilized' name than Squamish was needed, and chose the inspiring title Newport. Local people never liked this, so a few years later the railway invited school children to select a new name and win a $500 prize. The winning nomination was… Squamish.

British Columbia Sea to Sky Highway

Whistler and around ⊖⊘⋔⏾❀⏾▲⊟⏾ » pp172-181.

Garibaldi Provincial Park

Once you get beyond the sprawl emanating from Squamish, the journey to Whistler is a delight, giving an idea of the incredible scenery contained within Garibaldi Provincial Park to the east. This is the nearest thing to a wilderness park you'll find within such easy reach of a major city and two prime sporting centres. Too popular for some people's taste, it offers undeniably spine-tingling scenery packed with pristine lakes and rivers, alpine meadows, soaring peaks and huge glaciers. The hiking here is some of the best to be found outside the Rockies, and the trails are clearly signed and well maintained. For longer hikes, it is worth seeking further information from visitor information centres or investing in a good hiking guide before setting out. Walk-in campsites are primitive and tend to require self-registration, so take some cash. There is also a $3 per vehicle per day charge for parking at some trailheads.

Hikes in Garibaldi Provincial Park

▲ **Elfin Lakes/Mamquam Lake** ⓘ *22 km or 44 km, 915 m or 1555 m elevation gain. Trailhead: 3.1 km north of Squamish look for the Diamond Head sign, turn east (right) onto Mamquam Rd, and continue for 15 km.* This trail leads quickly to outstanding views of the mighty snowcapped Tantalus Range, so it's no surprise that it gets irritatingly overcrowded at weekends. The walk to Elfin Lakes is along an ugly road also open to cyclists. In winter it becomes a popular nordic skiing route. If possible, leave the crowd behind by continuing to Mamquam Lake. The campground here is in a wonderful setting (though you're unlikely to reach it in one day), and views from the ridge above are exceptional. The Elfin Lakes campground can be very busy. There is also a rudimentary overnight shelter with 34 bunkbeds and a stove (a fee is collected). A number of side-trips fan out from here, the best leading to Little Diamond Head: take the Saddle trail to the Gargoyles then ascend 170 vertical metres.

▲ **Garibaldi Lake/Taylor Meadows** ⓘ *35 km round trip, 2450 m elevation gain. Trailhead: Rubble Creek. 38 km north of Squamish or 20 km south of Whistler, turn east at the Black Tusk sign and proceed for 2.6 km.* This is one of the most rewarding areas for hiking in the park, with many options for making your own itinerary. Garibaldi Lake is huge, vividly coloured with glacial flour, and surrounded by sights like Guard Mountain and the Sphinx Glacier. You can camp here or at the flower-strewn Taylor Meadows a few kilometres away. Both are

The Whistler Valley is considered to be one of the world's top mountain-biking destinations, with stunning scenery, wildlife and plenty of lift-serviced downhill runs.

wonderful locations, but don't expect to be alone (remember to bring cash for camping fees). Be sure to do at least one side trip. The most highly recommended is Panorama Ridge, which affords expansive views of ice and peaks, including Mount Garibaldi and the Warren Glacier. The second option is the distinctive volcanic peak known as the Black Tusk. The trail passes through expansive meadows and leads to awesome views, but the summit requires serious scrambling.

▲▲ **Brandywine Meadows** ⓘ *13.6 km round trip, 600 m elevation gain. Trailhead: 15 km south of Whistler, 44 km north of Squamish, turn west onto Brandywine Forestry Rd. Park on the left at Km 4.4.* This is a popular, first-class hike to an alpine bowl full of wild flower meadows and set beneath towering cliffs. Early August is best for the flower show.

▲▲ **Cheakamus Lake** ⓘ *6.4 km return, 12.8 km with a loop of the lake, mostly flat. Trailhead: 7.7 km south of Whistler, 51.3 km north of Squamish, turn east onto a logging road and continue 7.5 km to the end of the road.* This is an easy hike and negotiable from early June to late October. The trail leads through patches of old-growth forest, and the big, beautiful turquoise lake itself is surrounded by ice-covered peaks that soar 1600 m over its shoreline. Bikes are allowed as far as the lake, where there is a campsite for those who wish to spend a bit of time at this gorgeous spot. The trout fishing is excellent.

▲▲ **Helm Creek** ⓘ *16 km round trip, 717 m elevation gain. Trailhead: same as Garibaldi Lake, above.* This is an alternative route into the Garibaldi Lake area, and the two hikes combine very well to make a 24-km one-way trip (though this requires a shuttle or hitching). Coming from the Helm Creek end is a longer and steeper route but consequently far less crowded, and the campground at the creek is smaller and much nicer than the more popular ones mentioned above. Day hiking from there to Garibaldi Lake is a recommended option.

▲▲ **Musical Bumps** ⓘ *19 km round trip to Singing Pass, 727 m elevation gain. Trailhead: at the top of Whistler Mountain gondola.* This is the nickname for Piccolo, Flute and Oboe summits. This is a ridge walk suitable for all levels. The gondola takes you up 1136 m, meaning almost anyone can enjoy the type of views usually only attained after hours of work. It's just a short ascent to the ridge, then the heart-stoppingly gorgeous views over a 360 degree panorama of peaks and glaciers are continuous. Cheakamus Lake and Glacier and Mount Davidson are the highlights, along with vast alpine meadows. For extra views of Brandywine Mountain, the glacier-clad Tantalus Range and the Pemberton Icefield, climb up Whistler Mountain first and descend on the Burnt Stew Trail rather than reaching the Musical Bumps via Harmony Lakes. Catch the earliest gondola possible (around 1000). Reaching Flute summit and returning in time for the last gondola should be possible, but getting to Oboe summit and back is tricky. Ideally, make it a 22-km one-way trip over the Bumps to Singing Pass then out via Fitzsimmons Creek Valley, though this means hitching or arranging a shuttle. Take plenty of water as the ridge is dry.

Blackcomb Peak ⓘ *9 km round trip, 355 m elevation gain. Trailhead: From Whistler Village car park take the Fitzsimmons Trail, then take the chairlift up 1174 m to Rendezvous Lodge.* The chairlift makes it easy to reach dizzying vistas. Almost immediately the Cheakamus and Overlord glaciers are visible, and soon you're strolling through fields of wild flowers. Ascend on the Overlord Summit Trail to Decker Tarn, then descend on the Outback Trail, making a nice loop. Scrambling higher from the tarn will lead to even better views.

Fitzsimmons Creek/Russet Lake ⓘ *19 km round trip, 945 m elevation gain. Trailhead: From Blackcomb Way follow signs to Singing Pass Trailhead, 5 km up a dirt road. This hike can be done one-way as a second leg of the Musical Bumps Trail above.* Or if you object to paying for the gondola, take this free route into the alpine. The path climbs at a reasonable grade and takes you through some gorgeous flower meadows, with views that include the stunning Cheakamus Lake. From an easily attained ridge just above the dramatic setting of Russet Lake, a dizzying, almost unparalleled array of ice is visible, including the Cheakamus and Overlord glaciers and the Pemberton Icefield.

Cougar Mountain Cedar Grove ⓘ *5 km round trip, 150 m elevation gain. Trailhead: 5 km north of Whistler turn west onto a dirt road signed Cougar Mountain Ancient Cedar Trail. Proceed 5 km.* This is less a hike than an experience. The short walk is nothing special, but the ancient cedars at the end are impressive and humbling.

Wedgemount Lake ⓘ *14 km, 1160 m elevation gain. Trailhead: 11.8 km north of Whistler, 20.6 km south of Pemberton, turn east at the Garibaldi/Wedgemount Lake sign and proceed 1.9 km up Wedge Creek Forestry Rd.* This steep, demanding climb leads to a beautiful lake in Garibaldi Provincial Park, passing a 300 m waterfall on the way. Take warm clothes as it tends to be chilly by the lake.

British Columbia Sea to Sky Highway

Renowned for its abundant light powder, flawless snowboarding parks and vast accessible backcountry terrain, Whistler does not disappoint.

British Columbia Sea to Sky Highway

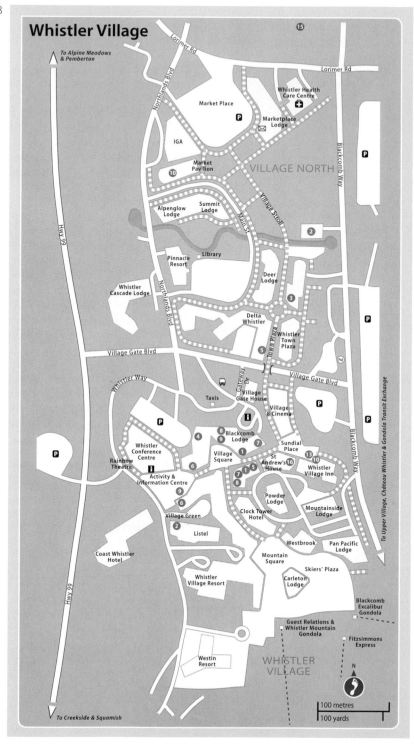

Whistler Village

To Alpine Meadows & Pemberton

Lorimer Rd

Hwy 99

Northlands Blvd

Lorimer Rd

Market Place

Whistler Health Care Centre

Marketplace Lodge

IGA

Market Pavilion

VILLAGE NORTH

Village Stroll

Alpenglow Lodge

Summit Lodge

Main St

Pinnacle Resort

Library

Deer Lodge

Whistler Cascade Lodge

Northlands Blvd

Delta Whistler

Whistler Town Plaza

Village Gate Blvd

Town Plaza

Village Gate Blvd

Whistler Way

Gateway Dr

Taxis

Village Gate House

Village 8 Cinema

To Upper Village, Château Whistler & Gondola Transit Exchange

Whistler Conference Centre

Blackcomb Lodge

Sundial Place

Village Square

St Andrew's House

Whistler Village Inn

Rainbow Theatre

Activity & Information Centre

Powder Lodge

Mountainside Lodge

Village Green

Listel

Clock Tower Hotel

Westbrook

Pan Pacific Lodge

Coast Whistler Hotel

Mountain Square

Skiers' Plaza

Whistler Village Resort

Carleton Lodge

Blackcomb Way

Blackcomb Excalibur Gondola

Guest Relations & Whistler Mountain Gondola

Fitzsimmons Express

Westin Resort

WHISTLER VILLAGE

N

To Creekside & Squamish

100 metres
100 yards

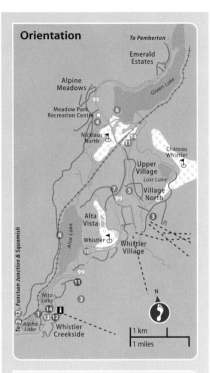

Orientation

To Pemberton

Emerald
Estates

Alpine
Meadows

Green Lake

Meadow Park
Recreation Centre

Nicklaus
North

Chateau
Whistler

Upper
Village
Lost Lake

Village
North

Alta
Vista

Alta Lake

Whistler

Whistler
Village

To Function Junction & Squamish

Nita
Lake

Alpha
Lake

Whistler
Creekside

1 km
1 miles

N

Sleeping ●
Brew Creek Lodge **12**
Cedar Springs B&B **4**
Edgewater Lodge **6**
Erin Lodge **5**
Haus Heidi Pension B&B **7**
HI Whistler **8**
Renoir's Winter Garden
  B&B **10**
Riverside Resort **11**
South Side Lodge Hostel **13**
UBC Whistler Lodge **3**
Whistler Resort & Club **1**

Camping ▲
Brandywine Falls **2**
Riverside RV Resort **14**

Eating ●
21 Steps **16**
Araxi & Pub **1**
Bearfoot Bistro **2**
Carambal **3**
Casa Tapas & Wine **13**
Gone Bakery & Soup Co **4**
Ingrid's Village Café **5**
Kypriake Norte **6**
La Bocca **7**
La Brasserie des Artistes **8**
Moguls Coffee Bean **9**

Pasta Lupino **10**
Rim Rock Café **11**
South Side Diner **12**
Uli's Flipside **14**
Wild Wood Bistro & Bar **15**

Bars & clubs ♠
Amsterdam Café **1**
Attic **10**
Buffalo Bill's **9**
Garfinkel's **5**
High Mountain
  Brewhouse **2**
Mallard Lounge **3**
Moe Joe's **6**
Savage Beagle **7**
Tommy Africa's **8**

British Columbia Sea to Sky Highway

Whistler is the largest ski area in North America and is consistently voted the continent's number one ski resort by many respected publications. The terrain is vast, the facilities state-of-the-art, and the management bend over backwards to make sure the visitor's every need is anticipated. Other winter sports include endless cross-country ski trails, backcountry skiing, heliskiing, dog-sledding, horse-drawn sleigh rides, snowmobiling, snow-shoeing and many other possibilities. With Garibaldi Provincial Park right next door, this is also a hiking haven in summer, when just about every kind of outdoor pursuit is available and plenty of tour operators.

Due to such considerable year-round prestige, and greatly exacerbated by the prospect of the 2010 Winter Olympics, Whistler has increasingly become the domain of the wealthy. Prices for everything, especially real estate, have risen astro-nomically. The atmosphere can be terribly posey and elitist: all designer ski labels and fancy sunglasses. Young jocks are the second predominant social group and, with so many of them getting pumped-up on the slopes all day and drunk in the evening, the atmosphere can get a little boisterous; single women may attract more attention than they would want. If you're looking for cheap, down-to-earth fun on the snow, consider heading to the Kootenays or Okanagan instead.

The purpose-built townsite centres on **Whistler Village**, where the ski lifts are located, with Village North and Upper Village both within walking distance. A toy-town maze of fancy hotels, bars, restaurants and sport stores, the resort has an unreal, Legoland appearance that might attract or repel, depending on your state of mind and predilections. The decision to keep all traffic out of the centre, leaving pedestrians to stroll around at leisure, reinforces the impression of being in a holiday camp, and the perpetual party atmosphere is helped along by several major seasonal festivals (see p176), with smaller events almost every weekend. On the outskirts are a few satellite suburbs, such as Function Junction and Creekside to the south, Alpine Meadows and Emerald Estates to the north; connected by local bus service, they contain much of the more affordable lodging.

Whistler's well-stocked **Visitor Information Centre** ⓘ *4230 Gateway Dr off Village Gate Blvd from Hwy 99, T604-9325922, www.whistlerchamber.com, daily 0830-1830*, is handy, especially for bookings. More conveniently central, is the **Activity and Information Centre** ⓘ *4010 Whistler Way, T604-9382769*, in the Conference Centre. For skiing information call T604-9323434, www.whistlerblackcomb.com. The website www.tourismwhistler.com is also very useful, especially for activities. A wealth of information, including maps, can be gleaned from the seasonal publication *99 North*, which is free and widely distributed around town. *Whistler Survival Guide* is useful for anyone planning to live or work here. You can download it at www.mywcss.org/survival_guide.htm. For further information about the 2010 Winter Olympics, call T604-9322010 or visit www.vancouver2010.com.

Pemberton to Lillooet ⊖🚻▲ ▶▶ *pp172-181.*

Pemberton and beyond

Beyond Whistler, the views open out as the highway approaches the steeper, more dramatic mountains to the north. Many people choose to stay in **Pemberton** and commute the half-hour to Whistler. The village is calmer, more picturesque and utterly free of the tourism-gone-mad that has blighted its popular sister to the south. And though there is little to Pemberton itself, the surrounding area is rich in possibilities for hiking, biking and fishing. There are also two fine hot springs within striking distance. The summer-only **Visitor Information Centre** ⓘ *7374 Hwy 99, T604-8946175, www.pemberton.net*, is on the way into town.

Just east of Pemberton a rough road strikes north from the wonderfully scenic Mount Currie, passing through D'Arcy and eventually making its own tortuous way to Lillooet. At Devine, a gravel road heads 18 km west to **Birkenhead Lake Provincial Park**, a remote destination with 85 primitive campsites for those seeking utter tranquillity. There's a good chance of spotting mountain goats, moose and blue herons, and the 3.5-km lakeshore trail is pleasant enough. More impressive for those in the area is **Place Creek Falls**, a 3-km return hike: at 21.4 km from Mount Currie take the dirt road right and proceed roughly 2 km.

A view down the cloud-filled valley from Whistler.

A storm gathers over the Pemberton Valley.

This is one of the best regions for hot springs, though they're characteristically hard to reach. **Meagre Creek Hot Springs** ($5) is the largest and one of the best in BC, although it is generally inaccessible except between May and October; even then you should seek advice before setting out. To get there follow Lillooet River logging road 64 km northwest of Pemberton. Also recommended are the free **Skookumchuck Hot Springs**. To get there follow Highway 99 east to Mount Currie, then take a very rough forestry road south along Lillooet River, passing various deserted homesteads and two native graveyards on the way; the 54-km drive takes about 1½ hours. Watch for small metal numbers attached to tree stumps by the road; the springs are between 22 and 21, close to Hydro Tower 682. Skookumchuck is less visited than Meagre Creek so nude bathing is much more likely.

Hikes around Pemberton (Accessible from Highway 99)

▲▲ **Stein Divide** ⓘ *28.6 km, 1265 m elevation gain. Trailhead: 10.3 km north of Mt Currie turn southeast onto the In Shuk-ch Forestry Rd. At Km 16.6 turn left onto Lizzie Creek Branch Rd. Most vehicles will want you to stop at Km 8 and walk.* This is one of the most rewarding hikes, but it is also the longest and most difficult to access. The trail through this region is extremely tough and demanding, but it provides access to a vast unspoilt alpine wilderness with a generous smattering of lakes, mountains and glaciers. Highlights are the views from Tabletop Mountain and the eerily beautiful colour of Tundra Lake.

▲▲ **Joffre Lakes Trail** ⓘ *11 km, 370 m elevation gain. Trailhead: 30 km north of Pemberton, 69 km south of Lillooet at Joffre Lakes Recreation Area.* This excellent and relatively easy hike leads to three gorgeous teal lakes set in exquisite mountain scenery. The first lake would be a worthy reward for hours of hiking but is reached after just five minutes. Whatever your fitness, don't drive by without stopping to hike at least this far. The only downside is the trail's popularity.

▲▲ **Rohr Lake/Marriott Basin Trail** ⓘ *9-16 km, 430 m elevation gain. Trailhead: 3.7 km north from the above, then 1 km down Cayoosh Creek Forestry Rd.* This considerably less busy trail is tough, narrow, steep and sometimes obscure, so suitable only for experienced hikers. The reward is solitude, a pristine meadow and an amethyst lake set beneath Mount Rohr.

▲▲ **Cerise Creek Trail** ⓘ *8 km round trip, 305 m elevation gain. Trailhead: 12.5 km north of Joffre Lakes, then 6 km southwest on Cerise Creek Main Forestry Rd.* This short, fairly easy hike leads to great views of the Anniversary and Matier glaciers and the peaks to which they cling.

North to Lillooet

The journey to Lillooet is much more of a commitment than the easy jaunt to Pemberton, but well worth the effort. The road narrows down and becomes more tortuous, with brake-destroying steep sections, narrow wooden bridges, the threat of landslides and ever more breathtaking mountain views. At Lillooet, Highway 99 meets the **Fraser River Valley**. As if in anticipation, the scenery changes about 20 km south of town with the arrival of a series of eye-catching bony rock faces, followed by an incredible downhill section, then the sudden appearance of **Seton Lake**, its water a striking milky aquamarine.

Lillooet

After all the raw splendour of the journey, Lillooet is disappointing, though its setting is spectacular. Should you feel like stopping, all the necessities are found on Main Street, including the **Visitor Information Centre** ① *790 Main St, T250-2564308, www.lillooetbc.com, Apr-Oct.*

Beyond Lillooet the scenery becomes even more extraordinary. The vast canyon, its cliffs dropping an impossible distance down to the Fraser River below, leads towards the harsh weather systems of the Cariboo and the Thompson Valley, both typified by vast, desert-dry landscapes in shades of yellow, red and ochre, dotted with lonely scraps of scrubby vegetation. Highway 99 intercepts Highway 97 just north of Cache Creek, from where the TransCanada heads east to Kamloops and beyond. Alternatively, Highway 12 follows the Fraser River south from Lillooet, picking up the TransCanada at Lytton and continuing south to Hope, from where you could head back to Vancouver to complete a very scenic loop.

● Sleeping

Squamish and around *p163*
A number of B&Bs, plus a couple of decent restaurants, are situated east of the Hwy, 4 km north of town, in an area called Garibaldi Heights.
B Coneybeare Lodge B&B, Garibaldi Heights, T1866-8159299 (mob), www.coneybearelodge.com. This is the pick of the bunch: a lovely house set in extensive gardens on the edge of an old growth forest with a salmon spawning stream. The 3 comfortable rooms have big windows to enjoy the wonderful views; there's a swimming pool and sauna, and the friendly hosts provide a great breakfast.
C Howe Sound Inn and Brewing Company, 37801 Cleveland Av, T604-8922603, www.howesound.com. The best choice Downtown, this beautiful wooden building contains stylish rooms as well as a great pub and restaurant with and views of the Stawamus Chief (see p163). Guests can use the sauna and climbing wall.
C Sunwolf Outdoor Centre, 70002 Squamish Valley Rd, Brackendale, 4 km off Hwy 99, 10 km north of town, T604-

8981537, www.sunwolf.net. Set on 2 ha at the confluence of the Cheakamus and Cheekeye rivers, this is the best place to see bald eagles. The owners organize eagle-spotting rafting trips, as well as whitewater rafting and kayaking, and offer good advice. Their 10 recently renovated riverside cabins are attractive and good value. There's a common room, café and volleyball court.
D-E Squamish Hostel, on the highway at the entrance to town, T604-8929240, www.squamishhostel.com. This large, brand new hostel has 4- to 6-bed dorms, plus private rooms with en suite bath. Facilities include a lounge with fireplace, a large kitchen and dining room, a TV room showing films, a games room, laundry, lockers and storage, a balcony with views of the Chief, internet access, BBQ, and a bouldering cave.

Camping
Alice Lake Provincial Park, 13 km north on Hwy 99. 108 wooded private sites, none of them very close to the beach. Pretty lake with fishing and swimming, showers and a big grassy area.

Klahanie Campground, 5 mins' south of Squamish, opposite Shannon Falls, T604-8923435. Fairly private sites with plenty of trees, showers and a restaurant.
Stawamus Chief Provincial Park, 5 mins' south. 45 walk-in sites and 15 ugly parking lot sites. No fires. Handy for hikers/climbers.

Whistler *p169, map p168*

Whistler Village is little more than a big hotel and condo complex, full of luxury choices that substitute comfort for character. It's best to book in advance, using www.whistlerchamber.com or www.whistler.ca, both of which have extensive listings. Reservations are particularly essential during the ski season or Canadian or US holidays, and for those seeking budget options. The few hostels catering to budget travellers fill up very quickly; it's a challenge to find a bed for less than $120. If you do just turn up, go to the visitor information centre for help or call **Central Reservations**, T604-6645625. Ski/accommodation packages can work out the cheapest option. Rates are greatly reduced in summer and double at Christmas. The satellite suburbs, such as Creekside (within walking distance of the gondola), offer better value.
A Cedar Springs B&B, 8106 Cedar Springs Rd, Alpine Meadows, 4 km north of Whistler Village, T604-9388007, www.whistlerbb.com. 8 attractive, varied rooms, all decorated in wood. There's a communal lounge, buffet breakfast, afternoon tea and free transport to the hill.
A Edgewater Lodge, 8030 Alpine Way, 3 km north of Whistler Village, T604-9320688, www.edgewater-lodge.com. This beautiful, quiet, seemingly remote lodge is situated on the shore of Green Lake, which can be admired from the 12 attractive lodge rooms, the patio, outdoor jacuzzi or the highly esteemed restaurant. Breakfast is included.
A Renoir's Winter Garden B&B, 3137 Tyrol Cres, near Alta Lake, T604-9380546, www.dualmountain.com/renoir. Possibly the nicest of Whistler's many B&Bs, which

is why you have to reserve so far ahead. 5 gorgeous en suite rooms, plus hot tub, views and a fantastic gourmet breakfast.
A Riverside Resort, 8018 Mons Rd, 1.5 km from the village via Blackcomb Way, T604-9055533, www.whistlercamping.com. Set in a spacious campground are these pretty, cosy log cabins, decked out in wood, and equipped with kitchenettes and small patios. Other facilities include a games room, playground, volleyball court and putting greens, plus they rent bikes, skis and other gear, arrange tours, and provide free shuttles to the gondolas.
B Brew Creek Lodge, 1 Brew Creek Rd, 22 km south of Whistler, 37 km north of Squamish, T604-9327210, www.brew creeklodge.com. A gorgeous, very private cluster of wood buildings nestled among the trees, offering a variety of choices such as lodge rooms, suites, cabins and guesthouses. There's an outdoor jacuzzi, and a wonderful guest lounge.
B Erin Lodge, 7162 Nancy Greene Dr, Village North, T604-9323641, www.pension edelweiss.com. The 8 en suite rooms in this charming house have a north European, uncluttered kind of sophistication. There's a whirlpool, sauna, mountain views and a hearty breakfast, plus free pick-up from town and bike rental. Great value.
B Haus Heidi Pension B&B, 7115 Nesters Rd, 15 mins walk from the Village, T604-9323113, www.hausheidi.com. A very attractive and distinctive European-style house, with 8 delightful en suite rooms, an outdoor hot tub, sauna, lovely balcony with views, and big breakfasts.
C Whistler Resort and Club, 2129 Lake Placid Rd, 6 km south in Creekside, T604-9325756, www.whistlerresortand club.com. Though not dramatically gorgeous, the rooms here are nice enough, good value for the price, and handily located. There's a hot tub, and canoes and bikes to rent.
E HI Whistler, 5678 Alta Lake Rd, opposite side of lake, T604-9325492. Not so easy to get to, but undoubtedly the budget option of choice, so reserve early.

On the banks of the lake, it's very quiet and scenic. Beds are mostly in dorms. There's a sauna, internet, canoes and bikes, and 5 buses per day to town.

E South Side Lodge Hostel, 6 km south in Creekside, T604-9323644, www.south sidelodge.com. 24 beds in recently renovated 4-bed dorms that are often rented by the week in winter and very popular with snowboarders. Shared kitchen, lots of useful info.

E UBC Whistler Lodge, 2124 Nordic Dr, 3 km south of the Village, T604-8225851, www.ubcwhistlerlodge.com. A student hostel with some beds available to the public in 2- to 4-bed dorms. Full kitchen facilities, common area with wood fire, separate TV lounge, sauna and hot tub, coin laundry, lockers, free parking, and lock-up shed. A great deal.

Camping

There are cheaper, more basic forestry campgrounds further out at Calcheak and Alexander Falls.

Brandywine Falls, 10 km south on Hwy 99. A standard park campsite.

Riverside RV Resort, 8018 Mons Rd, T604-9055533, www.whistlercamping.com. About the only real choice for campers within Whistler itself and open all year. Fairly private sites for tents, full service for RVs. Facilities include hot showers, laundry, and facilities at the Resort, see p173.

Pemberton *p170*

There are a couple of standard motels/ hotels in town but much better are the varied B&Bs, many of which cluster around Pemberton Meadows Rd.

B Log House B&B, 1357 Elmwood Dr, follow signs in town, T604-8946000, www.loghouseinn.com. 7 attractive wood-furnished rooms with en suite shower in a beautiful log home, with an outdoor hot tub, a wraparound deck with good views, and a guest lounge. Full breakfast included.

B Pemberton Valley Vineyard & Inn, 1427 Collins Rd, just off Pemberton Meadows

Rd, T604-8945857, www.whistlerwine.com. 3 large, light, airy and tastefully furnished rooms with en suite claw-foot tubs in a lovely home surrounded by a vineyard. There's a deck with mountain views, hot tub, and the breakfast is vegetarian.

Camping

Nairn Falls Provincial Park, 3 km south, T604-8983678. 94 reasonable sites, with hiking/fishing. 1.5-km walk to the falls.

Lillooet *p172*

C 4 Pines, 108 8th Av, T250-2564247. The most promising choice out of a few motels in Downtown, with big rooms and baths. It's worth paying the extra for newer rooms, which have kitchenettes.

E Reynolds Hotel, Main St, T250-2564202. Great value with big bathrooms, mountain views and bags of character.

Camping

To compensate for the building of the local dam, BC Hydro has provided a free campground with fairly nice sites on the creek to the south of town. Further south are some equally reasonable forestry campgrounds just off the highway.

● Eating

North to Squamish *p163*

♥ **Mountain WoMan Café**, Britannia Beach, by the museum. A kitchen-bus restaurant, good for fish 'n' chips and burgers.

Squamish and around *p163*

♥♥ **Howe Sound Brew Pub**, 37081 Cleveland Av, T604-8922603, www.howe sound.com. A lively and very tastefully decked out pub and restaurant serving creative West Coast food, salads and pizzas, as well as their own excellent beers. There are unbeatable views of the Stawamus Chief from the patio.

♥♥ **Pepe & Gringos** 40359 Tantalus Way, Garibaldi Heights. Handy for those staying in this area. A friendly little spot for tasty Mexican dishes and pasta.

♥ **Shady Tree Pub**, 40456 Government St, Brackendale, next to the bus station. Good pub-style food in a popular locals' hangout.

♥♥ **Wild Wood Bistro & Bar**, Tantalus Rd, Highland Village, T604-8154585. At last, fine dining in sophisticated surroundings at reasonable prices has arrived to perk up the stagnating Squamish culinary scene. West Coast food with an emphasis on seafood and Asian flavours.

♥♥ **Yianni Taverna**, 38043 Cleveland Av, T604-8929696. A good central option for Greek food, pizza and pasta.

♥ **Sunflower Bakery Café**, 38086 Cleveland Av. Good coffee and freshly baked goods.

Whistler *p169, map p168*

Most of Whistler's restaurants and bars are in and around Village Square, so it's easy to see where the action is.

♥♥♥ **Araxi Ristorante and Pub**, Village Sq, T604-9324540. With an excellent West Coast-influenced menu that concentrates on fresh, local meat, game, vegetables and fish, and an upbeat upmarket interior, this is widely considered the best in town.

♥♥♥ **Bearfoot Bistro**, 4121 Village Green, T604-9323433. Set in sumptuous surroundings. Taster menus are $90 for 3 courses, while the Champagne Bar has an à la carte menu featuring lots of game.

♥♥♥ **Rim Rock Café**, Whistler Creekside, south on Hwy 99, T604-9325565. This local favourite has a very comfortable, attractive and inviting interior, while the upmarket menu features such perennial favourites as crab and lobster.

♥♥ **21 Steps**, St Andrew's House, T604-9662121. An intimate and stylish place equally suitable for food or drinks. The menu concentrates on favourite international meat and seafood dishes, with a fine range of appetizers. There are cocktails, beer on tap and a good range of nicely-priced wines, many by the glass.

♥♥ **Caramba!**, 4314 Main St, Village North, T604-9381879. An incredibly popular venue, thanks to its lively, colourful atmosphere and good moderately priced Mediterranean dishes, such as calamari or wood-oven pizzas.

♥♥ **Casa Tapas & Wine**, T604-9359666, St Andrews House, 4433 Sundial Pl, Whistler Village. One of the hipper spots in Whistler, with a loungey atmosphere.

♥♥ **Kypriake Norte**, opposite the Listel, T604-9320600. Possibly the best Greek/Mediterranean food in town, with great specials, reasonable prices and a laid-back, friendly ambience.

♥♥ **La Bocca**, Village Sq, T604-9322112. With its funky, colourful interior dominated by a striking bar, and a menu that focuses on eclectic West Coast fusion cuisine, this is one of Whistler's more genuinely hip and sophisticated spots.

♥♥ **La Brasserie des Artistes**, Village Sq, T604-9323569. Stylish with a laid-back atmosphere, reasonable prices and a great breakfast menu.

♥♥ **Pasta Lupino**, Market Pavilion, Village North, T604-9050400. Homemade pasta dishes in a casual bistro-style setting.

♥♥ **Uli's Flipside**, Whistler Creekside, T604-9351107. Open and colourful interior with good art and an eclectic menu that covers anything from paella to perogies, with $10 specials daily 1500-1700. Huge portions, and good Martinis.

♥♥ **The Wild Wood Bistro & Bar**, 4500 Northlands Blvd, Village North in Whistler Racquet Club, T604-9354077. Calling itself an 'urban tapa parlour', this stylish and sophisticated spot features a broad menu of eclectic, Asian-influenced West Coast dishes, including plenty of seafood dishes, and stirfries to suit all budgets.

♥ **Ingrid's Village Café**, just off the Square, T604-9327000. Cheap breakfasts and lunches, homemade bread and yummy sandwiches. Very popular.

♥ **South Side Diner**, Whistler Creekside. Breakfast, lunch and dinner. A recently renovated institution, with big portions.

Cafés

Gone Bakery and Soup Co, behind Armchair Books, next to the liquor store.

Warm, cosy and down-to-earth. A great spot for coffee, baking, soups and salads. **Moguls Coffee Bean**, Blackcomb Lodge. Good for coffee.

Pemberton *p170*
♊ **Pony Espresso**, 1426 Portage Rd, T604-9381926. A popular hangout for locals, with good beer on tap, a deck on the roof and outdoor seating. The obvious choice for coffee, breakfast and melts. Tasty dinner menu of salads, pasta, and pizza.
♊ **Wicked Wheel Pizza Co**, 2021 Portage Rd, Mt Currie, on the way to Lillooet, T604-8946622. This is where locals go to treat themselves. Highly regarded and well worth the short drive from town.
♊ **The Wild Wood Bistro & Bar**, 101-1436 Portage Rd, T604-8940114. Sister company to the one in Whistler (see p175), this branch also serves Asian-influenced West Coast dishes, seafood and stirfries.

Lillooet *p172*
♊ **Dina's**, 690 Main St. Hands down the best choice in town. Popular and friendly, specializing in Greek cuisine.

☺ Bars and clubs

Whistler *p169, map p168*
There are plenty of busy pubs around the village, most offering live music every weekend in the winter. For weekly listings pick up a free copy of *This Week*.
Amsterdam Café, Village Sq, T604-9328334. Small, atmospheric and bursting with character, almost living up to its name.
The Attic, Main Village, T604-9662121. A cool, laid-back lounge with leather seating, music in the soul, jazz or funk vein, ice-wine Martinis... you get the idea.
Buffalo Bill's, 4122 Village Green, T604-9322323, www.buffalobills.ca. With its huge dancefloor and mainstream music, this is the most party-oriented club in town.
Garfinkel's, just north of the footbridge. Has the biggest stage in town, so gets a lot of the biggest acts.

High Mountain Brewhouse, by Blackcomb Way in Village North, T604-9052739. The patio here is a great place to relax and people watch. There's also a decent selection of microbrews, pool tables and quite good food.
Mallard Lounge, in the Château, T604-9388000. A predictably upmarket, chic spot for a quiet Martini.
Moe Joe's, Village Sq. A small but fun spot playing funky dance tunes.
Savage Beagle, Village Sq. Upstairs is a laid-back lounge and dining room, while below is a heaving dancefloor.
Tommy Africa's, 4216 Gateway Dr, T604-9326090. Attracts a younger crowd with hip-hop style sounds.

☺ Festivals and events

Squamish *p163*
Jan The Brackendale Winter Eagles Festival will enjoy its 20th year in 2006. In 1994, 3769 eagles were spotted in one day. Contact the Brackendale Art Gallery (see p164) for details.
Jun Towards the end of the month is the **Test of Metal Mountain Bike Race**, T604-8985195, www.testofmetal.com. This is one of the most exciting and prestigious mountain bike events in the world.
Jul The annual **Squamish Days Logger Sports**, T604-8929244, www.squamish days.org, at the end of Jul is the biggest chainsaw bonanza in Canada, featuring competitions, races, beef BBQ, gospel singing, a parade and Haddon.

Whistler *p169, map p168*
Throughout the winter, Whistler plays host to a stream of ski and snowboard competitions. In summer, the spirit is kept alive with a number of mountain bike competitions and various smaller events. The best place to find out exactly what's going on is **Whistler-Blackcomb**, T604-9323434, www.whistlerblackcomb.com.
Feb Early Feb sees the **Peak to Valley Race**, T604-9052034. Not long after,

Altitude, www.ontheslopes.com, is a week-long gay-pride event.

Apr The **International FIS Juvenile Ski Races** are held in early Apr. In mid-Apr is the biggest annual winter sports event in North America, the **Telus World Ski and Snowboard Festival**, T604-9383399, www.whistler2006.com. This huge 10-day party features free outdoor concerts, the world snowboarding championship and downhill ski freestyle events.

Aug Crankworx, www.crankworx.com, is a freeride mountain bike festival.

Nov In the 2nd week, **Cornucopia**, T1888-9994566, www.whistlercornucopia.com, is a week-long food and wine festival.

Dec In early Dec, the annual **Whistler Film Festival**, T604-9383200, www.whistler filmfestival.com, gets everyone in the mood with a showing of mountain films, as well as other independent productions. The **Snowscene**, T604-7877770, www.snowscene.ca, in mid-Dec, features the Snowboard FIS World Cup.

◉ Shopping

Squamish *p163*
Valhalla Pure Outfitters, Squamish Station Shopping Centre, T604-8929092. The best place for camping gear, outdoor clothing and climbing equipment.

Whistler *p169, map p168*
The **market place** in Village North has the most useful selection of shops, including an **IGA** supermarket. In Whistler Village, the grocery store, liquor store and **Armchair Books**, are grouped together under one roof close to the square. There are a number of art galleries in Whistler, many of them in hotels.

Black Tusk, Whistler Village, 106-4050 Whistler Way, T604-9055540, www.black tusk.ca, has a wonderful collection of quality First Nations pieces worth seeing even if you're not looking to buy.

▲ Activities and tours

For all types of activities along the Sea to Sky Highway, the free *99 North* magazine has excellent maps and listings.

North to Squamish *p163*
Diving
There are 10 dive sites accessible from the coast between Horseshoe Bay and Britannia Beach, the most celebrated being **Whytecliff Park** at Horseshoe Bay and **Porteau Cove Provincial Park**. See p163 for more details and Vancouver listings, p90, for operators.

Golf
Furry Creek Golf and Country Club, just south of Britannia Beach, T604-8962224. Great views, lots of water, and a good (expensive) restaurant.

Squamish *p163*
Climbing
Almost 300 routes traverse the 625-m face of the **Stawamus Chief**, including the **University Wall**, considered Canada's most difficult climb. But the Chief is only one of many climbing venues around Squamish. The **Smoke Bluffs**, across from the entrance to town, also have over 300 routes of all levels, and **Murrin Provincial Park**, 8 km south, has many more.

Squamish Select by Marc Bourdon is a useful book with maps and descriptions of climbing and bouldering routes in the Squamish/Whistler area. A handy online guide is www.squamishclimbing.com. In winter, some challenging excellent ice-climbing routes are found at **Olesen Creek**. **Slipstream Rock and Ice**, T604-8984891, www.getclimbing.com. Rock/ice-climbing at Paradise Valley Crags north of Squamish. **Squamish Rock Guides**, T604-8151750, www.squamishrockguides.com. Guiding and instruction with certified guides. **Vertical Reality Sports Store**, 37835 2nd Av. A good source of information; also rents equipment.

Eagle spotting

Elaho Adventures, T1800-7137238, www.elahoadventures.com. Whitewater rafting and eagle safaris.

Sunwolf Outdoor Centre, 70002 Squamish Valley Rd in Brackendale, 4 km off Hwy 99, 10 km north of town, T604-8981537, www.sunwolf.net. Watch the eagles from dry land or from the river. Whitewater rafting/kayaking also arranged.

Golf

Garibaldi Springs, just north of Squamish, T604-8988356, www.garibaldispringsgolf resort.com. Very scenic, incorporating salmon streams, waterfalls and rock faces.

Mountain biking

There are countless trails around Squamish, suitable for all levels up to the most extreme. The majority are concentrated in the **Smoke Bluffs** and **Crumpit Woods** area east of town, or around **Alice Lake** and the **Garibaldi Highlands** further north. **Squamish Bike Guides**, T604-8151311, www.squamishbikeguides.com. Guided mountain bike trips and instruction. **Tantalus Bike Shop**, 40446 Government Rd/Hwy 99. Rents bikes, and can offer good advice/information.

Watersports

See also under Eagle spotting, above. A popular spot for windsurfing and whitewater kayaking is **Squamish Spit** just past the Railway Heritage Park about 3 km from town. It's maintained by the **Squamish Windsports Society**, T604-8922235, www.squamishwindsurfing.org, who charge a small fee ($15). On a good day, this makes for a great spectator sport. **Sea to Sky Ocean Sports**, 37819 2nd Av. Kayak rentals, $45 per 4 hrs.

Whistler *p169, map p168*

Whistler is all about outdoor activities; the only difficulty is in choosing what to do. www.tourismwhistler.com lists activities, tours operators, and rental companies; www.whistlerblackcomb.com is also

invaluable. Besides the activities listed below, operators will take you horse riding, bungee jumping, jet-boating, bear-viewing, windsurfing, ATV-ing, even on a 4WD hummer tour. Helicopter sightseeing tours start at about $640 for 20 mins.

Climbing

Nordic Rock, in Nordic Estates between the Village and Creekside, and **Cal-Cheak**, 13 km south of Whistler, are the key sites for rock climbing. Ice climbing with **Alpine Guides** (see Tour operators, p180) on a glacier is also available Jun-Oct. **The Great Wall Underground**, T604-9057625, www.greatwallclimbing.com, has 2 walls, 1 indoors at the **Westbrook Hotel**, another outside at the base of **Blackcomb Mountain**. The 'Youth Climb and Dine' gives parents a night off, and by providing climbing instruction and dinner for $65 per child.

Fishing

99 North's summer edition lists 28 lakes and 11 rivers that are prime spots, mostly for trout and Dolly Varden. You need a non-tidal angling licence (see p14), and should be aware of quotas, regulations and closures. Contact T604-6660384, www.dfo-mpo.gc.ca for further information.

Golf

Whistler has a lot of courses, many of them are world class, as well as spectacular. **Chateau Whistler** , T604-9382095, www.chateauwhistler.com. Beautifully merges with the surrounding countryside. **Nicklaus North**, T604-9389898. Designed by the pro; one of the best and most scenic. **Whistler Golf Club**, T604-9323280, www.whistlergolf.com. Designed by Arnold Palmer, with 9 lakes and 2 creeks.

Hiking

Hiking around Whistler is prime. You don't have to be fit to hike in the alpine around here. Throughout the summer, the gondola ($25/20) whisks hikers up to breathtaking views of Black Tusk,

Cheakamus Glacier and Cheakamus Lake, and the start of numerous hikes. The Peak chair ($35/$27 with gondola) then ascends another 1000 m to the top of Whistler Mountain and 48 km of elevation trails. Whistler/Blackcomb arrange guided tours, $89/$59 for 2½ hrs, including lunch.

Mountain biking

There are hundreds of bike trails in the valley, particularly around **Lost Lake**. Bikers can also carry their steeds on the lift ($41) up to **Whistler Mountain Bike Zone**, open May-Sep, daily 1000-1700 which consists of 200 km of single-track trails and 4800 ft of vertical drop. Half-day mountain bike tour $95.

Cross Country Connection, Lost Lake Park, just off Lorimer Rd, T604- 9050071, www.crosscountryconnection.bc.ca. Rentals, tours, instruction and information.

Ticket2RideBC, 7162 Nancy Greene Dr, Whistler, T604-9386230, ticket2 ridebc.com. Tailored mountain-biking holidays for all levels, guided adventures including heli-drops, instruction and accommodation. Recommended.

Whistler Bike Company, 4050 Whistler Way. Rentals.

Rafting

Whistler River Adventures, Whistler Mountain gondola, T604-9323532, www.whistler river.com. $70 per 2 hrs.

Skiing

Between them, the mountains of Whistler and Blackcomb offer skiers over 3300 ha of terrain, featuring 12 bowls, 3 glaciers and 200 marked trails. The state-of-the-art network of lifts has a capacity of over 59,000 skiers per hr. There are at least 12 restaurants on the mountains.

Each mountain has its own character. **Whistler** is more laid-back, has a family zone, and is suitable for beginners and intermediates. The breakdown is 20% beginner, 55% intermediate and 25% advanced. **Blackcomb** (15%/55%/30%) boasts the 2 longest lift-serviced vertical

falls in North America, one of the biggest terrain parks in the world, a superpipe, tube park, and an expert park (with a 485-ft vertical drop), which you can only enter with a helmet and a special endorsement on your pass. Night skiing is available at 'Night Moves' on Wed, Fri and Sat only.

Whistler Ski School, T1866-2189681, is one of the best in North America. Prices are about $99 per day, $143 with lift pass and rentals, $579 per day with a private instructor. **Mountain Hosts** runs free ski-guiding at 1130. Basic avalanche awareness courses are also available. Equipment can be rented from stores, hotels or on the mountain.

On a fresh powder day the **Fresh Tracks Breakfast** is highly recommended. Tickets, $15.50 on top of the regular lift pass, can be reserved or bought at the lift. Turn up at 0700; you are taken up to the Roundhouse for breakfast then let out onto the fresh snow at 0800, 50 mins before the regular crowds arrive.

The **Whistler Express**, **Fitzsimmons Express** and **Blackcomb Excalibur** gondolas leave from the south side of the Village. The **Wizard Express** and **Magic Chair** lifts both head up to Blackcomb from the Upper Village. A day pass for all lifts is $75/$64/$41, free for 6 years and under. You can ski between the hills and there are plans to connect them with a gondola. The hills are open daily 0830- 1500, from mid-late Nov depending on conditions. Blackcomb closes in Apr, Whistler continues till early Jun. For weather, snow and lift reports, call T604- 9323434, www.whistlerblackcomb.com.

Backcountry/cross-country skiing

Backcountry skiing is available all around Whistler, especially in **Garibaldi Provincial Park** (see p165), but only for those with experience or a guide. Also available is cross-country skiing, cat skiing and heli-skiing. **Lost Lake Park**, Lorimer Rd, T604-9050071, www.crosscountry connection.bc.ca, offers 32 km of cross-country trails, open daily in winter until 2000 ($10) and illuminated at night. The **Valley**

Trail links the Village, Lost Lake, Alta Lake, Alpha Lake and beyond. There are also some good trails at the **Château Whistler** and **Nicklaus North** golf courses.
Powder Mountain Cat Skiing, T604-9320169, www.pmcatski.com. $450 for a full day of untracked skiing or snowboarding far from the madding crowd.
Whistler Heli-Skiing, T1888-4354754, www.whistlerheliskiing.com. Starts at about $640 for 3 runs.

Swimming
For indoor swimming, **Meadow Park Recreation Centre**, 6 km north on Hwy 99, T604-9357529, has a pool, exercise room, skating rink, sauna and hot tub. For outdoor swimming, there are plenty of lakes, including **Lost Lake**.

Tour operators
Cougar Mountain, 18-4314 Main St, T604-9324086, www.cougarmountain.ca. Wide range of backcountry adventures including snowmobile tours, snow shoeing, dog sledding, fishing and horse riding.
Whistler Activity and Information Centre, 4010 Whistler Way off Hwy 99, T604-9382769, daily 0900-1700. Can arrange any activity for you.
Whistler Alpine Guides Bureau, T604-9383228, www.whistlerguides.com. Arranges tours and instruction for back-country winter and summer touring; skiing, snowboarding, ice climbing and mountaineering.

Winter sports
Green Lake is a popular spot for ice skating. Snowmobiling tours for all levels start at $89 per 2 hrs for a double. Snowshoeing is possible just about anywhere; **Lost Lake** is the obvious choice, tours start at $69 per 1½ hrs. Dog-sledding tours of the **Soo Valley** cost $280 per person for 2½ hrs and leave twice daily. Horse-drawn sleigh rides leave hourly from 1700-2000 and cost $45 per person for 30 mins.

Ziplining
Ziptrek Ecotours, inside **Essentially Blackcomb** across from Whistler Village Gondola, T604-9350001, www.ziptrek.com. Carreen down Fitzsimmons Creek attached to a zipline. The highest is 1100 ft up. Open year round. $98/$78 for a 2½-hr tour. They also arrange treks through the tree tops along suspension bridges and boardwalks, $39/29 for a 1½-hr tour.

Pemberton *p170*
Fishing
There are plenty of spots for fishing. **Joffre Lake** (see p171) and **Blackwater Lake** (south of D'Arcy) contain rainbow trout.

Tour operators
Coast Range Heli-skiing, T1800-7018744, www.coastrangeheliskiing.com. A 4-run package is $739.
High Line Cycles, 1392 Portage Rd. Rentals and information.
Pemberton Soaring Centre, Airport Rd, T604-8945727.

Lillooet *p172*
Fishing
Seton Lake and the **Fraser River** are both good for rainbow trout, and sturgeon.

⊖ Transport

Squamish *p163*
Air
Sea to Sky Air, T604-8981975, www.seatoskyair.ca. Flights between **Nanaimo** and Squamish (and sightseeing tours).

Bus
Squamish bus station is at Garibaldi Highlands, 1 km north on Hwy 99 but most buses also stop in Downtown. **Greyhound**, T1800-6618747, www.whistlerbus.com, runs 8 daily buses to **Vancouver** and **Whistler**, and 4 to **Pemberton**. The 0800 and the 1300 **Perimeter** buses from **Vancouver Airport** (see Whistler, below) also stop in Squamish.

Whistler *p169, map p168*

Bus

Local Whistler Village is small enough to get around on foot, but for the periphery there's an efficient local transit system, **The Wave**, T604-9324020, www.busonline.ca, links the many satellite suburbs, with all routes converging on Village Gate Boulevard. The free **Village Shuttle** runs around the village and to the gondolas all day. **Lost Lake Free Shuttle**, Jul-Aug, goes from the gondolas to Lost Lake.

Long distance The bus station is at 2029 London Lane, T604-9325031, www.whistlerbus.com. **Greyhound**, T1800-6618747, runs 9 daily buses from **Vancouver**, $19 one-way. Their non-stop Ski Express leaves Vancouver at 0630 arriving at the Village 0830. **Moose Travel Network**, T604-7779905, www.moose network.com, offers buses from $35 one way, $65 return to/from hostels in **Vancouver**. If it's still running, the Snowbus, T604-6857669, www.snow bus.ca, is the cheapest bus at $30 return, $20 one way. It leaves hostels in **Vancouver** at about 0550, arriving in Whistler at 0845. **Perimeter Whistler Express**, T1877-3177788, picks up at the airport and major hotels and charges $65, $45 one-way.

Car

The highway to Whistler is overcrowded, and works will be in progress intermittently to widen the road in time for 2010. For up-to-the-minute information, call T1877-4723399, or visit www.tourismwhistler. Com/downloads/hwy99_construction. Parking in Whistler is about $10/night. **Avis Rent-a-car**, Whistler Cascade Lodge, 4315 Northlands Blvd, T604-9321236. **Budget Car Rental**, Coast Hotel, 4005 Whistler Way, T604-9354122.

Taxi

Whistler Resort Cabs, T604-9381515.

Train

Rocky Mountaineer, T604-6067245, www.whistlermountaineer.com, is a picturesque 3-hr train journey to/from **North Vancouver**, with an open-air observation car. Leaves Vancouver daily 1 May-16 Oct at 0730, $99/$49 one-way, $179/$89 return, including bus transport from Downtown to North Vancouver, and into Whistler Village from Whistler railway station.

ⓘ Directory

Squamish *p163*
Canada Post Cleveland Av/Victoria St. **Laundry** Cascade Laundry, 38921 Progress Way. **Medical services** Sea to Sky Walk In Clinic, 40147 Glenalder, next to Canadian Tire, T604-9895555, daily. Squamish General Hospital, 38140 Behrner, T604-8925211.

Whistler *p169, map p168*
Banks TD Bank and Thomas Cook are found in Market Place, Village North. **Canada Post** Market Place. **Emergencies** Fire, T604-9358260. **Internet** Whistler Java Boutique Café, in the Summit Lodge, 4359 Main St. Free at the library. **Laundry** Nesters Laundromat, 7009 Nesters. **Library** by the car park off Main St, Village North. **Medical services** Town Plaza Medical Clinic, 4314 Main St, across from the library, T604-9057089, daily, no appointment necessary. For emergency services, **Whistler Health Care Centre**, 4380 Lorimer, T604-9324911. **Aarm Dental Group**, Timberline Lodge, 4122 Village Green, T604-9660599. **Photography** Whistler One Hour Film Processing, in the Crystal Lodge, close to the Village Sq. **Police** Village Gate Blvd/Blackcomb Way, T604-9323044.

Heading east from Vancouver, Highway 1 splits in three at Hope. Highway 5 (the Coquihalla Highway) is a high-speed, less attractive route to Kamloops or Kelowna – via Highway 97C – with a $10 toll. Highway 1 (the TransCanada Highway) is the most direct route to the Rockies; there are few reasons to stop but it's a beautiful drive through some wonderfully varied landscapes: the steep walls and thrashing water of the Fraser Canyon; the arid vistas of the

⊘ **Getting there** Bus or car.
⊖ **Getting around** Bus or car.
⊖ **Time required** 2-4 days.
⊛ **Weather** Extremely varied.
⊜ **Sleeping** A broad range but limited quality options.
⊘ **Eating** Mostly limited.
▲ **Activities and tours** Rafting, skiing, biking, hiking.
★ **Don't miss...** Trying some outdoor pursuits in the friendly, town of Revelstoke ›› p185.

Thompson Valley; weirdly-shaped expanses of water in the Shuswap; and increasingly sublime mountain scenery in the Columbia Mountains. Highway 3 – the Crowsnest Highway – is mostly scenic with some boring stretches. It skirts the US border, offering direct access to Nelson (West Kootenays) and Osoyoos (Okanagan), with a few highlights of its own, such as Manning Provincial Park and the ski villages of Rossland and Fernie.

Ins and outs

Getting there and around

There are airports for internal flights in Kamloops, Castlegar and Cranbrook. **Greyhound** runs four buses daily between Vancouver and Calgary, serving most of the destinations in this chapter, as well as Banff. It also runs daily buses from Vancouver to the Alberta border, serving most of the Crowsnest Highway destinations in this chapter. The route is: Vancouver to Hope (Highway 1) to Merritt (Highway 5) to Kelowna (Highway 97C) to Rock Creek (Highway 33) to the Alberta Border (Highway 3) via Nelson. **Via Rail**, T1800-5618630, www.viarail.ca, runs trains from Vancouver to Jasper via Kamloops three times weekly. ⊖ ›› p198.

Tourist information

All but the smallest towns on these routes have visitor information centres. The most useful are in Hope, Kamloops, Revelstoke, Salmon Arm and Castlegar, and at the Highway 5/Highway 5A junction at Merritt.

TransCanada Highway ⊜⊘⊘⊘⊛⊛▲⊖⊘ ›› pp189-199.

Vancouver to Hope

The string of sprawling suburbs that line the TransCanada as it follows the Fraser River east from Vancouver barely lets up until you clear Chilliwack, some 120 km from Downtown. This suburban corridor is the main artery of the Lower Mainland, which contains most of BC's population. The first real diversion, north to **Harrison Hot Springs**, is only really worthwhile in September, when international sculptors create giant, intricate works of art at the annual Sandcastle Festival, or during the annual Festival of the Arts in July. A quicker, easier diversion is to the spectacular **Bridal Veil Falls**, a 15-minute leg-stretch reached via exit 135.

Hell's Gate

Background

Along the TransCanada Highway, you can find out the history of Simon Fraser, after whom the river is named. One of the greatest early explorers of North America, he was seeking a route to the Pacific, and followed the river along its whole 1300-km course thinking it was the Columbia. The hellish canyon section, driven today in a couple of hours, cost him 35 days of hard labour to cross.

For a long time it was believed that the canyon was impassable, and indeed it feels like a miracle of engineering and sheer audacity that the nation's major highway and railway go through it. In places the rock had to be blasted out. It has been estimated, for instance, that the Hell's Gate section of Fraser Canyon cost the lives of three Chinese workers for every kilometre of line that was laid.

Most people drive right past **Hope** on their way somewhere else, but there's some good hiking and biking around, including the **Othello Quintette Tunnels**, a 90-m-deep solid granite wall that was blasted through in 1911 as part of the Kettle Valley Railway (see p203). Ask for details at the **Hope Visitor Information Centre and Museum Complex** ⓘ *919 Water Av, T604-8692021, www.hopebc.ca.*

Fraser Canyon

Between Hope and Lytton, the tumultuous Fraser River's massive volume of water is forced through a narrow channel between the sheer rock faces of the Cascade and Coast mountains, gouging out a steep, awe-inspiring canyon. Since the Fraser was the only river in southern BC to penetrate the mountain barrier, road and railway builders were obliged to follow this unlikely route (see box above). By either means, the journey is breathtaking.

The prettiest part of this spectacular drive is around tiny **Yale**, which is surrounded by sheer cliffs. It's hard to believe, but, during the Fraser Valley Gold Rush, this sleepy village of less than 200 was a steamship navigation capital, and one of North America's largest cities, with a population of over 20,000. You can find out all about it at the small **Yale Museum** ⓘ *31187 Douglas St, T250-8632324, Jun-Sep 0900-1800, by donation,* on the highway. Also here is the summer-only visitor information booth.

Fraser River reaches its awesome crescendo at **Hell's Gate**, where it is forced through a gorge 38 m wide and 180 m deep. The thrashing water reaches a depth of 60 m and thunders through with incredible power. The **Hell's Gate Airtram Gondola** ⓘ *T250-8679277, www.hells gateairtram.com, summer 0930-1730, otherwise 1000-1600, $15, $9 child,* carries up to 2500 people a day across the canyon for up-close views. Free canyon views can be had 8 km south at **Alexander Bridge Provincial Park**.

Heading north, the scenery remains spectacular, slowly taking on the dry, Wild West characteristics of the Thompson Valley, which the highway follows from Lytton. There's little to recommend the remaining towns, except as bases for some of the province's best rafting. There are excellent adrenaline-charged rapids just north of **Boston Bar**, and further north between Spences Bridge and Lytton, with rapids such as the Jaws of Death.

At **Cache Creek**, Highway 1 veers eastwards. This funny little town, which has retained a distinctive 1950s feel, is surrounded by exceptional scenery, an arid, rocky moonscape of vast wrinkled mounds in shades of yellow and red, practically vegetation-free. The 'Painted Bluffs' between Savona and Ashcroft offer the best example of these colourful rock formations.

The Fraser Canyon is one of just three rivers to forge its way through the formidable Coast Mountains.

Kamloops

The sublime Thompson Valley landscape between Cache Creek and Kamloops provides a magnificent setting for this bland city. The endless hills of semi-desert, with their subtle hues and weird shapes, are an unlikely location for the second largest city in BC's interior, but a chance meeting of valleys has made this an important transport hub ever since the days when the canoe was the vehicle of choice; in fact, the Shuswap name Cumloops means 'meeting of the waters'. Today the Canadian Pacific and Canadian National railways, as well as two major highways connecting Vancouver, the Rockies and points east, south and north all converge here. It's a tough place to avoid, but there's little reason to stop, except in August, when one of the best **pow wows** in the country takes place (see Festivals and events, p195).

Five minutes north on Highway 5, **Secwepemc Museum and Heritage Park** ① *T250-8289801, Mon-Fri 0830-2000, Sat-Sun 1000-1800, $6, $4 child*, is an interesting place to learn more about the Secwepemc, or Shuswap, whose culture thrived here for thousands of years. A full-size replica of a 2000-year old village contains traditional pit houses.

If you want to explore the surrounding area, a two-hour walk, starting 4 km west on Tranquille Road, leads to the **Hoodoos**, tall sandstone sculptures carved by wind and water. Alternatively, go hunting for semi-precious stones and fossils with a guided geological tour, or visit **Sun Peaks Ski Resort**, www.sunpeaksresort.com, one of the interior's best (see p196).

The Shuswap

East of Kamloops, the arid vistas of the Thompson Valley give way to duller scenery and an abundance of water. The strangely shaped **Shuswap Lake** provides 1130 km of shoreline, beaches and waterways to explore. Of the many provincial parks in the Shuswap, the most popular and dramatic is **Cinnemousun Narrows**. The classic way to see the lake is in a houseboat (see Activities and tours, p196); the alternative is to rent a canoe and take a tent.

In summer, the Shuswap can get incredibly busy and booked up. The further you get from the highway, the smaller the hordes, but it is debatable whether the rewards justify the effort. One undeniable draw is **Roderick Haig-Brown Provincial Park** on the north shore (5 km north of an excellent hostel in Squilax), which is the province's best place to witness the autumn return of migrating salmon, especially every fourth year (2006, 2010 etc) when some 1.5 million fish turn the Adams River a brilliant red.

The Shuswap's rapidly expanding main resort town, **Salmon Arm**, is a disappointment, but there's a pleasant 9-km boardwalk trail along the lake in Waterfront Park, starting at the **Visitor Information Centre** ① *751 Marine Park Dr (follow signs), T250-8322230, www.sac hamber.bc.ca*; pick up the very informative *Trail Guide*. Between May and September you're likely to see one of the 250 pairs of endangered western grebe performing their extraordinary mating dance. Rock-climbing is big at nearby **Haines Creek**. There's a stunning historical suspension bridge at **Malakwa**, 17 km east of Sicamous.

Revelstoke

As the TransCanada enters the lofty Columbia Mountains, the scenery takes a dramatic upswing with increasingly frequent glimpses of the majestic Rockies beyond. Situated amidst giant trees halfway between Sicamous and Revelstoke, the **Enchanted Forest** ① *T250-8379477, www.enchantedforestbc.com, May-Sep 0900-dusk, $7.50, $5.50 child*, is a must for kids, featuring hundreds of fairy-tale settings and characters, and some crazy tree houses. **Revelstoke**, besides its splendid location, is a friendly, attractive town with top-notch outdoor pursuits and lots of heritage buildings sporting turrets and wraparound balconies. A self-guided tour brochure is available from the two **Visitor Information Centres** ① *204 Campbell Av, T250-8375345, www.revelstokecc.bc.ca, year-round; and corner of hwys 1 and 23 N, T250-8373522, summer only*. The town's only real sight is **Revelstoke Railway Museum** ① *Victoria Rd, opposite the bears, T250-8376060, www.railwaymuseum.com, Apr-Oct Mon-Sat 0900-1700, Jun-Jul daily 0900-2000, Nov-Apr 1300-1600, $6, $3 child*, whose highlights include an entire passenger car, a locomotive and an interactive diesel simulator. **Mount Revelstoke National Park** has some popular walking trails and fabulous wild flowers in July and August.

Glacier National Park

With the Rockies so close, not many people stop to admire this chunk of the Selkirk Mountains, yet the peaks here are just as impressive and even more snow-laden. As its name suggests, Glacier National Park's defining feature is the 422 fields of permanent ice that cloak an incredible 14% of its area year-round. Whereas most of the world's glaciers are rapidly retreating, the largest one here, **Illecillewaet Neve**, is still growing and some 70 new glaciers have recently been identified. The weather that fuels this ice-factory is wet and frequently abysmal.

Rogers Pass is recognized as one of the best backcountry skiing areas in the world, with some 1349 sq km of terrain featuring descents of up to 1500 m. For all but the most experienced, a professional guide is essential as avalanches are very common. For daily updated information about snow conditions phone **Backcountry Report**, T250-8376867. Hikes in the park tend to be short and striking. Unfortunately, you're never very far from the highway. *Footloose in the Columbias* is a useful hiking guide to Glacier and Revelstoke national parks. There is a very helpful **Visitor Information Centre** ① *1 km west of Rogers Pass, T250-8376274, Jun-Sep 0900-2100, otherwise 0900-1700*. As well as trail maps and information it has a number of impressive and entertaining hi-tech displays, and run guided walks in the summer. There's a very helpful map of the park in *The Mountain Guide*, available throughout the Rockies at visitor information centres.

▲ **Glacier Crest** ① *10.4 km return; elevation gain 1005 m. Trailhead: turn into Illecillewaet Campground and proceed just over 1 km to car park*. This glorious trail takes you up the ridge between the park's two major glacier-bearing valleys, Illecillewaet and Asulkan, with ample views of both. You start in an old-growth forest, follow a burbling stream, ascend a steep canyon wall into a land of icy peaks, and top out at a viewpoint offering dramatic 360 degree views. The last stretch is dangerous when wet, so do not attempt after recent rain.

▲▲ **Perley Rock** ⓘ *11.4 km return, 1162 m gain. Trailhead: as above.* This steep and challenging trail would be a torment without the well-built switchbacks. The Illecillewaet Glacier is again on full display, along with the polished bedrock beneath its receding tongue. The higher you go, the better the views get, and on the way back they're even better.

▲▲ **Hermit Basin** ⓘ *5.6 km return, 770 m gain. Trailhead: 1.4 km northeast of Rogers Pass Information Centre.* Even steeper than the above but well maintained, this trail leads to a tiny alpine shelf with great views of the peaks and glaciers on the park's south side. There are four tent pads for overnight stays.

▲▲ **Bald Mountain** ⓘ *35.2 km return, 1354 m gain, 3 days. Trailhead: 11 km northeast of Rogers Pass; or 11.5 km south of northeast park entrance, turn onto Beaver Valley/ Copperstain Rd. Go left after 1.2 km and proceed 200 m.* This long and little-used trail slogs through old-growth forest for most of the first day, but then rewards you with an 8-km-long ridge covered in wild flower meadows (prime grizzly bear habitat). The scenery is gobsmacking, with the glacier-supporting massif in full view across the valley.

Golden

Golden's location could hardly be more fortuitous: halfway between Glacier and Yoho national parks at the junction of the Columbia and Kicking Horse rivers, with the Selkirk and Purcell ranges to the west and the Rockies to the east. Naturally enough, this is a magnet for adventure enthusiasts and, with the arrival of **Kicking Horse Ski Resort**, the area is booming. Inevitably, the town fails to live up to its setting, though the ugly stretch of services on the highway bears no relation to the small, fairly pleasant centre. The **Visitor Information Centre** ⓘ *500 10th Av, T250-3447125, www.goldenchamber.bc.ca*, is open year-round.

Bugaboo Provincial Park

Reached by a good 45-km gravel road from Spillimacheen, 65 km south of Golden, Bugaboo Provincial Park is famous in rock-climbing circles for its spectacular granite spires. Though the long access is off-putting, a couple of good trails allow hikers to enjoy the park's rugged beauty and extensive glaciers. **Bugaboo Spires Trail** (10 km return, 660 m elevation gain. Trailhead: parking lot at Km 43.3) leads to the base of the spires and Conrad Kain Hut, which sleeps 40 people and is equipped with propane stoves. Exploring beyond is recommended. **Cobalt Lake Trail** (17.4 km return, 930 m elevation gain. Same trailhead) involves a lot of hard work before mind-expanding views take over. A shorter trail (10 km return) leads from Bugaboo Lodge, which is operated by **Canadian Mountain Holidays**, T250-7627100. Climbers should get the *Nat Topo Map 82K/10* and/or *82K/15*, and might enjoy *Bugaboo Rock: A Climber's Guide* by R Green and J Benson.

Crowsnest Highway ⊖◑◍❁✹▲⊖◐ ▸▸ *pp189-199.*

Manning Provincial Park

From Hope, Highway 3 climbs quite steeply into the Cascade Mountains, through a vast area of wilderness with no communities to speak of until Princeton, 126 km away. This area is liable to have snow most of the year and, in winter, is excellent for cross-country skiing, with some 130 km of ungroomed backcountry trails, a small ski hill and 30 km of groomed trails. Most of the hiking trails begin around the park's only accommodation, the Manning Park Resort (see

With its warm, clear water Christina Lake is popular for swimming, fishing and watersports.

p191), also a good source of information. Some other good trails are accessed from Lightning Lake, including the 7½-hour return hike to the east peak of **Frosty Mountain**, the park's highest point; it's a steep climb, rewarded by a ridge walk with fantastic views. **Princeton** is renowned in angling circles, boasting 48 trout-fishing lakes within 60 km, 15 of them clustered together about 37 km north on Highway 5A.

Hedley

As the landscapes tend increasingly toward the arid, rolling hills of the Okanagan, the stretch east to Osoyoos is one of the most scenic sections of this highway (see p206 in the Okanagan). The tiny village of Hedley was once one of the most important gold-mining towns in BC. The museum, which doubles as a **Visitor Information Centre** ① *712 Daly St, signed from the highway, T250-2928422, www.hedleybc.ca, summer daily 0900-1700, rest of the year Thu-Mon, by donation*, has photos, artefacts and information about the interesting remains and historic buildings around town. Borrow their binoculars to see from the porch the remains of **Mascot Gold Mine** ① *T250-2928733, www.mascotmine.com, $30, $22.50 child, 3 shuttles leave the museum daily, less off-season*, set amongst dramatic swirls of rock. The **Upper Similkameen Native Band** runs three-hour tours up to the mine including a 200 m underground tunnel, fabulous views of the valley and details about the history of mining in the area, and the Similkameen people.

East to Christina Lake

East of Osoyoos (p204), the highway runs through some fascinating rocky landscapes, the scenery slowly shifting from the barrenness of the Okanagan to the densely forested mountains of the Kootenays. The best reasons to stop are the **Kettle River Museum** ① *T250-4492614, $2*, in Midway, which celebrates the Kettle Valley Railway, and the quaint town of **Greenwood**, whose Wild West appearance is more natural than contrived.

The town of **Christina Lake** has few facilities and poor lake access. Fortunately over half of the beautiful, very warm lake is contained within **Gladstone Provincial Park** and easily accessed via the Texas-Alpine turning, 5 km north on the highway; turn onto Alpine Road and continue to the end for the campground (see Sleeping, p192). A very satisfying hiking and biking trail begins here, hugging the lake to its northern tip. A right fork then continues deep

An aerial view of the Rockies, east of Cranbrook.

into the park, the left leading to more private wilderness campsites, one close by on Christina Lake, another on Xenia Lake further west. You could also hire a canoe and cross the main lake to one of the remote wilderness campgrounds on the west shore.

East to Rossland

At the junction with Highway 3B, **Nancy Greene Provincial Park** contains a lovely lake you can ski round, with a beach for summer swimming and fishing. Highway 3 carries on to Castlegar, but it's well worth making a diversion down Highway 3B to **Rossland**, one of the great unsung skiing meccas and 'mountain bike capital of Canada'. Most people who live here are obsessed with one or both of these activities, so the atmosphere is saturated with an outdoor mentality. In winter the population doubles, as the town fills up with ski-bums. Besides being young, lively and friendly, with a perpetual party atmosphere in winter, this is also an exceptionally picturesque little town with wide, impossibly steep streets, mountains all around and views above the clouds.

In the 1890s, Rossland was a booming gold-mining town, with 7000 people, 42 saloons and four local newspapers. The **Rossland Museum** ⓘ *junction hwys 22 and 3B, T250-3627722, www.rosslandmuseum.ca, mid-May to mid-Sep 0900-1700, $8, $3 child including tour,* which doubles up as the **Visitor Information Centre**, offers interesting tours through a spooky (and chilly) turn-of-the-20th-century mine, filled with old equipment.

Fort Steele Heritage Town

At dreary Castlegar, you're advised to take Highway 3A to Nelson (see p219), then north through Nakusp to Highway 1. Highway 3 east via the Salmo-Creston pass is mostly a dull drive, as is Highway 93 north from dismal Cranbrook. If headed this way, however, it's worth stopping at the reconstructed late 19th-century town of **Fort Steele** ⓘ *9851 Hwy 93/95, 16 km northeast of Cranbrook, T250-4176000, www.fortsteele.bc.ca, Jul-Sep 0930-1900, Nov-Apr closed; $9, $2 child; steam train $6/$3; live 1890s variety shows in the Wild Horse Theatre, at 1400, $8/$3; all-inclusive pass for 2 days $22.50/$9,* one of the best 'living museums' in BC. There are over 50 buildings, some original, some replicas and some brought in from elsewhere. The overall effect is a convincing step back in time. All the requisite shops and services are represented, with costumed staff acting out their roles, while also filling in historical details and anecdotes. The blacksmith shoes horses, the candy shop and bakery sell wares that are made on the spot, the restaurant with its wood-fired brick oven serves meals. There's a working printer, a tinsmith shop, general store, farm animals, street dramas and live shows in an old-time music hall. You can even get taken round in a steam train or horse-drawn wagon.

Fernie

Towards Fernie, the Crowsnest finally rewards its faithful with titillating previews of the Rockies. Surrounded by the soaring, jagged mountains of the **Lizard Range**, Fernie doesn't exactly do the setting justice, but it comes closer than most. Recent expansion of its excellent ski hill has resulted in a fair amount of development; hotels have sprung up along the highway but the pretty little Downtown has been almost entirely spared. Most buildings here were constructed in brick or stone after a fire in 1908 wiped out the whole town in 90 minutes. A historical walking tour highlights these heritage buildings, many of which are clustered around 6th Street and 4th Avenue. A map is available at the **Visitor Information Centre** ⓘ *102 Commerce Rd, T250-4236868, www.ferniechamber.com.*

Until quite recently the copious challenging runs and plentiful powder of **Fernie Alpine Resort** were a fairly well-kept secret, along the lines of Red Mountain in Rossland. Like that town, Fernie is equally fine for skiing and mountain biking, resulting in a dynamic energy that helps save it from the backwater red-neck ambience of most of the East Kootenays.

⬤ Sleeping

Fraser Canyon *p183*

C Chrysalis Retreat B&B, 31278 Douglas St, Yale, T250-8630055. 3 nice rooms in a beautiful cottage with lovely gardens, hot tub and sauna, also offering and massage and hydrotherapy. Breakfast included.

C-D Bear's Claw Lodge, 1492 Hwy 97 N, Cache Creek, T250-4579705. Far and away the nicest place to stay and eat on this stretch, this striking log-built lodge has comfortable rooms, a spacious guest lounge and a decent restaurant.

D Teague House B&B,1 km west of Yale on Hwy 1, T250-3637238, www.teague house.com. Built in 1864, this quaint little blue house has 3 nice bedrooms, a full kitchen and a comfortable sitting room, all furnished with historical artefacts. There's a covered deck from which to enjoy the views over a full breakfast.

Camping

Skihist Provincial Park, 6 km north of Lytton. 56 decent sites, some dramatic views of the Thompson Valley and hiking trails on part of the Cariboo Wagon Rd.

Yale Campground, 28800 Hwy 1. Large leafy sites, hot showers and trails.

Kamloops *p184*

The upmarket accommodation is to be found near the junction of Rogers Way, on the highway above town. Columbia St, the road into town has lots of mid-range options.

B Sun Peaks Lodge, T250-5787878. One of several lodges at the Ski Hill, with balconies, a spa and breakfast included.

C The Plaza, 405 Victoria St, Downtown, T250-3778075, www.plazaheritage hotel.com. The most appealing downtown choice. Rooms in this 1926 building are small, newly renovated and full of character.

D Econo Lodge, at 775 Columbia St, T250-3728235. Very nice rooms with large beds, balconies and new furnishings and carpets. Ask for a room with a view.

E Old Courthouse HI Hostel, 7 West Seymour St/1st Av, T250-8287991. This large heritage building really is housed in a former courthouse, with lots of character and space, though the dorms are a bit confined. There are kitchen and common areas, and the dining room still contains the jury seating and judge's podium.

E Sun Peaks Hostel, T250-7630057, www.sunpeakshostel.com. Yes, there's a budget option at the Ski Hill, with all the usual facilities, including a kitchen, common room, internet, canoes and skiing right out of the door. Phone ahead for transportation from Kamloops.

Camping

Paul Lake Provincial Park, 17 km east off Hwy 5 N. There is no decent camping in town, but you might find this secluded spot on a lovely lake worth the drive. There's good fishing and a steep hike to the top of Gibraltar for views.

The Shuswap *p184*

B-C Trickle Inn B&B, Tappen, T250-8358835, www.trickleinn.com. 5 unique, sumptuously decorated rooms in a gorgeous Victorian heritage home, overlooking the lake and surrounded by landscaped gardens. There's a superb restaurant by prior reservation only.

C Villager Motor Inn, 61 10th St, Salmon Arm, T250-8329793. There are plenty of chain hotels and functional motels on the TransCanada in Salmon Arm. None particularly stands out but this one is at least handy for the bus station.

C-D The Artist's House, 20 Bruhn Rd, 1 km west of Sicamous, T250-8363537, www.artistshouse.ca. A friendly, colourful, antique-filled B&B right on the lake, with 3 rooms, 1 with en suite shower, plus a library, living room, den, sun porch and a lovely big patio with views over the lake.

D Alpiner Motel, 734 Hwy 1, Sicamous, T250-8362290. Cabins with large beds and kitchenette, and some very cheap tenting sites. Great value.

E Caboose Hostel, Squilax, T250-2752977. The main building is a historic General Store on the lake and the dorm beds are in old cabooses (railway cars), each with its own kitchen and bathroom. There is kayaking, bat watching, bike rentals, pet llamas, an authentic sweat lodge, plus cross-country skiing and ice-skating in winter. Phone ahead to arrange pick-up.

Camping

There are remote campgrounds at **White Lake Provincial Park** and **Herald**

Provincial Park, which has a sandy beach and an easy trail to Margaret Falls.
Bush Creek Provincial Park, Adams Lake, 5.5 km up a rough logging road. One of the nicest, most peaceful and scenic places to camp in the area.
KOA, junction of hwys 1 and 97B, T250-8326489. A well-equipped campground with laundry, showers and a pool.
Shuswap Lake Provincial Park, 1210 McGill Rd, east of Squilax at Scotch Creek. 270 nicely wooded, private and well-equipped sites, as well as a large beach.
Silver Beach Provincial Park, Seymour Arm. A remote but spectacular location at the northernmost extremity of the lake.

Revelstoke *p185*

B Mulvehill Creek Wilderness Inn B&B, 4200 Hwy 23, 19 km south towards Shelter Bay ferry, T250-8378649, www.mulvehillcreek.com. A fabulous option for those with transport. This beautiful wood lodge stands on 40 ha of peaceful private land on the shore of Upper Arrow Lake. 9 rooms with en suite bath, plus an outdoor hot tub, common room and library, games room with billiards, canoes. Friendly, interesting hosts and a full breakfast.

B The Regent Inn, 112 1st St, T250-8372107, www.regentinn.com. Large, comfortable rooms with big beds and baths. Centrally located, with an outdoor hot tub, sauna and gym access.

C Minto Manor B&B, 815 Mackenzie Av, T250-8379337, www.mintomanor.com. 3 plush en suite rooms decked out with period furniture. The 1905 Edwardian mansion has a veranda, large gardens, a sitting room, music room and TV room.

D Monashee Lodge, 1601 3rd St W, T250-8376778, www.monasheelodge.com. A quiet good-value motel, with hot tub, and a light breakfast included.

E Samesun Backpacker Lodges, 400 2nd St, T250-8374050, www.samesun.com. One of the great hostels. 76 beds in clean, bright, wood-finished dorms of up to 4, or doubles at no extra charge. 6 kitchens, common room, free internet, bike rentals. $99 ski package including lodging and lift tickets, plus great cat skiing deals.

Camping
Blanket Creek Provincial Park, Hwy 23 S, halfway to Shelter Bay. 64 sites on Arrow Lakes by Sutherland Falls.
Williamson Lake Campground, T250-8375512, 818 Williamson Lake Rd, 5 km south on 4th St/Airport Way. Well located on a warm lake away from the highway, with plenty of trees and greenery, a playground, canoe and rowboat rentals, showers and laundry.

Glacier National Park *p185*
B **Best Western Glacier Park Lodge**, right on Rogers Pass, T250-8372126, www.glacierparklodge.ca. The only beds in the park. Heated outdoor pool, 24-hr café and service station. Otherwise, there are a number of lodges on the way to Golden.

Camping
Illecillewaet Campground, 3.7 km east of Rogers Pass. In the park are back-country campsites and cabins. You can also camp southeast of the park boundary where no fees or restrictions are in place.

Golden *p186*
Golden's mountain setting has led to a proliferation of log-built lodges, mainly west of the TransCanada, many of them accessed by helicopter only.
C **Goldenwood Lodge**, 14 km west, then 6 km east on Blaeberry School Rd, T250-3447685, www.goldenwoodlodge.com. This rustic but handsome wood lodge offers tranquillity, glorious surroundings and a variety of sleeping options, such as family lodges, cottages with or without kitchenette, and tipis (**E**). Vegetarian meals and bikes available, canoeing and horse-riding trips arranged.
C **HG Parson House B&B**, 815 12th St, T250-3445001, www.hgparsonhouse bb.com. 3 rooms in a heritage home. Ask about summer and winter packages.

C **Mary's Motel**, 603 8th Av, T250-3447111. With so little accommodation in Golden, apart from the undesirable strip on the highway, this makes a good, if slightly overpriced, standby, with 2 pools, sauna, hot tub and 81 rooms.
E **Kicking Horse Hostel**, 518 Station Av, take Hwy 95 exit off Hwy 1 then 1st left before the overpass, T250-3445071, www.kickinghorsehostel.com. Dorms plus kitchen, sauna and camping spots.

Camping
Waitabit Creek, 23 km to the west. Turn north onto Donald Rd for 500 m then left down Big Bend Rd for 2 km. Far away, but the best camping, right on the rivers.
Whispering Spruce Campground, 1430 Golden View Rd, off Highway 1 E, T250-3446680. 135 reasonable sites.

Manning Provincial Park *p186*
B **Manning Park Resort**, on the highway, T250-8408822, www.manningpark.com. An impressive log building decorated inside and out with artfully crafted chainsaw carvings, after which the rooms and cabins fall rather flat. Still, it's a great location, with all you need: a café, restaurant and lounge to warm up in, plus bike, ski, canoe and kayak rental.

Camping
Lightning Lake, 5 km from resort. Most convenient of the park's 4 campgrounds, with 88 sites, canoeing and access to trails.

Hedley *p187*
C-D **Colonial Inn B&B**, Colonial Rd, T250-2928131, www.colonialinnbb.ca. Bursting with character from the outside, this historic house is spectacular inside, too, with its immaculate antique furnishings, oak staircase, chandeliers and hardwood floors. The 5 nice rooms (3 en suite) are equally impressive and a steal at this price. Full breakfast included.
D **Gold House B&B**, 644 Colonial Rd, T250-2928418, www.thegoldhouse.com. A fabulous historic house, occupying the

mine's former office and storage room, built in 1904. The 4 lovely rooms, some sharing a bath, have access to the wrap-around balcony, with views of the mine and mountains. Behind here are the scenic remains of a crushing plant, known as the Stamp Mill.

Camping

Stemwinder Provincial Park, just west of town. 27 nicely wooded and fairly private campsites on the river.

Christina Lake *p187*

B Sunflower Inn B&B, Alpine Rd 159, T250-4476201, www.sunflowerinnbb.com. Well situated next to the lake and park, with a private beach, canoes and 3 pleasant rooms with shared bath.
C Hummingbird Haven B&B, 255 1st Av, T250-4479293. 3 very nice rooms in a spacious house enjoying a peaceful location right next to the golf course.
D Parklane Motel, 31 Kingsley Rd, T250-4479385. There are lots of unimpressive motels in town. This one is at least away from the highway.

Camping

Gladstone Provincial Park, accessed via the Texas-Alpine turning, 5 km north on the highway. A large and extremely busy campground by the lake, with access to several beaches and hiking trails. Reserve early, or keep your fingers crossed.

Rossland *p188*

AL-B Rams Head Inn, Red Mountain Rd, 400 m before ski hill, T250-3629577, www.ramshead.bc.ca. By far the best option around. The beautiful rooms are comfortable and homely, plus there's a common room with a big stone fireplace, sauna, outdoor hot tub with views, a games room and full breakfast included. Prices drop considerably in summer.
B Angela's Place B&B, 1520 Spokane St, T250-3627790, www.visitred.com. A classic renovated 1920s house, with 2 suites that

are more geared to bigger groups but may suit a couple, if available. Extras include hot tub, fireplace and garden, with a creek running through the property.
B Prestige Inn, 1919 Columbia Av, T250-3627375, www.prestigeinn.com. Recently taken over by yet another chain hotel but little has changed. It's still a convenient downtown choice, with decent rooms, jacuzzi and fitness centre, restaurant, lounge, and noisy bar that hosts frequent bands.
B-C Red Mountain Village, 3 km north on Hwy 3B at the base of the hill, T250-3629000, www.redmountainvillage.com. A wide range of options, from luxury chalets to large cabins and motel rooms. Prices drop by 50% in summer.
E Mountain Shadow Hostel, 2125 Columbia Av, T250-3627160. Dorms and private rooms, common room and kitchen, internet access.

Camping

Rossland Lions Park, Red Mountain Rd, 1 km north on Highway 3B. 18 sites, some with hook-ups. Summer only.

Fort Steele Heritage Town *p188*
Camping

Fort Steele Original Campground, 2 km south, T250-4265117. 60 quiet wooded sites, heated pool, showers, RV hook-ups.
Fort Steele Resort and RV Park, T250-4894268. 200 sites right by the town, heated pool, showers, hook-ups.

Fernie *p189*

Fernie has lots of accommodation. Check www.fernie.com/lodging for information. You can also book what you need through **Fernie Central Reservations**, T1800-6225007. Note that these prices are for the peak ski season, with rates up to 50% less during summer.
B Park Place Lodge, 742 Hwy 3, T250-4236871, www.parkplacelodge.com. Spacious and stylish rooms, some with balconies or kitchenettes, plus an indoor pool, hot tub and sauna, pub and bistro.

C **Griz Inn**, 5369 Ski Hill Rd, at the hill, T1800-6610118, www.grizinn.com. One of several decent lodges at the ski hill, offering rooms, studios and suites. Indoor pool, 2 outdoor hot tubs and sauna.
D **Barbara Lynn's B&B**, just off the highway close to town, T250-4236027. 10 small rooms, hot tub, mainly shared baths.
D **Snow Valley Motel**, Hwy 3/10th St, T250-4234421, www.snowvalleymotel.com. One of many motels on the highway downtown, with recently renovated rooms, suites and kitchenette rooms.
E **Raging Elk Hostel**, 892 6th Av, T250-4236811, www.ragingelk.com. An excellent hostel, with dorms, semi-private and private rooms, and a sauna.
E **SameSun International Lodge**, Hwy 3, T250-4234492, www.samesun.com. One of the finest hostels you will ever see. A beautiful, spacious building with dorms and nice private rooms with en suite baths, plus all facilities including a games room, hot tub, sauna and even a piano.

Camping
Mount Fernie Provincial Park, 2 km west on Park Rd, 40 nice sites, wooded and private.

⊘ Eating

Kamloops *p184*
♕♕♕ **Chapters Viewpoint**, 610 W Columbia St, Panorama Inn, T250-3743224. A long-term favourite, offering fantastic views, outdoor seating and a menu that ranges from steak and seafood to salad and pasta, with an equally wide price range.
♕♕♕ **This Old Steak and Fish House**, 172 Battle St, T250-3743227. A heritage house with a romantic atmosphere, a lovely garden patio and a good menu that again focuses on seafood and steak.
♕♕ **Hot House Bistro**, 438 Victoria St, T250-3744604. Vegetarian cuisine with a laid-back atmosphere, and international food from Mexican to Indian.

♕♕ **Warunee's Thai Restaurant**, 413 Tranquille Rd, north shore, T250-5547080. Excellent Thai food, friendly service.
♕ **Cowboy Coffee**, 229 Victoria St. The best coffee. Try the cambozola panini.

The Shuswap *p184*
♕♕ **Mino's**, 720 22nd St, Salmon Arm. Good Greek fare.
♕♕ **Moose Mulligans**, Super 8 Motel on the marina, Sicamous. Good pub food and draft beer.

Revelstoke *p185*
♕♕♕ **112 Restaurant**, Regent Inn, 112 1st Av, T250-8372107. The best choice for fine dining.
♕♕ **Bad Paul's Roadhouse Grill**, 114 Mackenzie Av, T250-8379575. One for the carnivores, specializing in prime rib.
♕♕ **Woolsey Creek**, 600-2nd St, T250-8375500. The number one choice for food that is international, imaginative and well-executed. The interior is colourful and comfortable, with couches and good art on the walls, and there's a patio.
♕ **The Ol' Frontier**, corner Hwy 1 and Hwy 23 N, T250-8375119. With its Wild West saloon theme, this is a fun place for a large breakfast.

Golden *p186*
♕♕♕ **Cedar House**, about 4.5 km south at 735 Hefti Rd, T250-3444679. Casual Pacific Rim-style fine dining in a quiet, forested area with a lovely patio.
♕♕♕ **Eagle's Eye View**, T1866-7545425. At the very top of the ski hill, accessible via the gondola (free with reservation), this is the highest restaurant in Canada, offering fine dining and even finer views from a timber-frame building with masses of glass and a stone fireplace.
♕♕ **Apostoles Restorante**, 427 9th Av, T250-3444906. Authentic Greek cuisine at very reasonable prices.
♕♕ **Kicking Horse Grill**, 1105 9th St, T250-3442330. International fusion cuisine.
♕ **Jenny's Java Express and Internet Café**, 420 9th Av. Coffee and internet.

Hedley *p187*

¶ **Gold Dust Pub**, off Hwy 3 east of town. The best bet for food and drink.

Christina Lake *p187*
¶ **Jimmy Beans**, 9 Johnson Rd, T250-4476610. Great coffee and light food, internet access, and a pleasant garden and deck. A good place to stop for a break if you're driving through the area.

Rossland *p188*
¶¶ **The Grind**, Columbia/St Paul, T250-3622280. Excellent good-value food, prepared by a top chef, great coffee too. Open for breakfast and lunch, with views from the deck.
¶¶ **Gypsy at Red**, 4430 Red Mountain Rd, at the ski hill, T250-3623347. World cuisine with a West Coast edge.
¶¶ **Idgies**, Washington/2nd Av, T250-3625333. A long-standing favourite with a mixed menu that covers meat, seafood and pasta dishes.
¶ **Goldrush Café**, 2063 Washington St, T250-3625333. A bakery with sourdough bread, a decent bookstore and internet.
¶ **Sunshine Café**, 2116 Columbia St, T250-3627630, 0730-1500 only. Good for breakfast and panini.

Fernie *p189*
¶¶¶ **Lizard Creek Lodge**, Fernie Alpine Resort, T250-4232057, www.lizard creek.com. With a dress code of 'smart casual' and a menu to match, this joint includes the usual kind of steak and sea-food options, plus some more interesting choices, such as buffalo and duck.
¶¶¶ **The Old Elevator**, 291 1st Av, T250-4237115. A down-to-earth but exciting option featuring a range of dishes with an emphasis on creative sauces, plus tapas in the lounge.
¶¶ **The Curry Bowl**, Hwy 3 W. Indian, Japanese, Vietnamese and Thai food.
¶ **Mug Shots Bistro**, 592 3rd Av. Good breakfast and coffee, fresh juices, used books, internet ($5 per hr).

🍸 Bars and clubs

The Shuswap *p184*
Hideaway Pub, 995 Lakeshore, Salmon Arm. A nice spot where connoisseurs can sample excellent locally-brewed Crannog organic beers on tap.

Revelstoke *p185*
Big Eddy Inn, 2108 Big Eddy Rd. The best pub in town, with decent food.

Rossland *p188*
Flying Steamshovel Inn, Washington/ 2nd Av, T250-3627373. More of a day-time pub than the **Powder Keg** and a more pleasant space. Small, intimate and very light, with a pool table, a good selection of beer on tap, drink specials and good pub food.
Powder Keg Pub, Prestige Inn, 1919 Columbia Av. The most happening spot in town, with frequent live music and pool tables. Frequently packed to the gills.
Rock Cut Neighborhood Pub, 3052 Highway 3B, across from ski hill, T250-3625814. Patio with great view, pub food, no smoking.

Fernie *p189*
Eldorado Lounge, 2nd Av, Downtown. The best choice for dancing.
Grizzly Bar, above the Daylodge at the ski hill. The après-ski bar of choice.
Pub Bar and Grill, Park Place Lodge. A watering hole for locals and ski-bums alike

🎵 Entertainment

Kamloops *p184*
For information and tickets, call **Kamloops Live!** on T250-3745483.
Kamloops Art Gallery, 465 Victoria St, by the library, www.galleries.bc.ca/kamloops, Tue-Sat 1000-1700, $3. One of the town's finest features, with a large collection of quality works by inspiring artists.

☸ Festivals and events

Kamloops *p184*
Aug Kamloops Pow Wow, T250-8289700, 3rd weekend at the Special Events Facility. One of the best pow wows in the country. Everyone is welcome and it's the most enjoyable way to get an authentic taste of contemporary aboriginal culture. Brightly clad dancers from over 30 different bands across Canada and northern US perform to the rhythms of drumming and singing.

The Shuswap *p184*
For 3 weeks in summer, the excellent 30 year-old **Caravan Farm Theatre**, T250-5468533, www.caravanfarmtheatre.com, stages daily outdoor shows at Knob Hill, east of Enderby to the south. For 10 days before New Year's Eve they also put on a touring play, which involves a sleigh ride to different sets throughout the forest.
Aug For 3 days in late Aug, the superb **Roots and Blues Festival**, T250-8334096, www.rootsandblues.ca, brings Salmon Arm to life, with acts performing on 6 stages, $125 at gate, $40-55 per day. Camping is available.

Revelstoke *p185*
Jun Blues Festival, T250-8375500, www.mountainbeats.com. 3rd weekend.
Sep Mountain Arts Festival, T250-8375345, www.mountainfest.com. 3 days of events including street performers and craft fairs.

Fernie *p189*
Apr The **Powder, Peddle, Paddle Relay Race** marks the closure of the ski hill and is an excuse for a big party, disguised as a fun variation on the gruelling triathlon.
Sep Taste of Fernie, T250-4234842, gives attendees a chance to sample the fare of local restaurants, with live entertainment throughout the day.

▲▲ Activities and tours

Fraser Canyon *p183*
Rafting
Fraser River Raft Expeditions, on the riverside at the south end of Yale, T1800-3637238, www.fraserraft.com. A small, friendly company offering 1- to 8-day rafting tours anywhere in the valley, starting at $120 a day.
Kumsheen Raft Adventures, T250-4552296, www.kumsheen.com. The most professional operation around, with every type of trip on all the local rivers, plus gear rental. All-inclusive packages involve a stay at their beautiful **Adventure Resort**, 5 km north of Lytton, which has deluxe cabin tents, a campground, trails, restaurant, fabulous pool and spa.

Kamloops *p184*
Fishing
This area is famous for its trout fishing, with over 200 nearby lakes. Among the closest and best are **Paul Lake**, 23 km northeast, and **Lac Le Jeune**, 35 km south.

Fossil hunting
Kamloops Geological-Palaeontology Tours, 1075 Calmar Pl, T250-5542401. Guided tours in the mountains, looking for crystals, fossils and minerals.

Golf
There are 11 golf courses in the area, including **Rivershore**, T250-5734622, and **The Dunes**, T250-5793300. Visit www.golfkamloops.com for more information.

Mountain biking
There are a lot of good trails around Kamloops and it's a great way to explore the weird landscapes. The best places are **Sun Peaks** and **Lac Dubois**.
Full Boar Bike Store, 310 Victoria and at Sun Peaks Resort, rents out bikes and can provide information.

Sun Peaks Ski Resort, www.sunpeaks resort.com. Follow Hwy 5 north for 19 km to Heffley Creek, then right for 31 km at the Sun Peaks sign. There is a shuttle bus from Kamloops airport, $34 one way, T1800-8073257, daily Nov 19-Apr 17, 0830-1530. With 117 runs up to 8 km long on 1500 ha of skiable terrain, which includes vast alpine bowls and a 881-m vertical drop, Sun Peaks is BC's second largest ski area, serviced by 11 lifts capable of handling 11,000 skiers per hr. The breakdown favours experienced skiers and snowboarders, with 58% of runs intermediate and 33% expert. There's also a kids' terrain garden, 40 km of cross-country trails and the bonus of 2000 hrs of sun per year (thus the name). The village has 15 cafés and restaurants. There's also lift-assisted mountain biking and hiking in the summer. Lift passes are $59/$49/$40 per day, $10 for cross country.

The Shuswap *p184*
Houseboats
All the rental companies are clustered together on the marina in Sicamous, so you can shop around and see what you're getting. Unfortunately, they're prohibitively expensive, unless you're with a group, and can only rented by the week.
Bluewater Houseboat Rentals, T250-8362255, www.bluewaterhouseboats.ca. There are so many houseboat rental companies, but this outfit is as good as any. Best value is the 4-day midweek rate of $995 for up to 8, with kitchen.

Watersports
Adams River Rafting, 3993 Squilax-Anglemont Rd, Scotch Creek, T250-9552447, www.adamsriverrafting.com. $52 for a 3-hr trip on the Adams River.
Get Wet Rentals Ltd, 1130 Riverside Av, Sicamous, T250-8363517. All kinds of water toys for rent, including jet-skis for $250 per day and canoes for $40 per day.

Sicamous Water Tours and Charters, T250-8364318. 2-hr tours with narrative and petroglyph-viewing, $80 for 4 people. They also act as a water taxi.

Revelstoke *p185*
Hiking
A 10-km trail up Mt Revelstoke starts behind the Railway Museum. It can also be snowshoed in winter. **Keystone and Standard Basins** is a first-class 14.6- or 22-km hike with grand views of the Columbia Range, but the trailhead is 63 km away. Ask at the information centre if interested.
Arrow Adventure Tours, T250-8376014, www.arrowadventuretours.com. Tours in the Selkirk and Monashee Mountains.

Mountain biking
Revelstoke has some great trails. Get a map from the information centre.
High Country Cycle and Sports, 188 MacKenzie Av. Rentals, tours and advice.

Skiing
Powder Springs, 4 km south of town, T1800-9914455, www.catpowder.com. Very small and low-profile, with only 1 lift, it's practically free if you're staying at the hostel. Otherwise a lift pass is $28. Most locals go backcountry skiing across the river on the 'Five Fingers' of Mt McPherson. This is the best, most convenient spot, with northern exposure insuring good snow conditions.
Canadian Mountain Holidays, T250-7627100, www.cmhski.com, serv es one of the biggest heliskiing terrains in the world, covering 14,000 sq km ($800 a day).
Cat Powder, 200 3rd St W, T250-8375151, www.catpowder.com. Cat-skiing is huge around here. Book before Jul and pay about $850 for 2 days of skiing, including food and accommodation.
Freespirit Sports, 203 1st St W. All manner of winter sport rentals.
High Country Sports, 118 Mackenzie Av, T250-8140090. Cross-country and back-country gear rentals.

Golden *p186*
Hang-gliding
Mt Seven is considered Canada's premier site, hosting the annual Western Canadian Hang Gliding Championships and the Canadian National Paragliding Championships in Aug.

Rafting
Between May and Sep the aquamarine untamed **Kicking Horse River** provides class III and IV rapids for exciting rafting and kayaking. Gentler trips explore the unique wetlands of the **Columbia River**. **Kootenay River Runners**, T250-3476595, www.raftingtherockies.com. **Wet'n'wild**, 1509 Lafontaine Rd, T250-3446546, www.wetnwild.bc.ca.

Skiing
Kicking Horse Ski Resort, 13 km from Golden, T250-4395424, www.kicking horseresort.com, open mid-Dec to mid-Apr, $59/49/27. The most recent large ski hill to be built in BC, offering 1112 ha of award-winning powder, a pair of alpine bowls and a vertical rise of 1260 m. The state-of-the-art 8-person Golden Eagle Express Gondola whisks skiers up 3413 m in 12 mins to the highest peak, from where 106 runs (20% beginner, 20% intermediate, 45% advanced and 15% expert) fan out into the wide-open spaces. There are several lodges on the hill for those who want to stay, and all the usual services. In summer the lifts stay open for alpine hiking and diners. **Mount Seven Taxi**, T250-3445237, runs a shuttle from town ($6 return) in winter and summer.

There are 14 km of cross-country skiing trails at **Dawn Mountain**.

Tour operators
Alpenglow Aviation Inc, 210 Fisher Rd, T250-3447117. $145 for 45-min flightseeing tours over the Rockies. **Higher Plateau**, 804 Park Dr. Used ice-climbing equipment and rentals. There are over 60 routes in the area.

Golden Mountain Adventures, T403-2444795, www.adventurerockies.com. A big company covering many needs: rafting, biking, hang-gliding, snow mobiling, birdwatching, skiing. **Selkirk Source for Sports**, 504 9th Av, T250-3442966. Mountain bike rentals, service and information on local trails.

Christina Lake *p187*
Wild Ways Adventure Sports, 1925 Hwy 3, T250-4476561, www.wildways.com. Bikes and general outdoor gear to buy or rent, and mountain-biking tours. Kayak rentals, tours, instruction and information.

Rossland *p188*
Mountain biking and hiking
There are several good hiking and skiing trails right from town but Rossland is especially famous for its biking, with over 100 km of trails. **Old Glory** is a great 8-hr return hike to 360° views of the mountain ranges. The trailhead is 11 km north of town on Highway 3B. **High Mountain Adventures**, T250-3625342, www.highmtntours.com. Biking, hiking and snowmobile tours. **Revolution**, 2044 Columbia Av, T250-3625688. Information and rentals.

Skiing
Red Mountain Ski Hill, 3 km W on Hwy 3B, T250-3627384, www.redresort.com. Open Nov-Apr. A day pass is $52. This is a great hill for experts with 45% black diamond runs and lots of tree skiing. The vertical gain is an impressive 880 m but a relatively low elevation can cause problems when the weather is uncooperative. The **Paradise** area is good for beginners and very pretty, with lots of views and sun. Much development is planned, including 1400 sleeping units and 70,000 sq ft of commercial space plus new lifts.

For cross-country skiing there are the **Black Jack** trails across from Red Mountain, T250-3645445, www.skiblack jack.ca, $9 day pass. Rentals available at the hill, or at **Powder Hound**, 2040

Columbia Av, who also rent bikes. Shuttles to the hill leave the **Prestige Hotel** from 0825, the last one returning at 2115. Hitching is fairly easy.
Adrenaline Adventures, T250-3627421, www.adrenalineadventures.ca. Runs a shuttle from Spokane and Castlegar to Rossland and Red Resort, multi-day tours.
Rossland Mountain Adventures, T250-3687375, www.rosslandmt adventures.com. Ski touring and hiking.

Swimming

Trail Aquatic and Leisure Centre, 1875 Columbia Av, Trail, T250-3686484. The best facilities in the Kootenays, including a large, unchlorinated pool, plus sauna, hot tub and fitness room.

Fernie *p189*

Mountain biking

Fernie is famed for its biking and hiking, much of it in **Mt Fernie Provincial Park**, and at the ski hill.
Bike and Ski Base, 442 2nd Av. Rentals.
Fernie Fat Tire Adventures, T250-4237849, www.ferniefattire.com. Back-country tours in BC and the Rockies.

Rafting

Mountain High River Adventure, T1877-4234555, www.raftfernie.com. Gentle or whitewater rafting and kayak trips on the Elk River, from $89/day.

Skiing

Fernie Alpine Resort, T250-4234655, www.skifernie.com. 7 km from town, connected by a convenient shuttle bus, the hill has been a secret among ski-bums for some time and remains a great choice for those who know their skiing and would rather stay in a real town, with good restaurants and bars and excellent cheap accommodation, rather than a purpose-built resort. A ski pass is $69/$56/$50.
Fernie Wilderness Adventures, T250-4236704, www.fernieadventures.com. Backcountry skiing, cat-skiing, hiking, fishing and lodge accommodation.

Mountain Pursuits, T250-4236739, www.mountainpursuits.com. Year-round guided hiking, skiing and climbing.

 ## Transport

TransCanada Highway *p182*
Bus
Buses leave **Vancouver** at 0630, 1345 and 1845, and travel along the Coquihalla Hwy to Kamloops, then the TransCanada east, stopping at **Hope** (2 hrs), **Kamloops** (4.5 hrs), **Salmon Arm** (7 hrs), **Revelstoke** (8.5 hrs), **Golden** (11.5 hrs).

In the other direction, buses leave Banff at 0055, 0900, 1500 and 2100, stopping at **Golden** (2 hrs 20 mins), **Revelstoke** (3 hrs 40 mins), **Salmon Arm** (5 hrs), **Kamloops** (7 hrs) and **Vancouver** (12 hrs). The 0055 bus is via **Kelowna**.

Fraser Canyon *p183*
Greyhound runs 2 daily buses from **Vancouver** to **Cache Creek**, stopping at all towns along the way. They leave at 0800 and 1745.

Kamloops *p184*
Air
The airport is 6 km northwest of town on Tranquille Rd. The **Airport Shuttle**, T250-3144803, runs to Downtown, $10. **Air Canada**, www.aircanada.com, flies daily to **Vancouver** and **Calgary**; **Central Mountain Air**, T1888-8658585, www.flycma.com, flies daily to **Vancouver** and **Prince George**.

Bus
Local BC Transit bus No 1 (Tranquille) goes to the North Shore, airport and city park; bus No 6 (Cityloop) runs round town to the youth hostel and Greyhound station.

Long distance The Greyhound station is at 725 Notredame Dr, T250-3741212, with 7 daily buses to **Vancouver**, $55; 4 to **Calgary**, $89; 4 to **Prince George**, $77; and 5 to **Kelowna**, $30.

Train

Via Rail, T1800-5618630, www.viarail.ca , runs west to **Vancouver** on Thu, Sat and Mon, $65; to **Jasper** and east on Wed, Sat and Mon.

Taxi

Kami Cabs, T250-5541377; **Yellow Cabs**, T250-3743333.

The Shuswap *p184*
Bus

Salmon Arm receives 4 buses daily to/ from **Kamloops** or **Kelowna**, $21, and several to/from **Vancouver**, $68.

Revelstoke *p185*
Bus

The Greyhound station, T250-8375874, is on Fraser Dr, just off Hwy 1. There are 4 buses daily to **Vancouver**, $83, and 4 to **Calgary** via **Banff**, $55.

Golden *p186*
Bus

The Greyhound station is at 1050 Hwy 1, T250-3442917, with 4 buses daily to **Vancouver** (1 via Vernon), $105; 3 to **Calgary**, $45; and 1 to **Invermere**.

Crowsnest Highway *p186*
Bus

Greyhound runs 2 daily buses which take the Coquihalla Hwy to Kelowna, then join Hwy 3 at Rock Creek, and follow the Crowsnest east to Fernie and beyond, via Nelson. Journey times from Vancouver are: **Kelowna** (5½ hrs), **Rock Creek** (9 hrs), **Midway** (9 hrs 10 mins), **Greenwood** (9 hrs 25 mins), **Grand Forks** (10 hrs), **Christina Lake** (11 hrs), **Castlegar** (12 hrs), **Nelson** (13 hrs), **Creston** (16½ hrs), **Cranbrook** (18 hrs), **Fernie** (19.5 hrs).

Rossland *p188*
Bus

The Greyhound station is in Trail at 1355 Bay Av, T250-3688400. Local buses

between Rossland and **Trail** leave every 1½ hrs from Cedar/Spokane in Trail, from Jubilee/St Paul in Rossland. The bus times tend to be at inconvenient times, so you might need a taxi; **Champion Cabs**, T250-3643344, charge about $15.

Fernie *p189*
Bus

The **Greyhound** station is at **Parks Place Lodge**, 742 Hwy 3, T250-4236871, with 2 buses daily in each direction. A shuttle to the ski hill leaves from several spots in town including the hostels. **Rocky Mountain Sky Shuttle**, www.rocky mountainskyshuttle.com, runs a shuttle to Fernie from **Calgary** and **Cranbrook** airports.

❶ Directory

Kamloops *p184*

Canada Post 217 Seymour St. **Internet** free at the library. **Laundry** McCleaners Laundromats, 437 Seymour. **Library** 465 Victoria St. **Medical** Royal Inland Hospital, 311 Columbia St, T250-3745111.

Revelstoke *p185*

Canada Post 301 3rd St. **Internet** Samesun Hostel (see Sleeping, p190), free for guests. **Laundry** Family Laundry, 409 W 1st St. **Medical services** Queen Victoria Hospital, 1200 Newlands Rd, T250-8372131.

Rossland *p188*

Canada Post 2090 Columbia Av. **Internet** Goldrush Café, 2063 Washington. **Laundry** Beside the Goldrush. **Medical services** Trail Regional Hospital, 1200 Hospital Bench, Trail, T250-3683311.

Fernie *p189*

Canada Post 491 3rd Av. **Internet** Mug Shots Bistro. **Library** 492 3rd Av. **Medical services** Sparling East Medical Centre, 402 2nd Av T250-4234442.

Okanagan

Sitting in the rain shadow of the Cascade and Coast Mountains, the Okanagan Valley receives the most sun and least rain in Canada. The barren hills, rocky bluffs and subdued but striking colours caused by such aridity possess an eerie beauty that intensifies towards the south, where Osoyoos contains Canada's only functioning desert ecosystem. The climate is ideal for the beach and watersports, as well as for orchards and vineyards, with plenty of great wineries to tour. The

⊘ **Getting there** Bus or car.
⊖ **Getting around** Bus or car.
⊖ **Time required** 2-4 days.
⊛ **Weather** Hot in summer, cold in winter.
⊜ **Sleeping** All bases covered.
⊘ **Eating** Disappointing.
▲▲ **Activities and tours** Wineries, watersports, skiing.
★ **Don't miss** Touring the wineries ▶▶ *p205*.

combination of sun, warm water and ample stretches of lakefront naturally transforms the region into one big holiday resort every summer, as well as attracting a sizeable retirement community. As ever, those who thrive on outdoor activities will find plenty on offer, including three major ski-hills. Kelowna is the main town and obvious destination, though sleepy Naramata might appeal to those who value tranquillity.

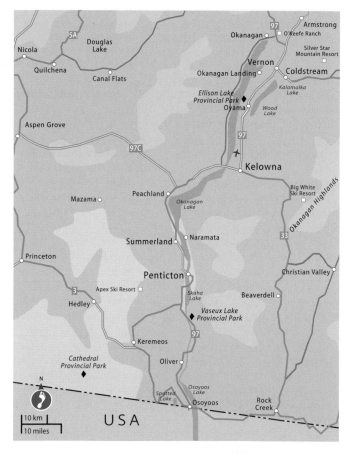

Ins and outs

Getting there and around

Kelowna International Airport (YLW), T250-7655125, 10 km north on Highway 97, receives daily flights from Vancouver, Victoria, Calgary and Seattle. Regular shuttles and city buses run to Downtown. Osoyoos receives daily buses from Vancouver via Keremeos and Penticton.

Kelowna's Downtown is small enough to explore on foot, but some of the attractions require transport. A network of local buses operates from a depot on Queensway between Ellis and Pandosy. All other towns are small enough to walk around. ● ⟩⟩ *p216.*

Best time to visit

Most people flock to the Okanagan's beaches in summer but spring and autumn are even better, not only to avoid the excessive summer crowds, but also to catch blossom and harvest times. The former runs from roughly mid-April to mid-May, the latter continues as late as the end of October. Coinciding nicely with these periods are the **Spring Wine Festival** in early May and the **Fall Wine Festival** in late September. ● ⟩⟩ *p211.*

Climate

The Okanagan's tinder-dry conditions make this region particularly vulnerable to the numerous and devastating forest fires that plague BC every summer. In August 2003, the Okanagan Mountain forest fire reached the very edge of Kelowna, destroying many homes as well as 10 of the 16 historic Myra Canyon Tresles (see p203).

Tourist information

Each of the Okanagan towns has its own visitor information centre, the biggest and best being the handily located **Tourism Kelowna** ⓘ *544 Harvey Av, T250-8611515, www.tourism kelowna.com; summer Mon-Fri 0800-1800, Sat-Sun 0900-1800; winter Mon-Fri 0800-1700, Sat-Sun 1000-1500.* **Penticton's Centre** ⓘ *553 Railway St, T4934055, www.penticton.ca,* contains a wine centre. There are also a number of useful free magazines available, including the tourist board's guide and a *Where* guide.

Kelowna ●●●●●●●▲●● ⟩⟩ *pp207-216.*

The Okanagan's biggest and most central town, Kelowna offers more recreational and cultural possibilities than its neighbours, but also more of the crowds and brash commercialism that can detract from the region's natural charms. Once you get away from the ugly highway (here called Harvey) and escape the characterless grid of malls and housing estates, there is plenty to discover. Beyond the pretty Downtown is a green belt of orchards, vineyards and golf courses, with some decent walks including the outstanding Myra Canyon section of the Kettle Valley Railway (see p214). There are wineries in town, more nearby in Westbank, and the major ski hill at **Big White Ski Resort** is within striking distance (see p213).

Downtown and Cultural District

Kelowna's Downtown, decorated in summer with hanging flower-baskets, is a pleasant place for a stroll. Most of the shops and restaurants cluster around Bernard Avenue, which heads west to meet the lake close to three of the city's landmarks: a white sculpture called *The Sails,* a model of the legendary lake monster, *Ogopogo,* and the *MV Fintry Queen,* a 1948 paddle-wheeler. To the south is the lakefront **City Park**, a big green area fronted by a beach, perfect for enjoying the stunning views across the lake, with frequent events and live music.

North of Bernard, a waterfront walkway leads past the yachts and sailboats in the marina to an area roughly bounded by Water and Ellis streets and Queensway and Cawston avenues, known as the **Cultural District**. Old warehouses and other interesting buildings are being reclaimed by artistic causes or replaced by modern cultural institutions. Within a few blocks are the impressive library, the main sports and music venue, **Skyreach Place**, a new **Community Arts Centre**, plus several museums, theatres and art galleries. ⊕ ►► *p211*.

The **BC Orchard Industry Museum** ⓘ *1304 Ellis, T250-7630433, by donation*, and **Wine Museum**, T250-8680441, are situated together in the restored brick Laurel Packinghouse, built in 1917. The former has displays on the history of the fruit business and a model railway. The latter is the best place to find out about local wines and which wineries to visit.

The lakeside promenade runs without interruption from City Park north to **Waterfront Park**, an area of lagoons, beaches, trails and lawns, and an outdoor stage that is the main focus for live music and events during the summer. Further north at the end of Ellis Street, are the **Rotary Marshes**, a good place for birdwatching, and the 235-ha **Knox Mountain Park**, with a trail that climbs high up to yield unbeatable views of the town, lake, floating bridge and valley.

Lakeshore

Considering the length of its lakefront, Kelowna has a disappointing lack of decent public beaches. Apart from City Park, the town's most popular beaches are south of the centre along Lakeshore Road, via Pandosy Street. **Gyro Beach**, popular with youngsters and posers, is where you're most likely to hire waterskis, jet skis and other watersports equipment. **Rotary Beach** is popular with windsurfers. Both are small and crowded. For something more private, look out for the public beach access signs, leading to tiny patches between the private beaches that have snapped up most of the sand.

Further south is one end of the **Mission Creek Greenway**, a lovely 18-km pathway that follows the course of the lake's main artery right through the **Father Pandosy Mission** ⓘ *3685 Benvoulin Rd, Apr-Oct*, which preserves eight hand-hewn log buildings, four dating back to the original settlement. At the very end of Lakeshore Drive is the 10,500- ha **Okanagan Mountain Provincial Park**. Many trails lead through the semi-arid hillsides to some superb sub-alpine forests.

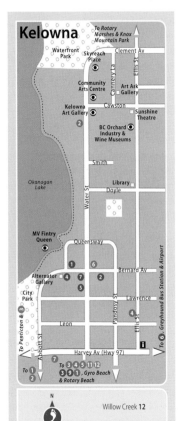

Kelowna

100 metres
100 yards

Sleeping
Abbott On The Lake 2
Beach House B&B 1
Kelowna International
Hostel 3
Lakeshore Inn 4
Royal Anne 6
Same Sun International
Hostel 7

Camping
Hiawatha RV Park 11

Willow Creek 12

Eating
Bean Scene 1
Bohemian Café 2
Fresco's 5
Joey Tomato's 6
Lakeside Dining 3
Siam Orchid 7
The Teahouse 9
Vintropolis 4

Bars & clubs
McCulloch Station 1
Pier Pub 3
Rose's Pub 2
Tonics Pub & Grill 4

British Columbia Okanagan

Background

Kettle Valley Railway

When silver was struck in the Kootenays, a railway was needed to help exploit the finds. The Kettle Valley Railway (KVR) became 'the most expensive railroad ever built' due to the virtually impenetrable terrain that had to be conquered, using tools no more sophisticated than hand-picks and shovels. Completed in 1916, this outstanding accomplishment was plagued by heavy snow and avalanches in winter, then washouts and rockslides in spring. Like most of Canada's great rail lines, the modern obsession with cars eventually left it redundant, with the last train running in 1989.

Today some 600 km of the KVR are suitable for hiking. The best sections are between Penticton and Kelowna, especially Myra Canyon Trestles just outside the latter. Also worthy of note are the Othello Tunnels just outside Hope. For more information, visit the Kettle River Museum in Midway (see p187), or www.kettlevalley railway.org. Useful books include B Sanford's McCulloch's *Wonder* and D & S Langford's *Steel Rails and Iron Men*, and *Cycling the KVR*.

British Columbia Okanagan

Vernon and around 🍴🏃🚴🏕️🏛️🎭 » *pp207-216.*

If moving north from Kelowna, Highway 97 is a pleasant enough drive, half of it right alongside Wood and Kalamalka Lakes. However, for a real taste of the Okanagan, away from the hustle and bustle, a highly recommended route is the much slower road along the west bank of Okanagan Lake (cross the floating bridge then follow signs to Bear and Fintry provincial parks). On this route, it might be tempting to bypass **Vernon** altogether: oldest of the Okanagan towns it is also the least interesting. Apart from a first-class hostel, all the things worth noting here are far from town. **Ellison Lake Provincial Park**, T250-4922424, has some of the least spoilt beaches around Okanagan Lake. **Silver Star Mountain Resort** (see Activities and tours, p214) is one of the province's most charming ski hills. The **Okanagan Highlands**, east of Oyama, offer a wealth of wilderness hiking and camping around small trout-filled lakes. And 12 km north on Highway 97 is the **O'Keefe Ranch** ① *T250-5421415, www.okeeferanch.bc.ca, May-Oct 0900-2000, $10, $8 child*, a popular 20-ha site with original buildings and furnishings from 1867, as well as animals, a restaurant and a decent gift shop. For more details on any of these, ask at the **Visitor Information Centre** ① *701 Highway 97, south of town, T250-5421415, www.vernontourism.com*. An additional summer-only information centre is north at 6326 Highway 97, T250-5452959.

South of Kelowna ⊖⊘⊕⊗⊛⊙▲⊡⊙ ›› *pp207-216.*

Penticton and around

Every summer, the otherwise bland town of Penticton transforms into a hectic, throbbing beach-fest, attracting both families and a younger crowd, who come to party and show off their tans. Sandwiched between two lakes, the town has plenty of sand and water to go round, and temperatures regularly exceed 35°C, sometimes reaching up to 45°C. Most of the action happens on **Okanagan Beach** around the **Lakeshore Resort**, where gear can be rented for a multitude of watersports, see Activities and tours, p214. The beaches around **Skaha Lake** to the south are more family orientated, and there's a nude beach at **3 Mile** towards Naramata.

Those bored of the beach scene will find plenty of other activities: tubing down the channel between the two lakes, skiing at **Apex Ski Resort** (33 km to the west), watching for birds, bighorn sheep and rattle-snakes at **Vaseux Lake Provincial Park** (15 km south), or rock-climbing at **Skaha Bluffs**. Seek advice at the helpful **Visitor Information Centre** ① *553 Railway St, T250-4934055, www.penticton.ca, www.penticton.org, daily 0800-1800*. Also here is the **Wine Centre**, T250-4902006, whose extremely knowledgeable staff will advise you on local wineries. They also stock a broad range of Okanagan wines and do daily tastings.

The only local sight is the **SS Sicamous** ① *1099 Lakeshore Dr, on the beach, T250-4920403, summer 0900-2100, otherwise 1000-1600, $5, $1 child*, a fully restored and decked out 1914 paddle-steamer. For railway buffs the highlight is a working model of the Kettle Valley Railway (see p203). The only section of that line still in use is 15 km north in Summerland. From late May to early October the **Kettle Valley Railway Steam Train** ① *T250-4948422, www.kettlevalleyrail.org, $18 return, $11 child, $14 one-way for cyclists and hikers*, leaves Prairie Valley Station (take Prairie Valley Road from the Highway) at 1030 and 1330 on Saturday, Sunday and Monday, and on Thursday and Friday from July to September, covering just 10 km in two hours.

Naramata

For those who understandably love the Okanagan's climate, scenery, orchards and vineyards, but feel that its towns are all a little brash and overcrowded, the answer is Naramata, a sleepy little village about 16 km north of Penticton on the east side of Okanagan Lake, away from the highway. Its only drawback is the lack of a decent public beach. Surrounded by vineyards, this is the perfect place for a winery tour, which energetic visitors could even manage on foot. See p215 for a list of wineries.

Osoyoos

As Highway 97 heads south through the **Okanagan Valley**, the climate and scenery becomes increasingly arid. Osoyoos, a disappointingly ugly town set in a gloriously weird desert landscape of barren, scrub-covered hills, has Canada's lowest rainfall, highest temperatures and warmest water. Those entering from the Crowsnest Highway (see p186) have to descend rapidly via a series of steep switchbacks to the bottom of the valley. Views from the top highlight the town's superb position on **Osoyoos Lake**.

Driving on Highway 97, it's hard not to be charmed by the endless parade of highly successful orchards and wineries. Yet, before irrigation, most of this land was occupied by Canada's only living desert, an extension of the Great Basin Desert in the US, and part of the Sonoran Desert ecosystem that runs right down into Mexico. The **Desert Centre** ① *north of town, off Hwy 97 to Oliver, T250-4952470, www.desert.org, mid-Apr to mid-Oct, $6, $3 child*, aims to protect the small, fragile pocket that remains, supporting over 100 rare plants and

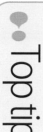

Top tips

Wine not?

A tour of some of the Okanagan's 65 or so wineries is highly recommended. The areas with the greatest concentration are Kelowna, Naramata and the 'golden mile' in Oliver, see Activities and tours, p212. Besides offering tours and tastings (usually open from spring to autumn), many of the wineries have gourmet bistros. Going on a tour rather than driving means that you can drink. If going alone, stop in at Kelowna's Visitor Information Centre or Wine Museum, or at Penticton's Wine Centre, for maps and a wealth of information; www.owfs.com is also useful, as is John Schreiner's book, *The Wineries of British Columbia*.

With the exception of some of the more southern vineyards, the Okanagan's growing season is too short for red wines. The region's reputation has been built on its German-style whites, Chardonnays, Pinot Noirs, sparkling wine and, increasingly, on its prize-winning ice wines. Made from grapes harvested at -8°C and pressed while still frozen, this dessert wine is sweet, strong and expensive.

British Columbia Okanagan

over 300 rare invertebrates, including about two dozen that are unique to the area. Fauna includes the great basin spadefoot toad, western rattlesnake and tiger salamander. The dominant flora are antelope brush and wild sage. There is over a mile of boardwalk from which to observe the desert's features but these are often so subtle that only the genuine enthusiasm of the guides brings the experience to life. Tours run every hour on the hour, the first and last offering the best chance of seeing animals. Night tours are offered once a month in summer. Many special tours are run, such as a birdwatching tour at 0630 on Wednesdays. The **Nk'mip Desert and Heritage Centre** ① *1000 Rancher Creek Rd, T250-4957901, www.nkmipdesert.com, May-Sep daily 0900-1900, otherwise 1000-1600, $7, $5 child*, links this unique desert environment to the aboriginal culture that flourished there. For more information contact the helpful **Visitor Information Centre** ① *9912 Hwy 3, T250-4955070, www.destinationosoyoos.com.*

Hiking in the Cathedral Lakes Park near Keremeos.

Some 11 km west of Osoyoos is the highly photogenic **Spotted Lake**, whose unusually high level of epsom salts, calcium and magnesium has resulted in large, almost circular blotches, which change colour dramatically according to weather conditions. Mud from the lake was used by natives to alleviate aches and pains, and was believed to heal the spirit, bringing youth and wisdom. Warring enemies met here in peace to soothe battle wounds. For commanding views of the Okanagan Valley head 20 km up Kabau Forestry Road, just west of here, to the 1-km **Mount Kabau Lookout Trail** or the **Tuculnuit Trail**, a 4-km loop.

Keremeos

Set within the most stunning stretch of Highway 3, 46 km west of Osoyoos, Keremeos enjoys a classic Okanagan landscape, surrounded by orchards, and is especially beautiful when the trees are in blossom. Justifiably dubbed the 'fruit stand capital of BC', the selection, quality and prices here are exceptional even by local standards. There is good golfing in the area and mountain biking at nearby Cawston but the major attraction in town is the **Keremeos Grist Mill and Gardens** ① *2 km north on Hwy 3A, T250-4992888, www.keremeos.com/gristmill, mid-May to mid-Oct 0930-1700, $5 including tour*. First built in 1877 to supply gold-rush pioneers travelling the Dewdney Trail, this mill has been lovingly restored as a very popular 'living museum'. Everything still functions as it did over a century ago: ancient strains of wheat grown on the premises are ground by the water-powered mill and baked into bread, which is sold in the café. People in costume do the work and give tours of the operation.

Cathedral Provincial Park

From the highway, 3 km west of Keremeos, Ashnola River Road leads over a historic red covered bridge and follows this pretty waterway 23 km to the Lakeview trailhead. This is the most direct of three routes into the spectacular 33,200-ha **Cathedral Provincial Park**. It is a steep six- or seven-hour hike (or $85 return transfer with Cathedral Lakes Lodge, see Sleeping, p209), with 1300 m elevation gain in 16 km. From the near desert of the Okanagan, the landscape changes to lush cedar and Douglas fir, then to pine, spruce, balsam fir and larch, finally climbing above the tree line to gain magnificent uninterrupted panoramas of the Cascade Mountains. It is well worth the effort for this is a chance to view paradise. Seven beautiful alpine lakes, their turquoise waters emphasized by the surrounding sharp granite peaks, are within easy walking distance; the trout fishing is excellent, and there's a good chance of seeing mountain goats, bighorn sheep and marmots.

Around **Quiniscoe Lake** are the main wilderness campground, a ranger station and a private lodge. From here a network of trails leads to the other lakes; **Ladyslipper Lake**, the furthest and prettiest, is a mere 2.5 km away. Beyond are a number of strange rock formations that can all be seen on a 10-km round trip. The **Devil's Woodpile** is a series of upright jointed basalt columns. **Stone City** is a bizarre moonscape of eroded quartz monoliths. The **Giant Cleft** is a massive split in the granite mountain face. **Quiniscoe** and **Pyramid** mountains can both be reached via **Glacier Lake**, each a 7-km round trip. A day's hike away is a wilderness campground at the **Haystack Lakes**. There is also a four-day hike to **Manning Park**.

● Sleeping

Kelowna *p201, map p202*
Kelowna has plenty of beds, though the mid-range choices and campgrounds are limited. Best of all are its 2 excellent hostels. If you're looking for a cheap motel, there are dozens stretching along the main drag on Harvey Av, but none stand out.
A Lakeshore Inn, 3756 Lakeshore Rd, T250-7634717, www.lakeshoreinn.com. Comfortable, pleasant rooms right on the lake, with a private stretch of sand, a swimming pool and kitchenettes.
A-B Beach House B&B, 188 Beach Av, T250-7632321, www.beachhousebedand breakfast.ca. 2 lovely rooms and 1 suite in a romantic historic house near Downtown. Private beach and wraparound deck.
B Abbott On The Lake, T250-7620221, 1986 Abbott St, www.abbottonthelake.com. A heritage house right on the lake close to Downtown, offering 2 suites and 2 rooms tastefully decorated with antiques. Full breakfast, private beach and hot tub.
B Royal Anne Hotel, 348 Bernard Av, T250-7632277, www.royalannehotel.com. Big rooms with balconies (best on 2nd floor) and views, in a handy Downtown location. Exercise room and saunas.
E Kelowna International Hostel, 2343 Pandosy St, T250-7636024, www.kelowna-hostel.bc.ca. Well located close to Downtown and the beach, this clean, friendly and helpful little hostel has dorms and private rooms with shared bath. Kitchen, lounge, laundry, internet, free pick-up from the bus station, even a free coffee and pancake breakfast.

E Same Sun International Hostel, 245 Harvey Av, T250-76 9814, www.same sun.com. This vast, very central building has 30 private rooms and 100 dorms with top facilities, including kitchen, common room, lockers and laundry. Shuttles run to **Big White Ski Resort**, for $18/$25 return, or they have a sister hostel in the Alpine Centre at the resort, see p213.

Camping
Hiawatha RV Park, 3787 Lakeshore Rd, T250-8614837. Open Mar-Oct. With heated pool and hot tub.
Okanagan Lake Provincial Park, 11 km north of Summerland, 45 km from Kelowna. North and south sites have different characters, but both are on the lake, with private pitches, and showers. In the 1950s thousands of non- native trees were planted here, such as Russian olive, Chinese elm and Lombardy poplar.
Provincial Park Campgrounds. For the best camping, head to 2 parks to the north on the lake's west shore. Cross the bridge and follow signs. Both are open Apr-Oct and extremely busy. **Bear Creek** at Km 9, has 122 sites on the lake, with showers. **Fintry**, at Km 32, has 100 sites amidst big trees on the lake.
Willow Creek Family Campground, 3316 Lakeshore Rd, T250-7626302. Open year-round and has its own beach.

Vernon and around *p203*
B Best Western, 3914 32nd St, T250-5453385. The best place to stay, with a beautiful, tropical courtyard, pool and restaurant with a genuine creek running

through the middle. $10 extra for a room with balcony overlooking the creek.

D Richmond House 1894 B&B, T250-5491767, 4008 Pleasant Valley Rd, www.richmondhousebandb.com. 3 pretty en suite rooms in an old house close to Downtown, with antique furnishings, lounge, veranda and hot tub.

D Schell Motel, 2810 35th St, T250-5451351. Good-value rooms with kitchenettes. Outdoor heated pool and hot tub. Close to Downtown.

E Lodged Inn HI Hostel, 3201 Pleasant Valley Rd, T250-5493742. A huge and beautiful 1894 home surrounded by gardens and trees. Fantastic interior with hardwood floors, a library, lounge, meeting room and kitchen. Dorms and private rooms. Activities arranged. Highly recommended.

Camping

Dutch's Tent and Trailer Court, 15408 Kalamalka Lake Rd, T250-5451023. Reasonable setting, conveniently close to the lake and Kal Beach. Open year round.

Ellison Provincial Park, 16 km southwest on Okanagan Lake. Take 25th Av west from Downtown and keep going straight. 71 private, wooded sites in a gorgeous park with hiking trails, great beaches, a playing field, and even an underwater park for snorkelling and diving.

Penticton and around *p204*

Penticton has a lot of hotels and motels so, though most are pretty dreary, finding a room shouldn't be a problem except during the Ironman Triathlon in Aug.

AL Penticton Lakeside Resort, 21 Lakeshore Dr, T250-4938221, www.rpb hotels.com. Luxury option in the best location, with pool, hot tub, balconies, bar, casino and a first-class restaurant.

A-B Sandman Hotel, 939 Burnaby Av W, T250-4937151, www.sandman.ca. Standard, reliable and well located. Kitchenettes, pool and hot tub.

C Crown Motel, 950 Lakeshore Dr, T250-4924092, www.crownmotel.com. Best

value of the many motels rubbing shoulders opposite the main beach. Reasonable-sized rooms with patios and BBQs and a heated outdoor pool.

E Penticton HI Hostel, 464 Ellis St, T250-4923992, www.hihostels.bc.ca. Friendly, well-run hostel in a Downtown building full of character. Dorms and private rooms with shared bath, kitchen, TV lounge, laundry, lockers, BBQ. Good for information.

Camping

Camp-Along Resort, 6 km south on Hwy 97, T250-4975584, www.campalong.com. Set in an apricot orchard, with a pool and good views of Skaha Lake.

Wright's Beach Camp, 4071 Skaha Lake Rd, T250-4927120. Quite ugly and cramped, despite trees and beach, but still about the best of the many in town around Skaha Lake.

Naramata *p204*

L Naramata Heritage Inn and Spa, T250-4966808, www.naramatainn.com. Hands down the finest place to stay in the valley, this lovingly restored historic building has a gorgeous interior, featuring hardwood floors and period furnishings. The 12 classic rooms have clawfoot tubs, and semi-private decks with wrought-iron furniture. Breakfast included.

C The Village Motel, 244 Robinson Av, T250-4965535. Very pleasant and friendly.

D BC Motel, 365 Robinson Av, T250-4965482. Another perfectly decent option.

Osoyoos *p204*

Osoyoos's rooms are greatly overpriced in summer and fill up quickly. The cheaper motels, mostly along the strip on Hwy 3, still sport 1970s decor and brown carpets.

A Burrowing Owl Winery, near Oliver, 8 km north of Osoyoos, then 3 km east, T1877-4980620, www.bovwine.ca. A new guesthouse featuring a swimming pool, patio and 10 luxurious suites whose private balconies offer views over the vineyards and valley. Breakfast included.

B Avalon Inn, 9106 Main St, T250-4956334. Small suites with kitchenettes and decks. New rooms are worth the extra.
C Spanish Fiesta/Falcon Motels, 7104/6 Main St, T250-4956833. Small reasonable rooms with kitchenettes, right on the lake with private stretch of beach. Swimming pool and jacuzzi.
D Villa Blanca B&B, 23640 Deerfoot Rd, 10 km east on Hwy 3, T250-4955334. Situated on the hilltop facing out over the valley, this is definitely the place to stay if you have transport and are happy to be out of town. The 3 rooms have private baths and great views.
D White Horse B&B, 8000 Hwy 3 W, T250-4952887. Another great location, just out of town. 3 rooms with private bath, patio and views.

Camping
Brook Vale Holiday Resort, 1219 Lakeshore Dr, T250-4957514. The last of many RV parks along this road, also with simple cabañas, bedding not supplied.
Haynes Point Provincial Park, follow Hwy 97 S, then look for signs. Beautifully located on a sand spit reaching out into the lake. Showers, flush toilets but sites are a bit too closely packed. The busiest provincial campground in BC, so reservations are essential.

Keremeos p206
D Login B&B, Hwy 3 W, T250-4992781, www.loginbnb.com. An attractive log house with pleasant rooms and views.
E Similkameen Back-Pack Shack, River Road, T250-4992318, www.hostelbc.com. Very handsome old farmhouse in a highly scenic but remote location, with 8 dorm beds in 2 rooms, and a shared kitchen. Pick up from the bus station.

Cathedral Provincial Park p206
LL-AL Cathedral Lakes Lodge, T250-4921606, www.cathedral-lakes-lodge.com. Unless you're camping, this is the only place to stay in the park. Rooms are $200 per person, including all meals, which are

all-you-can-eat style. A jeep ride to the top is $85 return per person, free if you get a room. Hot tub, and use of canoes. Open Jun to mid-Oct, reservations required. Campers can buy meals at the lodge.

Camping
There is wilderness camping at **Quiniscoe Lake**. There are also campsites below the Lakeview trailhead at **Buckhorn**, 2 km further down Ashnola River Rd (vehicle accessible), and at **Lake of the Woods**. Visitors should be prepared to rough it.

⊘ Eating

Kelowna p201, map p202
Some of the best dining is at the winery bistros, which often have great views but usually only offer lunch, see p213.
¶¶¶ **Fresco's**, 1560 Water St, T250-8688805. Exquisite fine dining usually ranked as the town's finest.
¶¶¶ **Lakeside Dining**, 500 Cook Rd, at the Eldorado Hotel, T250-7637500. A very satisfying eating experience in an intimate and atmospheric room with hardwood floors and an air of understated sophistication. Seafood and steaks but also some very reasonably priced pasta dishes and salads. There are views of the lake, especially from the summer patio, which is right on the water.
¶¶¶ **The Teahouse**, 3002 Dunster Rd, via Kelowna and east, T250-7129404. Far from Downtown but nicely set in an orchard, with a patio offering bucolic views, and a fine menu of French-influenced haute cuisine. Open for lunch and dinner.
¶¶ **Joey Tomato's**, 2475 Hwy 97 N, T250-8608999. Upbeat and popular, with a varied menu that touches most key bases, decent beer and a summer patio.
¶¶ **Siam Orchid Restaurant**, 279 Bernard Av, T250-8605600. Consistently good Thai food and large portions.
¶¶ **Vintropolis**, 231 Bernard Av, T250-7627682. Tapas dishes, and a large selection of wines by the bottle or glass.

Bean Scene, 274 Bernard Av. Casual, central and agreeably downbeat. Outside seating close to the beach.

Bohemian Café, 363 Bernard Av. Attractive and popular Downtown purveyor of good breakfasts and coffee.

Vernon and around *p203*

The Eclectic Med, 3117 32nd St, T250-5584646. Lives up to its name. The menu is impressively broad and varied; the decor is simple, tasteful and quite romantic. A little overpriced though.

DiVinos Ristorante Italiano, 3224 30th Av, T250-5493463. Fresh pasta and some exciting choices, such as sambuca prawns.

Merona's, 2905 29th St, T250-2604257. Intimidatingly large portions of good Greek food and cheap beer in surroundings that are nicer than the exterior suggests.

Bean Scene, 2923 30th Av. Casual Downtown spot for good coffee.

Little Tex, 3302 B 29th St, T250-5581919, www.littletex.ca. A cute and colourful, very casual café-style joint for fajitas, quesadillas and pizza.

Portillo, 2706 30th Av. Comfortable and attractive coffee shop slightly out of the centre. Good snacks and cakes. Nice views from the patio.

Penticton *p204*

Magnum's, Lakeside Resort, T250-4938221. An excellent reputation for fine dining in luxurious surroundings, with attentive service and prices that are surprisingly reasonable.

Salty's Beach House, 1000 Lakeshore Dr, T250-4935001. An eccentric, pricey, but extremely popular spot, resembling a beach shack, serving tasty seafood specialities from Mexico to Thailand.

Theo's, 687 Main St, T250-4924019, www.eatsquid.com. A Penticton institution. Vast and very popular, yet intimate and personal. Big portions of tasty, authentic Greek cuisine. An extensive wine list, good service and a patio for summer dining.

Elite, 340 Main St. An authentic diner, worth visiting for the atmosphere alone: horseshoe booths and decor that looks as if it hasn't changed since the place opened in 1927. Cheap breakfasts and other perennial favourites like grilled cheese sandwiches.

Green Beanz Café, 218 Martin St. The undisputed best choice for coffee, with an arty, downbeat atmosphere.

Naramata *p204*

Rock Oven Dining Room, Naramata Heritage Inn, T250-4966808. A very sophisticated location with tasting menus $60-90 and occasional live music. Enjoy a drink in the **Cobblestone Winebar**.

Mahinda's, at Lake Breeze Vineyards, 930 Summit Rd, T250-4965619, www.lake breezewinery.ca, Jul-Aug 1330-1530. Mediterranean-inspired dishes served on a lovely patio.

Naramata Pub, 986 Robinson. A local favourite, with a Kettle Valley Railway theme.

Osoyoos *p204*

The 2 pubs mentioned in Bars and clubs, below, are also good mid-range options.

The Sonora Room, Burrowing Owl Winery, T1877-4980620, summer only. A setting to die for, and a handsome room with vaulted wood ceiling, serving gourmet food.

Campo Marina, 5907 Main St, T250-4957650. Tue-Sun from 1700. Serves Italian cuisine.

Wildfire Grill, 8523 Main St, T250-4952215. Global cuisine, with a coffee bar-bistro next door.

Big Banana Juice and Smoothie Bar, 6511 Main St. Health food and juices.

Keremeos *p206*

Pasta Trading Post, 629 7th Av, T250-4992933. Antiques-store turned restaurant, specializing in steak and seafood, with a garden patio, and a couple of B&B-style rooms (**C**).

ⓘ Bars and clubs

Kelowna *p201, map p202*
McCulloch Station, McCulloch Rd. Out of the way but pleasant and old-fashioned.
Pier Pub, cross the floating bridge, then take the first left. Appealing waterside location and patio. Good food, often involving great lobster/crab/steak deals.
Rose's Pub, Grand Hotel, Water St. With an attractive patio overlooking the lake and marina, perfect for summer drinking.
Tonics Pub and Grill, 1654 Ellis St, T250-8602997. A new bar with a patio, and an extensive wine list and Martini selection.

Penticton *p204*
In summer, Penticton is a very lively town, and it doesn't take long to find where the action is. The crowd's loyalties depend on variables like happy hours, drinks specials, favoured DJs and live music.
Barking Parrot Lounge, Lakeside Resort. Most evenings begin at this sophisticated but laid-back bar which is certainly the town's nicest.
Blue Mule Country Club, 218 Martin St, T250-4931819. A club usually specializing in country music.
The Element, 535 Main St, T250-4931023. A typical small-town club, mainly attracting a younger crowd.

Osoyoos *p204*
The Owl Pub, 7603 Spartan, T250-4953274. Big food portions, good beer on tap and a pool table.
Ridge Brewing Co, junction of hwys 3 and 97. Brews its own beers. Pub food.

ⓘ Entertainment

Kelowna *p201, map p202*
Art
Alternator Gallery, 421 Cawston Av, T250-8682298. Contemporary works, mostly by local artists.

Art Ark Gallery, 135-1295 Cannery Lane, T250-8625080, www.theartark.com. The best of the private galleries, with some exceptionally beautiful items.
Geert Maas Sculpture Gardens and Gallery, 250 Reynolds Rd via Hwy 97 N and Sexsmith Rd. May-Oct Mon-Sat. Bronze sculptures and other works by this well-known and respected artist.
Kelowna Art Gallery, 1315 Water St, T250-7622226. Tue-Sat 1000-1700, Thu till 2100, Sun 1300-1600, $4. For excellent Canadian exhibits.
Rotary Centre for the Arts, Cawston Av, T250-7175304, www.rotarycentrefor thearts.com. 0800-2300. Free. Watch works of art in the making. There's also a theatre available to local performing groups, as well as 8 resident artists and a potter, whose studios can be visited.

Music and theatre
Okanagan Symphony, T250-7637544, various venues.
Skyreach Place, on Water St, T250-9790888. The major arena for big-name concerts and sporting events.
Sunshine Theatre, 1304 Ellis St, T250-7634025, www.sunshinetheatre.org.

Vernon and around *p203*
Vernon and District Performing Arts Centre, T250-5497469, www.ticket seller.ca. One of the valley's best venues for live music, theatre and dance.
Vernon Public Art Gallery, 31st St/31st Av, www.galleries.bc.ca/vernon.

Penticton *p204*
Art Gallery of the South Okanagan, 199 Front St, T250-4932928. Tue-Fri 1000-1700, Sat-Sun 1200-1700. $2, Sat-Sun free. An attractive space, intelligently managed, with a good little gift shop.

ⓘ Festivals and events

Kelowna *p201, map p202*
Kelowna is the natural main focus of the valley-wide **Spring Wine Festival** in early

May and the **Fall Wine Festival** in late-Sep/ Oct. About 90,000 people attend over 100 events at various locations, including dinners, parades and grape stomps. For information on both festivals, T250- 8616654, www.owfs.com.
Jul Cherry Fair at the BC Orchard Industry Museum. The 3-day **Kelowna Regatta** takes over the marina and City Park in mid-Jul and features the popular **Mardi Gras Street Festival**.
Sep The International Dragon Boat Festival is a 3-day event.
Oct Apple Fair at the BC Orchard Industry Museum.

Penticton *p204*
Jul Perhaps the most entertaining event of the year is the **Beach Blanket Film Festival**, www.beachblanketfilmfest.ca, when various movies are shown through the evening on Okanagan Beach.
Aug As well as taking part in the **Spring and Fall Wine Festivals** (see Kelowna, above), Penticton hosts a massive **Peach Festival** in early Aug, T1800-6635052, www.peachfest.com. The last weekend of Aug is the busiest in Penticton's calendar, with every room in town reserved months ahead. The **Ironman Triathlon**, www.ironman.ca, is taken seriously, requiring the help of 4000 volunteers, and attracting 1000 iron men from over 30 countries.

O Shopping

Kelowna *p201, map p202*
There is a whole strip of gift shops on Ellis St, north of Bernard.
Art Ark Gallery (see p211) always has lots of extremely desirable gifts.

Penticton *p204*
There's a string of craft stores along the cute but disappointingly short Front St, which is trying very hard to bring a bit of colour and culture to Downtown. The **Art Gallery** (see p211) also has a nice gift shop.

The Bookshop, 242 Main St. An excellent used-book store, arguably one of the best in the country for its breadth, organization of stock, and knowledgeable staff.

▲ Activities and tours

Kelowna *p201, map p202*
Cheese tasting
Carmelis Alpine Goat Cheese, 170 Timberline Rd, T250-7700341, www.carmelisgoatcheese.com. Summer daily 1000-1800. 20 different goat's cheeses including blue cheese and brie. Book ahead for a tour ($4), which includes tasting. Combines well with a wine tour.

Golf
Gallagher's Canyon, 4320 Gallagher's Dr W, T250-8614240. Narrow fairways run harrowingly close to a steep ravine.
Harvest Golf Club, 2725 Kelowna, T250-8623103. Set among orchards, lake views.
Okanagan Golf Club, 3200 Via Centrale, T250-7655955. 2 championship courses.

Hiking
Mission Greenway right in town, makes a pleasant stroll. The trail up **Knox Mountain** is more demanding and satisfying, leading to spectacular views of the town, lake, floating bridge and valley. More difficult to reach, but the most recommended hike/bike in the area, is the **Myra Canyon Trestles** section of the Kettle Valley Railway (see p203 and also Monashee Adventures under Tour operators, below). This 12-km trail takes you through tunnels and over bridges, affording magnificent views. Take KLO Rd to McCulloch Rd; 2 km after the pavement ends, take Myra Forest Service Rd to the right and climb about 8 km uphill. Sadly, 10 of the 16 trestles were destroyed in the 2003 fire but reconstruction should be completed by Autumn 2006. A perfect afternoon would combine the trestles with a meal at the **Teahouse** (see p209), a tour of their

orchards, and a pint in the **McCulloch Station Pub** (p211). You can hike-bike the KVR all the way to Naramata/Penticton via Chute Lake, where you can fish for rainbow trout, and stay in a tent or rustic cabin (**D**) at **Chute Lake Resort**, T250-4933535.

Okanagan Mountain Provincial Park also has some good longer trails, including the **Mountain Goat Trail**, which climbs through a granite obstacle course to Divide Lake; and the **High Rim Trail**, a 50-km wilderness route to Vernon, which offers a smorgasbord of the Okanagan's many diverse landscapes.

Skiing

Big White Ski Resort, T250-7653101, www.bigwhite.com. One of BC's most significant ski resorts is 56 km from Kelowna via Hwy 33. Its 1130 ha of skiable terrain get a lot of snow, particularly the light and fluffy powder most skiers dream about. Its 118 runs are extremely varied, with a breakdown of 18% beginner, 56% intermediate, 26% expert. The resort has plenty of eating and sleeping options and all kinds of facilities, including 3 snowboard parks, night skiing (Tue-Sat 1700-2000), 15 lifts (including a high-speed gondola) with a 25,400 person per hr capacity, North America's largest Tube Park ($15/13 for 2 hrs), 25 km of cross-country trails ($12), snowmobiling, ice-skating, tobogganing, lessons (T250-7653101), gear rental (T250-7653101), ATM, and so on. It's especially well suited for families. The hill is open late-Nov to Apr, ski passes $64/$55 youth and senior/ $32 child.

Telus Park shuttle, T250-7653101, picks up at various downtown spots (eg McDonalds, Harvey & Water at 0730). daily throughout the Christmas and spring breaks, returning at 1600, $19 return. The hill runs 7 shuttles daily to/from Kelowna Airport, T1800-6632772, $65/46 return.

Big White can sleep an impressive 8900 people, mostly in quite expensive lodges.

Ski packages can be the best deal, T250-7658888. **Same Sun Ski-In Hostel**, in the Alpine Centre, T250-7657920, www.same sun.com. Dorms and private doubles (**E**), hot tubs, internet, laundry, kitchen, free pancake breakfast. They also have a hostel in Kelowna see p207.

Tour operators

Kelowna Parasail Adventures Ltd, T250-8684838, www.parasailcanada.com. **Monashee Adventure Tours Inc**, 470 Cawston Av, T250-7629253, www.monasheeadventuretours.com. Bike, hike, snowshoe, winery, canoe, and skiing tours. Their speciality is in combined bike and wine/food tours. They also operate a shuttle service around Myra Canyon. **Scenic Boat Tours of the Okanagan**, T250-8610691, www.okanaganboat tours.com. A variety of tours, including a 1-hr twilight tour at $20 per person.

Watersports

Sparky's, Grand Hotel, 1310 Water St, T250- 8622469, www.sparkyrentals.com. Rental of everything from power-boats to baseball gloves. **Sports Rent**, 3000 Pandosy St, T250-8615699. Bikes, skis and all manner of water toys.

Wineries and tours

If you want to visit the wineries on a tour, the following are recommended: **Distinctly Kelowna Tours**, T250-9791211, www.wildflowersandwine.com, $50 for ½-day wine tour, also hiking and walking tours, stopping at a couple of wineries; **Okanagan Wine Country Tours**, www.okwinetours.com, ½-day tour for $65, plus full days and overnight stays; **Winds and Rivers Escapes**, T250-5454280, www.windrivers.bc.ca, combined canoe and winery tours, plus some hiking tours. **Calona**, 1125 Richter St, T250-7629144, www.calonavineyards.ca. BC's oldest winery, and the most central in Kelowna.

Cedar Creek Estate Winery, 5445 Lakeshore Rd, T250-7648866. Lunch offered in their very nice bistro.

Hainle, 5355 Trepanier Bench Rd, south on Hwy 97 near Peachland, T250-7672525, www.hainle.com. One of the few organic wineries. Their **Amphora Bistro** is recommended for lunch, Tue-Sun 1100-1700.

Mission Hill, 1730 Mission Hill, T250-7685125, www.missionhillwinery.com. A gorgeous property with views over the whole valley, newly expanded to include a bell tower that rings on the hour, and a classic arched barrel room.

Quail's Gate, 3303 Boucherie Rd, T250-7694451, www.quailsgate.com. A good selection of wines sampled in a turn-of-the-20th-century storehouse. Their **Old Vines Patio** is a nice spot for gourmet lunches and dinners, from 1130.

Raven's Ridge Cidery, 3002 Dunster Rd, T250-7631091. First in the province to make ice cider.

Sumac Ridge, Hwy 97, further south near Summerland, T250-4940451, www.sumacridge.com. Experts in sparkling wines, with the **Cellar Door Bistro**, open daily in summer from 1130 for lunch, from 1730 for dinner.

Summerhill Estate, 4870 Chute Lake Rd, T250-7648000, www.summerhill.bc.ca. Possibly the most interesting and progressive organic winery, where bottles are aged in a giant pyramid. There's a settlers' cabin to visit, and the **Sunset Bistro** open daily 1130-2000.

Vernon and around p203
Skiing
Silver Star Mountain Resort, T250-5420224, www.skisilverstar.com. Fairly close to town, 22 km on Silver Star Road from Hwy 97 North, Silver Star is smaller, more relaxed and much prettier than most other resorts; its buildings all painted bright, cheerful colours. Skiing here (Nov-Apr) is good for beginners and intermediates, with 1240 ha of terrain, over 100 runs and a snowboard park.

There are also 100 km of cross-country ski trails in the area ($18). A lift pass costs $64 per day. In summer (Jun-Sep) the hill stays open for great biking and hiking. There is an information kiosk in the village centre, T250-5586092, and a free shuttle bus around the resort. On Sat and Wed, a shuttle bus also runs between Big White, Kelowna airport and Silver Star ($68), T1800-6632772 for details.

Of the village's 8 resident hotels the best deal is **B Silver Lode Inn** on the upper side, T250-5495105, www.silverlode.com The budget option is **E Same Sun Hostel**, the uppermost building, T250-5458933, www.samesun.com, which has dorms and private doubles with shared bath, kitchen, common room, hot tub and a free pancake breakfast. There is also an RV parking lot (**E**). As usual, package deals are a good bet. Contact **Central Reservations**, T250-5586083. There are several places to eat.

Penticton p204
Birdwatching
Vaseux Lake Provincial Park, 15 km south, is renowned for its birdwatching, bighorn sheep and rattlesnakes. Birdwatchers should check out **Rave**, 27a Front St, Penticton, for advice.

Hiking and biking
The total Kettle Valley route is 600 km. The most challenging section of the trail is north of Penticton, climbing 900 m through 2 tunnels and past Chute Lake on the way to the Myra Canyon on the edge of Kelowna. Access is where the rail crosses Naramata Rd, or right from this road to the top of Arawana or Smethurst roads.

Campbell Mountain and **Ellis Ridge Canyon** are also recommended for hiking, while **Munson Mountain**, of volcanic origin, is a nice walk and the obvious place for views.

The Bike Barn, 300 Westminster Av W. Everything a cyclist could desire, including rental and trail information.

Rock-climbing

Skaha Bluffs has world-class rock-climbing, with 260 climbs and 400 bolted routes. **Skaha Rock Adventures**, T250-4931765 www.skaharockclimbing.com. Provides lessons and will take you out.

Skiing

Apex Ski Resort, 33 km west of Penticton, T1877-7772739, www.apex resort.com. With just 450 ha of skiable terrain, Apex village is dwarfed by Kelowna's Big White and even Vernon's Silver Star, but its small size is its strong point. The 67 runs, which break down as 16% beginner, 48% intermediate and 37% advanced, are serviced by just 4 lifts. There's also night skiing (1630-2100 Fri-Sat), tube park, snowshoeing and ice skating. Day passes are $53/43/32, T250-2928222. Carmi Rd runs east of Penticton to the Carmi cross-country ski trails.

There are some nice but expensive lodges, plus **E Double Diamond Hostel**, T250-2928256, www.doublediamond hostel.com, with dorms and private rooms, ski lockers, internet, kids' play area, laundry. **Nickel Plate Nordic Centre**, 6 km away, has excellent cross-country skiing, with 30 km of groomed and track-set trails, plus 20 km of backcountry trails, a hostel at Apex and an RV parking lot (**F**). The **Gunbarrel Saloon and Restaurant** in the **Saddle Back Lodge** is a very popular no-smoking spot for grub and pints. Equipment rentals and lessons are available at the hill.

Tubing

In town, a path has been made along the 8 km river channel that connects the 2 lakes. Most people prefer to float down the channel on a giant inner-tube. **Coyote Cruises**, 215 Riverside Dr, T250-4922115. Jun-Sep 0900-2000. For $10 they will rent you a tube and transport you back.

Winery tours

Bacchus Tours, T250-7708282. You drink, they drive, on a tour of some of the neighbouring wineries.

Naramata *p204*
Wineries
Hillside Estate, 1350 Naramata Rd, T250-4936274. Hourly tours 1215-1515 and lunch from 1130-1500.
Lake Breeze, 930 Sammet Rd, T250-4965659.
Poplar Grove Winery, 1060 Poplar Grove Rd, T250-4924575. Also makes some yummy cheeses.
Red Rooster Winery, 891 Naramata Rd, T250-4922424, www.redrooster winery.com. Fine wines, tours, restaurant and picnic area. Some of the valley's finest reds, recently visited by Queen Elizabeth II.

Osoyoos *p204*
Golf
Osoyoos Golf and Country Club, 12300 Golf Course Dr, T250-4957003.

Watersports
Wakepilot, T250-4954195, www.wake pilot.com. Wakeboarding, waterskiing, tubing, etc.

Winery tours

Wine and food tours of the Okanagan are run by **Desert Country Wine Tours**, T250-4987316, www.desertwinetours.com. **Burrowing Owl Vineyards**, T250-4980620, Oliver, www.bovwine.com. Great wines, a lovely site and a fine restaurant. **Osoyoos, Nk'mip Cellars**, 1400 Rancher Creek Rd, T250-4952985, www.nkmip cellars.com. The first aboriginal winery in North America, using grapes only from their own vineyard.

Keremeos *p206*
Wineries
Crowsnest Vineyards, Surprise Dr, Cawston, T250-4995129, www.crowsnest vineyards.com. Tours, tastings and a restaurant.

⊖ Transport

Kelowna *p201, map p202*
Air
Kelowna airport, 10 km north on Hwy 97, T250-7655125, has daily flights to **Vancouver**, **Victoria**, and **Calgary** with West Jet, T1800-5385696, www.west jet.com; to **Vancouver** and **Calgary** with Air Canada Jazz, T1888-2472262, www.aircanada.com; and to **Seattle** with **Horizon Air**, T1800-5479308, www.alaska air.com. The **Airporter Shuttle**, T250-7650182, runs regularly to Downtown, $15. For Orchard Park or Downtown by city bus, take No 23, then transfer to No 8.
   Airline offices Air Canada, T250-7658777; WestJet, T4915600; Horizon Air, T1800-5479308.

Bus
Local BC Transit, T250-8608121, www.busonline.ca
   Long distance Greyhound, T250-8603835, www.greyhound.ca, runs 7 daily buses to **Vancouver** ($62), 4 to **Banff** ($75) and **Calgary** ($87), 4 to **Kamloops** ($28), 7 to **Vernon** ($13) and 2 to all points east on Hwy 3 via **Rock Creek**, including **Nelson** (7.5 hrs). The station is at 2366 Leckie Rd, off Hwy 97. City bus No 8 runs to town.

Taxi
Kelowna Cabs, T250-7622222

Vernon and around *p203*
Bus
Local Vernon Regional Transit System, T250-5451361, www.busonline.ca .
   Long distance The Greyhound station is at 30th St/31st Av, T250-5450527, with 7 buses daily to **Kelowna** ($13), 3 to **Kamloops** ($21), 4 to **Salmon Arm** ($13).

Penticton *p204*
Bus
Local Transit buses, T250-4925602, run from Downtown to Skaha Lake/Naramata.

Long-distance The Greyhound station, T250-4934101, is just off Main at Nanaimo/Ellis, with 4 buses daily to **Vancouver** ($60), 3 to **Calgary** ($96), 4 to **Kamloops** ($40), and 3 to **Osoyoos**.

Osoyoos *p204*
Bus
The **Greyhound** stop is at 9912 Hwy 3, T250-4957252, with 3 daily buses from **Vancouver** via **Penticton** ($70), 2 to **Kelowna** ($23) and 2 to **Calgary** ($110).

Keremeos *p206*
Bus
Greyhound buses stop in Downtown, with 3 services daily to **Vancouver** and 1 to **Kelowna**.

❶ Directory

Kelowna *p201, map p202*
Canada Post Kelowna Stationers on Bernard. **Internet** Free at the library. **Laundry** Minella Cleaners, 559 Bernard Av. **Library**, 1380 Ellis St. **Medical services** Kelowna General Hospital, 2268 Pandosy St, T250-8624222. **Walk-in clinics** at 515 Harvey Av, 605 KLO Rd, 1990 Cooper Av.

Vernon and around *p203*
Canada Post 3101 32nd Av/31st St. **Medical services** Vernon Jubilee Hospital, 2101 32nd St, T250-5452211.

Penticton *p204*
Banks Banks cluster around Main/Nanaimo. **Canada Post** Plaza Card and Gifts, 1301 Main St. **Internet** Several cafés, such as the **Mousepad Café**, 320 Martin St, and **Net Werx**, 151 Front St.

Osoyoos *p204*
Canada Post Spartan Dr/78th St. **Internet** Free at visitor centre or library. **Library** Main St. **Medical services** The nearest hospital is in Oliver, 20 km north.

West Kootenays

Surrounded by mountains, the West Kootenays comprises a ruggedly beautiful and undiscovered collection of small communities, connected by tortuous roads winding through lake-filled valleys, lined with jagged mountains, rocky bluffs, and icy creeks. Their focal point, scenic and culturally vibrant Nelson, combines perfectly with Kaslo and New Denver to make a trio of pretty former mining towns that can be easily visited as a loop. Sporting activities are rewarding here, particularly skiing, mountain biking and hiking, with thin crowds, plus a few good, accessible hot springs, and the odd atmospheric ghost town. As on the Gulf Islands, counter-culture thrives here, meaning plenty of arts and crafts, healthy living, organic farming (including less than legal crops), music, spirituality, colour and dogs.

⊘ **Getting there** Bus, car or air.
⊘ **Getting around** Car recommended.
⊖ **Time required** 3-7 days.
⊛ **Weather** Hot dry summers, coldish, snowy winters.
⊜ **Sleeping** Camping and mid-range options. Some nice B&Bs. Little choice outside Nelson.
⊘ **Eating** Excellent range in Nelson, limited elsewhere.
▲ **Activities and tours** Skiing, hiking, mountain biking, kayaking … everything.
★ **Don't miss...** Driving the Nelson-Kaslo-New Denver circuit ▸▸ *pp219-223*.

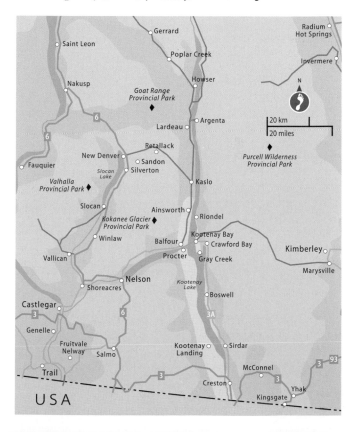

There is a **Greyhound** bus from Kelowna to Nelson. Getting around the Kootenays without your own vehicle is possible, but challenging. Nelson has the most useful visitor information centre, but there are others in Kaslo, New Denver and Nakusp. Also check www.kootenays-bc.com, a very useful site. 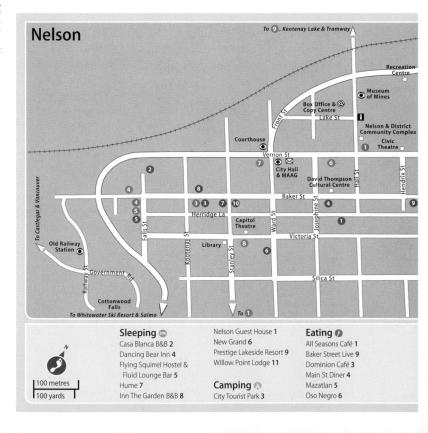» p233.

Nelson and the East Shore ⬛🅿🚻🍴❄♨⛺🚏🚻ℹ️ » pp224-233.

Beautifully situated on **Kootenay Lake** in a natural amphitheatre of rolling hills, Nelson is the obvious hub of the West Kootenays and arguably the most interesting small town in BC. The focal point for dozens of small communities scattered through the surrounding valleys, it caters to a large population without having to house or employ it, thus combining the positive facilities of a large town with the charm and friendliness of a small one. In particular, Nelson has a good range of quality restaurants, live music venues, cafés, and craft stores. Benefiting from the creativity of the many satellite villages, it is one of the best small arts towns in the country.

Nelson developed following the discovery of large deposits of copper and silver ore in the surrounding mountains. Incorporated in 1896, with a population of 3000, a hydro-generating station, streetcars, a sewer system and police force, this is an old town by BC standards. Thanks to intelligent planning, it has managed to retain an overall appearance that has barely changed in 100 years, with over 350 well-looked-after heritage buildings,

British Columbia West Kootenays

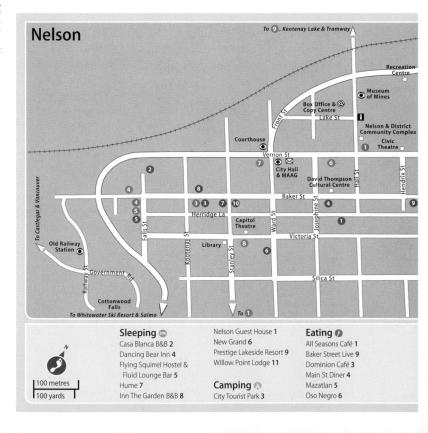

Sleeping
Casa Blanca B&B 2
Dancing Bear Inn 4
Flying Squirrel Hostel &
Fluid Lounge Bar 5
Hume 7
Inn The Garden B&B 8

Nelson Guest House 1
New Grand 6
Prestige Lakeside Resort 9
Willow Point Lodge 11

Camping
City Tourist Park 3

Eating
All Seasons Café 1
Baker Street Live 9
Dominion Café 3
Main St Diner 4
Mazatlan 5
Oso Negro 6

100 metres
100 yards

including the **Courthouse**, **City Hall**, the **Hume Hotel** and the old **Railway Station**. The **Visitor Information Centre** ⓘ *225 Hall St, T250-3523433, www.discovernelson.com*, can supply a *Heritage Walking Tour* pamphlet, which takes in the major sights. The town is a delight to explore, especially as everything is on or near Baker Street, where even the most pedestrian of businesses tends to be housed in a distinctive, historic building.

Those interested in the local history should talk to the curator of the **Museum of Mines** ⓘ *daily 0900-1700, free*, next to the visitor centre. For accounts of the town's general history, visit the **Museum-Archives-Art Gallery (MAAG)** ⓘ *City Hall, 502 Vernon St, www.museum.kics. bc.ca, summer Mon-Sat 1300-1800, winter 1300-1600, $2, $1 child*. The historic tramway, **Streetcar 23** ⓘ *summer 1200-1800, $2, $1 child*, runs along the waterfront by the mall.

Nelson has many faces: arts town, cultural oasis, well-preserved historic relic. It's also a paradise for outdoor enthusiasts, with a ski-hill down the road, backcountry skiing and hiking in the surrounding mountains, paddling and fishing in many local lakes and rivers, and a whole network of trails famous in mountain-bike circles. This is also a magnet for all kinds of alternative types, neo-hippies, rainbow children and pot-heads, who hang out around the Kootenay Co-op and Oso Negro, playing drums and guitars.

East Shore

From Nelson, Highway 3A follows a minor arm of Kootenay Lake towards Kaslo (an hour's drive), meeting the lake proper at **Balfour**, little more than a landing stage for the longest free ferry ride in the world, to Kootenay Bay on the East Shore. If travelling south to **Creston**, Highway 3A via the ferry at Balfour is a slower, but infinitely more enjoyable than the obvious route via Salmo. The road hugs Kootenay Lake tightly as it meanders through wonderfully dramatic scenery, passing a series of sleepy villages collectively known as the East Shore. On the road to Riondel, near the ferry-landing of **Kootenay Bay**, are the highly respected yoga retreat centre, **Yasodhara Ashram** (T250-2279224, www.yasodhara.org), and the **Tara Shanti** retreat (T250-2279616). If not Creston-bound, a good excuse to take the ferry is the artisan scene that is transforming **Crawford Bay**, 5 km to the south. The original blacksmith, glass blower and old-style broom maker are joined by more newcomers every year. There's a summer-only **Visitor Information Centre** ⓘ *just off the highway, T250-2279267, www.kootenaylake.bc.ca*.

Further down the lake, near Boswell, is the **Glass House** ⓘ *T250-2238372, May-Oct, $5*. Constructed entirely from 500,000 embalming fluid bottles assiduously collected from colleagues by a retired mortician, it's a truly fascinating oddity, all the more so as it was built as a home, not a tourist attraction. After a long descent, the highway enters a wide, flat valley, created by the flood plain of the Kootenay River.

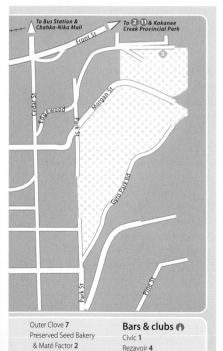

Outer Clove **7**
Preserved Seed Bakery
& Maté Factor **2**
Rice Bistro **8**
Sidewinders **9**
Stanley's on Baker &
Boomtown Emporium **10**

Bars & clubs 🍷
Civic **1**
Rezavoir **4**
Royal on Baker **3**

Around Kaslo ⊜⊘⊕⊕⊛⊛▲⊜⊕ ⟫ *pp224-233*.

Ainsworth Hot Springs

Highway 31 continues north from Balfour, shortly coming to **Ainsworth Hot Springs** ⓘ *1000-2130, $11 day-pass; free for guests at the resort pools and open from 0830*, the oldest village and first commercial hot springs in the mineral-rich Kootenay Arc. Today's resort features a horseshoe-shaped cave, the site of a mining shaft that had to be abandoned when miners struck hot water. There is also an icy-cold dipping-pool.

High in the Selkirk Mountains above Ainsworth, **Cody Caves Provincial Park** ⓘ *402 Anderson St, T250-3529813, Jul-Aug daily 1300-1800, otherwise Mon-Sat 1300-1600, $2, $1 child*, protects a natural limestone cave system sculpted by a glacier-fed stream that continues for over 1 km underground. Access is on a steep and rough 10 km gravel road, 2 km north of Ainsworth; or via a 15 minute walk on a clear trail. For carving trips, see Activities and tours, p232.

Kaslo

With an idyllic setting on Kootenay Lake, surrounded by parks and some of the highest mountains in the province, Kaslo is the quintessential small Kootenay town. So pretty, in fact, that surely only its remoteness has protected the charming atmosphere of its wooden houses and friendly, laid-back inhabitants against rampant tourism. A perfect base from which to explore the great outdoors, there's little to do in town but the lake offers fishing, boating and waterskiing, and the views never disappoint.

Like so many of its neighbours, this formerly sawmill-driven town boomed with the discovery of silver in 1893. Originally called Kane's Landing, it was the region's first incorporated city with 27 saloons (now it has two pubs). It survived the bust when the ore ran out thanks to agriculture, steamships that served the mining industry and, one suspects, the determination of inhabitants not to leave so idyllic a spot.

A fitting relic from the glory days, the **SS Moyie** ⓘ *324 Front St, T250-3532525, www.klhs.bc.ca, mid-May to mid-Oct 0930-1700, $5, $2 child*, built in 1890, is the oldest surviving paddle steamer in North America. Able to operate in extremely shallow waters, such vessels were vital for the economy of the Kootenays, carrying men, provisions and ore to and from the mines before the advent of roads. Retired in 1957, the *Moyie* was bought by the village of Kaslo from the Canadian Pacific Railway for $1. Now she is a designated National Historic Site and BC landmark, complete with artefacts, models and some eerie sound effects. Next to the *Moyie* is the summer-only **Visitor Information Centre** ⓘ *324 Front St, T250-3532525, www.klhs.bc.ca*.

Purcell Wilderness Provincial Park

Much of Highway 31, which follows the west bank of Kootenay Lake north from Kaslo to Galena Bay, is a demanding dirt road whose rewards do not justify the effort. But the paved section to **Howser** makes a nice excursion from Kaslo, passing scattered no-nonsense farming communities that have retained a frontier homesteader feel. The snow around here is possibly the finest in the province, with unbeatable cat-skiing out of Meadow Creek and a planned ski hill, called Jumbo Ski Resort, that has come up against extensive local resistance.

About 35 km from Kaslo, a bridge crosses the Duncan River to access the small, idiosyncratic communities of **Argenta** and **Johnson's Landing** and a number of excellent hikes in the vast and remote Purcell Wilderness Provincial Park.

▲▲ **Fry Creek Canyon Trail** Starting beyond Johnson's Landing, this is a fairly easy, thoroughly rewarding 10- to 19-km return hike, taking four to seven hours. The canyon walls rise vertically over 1 km from the creek waters, an awesome spectacle.

66 99 Kaslo is so pretty that surely only its remoteness has protected the charming atmosphere of its wooden houses and friendly, laid-back inhabitants against rampant tourism...

▲ **Earl Grey Pass Trail** (or Hamill Creek) Starting from Argenta, this is a tough but rewarding 61-km, three- to five-day one-way trek along the route by which Chief Kinbasket of the Shuswap Natives led his people to their present home near Invermere. Though the path is distinct, it is full of obstacles and very demanding, so consult a hiking guide and get local information before attempting it. You're not likely to see another soul, and the stands of ancient giant cedars are magnificent. It's worth doing the 1-hr scramble up Slate Peak north of the pass for 360° views that rival anything in the Rocky or Coast mountains.

▲ From Duncan River Bridge, continue straight for the trailheads of three more highly recommended hikes. Ask in Kaslo or consult a hiking guide for exact directions. **Monica Meadows** is an easy 8-km round-trip, about five hours, with 579 m elevation gain. This beautiful alpine meadow, surrounded by glacier-clad mountains, is full of bright flowers at the height of summer. Access is difficult and a 4WD is needed. Easier to reach and preferable for views is the more challenging **Jumbo Pass Trail**, 8.4 km, six to seven hours with 686 m elevation gain. The view from the pass is stunning. There's a hut for overnight stays; T250-3424200 for reservations. Access is also easy to the **Macbeth Icefield Trail**, which usually takes nine or ten hours, with 874 m elevation gain, but the final section could add an extra 3.6 km to the 12-km round-trip. This is harder still, though the views of the dual waterfalls cascading down from the glacier surrounded by a sea of ice are worthy rewards.

West of Kaslo

From Kaslo, Highway 31A continues to New Denver in the Slocan Valley (see p223). Clinging to the side of the fast-flowing Kaslo River as it winds its way through the steep cliffs of the Selkirk Mountains past a series of charming little lakes, this is one of the most scenic routes in the Kootenays. Halfway down is the abandoned mining townsite of **Retallack** and the **Retallack Ski Resort**. There is some exceptional summer hiking nearby in **Goat Range Provincial Park**. Further down the highway, a signed gravel road leads 13 km to the quintessential mining ghost town of **Sandon**. At its peak, Sandon had electricity (before Vancouver), an opera house and a red-light district, 24 hotels and 23 saloons. After a fire and two floods, there is little left to evoke that heady history, but the location and dilapidated remains are worth the diversion, especially since some excellent hikes begin here. In addition, a steep but manageable gravel road leads 18 km to a car park from where it is just a 1.4-km walk to Idaho Peak, an easy way to reach stunning views.

▲ **Mount Brennan** This challenging 14.6-km round-trip (seven to 10 hours, 1463 m elevation gain) starts 5 km from Retallack, leading to a jaw-dropping panorama that takes in glaciers, ice fields, and countless peaks of a few ranges, including the Rockies.

▲ **White Canyon Trail** A moderate 13.5-km round-trip starting 2.7 km from Retallack, taking eight to nine hours, with 893 m gain.

▲ **K&S Railway/Galena Trail** Combines views of the Valhalla Range with a pleasant forest hike and a history lesson that follows on nicely from a visit to Sandon. The summer-only visitor information centre there can provide a leaflet, which talks you through the glory-days of 'Silvery Slocan', along the 14.5-km trail (one-way), which passes old mine works and numerous artefacts on its way to New Denver (via Three Forks). It follows the old ore-carrying railway line. If you parked in Sandon, you have little choice but to hitch back.

Kokanee Glacier Provincial Park

Established in 1922, this 32,000-ha park is one of BC's oldest. Radiating out from the eponymous glacier and **Mount Cond**, which at 2775 m is the park's highest peak, are a number of creeks whose deep valleys provide the park's access routes. Out of the drainage patterns has evolved a complete network of trails, most of them originally built to service the small mines whose remains are still visible. There are three glaciers, over 30 lakes and endless forested valleys to admire. The historic **Slocan Chief Cabin** now houses an interpretive centre, with displays on local geography, flora and fauna, which includes black and grizzly bears, mountain goats, marmots, pikas and ground squirrels. **Kokanee Glacier Alpine Cabin**, always full in winter, operates on a first-come first-served basis in summer. Many trails start here, including the popular hikes to Smuggler Ridge and Kokanee Glacier.

▲▲ **Keen Creek** Turn south off Highway 31A, 6.4 km northwest of Kaslo. This 24-km rough road requires 4WD in all but peak conditions, but gives deepest entry into the park. Many trails lead from the car park at Joker Millsite, including a 4.8-km, three-hour hike to the Slocan Chief, or one of similar length to Joker Lakes.

▲▲ **Kokanee Creek** Turn north off Highway 3A, 19.2 km east of Nelson. This easier 15.2-km road leads to a car park at Gibson Lake. There is a short loop round the lake. The 8.8-km, 4.5-hour hike to the Slocan Chief passes four major lakes and gives easy access to extreme wilderness conditions. The Glory Basin Circuit is a moderate 24-km hike taking in most of the park's key sights. Possible in 10 hours, but better as a two-day trip camping at Kaslo Lake.

▲▲ **Woodbury Creek** Turn west off Highway 31, 6.4 km north of Ainsworth. Parking area is at 13.2 km. Two huts are accessible, both a four-hour walk: Woodbury Hut is a moderate 8-km hike; Silver Spray is shorter but harder. Above it is an old mine site and some interesting relics.

▲▲ **Lemon Creek** Turn east off Highway 6 at Lemon Creek, 14.4 km south of Slocan. Park off the road at a signed trailhead after 16 km. A varied hike of 9.6 km, five hours, not all of it well marked, leads to the beautiful Sapphire Lakes.

Slocan Valley ⊜⊘⊗⊙▲⊜❶ » *pp224-233.*

Running north to Nakusp from a point midway between Castlegar and Nelson, the Slocan Valley remains one of the best-kept secrets of the Kootenays. Clinging to the course of the enchanting Slocan River, sandwiched between Valhalla and Kokanee Glacier provincial parks, the road weaves between undulating green hills, rugged bluffs and icy creeks.

Slocan and around

Across the bridge in **Slocan**, where the winding river turns into a lake, a lovely 8-km **Slocan Lake Trail** leads to Evans Creek and the **Valhalla Retreat and Tipi Lodge**, T250-3653226, also accessible by canoe from Slocan (see p233). From here the **Cahill/Beatrice Lake Trail** offers relatively easy access (12 km, six hours) to the rugged Valhalla Provincial Park (see p223), where there is wilderness camping.

Above Slocan, the road climbs steeply towards a fine viewpoint. This stretch of road is particularly dramatic, clinging to cliff faces, taking hairpin curves, crossing rickety wooden bridges and losing sight of the lake until a bend is turned and it suddenly fills the whole panorama. Almost 3 km north of here, a steep dirt road winds down through a gravel pit, from where well-trodden paths lead to **Bannock Point**, a beautiful, clothing-optional beach.

Valhalla Provincial Park

This 49,000-ha park was designated in 1983 after years of campaigning and protest on the part of locals who sought to protect such an extraordinary area from the whims of logging companies. It is easy to see how the jagged, snow-capped peaks inspired association with the dwelling place of the nordic pantheon. There is plenty here to satisfy professional adventurers and climbers, but from June to October beginners can also gain easy access to areas of extreme wilderness. The routes are long and confusing, so make sure you seek thorough instructions before setting out.

▲▲ **Gwillim Lakes** via Drinnon Pass. Signed access from Highway 6 is at Passmore, south of Winlaw, or from Slocan City. From the former, turn left at Km 25.3; from the latter turn right at Km 20.3, onto Hodder Creek Forestry Road. Follow for 18.8 km and turn right for the last rough 2.4 km. This 11.6-km round-trip, with 701 m elevation gain, is the most popular route and could be accomplished as a 10-hour hike. It's possible to stay at the lovely meadow campground, giving time to explore Lucifer Pass, a further 3-km, three-hour hike with a scramble at the end and even better views.

▲▲ **Mulvey Basin** is most people's second choice. From Slocan, follow signs down the Little Slocan Lakes Forestry Road for 10.9 km, then turn right onto Bannock Burn and follow for 12.9 km. This 9.7-km round-trip (five or six hours, 765 m elevation gain) is more difficult, but the rewards are incredible: glacial sculptures and world-class mountaineering.

Silverton and New Denver

Soon enough, the highway rejoins the lake and passes through a duo of picturesque old mining towns, settled when silver and lead were found in nearby Idaho Mountain. **Silverton** contains a surprising number of artists' galleries and studios, and a museum with displays of old mining equipment.

New Denver is the valley's most worthwhile stop, and similar in many ways to Kaslo: a pretty little lakeside town of quaint wooden houses that still resembles the mining boomtown it once was. To learn more about this rich history, take a hike along the old mining railway to **Sandon** (see p221), with historical details supplied along the way, or visit the **Silvery Slocan Museum** ⓘ *1202 6th Av, T250-3582201, summer 1000-1600, $2*.

Another slice of local history is explored at the **Nikkei Internment Memorial Centre** ⓘ *306 Josephine St, T250-3587288, May-Sep 0900-1700, $4, $2 child*. In early 1942, in the wake of the Japanese bombing of Pearl Harbour, Japanese-Canadians, most of them living in Vancouver, were dispossessed of their belongings and herded into internment camps. This interesting museum is housed in one such camp and contains a lovely formal Japanese garden. There's another Japanese garden, the **Kohan Reflection Garden**, on 1st Avenue.

Almost everything else of interest is located on 6th Avenue, which leads to **Greer Park**, with a shady picnic area, lakeside trail and beaches. On Fridays there's a splendid market selling local crafts and produce. The summer-only **Visitor Information Centre** ⓘ *101 Eldorado Av, T250-3582719, www.slocanlake.com*, and the **Valhalla Nature Centre** at 307 6th Avenue, can provide trail maps of Valhalla and White Grizzly provincial parks.

Nakusp

Attractive enough in its lakeside setting, Nakusp cannot rival some of the other Kootenay towns for picturesque qualities, but the many local hot springs (see p224) make this a good stopover for those heading from the Okanagan or Nelson to the TransCanada Highway. In town, the biggest attraction is the lake itself, best admired from a pleasant promenade which takes in a small but pretty **Japanese Garden**. Almost everything of importance is found on or near the main street, Broadway, including the **Visitor Information Centre** ⓘ *92 6th Av, T250-2654234, www.nakusphotsprings.com*, which is disguised as a paddlesteamer.

Top tips

Nakusp's hot springs

The hot springs around Nakusp have been used by native peoples for centuries. In 1897 the first private sanitarium was opened and enjoyed tremendous success until it burnt down in 1955. It was reopened in 1997 as **Halcyon Hot Springs** ⓘ *34 km north on Hwy 23, T250-2653554, www.halcyon-hotsprings.com, 0800-2200, $7.95 for a dip, $12.50 day pass*, the best private resort in the area, with sulphur-free and lithium-rich water. The three pools, hot (42°C), warm (35°C) and cold (13°C), overlook the Arrows Lake. There is accommodation on site (see p227)

Alternatively, from the outskirts of Nakusp, a scenic 12-km road leads to the **Nakusp Hot Springs** ⓘ *92-6th Av NW, T250-2654528, summer 0930-2200, winter 1000-2130, $7.50 for a dip, $11 day pass, $3 on Wed in winter*, cheaper and closer than Halcyon, but not as appealing. A simple, round pool is divided in two, with temperatures of 37°C and 41°C. A bus to the springs leaves from the Seniors' Lodge in town on Monday at 1000, and from Overwaitea on Wednesday at 1100.

There are a few smaller, free hot springs reached by logging roads about 24 km north of Nakusp on Highway 23. **Saint Leon** and **Halfway** are most peoples' favourites, the former situated amidst giant old-growth trees. Nudity is common at both. Neither is easy to find. Ask around for directions.

By car it is 49 km north (past the hot springs) to the free **ferry** at Galena Bay, and a further 49 km to Revelstoke and the TransCanada Highway (see p185). Highway 6 heads west from Nakusp towards Vernon (p203) and the Okanagan, via the free ferry (every ½ hr 0500-2200) at **Fauquier**. The 135-km road to Vernon is a lonely, tortuous drive with few buildings or services, and lots of deer on the road at night. ● ›› *p198.*

● Sleeping

Nelson *p219, map p218*
AL Prestige Lakeside Resort, 701 Lakeside Dr, T250-3527222, www.prestige inn.com. The only lodging right on the lake. All rooms have views and kitchennettes, plus there's an indoor pool and breakfast included.

B Willow Point Lodge, 2211 Taylor Dr, 6.5 km north on Hwy 3A, T250-8259411 www.willowpointlodge.com. Ideal for those with a car who want to be close to town but immersed in the glorious countryside, this attractive 1920s lodge nestled in mountainside forest is surrounded by beautiful flower-filled gardens featuring creeks, waterfalls and a gazebo. The 4 unique en suite rooms and 2 honeymoon suites are furnished with antiques. There's a hot tub and breakfast.

C Casa Blanca B&B, 724 2nd St, T250-3544431, www.casablancanelson.com. 3 rooms in an elegant, wood-finished art-deco home in a quiet area close to Downtown, overlooking the lake. Guests have their own living room.

C Hume Hotel, 422 Vernon St, T250-3525331, www.humehotel.com. Recently renovated, this good-value centrally located hotel has bags of character, with a lounge, pub and restaurant downstairs. Rooms are spacious and comfortable, with antique furniture and feather duvets. Breakfast included.

C Inn the Garden B&B, 408 Victoria St, T250-3523226, www.innthegarden.com. Thanks to its handy location, 1 block from Baker St, and attractive gardens, the 6 pleasant rooms in this Victorian home are heavily booked, so reserve ahead. There is also a 3-bedroom guesthouse.

C Nelson Guest House, 2109 Fort Sheppard Dr, T250-3547885, www.nelson guesthouse.com. This beautiful hand-crafted cedar West Coast-style home is a little removed from Downtown but has tasteful, wood- finished rooms and 2-bedroom apartments, pleasant surroundings, wonderful views from the balconies and an outdoor hot tub.

D-F New Grand Hotel, 616 Vernon St, T250-3527211, www.newgrandhotel.ca. Dating from 1913, this funky Downtown boutique hotel has 30 tasteful rooms with 1940s-style decor, and hardwood floors. There are also 15 private hostel-style rooms for 2 to 3 people, with shared bath, a common room, and basic kitchen. There's a steakhouse and lounge downstairs, and breakfast is included.

E Dancing Bear Inn, 171 Baker St, T250-3527573, www.dancingbearinn.com. A superior hostel, very clean and comfortable, with 2-bed dorms and private rooms that have nice shared bathrooms. Facilities include a kitchen, lounge area, laundry, storage and lockers.

E Flying Squirrel Hostel, 198 Baker St, T250-3527285, www.flyingsquirrel hostel.com. Colourful and friendly, dorms and rooms have private bathrooms. Kitchen and common area, laundry, lockers and internet.

Camping

City Tourist Park Campground, High St, T250-3527618. Small and not very private, but wooded and handy, with showers and a laundry.

East Shore *p219*

B Kootenay Lake Lodge, Hwy 3A, 30 km south of Crawford Bay in Boswell, T250-2238181, www.kootenaylakelodge.com. A beautiful log house with antique furniture, balconies, views, friendly owners and various animals. 5 spacious and attractive rooms, plus a suite, chalets and RV sites. Breakfast, and use of boat and bikes, included. Canoes and kayaks for rent.

B Wedgwood Manor, 16002 Crawford Creek Rd, T250-2279233, www.wedgwood countryinn.com. This exquisite heritage house, built for Wedgwood's daughter, is set on 20 ha of landscaped grounds. The 6 rooms are very tasteful, with hardwood floors, en suite baths and antique furnishings. Guests can enjoy the library, parlour, dining room and a self-guided historical tour of the grounds.

D Kokanee Chalets, 15981 Hwy 3A Crawford Bay, T250-2279292. 1-bedroom motel-style rooms and nice 3-bedroom chalets, plus campsites with hot showers, a hot tub and hook-ups.

Camping

Lockhart Creek Provincial Park, 13 km south of Gray Creek. Apr-Oct only. 18 basic but wooded and private campsites, with a beach and trail.

Ainsworth Hot Springs *p220*

B Ainsworth Hot Springs Resort, T250-2294212, www.hotnaturally.com. Decent rooms and a fairly expensive restaurant overlooking the pools. Price includes free multiple entry to the pools.

D Ainsworth Motel, Hwy 31, T250-2294711. A nice, economical alternative, with lake views and kitchenettes.

Camping

Kokanee Creek Provincial Park, 20 km east of Nelson on Hwy 3A, T250-8253500. A beautiful campground with lots of trees, sandy beaches and hiking trails.

Kaslo p220

B Dayspring Lodge B&B, 4726 Twin Bays Rd, 10 km south of Kaslo, T250-3532810, www.dayspringlodge.com. A gorgeous Southwestern-style building in striking waterfront surroundings, with 3 large and stylish suites.

C Lakewood Inn, 6 km north on Hwy 31, T250-3532395, www.lakewoodinn.com. One of a long string of cabins and camping spots on Kootenay Lake, north of Kaslo. Cabins of varied age and size right on the lake, among trees and gardens. Kitchenettes and patio, use of sauna, marina and beach. Steep access.

D Beachcomber's Resort and Marina, 551 Rainbow Dr, at the Marina on other side of bay, reached by Hwy 31, T250-3537777. Rooms for up to 6 people, with kitchenettes, decks, views and BBQs, most with showers not tubs.

D Kaslo Motel, 330 D Av, T250-3532431, www.kaslomotel.ca. Standard but handy. Ask for one of the refurbished rooms.

D Edge of the Woods B&B, 116 C- Av, T250-3532600, www.edgewoods.com. A lovely handmade wooden house brimming with character, in a peaceful spot just outside Kaslo. 2 pleasant rooms and use of living area and deck. A bargain.

E Kootenay Lake Backpackers Hostel, 232 Av B, T250-3537427. Dorms and 4 private rooms with shared baths, kitchen, living room and sauna. Friendly and homely. Bikes, canoes and kayaks for rent, and internet access. The owner can advise about local hiking, biking and skiing trails.

Camping

Mirror Lake Campground, 5777 Arcola Rd, 5 km south on Hwy 31, T250-3537102. Not particularly attractive but a nice location with a beach. Good for kids. Showers, boat rentals. 5 mins' drive further south are the very attractive **Fletcher Falls**, where a Forestry Site has free wilderness camping.

Municiple Campground, close to SS *Moyie* on Front St. Basic but handy.

Purcell Wilderness Provincial Park p220

The first stretch of Hwy 31 north is thick with cabins, B&Bs and campgrounds.

C White Grizzly Lodge, 110 Duncan Dam Haul Rd, just north of Meadow Creek, T250-3664306, www.whitegrizzly.com/alpinelodge_bb. A beautiful log house with stone fireplace, hot tub, breakfast included and other meals available. The owners also run a cat-skiing tour operation, and can arrange hiking, biking, fishing and mountaineering.

Camping

Kootenay Lake Provincial Park. 2 sites: **Lost Ledge**, Km 25, has 12 sites on the lake with calm, privacy and a large beach; **Davis Creek**, at 28 km, has 12 even more private and primitive sites, but a rockier beach and no drinking water.

Howser Campsite, 8 km beyond Meadow Creek. A pretty, forested spot on Duncan Lake with drive-in and walk-in sites and a big sandy beach.

Slocan Valley p222

C Arica Gardens B&B, 6307 Youngs Rd, Winlaw, T250-2267688, www.aricagardens.com. An exquisite straw-bale and timber-frame house with 2 spacious, luxurious rooms – a steal at this price. Knowledgeable hosts can also arrange activities to help you get the most out of the area. Book early.

C Lemon Creek Lodge, 7680 Kennedy Rd, Lemon Creek, T250-3552403, www.lemoncreeklodge.com. Lodge rooms with shared bath, or fully-equipped cabins that are great value, especially for families. Sauna and breakfast included. There's also a good restaurant and poor campsites.

D-E The Artful Lodger, 6676 Appledale West Rd, Winlaw, T250-2267972, www.artfullodger.ca. 2 pretty strawbale cottages on 2 ha of land bordering the Slocan River, surrounded by organic gardens, flowers, decks and art created by the very interesting owner. Peaceful, warm and very inspiring.

D-E Little Slocan Lodge, 6.5 km from Slocan, T1800-5056788, www.little slocanlodge.com. Follow directions to Valhalla Provincial Park (see p223). Occupying 100 beautiful ha on the edge of the park, this brand new hostel incorporates straw-bale and timber-frame elements. There are dorms, private and family rooms, 2 common rooms, kitchen, a licensed café, lockers, laundry and a lovely deck. Great for hiking, climbing, mountain biking, canoeing or skiing.

Camping

Springer Creek Campground, 1020 Giffin Rd, Slocan, T250-3552226, May-Sep only. Certainly the valley's best campground, featuring 25 surprisingly private sites in a heavily wooded area right in town. Some hook-ups, showers, information.

Silverton and New Denver *p223*
C William Hunter Cabins, 303 Lake Av, Silverton, T250-3582844, www.william huntercabins.com. 6 suites with decks and kitchenettes, in 3 handsome, handcrafted log cabins on the lake. Canoe rental.

D Glacier View Cabins, 426 8th Av, New Denver, T250-3587277, www.glacier cabins.com. Not the most attractive cabins, but recently renovated and clean with full kitchens. Near the lake and certainly good value.

D Mistaya Country Inn B&B, 10 km south of Silverton, signed from highway, T250-3587787, www.mistayaresort.com. Nice rooms with shared bath in a gorgeous,

very remote spot by the lake. Hot tub and breakfast. Horse riding trips are the speciality ($35 for 2 hrs, $65 for ½ day with lunch). You can also stay in a tipi.

D Sweet Dreams Guesthouse, 702 Eldorado Av, New Denver, T250-3582415. 5 comfortable rooms in an attractive heritage house near the lake, with reservations-only restaurant. Kayak rentals. Breakfast included.

Camping

New Denver Municipal Campground, south side of village, T250-3582316. Right on the beach but pretty dingy.

Rosebery Provincial Park, 6 km north of New Denver. May-Sep only. 33 very nice, private sites on the banks of a creek.

Silverton Municipal Campground, Leadville/Turner. A primitive but attractively wooded location on the lake, with a beach and boat dock.

Nakusp *p223*
AL-B Halcyon Hot Springs Resort, 34 north on Hwy 23, T250-2653554, www.halcyon-hotsprings.com. A great place to stay with cosy cottages or lovely log chalets with full kitchens and living area with TV and covered sundecks. There's a restaurant and spa on site, and passes to the hot springs are included. There are also unattractive RV and tent sites, the latter overlooking the lake. All kinds of rentals and tours available.

C O'Brien's, 2.5 km west on Hwy 6, T250-2654575, www.obriens.kootenays.com. 3 fully-equipped, handcrafted log cabins. One of many resorts and campgrounds on Hwy 6 heading west. A quiet and scenic choice if you have your own transport.

D Huckleberry Inn, 1050 Hot Springs Rd, T250-2654544, www.huckinn.cjb.net. 4 comfortable theme rooms decorated with tasteful kitsch, showers not baths. Good value.

D Kuskanax Lodge, 515 Broadway, T250-2653618, www.kuskanax.kootenays.com. A heli-skiing base, sometimes fully occupied, otherwise hands down the

British Columbia West Kootenays Listings

best option in town, with decent rooms, and a good restaurant and bar.
D-E Selkirk Inn, 210 6th Av W, T250-2653666, www.selkirkinn-nakusp.com. Standard rooms, but spacious and clean.
E Windsor Hotel, Trout Lake near Galena Bay, T250-3692244, www.windsor-troutlake.com. A bit off the beaten track, but those with a taste for the quirky will relish this wonderfully eccentric establishment, which looks just as it must have when built in 1892.

Camping

McDonald Creek Provincial Park, 10 km west on Hwy 6. Apr-Oct only. 38 wooded and private sites close to the beach. No showers or hook-ups.
Nakusp Village Campground, 381 8th St northwest. Wooded sites in a quiet part of town with fire-pits and showers.
Summit Lake Provincial Park, 13 km south on Hwy 6. May-Sep. 35 sites with toilets and water taps but no hook-ups (there's a private RV park next door). With fine views of the Selkirk Mountains, good fishing, sightings of mountain goats and an agreeable climate, this is a popular spot. At the end of summer, thousands of migrating toads flood from the lake.

🍴 Eating

Nelson *p219, map p218*
Nelson has a surprising volume of restaurants and also quite a turnover. Those listed are tried and tested survivors, but it's always worth strolling along Baker St to check out the latest contenders.
All Seasons Café, 620 Herridge Lane, T250-3520101. A long-term favourite with locals when it's time to celebrate or splash out. The menu is small and intelligently conceived; the food is influenced by European and West Coast cuisine, and beautifully prepared and presented, though servings are on the small side, and the tables a little cramped. There's a small courtyard for romantic

summer evenings and an impressive selection of wines and malt whiskies.
Baker Street Live, 802 Baker St, T250-5055483, www.bakerstreetlive.com. Located in the beautiful Old Scandinavian Church, this brand new venue has resurrected the concept of the supper club. Tapas, West Coast-style entrées and cocktails are combined with cabaret acts, nightly music in a jazzy vein, singing waitresses and a lot of style.
Mazatlan, 198 Baker St, T250-3521388. Authentic Mexican favourites in bright, attractive surroundings. Extremely popular and lively. The portions are large, as are the dangerously strong Margaritas.
Outer Clove, 536 Stanley St, T250-3541667. Everything on the menu, even the ice cream, revolves around garlic at this long-standing favourite, which has stood the test of time simply because the food never disappoints.
Rice Bistro, 301 Baker St, T250-3520933. Open from 1600. Oriental tapas and sushi, plus creative brunches, fancy cocktails and sake, in elegant surroundings.
Main St Diner, 616 Baker St, T250-3544848. The best place to go for burgers, fish and chips, and Greek entrées. Good portions and prices, fine beers on tap and a summer patio.
Stanley's on Baker, 401 Baker St, T250-3544458. Recommended for breakfast and the lunch specials are often the best deal in town. Impeccable service.

Cafés

Dominion Café, 334 Baker St. An elegant New York-style coffee shop, with wooden interior and an attractive patio.
Oso Negro, 604 Ward St. This famous coffee-roasting company had to move to larger premises to keep up with demand. The new wood-dominated building has an upbeat West Coast vibe and a nice patio. Needless to say, the coffee is excellent and there's good light food, like bagels and muffins.
Preserved Seed Bakery and Maté Factor, 202 Vernon, T250-3520325.

This relaxing little health-conscious bakery- café is a lovely spot for delicious cakes and cookies, salads and wraps.

East Shore p219
¶ **Abracajava Café**. Apr-Oct Thu-Sun. Healthy, tasty dishes and good coffee in a colourful little room full of decent art, with a small patio.

Kaslo p220
¶¶¶ **Rosewood Café**, 213 5th St, T250-3537673. Kaslo's European fine-dining option. Intimate seating in a pretty house, with a garden patio and BBQ.
¶¶ **Crooked Café**, 4th/Front St. A warm and friendly pizza joint, with a licensed summer patio, making it about the nicest place in town where you can get a drink.
¶¶ **The Treehouse**, 419 Front St, T250-3532955. A popular meeting place for locals, serving a variety of good value, home-cooking-style food, and plenty of it.
¶ **Silver Spoon Bakery**, 301 Front St. Good coffee and sandwiches, fresh bread, croissants and breakfasts, in a summer house-style room.

Slocan Valley p222
¶¶ **Cedar Creek Café**, 5709 Hwy 6, Winlaw. The usual range of comfort food, prepared with a little extra thought. Open from breakfast to dinner, with beer on tap, wine by the glass and occasional live music.
¶¶ **Lemon Creek Lodge**, 7680 Kennedy Rd, Lemon Creek, T250-3552403. This place has long been considered the best eating option for miles around, especially for something a bit special or romantic.
¶ **Herald Street Café**, Herald St, Slocan. Burgers, breakfasts, pizza and grilled cheese sandwiches, with pictures of logging trucks on the walls.
¶ **Sleep is for Sissies**, on the highway as you enter Winlaw. The liveliest of a number of coffee shops.

Silverton and New Denver p223
¶¶ **Apple Tree Sandwich Shop**, 210 6th Av, New Denver. Only till 1600. A

long-standing favourite, on the strength of its varied menu of creative sandwiches. There's some seating in the secluded little garden at the side.
¶¶ **Panini**, 306 6th Av, New Denver. An appealingly bright and comfortable spot, offering the town's best coffee, breakfast, lunches and some creative paninis. It's one of the few places selling wine and beer.
¶¶ **Wild Rose Mexican Restaurant**, Rosebery, 5 mins' north of New Denver, T250-3587744. Daily 1700-2100 in summer. The best choice for dinner. First-class Mexican food, attractive surroundings and good service.

Nakusp p223
¶¶ **Kuskanax Lodge Restaurant**, 515 Broadway, T250-2653618. The usual range of burgers/pasta but also some more exciting main courses, very well presented. The menu is also available in the lounge, which is a nicer environment, with a good selection of beers on tap.
¶¶ **Wylie's Pub**, T250-2654944, and **Picardo's**, T250-2653331, share a location, 401 Broadway, and a menu, which concentrates on southern favourites like ribs and lots of appetizers. The pub, favoured by a younger crowd, is a preferable location, if only for the fish tank.
¶ **Broadway Deli Bistro**, 408 Broadway. The best bet for breakfast.
¶ **What's Brewing on Broadway**, 420 Broadway. The best coffee in town.

❶ Bars and clubs

Nelson p219, map p218
Civic, 705 Vernon St, T250-3525121. Rough-and-ready but gets some good bands. The beer and cover charge are cheap, you can smoke if you want and there's a deck out back.
Fluid Lounge, 198 Baker St, T250-3544823. A great little basement club whose funky, stylish interior shows off the work of some local artisans. Friendly and unpretentious atmosphere, with plush

armchairs, quality Nelson beers and a good range of Martinis. Well-chosen bands or DJs perform most nights, playing anything from jazz to house to kids' shows, often with a funky edge.
Hume Hotel, 422 Vernon St, T250-3525331, has 2 bars: **The Library** is the nicest place for a quiet drink and also has good food. **Mike's Place** is the most typical boozer in town, its 3 levels usually packed solid and hazy with smoke. Nelson Brewery beers on tap, reasonable pub food, big screens for sports fans and 3 pool tables.
Rezavoir, 198 Baker St. Next door to **Fluid** and owned by the same people, this is an upmarket, drinks-after-work kind of pub, with comfy leather chairs and a big TV. Martinis and beer on tap.
Royal on Baker, 330 Baker St, T250-3521269. A straight-ahead gritty pub that has live music most nights, traditionally of a bluesy nature. Nice patio.

Kaslo *p220*
Fisherman's Tale Pub, 551 Rainbow Dr, across the bay on the marina (Hwy 31). Much better than the pub in town: it's quieter and there's outdoor seating by the water, with great views.

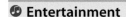 **Entertainment**

Nelson *p219, map p218*
Cinema and theatre
The Capitol, 421 Victoria St. Opened in 1927, and one of the finest in the country at the time, this attractive little venue is still going strong with regular plays and live music.
Civic Theatre, 104-719 Vernon St. Mostly first-run films, often with more interesting choices on Thu night.

Music
David Thompson Cultural Centre, 621 Baker St, T250-3521888. This relatively new centre is now the biggest venue in town for live music and consequently snags many of the biggest acts, as well as

hosting a wide range of visual, literary and theatrical events.

Kaslo *p220*
Langham Cultural Society, Av A, opposite the post office, T250-3532661. An arts centre that hosts consistently fine displays for such a small town, as well as an array of historic photos and artefacts upstairs, documenting such things as the local Second World War Japanese internment camps.

⊗ **Festivals and events**

Nelson *p219, map p218*
Jul-Sep Artwalk, T250-3522402, local artists display their works in numerous restaurants and shops, galleries and workshops around the town.
Aug Shambhala, T250-3527623, www.shambhalamusicfestival.com. Held at Salmo, south of Nelson, this has become the most important annual festival in the Kootenays. The non-stop 3-day orgy of music and mayhem gets bigger and more ambitious each year. All kinds of techno and live music takes place on unique and imaginatively conceived stages/dance areas dotted around in the forest.

East Shore *p219*
Jul Starbelly Jam Global Music Festival, www.starbellyjam.org. Held in Crawford Bay over a weekend in mid-Jul this 2-day open-air bonanza of major and minor world, folk and roots bands, plus an assortment of other acts, is always lots of fun and very kid-friendly. Most of the serious action is rumoured to happen at the after-party, usually at the beach.

Kaslo *p220*
Aug This sleepy town bursts into life in with the **Kaslo Jazz Fest**, T250-3537538, www.kaslojazzfest.com, a fabulous event that attracts some major acts to play on a floating stage on Kootenay Lake.

New Denver

Jul-Aug The small communities around New Denver host **Slocan Lake Art Walk**, with maps available from visitor centres. **Sep** On the 2nd Sun, New Denver (not Hills) hosts the celebrated 1-day **Hills Garlic Festival**, a very popular event that's really all about the food.

⚙ Shopping

Nelson *p219, map p218*
Books and crafts
The Craft Connection, 441 Baker St. An impressive collection by local artisans. **Pack Rat Annie's**, 411 Kootenay St. Wide range of used books, as well as new and used CDs, and a good café/restaurant, whose homemade spatzle is one of the best and most filling lunch options around.

Camping equipment
Valhalla Pure Outfitters, 626 Baker St. **Snowpack Outdoor Experience**, 333 Baker St. A Patagonia outlet.

Food
Kootenay Co-op, 295 Baker St. The best place for healthy, organic local produce and people-watching. **The Rising Sun French Artisan Bakery**, 281 Herridge Lane, behind the Bank of Montreal, has caused quite a stir among locals with the quality of its breads. **The Tree of Life Market** is held on Sat in Cottonwood Falls Park, near the old railway station. Locally grown produce, music and more good people-watching.

Sports
Boomtown Emporium, 104-402 Baker St, the only place for used equipment; **Gerick Cycle and Sports**, 702 Baker St; **Kootenay Experience**, 306 Victoria St, for skiing equipment; **The Sacred Ride**, 213 Baker St, for mountain-bike and snowboard equipment; **Village Ski Hut**, 357 Baker St.

East Shore *p219*
Crawford Bay's vibrant artisan scene currently includes: a blacksmith and an artist working with copper and glass at **Kootenay Forge**, T250-2279467, www.kootenayforge.com; a glass blower at **Breathless Glass**, T250-2279598; a traditional broom maker at **North Woven Broom**, T250-2279245, www.northwoven broom.com; traditional weavers at **Barefoot Handweaving**, T250-2279655, www.barefoothandweaving.com; and hand milled soaps at **The Soapstone**, just up from the ferry, T250-2278905.

Slocan Valley *p222*
Arts and crafts can be bought directly from the several artists and artisans in Silverton or at the Fri market in New Denver.

Books
Jennie's Book Garden, Winlaw. A small shop packed with an intelligently selected range of desirable fiction and non-fiction. **Earth Spirit**, almost next door. Metaphysical books, artefacts and New Age music.

Clothing
Valhalla Pure Outfitters, 101 Eldorado/ 6th Av, New Denver. Outdoor clothing, equipment and information.

⚑ Activities and tours

Nelson *p219, map p218*
Nelson and District Community Centre, 305 Hall St, T250-3544386. A brand new facility with a good swimming pool, fitness centre and ice rink.

Climbing
Gravity Climbing Club, 513 Victoria St, T250-3526125. The best place for information, equipment and practice on an indoor climbing wall.

Mountain biking

Nelson is a mecca for this sport, with dozens of trails. A useful map put together by the **Nelson Cycling Club** is for sale at bike shops. For information, follow links from www.discovernelson.com.

The Sacred Ride, 213 Baker St. Equipment and information.
Wright Wheels, T250-3529236, www.biketourbc.ca. Road bike tours of the Selkirk Loop.

Skiing

Baldface, T250-3520006, www.baldface.net. 5 mins in a helicopter from Nelson, this increasingly revered cat-skiing operation has 14,500 ha of perfect snow, plus luxurious lodging and gourmet food. $700 per person per day all-inclusive.
Whitewater Ski Resort, T250-3544944, www.skiwhitewater.com. With a 1640-m base elevation, Whitewater regularly gets over 10 m of dry snowfall per season, making for powder a plenty without the crowds. The terrain is for fairly advanced skiers, with lots of tree skiing. A lift pass costs $44. A discounted lift price is available if you're just going up once to ski the bowls. There is no accommodation but the lodge has a very good restaurant, a pub and ski rentals. Head south on Hwy 6 for 15 km to the steep Whitewater Ski Rd. For information visit the office upstairs at 513 Victoria St. **Village Ski Hut**, 367 Baker St, T250-3526326, rents equipment.

There's also cross-country skiing on beautiful groomed trails across the highway in the **Nordic Ski Club**.

Tour operators

Go Wild Tours, T250-3521164, www.gwt.com. Tours of the Kootenays
Gravity Adventures Unlimited, T250-3526125, www.gravityadventures.net. Mountain bike shuttle and guiding service; 2- to 6-day ice climbing adventures and hiking tours.
Summit Reflections Hiking & Climbing Adventures, 414 Beasley St, T250-3544884, www.summitreflections.com.

Ainsworth Hot Springs *p220*

Caving

Hiad Venture, T250-3537364, www.codycaves.ca. Tours of Cody Caves with trained guides, 1-hr tours cost $15/10 and more extensive 3-hr tours cost $50/40.

Kaslo *p220*

Hiking and biking

Kaslo is the best base for trips into **Kokanee Glacier Provincial Park**, via Keen Creek. For a short walk to 360° panoramas of lake and mountain ranges, do the 2-km loop to **Buchanan Lookout**. Follow Hwy 31A west for 9.2 km then take the rough Buchanan Forest Service Rd to the right for 11 km. An extreme mountain bike trail heads straight down 1220 m from here. There are 2 launch sites for hang-gliding.

Skiing

Kaslo is also gateway to arguably the best in backcountry skiing in BC. Cat-skiing and heli-skiing packages, about the only way to access it, are rather expensive, see www.kootenayexperience.com.
Outdoor Adventure Centre, 331 Front St, T250-3537349, www.discoverycanada.ca. For the best advice on skiing and other outdoor pursuits. Also rents kayaks.

Purcell Wilderness Provincial Park *p220*

Catskiing

White Grizzly, Meadow Creek, T250-3664306, www.whitegrizzly.com
Selkirk Wilderness Skiing, Meadow Creek, www.selkirkwilderness.com.

West of Kaslo *p221*

Skiing

Retallack Ski Resort, T250-2267784, www.retallack.com. One of the best and easiest bases for cat-skiing, with 5000 ha of terrain including 600 m runs and some of BC's steepest tree skiing. The cost is $525 per day including luxury and gourmet meals, with a standby rate of $275 for skiing and lunch only.

Slocan Valley *p222*

There's a 50-km trail for mountain biking or cross-country skiing along the old rail bed, following the river all the way up the valley. For rock climbing, there are some good cliff faces just past the mill in Slocan.

Paddling
Slocan River is mostly leisurely but there are some rapids around Lemon Creek. Most people put in at the **Winlaw Bridge** and take out at **South Slocan**.
Race Track Gas Station, Slocan Park. Rents inner tubes for floating down the river; a popular summer activity.
Smiling Otter, 8846 Slocan West Rd, Slocan, T250-3552373. Tours and lessons.
Wild Ways, 1286 Hwy 6, Crescent Valley, T250-3598181. Rentals, lessons and tours.

⊖ Transport

Nelson *p219, map p218*
Bus
Local Nelson is small enough to explore on foot. All bus routes, T250-3528201, www.busonline.ca, converge at the junction of Baker and Ward Sts. Buses go as far as Balfour. There is 1 weekly shuttle to **Kaslo** (see below), 1 to **Nakusp**, and a few daily to the **Slocan Valley**.
Long distance Greyhound, T250-3523939, www.greyhound.ca, has 2 daily buses west to **Kelowna** for connections to **Vancouver** and **Kamloops**, and east to **Cranbrook** for connections to **Banff** and **Calgary**. The station is in the lakeside mall.

East Shore *p219*
Ferry
The 9-km ferry from **Balfour** to **Kootenay Bay** takes 40 mins, leaving every 50 mins in summer, otherwise every 2 hrs. Free.

Kaslo *p220*
Kaslo is difficult to reach without your own transport. A single shuttle for **Nelson** leaves Wed morning at 0900, returning in the afternoon at 1500.

Slocan Valley *p222*

ASLCS, T1877-8432877, www.aslcs.com, runs 3-4 minibuses per day between **Slocan** and **Nelson**, with 4 others between Nelson and **Passmore** at the southern end of the valley; call for schedules. A ticket is $1.50-3 on a zone system. Buses from **Nakusp** pass through Slocan on Tue and Thu, and can be flagged down. Otherwise, hitchhiking is a way of life.

Nakusp *p223*
Bus
Nakusp Transit, T250-2653674, provides local services and runs to **Nelson** Tue and Thu at 0815, returning at 1445.

Ferry
Ferries from Galena Bay to **Shelter Bay** leave hourly 0530-0030; returning hourly 0500-2400.

⊖ Directory

Nelson *p219, map p218*
Canada Post 514 Vernon St. **Internet** Box Office & Copy Centre, 622 Front St; or at the library. **Laundry** Plaza, 616 Front St Library, 602 Stanley St. **Medical services** Kootenay Lake Regional Hospital, 3 View St, T250-3523111. Dentist, Dr RD Clarke, 110 Baker St. **Pharmacy**, Pharmasave Drugs, 685 Baker St. **Useful addresses** Police, 606 Stanley St, T250-3543919; Fire 919 Ward St, T250-3523103; Ambulance T911.

Kaslo *p220*
Canada Post 312 5th St. **Medical services** Victorian Community Health Centre, 673 A Av, T250-3532291. **24hr emergency line** T250-3532211.

Slocan Valley *p222*
Canada Post Winlaw, on Hwy 6; 219 6th Av, New Denver. **Medical services** Slocan Community Hospital, 401 Galena St, New Denver, T250-3587911. **Arrow Lakes Hospital**, 97 1st Av, Nakusp.

British Columbia West Kootenays Listings

Northern BC

Heading north, your chances of encountering wildlife, First Nations culture and solitude increase, but so do the distances, while good food, sights, sleeping options and the scenery-to-distance ratio all decrease. The Wild West-style Cariboo offers ranches, gold rush history, excellent canoeing on Bowron Lakes, and the ultimate living museum of Barkerville. The Chilcotin includes beautiful but remote town of Bella Coola, and the vast wilderness of Tweedsmuir Provincial Park. Nisga'a Memorial

◐ **Getting there** Plane, car, bus.
◐ **Getting around** Car, bus.
◐ **Time required** 4-7 days.
◐ **Weather** Colder and wilder.
◐ **Sleeping** Limited.
◐ **Eating** Limited.
▲ **Activities and tours** Fishing, canoeing, hiking, biking, kayaking, gold-panning.
★ **Don't miss...** Visiting one of the abandoned villages of the Haida Gwaii ▶▶ p244.

Lava Bed Park is the highlight of a mostly dull drive west from Prince George to Prince Rupert, the north's most interesting town, with many worthwhile excursions. Haida Gwaii – the Galápagos of the North – is an extraordinary set of rugged islands, containing several abandoned Haida villages. The Cassiar Highway heading north passes through magnificent scenery, with a short diversion via the stunning blue Bear Glacier to Stewart and Hyder, where you can watch grizzlies fishing for salmon.

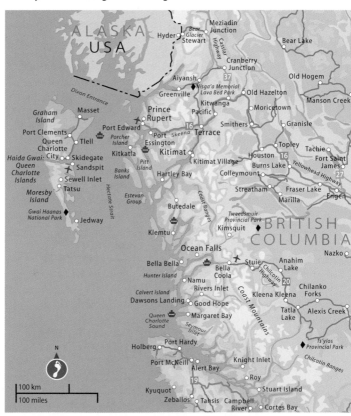

Ins and outs

Getting there and around

Given the vast distances involved, unless you have a vehicle it's definitely worth considering a flight north, which is a lot faster than the bus and not necessarily more expensive. **Pacific Coastal Airlines** flies to Bella Coola and Williams Lake from Vancouver, Victoria, Powell River and Port Hardy. **WestJet** flies to Prince George and Prince Rupert from Vancouver, Kelowna and Calgary. **Air Canada Jazz** flies to Prince George, Prince Rupert and Haida Gwaii from Vancouver. **Hawk Air** flies to Prince Rupert from Vancouver.

An even better idea is to take one of the sailings from Port Hardy (see p144), such as the Inside Passage to Prince Rupert, or the Discovery Passage to Bella Coola. These are tantamount to a cheap cruise through spectacular scenery, and take you straight to the most worthwhile destinations. **BC Ferries**, www.bcferries.com, also operates a service from Prince Rupert to Haida Gwaii.

Greyhound operates three daily buses from Vancouver or Kamloops to Prince George via the Cariboo. There are two daily buses between Prince George and Prince Rupert and between Prince George and Dawson Creek; and three weekly buses up the Alaska Highway from Dawson Creek to Whitehorse, Yukon. There is no public transport on the Chilcotin or Cassiar Highways. **Seaport Limousine**, T250-6362622, runs a daily bus from Terrace to Stewart.

VIA Rail, T1800-5618630, www.viarail.ca, runs three weekly daylight-only trains from Prince Rupert to Jasper, with an overnight stop in Prince George. ⊖ ▸▸ p261.

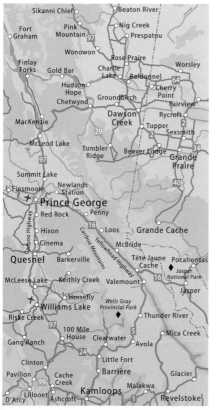

Best time to visit

The best time to visit is in summer as the winters can get pretty cold. Grizzlies bears are best seen between April and September. May to July is the best time for orcas. The **Williams Lake Stampede** is held around 1 July (see p257). August to October is the best time for humpback and grey whales. September to early October is best for those elusive white Kermode Spirit bears.

The Cariboo ⊖✳▲⊜ ▸▸ pp251-263.

The most obvious road to Northern BC follows the historic route of the Cariboo Wagon Road through the middle of a vast plateau between the Coast and Cariboo mountain ranges. This is dry ranching country, whose broad horizons are laden with endless pine forests and literally thousands of lakes. Apart from anglers, for whom this is a paradise, most people find that its scenic appeal runs thin fairly quickly and, without a single town of any interest, the monotony is only broken by constant reminders of the area's gold-mining past. The region's most useful base is Williams

Heritage buildings and church, Barkerville.

Lake, but the only real attraction is Barkerville, an extensive reconstruction of that Gold Rush town. Nearby are **Bowron Lakes**, which have been voted one of the world's top ten canoeing destinations.

Clinton and around

Today's **Cariboo Highway** (Highway 97) begins at Cache Creek, whose dry bluffs and colourful rock formations set the tone for the drive to come. **Clinton**, 40 km north, is one of the better places for anyone who would like to experience the cowboy lifestyle first-hand by staying on a working guest ranch (also known as dude ranches; T250-4592640 for information). ● ⟫ *p251*.

Williams Lake and around

Williams Lake is an uninspiring town but a useful springboard to many activities, with the area's best year-round **Visitor Information Centre** ① *1148 Broadway St, T250-3925025, www.landwithoutlimits.com*. Ask about the excellent local mountain biking, or hiking in the Williams Lake Valley. Rafting and whitewater kayaking trips are operated down the Farwell Canyon to the west. Williams Lake is also the place to pick up supplies if tackling the 456 km drive west to Tweedsmuir Provincial Park and Bella Coola (see pp237-238).

  Xats'ull Heritage Village, T250-9892323, is situated on a plateau overlooking the Fraser River, 33 km north of Williams Lake in Soda Creek. The first of its kind in North America, it features pit houses, petroglyphs, tipis and native artefacts, and operates a series of one-to 12-day cultural programmes where native crafts and skills are taught, and food and lodging are provided.

  Continuing north, the Fraser River breathes fresh life into the scenery, but the forests in these parts have been horribly decimated, so it comes as no surprise that **Quesnel** is just another ugly logging town. Gold Rush enthusiasts might enjoy the four-day **Billy Barker Days Festival** held in the third week of July, and a visit to the **Quesnel Museum and Archives** ① *703 Carson Av, T250-9929580, year-round*, the best museum in the Cariboo. It's located in Le Bourdais Park along with the **Visitor Information Centre** ① *T250-9928716, www.northcariboo.com*.

The main reason to stop anywhere in the Cariboo is **Barkerville Provincial Historic Park** ① *82 km east of Quesnal, May-Sep 0800-2000, $12.50, $3.50 child; stage coach ride $8, $6 child; theatre $12.75, $6.50 child*. The most impressive monument to local history, it's set in the refreshingly beautiful scenery of the Cariboo Mountains. Billy Barker struck it lucky here in 1862 and, for the next 10 years, Barkerville became the biggest town north of San Francisco and west of Chicago. Today it is the biggest and best of many reconstructed heritage towns scattered around the country, with historic displays and demonstrations, and 125 restored buildings full of costumed, role-playing staff. The Theatre Royal features live vaudeville shows, old-style shops sell authentic wares and there are plenty of restaurants. You can pan for gold, get photographed in period costume, tour the cemetery and ride in a stage coach. There is no public transport from Quesnel apart from **Gold Safari Tours**, T250-9943302.

Barkerville provides the easiest access to **Bowron Lakes Provincial Park**, 24 km further east. This mountain wilderness, the top of a protected belt that runs north from Wells Gray Provincial Park, offers swimming, hiking and camping, but is especially renowned as one of the ten best canoe routes in the world (see p258). Again, **Gold Safari Tours**, T250-9943302, provide the only transport.

The Chilcotin ⊜◑❂🔱⊖ ▸▸ *pp251-263.*

One of Canada's most unlikely roads, the **Chilcotin Highway** (Highway 20) heads 456 km west from Williams Lake to Bella Coola, one of the last great wilderness settlements, whose only other access is by ferry from Port Hardy at the northern tip of Vancouver Island. The first 350 km passes through the remote but flat, monotonous scenery of the Chilcotin Plateau. Heckman Pass (1524 m) marks the end of the plateau and start of a 30-km section of narrow, winding, unpaved road, culminating in 'The Hill', 10 km of steep, brake-grinding switchbacks with up to 18% grades. The highlight along the way is the exceptional **Tweedsmuir Provincial Park**, which has some of the most remote trails in the Coast Mountains.

Chilcotin Plateau

As in the Cariboo, those excited by this kind of country will find much to explore on the back roads mostly to the south. **Bull Canyon Park**, 10 km west of Alexis Creek, is a good spot to admire the glacial blue water of the Chilcotin River and some fine rock walls. A little further west, a rough road leads to **Nazko Lakes Provincial Park**, where a 20-km canoe trip can be made between six lakes with easy portages. At Chilanko Forks, a fair 12-km road leads to scenic **Puntzi Lake**, with good fishing, visiting pelicans and trumpeter swans, and 360° views.

From **Tatla Lake**, helicopter companies whisk hardcore enthusiasts to the Coast Mountains' highest peak, **Mount Waddington** (4016 m), or its largest body of water, **Chilko Lake**, contained by the vast wilderness of **Ts'ylos Provincial Park**, which can also be reached via 60 km of rough roads. The **Chilko River**'s Lava Canyon is well known for its river rafting with a drop of 19 m/km over a 24-km stretch, including the infamous 'White Mile'.

Tweedsmuir Provincial Park

British Columbia's largest park, Tweedsmuir contains 8967 sq km of breathtaking wilderness, spanning the full gamut of peaks, glaciers, wild flower meadows, waterfalls, forests and lakes, and is home to thriving populations of black and grizzly bears, moose and caribou. On its eastern edge, the plateau gives way to the **Rainbow Range**, named for the wonderful spectrum of reds, oranges, yellows and purples in the fragmented layers of rock and eroded lava. A number of hiking trails lead from the trailhead here. 🔺 ▸▸ *p259.*

Rafting the Chilcotin River.

On the highway, midway through the park at Atnarko River, is the main campsite, with water, toilets and wood. Nearby, an old tote road, suitable only for high-clearance vehicles, leads 13 km to the **Hunlen Falls/Turner Lake Trailhead**. The spectacular **Hunlen Falls** is a major draw, plummeting 260 m and disappearing in a cloud of spray. But the trail to get there is a difficult 16.4-km hike with an elevation gain of 2000 m. Just to the south is **Turner Lake**, starting point of an excellent 19-km canoe route whose chain of seven lakes is connected by easy portages, with six campsites and great fishing; rentals are available at the lake. Further west, towered over by a wall of giant granite Coast Mountain peaks that mark the park's western boundary, is **Stuie**, the only village in the park. Nearby is the best of the park's short hikes, the two-hour **Burnt Bridge Loop**.

Bella Coola

Sitting at the end of a long, saltwater fjord, Bella Coola's chief asset is its stunning scenery. The town is surrounded by utter wilderness, home to some of the healthiest animal life in the country, including particularly large grizzlies. Rafting, kayaking or canoeing down the river are all great ways to appreciate the surroundings. Salmon fishing is also particularly good. Otherwise, there's little to do but watch the activity around the marina or go for a hike, unless your visit coincides with the **annual rodeo** at the end of June, or the **Discovery Coast Music Festival** at the end of July. Information can be obtained at www.centralcoastbc.com.

The Bella Coolas, or Nuxalk Natives, depended for thousands of years on the abundance of salmon in their rivers. Today their descendants can still be seen catching and smoking fish in the age-old way. About half of today's non-aboriginal population can trace their heritage back to the first white settlers, a group of 120 Norwegians who were led here from Minnesota by Pastor Christian Saugstad in 1894, in order to found a Utopian society. Unlike many similar attempts, the hard-working Scandinavians managed to survive the challenge. Their story can be read at www.nordicfolks.com.

Bella Coola Museum ⓘ *on the highway, T250-7995767, $2*, is housed in a 19th-century Norwegian school-house and contains many settler relics, as well as aboriginal and Hudson's Bay Company artefacts. In Hagensborg, 23 km east, there are more signs of the Norwegian past at the **Sons of Norway Heritage House** ($2), on the highway. The **Thorsen Creek Petroglyphs**, halfway between the towns, are a hundred or so aboriginal rock drawings.

Highway 5 to Prince George ⊕🐟🎵⊙▲⊕🌙 » *pp251-263.*

Highway 5 is a longer route north than the Cariboo Highway. Passing between the Cariboo and Rocky mountains, its scenery is stimulating enough, but none of the towns offer much of interest. **Wells Gray Provincial Park**, however, is one of the most rewarding parks in BC, and relatively underused thanks to the proximity of the high-profile Rockies. **Valemount** is a good base for the classic Mount Robson/Berg Lake hike (see p316), with plenty of places to stay; ask at the **Visitor Information Centre** ⓘ *99 Gorse St, T250-5664846, www.valemount-bc-org.* At Tête Jaune Cache, Highway 5 meets the Yellowhead Highway, which heads east to Jasper, and northwest through duller scenery to Prince George.

Wells Gray Provincial Park

Thanks to its location in the Cariboo Mountains, the scenery in Wells Gray is extremely varied, including large lakes and river systems, some impressive waterfalls, extinct volcanoes, lava beds and mineral springs. Deer, caribou, moose and bears are frequently seen and there's good fishing in most of the lakes and rivers. The south of the park has alpine meadows, while the inaccessible north and east edges are lined with peaks and glaciers. As in the Rockies, summers can be quite wet, the driest month being April. While there are many first-class hiking and canoeing trails, you don't have to walk far to see some of the most impressive natural phenomena.

The park entrance is at **Hemp Creek**, 40 km from Clearwater on the mainly paved Clearwater Valley Road. There's no public transport to the park. At the junction with Highway 5 is the very helpful **Visitor Information Centre** ⓘ *T250-6742646,* which can put you in touch with operators for horse riding, float planes, canoeing and whitewater rafting. On the way to the park is **Spahats Creek/Falls**, where the creek has carved a 122-m-deep canyon through layers of lava. There's a campground here and a viewpoint of the canyon and 61-m falls.

Beyond Hemp Creek, a side road leads to Green Mountain Viewing Tower and a chance to take in the full extent of the surrounding wilderness. Further along, the wide and powerful Murtle River crashes down **Dawson Falls**, which can be observed from vantage points along a short trail. Where the road crosses the river, the **Devil's Punch Bowl** (or Mush Bowl) is the dramatic result of fierce water cutting its way through a narrow gorge. A little further on, a

British Columbia Northern BC

Trekking in the Coast Range above Chilko Lake.

King of the fish

All five species of Pacific salmon are born in gravel beds in streams. Laid in the autumn, their eggs are incubated through the winter by ice and snow up to several feet deep. In spring they emerge as inch-long fry, then spend up to a year or more in a nearby river or lake before heading downstream to the ocean. One early summer day, after about three to five years, an unknown impulse compels them to return to their birthplace. Some species cover distances of up to 1600 km, at speeds of more than 50 km per day. For weeks the salmon struggle upstream, jumping up steep waterfalls and negotiating fierce rapids. What's more, the entire journey is undertaken without food. On the way, they change colour from their normal blue-tinged silver to varying shades of red. By late summer they reach the exact place of their birth and, after enacting the reproductive stage of the life cycle, promptly die.

The best places to see the salmon are on the Adams River in the Shuswap, Campbell River on Vancouver Island, or around the Skeena River between Prince George and Prince Rupert in Northern BC.

10-km side road heads left to the most impressive sight of all, the 137-m **Helmcken Falls**.

The main road continues for 23 km, passing three more vehicle-accessible campsites and the homestead remains of **Ray Farm** on the way to **Clearwater Lake**. Linked by a short portage to Azure Lake, this is ideal canoeing country, with a possible 102-km round-trip that has fishing and campsites all the way. A 2-km trail leads from Clearwater Lake campground to the **Dragon's Tongue** lava flow, while the 12-km Chain Meadow Loop has numerous viewpoints.

Prince George

Situated at the crossroads of the only highways heading north (Highway 97 and Highway 16), Prince George is the main service centre and transport hub for an incredibly vast region, and almost impossible to avoid. It is also the focus for some of the most heavily logged land in Canada and no place to linger. There's a **Visitor Information Centre** ⓘ *1300 1st Av, T1800-6687646, www.tourismpg.com, Mon-Sat 0900-1600, longer in summer.*

If you have time to kill, the best place to head is **Fort George Park**, on the Fraser River about 10 minutes' walk southeast of Downtown. As well as a miniature railway, water park and native cemetery, it contains the museum and science centre of **Exploration Place** ⓘ *333 Becott Place, end of 20th Av, T250-5621612, www.theexplorationplace.com, summer daily 1000-1700, otherwise Wed-Sun, $11, $9 child*, which includes seven different galleries devoted to themes as diverse as palaeontology, children and First Nations.

From here, the pleasant Heritage River Trail, an 8-km loop that connects a number of parks, follows the Fraser 2 km to **Cottonwood Island Nature Park**, which contains several interpretive trails and the **Railway and Forestry Museum** ⓘ *take River Rd from 1st Av, T250-5637351, www.pgrfm.bc.c, May-Oct daily 0900-1730, $6/5/3*, where a collection of steam engines, assorted railway relics and forestry artefacts are presented mostly in the open air.

There are also a couple of galleries that are worth a visit: the **Native Art Gallery** ⓘ *1600 3rd Av, T250-6147726*, has a good collection of quality local and national native works for sale. **Two Rivers Gallery** ⓘ *725 Civic Plaza, T250-6147800, www.tworiversartgallery.com, daily 1000-1700, Sun from 1200, Oct-Apr closed Mon, $4, $3 child*, has consistently impressive exhibitions.

Prince George to Prince Rupert ⚡️⛰ ⟫ pp251-263.

West to Smithers

The eastern section of the Yellowhead Highway is a monotonous drive with few reasons to stop, but the Lakes District, west of Prince George, between Fraser Lake and Houston has good wilderness fishing in over 300 lakes, and there's prime birdwatching at the **Vanderhoof Bird Sanctuary**, on the Pacific Flyway. Drivers should head to **Telkwa**, 360 km west of Prince George, a pretty riverfront village full of heritage buildings, with a charming pioneer museum.

There's plenty of hiking, biking and skiing close to **Smithers** in the Babine Mountains Recreation Area, 15 km east, and at Hudson Bay Mountain. Ask at the **Visitor Information Centre** ① *1411 Court St, T250-8475072, www.tourismsmithers.com*. There are also fossil beds to explore at Driftwood Canyon Provincial Park, 11 km northeast. The Babine and Bulkley rivers are good for canoeing, kayaking or river rafting.

Hazeltons

For 4000 years, the region has been home to the Gitxsan Wet'suwet'an people, the most easterly of the West Coast First Nations. Like all Native American groups, their way of life was irrevocably disrupted by the white man's arrival, but a decision by the tribe's elders in the 1950s to preserve what remained of their legacy has made this one of the best places in Western Canada to encounter aboriginal culture. At the summer-only **Visitor Information Centre** ① *on the highway, New Hazelton, T250-8426071*, you can pick up a copy of the *Hands of History* self-guided driving circuit, which covers many First Nations villages. Among the most interesting are **Kispiox**, **Gitwangak** (Kitwanga) and **Gitanyow** (Kitwancool).

Old Hazelton, 8 km north of Highway 16 on a secondary road that crosses the a single-lane suspension bridge 76 m above the Bulkley River, is a well restored 19th-century sternwheeler terminus full of heritage buildings. A pair of totems mark the entrance to the regional highlight, **'Ksan Historical Village** ① *T250-8425544, www.ksan.org, summer only, $10/8.50, summer 0900-1700, giftshop and museum open year-round*. This 1970 reconstruction of a settlement that had stood on the site for centuries until 1870, was the main focus of attempts to resurrect the dying culture. The grounds contain seven colourful longhouses,

Log sort in Prince George.

British Columbia Northern BC

Longhouse in Nisga'a Memorial Lava Bed Park.

many totems, an art gallery, a gift shop and a carving studio where skilled artists can be seen working on plaques, poles, masks and bowls. The museum contains a host of artefacts such as robes and headdresses. Performances by the fabulous **'Ksan Performing Arts Group** take place on at 1830 on Fridays from 4 July to 8 August, $8/5.

Terrace and the Nisga'a Memorial Lava Bed Park

With the entrance of the **Skeena**, a river capable of rising 5 m in a day and fluctuating 18 m between low and high tide, the scenery suddenly comes alive and remains riveting most of the way to Prince Rupert. The broad valley is framed within magnificent mountain peaks such as the photogenic **Seven Sisters**, which dominate the southern skyline west of Kitwanga. While **Terrace** is another uninspiring logging centre, its surroundings are quite the opposite.

Salmon fishing in the Skeena and its many tributaries is a major obsession, and this is one of the best places to see the creeks turn red in spawning season, see p240. It's also a good region for thermal waters, such as the easily reached **Mount Layton Hot Springs** ⓘ *16 km south on Hwy 37 to Kitimat, T250-7982478, www.kermode.net/mountlayton, Mon-Fri 1400-2200, Sat-Sun 1100-2200, $4.50, $2.50 child*. They also have rooms (C). In winter, the fairly undeveloped **Shames Mountain** ⓘ *T250-6388754, www.shamesmountain.com*, 35 km away, has good skiing with lots of powder. In autumn, this area is unparallelled for wild mushroom picking (see box, p250). The helpful **Visitor Information Centre** ⓘ *4511 Keith Av, T250-6352063, www.terracetourism.bc.ca*, can provide a list of local hikes.

Just west of town, the Nisga'a Highway heads north to pretty **Kitsumkalum Lake** and the remarkable **Nisga'a Memorial Lava Bed Park**, hands down the area's top attraction. In the mid-18th century the most recent of several volcanic eruptions wreaked havoc here, burying several villages and killing some 2000 Nisga'a. The whole area is now a fascinatingly eery lunar landscape, with exquisite blue-green ponds and streams, good for spotting salmon in season. The only way to visit the volcano is as part of a tour run by **Northwest Escapes**, T250-6388490, www.nwescapes.ca. The four-hour (6 km round trip) tours, led by Nisga'a guides, leave at noon on weekends from May to August, $25, $15 child. The **Park Visitor Centre and headquarters**, T250-6389589, is in a striking longhouse at Vetter Creek, 26.5 km from the tour start. Pick up one of the self-guided auto tour brochures ($1.50). In 1999 the Nisga'a made history as the first Native band to negotiate legal ownership of their traditional land in the Nass Valley.

Prince Rupert ⊜🚲🏍🚗❄🚌🚐🔺🚈🚢 ›› *pp251-263.*

Most travellers will be passing through Prince Rupert on their way somewhere else, but this picturesque fishing town, at the mouth of the Skeena River, is worth a stop. First Nations history, art and culture are integral to this region and the town contains one of the largest collections of totem poles in the north. **Cow Town**, a pretty little harbour area dotted with gift shops and restaurants, is the place to relax. A large number of Chinese and Vietnamese descendants lend the town a cosmopolitan flavour that is unusual in the north. Plenty of tours and excursions run to abandoned native villages, or to see whales or grizzlies. Sport fishing is also a big draw. For further details, contact the helpful **Visitor Information Centre** ① *215 Cow Bay Rd, T1800-6671994, www.tourismprincerupert.com, www.rupert.bc.ca, summer Mon-Sat 0900-2000, Sun 0900- 1700, winter Mon-Sat 0900-1700.* 🔺🔺 ›› *p260.*

Museum of Northern BC
① *100 1st Av W, T250-6243207, www.museumofnorthernbc.com, summer Mon-Sat 0900-2000, Sun 0900-1700, winter Mon-Sat 0900-1700, $5, $1 child.*
This is hands down Prince Rupert's major attraction, illustrating the history and culture of the Northwest Coast back to the end of the last ice age, through exhibits and ancient artefacts. The museum showcases the superb artworks for which the local aboriginal peoples are famous, as well as the cultures of other First Nations. The gift shop is stocked with locally made articles such as carved masks, silver Haida jewellery and books on art and culture. In summer there are tours of the museum at 1400, as well as the Heritage Walking Tour and Totem Pole Walking Tour around town. There is also an Archaeological Harbour Tour and presentations of the Prince Rupert Story, a one-hour dramatization and slide show.

One block away at Market Place is the **Museum Carving Shed**, T250-6242421, where Haida, Nisga'a and Tlingit artists can be seen at work from June to August. Nearby, the new **longhouse** hosts drama, dance and song performances by the Gwisamiikgigot Dancers. The **Prince Rupert Archives**, with 20,000 historic photos, are at 100 1st Avenue East. Another important part of Prince Rupert's past is the story of the railway, thoroughly explored in the **Kwinitsa Railway Station Museum** ① *Bill Murray Way, T250-6245637, Jun-Aug 0900-1700, by donation*, housed in the original 1911 station in Waterfront Park.

The harbour at Prince Rupert.

British Columbia Northern BC

Other than those offered by the museum, most tours involve wildlife viewing or a trip to **Laxspa'aws** (**Pike Island**), which contains three abandoned First Nations villages dating back as far as 1800 years. Whale watching is big business here, with high concentrations of humpback whales to the north, as well as grey whales and orcas. The best time is August to October, or May to July for orcas. You're also likely to see bald eagles and sea lions. **Khutzeymateen Grizzly Bear Sanctuary**, the only protected grizzly habitat in Canada, is 45 km to the northeast, and only accessed by water. The best time to visit is late April to September. People get very excited about the possibility of seeing one of the rare and elusive white Kermode (Spirit) bears. While the chances are slim, the best place to catch a glimpse is at **Princess Royal Island** far to the south. The best time is September to early October.

North Pacific Cannery and Fishing Village ⓘ *T250-6283538, www.cannery.ca, May-Sep 0900-1800, several tours daily, $12/10*, 30 minutes away in Port Edward, is very popular. The cannery was operational from 1889 to 1981. Now the whole village has been restored and opened as a living museum with tours, exhibits, live performances, a restaurant and a hostel in the atmospheric old bunkhouse. In summer, Prince Rupert buses run all the way here; call **Prince Rupert Transit**, T250-6243343 for details.

Haida Gwaii: Queen Charlotte Islands ⬛🔾⬛▲🔾🔾 ↠ *pp251-263.*

This 300-km long, horn-shaped archipelago 150 km west of Prince Rupert consists of two big islands and the 200 or so islets that surround them. One of only two places in Western Canada to have avoided glaciation during the last ice age, Haida Gwaii (also known as the Queen Charlotte Islands) harbours many species of flora and fauna not found anywhere else, prompting associations with the Galápagos. The world's largest black bears live here, as well as its greatest populations of Peale's peregrine falcons and black-footed albatross. Marine life is equally abundant, making for excellent fishing and whale watching. Fin, sperm, right, humpback and grey whales migrate through, and resident pods of orca can be seen almost anywhere, even coming right up to the shores of Queen Charlotte City.

Another reason to visit is the Haida themselves, who have thrived on these islands for over 10,000 years (see p41). Widely recognized as being one of the most sophisticated aboriginal peoples on the continent, they are consummate artists and craftsmen. Like few other spots in Canada, this still feels like native land, inhabited by a mere 6000 predominantly aboriginal souls.

A fault line stretching from California to Alaska passes close to the west coast of Haida Gwaii, adding occasional earthquakes to the most wind- and tide-lashed coastline on the Pacific. **Cape St James** at the southern tip is the best place for storm watching, with an average wind-speed of 34 kph. It is little wonder that the communities cling to the protected east coast with its fine beaches. The warm streams of the so-called Japanese Current keep temperatures surprisingly mild here, even in winter. Combined with the copious amounts of rain that perpetually shroud the islands, this has resulted in a lush covering of ancient rainforest.

Ins and outs

Ferries arrive at Skidegate on **Graham Island**, from where it's 5 km to Queen Charlotte City, the main base on the island with the most useful visitor centre; see also www.qcinfo.com for information. Apart from the museum at Skidegate, the main attraction on Graham Island is Naikoon Provincial Park. South of the Skidegate Narrows, connected by ferry, is the long, tapering **Moresby Island**, whose name also embraces the myriad tiny islets that surround it. Barely populated, it is an almost inaccessible wilderness, the whole southern half of which is now protected as Gwaii Haanas National Park, whose abandoned Haida villages are one of the main highlights of the islands.

Haida Gwaii

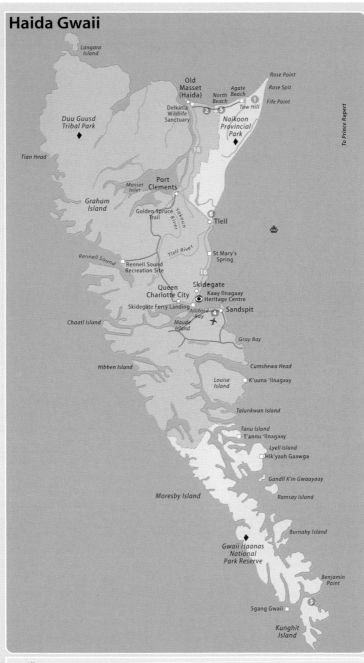

Langara Island

Duu Guusd Tribal Park

Tian Head

Old Masset (Haida)

Rose Point
Rose Spit
Fife Point

Agate Beach
North Beach

Delkatla Wildlife Sanctuary

Tow Hill

1
2 **5**

Naikoon Provincial Park

To Prince Rupert

16

Masset Inlet

Port Clements

Graham Island

Golden Spruce Trail

Yakoun River

6 Tlell

Tlell

Tlell River

Rennell Sound

Rennell Sound Recreation Site

St Mary's Spring

Skidegate

16

Queen Charlotte City

Kaay Ilnagaay Heritage Centre

Skidegate Ferry Landing

Alliford Bay

Sandspit

Chaatl Island

Maude Island

Gray Bay

Hibben Island

Cumshewa Head

Louise Island

K'uuna 'Ilnagaay

Talunkwan Island

Tanu Island

T'annu 'Ilnagaay

Lyell Island

Hlk'yaah Gaawga

Gandll K'in Gwaayaay

Moresby Island

Ramsay Island

Burnaby Island

Gwaii Haanas National Park Reserve

Benjamin Point

3

Sgang Gwaii

Kunghit Island

N

10 km
10 miles

Sleeping ⬭
Alaska View Lodge **2**
Gwaii Haanas Guest House **3**
Moresby Island Guesthouse **4**

Rapid Richie's Rustic Rentals **5**

Camping 🏕
Agate Beach Campground **1**

Misty Meadows Campground **6**

British Columbia Northern BC

The weathered totem poles on Haida Gwaii have stood the test of time.

Graham Island

Graham Island contains almost all of Haida Gwaii's inhabitants in a few communities connected by a single paved road. Ferries arrive at Skidegate Landing. The **Haida Gwaii Museum** ① *500 m east of the terminal at Kaay Ilnagaay (Sea Lion Town), T250-5954643*, is a fine introduction to the human and natural history of the islands, with many fine artworks including an excellent assortment of argillite carvings. It's part of the **Kaay Ilnagaay Heritage Centre**, a multi-million dollar project currently nearing completion, which will also include a Greeting House, Performance House, café and gift shop. Six monumental cedar totem poles have already been raised. The nearby **Canoe Shed** contains the famous 50-ft cedar canoe *Loo Taas* (Wave Eater) designed by the latter-day Haida genius Bill Reid, see box p62. **Skidegate Village**, 2 km east, has an arts co-operative, a carving shed where artists can be seen at work, a totem pole by Bill Reid, the gravity-defying Balance Rock and the interesting circular 3-km Spirit Lake Trail. For more information, visit www.skidegate.ca.

The picturesque fishing village of **Queen Charlotte City**, 5 km west of the ferry, is centred around a pretty harbour and marina. The excellent **Visitor Information Centre** ① *3220 Wharf St, T250- 5598316, www.queencharlotte.ca, May-Sep 1000-1900*, can arrange tours and permits to the abandoned villages on Moresby Island (the only way to get there is on a tour). The **Parks Canada Office** ① *above City Centre Grocery Store, T250-5598316, www.pc.gc.ca/pn-np/bc/gwaiihaanas, Mon-Fri 0800-1630*, provides information on Gwaii Haanas National Park. The **Ministry of Forests** ① *3rd Av, T250-5598447*, can give information on the forestry campgrounds dotted around both islands. If planning to drive on the logging roads, get up-to-date details from **McMillan Bloedel**, T250-5594224. One destination reached by such roads from Queen Charlotte City is **Rennell Sound Recreation Site**, the best place to experience the wild west coast, with wilderness campgrounds and paths through rainforest to sandy beaches.

Highway 16, the island's only paved road, runs north through Skidegate to Tl'ell, Port Clements and Masset. Halfway to Tl'ell a wooden carving marks the site of **St Mary's Spring**. According to legend, those who drink from here are destined to return. **Tl'ell** itself is a tiny artist community and home to the Naikoon Park HQ and interpretive centre (see below). Trails along the Tl'ell River lead to endless beaches and dunes, and the shipwreck of the

Pezuta (two hours each way). At **Port Clements**, www.portclements.com, a small museum explores the pioneer history of the islands. A trail leads through temperate rainforest to the erstwhile site of the **Golden Spruce**, sadly chopped down by a crazed logger in 1997. A few kilometres further is the site of the partially carved **Haida Canoe**.

The island's most populated town, **Masset** is an ex-military base that lacks QCC's picturesque qualities, but its summer-only **Visitor Information Centre** ① *1455 Old Beach Rd, T250-6263995, www.island.net/~masset*, can point you towards the local attractions. To the north is **Delkatla Wildlife Sanctuary**, the best place for birdwatching on Haida Gwaii, with more than 140 visiting species, and a new interpretive centre. **Old Masset**, or Haida, is 2 km west, with old and new totem poles, a small museum and some canoe and carving sheds. The **Village Office** on Eagle Road, T205-6263337, is the place to ask for permission to visit ancient village sites within **Duu Guusd Tribal Park** to the northwest.

From Masset, the road leads 26 km east to the **Naikoon Park** trailhead at Tow Hill, a 130-m volcanic cliff with amazing rock formations created by lava flows. These are best appreciated at its base, reached by a 1-km trail, where a blowhole springs into action when the tide comes in. Two other beautiful paths lead to the top of Tow Hill. From here you can take in the full extent of North Beach, which follows the whole strip of coast from Old Masset to Rose Spit. This is a good place to collect razor clams, scallops and crabs (a saltwater fishing licence is needed for the latter). Just west of Tow Hill is Agate Beach with great camping, and beachcombing. A 10-km hike from Tow Hill leads to **Rose Spit**, a sacred Haida site and ecological reserve at the northeast corner of Naikoon Park. This 12-km sand peninsula can be walked or biked on a 40-km loop. A longer two day circuit involves taking the **Fife Point Trail** from Tow Hill to the east side of the park, then walking around Rose Spit and back to Tow Hill. It's a good idea to get a tide chart before setting off.

Gwaii Haanas National Park

Before entering the park you must buy a permit and attend a 90-minute orientation session. These take place daily at 0800 and 1930 in summer. A limit is placed on the number of visitors. To make a reservation ($15), call T250-3871642, or show up at the 0800 orientation session at the **Queen Charlotte City Information Centre** and hope for one of the six daily standby spots. For up to date requirements and information, contact the

The west coast of Haida Gwaii bears the brunt of the wind and rain sweeping in from the Pacific.

British Columbia Northern BC

Background

The Haida

The art of the Haida is utterly distinctive due to their particular style of representing animals and mythical creatures, often in red and black. Prolific carvers of totem poles, they also used the giant red cedars that once flourished on the islands to make huge dug-out canoes and ornately decorated houses. For many, the highlight of a visit to Haida Gwaii is the opportunity to buy authentic Haida art such as beautiful masks and jewellery or delicate carvings in argillite, a black, slate-like rock only found on these islands.

As well as being artists, the Haida had a reputation as fearful warriors; their unsurpassed sea-faring skills gained them the label 'Vikings of the Pacific Northwest'. More recently, they have proven themselves powerful negotiators in their dealings with logging companies and politicians. All this despite the decimation of their population by smallpox and other epidemics brought by the first Europeans: estimated at around 8000 in 1835, their number had dropped to 588 by 1915. This tragedy forced the Haida to abandon almost all of their villages, especially on the southern island, and today many of these can be visited on tours, the houses and totems slowly returning to the earth. Only one, Sgan Gwaii (Ninstints) at the southern tip of Moresby Island, has been preserved and declared a UNESCO World Heritage Site.

Queen Charlotte City or Sandspit information centres, or call the Watchmen on T250-5598225. Park fees are $10 per day, $10 per night, with a flat rate of $60 for six to fourteen nights. Camping is allowed anywhere but cultural sites. The beach is best so that the water will erase any traces, but check tide times.

Ferries from Skidegate run south to the virtually uninhabited **Moresby Island**, docking at **Alliford Bay**. The island's only village, **Sandspit**, is 15 km east and little more than an airport with a **Visitor Information Centre** ⓘ *T250-6375362, www.sandspitqci.com, May-Sep 0900- 1800*. To the south is **Gray Bay**, a large sandy beach with a great forestry campsite. A four-day trek leads south to Cumshewa Head, with beautiful beaches on the way.

Half of Moresby Island is protected by the extraordinary **Gwaii Haanas National Park Reserve**, which includes 1600 km of coastline and 138 islands. There are no hiking trails, and entry is by boat or float plane only, involving a potentially expensive tour for all but experienced kayakers, who have endless scope for exploration and whale watching. Most visitors come to see the abandoned villages and over 500 important archaeological features that are evidence of 10,000 years of occupation. Today these are co-managed by the government and the Haida Nation. The five most culturally significant sites are manned by Watchmen, traditional guards sometimes seen on top of totem poles, wearing distinctive tall hats. They live at the sites in the summer and are very liberal with information.

K'uuna 'Ilnagaay (Skedans) on Louise Island, the easiest village to access, was painted by Emily Carr (see p104) in 1907 before most of the buildings and totems returned to the earth. A trail meanders through the eerie but beautiful remains of the ancient village and cemetery. Look out for abandoned logging equipment now covered with moss. **T'annu**

66 99 the famous Bear Glacier is an eerie
blue sheet of ice that comes right down to
the road, glows in the dark, and cracks and
groans like a living thing....

'Ilnagaay (**Tanu**) on T'anuu Island is a beautiful spot facing two beaches. **Hlk'yaah Gaawga**
(**Windy Bay**) on the eastern shore of Lyell Island is where the Haida blocked the road in 1985,
bringing an end to logging in South Moresby, hopefully forever. A longhouse where the
Watchmen now live was built in commemoration. There are trails here through
1000-year-old trees that are 70 m tall. **Gandll K'in Gwaayaay** (**Hot Spring Island**) is a
gorgeous place with a dozen hot pools. A bath house is provided for rinsing off before
dipping in. **Sgang Gwaay** (**Ninstits**), off the west coast of Kunghit Island, is a UNESCO World
Heritage Site and the only village that has been preserved. Facing the beach are over two
dozen totem poles, a magnificent display of standing Haida mortuary poles.

Cassiar Highway ●❶❷❸ » *pp251-263.*

Back on the mainland, joining the Yellowhead Highway at Kitwanga and running to just west
of Watson Lake in the Yukon, Highway 37 is one of the West's last great frontier roads, and the
section between Meziadin Junction and Iskut has some of the best scenery in BC, with the
sharp peaks and vast glaciers of the Coast Mountains almost tapping on your windshield.
Outside the tourist season, you're almost as likely to see a black bear as another car. There are
few towns or services, and on either side of the road nothing but wilderness for hundreds of
kilometres. A full list of facilities is available from visitor information centres in Prince Rupert,
Terrace and Meziadin Junction. This windy, often narrow road is now mostly paved but some
portions are gravel and others are pot-holed. It's advisable to carry two good spare tyres.
Snow can occur at almost any time of the year; for up-to-date road conditions visit
www.th.gov.bc.ca/roadreports. It is important for drivers to fill up with petrol when they get
the chance, especially as prices rise quite steeply the further you go. If doing a circuit, it would
be better to drive this road from north to south.

Stewart, Hyder and the Bear Glacier
Just north of the Yellowhead-Cassiar junction, the villages of **Gitwangak** (**Kitwanga**) and
Gitanyow (**Kitwancool**) have some interesting old and new totem poles; and Meziadin
Junction, 90 km further on, has a pleasant lake and campsite (T250-8477320), good fishing,
and a small summer-only visitor information centre. Only here, however, does the Cassiar
start to show its worth, with some of the province's most awe-inspiring scenery opening up
both north, and on Highway 37A which runs 65 km west to Stewart and its Alaskan twin,
Hyder. You'd be mad to come this far and not at least detour 28 km west to the famous **Bear
Glacier**, an eerie blue sheet of ice that comes right down to the road, glows in the dark, and
cracks and groans like a living thing.

The ramshackle, photogenic town of **Stewart** is another slice of Wild West life. At the
Stewart Historical Museum ⓘ *Columbia and 6th Av, T250-6362568, summer 1100-1900, $3,*
you can learn all about the twists of fortune that constitute the town's interesting history,
including a spell as North America's largest gold mine town. Film-makers (*Insomnia, The*

Top tips

Mould rush

If driving the Cassiar Highway in September or October, look out for The Zoo, about 70 km from Kitwanga. In season, this shanty town of makeshift tarpaulin huts houses hundreds of mushroom- pickers, along with shops, restaurants, buyers, even a bar. The whole unofficial industry that surrounds the harvesting of wild and valuable Pine Mushrooms (*masutake*) is the closest modern equivalent to the Gold Rush, with some people making a small fortune, others barely scraping together the bus fare home, and everyone hoping to stumble upon the mother lode. The Zoo could be seen as the Dawson City of its day, as raw and authentic a slice of life as you could ever hope to encounter. Don't expect anyone to tell you where the mushrooms are though!

Thing, and *Leaving Normal* are among those films shot here) agree that Stewart's most reliable natural resource is its incredible setting at the heart of an amphitheatre of mountains, whose steep rocky peaks rise almost vertically from the Portland Canal, one of the world's longest fjords.

There's not much to do, but the summer-only **Visitor Information Centre** ⓘ *222 5th Av, T250-6369224, www.stewart-hyder.com*, can recommend local hikes, and provide pamphlets for the Heritage Walking Tour around town and the Salmon Glacier Auto Tour. The latter follows the Salmon River through mining country in BC and Alaska to the massive **Salmon Glacier** and **Summit Lake**. In mid-summer, this entire lake drains under the glacier leaving behind a weird landscape of scattered icebergs.

On the other side of the fjord, **Hyder** draws a lot of tourists just by being such an easily accessed part of Alaska. A surprisingly popular ceremony has built up here. It's almost compulsory to get 'Hyderized', which entails downing a shot of incredibly hard liquor in one of the town's two almost permanently open bars. A much more legitimate draw is the viewing platform at **Fish Creek**, about 7 km away, possibly the best and most reliable place to safely enjoy the awesome spectacle of grizzly and black bears fishing for salmon. You'll see grizzly mothers showing their cubs the ropes, and observe the different strategies these fascinating animals adopt according to their personalities.

● Sleeping

Clinton and around *p236*

There are plenty of guest (dude) ranches around Clinton, offering a genuine Wild West experience, guided horse riding, and often gourmet food or spa/health packages. Follow links from www.hellobc.com or visit www.bcgra.com for a selection.

AL Big Bar Guest Ranch, 9 km north of Clinton, turn west on Big Bar Rd for 45 km, T250-4592333, www.bigbarranch.com. One of the best and most affordable ranches, with highly rated riding, lodge rooms, cabins, tepees and RV sites.

C Red Coach Inn, 170 Hwy 97 N, 100 Mile House, T250-3952266. There are plenty of motels (**D**) in town, but it's worth paying a little extra for to stay here, with its indoor pool and hot tub.

C Spring Lake Ranch, 15 km north of 100 Mile House on Spring Lake Rd, T250-7915776, www.springlakeranch.com. This hand-built log cabin is set by a lake in extensive grounds. There is 1 chalet and 4 cabins, all with kitchen facilities, though (very good) meals are also available. There's a games room and plenty of scope for activities in the area.

Camping

Municipal RV Park, 385 Birch Av, Clinton, T250-3952434.

Williams Lake and around *p236,*

C Drummond Lodge and Motel, 1 km south at 1405 Hwy 97, T250-3925334, www.drummondlodge.com. Decent rooms with decks in a nice lakeside setting.

C Neilsen's Lakeshore Cabins, 6071 Cedar Creek Rd, 5 km from Likely, T250-7902258. Cabins on Quesnel Lake and RV sites.

D Rowat's Waterside B&B, 1397 Borland Rd, T250-3927395, www.wlakebb.com. 5 rooms in a pleasant house on the lake, with guest lounge, decks, en suite baths and full breakfast.

D-E Moreshead Lake Resort, Likely Rd, 15 km from Likely, T250-7902323. Basic cabins with kitchenettes, plus 8 campsites. Rowing boat, canoe and kayak rentals.

Camping

Williams Lake Stampede Campground, at 850 Mackenzie St, T250-3986718. A handy choice for town.

Wildwood Campsite, 13 km north on the highway, T250-9894711. Much nicer sites.

Barkerville and Bowron Lakes *p236*

A St George Hotel, 4 Main St, right in Barkerville Heritage Park, T250-9940008, www.stgeorgehotel.bc.ca. 7 rooms in a restored 1890s house with antique decor, some with en suite. Gourmet breakfast.

A-D Beckers Lodge Resort, Bowron Lake Rd, T250-9928864, www.beckerslodge.ca. This is the ideal place to relax at the start and end of the Bowron Lakes circuit, with a range of chalets and cabins right on the lake, plus campsites, a great restaurant, a store, a very broad array of kayaks and canoes to rent, and full tours.

B-D Bowron Lake Lodge, Bowron Lakes, T250-9922733, www.bowron lakelodge.com. The cabins here aren't nearly as nice as the Beckers Lodge Resort, above, but they're also on the lake and have campsites, rentals and a restaurant.

C Kelly House B&B, Hwy 26, Barkerville, T250-9943328, www.kellyhouse.ca. 3 nice rooms with shared or private bath and antique furniture. Full breakfast.

C The Wells Hotel, 2341 Pooley St, Wells, T250-9943427, www.wellshotel.com. Set in a charming, picturesque little town 8 km west of Barkerville, this homely heritage inn has comfy rooms, a pub and restaurant, and breakfast is included.

Camping

Barkerville Provincial Park, 3 km east, T250-3984414. 168 sites in 3 campgrounds, reservations recommended in summer. Showers and hiking trails.

Chilcotin Plateau *p237*

D **Puntzi Lake Resort**, T250-4811176, www.puntzilake.com. 1 of 5 such resorts, with lakeside cabins and campsites, canoe and boat rentals, and a campsite with hookups, showers and a laundry.

Tweedsmuir Provincial Park *p237*

A-B **Tweedsmuir Lodge**, Stuie, T250-9822402, www.tweedsmuirpark lodge.com. A variety of lovely wood cabins and chalets, some with kitchenettes, in gorgeous forested surroundings. Also has campsites and buffet-style meals for $65.

Bella Coola *p238*

C **Bella Coola Valley Inn**, Mackenzie St, T250-7995316, www.bellacoolavalley inn.com. The most upmarket choice and handy for the ferry, with an atmospheric turn-of-the-20th-century-style lobby and lounge, a restaurant, patio, a nice pub, and some fairly attractive rooms.

C **Tallheo Cannery Inn**, 10 mins' from the wharf in a water taxi, free for guests, T250- 9822344. The most interesting choice by far. 15 rooms with shared bath in a classic restored 1920 bunkhouse that was part of a cannery village. Meals and canoe/kayak tours available. There's also lots of hiking on the 68-ha grounds, a stream with salmon and trout, and a private beach.

C-D **Bella Coola Motel**, Clayton St, T250-7995323. Reasonable rooms with kitchens, and rental of scooters, bikes and canoes.

D **Sinclair House**, 10 km east of Hagensborg, T1888-8676668. 3 lovely rooms in a fine house surrounded by flowers and gardens. Private baths, guest lounge, library, jacuzzi, breakfast included, and dinners by arrangement.

Camping

Bailey Bridge Campsite, off Hwy 20, Salommpt Rd, Hagensborg, T250-9822342. The nicest camping option,

located on a river with showers and 4 basic cabins with kitchenettes (**E**).

Hagen Haven RV Park and Campground, 8 km east on the Hwy, T250-7995659. On a creek with showers, laundry and hook-ups.

Wells Gray Provincial Park *p239*

B **Clearwater Lodge**, 331 Eden Rd, Clearwater, T250-6743080. The nicest of many choices in Clearwater, with kitchenettes, pool, hot tub, sauna and restaurant.

B **Helmcken Falls Lodge**, by the park entrance, T250-6743657, www.helmcken falls.com. Decent rooms, dining, trail rides, guided hiking and canoeing.

C **Wells Gray Guest Ranch**, 9 km before entrance, T250-6742792, www.wellsgray ranch.com. Log cabins with kitchens and shower on an authentic working ranch.

D **Trophy Mountain Buffalo Ranch**, 4373 Clearwater Valley Rd, 20 mins from the park, T250-6743095, www.buffalo ranch.ca. A working buffalo ranch with rustic log buildings, friendly owners and a peaceful setting. Recommended.

Camping

North Thompson River Provincial Park, T250-8513000, just west of the park entrance is the nicest and closest of several provincial park and private campgrounds in the area.

Park Campgrounds, T250-8513000. There are a few vehicle-accessible campgrounds in the park, but they all fill up in summer, so it's a good idea to reserve in advance. A small fee is charged for wilderness camping.

Prince George *p240*

For B&B options, try www.pgonline.com/ bnb/hotline.

A **Coast Inn**, 770 Brunswick St, T250-5630121, www.coasthotels.com. The nicest hotel in town, with a pool, sauna, gym, lounge, pub and 3 restaurants.

D **Credo Manor B&B**, 6872 O'Grady Rd, T250-9648142. Spacious, comfortable rooms, with breakfast included.

D **Downtown Motel**, 650 Dominion, T250-5639241, www.downtownmotel.ca. About the nicest of many conveniently central budget options.

D **Laura's Roof Garden B&B**, 261 Moffat St, T250-5648598, www.roof gardenbb.com. A very nice spot with gorgeous flowers everywhere, patios and jacuzzi tub, but only 2 rooms.

E **National Hotel**, 1201 1st Av, T250-5647010. A hostel-type joint but private rooms only, with shared bath, kitchen, and common room.

Camping

Blue Spruce RV Park, 5 km west on Hwy 16 from Hwy 97 junction at 4433 Kimball Rd, T250-8647272. Pool, laundry, showers, playground.

Fraser River RV Park, Highway 97 south, T250-3304453. One of the better campgrounds, with wooded sites on the river, and showers.

West to Smithers *p241*

A-B **Hudson Bay Lodge**, 3251 Hwy 16 E, Smithers, T250-8474581, www.hudsonbaylodge.com. The nicest option, this attractive hotel has a broad range of rooms and suites, plus a restaurant, pub and café.

C **Douglas Resort Motel**, Hwy 16 W, Telkwa, T250-8465679, www.douglas resortmotel.com. Nice log cabins with fireplaces, kitchens and views of the Bulkley River rapids from the balconies and patios. Sauna and hot tub.

D **Stork Nest Inn**, 1485 Main St Smithers, T250-8473831, www.stork nestinn.com. There are plenty of fairly characterless motels in town. This one is clean, handy and good value, with breakfast included

E **Smithers Guesthouse & Hostel**, 1766 Main St Smithers, T250-8474862, www.smithershostel.com. Dorms and private rooms, with shared bath, common room, kitchen, internet and laundry.

Camping

Tyhee Lake Provincial Park, Telkwa, T250-8477320. 59 nice forested sites, trails and a beach.

Hazeltons *p241*

E **Bulkley Valley Motel**, 4444 Hwy 16, New Hazelton, T250-8426817, www.bulkley valleymotel.com. The most promising of a couple of motels here, with kitchenettes.

Camping

'Ksan Campground, T250-8425297. A pretty site on the banks of the river, handy for visiting the main sites of interest. Showers and hook-ups.

Terrace and the Nisga'a Memorial Lava Bed Park *p242*

B-C **Coast Inn of the West**, 4620 Lakelse Av, T250-6388141, www.coasthotels.com. The most comfortable option.

D **Costa-Lessa Motel**, 3867 Hwy 16 E, T250-6381885. The best value of many budget motels that line Hwy 16 on both sides of town.

Camping

Ferry Island Campground, in Terrace, follow signs from Hwy 16, T250-6152951.

Kleanza Creek, 15 km E on Hwy 16. A small campground beautifully located on a creek cascading through a canyon.

Nisga'a Park Visitor Centre, see p242, T250-6389589. There's a simple but pretty campground here, and it's also the place to ask about B&Bs in local Nisga'a homes, such as in New Aiyansh.

Prince Rupert *p243, map p254*

A **Crest Hotel**, 222 1st Av W, T250-6246771, www.cresthotel.bc.ca. The most luxurious option in town, with harbour views, hot tub, gym, sauna, sundeck, restaurant and lounge.

C **Inn on the Harbour**, 720 1st Av W, T250-6249107, www.innontheharbour.com. Slightly more stylish than most downtown options. Ask for a room with harbour views. Continental breakfast.

C Java Lodge, 516 3rd Av, T250-6222833, www.citytel.net/javalodge. 4 stylish and large rooms above an internet café in central downtown, with TVs and internet, deck, laundry, shared bath.

D Aleeda Motel, 900 3rd Av W, T1888-4602023, www.aleedamotel.bc.ca. Comfy, clean and spacious rooms, some with kitchenette.

D Andrée's B&B, 315 4th Av E, T250-6243666, www.andreesbb.com. 3 very attractive rooms with hardwood floors and harbour views. Guests can enjoy the living room, library, garden and deck.

D Eagle's Bluff B&B, 201 Cow Bay Rd, in Cow Bay, T250-6274955. 7 rooms with lots of character, mostly en suite, in a historic house located right on the harbour with great views.

E Pioneer Hostel, 167 3rd Av E, T250-6242334, www.citytel.net/pioneer. Well situated in a charming clapboard house close to town and Cow Bay, this friendly little hostel has dorms and private rooms, shared baths and kitchen facilities, internet, bikes, laundry, and a backyard with BBQ.

E The Waterfront Inn, North Pacific Cannery (see p244), T250-6283538, www.cannery.ca. A hostel in the atmospheric old bunkhouse.

Camping

Park Avenue Campground, 1750 Park Av, T250-6245861. A big ugly parking lot, but close to the ferry terminal.

Prudhomme Lake Provincial Park, 15 km E on Hwy 16, T250-7982277. Much nicer, with 24 wooded sites by the lake.

Haida Gwaii: Graham Island
p244, map245

A-C Gracie's Place, 3113 3rd Av, T250-5594262, Queen Charlotte City. 5 units ranging from a 2-bedroom suite with kitchen and bathroom to a closet-like room. Antiques and patio. Airport pick up.

C Sea Raven Motel & Restaurant, 3301 3rd Av, Queen Charlotte City, T250-5594423, www.searaven.com. Regular motel room, balcony, good for breakfast.

C-D Alaska View Lodge, No 12291, 11 km from Masset, Tow Hill Rd, T250-6263333, www.alaskaviewlodge.ca. 4 rooms on the ocean in a very remote setting in Naikoon Park, with shared or private bath, balconies, and breakfast.

C-D Dorothy & Mike's Guesthouse, 3127 2nd Av, Queen Charlotte City, T250-5598439, www.qcislands.net/doromike. 4 beautiful suites with kitchens and living rooms, plus a couple of cheaper rooms, in a gorgeous house, with use of living

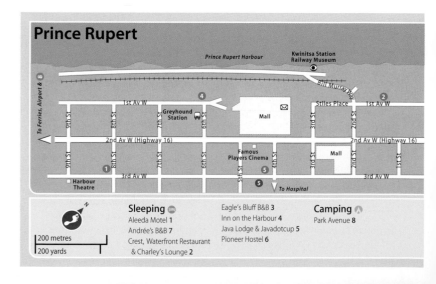

Prince Rupert

Sleeping
Aleeda Motel 1
Andrée's B&B 7
Crest, Waterfront Restaurant
& Charley's Lounge 2

Eagle's Bluff B&B 3
Inn on the Harbour 4
Java Lodge & Javadotcup 5
Pioneer Hostel 6

Camping
Park Avenue 8

room, library, decks and patio with views of the water. Breakfast included.

D **Riverside B&B**, Richardson Rd, Tl'ell, T250-5574418, www.qcislands.net/ margaret. 4 spacious rooms in an attractive wood building, with sliding doors to balconies with views of the river.

D **Spruce Point Lodge**, west end of town, near the school, Queen Charlotte City, T250-5598234, www.qcislands.net/ sprpoint. A striking wood lodge in a dramatic, very peaceful waterfront setting on a point, with decent but plain rooms.

D-E **Premier Creek Hostel and Lodging**, 3101 3rd Av, T250-5598415, Queen Charlotte City, www.qcislands.net/premier. A very interesting restored 1910 building fronted with long balconies, and surrounded by gardens. Spacious rooms have large windows with great views of the harbour. There's also a separate hostel with common room and cooking facilities.

D-E **Rapid Richie's Rustic Rentals**, No 15900, 16 km from Masset, Tow Hill Rd, T250-6265472, www.beach cabins.com. Sweet cedar-shake cabins on the beach, with lots of windows facing the sea and a very relaxed vibe. Definitely a place to kick back and unwind. Wood stove, cooking facilities,

very comfy but no flush toilet (private outhouse). Useful website.

Camping

Agate Beach Campground, Tow Hill Rd, 26 km east of Massett near Tow Hill. On the beach.

Misty Meadows Campground, 0.5 km north of Tl'ell in Naikoon Park. 64 km of beach. No reservations.

Haida Gwaii: Gwaii Haanas National Park *p247, map245*

AL **Gwaii Haanas Guest House**, Rose Harbour, T250-5598638, www.gwaii haanas.com. Expensive and remote, accessible only by floatplane or boat. Check the website and consider the package with a visit to Hot Spring Island. The setting is spectacular, however, if rustic, and this price includes 3 organic meals a day. They also arrange kayak and floatplane tours of the park. The kind of experience that could make your trip.

D **Sandspit Inn Hotel**, 200 m from airport, T250-6375334. Restaurant and pub.

E **Moresby Island Guesthouse**, 385 Alliford Bay Rd, 1 km from airport, T250-6375300, www.moresbyisland-bnb.com. 10 rooms with shared bath, kitchen and 2 lounge areas, laundry, and bike rentals. Basic breakfast included.

Stewart, Hyder and the Bear Glacier *p249*

C **Ripley Creek Inn**, 306 5th Av, Stewart T250-6362344, www.ripleycreekinn. homestead.com. Reasonable rooms in a number of interesting historic houses, one of which was the home of legendary Klondike Kate. Sauna, common room, bikes, and the best restaurant in town.

C-D **King Edward Hotel and Motel**, 405 5th Av, Stewart, T250-6362244, www.king edwardhotel.com. The motel rooms are slightly nicer, and have kitchenettes. The hotel contains almost the only restaurant, pub and coffeeshop in town.

D **Sea Alaska Inn**, Hyder Dock Rd, Hyder, T250-6369006, www.sealaskainn.com.

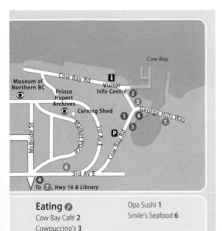

Eating
Cow Bay Café 2
Cowpuccino's 3
Green Apple 4
Macey's 5

Opa Sushi 1
Smile's Seafood 6

Bars & clubs
Breaker's Pub 1

Several types of room plus a campsite (Camp Run-a-muck) bar, and one of the town's 2 restaurants.

Camping
Rainey Creek Campground, 8th Av, Stewart, T250-6362537, Nicely placed on a salmon stream at the edge of town, and the starting point for a few local trails.

🕐 Eating

You're often left with slim pickings for food in the north. The official brochures and websites tend to ignore the question altogether and hope you won't notice. If nothing is listed here, it means there was nothing to be recommended. Try restaurants in the hotels, see Sleeping.

Bella Coola *p238*
Cozy Corner Café, Cliff St/Burke Av. One of the only places for food and coffee.

Prince George *p240*
Cimo Mediterranean Grill, 601 Victoria St, T250-5647975. Pasta, seafood and desserts are all made from scratch at this central, Mediterranean-inspired eatery.
Log House, 11075 Hedlund Rd, T250-9639515. Fine European-style cuisine in a very romantic location right on Tabor Lake, with lots of big windows from which to admire the view.
North 54, 1493 3rd Av, T250-5645400. A European-inspired fine dining menu that changes daily according to available ingredients and inspiration, together with a good wine list and attentive service make this the number one choice.
The Waddling Duck, 1157 5th Av, Smithers, T250-5615550. A charming pub and restaurant with 18th century decor, and an internationally inspired menu.

West to Smithers *p241*
Mountainside Café, 3763 4th Av, T250-8473455. Wholesome food in a friendly atmosphere.

Mountain Eagle Books and Cappuccino, 3775 3rd Av. Café.

Terrace *p242*

Don Diegos, 3212 Kalum St, T250-6352307, open till 2100. Hands down the best place in town, with an excellent reasonably priced menu that's more international than Mexican. Colourful, very popular, quite romantic, with decent portions, sangria and a good wine list.

Prince Rupert *p243, map p254*
The Waterfront, in the Crest Hotel, see above. Steak and seafood, with a good wine list and ocean views.
Cow Bay Café, 205 Cow Bay Rd, T250-6271212. Don't be fooled by the casual café-style appearance: this place serves creative seafood dishes with an international edge and Pacific Rim leanings. The menu changes daily, and there are fine harbour views and a good wine list. It's very popular, so be sure to reserve.
Opa Sushi, 34 Cow Bay Rd, T250-6274560. Japanese food in understated surroundings.
The Salmon House, at the North Pacific Cannery (see p244), T250-6283273.
Smile's Seafood, 113 Cow Bay Rd, T250-6243072. A c1934 diner-style joint with a good reputation for its seafood dishes and a deck over-looking the marina.
Cowpuccino's, 25 Cow Bay Rd, T250-6271395. Funky café with bohemian atmosphere, good coffee, soups, bagels and fabulous baking.
Green Apple, 301 McBride St. A local institution for cheap, tasty fish and chips.
Javadotcup, 516 3rd Av. Stylish, trendy and spacious café, with baking, speciality coffees and internet.
Macey's, 519 3rd Av. One of the many Asian joints Downtown. The food is good, authentic and inexpensive. Vietnamese, Chinese and Thai, cheap breakfasts.

Traveller's tale

If you go down to the woods today...

We'd hiked into an unfamiliar forest from the end of a logging road east of the Cassiar Highway, looking for pine mushrooms. With daylight fading, it became clear that our compass bearing had not led us back to the road. Which way to turn? Make the wrong choice, and we could literally walk for weeks without hitting any sign of civilization. The only sure thing was to keep heading west, knowing that eventually we'd hit the highway. It took two full days of hard bushwhacking: through marshes, around lakes, over mountains. Luckily we had some matches in a plastic bag. At night we started fires, using wood from the dry underside of fallen cedar trunks. We ate as many roasted mushrooms as we could stomach and snatched fragments of hallucinatory sleep. On the second day, fresh piles of berry-rich faeces made it clear that we were being circled by a bear. On day three, we finally hit a logging road and managed to hitch a lift back to 'the Zoo'. We were the fourth party to get lost in the woods that season. Not all the others made it back. *Roger Taylor*

Haida Gwaii: Graham Island
p244, map245

Howler's Bistro and Pub, centre of town, Queen Charlotte City, T250-5598602. Great views of the ocean, good selection of beer on tap, pool tables and a menu of burgers, steaks and seafood.

Dress For Les, Tl'ell, on the highway, T250-5572023. A funky café with good coffee, used clothes, local news and art.

Golden Spruce Breakfast Room, 2 Grouse St, Port Clements, T250-5574325.

Myles from Nowhere, Port Clements. Coffee shop with great books and crafts.

Queen B, 3211A Wharf St, Queen Charlotte City. Good coffee and light homemade dishes in this café.

Stewart *p249*

Bitter Creek Café, in Ripley Creek Inn, 311 5th Av, T250-6362166. By far the best place to eat, with a broad menu covering pizza, burgers, Mexican dishes, steaks, fish, plus some more unusual possibilities.

King Edward Hotel, Columbia/5th Av, T250-6362244. This is where the locals usually go, specializing in fish and chips and king crab.

Bars and clubs

Prince Rupert *p243, map p254*
Breaker's Pub, 117 George Hills Way, Cow Bay. Huge windows and harbour views.
Charley's Lounge, Crest Hotel (see Sleeping p253). A comfy spot for Martinis, cocktails and a good range of draft beers.

Entertainment

Prince Rupert *p243, map p254*
Performing Arts Centre, 1100 McBride St, T250-6277529. A state of the art venue, hosting a wide variety of performances.

Festivals and events

Williams Lake and around *p236*
Jul The Williams Lake Stampede, T250-3926585, www.williamslake stampede.com. Held on the weekend closest to 1 Jul, this major event was first held in 1919 and is one of the biggest and oldest of its kind in BC, with over 13,000 spectators for events like steer wrestling and chuck wagon racing.

Bella Coola *p238*

There's no visitor information centre, but information can be obtained at T250-7995919, or www.centralcoastbc.com.
Jun Annual **rodeo** at the end of Jun.
Jul Discovery Coast Music Festival at the end of Jul.

Prince Rupert *p243, map p254*
Feb The All Native Basketball Tournament, T250-6278997, will celebrate its 47th year in 2006. It's a massive event, attracting over 10,000 spectators to watch basketball all day every day for a week.
May The BC Annual Dance Competition attracts plenty of competitors with $50,000 in cash prizes.
Jun Seafest, T6249118, involves 4 days of various small events.

○ Shopping

Prince George *p240*
Centre City Surplus, 1222 4th Av. A very impressive range of outdoors equipment/clothing, and camping supplies.

Prince Rupert *p243, map p254*
Cow Bay is the place to go for interesting boutiques and gift shops. For aboriginal art go to the museum, or the **Ice House Gallery**, in the historic Atlin Terminal on the harbour in Cow Town, which contains the **North Coast Artists' Co-op**. Locally smoked salmon is available at **Dolly's Fish Market**, 7 Cow Bay Rd, and fresh fish can usually be bought at the dock.

Haida Gwaii: Graham Island
p244, map245
There are gift shops, studios and galleries all over Graham Island. The best are the **Arts Co-op** in Skidegate, the gift shop in the Heritage Centre, and **Haida Art & Jewellery**, 387 Eagle Av, Old Masset, T250-6265560.

▲ Activities and tours

Clinton and around *p236*
Horse riding is popular in the area; check www.landwithoutlimits.com to find out about guest ranches and working ranches.
Stillwater Angling Adventures, 4 Eagle Creek, Canim-Hendrix Lake north, T250-3974121, www.stillwateradventures.com. All inclusive guided fly fishing packages, hiking, horse riding.
XH Buffalo Ranch, 938 S Green Rd, 70 Mile House, T250-4562319, www.xhbuffalo ranch.com. Buffalo viewing from atop a hay wagon.

Williams Lake and around *p236*
Big Canyon Rafting, 120 Lindsay St, Quesnel, T250-9927238, www.bcraft.bc.ca. A variety of whitewater rafting trips from $120 for 4 hrs.
Caribou Wilderness Adventures, 150 Mile House, T250-2964216, www.cariboo wildernessadventures.com. Canoe and kayak tours on Cariboo lakes ($85 half-day), hiking/backpacking tours, fishing and wildlife viewing.

Mountain biking
There are over 50 established mountain-biking trails in the area of all levels and lengths. Pick up a copy of the excellent *Bike Trails* map for full details, or visit www.puddlebike.com.
Red Shreds Bike Store, 95 1st Av, Williams Lake, T250-3987873, www.red shreds.com. A bike and board shop for gear, rentals and information.

Barkerville and Bowron Lakes *p236*
Canoeing
The 116-km Bowron Lakes canoe circuit consists of 11 lakes with 8 portages, and takes a minimum of 7-10 days. Access is limited, with reservations and a registration fee of $55 per person paid at the **Visitor Centre** at the campground, T250-4355622.
Beckers Lodge Resort, Bowron Lake Rd,

T250-9928864, www.beckerslodge.ca, is the best place to get kitted out.

Chilcotin Plateau *p237*
Hyak Wilderness Adventures, T1800-6637238, www.hyak.com. River rafting in the Chilko River's Lava Canyon. **White Saddle Air**, T250-4761182. Helicopter trips from Tatla Lake to Mt Waddington.

Tweedsmuir Provincial Park *p237*
For guided horse riding trips, contact **David Dorsey Jr**, Anahim Lake, T250-7423251.

Hiking
From the Rainbow Range trailhead, **Octopus Lake Trail** is an easy 16-km hike (one-way) to a campsite. **Crystal Lake Trail** is a difficult 25-km hike with 1000 m elevation gain, leading to the Mackenzie Valley close to the Rainbow Cabin. Both can be extended to a cabin and campsite at Tanya Lakes, 25 km further on.

Bella Coola *p238*
Bailey Bridge Fishing & Guiding Services, Hagensborg, T250-9822470. Fishing, sightseeing, wildlife viewing and river drifting. **Bella Coola Air**, Hagensborg, T250-9822545, www.bellacoolaair.com. Flightseeing tours in Cessna planes from 1 hr. **Heritage River Rafting**, Fishing Bailey Bridge, T250-9822972, www.centralcoastbc.com/rafting. Gentle floats down the river in a 4-passenger raft. A great way to enjoy the awesome scenery. **Kynoch West Coast Adventures**, 1900 Hwy 20, Hagensborg, T250-9822298, www.kynochadventures.com. All kinds of trips are run or arranged by these guys, including kayaking and rafting, interpretive hikes, mountain biking and snorkelling with salmon. **Northern Natural Tours**, Hagensborg, T250-9822326. Plant identification and wildlife-habitat viewing tours.

Hiking
The Clayton Falls logging road, heading southwest from the Marina, leads to the 2.7 km M**Gurr Lake Trail**, a good place to view local fjords and the Coast Mountains. Further on, a trail leads to **Blue Jay Lake**, with a campground and a boardwalk trail around peat bogs, and on to **Gray Jay Lake**. A further drive leads to the **Big Cedar**, which at 4.6 m across, is one of BC's biggest trees. From Hagensborg, Nusatsum Valley leads 25 km south to a trail and campsite at **Odegaard Falls**, and 34 km to the longer **Hammer Lake/Ape Lake Trail**.
Doug on the Trail, T250-9822537, www.centralcoastbc.com/dougonthetrail. All manner of guided hikes and walks with a local guide

Wells Gray Provincial Park *p239*
Clearwater Visitor Information Centre, T250-6742646. Well informed and can hook you up with operators for horse riding, float planes, guided canoeing, whitewater rafting and other activities. **Helmcken Falls Lodge**, by the park entrance, T250-6743657, www.helmckenfalls.com. Also arranges most activities.

Prince George *p240*
Mountain biking
McBike, 2095 5th Av, T250-5636001, www.mcbike.bc.ca. Tours, sales, rentals and information. Their website has lots of useful information; also visit www.trailbombers.com.

West to Smithers *p241*
McBike & Sport, 1191 Main St, T250-8475009, www.mcbike.bc.ca. Sales, repairs, tours and rentals. **Suskwa Adventure Outfitters**, T250-8472885, www.suskwa.bc.ca. Rafting daytrips on the Bulkley River, featuring over 30 rapids, and canoeing or kayaking trips on the Stikine or Babine Rivers.

British Columbia Northern BC Listings

There are 2 great options for hiking the Hudson Bay Mountain: a very steep 4-km route via **Glacier Gulch** with 927-m elevation gain, and the much gentler 9-km hike via **Crater Lake**, much of it through meadows, with 1,076 m gain. **Bear Mountaineering**, T250-8472854, www.bearmountaineering.ca. Mountain climbing, ice climbing, hikes and treks, and access to the Burnie Glacier Chalet.

Skiing

Hudson Bay Mountain, T250-8472058, www.skismithers.com. 121 ha of skiable terrain, 34 runs (25% novice, 55% intermediate, 20% advanced), a vertical drop of 1750 ft, 4 lifts, plus lodging, food, lessons and rentals, and a freestyle park. Lift passes $36, $19 child.

Hazeltons *p241*

Skeena Eco-Expeditions, T250-8425249, www.kispiocadventures.com. Guided hiking and cultural tours, canoe rentals, fishing guides and/or river rafting trips.

Terrace and around *p242*
Skiing

Shames Mountain, 35 km west on Hwy 16, T250-6388754, www.shames mountain.com. 57 ha of skiable terrain, 28 trails (21% novice, 60% intermediate, 19% advanced), 1600 ft vertical rise, 4 km longest run, 3 lifts. Day lodge, café, lessons and rentals. Wed-Sun 0900-1530, $39, $19 child.

Prince Rupert *p243, map p254*
Bear watching

Palmerville Lodge, T250-6248243, www.palmerville.bc.ca. Flights to the bear sanctuary in a helicopter or seaplane, starting at $375 per person for 3 hrs, including 1 hr of flight, 2 hrs watching the bears graze on freshwater sedge from a zodiac. In 2005, 90% of tours saw bears. **West Coast Launch**, T250-6279166, www.westcoastlaunch.com. Boat tours to **Khutzeymateen Bear Sanctuary**, $145 for

6 hrs. They also offer whale watching tours, $90 for 4 hrs, Kaien Island tours.

Boat tours

As well as whale watching and Pike Island, a popular excuse to get out on the water is on tour around Kaien Island, also taking in various sights such as Prince Edward, Seal Cove and Butzke Rapids. Tours average $45 for 1½-2 hrs.

Fishing

A long list of charter companies is available from the visitor centre. All 5 species of salmon, as well as halibut and lingcod, are plentiful in local hot spots such as **Chatham Sound** and **Work Channel**. The season for salmon is May-Sep, peaking in Jul-Aug. Halibut is May-Sep. There's freshwater trout fishing in the rivers May-Oct, and steelhead Mar-Apr. **Seashore Charters**, T250-6243323, www.seashorecharters.com. **Trayling's Tackle Shop**, 635 2nd Av, T250-6249874. Supplies.

Flightseeing

North Pacific Seaplanes, T250-6241341, www.northpacificseaplanes.com. A variety of set tours available.

Hiking and biking

Mt Oldfield is a challenging 8.4-km return hike with good views; it's a continuation of the shorter Mt Oldfield Meadows boardwalk trail. Another 5-km hike leads through old-growth forest to **Butze Rapids**, 6 km east of town. Maps and info are available at the visitor centre. **Farwest Sport and Cycle**, 212 3rd Av W, bikes for hire.

Kayaking

Butze Rapids are reversing tidal rapids excellent for whitewater kayak surfing, though the 4.5-6 m tides are for the experienced only. **Skeena Kayaking**, T250-6245246, www.skeenakayaking.ca. Rentals and tours. They also run a B&B.

Excursions from Prince Rupert: Pike Island *p244*

Tour operators
Rave-On-Charters, 655 4th Av E, T250-6249842, www.worldwidefishing.com. Fishing and sightseeing on a 48-ft yacht.
Seashore Charters, T250-6245645, www.seashorecharters.com. Tours led by native guides to 3 abandoned old native villages and 5 other significant archeological sites on **Laxspa'aws**, leaving daily May-Sep. They also do whale watching, sightseeing tours, bear viewing, Tsimshian cultural kayak and traditional canoe trips, cultural evenings, fishing charters and Kaien Island tours.
West Coast Launch, T250-6279166, www.westcoastlaunch.com.

Haida Gwaii *p244, map245*
Bike hire
Moresby Island Guest House, Sandspit, T250-6375300. Bike rentals.
Premier Creek Lodging, Queen Charlotte City, T250-5598415. Bike rentals.

Kayak
This the obvious activity, with plenty of islands to explore, and a good chance of seeing whales (including orcas), sea lions, and otters. Stay away from the west coast, and remember that sea lions can be dangerous. It's also the best way to visit the abandoned Haida villages of Gwaii Haanas Park. Experience – or a guide – is necessary. Peter McGee's *Kayak Routes of the Pacific North West* is recommended by BC Parks.
Anvil Cove Charters, T250-5598207, www.queencharlottekayaking.com. 6- to 10-day kayak tours in small groups, using a 53-foot schooner as a mother ship. Licensed for Gwaii Haanas National Park.
Butterfly Tours, T604-7407018, www.butterflytours.bc.ca. A variety of 6- to 10-day tours, using a mother ship, an accommodation base or just kayaks and tents. Some suitable for novices.

Ecosummer Expeditions, T1800-4658884, www.ecosummer.com. Long, expensive and life-altering kayak trips, with one of the companies who pioneered ethical, ecologically friendly touring of the park.

Tour operators
Blue Water Adventures, T250-9803800, www.bluewateradventures.com. 8- to 10- day trips around Gwaii Haanas Park in a yacht, with a crew of trained naturalists. Possibly the trip of a lifetime, but very expensive.
Delkatla Bay Birding Tours, Masset, T250-6265015. Birdwatching.
Haida Gwaii Ecotours, T1877-5598333, www.gwaiiecotours.com. From 1 day to several days, these ecologically friendly tours can be done by bike, canoe, kayak or on foot. All have a First Nations spiritual flavour.
Haida Soul Fishing Charters, Skidegate, T250-5598397, www.qcislands.net/chinihar.
QCI Ocean Charters, Port Clemens, T250-5574541. Diving in Rennell Sound on the west coast.

⊙ Transport

Williams Lake and around *p236*
Air
Pacific Coastal Airlines, T250-9822225, www.pacific-coastal.com, has regular scheduled flights to **Vancouver**, **Victoria**, **Powell River**, **Bella Coola** and **Port Hardy**. Central Mountain Air, www.flycma.com, also has regular flights to **Vancouver**. The airport is 14 km north, with frequent city buses into town.

Bus
Greyhound station is at 215 Donald Rd, T250-3987733, www.greyhound.ca. There are up to 3 daily buses from **Vancouver** to **Williams Lake** (8½ hrs) via the Fraser Valley and **Cache Creek**, continuing to **Quesnel** and **Prince George** (12½ hrs).

British Columbia Northern BC Listings

Bella Coola *p238*

Air

The airport is 20 km east in Hagensborg. **Pacific Coastal Airlines**, T250-9822225, www.pacific-coastal.com, has regular flights to **Vancouver**, **Victoria**, **Powell River**, **Williams Lake** and **Port Hardy**.

Ferry

BC Ferries, T250-3863779 or T1888-2233779, www.bcferries.com, operates the **Discovery Coast Passage** between **Port Hardy** and **Bella Coola**, with some services also stopping at the tiny coastal communities of **McLoughlin Bay** (**Bella Bella**), **Namu**, **Shearwater**, **Klemtu** and **Ocean Falls**. Summer only, reservations essential. See box p144 for details.

Prince George *p240*

Air

Prince George's airport, 4141 Airport Rd, T250-9632400, is 10 km east of town, off Hwy 16 on the Old Cariboo Hwy, T250-9632400. The **Airporter** shuttle, T250-5632220, stops anywhere in town, $8, $2.50 child. **Emerald Taxi**, T250-5633333. There are at least 12 flights daily, often cheaper than the bus. **WestJet**, T250-9638123, www.westjet.ca, has 5 daily flights to **Calgary** and 2 to **Vancouver** via **Kelowna**. **Air Canada Jazz**, www.flyjazz.ca, has several daily flights to **Vancouver**.

Bus

For regional transit information, call T250-5630011. The **Greyhound** station is at 1566 12th Av, about 5 blocks from Downtown, T250-5645454, www.grey hound.ca. To get there, take buses No 3 or No 4 from Victoria St. There are 3 daily buses to **Vancouver** (12½ hrs, $115), 4 to **Kamloops** (7½ hrs, $80), 1 of which continues east to **Jasper** (5 hrs, $56), and 2 to **Prince Rupert** (10½ hrs, $106).

Train

VIA Rail, T1800-5618630, www.viarail.ca, runs 3 trains weekly to and from **Jasper** (7½ hrs, $93) and **Prince Rupert** (12½ hrs, $120), cheaper if booked 7 days ahead. The station is Downtown on 1st Av (Hwy 16), reached by buses No 1 and No 3.

Prince Rupert *p243, map p254*

Air

Prince Rupert's airport is located on Digby Island. A bus/ferry service, T250-6243355, meets scheduled flights, $11 one-way to Downtown. The return service leaves from Rupert Sq Mall. **Air Canada Jazz**, www.fly jazz.ca, flies twice daily to **Vancouver**. **Hawk Air**, T1800-4871216, www.hawk air.ca, also flies to **Vancouver** and is often cheaper, especially one-way.

Bus

Local buses are operated by **Prince Rupert Transit System**, 225 2nd Av W, T250-6243343. The **Greyhound** station is at 112 6th St, T250-6245090, www.grey hound.ca, with 2 daily buses to **Prince George**.

Ferry

Prince Rupert Water Taxi, T250-6243337, runs 4 times daily Mon-Fri from the visitor information centre to the native village of **Metlakatla** across the harbour ($6). Local ferries go 3 times weekly to **Port Simpson**, T250-6245411, and twice weekly to **Kincolith**, halfway up Portland Inlet, T250-6246116, 6½ hrs.

   BC Ferries, www.bcferries.ca, operates the Inside Passage to **Port Hardy** on Vancouver Island (see p144 for details), and a daily service to **Haida Gwaii** . Alaska Marine Highway, T1800-6420066, www.ferryalaska.com, have at least 4 weekly sailings most of the year to Skagway, **Alaska**, with daily sailings in peak season. They stop in some or all of: Keichikan, Wrangell, Petersburg, Sitka, Hyder, Stewart, Juneau, Haines and Hollis.

Train

VIA Rail, T1800-5618630, www.viarail.ca, runs 3 weekly trains to **Jasper** with an overnight stop in **Prince George**.

Haida Gwaii *p244, map 245*

Air

The airport is in Sandspit, T250-6375660.
Air Canada Jazz, T1888-2472262, www.fly
jazz.ca, has regular flights to **Vancouver**.
A **shuttle**, T1877-7474461, meets flights
and charges $14 to Queen Charlotte City.

North Pacific Seaplanes, T1800-6894234,
www.northpacificseaplanes.com, runs a
float plane service from Masset to **Prince
Rupert**, and 3 times weekly from Sandspit/
QCC. **Pacific Coastal Airlines**, www.pacific-
coastal.com, flies daily from Masset during
the summer, winter 3 times weekly.

Ferry

BC Ferries runs between **Skidegate**
(Graham Island) and **Alliford Bay**
(Moresby Island), 12 times daily each
way, $4.75 return, $16.75 with vehicle.

BC Ferries, T250-3863431, www.bc
ferries.com, operates a service from
Skidegate to **Prince Rupert** (usually
6½ hrs). Reservations recommended.
Summer: departs Skidegate Mon-Tue
1100, Wed-Sat 2300; departs Prince
Rupert Thu-Sun 1100, Mon 2100, Wed
1300; $26 per person, plus $98 with car.
Rest of year: departs Skidegate Sun and
Mon 0600 and Thu 2000; departs Prince
Rupert at Sun and Mon 2300, Thu 1330;
$21.50, plus $78 with car. Kayak/canoe $7,
bike $6. Cabins available.

Bus

In summer, 3 buses travel each way
between **Masset** and **Sandspit** via
Queen Charlotte City, stopping at
the airport only on weekends at 0945.
Fares range from $5-30 including
ferry costs.

Car

Other than the paved road from Queen
Charlotte City to Masset, all driving is on
logging roads, which require much care.
Give way to logging trucks and call
Weyerhauser, T250-5576810, to make
sure the road isn't active.

For car rental try: **Budget**, T6375688, and
Thrifty, T250-6372299 in Sandspit; **Rustic
Rentals**, T250-5594641 in Skidegate.

Taxi and water taxi

Bruce's Taxi in Sandspit, T250-6375655;
Pete's Taxi in Skidegate, T250-5598622.
Water taxis available from: **SMC Water
Taxi and Sea Bus**, T250-5598383; and **T&S
Water Taxi**, T250-5598689, in Skidegate.

Stewart *p249*

Seaport Limousine, T250-6362622, runs a
bus from Stewart to **Terrace**, Mon-Fri,
$29/14 one-way. Leaves Terrace at 1700,
leaves Stewart at 1000 (4 hrs).

❶ Directory

Prince George *p240*
Banks Scotiabank, 390 Victoria; TD Bank,
299 Victoria. **Internet** Isle Pierre Pie Co,
409 George. **Laundry** White Wash, 1-231
George. **Library** 887 Dominion. **Medical
services** Prince George Regional
Hospital, 2000 15th Av, T250-5652000.

Prince Rupert *p243, map p254*
Canada Post 365-500 2nd Av W.
Internet At the library and Javadotcup,
516 3rd Av W. **Laundry** King Koin,
745 2nd Av W. **Library** 101 6th Av W.
Medical services Hospital, 1305
Summit, T250-6242171.

Haida Gwaii *p244, map245*
Banks ATMs and credit unions at Queen
Charlotte City and Masset. **Canada Post**
117 3rd Av, Queen Charlotte City; 1633
Main St, Masset. **Internet** At libraries and
Northwest Community Colleges in Queen
Charlotte City and Masset. **Laundry**
City Centre Store, Queen Charlotte City.
Library 138 Bay St, Queen Charlotte City;
2123 Collison, Masset. **Medical services**
Queen Charlotte Islands General Hospital,
3209 3rd Av, Queen Charlotte City,
T250-5594300; 1760 Hodges, Masset,
T250-6264700.

Canadian Rockies

An elk grazes in a pine forest

Don't miss...

1 Glenbow Museum, Calgary ▶▶ *p273.*

2 Badlands landscapes & Royal Tyrrell Museum of Palaeontology ▶▶ *p278.*

3 Skiing Lake Louise ▶▶ *p297.*

4 Icefields Parkway ▶▶ *p299.*

5 Lake O'Hara ▶▶ *p325.*

30 km
30 miles

Introduction

The Canadian Rockies are like the Egyptian Pyramids: it's hard to imagine why anyone would visit the country without seeing them. If you go feeling that the reality will never live up to the hype, you'll be proved wrong: the Rockies deserve their reputation as Canada's premier attraction and one of the natural wonders of the world. You can make a trip here whatever you want: there are luxury resorts and the option of viewing heavenly scenery without straying from your vehicle, or remote campsites beside waterfalls and emerald lakes that can only be reached through days of trekking across the mountain wilderness. Hiking is the obvious activity in the parks and the best way to commune with the exceptional scenery and wildlife, but every other major outdoor activity is pursued here: canoeing, whitewater rafting, mountain biking, climbing, fishing, caving, skiing, skating, golf, and soaking in hot springs.

Calgary is the most convenient entry point for visiting the parks. Most people concentrate on Banff, which contains the lion's share of scenery and hikes; Jasper is further away, less busy, much bigger and wilder; between the two is the astonishing Columbia Icefield; Yoho, a compact jewel, combines with Kootenay to make a nice loop back to Banff.

Ratings

Culture
★★

Landscape
★★★★★

Wildlife
★★★★★

Activities
★★★★★

Relaxation
★★★

Costs
$$$-$$$$

Ins and outs

Getting there and around

Calgary has the closest major airport to the Rockies, a mere 128 km east of Banff, receiving international and domestic flights (see p19 and p272). Several shuttle services run directly from Calgary airport to Banff, Canmore and Lake Louise. **Greyhound** runs daily buses to Banff from Vancouver and Calgary, and to Jasper from Prince George. **VIA Rail** operates three weekly trains to Jasper from Vancouver and Kamloops in the west.

The best way to get around the Rockies is with your own vehicle or bike (starting at Jasper is easier for cyclists). Be aware that some people are prone to slam on their brakes in the middle of the road if they spot a sheep or deer. Drive defensively! **Greyhound** buses connect Banff with Lake Louise, Field and Jasper. **Rocky Mountain Discount Travel**, T1888-2877638, **www.rmdtravel.com**, runs a hostel shuttle from Calgary to Vancouver ($85 one-way), with a stop-off in Banff or Lake Louise, as long as you return within a month.

Visitor information

There are first-class **visitor centres/park offices** in Banff, Lake Louise Village, Field (Yoho), and Jasper. Staff here are excellent sources of information about hikes and all other park activities, and usually keep a small library of key hiking guides. They hand out very useful maps with trail descriptions and backcountry guides, and issue compulsory wilderness passes for backcountry camping. They also organize guided hikes and other activities, and operate a voluntary safety registration programme for those engaging in potentially hazardous activities.

Friends of the Parks (www.friendsofyoho.ca, www.friendsrevglacier.com) sell an assortment of guide books and maps. The *DEMR 1:50,000* topographic maps are expensive and tend to cover a limited area; the *Gem Trek* maps cover more terrain, and so can be more useful. Most hikes are clearly marked, well maintained and much trodden, so finding your way is rarely an issue. **Parks Canada**, T1888-7738888, www.parkscanada.ca, produces two 1:200,000 maps - one for Banff, Yoho and Kootenay; one for Jasper - which are recommended as an overview.

Visitor centres keep track of local accommodation vacancies. If turning up without a reservation, their assistance can save a lot of time and hassle. They even have a courtesy phone. For a useful overview of all the parks, including maps that show the major trails, campgrounds and hostels, be sure to pick up the invaluable *Mountain Guide* from any visitor centre. Or visit www.parkscanada.ca. Weather information is available at T403-7622088 for Banff, Yoho and Kootenay national parks, and T780-8523185 for Jasper.

Best time to visit

Summer is best for most people, specifically July and August, when the days are warm and long and the trails most likely to be dry. Naturally, this is also when the trails and towns are at their busiest, which can be horrifying if you've come to get away from it all. Spring and autumn are much calmer, and certain trails can be hiked as early as mid-May and as late as October. The majority, however, are snow-bound until July, and in autumn the weather can be dangerously unpredictable. September is a favourite month for many people, as all the larches turn a glorious gold. Even at the height of summer, the Rockies receive a lot of rain, especially on the west of the divide. You could have clear blue skies every day for a week, or just as easily endure three weeks of solid downpours. At high altitude anything can happen any time, and snow is never out of the question. The **winter** ski season generally runs from mid-December to the end of May, but conditions are best in March when days are warmer and longer and the powder is most plentiful.

Activities in the Rockies

Hiking

There are over 3400 km of trails in the Rockies from the very short to the absurdly long. As a rule we have only mentioned the best, chosen from personal experience with the help of two excellent trail guides. *The Canadian Rockies Trail Guide*, by Brian Patton and Bart Robinson is the standard choice, providing a great deal of useful information and a comprehensive overview. *Don't Waste Your Time in the Canadian Rockies*, by Kathy and Craig Copeland is less detailed but straightforward and really helps

you choose from the daunting range of options. Brochures issued by parks offices are useful but devoid of opinion, though staff members are usually knowledgeable enthusiasts. They often have reference libraries for detailed research. The trail descriptions in this book are not intended to be sufficient to guide you through the hikes.

Winter sports

There are six ski hills in the Rockies. **Lake Louise** is the most significant, with the largest terrain in Canada and breathtaking views (but cold!). **Banff's Sunshine Village** is the second biggest, and receives 10 m per year of first-class powder, Canada's biggest snowpack. **Mount Norquay** is small, close to Banff Townsite, and well respected for its advanced runs. **Marmot Basin** in Jasper is cheaper and noted for its friendly atmosphere and uncrowded slopes. Canmore, Banff, Lake Louise and Jasper all have ample opportunities for cross-country skiing, while a wealth of operators and equipment renters can get you snowshoeing, skating, ice-climbing, canyon-crawling, dog-sledding, ice-fishing or curling.

Park fees

Banff and Jasper have booths on the main access roads collecting park fees. **Day passes** are $8, $7 senior, $4 youth, $16 family, valid for all the parks up to 1600 the following day. No fee is charged for through traffic. An **annual pass** costing $55-$109 is valid for entry to 28 national parks in Western Canada. If staying for a week or more, it is well worth getting one of these, as they also entitle you to discounts at a number of sights, and on certain tours. The annual **Discovery Package** pass will get you into these 28 national parks and 77 national historic sites for $69/$59/$35/$136. You can buy passes at information centres and some

Day hikes in the Rockies

Valley of the Ten Peaks/Sentinel Pass, Banff National Park ▸▸ *p298*
Cirque Peak, Icefields Parkway, Banff National Park ▸▸ *p300*
Wilcox Pass, Jasper National Park ▸▸ *p312*
Alpine Circuit, Yoho National Park ▸▸ *p326*
Iceline, Yoho National Park ▸▸ *p327*

campgrounds, or by credit card at T1800-7487275. Day passes can be bought at 24-hour automatic pass machines.

Mandatory Wilderness Passes for backcountry camping are $9 per person per night. An annual pass, good for unlimited wilderness camping in all Western Canada national parks, is $63. If you buy one, you still have to register. You can trade seven day-pass receipts for one of these. The fee for backcountry reservation (which is not mandatory, but necessary for Yoho) is $12. Front country campgrounds range from $33 with sewer and electrical to $9 for overflow. A campsite day use permit is $7. A fire permit is $7 per day, including firewood. Reservations can now be made at T1877-7373783, T1905-4264648 outside North America, or www.pccamping.ca. Fishing permits are $8 per day or $25 annual.

Flora and fauna in the Rockies

Flora

From mid-July to mid-August, the Rockies' many meadows come alive with an exciting display of multicoloured wild flowers, including Indian paintbrush of all shades, alpine forget-me-nots, lousewort, western anemone, buttercups, daisies, alpine fleabane, false azalea, arnica, columbine, spring beauty, pearly everlasting and many more. Several types of orchid bloom about a month earlier. Red and white heather, mosses and multicoloured lichens are present throughout the temperate months. In autumn, larches and deciduous trees brighten the predominantly evergreen forests with their spectacular golden hues. Other vegetation includes a host of berry bushes, rhododendrons, red elder, cinquefoil and several species of saxifrage.

Fauna

You are almost guaranteed a sighting of elk, deer and bighorn sheep, often on the roads or at campgrounds, causing a degree of excitement that after a while seems excessive. There's also a chance of seeing moose, black or grizzly bears, mountain goats and coyotes, as well as a host of smaller animals like otters, beavers, pikas and porcupines. Hoary marmots inhabit rocky slopes and make a distinctive whistling sound to warn each other of your presence. On rare occasions you'll catch a glimpse of a wolf, badger, wolverine, marten, cougar, caribou or lynx. Some first-class birdwatching spots attract all kinds of waterfowl, and there's a good chance of seeing jays, ptarmigans, finches, chickadees, ospreys, various eagles, and many other species.

There are only a couple of hundred grizzly bears left in the Rockies and the same number of black bears. As well as being much bigger, grizzlies have a dished face, a big, muscular shoulder hump, and long, curved front claws. You are more likely to see one by the side of the road than in the bush, but to minimize the chances of a scary encounter, take a few simple precautions (see p17 and p271). Any animal can be unpredictable and

Bear essentials

Bears are shy creatures who will usually take off if warned of your presence. In areas where forest limits visibility, especially if you are hiking into the wind or close to a stream, walk noisily and sing and shout loudly. Be particularly wary in areas where bears are known to live, if there are lots of berry bushes around, or if you have seen bear droppings (piles of mushed up berries). When camping, never leave food in or close to your tent (see Responsible tourism p17).

Only in very rare cases have bears preyed on humans, or attacked in a premeditated way. If you catch a bear by surprise, however, it may attack out of fear, especially if it's a sow with cubs to defend. If you see a bear, avoid looking it in the eyes, which could be construed as a challenge. Resist the temptation to run: like most animals, bears are more likely to pursue a fleeing target, and they run much faster than humans. They are also strong swimmers, and black bears are consummate climbers of trees. Generally the best advice is to stay calm and still, moving in slow motion if at all. Stand your ground making soothing, non-threatening sounds, then retreat slowly. If a lone black bear attacks, fighting back and screaming might be effective. If it's a grizzly, try climbing a tree, otherwise lie face down with your legs apart and your hands clasped behind your neck. This position makes it hard for the bear to flip you over. Once the bear feels you are no longer a threat, it is likely to leave you alone. Only move when you are sure the bear has left the area, then get up slowly and quietly and walk away.

dangerous if scared, so keep a respectful distance. More people are attacked by elk than by bears. Female elk are most aggressive during the May to June calving season; males are especially dangerous during the September to October rutting season. According to a po-faced notice at Lake Louise ski hill, the greatest number of injuries in Banff National Park result from people getting too close to squirrels!

Small creatures are indeed the ones most likely to prove a nuisance. At lower elevations, especially on dry overcast days, mosquitoes are sure to bug you. From early to mid-June ticks are prevalent, especially on sunny, grassy slopes. Check vigilantly for them at the end of the day, and ideally remove them using fine-pointed tweezers: grab hold of the mouth without squeezing the body and gently pull back until the tick lets go. Pull out any remaining parts like a splinter. Then there are black flies, deer and horse flies, and no-see-ums, so named because they're too small to see (see also p43).

Calgary

One of North America's youngest and most modern cities, Calgary possesses a youthful brand of energy and optimism. The Downtown area is a grid of sleek glass, chrome and granite skyscrapers, the result of an oil boom that began in the 1970s. While there's not much in terms of sights beyond the fine Glenbow Museum, Calgary has a decent selection of restaurants, bars, clubs, and entertainment, and a relaxed, friendly population who, during the famous Stampede, demonstrate how much they love to party. The obvious starting point for those

⊘ **Getting there** Plane, bus or car.
⊜ **Getting around** Bus or C-train.
⊗ **Time required** 1-2 days.
⊛ **Weather** Very hot in summer, very cold in winter.
⊜ **Sleeping** 5 star hotels to hostels.
⊘ **Eating** Varied and high quality.
▲ **Activities and tours** Tours to the Drumheller Badlands.
★ **Don't miss...** Glenbow Museum ►► p273.

whose primary focus is the Rockies, Calgary merits a day of discovery. With a day to spare, the fascinating Badlands and Dinosaur Museum of Drumheller, 148 km to the northeast, make a recommended day trip.

Ins and outs

Getting there

Calgary International Airport (YCC), T403-7351200, www.calgaryairport.com, is 10 km northeast of Downtown. **Calgary Transit** bus No 57 runs to Whitehorn C-train station for connections into town. **Airport Shuttle Express**, T403-5094799, www.airportshuttleexpress.com, goes to Downtown hotels. Three companies run regular shuttles from the airport to Banff, Canmore (both $51 one-way), and Lake Louise ($60): **Banff Airporter**, T403-7623330, www.banffairporter.com; **Sky Shuttle**, T403-7625200, www.rockymountainskyshuttle.com, runs to Emerald Lake ($74); and **Sun Dog Tours**, T1888-7863641, www.sundogtours.com, which continues to Jasper ($105). The **Greyhound** station is at 877 Greyhound Way SW. A free shuttle runs to the 7th Avenue/ 10th Street C-train from Gate 4. ►► ⊜ p286.

Getting around

Greater Calgary is a vast ever-expanding metropolis that is difficult to negotiate. The Downtown area, however, is small enough to tackle on foot. The **Plus 15 Walking System** is a maze of walkways connecting the many shopping centres, designed to avoid the cold outside in winter. **Calgary Transit**, www.calgary transit.com, runs a cheap and efficient system of buses and the electric C-train. The grid of streets is divided into quadrants, with Centre Street dividing east from west, and the river dividing south from north. In a three-digit street number, the first digit refers to the block, so 130 9th Av SE means that the building is No 30 on 9th Avenue in the block between Central and 1st streets southeast.

Driving in Calgary is difficult and parking is always a problem. Drivers should be aware that the **TransCanada Highway** runs north of Downtown as 16th Avenue Northeast. Highway 2, the major north-south artery, splits the town in two. **Macleod Trail** is Highway 2 heading south, **Deerfoot Trail** is Highway 2 heading north. Signs often refer to the highway's name and not its number.

Calgary's Downtown skyline, Centre Street Bridge.

Best time to visit

With an average low of -15.7°C in January, Calgary is too cold to visit in the winter. The best month is July, which has the Stampede, a microbrewery festival, the folk festival, and Shakespeare in the Park. September, which is also a great time to visit the nearby Rockies, has Art Week and the International Film Festival, and enjoys a climate that is midway between the too-cold winter and too-hot summer.

Tourist information

Calgary's main **Visitor Information Centre** ⓘ *101 9th Av SE, T403-2638510, www.tourism calgary.com*, is at the base of the Calgary Tower. There are also desks at the Arrivals and Departures levels at the airport. *Where Calgary*, www.where.ca/calgary, is a useful monthly magazine usually found at the visitor centres or high-end hotels. Also worth checking is www.downtowncalgary.com.

Downtown Calgary ⊖🍴🏨 ▸▸ *pp280-286.*

Glenbow Museum

ⓘ *130 9th Av SE, T403-7775506, www.glenbow.org, daily 0900-1700, Thu till 2100, $12, $2 Sun am.* Spread over three floors, the large and varied collection of the Glenbow Museum represents Calgary's most compelling attraction. Besides **Many Faces, Many Paths: Art of Asia**, an impressive collection of Asian religious sculptures, the second floor is mostly devoted to an extensive temporary exhibition. These are always very varied, fascinating and educational. Their theme is taken up in the **Discovery Room**, where children are encouraged to explore the subject through interaction, and reveal their artistic side. The third floor presents an intense introduction to native Canadian culture. **Niitsitapiisinni: Our Way of Life** uses interactive displays, artefacts, and a circular narrative path to explore the history and culture of the Blackfoot. **We Are Still Here: First Peoples of the Four Directions** features artworks by various First Nations of the northwest. There are some fine examples of carving, beadwork, textiles, and even music, such as the eerie throat music of the Inuit. On the fourth floor is a section on minerals; a gallery exploring the cultures of West Africa; a display that traces the

Canadian Rockies Calgary

Calgary

Prince's Island Park

YMCA
Eau Claire Market
Chinese Cultural Centre & Museum
CHINATOWN

To Kensington
To Telus World of Science & Greyhound Bus Station

TD Bank
7 Av (Transit Mall)
Uptown
8 Av (Stephen Avenue Walk)
Globe
Canada Trust
Devonian Gardens
Art Gallery of Calgary
Calgary Tower

MISSION

Saint Mary's

Royal Av
Durham Av
Sydenham Rd

N
200 metres
200 yards

Sleeping 🛏
Auberge Chez Nous Hostel **8** *B5*
Calgary International Hostel **1** *C6*
Foxwood B&B **6** *E1*
Inglewood B&B **2** *C6*
Regis Plaza **4** *C5*
River Wynde Executive House B&B **7** *A1*
Sandman **5** *C2*

Eating 🍴
Belvedere **2** *C4*
Brava Bistro **16** *E2*
Buchanan's **6** *B2*
Catch Oyster Bar & Seafood **1** *C4*
Cilantro **9** *E3*
Divino Wine & Cheese Bistro **10** *C4*
Eiffel Tower Bakery **25** *E1*
Galaxie Diner **3** *D1*
Good Earth Café **12** *A4/C4*
Heartland Café **13** *A1*
La Chaumière **15** *E4*
Marathon **8** *A1*
Metropolitan Grill **24** *E1*
Piq Niq Wine Bar & Bistro & Beat Niq Jazz & Social Club **17** *C4*
River Café **18** *A3*
Roasterie Too **14** *A1*
Secret Café **26** *D3*
Sultan's Tent **19** *E1*
Teatro **21** *C4*
Thai Sa-On **22** *D3*
Verve & Martini Bar **7** *A1*
Wildwood Grill & Brewing Co **23** *F3*

Bars & clubs 🍸
Auburn Saloon **1** *C4*
Barley Mill **2** *A3*
Blind Monk **17** *F3*

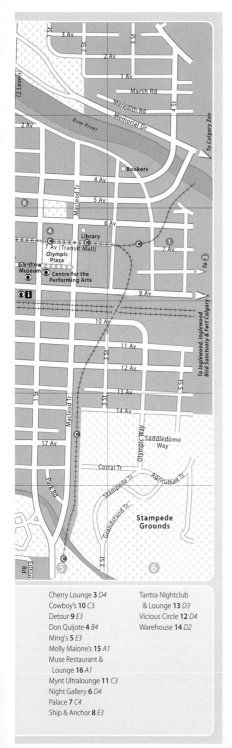

Cherry Lounge **3** *D4*
Cowboy's **10** *C3*
Detour **9** *E3*
Don Quijote **4** *B4*
Ming's **5** *E3*
Molly Malone's **15** *A1*
Muse Restaurant &
  Lounge **16** *A1*
Mynt Ultralounge **11** *C3*
Night Gallery **6** *D4*
Palace **7** *C4*
Ship & Anchor **8** *E3*

Tantra Nightclub
  & Lounge **13** *D3*
Vicious Circle **12** *D4*
Warehouse **14** *D2*

history of warfare across different cultures; 275
and **Learning Through Art: A Journey
Through Time II**, which examines the
differing cultural perspectives and social
values represented by diverse art forms. The
ground floor contains a gift shop and a café.

Around Stephen Avenue Walk

After the museum, those hungry for more
could check out the nearby **Art Gallery of
Calgary** or **Centre for the Performing Arts**
(see Entertainment, p283), or stroll down to
the 1905 sandstone **Cathedral Church of
the Redeemer** at 9th Avenue and 1st Street
Southeast, one of Calgary's most attractive
constructions. Those who don't object to the
unreasonable fee could ride the lift up
Calgary Tower ⓘ *9th Av/Centre St,
T403-2667171, www.calgarytower.com, 0700-
2300, $12, $7 child*, the city's most distinctive
landmark since it was built in 1968. At that
time, its 190-m height was unchallenged by
the surrounding structures and, even today,
great views of the city, with the Rockies as a
backdrop, can be enjoyed from the
Observation Terrace; there's also an
expensive revolving restaurant.

Otherwise, the obvious thing to do is
wander down **Stephen Avenue Walk** (8th
Avenue), a lively pedestrian street. Between
Macleod Trail Southeast and 3rd Street
Southwest, it is also the most intact turn-
of-the-20th-century Downtown street in
Western Canada, with many of Calgary's
finest and oldest buildings rubbing
shoulders with the brand new. At ground
level are pubs, restaurants, street vendors,
buskers and some funky shops. Up above is
a murky world of department stores, such as
the massive **Toronto Dominion Square**
between 2nd and 3rd streets, a block now
dominated by a new set of odd steel
sculptures called *The Trees*. Bizarrely, inside
on the fourth floor are some real full-sized
trees, as well as 20,000 varieties of plants,
plus fountains, ponds, bridges and art
exhibitions. Known as the **Devonian
Gardens** ⓘ *T403-2682489, 0900-2100, by
donation*, this is a perfect place to escape
whatever the Calgary weather is up to.

Canadian Rockies Calgary

17th Avenue and 4th Street

17th Avenue Southwest – just south of Downtown between 2nd Street and 14th Street – and **4th Street** are hands-down Calgary's most interesting night-time areas, with lots of good restaurants and pubs, and the highest concentration of clubs. While here, check out the nearby **St Mary's Church** at 1st Street and 18th Avenue, one of the latest Gothic-revival churches in Western Canada, with an incredibly striking symmetrical brick tower best appreciated at night. **Mission District** on 4th Street, southwest from 12th Avenue going south, was originally settled by French Canadian priests, and now has some classy restaurants and art galleries.

Along the Bow River ⊜⚙⚙ ⇥ *pp280-286.*

Apart from the sights concentrated in the Downtown core, most places of interest are to the north, scattered along the banks of the Bow River. These are presented below from west to east.

Kensington

Situated on the north bank, reached via a footbridge from Prince's Island Park (see below), or more directly from the 10th Street bridge, Kensington is a pleasant neighbourhood focused on 10th Street Northwest and Kensington Road Northwest. Colourful and culturally stimulating, the area has a bohemian flavour, with tasteful restaurants, lots of pubs, some interesting shops and the closest this town gets to an alternative scene. Those who dislike cities but are obliged to spend a day in Calgary should head straight here.

Telus World of Science

ⓘ *701 11th St SW, T403-2688300. C-train to 10th St station, www.calgaryscience.ca, summer 0930-1800, winter 1000-1600, $12, $9.50 child, including Discovery Dome show or Lego Mindstorms.*
Predictably enough, the Science Centre is aimed mostly at kids, with lots of hands-on stuff, mini experiments and intriguing information, as well as some interesting exhibits. The so-called Amazement Park is half-hearted, however, and the whole affair falls short of many similar venues elsewhere. The **Shaw Millennium Park** next door is a giant purpose-built skateboard park which also has a few volleyball courts.

Eau Claire Market and Prince's Island Park

Pleasantly situated on the Bow River between 2nd and 3rd streets, the **Eau Claire Market** brings together fruit and vegetable stalls, a food hall of fast-food joints, a few cinemas, and some tacky craft shops. Though this doesn't compare with Vancouver's Granville Market, it is worth a wander. Outside is an open area surrounded by pubs, which offers a welcome respite from Downtown Calgary's teeming streets, as well as acting as a meeting place and venue for cultural events. Across a pedestrian bridge is **Prince's Island Park**, a nice place for a stroll.

Chinatown

A few blocks east of the market, Calgary's Chinatown is small but clean, and packed with cheap bakeries and restaurants offering dim sum. The **Chinese Cultural Centre and Museum** ⓘ *197 1st St SW, T403-2625071, www.culturalcentre.ca, 1100-1700, $2, $1 child for museum, dome interior 0900-2100, bus No 31,* is its main attraction, featuring a magnificent dome copied from the c1420 Temple of Heaven in Beijing. Its interior features 561 individually crafted gold dragons and 40 phoenixes. There are temporary art galleries on the second and third floors (free) and a very worthwhile museum downstairs with a number of fascinating exhibits, such as a big picture of tigers made entirely of feathers, a 'transparent' bronze mirror, and a bronze bowl which spurts water when it's rubbed.

Background

The Calgary Stampede

In early July, the whole city goes cowboy crazy for 10 days during the Calgary Stampede. Locals don ten-gallon hats, leather boots and Wrangler jeans, and start affecting a John Wayne drawl. Shop windows are covered with cowboy cartoons, free breakfasts are offered throughout Downtown every morning, and the streets are choked with parties and drunken revellers.

Festivities begin with the Stampede Parade along 6th and 9th Avenues. Thereafter, the action takes place at the Stampede Grounds, on Macleod Trail Southeast and 14th Avenue. The major events are the Rodeo and the Chuckwagon races, involving nine days of heats building up to a final on the tenth day. Participants come from all over the world to compete for the $1.6 million of prize money. There is plenty of other entertainment put on during the stampede. Visitors are welcomed wholeheartedly.

Admission to the Stampede Grounds is $12. Tickets to the Rodeo are $25-180; and Chuckwagon races are $37-80, from the box office, T403-2699822. For general information, T403-2610101, www.calgarystampede.com. Getting there: C-train to Victoria Park or Erlton Stampede stations; bus No 10 or 433.

Fort Calgary and Inglewood

Fort Calgary ⓘ *750 9th Av SE, T403-2901875, www.fortcalgary.com, daily 0900-1700, $10, $9 child, bus No 1, 75 or 41 from Downtown,* is a reconstruction of the 1875 North West Mounted Police fort built to control the trouble caused by rogue whisky traders. It's staffed by costumed guides who supplement the exhibitions by telling the story of Calgary's roots. Just to the east, on 9th Avenue Southeast between 10th and 12th streets, is Inglewood, Calgary's oldest district, with some of the city's grandest houses and cottages, and a concentration of antiques shops. Still further east is **Inglewood Bird Sanctuary** ⓘ *2425 9th Av SE, T403-2214500, centre 1000-1700, paths open year-round till dark, by donation, bus No 411 from Downtown, No 1 back,* with 32 ha of paths, and an interpretive centre.

Calgary Zoo

Across from the fort, situated on St George's Island between two branches of the Bow River, are the **Botanical Gardens**, **Prehistoric Park** and **Calgary Zoo** ⓘ *1300 Zoo Rd, via Memorial Dr, T403-2329300, www.calgaryzoo.ab.ca, 0900-1700, $15, $9 child, take the C-train.* With over 1200 animals from all over the world, including the usual favourites, this is a nice place to spend the day, with lots of facts about the animals dotted around to make it an educational experience. The Prehistoric Park, entered via a suspension bridge across the river, has plastic life-sized dinosaurs in rather unconvincing settings. The conservatory, containing tropical, arid, and butterfly gardens, is well worth a visit.

Drumheller and the Badlands 🌐🚇🅿️ ▸ *pp280-286.*

Apart from the Rockies, the most worthwhile destination in Alberta is centred on the small, unexceptional town of Drumheller, an easy day excursion from Calgary. The Badlands scenery here is truly exceptional, easily enjoyed thanks to a circular driving route that connects some great vantage points, and takes in one of the world's finest palaeontology museums.

On the way to Drumheller, you'll pass **Horseshoe Canyon**, one of the most dramatic viewpoints for admiring the Badlands. Just before town **Reptile World** ⓘ *T403-8238623, summer 0900-2200, spring/autumn 1000-1700, $4.50, $3.50 child*, cashes in on the dominant theme, with a collection of snakes and toads that can be handled, and the 270-kg alligator, Fred. **Drumheller** itself remains hidden in the canyon until the last moment, no bad thing, as it's a fairly drab town. The nicest part of town is on its north side just over the bridge. As well as a wading pool, which offers some relief from the intense summer heat, and the 'World's Biggest Dinosaur' 25m tall ($3 to climb to the top), this is where you'll find the **Visitor Information Centre** ⓘ *60 1st Av West, T403-8238100, www.traveldrumbeller.com, 0900-2100*. If here in summer, ask about the celebrated **Passion Play** ⓘ *17th St SW/Dinosaur Trail, T403-8232001, www.canadianpassionplay.com*, held six times a year.

Royal Tyrrell Museum of Palaeontology

ⓘ *6 km northwest of Drumheller on Hwy 838 (North Dinosaur Trail), T403-8237707, www.tyrrell museum.com, summer daily 0900-2100, winter Tue-Sun 1000-1700, $10, $8 child.*

Half a million visitors per year flock to the Royal Tyrrell Museum to see the world's largest collection of complete dinosaur skeletons: over 35 in all, including the ever-popular Tyrannosaurus rex. With this many people you can expect it to be very crowded in summer, so think about arriving early or late. State-of-the-art technology is used to talk visitors through the Earth's history, from the primordial soup to the present. Displays explain matters such as evolution, plate tectonics and geology, how fossils are created, and how they are found and prepared. One engrossing exhibit deals with the findings at **Burgess Shale** in Yoho National Park, using a stunning display set in a dark tunnel to represent a deep-sea scene from 500 million years ago, with the bizarre prehistoric creatures blown up to 12 times their original size and floating around in a surreal, illuminated landscape.

Rock formations of the Drumheller Badlands.

Background

→ **The Great Canadian Dinosaur Rush**

Geological evidence suggests that 75 million years ago, at the time of the dinosaurs, this area was a lush coastal plain, supporting a wealth of plant and animal life. At the end of the last ice age, melting glaciers scraped away the upper layers of rock, gouging out a crazy jumble of odd sculptures and steep coulées (deep, narrow ravines). As the erosion continues, fossils are revealed in the Cretaceous layers beneath. So it is that one JB Tyrrell, looking for the coal deposits that fuelled a successful mining industry in these parts, stumbled instead across the skull of an Albertasaurus, thus sparking off the 'Great Canadian Dinosaur Rush'. More than 20 species of dinosaur, including many complete skeletons, have since been unearthed in one of the most fruitful beds of dinosaur remains in the world. Though these have found their way to museums around the globe, a large number are housed in the excellent Royal Tyrrell Museum just outside Drumheller.

The whole experience builds you up to the climax of the **Dinosaur Hall**, where a mind-blowing collection of skeletons is exhibited in front of artistic backdrops evoking the deltas, swamps and lush vegetation that would have constituted this valley's scenery 75 million years ago. The story is completed with a series of displays that deal with the extinction of the dinosaurs, the dawn of the Age of Mammals, and the occurrence of ice ages. As well as a museum, this is one of the world's premier palaeontological research facilities, and runs many educational programmes. In the summer, you can assist the experts (for a fee) on one of their Day Digs. Two trails, a one-hour and a 2½-hour loop, lead from the museum through the Badlands in Midland Provincial Park.

Dinosaur Trail and Hoodoo Trail

A perfect complement to the museum is the well-signed 48-km road circuit known as the **Dinosaur Trail**, an excellent way to see the stunning Badlands. Highway 838 is the North Dinosaur Trail, Highway 837 the South Trail. They join at the Bleriot Ferry. Which way you drive the loop depends on whether you want to visit the museum at the beginning or end. It's the first stop if you follow Highway 838. The next key attraction is **Horsethief Canyon**, which has superb views. Thereafter the road drops down to cross the river, with a lovely campground on the south bank. Views from this side have a different quality, so be sure to stop at the **Orkney Hill Viewpoint** on the way back to town.

The less essential **Hoodoo Trail** runs 25 km southeast along Highway 10 to a minor collection of hoodoos: mushroom-shaped sandstone pillars that would have appealed to Dr Seuss. On the way, you pass yellow canola fields dotted with nodding donkeys, a suspension bridge, and the **Atlas Coal Mine** ⓘ *1000-1800, $6*, one of many remnants of the once-booming local mining industry. You can hike up to the mine, tour the site and visit the museum. The detour to **Wayne** is a pretty drive, with 11 bridges along the way, and highly recommended on the first weekend in July, when the village hosts its annual **Harley Davidson Rally**, T403-8239189, a huge biker party with 4000 people and free camping everywhere.

Cowboy Trail

Southern Alberta's tourist board has put together a number of self-guided tours for visitors. The most tempting is the **Cowboy Trail**, most of which follows Highway 22, which can be picked up just west of Calgary. It runs south from Rocky Mountain House National Historic Site, some 180 km north, to Cardston near Waterton Lakes (see p334), via a number of ranches and heritage sites, including Cochrane's Western Heritage Centre, Longview's Bar U Ranch, and the Kootenai Brown Heritage Village in Pincher Creek. For more information call T1866- 6273051, or visit www.thecowboytrail.com.

● Sleeping

Downtown Calgary *p273, map p274*
There are disappointingly few options in Downtown Calgary. The major routes into town are lined with cheap chain motels, especially Banff Trail NW, which is known as Motel Village. Note that rates go up at least 50% during the stampede, when reservations are essential.
B Sandman, 888 7th Av SW, Downtown, T403-2378626, www.sandmanhotels.com. The best centrally located mid-range hotel, offering comfortable rooms, plus an indoor pool, hot tub, and fitness room.
C-D City View, 2300 6th St SE, T403-8705640, www.calgarycityview.com. 2 rooms and a studio near the Stampede Grounds, great views from the balcony.
D Regis Plaza, 124 7th Av SE, T403-2624641, www.regisplazahotel.com. About the cheapest option Downtown, offering a variety of plain but reasonable rooms, some with shared bath
E Auberge Chez Nous Hostel, 149 5th Av SE, T403-2325475, www.auberge-cheznous.com. Very central, and nicely decorated French style. Dorm rooms each have 5-6 beds (not bunks) separated by

lockers to afford some privacy. Shared living room and kitchenette.
E Calgary International Hostel, 520 7th Av SE, T403-2836503. Conveniently close to Downtown, with dorms and private rooms, shared bath, kitchen and common room, laundry facilities and free internet.

17th Avenue and 4th Street *p276*
C The Foxwood B&B, 1725 12th St SW, T403-2446693, www.thefoxwood.com. A beautiful Edwardian house furnished with antiques, close to the lively 17th Av district. 2 plush rooms, and a suite (**A**) with private bath and its own balcony, plus a large living room, cosy den, hot tub, a big veranda at the front, and gorgeous garden with a deck at the back.

Along the Bow River *p276*
B-C Inglewood B&B, 1006 8th Av SE, Inglewood, T403-2626570, www.inglewoodbedandbreakfast.com. 3 pleasant rooms in a Victorian-style house near the river.
C A Good Knight B&B, 1728 7th Av NW, T403-2707628, www.agoodknight.com. 2 attractive themed rooms with private

bath, plus an apartment in a pretty Victorian-style house close to Kensington.

C River Wynde Executive House B&B, 220 10A St NW, Kensington, T403-2708448, www.riverwynde.com. Lovely heritage home, featuring 4 unique themed rooms, some with hardwood floors and private balconies, and a small cottage in the garden. There's also a sunny patio, a pretty garden, library, and use of bikes.

Drumheller *p278*

B Best Western Jurassic Inn, 1103 Hwy 9 S, T403-8237700, www.bestwestern.com. The most reliable choice in town, with an indoor pool, hot tub, and exercise room.

C McDougall Lane B&B, 71 McDougall Lane, T403-8235379, www.bbalberta.com/mcdougall. A large house with 2 plush rooms and 1 suite, a very nice living room, and a fabulous sunken flower garden featuring fountains, ponds and decks.

C Newcastle Country Inn, 1130 Newcastle Trail, T403-8238356, www.virtually drumheller.com/nci. 11 pleasant rooms, plus a continental breakfast.

C Taste the Past, 281 2nd St, T403-8235889. A pretty old-brick home with 3 reasonable rooms, antique decor and a garden veranda.

D Badlands Motel, Hwy 838 on way to museum, T403-8235155. One of a few standard motels in town.

Camping

Bleriot Ferry Provincial Rec Area, 23 km west on the south side of the ferry crossing, on the Dinosaur Trail, T403-8231753. A pleasant little site right on the river, good for swimming. Great views of the landscape.

Dinosaur Trail RV Resort, 11 km west on Hwy 838 on Dinosaur Trail, T403-8239333. A nice spot with a swimming pool and canoe rentals. Reservations necessary in summer.

Little Fish Lake Provincial Park, T403-8231749, 25 km east of the Hoodoos off Hwy 10 on Hwy 573. A great

campground down a dirt road, with a nice lake setting.

River Grove Campground and Cabins, 25 Poplar St, off Hwy on north side of bridge, T403-8236655. The best of a few campsites right around town, with semi-private pitches on the river.

❼ Eating

Downtown Calgary *p273, map p274*

¶¶¶ **The Belvedere**, 107 8th Av SW, T403-2659595. Closed Sun. One of Calgary's longest-running and most respected restaurants, this upmarket New York-style dining room has a romantic atmosphere and an international menu.

¶¶¶ **Catch Oyster Bar and Seafood**, 100 8th Av SE, T403-2060000. With its hardwood floors, chandeliers, and classic furnishings, this long, elegant room is a beautiful place to enjoy international dishes prepared with French flair. There's also a handsome dark wood oyster bar, serving San Francisco-style seafood and draught beer.

¶¶¶ **Divino Wine and Cheese Bistro**, 113 8th Av SW, T403-4105555. A stylish, intimate little space to enjoy a glass of wine, and California-style cuisine, with an applewood oven for gourmet pizzas and wild salmon.

¶¶¶ **River Café**, Prince's Island Park, T403-2617670. The best location in town, with big views of the river and Downtown skyline beyond, and a wonderful interior reminiscent of a mountain fishing lodge, with an open fireplace. The menu is broad and very upmarket, with plenty of fish, and a West Coast-style emphasis on the freshness and locality of ingredients.

¶¶¶ **Teatro**, 200 8th Av, T403-2901012. Set in an elegant vintage bank building with sumptuous decor and a lively but romantic ambience, this long-standing favourite serves up European-style cuisine made using only the freshest ingredients, West-Coast style.

Canadian Rockies Calgary Listings

¶¶ Buchanan's, 738 3rd Av, T403-2614646. An old-fashioned chop house renowned for its steaks and burgers, and broad range (146) of malt whiskies.

¶¶ Piq Niq Wine Bar and Bistro, 811 1st St SW, T403-2631650. Gourmet food in an intimate setting genuinely reminiscent of a French bistro. Downstairs is a small venue for live jazz.

¶¶ Thai Sa-On, 351 10th Av SW, T403-2643526. For 15 years rated the best Thai food in town.

¶ Galaxie Diner, 1413 11th St SW, T403-2280001. Great breakfasts in an old-style diner, complete with booths and bar stools.

¶ Good Earth Café, several locations including Eau Claire Market and 119 8th Av SW. Casual atmosphere, speciality coffees, baking and vegetarian snacks.

¶ The Secret Café, 322 11th Av SW. Coffee, soup and salads.

17th Avenue and 4th Street *p276*

¶¶¶ La Chaumière, 139 17th Av SW, T403-2285690. French-style haute cuisine in almost excessively opulent surroundings.

¶¶¶ The Living Room, 514 17th Av, T403-2289830. The decor here is modern, sophisticated, minimalist and sleek. The food puts a contemporary twist on French and Italian cuisine, with fondues, shared meals, and encouraged wine pairings. There's also an outdoor patio.

¶¶¶-¶¶ Cilantro, 338 17th Av, T403-2291177. A long-standing favourite. California-fusion eclectic cuisine in a brick and wood setting with an outdoor patio.

¶¶¶-¶¶ Wildwood Grill and Brewing Co, 2417 4th St SW, T403-2280100. Downstairs is a pub that brews its own great beers, upstairs is a stylish restaurant with an eclectic West Coast fusion menu that concentrates on local ingredients including buffalo, caribou and rabbit. Good wine list.

¶¶ Brava Bistro, 723 17th Av SW, T403-2281854. French/Canadian cuisine with organic and vegetarian dishes, an excellent wine list, and a patio.

¶¶ The Metropolitan Grill, 880 16th Av SW, T403-8022393. New world cuisine such as wild mushroom gorgonzola scallopini. With its great Martini and wine list, and DJs and dancing Thu-Sat nights, this is also considered to be a bar-club.

¶¶ Sultan's Tent, 909 17th Av, T403-2442333. Delicious Moroccan dishes such as tagine, with decor made to resemble a Berber tent, including floor seating.

¶ Eiffel Tower Bakery, 1013 17th Av SW. French style breads, pastries and quiches.

Kensington *p276, map p274*

¶¶¶ The Verve Restaurant and Martini Bar, 102 10th St NW, T403-2832009. Sleek, trendy and dimly lit, sexy you might say. The menu features a broad variety of appetizers, some pasta dishes and seafood, and a lot of Alberta beef. Equally recommended just for a drink. Live music of a jazzy nature, Fri and Sat nights.

¶¶ Marathon, 130 10th St NW, T403-2836796. Delicious Ethiopian curries. Popular and intimate. Lunch buffet.

¶ Heartland Café, 940 2nd Av NW. Pleasant local hang-out with a wholefood attitude.

¶ The Roasterie Too, 227 10th St NW. Fresh roasted coffee, in a comfy spot with outdoor seating.

Drumheller *p278*

Eating choices in Drumheller are mostly family-dining joints catering to tour buses.

¶¶ Bernie and the Boys Bistro, 305 4th St W. A classic diner serving superior burgers and shakes.

¶¶ Sizzling House, 160 Centre St, T403-8238098. Excellent cheap Szechuan and Thai food minus the MSG and sugar. Great value, and a good veggie selection.

¶ Molly Brown's, 233 Centre St. Café serving good desserts.

¶ The Murray Tea House, next to the Homestead Museum on North Dinosaur Trail. Coffee and desserts.

¶ Whif's Flapjack House, 801 North Dinosaur Trail, in the Badlands Motel. Mostly breakfast but also lunch specials.

Bars and clubs

Downtown Calgary *p273, map p274*
Auburn Saloon, 712 1st St. An arty
Downtown spot with a loungey vibe;
cocktails on cosy couches.
Barley Mill. The most tempting choice
of many pubs around the courtyard
outside **Eau Claire Market**, whose inviting
summer patios offer a reprieve from the
Downtown traffic, as well as an absurd
range of beers on tap.
The Cherry Lounge, 1219 1st St SW. A
trendy and popular club with a minimalist
interior, and a cosy Martini lounge
upstairs. There's different DJs every night,
playing anything from underground funk
to hip hop to electronica.
Cowboy's, 826 5th St SW, www.cowboys
niteclub.com. Yes, it's a real hootenanny
cowboy bar, a huge one, with a gigantic
dance hall for line dancing.
Detour, 318 17th Av. A throbbing club
popular with Calgary's gay scene.
Don Quijote, 309 2nd Av SW. A Spanish
restaurant and tapas bar that turns into a
Latin dance club with tango/salsa Thu-Sat.
Mynt Ultralounge, 516C 9th Av SW,
www.mynt.ca This place is very chic, very
cool, combing brick walls and hardwood
floors with sleek, modern furnishings. The
many spaces include 2 lounges, dance
floors, and a rooftop patio set around a
circular illuminated bar. Martinis and
cocktails, tapas and sushi.
The Palace, 219 8th Av SW. This plush,
high-class club has a serious sound and
laser system, 2 main dance floors and an
intimate atmosphere. Music is hip
hop/R'n'B/house.
Tantra Nightclub and Lounge, 355 10th
Av SW. As the name suggests, a trendy,
sexy lounge and nightclub, with modern
decor interspersed with Asian sculptures.
Vicious Circle, 1011 1st St. A cosy
café/lounge with varied music.
The Warehouse, 733 10th Av SW,
entrance down a back alley, T403-2640535.
A long-lasting yet progressive rave-culture

favourite. Music is trance, jungle,
house etc. Cover charge. Open till
0600 at weekends.

17th Avenue and 4th Street
p276, map p274
Blind Monk, 2500 4th St SW. Club playing
deep house and ambient grooves.
Ming's, 520 17th Av SW. A very enticing,
trendy martini lounge with dim lighting,
an atmosphere of casual sophistication,
and good food.
Night Gallery, 1209 1st St SW. On the
way to 17th Av/4th St, 1st St between
12th and 13th Avs has a small but very
busy club scene. This is the most obvious
choice, with a small crowded dance floor,
and a mixture of DJ music and live bands.
Ship and Anchor, 534 17th Av SW. Very
popular with locals, and arguably the best
pub in town, with outside seating and an
unbeatable selection of draught beers,
including the whole range by excellent
local brewers Big Rock.

Kensington *p276, map p274*
There are far too many British-style pubs
here, all with very slight variations, so just
walk (or crawl) around. You can't knock
their vast selections of quality draught
beers. Happy hour is 1600-1900.
Molly Malone's, 1153 Kensington Cres.
A nice little Irish-style pub with seating
on the rooftop and live music.
Muse Restaurant and Lounge, 10710A
St NW, T403-6706873. An expensive
restaurant upstairs, and a sexy lounge
scene downstairs.

Entertainment

Calgary *p273, map p274*
Check the listings in *FFWD*,
www.ffwdweekly.com and *Straight*,
free from cafés and elsewhere.

Art galleries
Art Gallery of Calgary,117 8th Av SW,
T403-7701350, www.artgallery

calgary.org. Tue-Sat 1000-1800, Sun 1200-1600. By donation. A variety of artists exhibited in 4 different spaces. **Artspace Gallery**, 1235 26th Av SE, www.artspace.ca. Galleries, gift shops, a café and lounge, with 3250 sq m of exhibition space, and live jazz on Fri. **The New Gallery**, 516 9th Av SW, T403-2332399. An artist-run gallery conveniently close to **Calgary Art Gallery**. **Ranchman's**, 9615 Macleod Trail S, T403-2531100. An authentic cowboy saloon with live country bands Mon-Sat.

Cinema

The following show mainly first-run indie, foreign and art-house films.
Globe, 617 8th Av SW, T403-2623308.
Uptown, 612 8th Av SW, T403-2650120.
There is an **IMAX**, at 6455 Macleod Trail S, T403-2128994.

Live music

Beat Niq Jazz and Social Club, downstairs from **Piq Niq Wine Bar and Bistro**, 811 1st St SW, T403-2631650. Live music Thu-Sat at 2130, generally small, vocal-led acts, with a cover charge.
Bookers, 316 3rd St SE, T403-2646419. Cajun food. Blues and jazz Fri and Sat.
Centre for the Performing Arts, 205 8th Av SE, T403-4947455. Calgary's main venue for classical concerts.

Spectator sports

The Calgary Stampeders play **Canadian football** at McMahon Stadium, across from the NW Banff Trail C-train, T403-2890258. The Calgary Cannons play **baseball** at Burns Stadium, across Crowchild Trail from the NW Banff Trail C-train. There is **show-jumping** at Spruce Meadows, 3 km west of Macleod Trail on Hwy 22X, T403-9744200. **Horse racing** takes place at Stampede Park, 17th Av/2nd St SE, T403-2610214.

Theatre

Centre for the Performing Arts, 205 8th Av SE, T403-4947455, www.thearts

centre.org. Calgary's premier venue, with 5 theatres and concert halls; home to the **Calgary Philharmonic**, **Theatre Calgary** and other major companies.
Pleiades Theatre, 701 11th St SW, T403-2213735. Mystery plays.

✪ Festivals and events

Calgary *p273, map p274*
Calgary is famous far and wide for its sensational **Stampede** (see p277), but there are plenty of other events scattered through the calendar.
Feb The **Winter Festival**, T403-5435480, is a 10-day celebration of the cold.
May International Children's Festival, T403-2947414, www.calgarychildfest.org, runs for 5 days in late May.
Jun The **Jazz Festival**, T403-2332628, www.jazzfestivalcalgary.ca, runs for 10 days at various venues around town in mid-Jun, attracting some pretty big names. Later that month is the major 10-day **FunnyFest** comedy festival, T403-2287888, www.funnyfest.com.
Jul During the **Calgary Stampede** in early Jul the 3-day **Microbrewery Stampede**, at Telus Convention Centre, T403-2549204, adds to the revelry with samples of countless brews from across North America. Later that month is the 4-day **Folk Music Festival**, T403-2330904, www.calalgaryfolkfest.com, held in Prince's Island Park.
Jul-Aug Shakespeare in the Park, T403-2406821, early Jul to early Aug, with free performances of the Bard's plays, Tue-Sun at 1900, also in Prince's Island Park.
Aug A couple of good musical events take place in Aug in nearby towns: **Big Valley Country Music Jamboree** in Camrose, T403-6720224 www.bigvalleyjamboree.com; and the **Shady Grove Bluegrass Music Festival** in High River, T403-6525550, www.melmusic.com/sgrove.
Oct In late Oct is the 9-day International Film Festival, www.calgaryfilm.com.

◑ Shopping

Calgary *p273, map p274*
There are several antiques shops in Inglewood, 9th Av SE between 11th St and 13th St.
ABL Imaging, 238 11th Av SE, T403-2666300. Photography.
Alberta Boot Co, 614 10th Av SW, T403-2634623. One of the best things to buy in town is an authentic, handmade pair of cowboy boots.
Coast Mountain Outfitters, 817 10th Av SW. Sports and mountain equipment.
Fosbrooke Fine Arts, 2nd floor, Penny Lane, 8th Av/4th St. Rotating selection showcasing 15-20 artists.
The Hostel Shop and Abbot Pass Trading Co, 1414 Kensington Rd NW, T403-2838311. Books.
Lammle's, 11 shops including 209 8th Av SW, T403-2665226. Western wear.
Mountain Equipment Co-op, 830 10th Av SW. A massive store, with all the sport and camping equipment you need.
Pages Books on Kensington, 1135 Kensington Rd. Bookshop.
Riley and McCormack, 220 8th Av SW, airport, or Eau Claire market. Western wear.
Tramp's Music, 109 10th St NW. Loads of new and used CDs.

▲ Activities and tours

Calgary *p273, map p274*
Golf
Calgary has many fine courses. Among the best are **RCGA Golf Centre**, 7100 15th St SE, T403-6403555; and **McKenzie Meadows**, 17215 McKenzie Meadows Dr SE, T403-2572255.

Tour operators
Big Rock Brewery, 5555 76th Av SE, T403-7203239. Calgary's formidable brewery offers tours and tastings, Tue-Thu at 1330, $5.

Blue Moose Tours, T403-2752440, www.bluemoosetours.com. 1- to 10-day ecotourism trips to Drumheller and the Rockies, plus hiking and biking tours.
Chinook River Sports, T403-2637238, www.chinookkraft.com. Whitewater rafting on the Kicking Horse, Red Deer, Kananaskis, and other rivers. An easy ½-day float down the Bow River in Calgary is $45.
Creative Journeys, T403-2725653, www.legendarytravels.net. Historical walking tours of Downtown. They also do a bus tour of Calgary taking in all the sights, and a 10-hr tour to Banff.
Hammerhead Scenic Tours, T403-5906930, www.hammerheadtours.com. Bus tours of Calgary, the Rockies and the Drumheller Badlands.
Home On The Range, T403-2299090, www.homeontherange.ca. Cowboy tours geared to individual needs, including authentic western experiences like cattle drives, ranch stays, historic sites, powwows and rodeos, and multi-day horseback tours of the Rockies.
Inside Out Experience Inc, T403-9493305, www.insideoutexperience.com. A broad range of adventure tours, including whitewater rafting, hiking, biking, and horse riding.
University of Calgary Outdoor Centre, T403-2205038, www.calgaryoutdoor centre.ca. Whether you want instruction, tours, or gear rental, they have it all. Climbing, canoe trips, biking, kayaking, skiing… you name it.

Drumheller *p278*
Dinosaur Trail Golf Club, across from the museum, T403-8235622. One of the most interesting settings imaginable.
Mukwah Tours, T403-8230456, www.muk wah.com. Whitewater rafting trips on the Red Deer, Highwood and Ram rivers.
Wild West Jurassic Tours, T1888-8233118, www.wildwestjurassictours.com. Tours of the Badlands in an 8-passenger van, $35/ $25/$20 for a ½-day.

⊖ Transport

Calgary *p273, map p274*
Air
There are flights to all useful destinations within Canada. Example flights are to **Whitehorse**, $233 one-way with **Air Canada**, T1888-2472262, www.air canada.com; to **Kamloops** ($145 one-way) with **Air Canada Tango**, www.flytango.ca. To **Kelowna** ($105 one-way) or **Vancouver** ($142 one-way, with frequent discounted flights at $119) with **West Jet**, T1800-5385696, www.westjet.com.

Flight agents Travel Cuts, 1414 Kensington Rd NW, T403-5312070, travel agent offering student discounts.

Bus
Local Calgary Transit has its own information centre at 240 7th Av SW, T403-2621000, www.calgarytransit.com, Mon-Fri 0830-1700. They can provide very helpful maps. Tickets costing $2 or $5.60 can be bought here, on C-train platforms, or from shops with the **Calgary Transit** sticker. If you need to take more than one bus to complete a journey, ask the driver for a transfer. The C-train is free Downtown on 7th Av between Macleod Trail and 8 St SW.

Long distance Greyhound runs several daily buses to **Banff** ($24); **Vancouver** ($134); and **Prince George** ($150 or $111 with 1 day advance purchase). Various shuttles run from the airport to **Banff**, **Canmore**, **Lake Louise**, **Yoho** and **Jasper** (see Ins and outs, p272). Rocky Mountain Discount Travel, T403-5196594, www.rmdtravel.com, runs a hostel shuttle, $85 one-way from Calgary to **Vancouver**, with a stop-off in **Banff** or **Lake Louise**, as long as you return within a month.

Taxis
Calgary Cab Co, T403-7772222.
Associated Taxi, T403-2991111.

Vehicle rental
For car hire try: **Budget**, 140 6th Av SE, T403-2261550; or **Discount**, 444a 9th Av SW, T403- 2991224. **All Season Rentals**, 17a-416 Meridian Rd SE, T403-2041771, offers motorbike hire. For RVs try: **Canadream Campers**, 2508 24th Av NE, T403-2911000, www.canadream.com. **Cruise Canada**, 2980 26th St NE, T403-2914963, www.cruisecanada.com.

Drumheller *p278*
Roughly 150 km northeast from Calgary, Drumheller is reached on Hwy 9 north from the TransCanada Hwy. Daily buses leave **Calgary** at 1745 and 1945 ($32) and it's difficult to reach the museum without your own transport. For a taxi call T403-8237433.
Hammerhead Scenic Tours, T403-5906930, www.hammerheadtours.com. Tours to Drumheller and the Badlands leave Calgary at 0800, returning at 1730. $87, including museum entrance.

❶ Directory

Calgary *p273, map p274*
Banks Canada Trust, 751 3rd St SW; TD Bank, 902 8th Av SW. For foreign exchange: **Royal Bank Foreign Exchange**, T403-2923938; **Western Currency Exchange**, T403-2639000. **Canada Post** 207 9th Av S; 1702 4th St SW. **Embassies and consulates** American, T403-2668962. **Internet** At the library; **Cyber Center Internet Café**, 1602 Centre St NE. **Laundry** Avenue Coin Laundry, 333 17th Av SW. **Library** WR Castell Central Library, 616 Macleod Trail, T403-2602605, www.calgarypubliclibrary.com. **Medical services** Rockyview General Hospital, 7007 14th St SW, T403-5413000; Foothills Hospital, 1403 29th St NW, T403-6701110.

Banff National Park

Banff National Park, the oldest and most famous in the Canadian Rockies, and Canada's number one tourist attraction, receives some 4.7 million visitors per year. This is partly due to its 6641 sq km of jaw-dropping scenery, including 25 peaks over 3000 m and 1500 km of trails, many of which are accessed from the highway and gentle enough for almost anyone. Of equal significance is its location on the country's main highway, a mere 128 km from Calgary. The park's popularity is its only drawback.

⊘ **Getting there** Car or bus.
⊖ **Getting around** Car or bus.
⊖ **Time required** 2 days minimum up to 2 weeks.
⊛ **Weather** Extremely changeable.
⊜ **Sleeping** Camping and hostels to luxury hotels.
⊕ **Eating** Varied but limited.
▲ **Activities and tours** You name it!
★ **Don't miss...** Taking a day hike, such as Cirque Peak ▸▸ p300.

Banff Townsite is the park's main hub, a pleasant but absurdly busy place with services catering to every budget. A short hop north is Lake Louise, the single most famous location in the Rockies. From here, a nice loop leads through Yoho and Kootenay National Parks, while the incredible Icefields Parkway runs north to Jasper, lined with the most drool-inducing scenery of all, peaking around the extraordinary Columbia Icefields.

Ins and outs

Getting there and around

Banff Airporter, T403-7623330, www.banffairporter.com, and **Sun Dog Tours**, T1888-7863641, www.sundogtours.com, run regular shuttles from Calgary Airport (see p272) to Banff, Canmore (both $51 one-way) and Lake Louise ($60). The **Greyhound** station is downtown at 100 Gopher Street, with regular buses from Vancouver and Calgary. The TransCanada Highway connects Banff with Vancouver and all points east. Many trails in the south of the park start on the Smith-Dorrien Highway accessible from Canmore. The **Banff-Canmore Connector**, T403-7625200, runs three times daily ($6). **Brewster**, T403-7626767, and **Greyhound** run daily buses to Lake Louise ($14). Banff Townsite can be easily explored on foot; almost everything in town is on or near Banff Avenue. **Banff Transit**, T403-7621215, covers the whole town ($2). ▸▸ ⊖ p309.

Banff Townsite ⊜⊘⊙⊙⊛⊙▲⊜⊕ ▸▸ pp301-309.

Banff enjoys a stunning location and was once a pretty little village. Today, however, the 50,000 visitors it receives daily throughout the summer have taken their toll. The streets are perpetually heaving, the roads choked with tour buses. The relentless commercialism soon become tiresome and there is little to do but shop, eat and party. Those needing creature comforts will find it here but if you are camping or staying in hostels, there are nicer places to be. The main reason to visit is to use the excellent Banff Information Centre, see below. The nicest part of Banff lies at its west end, where a picturesque bridge over the Bow River gives an idea of how the village must have looked before its popularity got out of hand.

Banff National Park

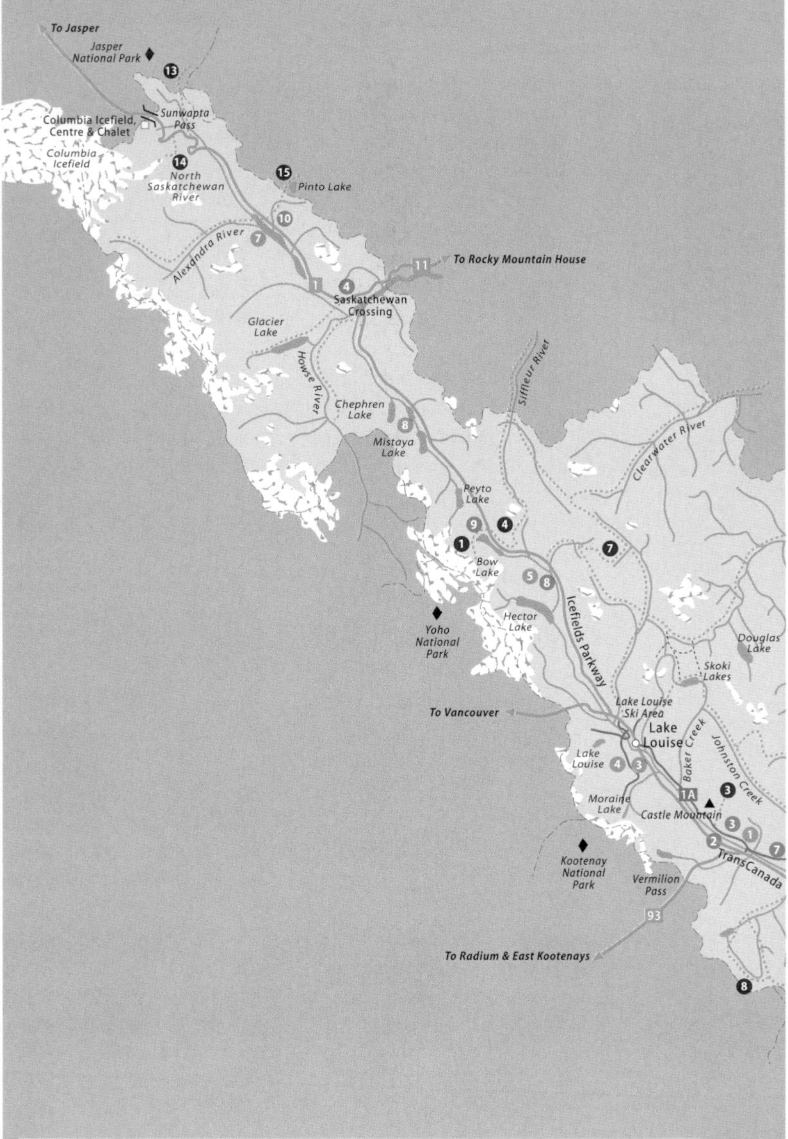

Sleeping
Castle Mountain Chalets **2**
Castle Mountain Hostel **3**
Crossing **4**
Johnston Canyon
  Resort **7**
Mosquito Creek Hostel **8**
Num-Ti-Jah Lodge **9**
Rampart Creek Hostel **10**

Camping
Castle Mountain **1**
Johnston Canyon **2**
Lake Louise Tent **3**
Lake Louise Trailer **4**
Mosquito Creek **5**
Rampart Creek **7**
Waterfowl Lake **8**

Trails
Bow Glacier Falls &
  Bow Hut **1**
Castle Crags **3**
Cirque Peak/Helen Lake **4**
Citadel Pass & Mount
  Assiniboine **5**
Fish Lakes/Pipestone
  Pass/Devon Lakes **7**

Healy Pass & Egypt Lake **8**
Johnston Canyon **9**
Lake Minnewanka **10**
Mount Assiniboine
  (via Bryant Creek) **11**
Nigel Pass, Jonas Pass
  & Poboktan Pass **13**
Parker Ridge **14**
Sunset Pass **15**

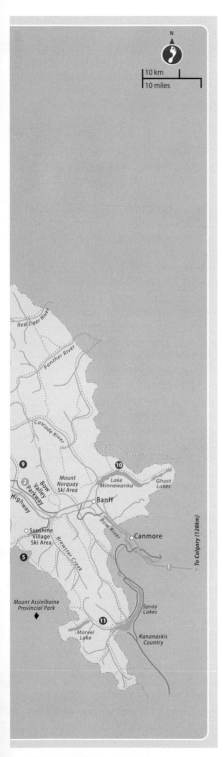

Tourist information

The **Banff Information Centre** ① *224 Banff Av, daily 0900-1700*, comprises the **Parks Canada Office**, T403-7621550, www.parks canada.ca/banff, and the **Banff Lake Louise Tourism Bureau**, T403-7628421, www.banff lakelouise.com. The former is an excellent source of information about hikes and all other park activities, and issues very useful maps for day-hikes, cycling, and one showing longer trails and backcountry campgrounds. To stay at one of these you must register here and buy a **Wilderness Pass** ($9 per person per night). The Tourism Bureau can help out with sleeping arrangements. It keeps track of which hotels, B&Bs and campsites still have spaces and provides a courtesy phone. It can also provide brochures for the *Banff Historical Walking Tour*. The **Friends of Banff National Park**, T403-7628918, www.friendsofbanff.com, sells maps and all kinds of books on hiking and other activities as well as and natural and cultural history. It also runs free guided walks throughout the summer. For park radio, tune in to 101.1 FM

Whyte Museum of the Canadian Rockies

① *111 Bear St, T403-7622291, www.whyte.org, daily 1000-1700, $6, $3.50 child.*
Created by artists Peter and Catherine Whyte, Banff's most worthwhile sight includes thousands of volumes of archives and Alpine Club records of early expeditions. Of greater significance to visitors is the fine collection of mountain-related art, much of it by the founders, and temporary exhibitions by local and international contemporary artists. Most fascinating of all is an excellent collection of photos that vividly documents the early days of the park and the changing attitudes that have prevailed regarding its wildlife. Countless black and white pictures depict fancily dressed Edwardian tourists standing next to their vintage cars, grinning stupidly as they feed a bear by hand; or a self-satisfied ranger standing smugly over some poor dead beast. The museum presents lectures and various tours. A 90-minute Historic Banff walking tour leaves once a day and costs $7.

Banff Park Museum

ⓘ *91 Banff Av, T403-7621558, summer 1000-1800, winter 1300-1700, $4, $3 child.*
The Banff Park Museum is housed in a splendid wood cabin built in 1895, its age explaining all the skylights, which compensated for the lack of electric light. Like the building itself, the interior is more a relic from the past than a place where the past is documented. A large collection of dusty, old stuffed animals pay their politically incorrect tribute to a time when people's idea of wildlife watching was taking high tea in a room lined with animal heads, and even the official park approach to wildlife preservation was to shoot all predators like cougars, lynx and eagles so that innocents such as elk, deer and sheep could multiply unhampered.

Across the river, the **Buffalo Nations Luxton Museum** ⓘ *1 Birch Av, T403-7622388, summer 0900-1900, winter 1300-1700, $8, $2.50 child*, has a small collection of First Nations artefacts like beadwork and headdresses, and a number of poorly executed tableaux. The gift shop is its best feature.

Cave and Basin Hot Springs

A couple of kilometres southwest of Banff centre, the **Cave and Basin Hot Springs** ⓘ *311 Cave Av, T403-7621566, summer 0900-1800, winter 1100-1600, $4, $2 child, tours daily at 1100*, is the site of the thermal waters whose discovery prompted the park's formation. The whole story is told through a collection of exhibits and the film *Steam, Schemes and National Dreams*. The cavernous, atmospheric setting of that first pool is the highlight, making you wish it were still open for bathing. The outdoor 'basin' pool is only slightly less enticing. The grounds are also attractive and contain a couple of short, popular walks. The 2-km interpretive **Marsh Loop Trail** leads on boardwalks around a wetland area whose warm microclimate has made it unusually lush and flower-filled and a rewarding spot for birdwatchers. The easy and popular 3.7-km **Sundance Canyon Trail** follows a paved path to the canyon mouth.

Banff Springs Hotel

After the discovery of the springs, the Canadian Pacific Railway quickly saw tourism as a means to pay for its expensive line and went about building a series of luxurious hotels. First of these was the Banff Springs Hotel, the largest in the world when finished in 1888. Unfortunately, the Gothic giant was constructed back to front, with wonderful views from the kitchens and none at all from the guest rooms. Since then it has been rebuilt and developed, its 250 rooms expanded to 770, all of which are full in summer, mostly with Japanese tour groups. Known as the 'Castle in the Rockies', it is now more village than hotel, a vast, confusing labyrinth of restaurants, lounges, shops and facilities. Utterly over-the-top, its sheer excessiveness makes it the only unmissable sight in Banff. Be sure to pick up a map from reception before exploring. It's a boring walk up Spray Avenue from the centre, so take the No 1 local transit.

Upper Hot Springs and Sulphur Mountain Gondola

If the Cave Springs have put you in the mood, head for the **Upper Hot Springs** ⓘ *end of Mountain Av, T403-7621515, May-Oct 0900-2300, Oct-May 1000-2200, $7.50, $6.50 child, reduced rates in evening and winter*, an outdoor thermal swimming pool with great views, whose very sulphurous water is cooled to 40° C. The **Hot Springs Spa** offers massage, aromatherapy, and a steam room.

Just down the road is the **Sulphur Mountain Gondola** ⓘ *end of Mountain Av, T403-7622523, summer 0730-2100, spring and autumn 0830-2000, winter 0900-1600, $22.50, $11.25 child, or take the local bus No 1 to Fairmont and hike up to the gondola*, which takes you up 700 m in eight minutes at a 51° angle. At the top is a restaurant, two observation terraces for taking in the exceptional panoramic views and a couple of short trails leading to even more vistas.

Vermilion Lakes and Lake Minnewanka

The **Vermilion Lakes**, just west of town off Mount Norquay Road, are easily explored by bike or car. The marshes around them are home to a wide range of birds, such as ospreys and bald eagles, as well as like muskrat, beaver, elk and coyote. **Lake Minnewanka**, north of the eastern highway junction, is a focus for hiking, biking, fishing and boating

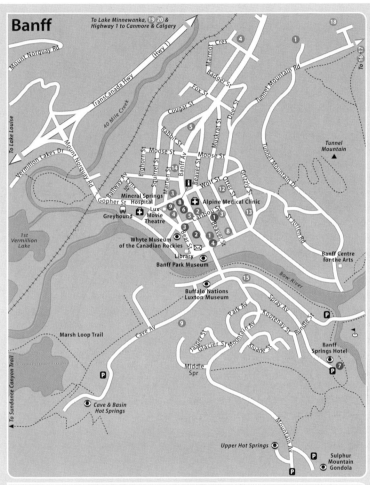

N

500 metres
500 yards

Sleeping
Banff Y Mountain Lodge
  & Sundance Bistro **15**
Blue Mountain Lodge **3**
Bumpers Inn **4**
Driftwood Inn &
  Caramba! Restaurant **14**
HI Banff Alpine Centre
  & Storm Cellar **1**
Mountain Home **8**
Pension Tannenhof **9**
Rocky Mountain B&B **12**
Samesun Hostel **5**

Tan-Y-Bryn **13**

Camping
Tunnel Mountain I **17**
Tunnel Mountain II **18**
Tunnel Mt Trailer Court **16**
Two Jack Lakeside **19**
Two Jack Main **20**

Eating
Aardvark Pizza & Sub **1**
Cassis Bistro, Maple Leaf
  Grille & Hoodoo Lounge **2**

Coyotes **3**
Evelyn's Coffee Bar **9**
Le Beaujolais **4**
Sukiyaki House **6**
Sunfood Café Vegetarian **8**
Waldhaus & Pub **7**

Bars & clubs
Aurora Night Club **1**
Lik Lounge **4**
Rose & Crown **2**
St James Gate **3**
Wild Bill's Legendary Saloon **5**

Scuba diving at Lake Minnewanka near Banff.

Hikes around Banff Townsite

▲ **Fenland Trail** ⓘ *access is from Mount Norquay Rd*. A 1.5-km loop through the wetlands near the first Vermilion Lake, a haven for birds and other wildlife.

▲ **Marsh Loop** ⓘ *access is from the Cave and Basin hot sprints*. This 2-km trail explores a similarly rich area for flora and fauna.

▲ **Tunnel Mountain** ⓘ *3.6 km return, 200 m elevation gain. Trailhead: St Julien Rd*. This short, steep but easily attainable hike leads to fine views of Banff Village.

▲ **C-level Cirque** ⓘ *8 km return, 455 m elevation gain. Trailhead: 3.5 km north on Lake Minnewanka Rd*. This is a short, easy hike leading to some heart-warming mountain scenery. You'll also see mining remains and wild flowers.

▲ **Lake Minnewanka** ⓘ *6-60 km return with little elevation gain*. This trail is suitable for anyone and is open even in April and November when most others are closed. You can also go as far as you like. The **Ghost Lakes** are at Km 24, with frequent campgrounds along the way. At Km 7.8, you can turn left for the steep climb to **Mount Aylmer Lookout/Pass** (23.6 or 27 km, 615 or 845 m elevation gain). This route also enjoys a longer season than most. From the lookout are great views of the lake and mountains towering above the opposite shore. From the pass the views are bigger but mostly limited to vast expanses of desolate grey rock.

▲ **Cory and Edith passes** ⓘ *13-km circuit, 960 m elevation gain. Trailhead: 0.5 km on Bow Valley Parkway after it leaves Highway 1, turn right and continue 1 km*. Cory Pass can usually be hiked by late June. An extremely tough trail involving steep sections and some scree slope scrambling, this is only for the fit and reasonably experienced but if you can manage it, the rewards are an adrenaline-pumping quest and some exhilarating views. Edith is less exciting but makes for an easier descent and a neat loop.

Around Banff ⊜🅿🛈🅾▲🚌🅒 ⓘ *pp301-309*.

Canmore

Though the highway around Canmore is now entirely engulfed by satellite suburbs of hotels and condos, its Downtown core, centred on Main (8th) Street, just about manages to retain the comfortable feel of an authentic small town, making this an attractive and cheaper alternative to the insanely busy and commercially-oriented Banff, just 21 km to the west.

There are some decent, down-to-earth pubs, fine restaurants and as many sports equipment shops as anyone could desire. Moreover, many fine hikes into Banff and Mount Assiniboine Parks are most easily accessed from Canmore, many tour operators are based here, and all kinds of outdoor activities are seriously pursued in the region, particularly climbing, Nordic skiing, and mountain biking (see Activities and tours, p306).

Across the bridge from town, past the Nordic Centre, a steep, rough road leads to the **Spray Lakes**, a nice quiet spot to camp. On the way, just about where its surface gives way to dirt, this road passes Canmore's most worthwhile attraction, **Grassi Lakes**. The unreal aquamarine/lime green colour of these lakes is extraordinary, even by local standards, and the whole area is a lovely, relaxing place. North of the lakes is a very popular spot for rock climbing; there's always plenty of action to watch for those who do not partake. Those who do will find lava cliff faces riddled with holes, and all levels of climb with routes already anchored by locals.

For maps and trail information, call in at **Tourism Canmore** ① *907 7th Av, T403-6781295, www.tourismcanmore.com*. They can provide a brochure for the self-guided *Historic Walking Tour* of the town. More useful for general enquiries is **Travel Alberta** ① *northwest of town at the junction of Hwy 1 and the Bow Valley Trail (Hwy 1A), T403-6785277, www.travelalberta.com, May-Oct 0800-2000, winter 0900-1800*. The national HQ of the **Alpine Club of Canada** is on Indian Flats Road, T403-6783200, a short drive from town. They are very helpful and knowledgeable about climbs and hikes and sell a good selection of maps and guidebooks. They also have a hostel (see Sleeping, p302) and backcountry huts dotted throughout the parks. For locations visit www.alpineclubofcanada.ca/rockymountain.

Mount Assiniboine Provincial Park

Canmore is the main jumping-off point for hikes into the south of Banff National Park. These are reached on the Smith-Dorrien Highway (No 742) beyond Spray Lakes. Just past the south end of Spray Lakes reservoir, turn right onto Watridge logging road and drive 5.3 km for Mount Shark trailhead, one of the starting points for hikes into Mount Assiniboine Provincial Park in BC. Mount Assiniboine is one of the most recognizable and visually gratifying peaks in the Rockies, a pyramid-shaped icon that has been compared to the Matterhorn in the Swiss Alps. The rest of the park is equally sensational, and certainly one of the top backpacking destinations in the range.

Rock climbing at Grassi Lakes near Canmore.

From Mount Shark, the easiest route is via **Bryant Creek** and the Assiniboine Pass. It is 27.5 km one way, with an elevation gain of 480 m. A strong hiker can do it in a day. Otherwise there is a campground at Km 9.7, and a warden hut, campground and shelter at Km 13.6. To stay at either, make arrangements with the Banff Visitor Centre. The easiest route back to Mount Shark, making a nice loop, is over **Wonder Pass** and by Marvel Lake. This is also 27.5 km, with an elevation gain of 230 m then a lot of downhill. A second access route, and probably the best, is over **Citadel Pass** from Sunshine Village. This is a delightful, slightly easier, 29-km hike with 450-m gain. The ultimate trip would be to enter this way and exit via Wonder Pass, but arranging a shuttle would be tricky. None of this should be done without a map and a more detailed trail description.

The core area of this triangular park is its southeast corner, which contains Mount Assiniboine, eight other peaks over 3000 m and several beautiful lakes. The main focus and campground is at **Lake Magog**. There is also a Park HQ/warden's cabin. Some excellent one-day hikes from here give the chance to see some of the park and recover from the trek in. **Nub Peak**, a moderate 11.6-km round-trip (from Magog), offers excellent views of the surroundings. **Windy Ridge**, a moderate 17.4-km round-trip, is one of the highest trail-accessible points in the Rockies, with even better views and wild flower meadows on the way. An easier excursion is the 8-km loop to **Sunburst**, **Cerulean** and **Elizabeth Lakes**, which can be extended to 18.6 km to take in the views from **Ferro Pass**. Whatever the skies are doing and the forecasts say, always come prepared for the worst the weather can throw at you.

Sunshine Village Ski Area

Bow Valley Parkway (see below) is the scenic route east from Banff to Lake Louise and beyond. Highway 1 is still a beautiful drive, but much faster with less chances to stop and hike. After 8 km, a road heads from the latter to **Sunshine Village Ski Area** ⓘ *T403-7626500, www.ski banff.com, lift pass$65, shuttles from bigger Banff Hotels $12*. Situated right on the Great Divide, this hill receives a much higher calibre of snow than nearby Mount Norquay, with 10 m per year of first-class powder, and is Canada's biggest snow-pack. The hill also has one of the longest seasons, running till late May. A high-speed gondola and 10 lifts whisk skiers up to 107 uncrowded runs. The highest elevation is 2730 m, with a vertical drop of 1070 m. As well as rentals and lessons, the hill has its own accommodation. Note that it's very cold up here.

Hikes from Sunshine Village

The beauty of ski hills is the speed with which you can be whisked to elevations that would take hours of hard walking to reach otherwise. Then you can maximise your time and effort because the views are already fantastic. Unfortunately the Sunshine gondola no longer runs in summer, though there is a shuttle bus run by **White Mountain Adventures**, T403-6784099, $21 return ($11 child) from the Sunshine parking lot, or $41 ($21 child) from Banff Townsite.

▲▲ **Sunshine Meadows** At the top of the gondola the meadows stretch for 15 km along the Great Divide, receiving copious amounts of rain and snow that feed one of the most glorious midsummer wild flower displays you'll ever see. Naturally, such an easily accessible Eden draws crowds of visitors. Most go only as far as **Rock Isle Lake**, an easy 1.6-km trail to a beautiful viewpoint. To avoid the crowds set a brisker pace towards **Citadel Pass**, 18.6 km return, 343 m elevation gain. On a clear day many of BC's mighty and rugged peaks are visible, including Mount Assiniboine. Continue a little further towards Fatique Pass, 2.5 km away, for even better views. This is a popular way to begin a multi-day backpacking trip into Mount Assiniboine Provincial Park in BC.

▲▲ **Healy Pass** ⓘ *18.4 km return, 360 m or 655 m elevation gain*. There are two ways to reach Healy Pass: from Sunshine Village via the shuttle and Simpson Pass, or from the Sunshine parking lot via Healy Creek. The distance is the same but the second option involves a lot more climbing, though at a gentle pace. If you are fit and don't want to pay the shuttle fare, go via Healy Creek. Either way, the flowers are wonderful. The pass itself is unexceptional but offers good views of Egypt and Scarab Lakes and the Pharaoh Peaks. You could also explore the Monarch Ramparts south of the pass. **Egypt Lake** campground and a basic, cheerless hut is 3 km further on. To stay here book at the **Banff Visitor Centre**, T403-7621550, $16 per person (including Wilderness pass). There are some worthwhile side-trips if you do. **Whistling Pass** is a fine 6.6-km round-trip, which could be extended to **Shadow Lake** beneath the lofty Mount Ball (26 km return from Egypt Lake).

A stunning vista of Lake Louise.

The Bow Valley Parkway leaves Highway 1 just west of Banff. Its speed limit is a sometimes frustrating 60 kph, but when drivers are liable to hit the breaks at any moment if a sheep appears, this is a good thing. Along the road are three campgrounds, a hostel, a few lodges, and numerous hikes and viewpoints. At Km 16 is **Johnston Canyon** and its eponymous trail of the same name (11.6 km return, 215 m elevation gain), which is the most worthwhile hike along the parkway. The chasms and waterfalls of this canyon are famous and perpetually flooded with tourists but it's a charming walk. The canyon is at its most beautiful in winter, when the waterfalls are frozen (see p306). You can continue beyond the falls to the multicoloured cold-water springs of the **Inkpots** and views of Johnston Creek Valley.

Castle Mountain, 30 km from Banff, marks the junction with Highway 93, which heads south through Kootenay National Park to Radium Hot Springs. The mountain itself is a magnificent and aptly named sight, worth pulling over to admire. The nearby **Rockbound Lake Trail** is more trouble than it's worth but **Silverton Falls** from the same trailhead is a nice 1.6-km jaunt. About 5 km to the west is the **Castle Crags Trail** (7 km return, 520 m elevation gain). This short but steep hike leads to an old fire lookout and an outstanding panorama of the Bow Valley from Banff to Lake Louise. It is also free of snow earlier and later than most trails. On the way up you'll pass wild flower gardens and a dilapidated old cabin.

Lake Louise ⊜𝟶𝟶◻▲⊜𝟶 ≫ *pp301-309.*

Magnificent Lake Louise is the single most famous icon in the Rockies and consequently receives far more visitors than any place of natural beauty should have to endure. This is the only focus in the park other than Banff Townsite, with a better assortment of trails and things to see, but far fewer facilities. There are actually four components to Lake Louise: the Village, the Lake, Moraine Lake and the Ski Hill.

The Village

You'll come to the village first, close to the important junction where Highway 1 veers west through Yoho towards Golden and Revelstoke. Highway 93 then becomes the sole route north, henceforth known as the **Icefields Parkway**. This 'village' is little more than the ugly, overpriced Samson Mall, though it does contain most of the limited local accommodation, including one of the best hostels in the country and the excellent **Lake Louise Visitor Centre** ① *T403-5223833, Jun-Sep 0800-1800, rest of the year 0900-1600 or 1700*. The parks office/ information centre helps out with hikes and accommodation, handing out brochures and maps and issuing backcountry permits. A number of interesting natural history exhibits explain some of the local geographical features, including displays on the Burgess Shale in Field (see p323).

The Lake

There are many lakes in the Rockies whose water has an opaque, milky quality due to the presence of glacial silt known as 'rock flour'; mineral deposits that glaciers have scraped from the mountain rock. These particles absorb all colours of the light spectrum except green and blue. Far and away the most famous is **Lake Louise**, whose milky water is of the most exquisite aquamarine colour (or colours, because the hue changes dramatically according to the time of year and angle of the sun). Add to this the lake's sheer size and dramatic location at the foot of an incredibly powerful, towering rock rampart and it is not difficult to understand why this is the definitive picture-postcard image of the Rockies, and the single most popular sight in the range.

Around 10,000 people come here every day in peak season, so if you want to see its shores crowd-free, arrive at sunrise. It comes as little surprise that this was the spot chosen by the CPR for the second of their giant hotels, the Château, originally built in 1890. Many visitors

Horse riding is a popular way to see the Rockies.

are shocked by this behemoth and consider its monstrous presence on the shores of the heavenly water an outrage that would never be allowed today. The best thing is to ignore it and go for a walk, or hire a canoe and go for a paddle. **Lake Agnes Tea House** and **Plain of the Six Glaciers Tea House** are each situated on popular trails about one or two hours' hike above the lake.

Moraine Lake

Lake Louise is 4.5 km from the Village up a steep hill (2.7 km on foot). Halfway up, a left fork leads 12.5 km to Moraine Lake, another striking emerald product of rock flour. Half the size of its sister, equally beautiful, and almost as popular, its location is maybe even more dramatic. Stretching away from its shores is the **Valley of the Ten Peaks**, a wonderfully scenic cluster of mighty mountains, also known as the **Wenkchemna**, the Stoney word for ten. Some excellent trails lead into the valley and up to viewpoints. Expensive canoes can be rented for a paddle ($27 per hour). Parking is often a problem.

Lake Louise Ski Area

Just before the Bow Valley Parkway crosses Highway 1 on its way to Lake Louise, it passes the turning to the **Ski Area**, T403-5223555, www.skilouise.com. This is the biggest ski hill in Canada, 40 sq km of terrain featuring vast open bowls. With excellent powder and stupendous views, it ranks for almost all ski aficionados as one of the best hills in North America. A high-speed gondola and 11 lifts service terrain that is 25% beginner, 45% intermediate and 30% expert. The top elevation is 2637 m, with a vertical drop of 1000 m. The only drawbacks are the low snowfall of 360 m and the fact that it is bitterly cold up there, not helped by the fact that most runs are above the tree-line. The lodges at the bottom are open year round, with restaurants, pubs and lounges, a cappuccino bar, equipment rentals and lessons. A day pass is $64.

In summer, the **Lake Louise Sightseeing Gondola** ⓘ *T403-5223555, May-Sep 0830-1800, $22, $11.50 child, $2 extra for breakfast buffet, $6 extra for lunch buffet*, runs people to the top of the hill to enjoy the views, though there's not much to do up there apart from that. The **Environmental Education Centre** runs guided nature walks several times daily, with a choice of themes, $5-7. A free shuttle bus to the hill leaves the Village every hour on the hour from 0800-1700, leaving the Château 30 minutes earlier.

Hikes around Lake Louise

From the Lake

▲▲ **Saddleback/Fairview Mountain** ① *7.4-10.6 km return, 600-1014 m elevation gain. Trailhead: by the canoe rental at northeast end of lake.* The hike to Saddleback, despite its steepness, is very popular, especially in September when the larches turn to gold. This is a great viewpoint; even better is Saddle Mountain, 90 m straight up above it. Best of all is Fairview Mountain, a further steep 1.6-km climb. The panorama from here is to die for, with gargantuan peaks all around Lake Louise 1000 m below.

▲▲ **Plain of the Six Glaciers** ① *13.8 km, 380 m elevation gain.* This popular trail takes you up to the Teahouse and is perpetually crowded. Go anyway, because the views are astounding, embracing the giant peaks of mounts Lefroy and Victoria and their extensive glaciers and icefalls. Try starting after 1600 to minimize the company.

From Moraine Lake Road

▲▲ **Paradise Valley/Lake Annette** ① *18.2-km circuit/11.4 km return, 400 m/250 m elevation gain. Trailhead: 2.5 km from junction with Lake Louise Drive, 10 km before Moraine Lake.* Though this is a valley hike, the views it offers are as good or better than most ridge walks, with plenty of peaks and sheer rock faces. A return hike to Lake Annette is phenomenal in itself, but the longer circuit is recommended, and best done in a clockwise direction. Horseshoe Meadow has a backcountry campground for those who want to take their time and extend it into a two-day trip. A possible worthwhile detour is to Giant Steps, where a river cascades slowly over some truly enormous slabs of quartzite. The paths there are confusing.

From Moraine Lake

▲▲ **Valley of the Ten Peaks/Sentinel Pass** ① *11.6 km return, 725 m elevation gain. Trailhead: past the lodge.* This wonderful, exhilarating trail leads through Larch Valley, a particularly popular spot in the autumn when the trees turn to gold. It is a fairly gentle hike most of the way until the final switchback ascent to the pass, which is not as hard as it looks. The view from the top is spectacular, taking in most of the ten peaks and looking down on the other side into Paradise Valley. This hike can be combined with the Paradise Valley one to make a 17-km one-way trip ending 10 km down Moraine Lake Road. The best bet is to leave a vehicle here and hitch or take the shuttle up to Moraine Lake. This is a very popular trail but only takes four or five hours so think about starting early or late.

▲▲ **Consolation Lakes** ① *6 km return, 60 m elevation gain.* Though no substitute for the above, this is a short and easy walk, and the cliffs that tower over the lakes are undeniably impressive. The rough trail beyond the first lake means that the second is always less busy.

From the Ski Area

▲▲ **Skoki Valley** ① *31.6 km, 785 m elevation gain. Trailhead: follow Whitehorn Rd towards the Ski Area, turn right at Km 2 onto Fish Creek Rd and follow for 1.1 km.* The high point of this hike are the alpine meadows and numerous lakes surrounded by rugged mountains with a romantically desolate air. The down-side is that many hikers come this way, meaning trails are muddy if it's been raining. At least the first 4 km are on a boring fire-road. Think of doing it as a day-trip and cycle that section. If camping, Merlin Meadows and Baker Lake are the best options, or you could stay at the **Skoki Lodge**, see p308. A fine day-hike from here is the 6.2-km round-trip to the beautiful Merlin Lake. A 1.6-km scramble up Skoki Mountain leads to 360° views. This is also a very popular area for cross-country skiing.

The road through Icefields Parkway.

Icefields Parkway ⊜🏃 ↠ *pp301-309.*

pp301-309

The 230-km road between Lake Louise and Jasper runs through some of the Rockies' most spectacular scenery, bridging the two major parks, and must qualify as one of the most exciting drives in the world. In fact, the endless parade of lofty snow-capped peaks and vast glaciers is likely to push you towards sensory overload. The climax comes just beyond the Sunwapta Pass that separates Banff and Jasper national parks. This is the Columbia Icefield, the single largest and most accessible area of ice and snow in the Rockies.

Distances given below are from Lake Louise. Dotted along the road at fairly regular intervals are five youth hostels, twelve campgrounds and a whole host of long and short trails. Pick up the Icefields Parkway map/guide from the visitor centre in Banff, Lake Louise or Jasper.

Lake Louise to the Columbia Icefield

Bow Lake, at Km 37, is a beautiful lake whose turquoise hue seems almost preternaturally vivid. Bow Summit (2069 m), 3 km further north, is the highest pass in the Rockies and the highest highway crossing in Canada. Just beyond, a short side road leads to the exceptional but very busy viewpoint above **Peyto Lake**, another of those Rocky Mountain icons whose undeniable beauty can get lost among the throngs and clamour. It's named after Bill Peyto, a legendary Rocky pioneer who was as famous for his exploits around town as for his wilderness exploration.

Saskatchewan Crossing, at Km 78, is a grim crossroads with Highway 11 but a useful service centre offering a rare chance to get gas and essential supplies. At 114 km the road enters a dramatic giant switchback known as the 'Big Bend'. At the top are the impressive **Panther Falls** and a couple of viewpoints where you can stop and enjoy the sweep of mountains back to the south. Look out also for the **Weeping Wall**, where water plunges down from a series of cracks in the apparently solid rock face.

Just beyond **Sunwapta Pass** (2023 m), which marks the border between the national parks, comes the highlight of the drive. For further information on the Columbia Icefield and the surrounding area, visit the **Icefield Centre** (see p312).

▲ Fish Lakes/Pipestone Pass/Devon Lakes Trail ⓘ *29.6-62.8 km, 762 m-1,116 m elevation gain. Trailhead: park at Mosquito Creek, at Km 28, then walk across the road and over the bridge.* This trail leads through mostly open terrain with scenery that is consistently

Canadian Rockies Banff National Park

Cirque Mountain.

wonderful. There are a few possible itineraries. North Molar Pass makes a good 23-km day-hike. On this route, a scramble east of the pass gives views of the Fish Lakes and Pipestone River valley. Upper Fish Lake is reached at Km 14.8, a day-trip for fast hikers. The campground, right on the lake beneath a towering rock wall, is a fine spot. To make it a four-day trip, continue to Pipestone Pass, with extensive views that include 19 km of the Siffleur River Valley, through the Clearwater Pass, and on to the quiet and remote Devon Lakes at Km 31.4.

▲▲ **Cirque Peak/Helen Lake Trail** ⓘ *15 km return, 1043 m elevation gain. Trailhead: Crowfoot Glacier viewpoint, at Km 34.* One of the best hikes in the Rockies, leading quickly to open sub-alpine meadows covered with heather and wild flowers, offering views of the impressive mountains. The marmots at Helen Lake are daring and entertaining. It's a long, slow scramble up a scree slope from here to Cirque Peak, but easier than you'd think and amply rewarded by 360° views of the Dolomite Valley, Bow and Peyto Lakes, and Crowfoot and Bow Glaciers.

▲▲ **Bow Glacier Falls** ⓘ *9 km return, 148 m elevation gain. Trailhead: Bow Lake at Km 37.* Stroll along the shore of this striking lake and witness the birthplace of the Bow River.

▲▲ **Bow Hut Trail** ⓘ *14.8 km return, 500 m elevation gain.* This follows the same trail as Bow Glacier, above, almost to the falls, then heads uphill through a canyon to a mountaineering hut close to the edge of the vast Wapta Icefield. The rock and ice views are wonderful but those scared of heights might baulk at the final ascent.

▲▲ **Bow Lookout Trail** ⓘ *6 km return, 260 m elevation gain. Trailhead: Peyto Lake at Km 40.* Leads up to a former fire lookout and gets you away from the crowds below. Commanding views take in the many lofty peaks and offer another perspective on the fabulous Bow Lake.

▲▲ **Sunset Pass Trail** ⓘ *16.4 km return, 725 m elevation gain. Trailhead: just north of Rampart Creek at Km 89.* This long expanse of pretty meadows is usually snow-free by late June but can be very wet and is prime grizzly habitat. The landscape climaxes at the north end with views of the deep-blue Lake Pinto.

▲▲ **Nigel Pass Trail** ⓘ *14.4 km return, 365 m elevation gain. Trailhead: Km 113.* A gentle hike offering constant expansive views. At the pass, look beyond to the more starkly beautiful, formidable peaks of the upper Brazeau Valley. This is the opening section of a multi-day trek to Jonas Pass and Poboktan Pass (80 km return, 1,913 m elevation gain). Among the best long hikes in the range, this network of trails presents many options and factors that require thought and research. The highlight of the trip is Jonas Pass, an 11-km high meadow valley with pristine mountain scenery. Poboktan Pass is also a delight to explore but both the loop via Brazeau Lake and the one-way exit along Poboktan Creek have major drawbacks. Better is to camp at Jonas Cutoff, day-hike to Poboktan Pass, pass another night at the Cutoff, then hike out the same way. The lack of camping throughout Jonas Pass means either hiking 33 km to the Cutoff campground, then 33km out on the third day, or breaking the journey by camping at Four Point (14 km), making it a five-day trip.

▲▲ **Parker Ridge Trail** ⓘ *4.8 km return, 270 m elevation gain. Trailhead: Km 117.* A hike whose rewards far outweigh the effort expended. Breathtaking views take in the awesome expanse of the 9 km-long Saskatchewan Glacier, the longest tongue of the Columbia Icefield.

▲▲ **Wilcox Pass Trail** ⓘ *8 km return, 335 m elevation gain. Trailhead: just south of Wilcox Creek campground.* A short and easy hike that everybody should do, quickly leading to views that many longer hikes fail to equal. After a brief ascent through mature forest, the Columbia Icefield is suddenly visible in all its glory. Wild flower meadows and resident bighorn sheep complete the idyllic picture. With so much to be gained from so little effort, don't expect to be alone.

● Sleeping

Banff Townsite *p287, map p291*
Accommodation in Banff is overpriced and heavily booked. On midsummer weekends, every single bed and vehicle-accessible campsite in the park will often be full, so reservations are strongly recommended. You can book through **Banff Accommodation**, T1877- 2263348, www.banffinfo.com. If you turn up without a reservation, head straight for the visitor centre; they know exactly what is left. To plan ahead, check www.bannflake louise.com, which has full details and links for just about everywhere in town.

A-B Mountain Home, 129 Muskrat St, T403- 7623889, www.mountainhome bb.com. 3 nice en suite rooms and a guest common room in a renovated home with antique furnishings.

A-B Pension Tannenhof, 121 Cave Av, T403-7624636, www.pensiontannen hof.com. 10 rooms, most with en suite bath, half with mountain views. Guests enjoy a large common room and breakfast.

B Blue Mountain Lodge, 137 Muskrat St, T403-7625134, www.bluemtnlodge.com. 10 small but attractive en suite rooms in a centrally located turn-of-the-20th-century building with period decor and shared lounge and kitchen.

B Bumpers Inn, Banff Av/Marmot Cres, T403-7623386, www.bumpersinn.com.

Fairly nice, spacious rooms. Situated on the edge of town and quiet as a result, with forest at the back, enjoyed from the large outside deck or 2nd floor balcony.

B The Driftwood Inn, 337 Banff Av, T403-7624496, www.bestofbanff.com. Reasonable, fairly spacious rooms with pine furnishings. Guests are allowed to use the spa and fitness room.

C Rocky Mountain B&B, 223 Otter St, T403-7624811, www.rockymtnbb.com. 9 decent rooms and a suite in an old house whose shared common room has a nice historic feel.

D HI Banff Alpine Centre, 801 Coyote Dr, Tunnel Mountain Rd, T403-7624122, www.hihostels.ca. 3 km from town but the Transit Bus passes by. Otherwise, this is the best budget option, with excellent facilities and plenty of choice: en suite rooms in a wood beam structure with a gorgeous lounge area, private rooms with shared bath, or dorms, some with en suite. There's also a nice kitchen, games room, deck, laundry, internet, lockers, a pub, and a cheap restaurant with good food and big portions. Be sure to book ahead.

D-E Banff Y Mountain Lodge, 102 Spray Av, T403-7623560, www.ymountain lodge.com. A cheap reliable option by the river at the pretty end of town. They have dorms and private rooms, a pleasant common room, kitchen, laundry, internet, and a bistro with a nice outdoor patio.

Canadian Rockies Banff National Park Listings

D-E Samesun, 449 Banff Av, T403-7625521, www.samesun.com. Not as well equipped as the HI but closer to town and more of a party atmosphere. Mostly 6-bed dorms, plus 1 semi-private double bed loft. Kitchen, small TV room, internet, courtyard, hot tub, sauna, lockers and bikes for rent. **D-E Tan-Y-Bryn**, 118 Otter St, T403-7623696, www.tan-y-bryn.zip411.net. 8 no-frills rooms at a great price.

Camping

There are 5 campgrounds around Banff Townsite. Sites can be reserved at T1877-7373783, www.pccamping.ca. On Tunnel Mt Road are the big and ugly **Tunnel Mountain I** and **Tunnel Mountain II**, with 618 and 188 crowded sites respectively, and showers. The latter is the only one open year-round. **Tunnel Mt Trailer Court**, is a big parking lot with full hook- ups for RVs. The nicest by far is **Two Jack Lakeside**, with 80 sites including some tent-only spots on the lake, and showers. **Two Jack Main**, across the road, has 381 fairly nice sites. Both are 12 km northeast of town on Lake Minnewaka Rd.

Canmore *p292*

Canmore has a dearth of decent hotels but there are dozens of nice, reasonably priced B&Bs. Many are close to Downtown on 1st and 2nd St. Call the **B&B Hotline**, T403- 6097224, www.bbcanmore.com, or check the Information Centre website. **A Hogs & Quiches**, 506 2nd St, T403-6785091, www.canmorebedandbreakfast.com. 2 tastefully decorated rooms in a handsome wood house on a residential street. Gourmet breakfast included. **B The Georgetown Inn**, 1101 Bow Valley Trail, T403-6783439, www.georgetowninn.net. 20 lovely rooms in a wonderful tudor-style inn with patios and gardens, a guest lounge and a restaurant/pub. **C Bow Valley Motel**, 610 Main St, T403-6785085, www.bowvalleymotel.com. Reasonable rooms, very central. **C By the Brook**, 4 Birchwood Pl, T403-6784566, www.bythebrookbandb.com.

2 big en suite rooms in a beautiful house with TV, sauna, hot tub and sundecks. **C Drake Inn**, 99 Railway Av, T403-6785231, www.drakeinn.com. The best Downtown option. Decent but standard rooms, with hot tub and sauna and a pub with patio. **C Riverview & Main**, 918-8 St, T403-6789777, www.riverviewandmain.com. 3 pleasant rooms with decks and mountain views and a very nice private sitting room. **E HI-Canmore Hostel**, Indian Flats Rd, a short drive east, no public transport, T403-6783200. Made up of 2 buildings, each one as a fully equipped kitchen, living room, fireplace, deck and BBQ, with a sauna available in the main building.

Camping

Spray Lakes Campground, T403-5915226. 16 km south on a rough and sometimes steep dirt road, with no public transport. But it's a wonderful campground that hugs the lakeside for 6 km, making for private sites right on the crystal-clear lake and surrounded by mountains.

Mt Assiniboine Provincial Park *p293*

E Naiset Huts, Lake Magog, T403-6782883. Bunk beds in this basic cabin can be booked and you're advised to do so. Despite the long walk-in, don't expect to have the place to yourself.

Camping

Lake Magog Campground. The park's main campground. There's a quieter one 6 km north at **Og Lake**. $5/night, cash only.

Bow Valley Parkway *p296*

AL Castle Mountain Chalets, T403-5222783, www.castlemountain.com. Very nice chalets and some rustic cottages. All have kitchens and bathroom and there's an exercise room, steam room, library and laundry on site. **A-B Johnston Canyon Resort**, T403-7622971, www.johnstoncanyon.com. A good alternative to staying in Banff. Large 2-bedroom cabins are very nice, modern and fully equipped, including a kitchen,

clawfoot tub, TV, porch and fireplace. A
great deal for 2 couples sharing. Smaller
cabins are less impressive and they are all
far too close together. There is a dining
room, coffee shop and tennis court.
E **Castle Mountain Hostel**, opposite
Castle Mountain Chalets, T403-6707580.
Fairly basic with 28 dorm beds, laundry
and kitchen. Cosy common room with a
wood-burning fireplace and bay windows.

Camping
Castle Mountain Campground. With just
44 sites, this is one of the smaller, nicer
sites in the park. No showers though.
Johnston Canyon Campground has
showers and 140 not very private sites.

Lake Louise *p296*
AL **Mountaineer Lodge**, 101 Village
Rd, The Village, T403-5223844,
www.mountaineerlodge.com. The most
reasonable of a hideously overpriced
collection of hotels in the village. Fairly
standard rooms, hot tub and steam room.
AL-A **Deer Lodge**, 109 Lake Louise Dr,
The Lake, T403-5223747, www.crmr.com.
Built in 'vintage national-park Gothic'
style, with antique furnishings, this hotel
has plenty of character but its rooms are
very small and rather ordinary. There's
a roof top hot tub and a decent but
expensive restaurant with a nice patio.
C-D **HI Lake Louise Alpine Centre**,
Village Rd, The Village T403-6707580,
www.hihostels.ca. A spacious, attractive,
well- equipped hostel, with dorms and
private double rooms, some with en suite
bath. Facilities include 2 kitchens, laundry,
library, lots of common places to relax,
map access, internet and an excellent
cheap restaurant. Some guided tours.
Reservations well in advance are essential.

Camping
Lake Louise Tent, The Village,
T403-5223833. 220 sites and showers.
Lake Louise Trailer, The Village, T403-
5223833. 189 sites with hook-ups.
Open year-round.

Icefields Parkway *p299*
L-A **Num-Ti-Jah Lodge**, T403-5222167,
www.num-ti-jah.com. In a prime location
on the shore of Bow Lake, this octagonal
construction was built in 1920 by Jimmy
Simpson, a legendary pioneering guide.
Age has lent a lot of charm to the rooms,
which include some cheaper options with
shared washroom. There is an outdoor
sauna, a fine restaurant and a coffee shop.
Its popularity is a little off-putting, and
makes advance booking a necessity.
C **The Crossing**, Saskatchewan Crossing,
T403-7617000, www.thecrossingresort.com.
An overpriced but heavily booked motel.
There's a fast-food cafeteria, restaurant,
grocery store and a tacky gift shop.
E **Mosquito Creek Hostel**, Km 28,
T403-6707580. 20 dorm beds, plus a few
private rooms, in 4 log cabins right by the
creek. Rustic with no running water but
with a kitchen, common room and sauna.
E **Rampart Creek Hostel**, Km 89, T403-
6706580, www.hihostels.ca. 24 beds in
2 cabins. Rustic with no running water.
Summer only.

Camping
Mosquito Creek Campground, at Km 28.
A small, basic year-round campground
with 38 sites, of which 20 are walk-in only.
Rampart Creek Campground, at Km 89.
Basic but pleasant, with 50 sites by the river.
Waterfowl Lake Campground, at Km 57.
116 nice sites close to the lake.

🍴 Eating

Banff Townsite *p287, map p291*
Banff's expensive restaurants often have
'tasting menus' which are 4- to 8-course
meals for around $90 per person.
🍴 **Cassis Bistro**, 137 Banff Av, T403-
7628289. An intimate and very stylish
cocktail bar with excellent tapas and a
good wine list. Lunch and dinner specials.
🍴 **Le Beaujolais**, Banff Av/Buffalo St,
T403-7622712. Set dinners for $65, as well

304 as à la carte. Very upmarket, with a dress code and an extensive wine list. The French- inspired menu features lots of game and seafood with delicious sauces.

Waldhaus, behind Banff Springs Hotel, T403-77606389. A beautiful setting and a very romantic interior. Fondues are a speciality, or try the roast duck or trout.

Aardvark Pizza & Sub, 304 Caribou St. Take-out menu, good pizzas, open till 0400.

Caramba!, 337 Banff Av, T403-7623667. Homemade pasta with innovative toppings, wood oven pizza, free range chicken. Nice patio but the lounge is more intimate.

Coyotes, 206 Caribou St, T403-7623963. Sophisticated southwest-style food such as orange chipotle prawns. Subtle decor with open kitchen and decent breakfast options.

Maple Leaf Grille,137 Banff Av, T403-7607680. The decor here concentrates on Canadiana, with lots of wood and leather and a genuine birch-bark canoe. The menu covers salmon, steak, pasta and other favourites, while the comfy lounge is a good spot for a quiet drink. Nice views from the dining room and a nice coffee corner that sadly doesn't open till 1100.

Sukiyaki House, 2nd floor, 211 Banff Av, T403-7622002. Sushi, hot pot and intimate tatami rooms.

Sunfood Café Vegetarian Restaurant, 215 Banff Av, T403-7603933. A friendly, relaxed spot for wild mushroom ravioli, curries, wraps, breakfast.

Evelyn's Coffee Bar, beside the cinema on Bear St, and in the town centre on Banff Av. Good coffee and baking.

Sundance Bistro, at the Banff Y Mountain Lodge. A charming bistro with a outdoor patio, the best value breakfast in town, wraps and salads.

Canmore *p292*

Tapas Restaurant, 633 10th St, T403-6090583. Spanish tapas, sangria, and special plates for 2 such as paella. Flamenco on Tue and Thu.

Crazyweed Kitchen, Main St. Espresso coffee and great food like Thai curries, gourmet sandwiches, pizzas and salads.

Grizzly Paw Brewing Co, 622 Main St. Fine ales brewed on the premises, and a great location to enjoy casual pub food like fish 'n' chips and burgers.

Quarry Bistro and Wine Bar, 718 Main St, T403-6786088. Bright and airy, sophisticated and modern, with an open beam construction and a long bar. The menu focuses on French and Italian bistro cuisine, with an emphasis on the freshness of ingredients.

Sunfood Café Vegetarian food, 743 Railway Av, T403-6092613. Tasty and varied vegetarian dishes.

Zona's, 710-9 St, T403-6092000. The place to eat, and understandably very popular. International food with a creative edge, like Moroccan lamb and molasses curry, served in a cosy house with a garden dining area. Licensed, open late.

The Coffee Mine, 802 Main St. Coffee, light food and outdoor seating.

The Summit Café, 1001 Cougar Creek Dr. The best breakfast in town.

Bow Valley Parkway *p296*

Baker Creek Bistro, at the Baker Creek Chalets, T403-5222182. Very good food, with a pleasant outdoor patio and a licensed lounge.

Lake Louise *p296*

Deer Lodge, Upper Lake Louise, T403-5223747. 'Rocky Mountain Cuisine' such as elk and wild mushrooms. Great patio.

Bill Peyto's Café, HI Alpine Centre. Cafeteria-style, good-value large portions, with great breakfasts, pasta and salads.

Lake Louise Station, 200 Sentinel Rd in the Village, T403-5222600. The interior is very nice, with lots of wood, high ceilings and big windows, and there's a lovely garden patio with BBQ in the summer. It's in a good location, a fine spot for a drink. The menu includes steak, pasta, fish and game. There's also a vintage railway car with an expensive menu, open 1800-2100.

Village Grill and Bar, in Samson Mall, T403-5223879. Family-style joint with all-day breakfast and sandwiches.

Canadian Rockies Banff National Park Listings

¶ Laggan's Bakery, in Samson Mall. Good bakery items and cheap sandwiches to go.

Icefields Parkway *p299*
¶¶¶ Num-Ti-Jah Lodge, (see above). The famous lodge has a good fine dining restaurant and a coffee shop.
¶¶ The Crossing, at Saskatchewan Crossing (see above). Contains a fast-food cafeteria and a second-rate restaurant.
¶¶ Icefield Centre (see above). An overpriced Chinese restaurant and a hamburger/hotdog cafeteria.

☊ Bars and clubs

Banff Townsite *p287, map p291*
Aurora Night Club, 110 Banff Av. Combines heaving DJ-led dancefloor action with an elegant Martini bar.
Hoodoo Lounge, 137 Banff Av. An energetic, somewhat youthful spot for DJ or live music every night.
The Lik Lounge, 221 Bear St. A lounge-style joint with cheap Martinis after 2130.
Rose & Crown, upstairs at 202 Banff Av. Good bands most nights, with jams on Sun nights and pub food.
St James Gate, 207 Wolf St. 31 beers on tap and upscale pub food. Really does feel like an Irish pub.
The Storm Cellar, at the HI Banff Alpine Centre. Just opened, this place has a no-smoking policy which is rare in Banff.
Waldhaus Pub, under the Waldhaus Restaurant at the Banff Springs Hotel. An authentic German-style boozer with low ceilings and Becks on tap. Sunshine, views and a good pub menu.
Wild Bill's Legendary Saloon, 2nd floor, 201 Banff Av, www.wbsaloon.com. A mix of different music that doesn't necessarily entail line dancing. Also a patio and food.

Canmore *p292*
Bandoleer's, Deadman's Flats, 5 mins east of Canmore, T403-6093006. A Tex-mex restaurant with live jazz on weekends.

Hooligan's Night Club, Lincoln Park, T403-6092662. DJ's and some live music.
Murrieta's Bar & Grill, 737 Main St. Live jazz Fri and Sat.
Rose and Crown, 749 Railway Av. 14 beers on tap, and a patio. Non-smoking.

☊ Entertainment

Banff Townsite *p287, map p291*
Banff Centre for the Arts, St Julien Rd, T403-7626301, www.banffcentre.ca/events. One of the most highly respected art schools in North America, with all sorts of cultural events, including art exhibitions, theatre, music and dance. Their **Walter Phillips Gallery**, T403-7626281, is open Wed-Sun 1200-1700 (free).
Canada House Gallery, 201 Bear St, T403-7623757, www.canadahouse.com. One of Alberta's most important private galleries, representing Canadian artists for over 30 years. Open 0930-2100 summer.
Lux Movie Theatre, 229 Bear St. Cinema.

☸ Festivals and events

Banff Townsite *p287, map p291*
Jan International Ice Sculpture competition.
May-Jun The Banff Centre for the Arts hosts the **Art Banff Jazz Festival**.
Jul-Aug Banff Festival of the Arts for over a month , featuring dance, theatre, film, visual art, lectures, music.
Oct The Banff Springs Hotel hosts the **International Wine and Food Festival**.
Nov The famous **Banff Mountain Film and Book Festival** showcases mountain/adventure films, the best 20 of which will then tour the rest of Canada and abroad.

Canmore *p292*
Aug Canmore Heritage Days Folk Festival, T403-6782524, in early Aug is the main annual event, with lots of acts on 3 stages in Centennial Park. 3-day pass $65.

○ Shopping

Banff Townsite *p287, map p291*

All along Banff Av are the often tacky gift shops offering souvenirs such as smoked salmon (which keeps well), maple syrup and copies of Aboriginal art.

Banff Book and Art Den, 94 Banff Av, in the Banff Springs. Big selection of outdoor recreation guides.

Friends of Banff, 214 Banff Av. Educational books and maps. All profits go to Banff Park.

The Glacier Shop, 317 Banff Av. Outdoor clothing, sports gear and ski equipment.

Mountain Magic Equipment, 224 Bear St. Massive selection of outdoor gear, rentals for camping, climbing and biking.

Home Hardware, 223 Bear St. Good for basic camping gear.

Weeds and Seeds, 211 Bear St. A health food store with bulk organic goodies.

Canmore *p292*

Canmore Rafting Centre, 20 Lincoln Park. Guide books and maps, gear rentals.

The Second Story Used Books, 713 Main St. Stock up here because used book stores in the Rockies are a rarity.

Sobeys, 950 Railway Av, in front of the **IGA** supermarket. The perfect place to stock up on healthy camping food.

Sports Consignment, 718-10 St. Good deals on used sports or camping equipment.

Valhalla Pure, 726 Main St, T403- 6785610. Camping gear and sports equipment.

Lake Louise *p296*

Wilson Mountain Sports Ltd, in the Village, T403-5223636, www.lakelouise wilsons.com. Camping and sports gear. Bike rental for $39 per day, climbing equipment, camping and fishing gear to buy or rent. $20 per day for tent, $9 per day for a back pack.

Village Grocery, Samson Mall. Overpriced, but essential for stocking up on food for your trip.

▲ Activities and tours

Banff Townsite *p287, map p291*

Ice-skating

Outdoor skating is possible on **Bow River** at the end of Wolf St; at **Banff High School**, Banff Av and Wolf St; and the **Banff Springs Hotel**. There's an indoor rink at **Banff Recreation Centre**, Mt Norquay Rd, T403-7621235.

Mountain biking

Mountain biking is possible on many of the local trails, though **Lake Louise** is better, and **Canmore** better still. Highest calibre is the **Brewster Creek Trail** which extends the **Sundance/Healy Creek trails** from Cave and Basin Hot Springs to a possible 37-km one-way ride to Allenby Pass. An exciting 5.2-km downhill run is the **Lower Stoney Squaw** at Mt Norquay Ski Area. The **Rundle Riverside** is a 14-km rollercoaster ride to Canmore Nordic Centre and more trails. Good gentle cycling can be had at Lake Minnewanka, Vermilion Lakes or Sundance Canyon.

Bactrax, 225 Bear St, T403-7628177. Offers tours, bike rental and information.

The Ski Stop, 203A Bear St, T403-7601650. Bike rentals, equipment and information.

Skiing

Banff is very much a year-round resort, with 2 ski hills right on its doorstep. As well as the excellent **Sunshine Village Ski Area**, T403-7627500, 18 km southwest of Banff off Hwy 1 (see p294), there's **Mt Norquay Ski Area**, T7624421, www.banff norquay.com, just 6 km to the north, which receives 300 cm of snow per year and employs a snow-maker. 5 lifts access terrain that is 11% beginner, 45% intermediate, 28% advanced and 16% expert. This has long been considered the domain of experienced skiers, with plenty of steep, deep runs. The season is early Dec to mid-Apr. Highest elevation is 2133 m, with a vertical drop of 497 m. A lift pass is $52. Rentals and lessons are available, and there's a shuttle from major Banff hotels ($10 return). It has the only night skiing in the Rockies on Fri 1600-2100 ($24).

Many local trails are groomed in winter for cross-country skiing. Pick up the *Nordic Trails* pamphlet from the visitor centre.
Performance Sports, 208 Bear St. Equipment rental.

Tour operators
Adventures Unlimited, 211 Bear St, T403-7624554, www.banffadventures.com. This activity booking centre can set you up with any kind of the activities available within the park.
Banff Fishing Unlimited, T403-7624936. Gear and licences can be obtained from Lake Minnewanka Boat Tours (see below). Also does ice fishing.
Bow River Canoe Docks, end of Wolf St. Rentals. Canoeing is possible on Two Jack Lake, Vermilion Lakes, Echo Creek, 40 Mile Creek, and Bow River.
Brewster, 100 Gopher St, T403-7606934, www.brewster.ca. Motorcoach tours to most destinations in Banff and the park.
Discover Banff Tours Ltd, T403-7601299, www.bannftours.com. Covers many bases including ice walks, sightseeing, snowshoeing, dog sledding, wildlife viewing, horseback riding, and so on.
Great Divide Nature Interpretation, T403-5222735, www.greatdivide.ca. Interpretive hikes led by naturalists.
Howling Dog Tours, T403-6789588, www.howlingdogtours.com. Dog sleds.
Hydra River Guides, T403-7624554, www.banffadventures.com. Rafting.
Icefield Helicopter Tours, T403-7212100. Tours of the icefields and glaciers, from $130 per person.
Lake Minnewanka Boat Tours, T403-7623473. Glass enclosed boat tours, $32, $15 child, for 1½- hrs. May-Oct 5 tours a day from 1030.
Mountain Magic Equipment, 225 Bear St, T403-7622591, www.mountainmagic.com. Arranges ice and rock climbing. They also have a climbing wall, and rent equipment such as ski gear, snowshoes and bikes.

Snowy Owl Sled Dog Tours, T403-6786369, www.snowyowltours.com.
Trail Rider Store, 132 Banff Av, T403-7624551. Horse-drawn sleigh rides.
True North Tours Ltd, T403-9345972, www.backpackertours.com/truenorth. In association with HI, they offer 3-day ($220) or 6-day ($440) tours of the park in a 15-passenger van, including accommodation (at hostels), and food. Drop-off in Calgary is also an option. This could end up being cheaper than going it alone using buses.
Warner Guiding & Outfitting, 132 Banff Av, the Trail Rider store, T403-7624551, www.horseback.com. Guided horse tours from ½-day to multi-day pack trips or trips in a horse-drawn carriage.
White Mountain Adventures, T403-6784099, www.whitemountainadventures.com. Tours through the beautiful frozen waterfalls of Johnston Canyon, highly recommended. They also give skiing lessons, run wildlife walks in snowshoes, and heritage tours of the Townsite.
Willow Root Nature Tours, T403-7624335. Walks and hikes with full interpretation from a professional naturalist.
Yamnuska, T403-6784164, www.yamnuska.com. Ice climbing.

Canmore *p292*
Climbing
This is Canmore's local speciality. There are climbs at **Grassi Lakes**, **Yamnuska**, on Hwy 1A E, and **Cougar Canyon** for a more challenging climb.
Alpine Club, T403-6783200, www.alpineclubofcanada.ca. The best place for advice and to find out about mountain huts.
Yamnuska Mountain Adventures, T403-6784164, www.yamnuska.com. Ice and rock climbing, backcountry skiing, mountaineering lessons and tours.

Hiking
Access to excellent long-distance hikes, mostly in the south of Banff Park, is via Spray Lakes Rd and its extension, the Smith-Dorrien Hwy, a distance of some 40 km. Follow signs to the Nordic Centre

and keep going up the steep, rough road, ignoring the right turn to Spray Lakes campground. Local hikes include the **Three Sisters** area, and **Ha Ling Peak**, across from the Goat Creek parking lot, both on Spray Lakes Rd; **Grotto Mountain** is accessed from the Alpine Club.

Mountain biking

There are excellent networks of trails at **Mt Shark** and **Mud Lake**, both on the Smith-Dorrien Hwy, and much closer at **Canmore Nordic Centre**. **Rebound Cycle**, 902 Main St. Rents bikes ($30/day) skis and snowboards.

Skiing

Cross-country Canmore Nordic Centre, off Spray Lakes Rd, well signed from town, T403-6782400, has some of the best trails in the Rockies, and hosts various events. **Trail Sports**, within the centre, www.trails ports.ab.ca, offers rentals/lessons.

   Downhill A shuttle from behind the ski hill takes you 10 km to the trailhead for an 11 km-ski-in to **B-C Skoki Lodge**, T1800-2587669, www.skoki.com. The log cabins here make an excellent base for getting into the backcountry, and have been used as such since the 1930s when the lodge put Lake Louise on the Nordic ski map.

Tour operators

Canadian Rockies Rafting Co, T403-6786535; www.rafting.ca. Whitewater rafting and kayaking on the Kananaskis. **Canmore Caverns**, T403-6788819, www.canadianrockies.net/wildcavetours. Caving tours of Rat's Nest Cave under Grotto Mountain. Trips last 4½-6 hrs; no experience necessary. **Canmore Rafting Centre**, 20 Lincoln Park, T403-6784919, www.canmorerafting centre.com. Trips on the Kananaskis River. **Cross Zee Ranch**, T403-6784171. Day horse-riding trips. **Gear Up**, 1302 Bow Valley Trail, T403-6781636. Kayak and canoe rentals. The Bow River makes for some mellow floating. Also climbing and camping gear and bikes.

Good Earth Travel Adventures, T403-6789358, www.goodearthtravel.com. Summer or winter sporting activities. **Halfway to Heaven Bird-Watching**, T403-6732542. **Mirage Adventure Tours**, T403-6785657, www.miragetours.com. Can arrange whatever activity you're looking for. **Rainbow Riders**, T403-6787238, www.rainbowriders.com. Whitewater rafting and kayaking trips. **White Mountain Adventures**, T403-6784099, www.canadiannatureguides.com. Walks, hikes, skiing, ice walks and so on.

Lake Louise *p296*

Canoes can be rented at both lakes. When the lake gets cold enough it provides an idyllic location for skating. **Monod Sports**, in the Château (see p296) for skate rentals. As well as top notch downhill skiing at **Lake Louise Ski Area** there is fine cross-country skiing in the **Skoki Valley**.

Mountain biking

Some local trails are ideal for riding. The 14.6-km return **Ross Lake Trail** starts behind the Château and leads through forest to a small lake beneath a steep rockwall. The more demanding 10-km **Moraine Lake Highline** leads from the Paradise Valley trailhead to the scenic lake; sometimes closed due to grizzly activity. The 13.4-km **Pipestone Trail** starts off Slate Rd just west of the Village and follows the Pipestone River to the valley. The 7-km **Bow River Loop** is a gentle trail on both sides of the river. The 10.5-km one-way **Great Divide Path** is a paved but traffic-free route starting at Km 3.6 on Lake Louise Drive and ending at Hwy 1 in Yoho.

Tour operators

Brewsters, T403-5223522. Sleigh rides on the lake when frozen. **Timberline Tours**, T403-5223743, www.timberlinetours.ca. 1- to 10-day trips. Will drop off or pick up at **Skoki Lodge** (see p308).

Wild Water Adventures, T403-5222212, www.wildwater.com. Trips on the Kicking Horse River.

⊖ Transport

Banff Townsite *p287, map p291*
Bus
Banff Transit, T403-7621200, runs 3 bus routes. One connects the Banff Springs Hotel with the Tunnel Mountain Trailer Court; another connects the Luxton Museum with the campgrounds on Tunnel Mountain Rd. Both run along Banff Av and cost $2, $1 child.

Greyhound, T403-7621092, www.grey hound.ca, has 5 daily buses to **Calgary** via the airport ($25), and to **Vancouver** ($118), with 3 daily to **Jasper** ($107). Sun Dog Tours, T1888 7863641, www.sundogtours.com, operates a shuttle to **Jasper** via **Lake Louise**.

Rail
Rocky Mountain Rail Tours, www.rocky mountaineer.com. Prohibitively expensive 2-day, 1-night trips from **Vancouver** to **Banff** or **Jasper**, with an option to continue on to **Calgary**. Prices start at $750 one way.

Taxi
Banff Taxi, T403-7624444.

Vehicle rental
Mopeds can be rented from the Shell station on Wolf St and Lynx St, T403-7609363, $11-25 per hr. **Dollar Rent a Car**, 600 Banff Av, T403-7603881, www.dollar.com.

Canmore *p292*
Bus
The Greyhound station is at 701 Bow Valley Trail, T403-6780832, with 4 daily buses to **Calgary** and **Banff** ($9). All 3 shuttle services stop here on the way from Banff to Calgary. **Banff/Canmore Connector**, T403-7623795, also runs a daily service to/from **Banff**.

Taxi
Canmore Taxi, T403-6784465.

Lake Louise *p296*
Taxi
Lake Louise Shuttle Service, T403-5222700.

❶ Directory

Banff Townsite *p287, map p291*
Banks Foreign Currency Exchange, Clock Tower Village Mall, 112 Banff Av, T403-7624698. But shop around. **Canada Post** 204 Buffalo St. **Internet** Cyber Web Internet Café. The library is cheaper. **Laundry** Cascade Coin Laundry, 317 Banff Av; Johnny O's, 223 Bear St. **Library** 101 Bear St, T403-7622661. **Medical services** Mineral Springs Hospital, 301 Lynx St, T403-7622222. Alpine Medical Clinic, 216 Banff Av, T403-7620460. **Useful numbers** For emergencies only: Police, T403-7622226; Medical and Fire T403-7622000; Banff Warden Office T403-7624506.

Canmore *p292*
Bank Bank of Montreal, 701 8th St; Royal Bank, 1000 Railway Av. **Canada Post** 801 Main St. **Internet** Free at the library. **Laundry** The Lost Sock Laundromat, 1000-7 Av. **Library** Canmore Public Library/Art Gallery, 8th Av, T403-6782468. **Medical services** Canmore Hospital, 1100 Hospital Pl, T403-6785536.

Lake Louise *p296*
Canada Post In Samson Mall, which also has internet machines and ATMs. **Medical Services** Lake Louise Medical Clinic, 200 Hector St, T403-5222184

Jasper National Park and around

Jasper National Park feels much closer to wilderness than Banff. Neither as famous nor as convenient to reach, it receives far fewer visitors, and has 10,878 sq km over which to spread them, an area bigger than Banff, Yoho and Kootenay National Parks combined. Vast tracts of this land are extremely remote and practically inaccessible, the overall emphasis being less on instant gratification, more on the long backcountry hikes that account for much of Jasper's 1000 km of trails. Apart from those on the Icefields Parkway, most of these are close to the pleasant town of Jasper, or around the attractive Maligne Lake, 48 km away.

Getting there Bus, car or shuttle.
Getting around Car.
Time required 3 days/1 week.
Weather Changeable.
Sleeping Camping, hostels, to 5-star hotels.
Eating A few stellar choices.
Activities and tours Hiking.
Don't miss... Hiking the Wilcox Pass Trail ▶ *p312*.

Ins and outs

Getting there and around

The airport closest to Jasper is in Edmonton (YEG), www.edmontonairports.com, 370 km to the west, about four hours' drive. The **Sky Shuttle**, T780-4658515, www.edmontonskyshuttle.com, $15, runs from the airport to the **Greyhound** station at 10324 103rd Street, T780-4138747, from where there are four buses daily to Jasper (five hours, $57). Trains run from the **Via Rail** station, 12360 121st Street, to Jasper three times a week (five hours, $127); to get there take a taxi.

Calgary Airport (see p272) is 412 km south of Jasper. **Sun Dog Tours**, T780-8534056, www.sundogtours.com, runs shuttles from the airport ($105 one way), also picking up at Banff and Lake Louise ($59); December to April only. The 281-km journey from Banff to Jasper is spectacular; for the best views, sit on the left-hand side. There are few services along what remains a region of extreme wilderness. Road closures are common from October to April after heavy snow. If cycling, note that Jasper is 500 m higher than Banff, so the journey is better made from north to south. Bikes can be rented in Jasper for one-way trips.

Jasper's train and bus stations are in the same attractive building, downtown at 607 Connaught St. **Greyhound**, T780-8523926, www.greyhound.ca, runs regular daily buses from Edmonton, Vancouver via Kamloops and Prince George. **VIA Rail** operates three trains per week from Edmonton and Vancouver and Prince Rupert via Prince George. **The Rocky Mountaineer** train, T604-6067245, takes three days and two nights from Vancouver, starting at $740 including accommodation. A beautiful journey. ▶ ⊖ *p322*.

Tourist information

The **Visitor Information Centre/Parks Canada** offices are situated in a pretty 1914 stone building in the city park at 500 Connaught Drive. Call T780-8526176 for general information, T403-8526177 for trail information, www.jaspercanadian rockies.com for general information, www.pc.gc.ca/pn-np/ab/jasper for parks information. Lines are open April to June 0900-1700, June to September 0830-1900, October 0900-1700, November to March 0900-1600. They have information on accommodation and trails, issue Park and Wilderness passes, and hand out a number of useful maps such as the *Backcountry Visitors' Guide*, the *Day-hiker's Guide* and a *Cycling Guide*. They also operate a voluntary safety registration system. **Parks Canada**, T780-8528487, runs guided walks around town at 1000 and 1400. **Friends of Jasper National Park**, T780-8524767, www.friendsofjasper.com, operates a number of free or cheap walking tours throughout the summer. There is also a Jasper National Park desk in the Icefield Centre (see p312).

Columbia Icefield 🛏🏕 ▸▸ *pp317-322.*

The northern hemisphere's most extensive glacial area south of the Arctic Circle, the Columbia Icefield provides a dramatic introduction to Jasper National Park. As well as feeding three giant watersheds, its melt waters are the source of some of the continent's mightiest rivers, including the Columbia, Saskatchewan and Athabasca, and drain into three oceans,

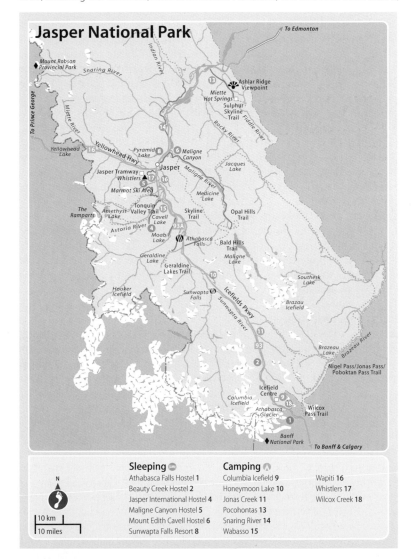

Jasper National Park

To Edmonton

Mount Robson Provincial Park

To Prince George

Indian River

Snaring River

Ashlar Ridge Viewpoint **13**

Miette Hot Springs

Sulphur Skyline Trail

Miette River

Rocky River

Fiddle River

14

Yellowhead Lake

Yellowhead Hwy **16**

Pyramid Lake **8**

Maligne Canyon **6**

Jasper

Jacques Lake

Jasper Tramway Whistlers **17**

Maligne River

5

Marmot Ski Area

The Ramparts

Amethyst Lake

Tonquin Valley Trail **15**

Cavell Lake

Astoria River

Moab Lake

93A

Athabasca Falls

Medicine Lake

Skyline Trail

Opal Hills Trail

Bald Hills Trail

Maligne Lake

Geraldine Lake

Geraldine Lakes Trail

10

Southesk Lake

Hooker Icefield

Sunwapta Falls

Icefields Pkwy

Sunwapta River

Brazau Icefield

11

93

2

Brazeau Lake

Brazeau River

Nigel Pass/Jonas Pass/ Poboktan Pass Trail

Icefield Centre **9** **18**

Columbia Icefield

Athabasca Glacier

Wilcox Pass Trail

1

Banff National Park

To Banff & Calgary

N

10 km
10 miles

Sleeping 🛏
Athabasca Falls Hostel **1**
Beauty Creek Hostel **2**
Jasper International Hostel **4**
Maligne Canyon Hostel **5**
Mount Edith Cavell Hostel **6**
Sunwapta Falls Resort **8**

Camping 🏕
Columbia Icefield **9**
Honeymoon Lake **10**
Jonas Creek **11**
Pocohontas **13**
Snaring River **14**
Wabasso **15**

Wapiti **16**
Whistlers **17**
Wilcox Creek **18**

the Atlantic, Pacific and Arctic. The only other icefield of equal scope and importance in the world is in Siberia. Most of the icefield's staggering 325 sq km terrain is high in the mountains out of view, but three of the six major glaciers are clearly visible from the road, including the huge **Athabasca Glacier** (6 km long, 1 km wide and 100 m thick), which you can walk or even be driven on (see below).

The ultimate way to see this spectacle is from the **Wilcox Pass Trail** that starts just south of Wilcox Creek Campground (8 km return, 335 m elevation gain). This is one hike that everybody should do. Short and easy, it quickly whisks you to views that many longer hikes fail to equal. After a brief ascent through mature forest, the Columbia Icefield is suddenly visible in all its glory, and from an angle far more gratifying than you'll get taking the Snocoach (see below). Wild flower meadows and resident bighorn sheep complete the idyllic picture. With so much to be gained from so little effort, don't expect to be alone.

A joint venture by Brewster and Parks Canada, the **Icefield Centre** ① *T780-8526288, Apr-Oct 0900-2100*, resembles an airport and totally takes the edge off the wondrous surroundings, although it is a fine vantage point from which to ogle the Athabasca Glacier. The Glacier Gallery contains well-mounted informative displays, explaining glaciation, the icefield, and the stories behind it. The Parks Canada desk is helpful and can provide maps and leaflets for whichever park you are entering. **Brewster's Snocoach** tours take you onto the glacier in a specially built bus (see Activities and tours, p321). Don't be tempted to walk on the glacier alone: people are killed and injured every year. Either they fall into one of its many crevasses, or injure themselves on the sharp sediment embedded in the ice.

North to Jasper

Distances below are from the Columbia Icefield, where many people choose to turn round anyway: understandable, as it is the high point of the drive. After so much rich fare, the easy 3.6-km **Beauty Creek Trail**, which starts 15.5 km to the north, provides a nice change. This tiny chasm and its chain of pretty scaled-down waterfalls can be an uplifting sight. The mountains along this stretch of highway are striated at a 45° angle, and resemble cresting waves.

At 53 km, a side road leads to **Sunwapta Falls**, which are mostly interesting for the canyon they have carved through the valley. **Athabasca Falls**, some 10 km further, are less worth a stop. At this point Highway 93A, the old Parkway, branches off from Highway 93 and runs parallel for 30 km, providing access to a campground, a hostel, Marmot Basin ski hill and a number of hikes.

Hikes from Highway 93A

▲ **Tonquin Valley** ① *43-km loop, 920 m elevation gain*. The Tonquin Valley is one of Jasper's most popular backpack trips, leading to the beautiful Amethyst Lakes and an incredible 1000-m rock wall known as The Ramparts that shoots straight up from their shores. Before considering this hike, be aware that it could easily turn into a nightmare. There are two possible routes to the valley, and both of them are used by operators whose horses churn up the trails. If it rains, or has done so in the last few days, the hike in is likely to be a long, frustrating trudge through ankle-deep mud. To do the trip by horse, see Tour operators on p321. If it's not raining, the mosquitoes and other biting insects are ferocious.

The easier, flatter route into the Valley is along the **Astoria River Trail** ① *7.2 km south on Parkway, turn west onto Highway 93A, continue 5.3 km south, then right onto Mount Edith Cavell Rd and 12.2 km to parking area just past the hostel*, known as the Tonquin Expressway. The more satisfying route is the **Portal Creek Trail** ① *2.5 km south on Highway 93A, right onto Marmot Basin Rd, 6.5 km to car park* over Maccarib Pass, which is steeper but consequently offers better views. Ideally, hike in on one and out the other, arranging a shuttle or hitching between trailheads. There are plenty of campsites to choose from, Surprise Point being a

Athabaska Valley.

good choice. Reserve sites well in advance. Nearby is the Wates-Gibson Hut, reserved through the **Alpine Club of Canada**, T403-6783200, www.alpineclubofcanada.ca. The best day-hike side-trip is into the narrow **Eremite Valley**, leading to more glacier-bearing peaks. In winter, you can ski 23 km into the valley and stay at the **Tonquin Valley Backcountry Lodge**, T780-8523909, www.tonquinvalley.com, $100 in winter, $135 in summer, including meals, canoe use and daily horse rides, in summer.

▲▲ **Geraldine Lakes** ① *10.5 km return to second lake, 13 km return to fourth lake, 407-497 m elevation gain. Trailhead: 1 km north of Athabasca Falls on Highway 93A, then 5.5 km up Geraldine Fire Rd.* The first lake is an easy hike to an unremarkable destination. After that, things get more difficult and more rewarding. It's a fairly tough climb to the second and biggest lake with ridge top views and a waterfall as compensation. Beyond there is no trail and much bushwhacking to reach pristine pools set in wild, alpine meadows.

▲▲ **Cavell Meadows** ① *8-km loop, 370 m elevation gain. Trailhead: 13 km south on Highway 93A, 14 km on Cavell Rd.* This easy hike leads to spectacular views of the giant Angel Glacier. In mid-summer, these are also some of the finest wild flower meadows in the Rockies. The pay-off is marching along with crowds of people.

Jasper Townsite 🚍🚲🏃🏠▲🚌☕ ⤳ *pp317-322.*

Jasper is a far more relaxed base than Banff, having managed to hold on to its small-town charm despite a turnover of some three million visitors per year. There is little in the way of out-of-control commercialism, and not much to do. Almost everything is on Connaught Drive, the road in and out of town, or Patricia Drive, which runs parallel to it. The only possible 'sight' in town is the **Yellowhead Museum and Archives** ① *400 Pyramid Lake Rd, T780-8523013, summer 1000-2100, autumn 1000-1700, $4, $3 child*, with a number of predictable displays exploring the town's fur trade and railway.

Around Jasper Townsite

There are many loop day-hikes around the Pyramid Bench area, some leading to Pyramid Lake. Start at the Activity Centre, 401 Pyramid Lake Road, and climb up to the bench. The Old Fort Point is a 3.5-km return trail leading to marvellous views of Athabasca River and Jasper. Take Highway 93A from town to the Old Fort Point access road. Turn left and cross the iron

bridge. You can continue from here on signposted No 7 trail to **Maligne Canyon** (9.5 km one
way), and return along the river for an easy 20.7-km loop.

Just 5 km east of town on Lodge Road are **Annette Lake** and **Edith Lake**, whose shallow waters are the warmest around in summer, making their beaches very popular for swimming and sunbathing. There is a wheelchair-accessible path around the former. The winding Pyramid Lake Road leads 8 km northwest of town to **Pyramid Lake** and **Patricia Lake**. Apart from good views of Pyramid Mountain, this duo offers a couple of alternatives to sleeping options in Jasper, plus fishing, boating and horse riding.

The longest and highest of its kind in Canada, **Jasper Tramway** ⓘ *3 km south on Hwy 93, then 4 km west on Whistler Mountain Rd, T780-8523093, www.jaspertramway.com, Apr-Oct 0830-2200, Nov-Mar 1000-dusk, $22, Sun Dog Tours run a shuttle $27, $11 child*, takes seven minutes to climb 1000 m in 2.5 km. Expect queues in summer. At the top are an expensive restaurant, an interpretive centre, and excellent views. A steep trail gains another 600 m to reach **Whistlers Summit** at 2470 m, and even more awe-inspiring vistas as far as Mount Robson, 80 km away. There's a cafeteria at the top.

Maligne Lake

The busy Maligne (pronounced 'maleen') Lake Road branches off Highway 16 east of town, leading 48 km to the most popular attraction in the park, with a few major sights on the way. In summer it is perpetually crowded with a stream of vehicles. The Maligne Lake Shuttle makes the journey several times daily (see Transport, below). **Maligne Canyon**, 11.5 km from Jasper, is a spectacular gorge, 55 m deep and almost narrow enough to jump across. A number of short walking trails and footbridges lead to viewpoints. Unfortunately, the area is far too busy and taking on the unpleasant feel of a tourist trap. The canyon is at its most

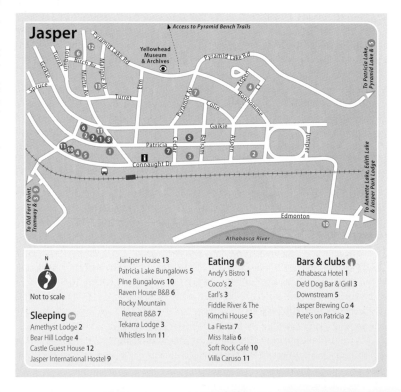

Not to scale

N

Sleeping 😴
Amethyst Lodge **2**
Bear Hill Lodge **4**
Castle Guest House **12**
Jasper International Hostel **9**
Juniper House **13**
Patricia Lake Bungalows **5**
Pine Bungalows **10**
Raven House B&B **6**
Rocky Mountain
  Retreat B&B **7**
Tekarra Lodge **3**
Whistlers Inn **11**

Eating 🍴
Andy's Bistro **1**
Coco's **2**
Earl's **3**
Fiddle River & The
Kimchi House **5**
La Fiesta **7**
Miss Italia **6**
Soft Rock Café **10**
Villa Caruso **11**

Bars & clubs 🍸
Athabasca Hotel **1**
De'd Dog Bar & Grill **3**
Downstream **5**
Jasper Brewing Co **4**
Pete's on Patricia **2**

beautiful in winter, when the water freezes into an ice palace with 30-m icefalls and
incredible, blue-ice caves. In winter a few operators (see below) run three-hour tours, with crampons, head lamps and other equipment provided. There is a hostel here, and the northern terminus of the famous Skyline Trail.

A further 21 km is the pretty **Medicine Lake**, whose water level fluctuates dramatically with the seasons because it fills and empties through sink-holes into an elaborate network of underground limestone caves. In summer the water is high, but in winter it sometimes disappears altogether. While such temporal variations fascinated Native Americans, the one-time visitor will see nothing but another lake.

At 22 km long, beautiful **Maligne Lake** is the largest lake in the Rockies, and the second largest glacier-fed lake in the world. Surrounded by white-peaked mountains, it is a sight to behold, though not as overwhelming as Lake Louise. The best views open up from the middle of the lake, accessible on cruises and tours (see below). Lots of hikes begin here, including the excellent Skyline Trail. For something shorter, the 3.2-km Schäffer Viewpoint loop leads along the east shore from Car Park 2. There is no accommodation at the lake apart from two backcountry campgrounds on the lakeshore that can only be reached by canoe (a four-hour trip), and must be booked at Jasper Information Centre.

Hikes from Maligne Lake

▲▲ **Skyline** ⓘ *44.5 km, 820 m elevation gain*. This is one of the all-time great backpack trips, offering everything you come to the Rockies for: drool-inducing views of lofty peaks, including some of the range's highest, and sweeping meadows full of wild flowers. Fast hikers can do it in two days, but three is more realistic. It is a one-way hike best started at Maligne Lake. If driving, leave your vehicle at the Maligne Canyon terminus and hitch or take a bus to the lake. Book sites in the backcountry campgrounds well ahead, because this is one hike that is almost impossible to get onto at short notice. Plan your trip for after late-July, when the steepest section of the trail, known as 'the Notch', should be snow-free. This is the only steep section of a hike that is surprisingly level, considering that almost all of it is above the treeline. This last fact means you're particularly at the mercy of the weather, so go prepared for anything.

▲▲ **Bald Hills** ⓘ *12.6 km return, 610 m elevation gain*. The Bald Hills are actually a 7 km-long ridge. The lack of trees that gave them their name makes for excellent views of the surroundings, including Maligne Lake and the Queen Elizabeth Ranges, with razorback ridges, gleaming glaciers, rugged rock faces, green forests, alpine meadows and extraordinary rock formations. After about 45 minutes, take the cut-off trail through the trees and look out for wild flowers. Most people stop at the old fire lookout but you can continue for greater panoramas and less company.

▲▲ **Opal Hills** ⓘ *8.2 km, 460 m elevation gain*. This trail is short but very steep. The rewards are gorgeous views of mountains and the lake, and a host of tiny wild flowers.

Miette Hot Springs

A favourite excursion from Jasper is to **Miette Hot Springs** ⓘ *T780-8663939, Jun-Sep 0830-2230, May-Jun and Sep-Oct 1030-2100, $6.25, $5.25 child, road closed winter*, 60 km east on Highway 16, then 17 km south on Miette Road. **Ashlar Ridge Viewpoint**, at 8.5 km on the latter, offers great views of this impressive rock wall. The springs are the hottest in the Rockies. Cooled from 54° C to 39° C, the water is chlorinated and runs into two large outdoor pools. Interpretive displays explain the local geology.

If you've driven this far, hike the short but steep **Sulphur Skyline**, an 8 km return trail, with 700 m elevation gain, offering views out of all proportion to the energy expended. It's also a good early-season hike.

Mount Robson National Park entrance.

Mount Robson Provincial Park 🚌🛺🚻 ›› *pp317-322.*

The Yellowhead Highway (Highway 16) accompanies the railway west from Jasper to the Yellowhead Pass (1131 m), which has been used as a route across the Continental (or Great) Divide by fur-traders and gold-seekers for over 150 years. This is the border between Alberta and British Columbia, Mountain and Pacific time zones (BC is one hour behind) and Jasper and Mount Robson parks. There are few facilities in the latter, so if planning to do the overnight hike discussed below, stock up in Jasper. The next closest town is **Tête Jaune Cache**, 16 km beyond the park's western boundary, though Valemount to the south is more substantial.

More than any other of the Rocky Mountain parks, this one is utterly dominated by its crowning feature. At 3954 m, **Mount Robson** is the highest peak in the Canadian Rockies and possibly the most spectacular. It was one of the last mountains in the Rockies to be climbed, and even today represents a difficult challenge. Whether you're approaching on Highway 16 or from Kamloops on Highway 5, the first sight of this colossal rock pyramid is likely to take your breath away: the perfection of its shape, highlighted by the pointed triangle of ice at its apex, and the distinct layering of rock which inspired the native name Yuh-hai-has-hun, 'Mountain of the Spiral Road'. The only way to fully appreciate the peak's awesome beauty is by doing the hike, which reveals the incredible vast glaciers that cover its north side.

The only public transport into the park is the Greyhound. Ask to be dropped at the Mount Robson viewpoint, also site of the **Visitor Information Centre** ⓘ *T250-5669174, May-Sep 0800-1700, Jul-Aug till 1900*. The nearby café/garage is about the only place to get food. The reservation fee for hiking Berg Lake ($6 per night up to $18 for three or more nights) is paid at the time of booking, which must be done by phone, T1800-6899025, so a credit card is essential. The camping fee ($5) is paid at the time of registration at the visitor centre, which also retains a few first-come, first-served sites: be there before it opens (0800) to get one.

Hikes in Mount Robson Provincial Park

🛺 **Mount Robson/Berg Lake** ⓘ *39.2 km return, 786 m elevation gain. Trailhead: 2 km north of the visitor centre on a side road*. This is the most popular and one of the very best backpacking trips in the range, and can be attempted as early as mid-June. Most people reach Berg Lake in a day, spend a day exploring, then hike out on the third. The trail is extraordinary and varied, leading through lush, flower-dotted rainforest, past open gravel

The snowy peak of Mount Robson.

flats, over suspension bridges in a rugged river gorge, through the Valley of a Thousand Faces, and past three powerful waterfalls, including the 60-m Emperor Falls. At Berg Lake, Mount Robson rises 2316 m directly from the shore, its cliffs wrapped in the vast ice-cloaks of Mist and Berg Glaciers. Huge chunks of ice regularly crash from the latter into the lake. There is a campground right here, a more private one 0.6 km further, and another 1.4 km further still. A recommended 9-km day-hike is to **Snowbird Pass**. The path leads to the toe of Robson Glacier and for the next 3 km the views of the glacier are stupendous.

▲▲ **Yellowhead Mountain** ⓘ *9 km return, 715 m elevation gain. Trailhead: 8.5 km west of the pass on Hwy 16, 1 km on a gravel road across Yellowhead Lake on an isthmus. Park below the railway where road splits.* Passing through meadows and aspen forest, this trail is particularly attractive in autumn. The best day-hike in the park, it offers wonderful views of Yellowhead Pass.

● Sleeping

Columbia Icefield *p311*
AL Columbia Icefield Chalet, T1877-4237433, www.brewster.ca ha. Spacious, comfy rooms with high ceilings, some with glacier views, some with lofts. Book ahead.

Camping
Wilcox Creek and **Columbia Icefield** campgrounds, right next to each other on the Jasper side, enjoy one of the prime locations in the Rockies, and are both predictably very crowded. The latter is for tents only, with very nice walk-in sites.

North to Jasper *p312*
AL Sunwapta Falls Resort, T780-8524852, www.sunwapta.com . Small but

very nice, cosy en suite rooms, some with sun decks, some with fireplaces. There's a reasonable restaurant, and bikes for rent.
E Beauty Creek Hostel, T780 8523215. A very basic, summer-only hostel with 24 beds in 2 cabins, no flush toilets or running water but showers and a small kitchen.
E Athabasca Falls Hostel, T780-8523215. 20 beds in 3 rustic cabins, with no running water, showers or flush toilets.

Camping
Jonas Creek Campground, 9 km beyond Beauty Creek. 25 nice sites by the creek, some walk-in only.
Honeymoon Lake Campground, a little further on. One of the nicer places to camp, with 35 spacious sites, some right on the lake.

Jasper Townsite *p313, map p314*

Jasper's hotels are not much better value than Banff's, and are just as likely to be full in summer. There are, however, plenty of private homes close to town with reasonably priced rooms (**C-D**). Check at the information centre or call **Accommodation Reservations**, T780-7620260. For all hostel reservations, call T780-8523215. Campgrounds close to town fill up very fast in summer, with queues starting about 1100, but you can reserve ahead at www.stayinjasper.com
AL Amethyst Lodge, 200 Connaught Dr, T780-8523394, www.mpljasper.com. Central location with big rooms, balconies, 2 outdoor hot tubs, restaurant and lounge.
AL Whistlers Inn,105 Miette Av, T780-8523361, www.whistlersinn.com. Standard rooms and much nicer suites in a very central property with an outdoor rooftop hot tub, a steamroom, 2 restaurants and a nice pub.
AL-A Tekarra Lodge, 1 km south off Hwy 93A, T780-8523058, www.maclab hotels.com. In a quiet spot in the trees by the confluence of the Athabasca and Miette rivers. Tasteful cabins with hardwood floors, stone fireplaces, balconies and kitchens, or plain B&B lodge rooms. Bike rentals. Hiking trails nearby.
AL-D Patricia Lake Bungalows, 6 km north towards Pyramid Lake at Patricia Lake, T780-8523560, www.patricialake bungalows.com. Lots of options in a quiet spot by the lake: attractive, spacious cottages with kitchen, luxurious suites and good value motel rooms. Facilities include hot tub, laundry and canoe rentals.
A Bear Hill Lodge, 100 Bonhomme St, T780-8523209, www.BearHillLodge.com. Good value bungalows with full bath, some with kitchenettes or gas fireplace.
B Raven House B&B, 801 Miette Av, T780-8524011, www.ravenbb.com. 2 pleasant rooms in a nice, private house in town.
B-C Pine Bungalows, close to where Connaught Dr meets Hwy 16 at the east end of town, T780-8523491, www.pine

bungalows.com. Reasonable and economical motel-style rooms and cabins, some with kitchenettes, and nicer 3-room cabins for 4 people at $155.
C Castle Guest House, 814 Miette Av, T780-8525768, www.bbcanada.com/1688. 2 comfortable rooms in an interesting modern wood house with a beautiful garden patio.
C Juniper House, 713 Maligne Av, T780-8523664, www.visit-jasper.com/juniperhouse. 2 very tasteful suites in a gorgeous, newly renovated heritage home, that's also very central. Good value.
D The Rocky Mountain Retreat B&B, 400 Pyramid Av, T780-8524090, www.bbcanada.com/rocky mountainretreat. 2 nice en suite rooms with high ceilings and mountain views, close to the centre.
E Jasper International Hostel, 7 km southwest, near gondola on Whistlers Mountain Rd, T780-8523215, www.hi hostels.ca. A chalet-style hostel with 84 beds, full kitchen, showers, laundry and bike rentals. Shuttles from downtown
E Maligne Canyon Hostel, 11 km east on Maligne Lake Rd, T780-8523215, www.hihostels.ca. 24 beds in 2 cabins near the canyon. Open year-round (closed Wed in winter). Rustic, with no running water or flush toilets.
E Mount Edith Cavell Hostel, Edith Cavell Rd, 13 km off Hwy 93A, 26 km south, T780-8523215, www.hihostels.ca. 32 beds in 2 cabins with views of the Angel Glacier. Handy for trails, and popular, with a sauna. No running water.

Camping

When the campgrounds are full, overflow sites are put into effect (cheaper, but not very nice). Jasper has over 100 backcountry sites. Wilderness Passes cost $9 per person per night, refundable till 1000 on proposed date of departure. Reservation (with $12 fee) at Info Centre or T780-8526177, up to 3 months before departure. Campsite Day use permit $7.

Whistlers, 3 km south off Hwy 93. 781 sites, including some with full hook-ups. Campers should try to get a walk-in site. **Wapiti**, 4 km south on Hwy 93. 362 sites, some with hook-ups. Showers. Open year-round. OK for being so close to town. **Wabasso**, 15 km south on Hwy 93A. 228 sites. Its inconvenient location tends to mean it's the last one to fill up. **Snaring River**, 15 km north off Hwy 16 on the road towards Celestine Lake. This is the nicest campground. When all others are full, there is overflow camping here with space for 500. **Pocahontas**, 45 km east then 1 km on Miette Hot Springs Rd. 140 reasonable sites.

Mt Robson Provincial Park *p316*
B **Mount Robson Lodge**, T250-5669899, www.mtrobson.com. Situated close to the trail (phone for directions), offering a couple of lovely log cabins with kitchen, and 4 rooms in the splendid wood lodge, with breakfast included.

C **Mount Robson Guest Ranch**, 2 km from the Hwy on Hargreaves Rd, T250-5664654, www.mountrobsonranch.com. 7 rustic cabins, some with kitchenettes, in a very quiet, private spot near the Berg Lake Trail. Also RV sites, and a restaurant offering all meals.

Camping
Emperor Ridge Campground, within walking distance of the visitor centre on Kinney Lake Rd, T250-5668438. 37 decent sites, and hot showers.

Robson River and **Robson Meadows**, Provincial Park campgrounds, are both close to the visitor centre, with 144 sites between them, and showers.

Robson Shadows Campground, 5 km west of the park boundary on Hwy 16, T250-5664821. Nice sites on the river, and showers.

⊘ Eating

Jasper Townsite *p313, map p314*
⦙⦙⦙ **Andy's Bistro**, 606 Patricia St, T780-8524559. European-influenced cuisine in an intimate setting, with a frequently changing menu that focuses on meat dishes and fondue. Chef Andy is undoubtedly one of the best in town.
⦙⦙⦙ **Fiddle River**, 620 Connaught Dr, T780-8523032. The place to go for seafood, immaculately cooked in a variety of imaginative or tried and tested ways. Also has a big wine list.
⦙⦙⦙ **The Pines** at Pyramid Lake, T780-8524900. Sumptuous dishes like smoked trout chowder and seafood pasta flavoured with black sambuca, served in a comfortable interior, or on a patio overlooking the lake.
⦙⦙⦙ **Villa Caruso**, 640 Connaught Dr, T780-8523920. A classic steak and seafood style menu, in a downtown spot with a nice atmosphere and balcony seating.
⦙⦙ **Earl's**, 600 Patricia St, T780-8522393. The standard broad menu covering many popular bases, with good views from the 2nd-floor balcony. One of the nicest locations in town.
⦙⦙ **Kimchi House**, 407 Patricia St, T780-8525022. A real cultural experience, serving authentic Korean BBQ dishes that are big enough for two. Choose between the cosy interior or outdoor patio.
⦙⦙ **La Fiesta**, 504 Patricia St, T780-8520404. A colourful little spot specializing in paella and Spanish tapas.
⦙⦙ **Miss Italia**, upstairs at 610 Patricia St, T780-8524002. A sweet spot with little tables on the balcony, lots of plants, and good pasta dishes.
⦙ **Coco's**, 608 Patricia St. A nice place to hang out, with good coffee and music, magazines, and some vegetarian food.
⦙ **Soft Rock Café**, 632 Connaught Dr. Good breakfast and grilled sandwiches, internet access.

🍸 Bars and clubs

Jasper Townsite *p313, map p314*
Most of Jasper's hotels have 'lounges' for a quiet drink, but with big screen TVs.
Athabasca Hotel, 510 Patricia St. Sleazy nightclub with DJs and live music.
De'd Dog Bar and Grill, Astoria Hotel, 404 Connaught Dr. Fairly good ale on tap, pool table and darts.
The Downstream Bar, 620 Connaught Dr. A cosy spot for a glass of wine.
Jasper Brewing Co, 624 Connaught Dr. A decent pub that brews its own beers and serves contemporary pub food.
Pete's on Patricia, 614 Patricia St. Dancing, and occasional live music.

⚙ Festivals and events

Jasper Townsite *p313, map p314*
Aug Heritage Folk Festival, T780-8523615, www.jasperfolkfestival.com. A major folk music festival held biennially (next in 2007, 2009). **Jasper Heritage Pro Rodeo**, www.jasperheritagepro rodeo.com, in mid-Aug attracts top cowboys and stock from around the world, with events like bullriding, bareback and saddle bronco riding, steer wrestling, calf roping, barrel racing and more. Dances on Fri and Sat nights featuring top Country entertainers.

🛍 Shopping

Jasper Townsite *p313, map p314*
Friends of Jasper National Park, opposite the visitor centre on Connaught Rd, T780-8524767 www.friendsofjasper.com. Profits go to the park. Camping/hiking gear
Everest Outdoor Stores, 414 Connaught Dr. Gear, maps and outdoor clothing.
Gravity Gear, 618 Patricia St. Climbing gear.
Jasper Source for Sports, 406 Patricia St. Fishing equipment, boat rentals, bike and camping gear rentals.

Nutters, 622 Patricia St. Health food and hiking snacks, good salamis and cheeses.

🔺 Activities and tours

Columbia Icefield *p311*
Brewster's Snocoach, T403-7626700, www.columbiaicefield.com. Runs tours onto the glacier in a specially built bus that moves at a snail's pace, doing the 5-km round trip in 55 mins. Tours leave every 15 mins, Apr-Oct daily, and cost $32, $16 child.

Jasper *p313, map p314*
Biking
Pick up the *Jasper Cycling Guide* at the visitor centre. There are several good trails starting from town. Experienced bikers will enjoy the **Saturday Night Lake Loop**, 27 km, starting at the Cabin Lake Rd parking lot, west end of town, with views of Miette and Athabasca Valley. There is some good riding across the river at **Old Fort Point**, which is also the start of the 23-km **Trail No 7**, a good all-level ride passing through Maligne Canyon.
Freewheel Cycle, 618 Patricia St, T780-8523898, www.freewheeljasper.com. Trail-maps, rentals ($24-30/day) and information.

Climbing
Gravity Gear, 618 Patricia St, T780-8523155, www.gravitygearjasper.com. Ask them about climbing at Maligne Canyon, Rock Gardens and Boulder Garden. Hidden Valley, 30 km east, is good for the experienced.
Jasper Activity Centre, 303 Pyramid Av, has an indoor climbing wall.
Paul Valiulis, T780-8521945. Guided trips to Morro Slabs.

Ice Skating
Ice-skating on **Lac Beauvert** by Jasper Park Lodge, on **Pyramid Lake**, and on an indoor rink at **Jasper Activity Centre**, 303 Pyramid Av, T780-8523381.

Rafting

Athabasca River is for mellow Grade II runs, Sunwapta and Maligne Rivers offer more dramatic Grade III trips. Usually 2-3 hrs, $45-70 per person.

Maligne Rafting Adventures, T780-8523370, www.mra.ab.ca. Sunwapta trips, also wilderness tours on the Kakwa/Smoky rivers.

Raven Rafting, T780-8524292, www.raven adventure.com. Mild to wild trips.

Rocky Mountain River Guides, T780-8523777, www.rmriverguides.com.

Whitewater Rafting Ltd, T780-8527238, www.whitewaterraftingjasper.com.

Skiing

Visit www.skijaspercanada.com for general information.

Downhill Marmot Basin, T780-8523816, www.skimarmot.com. Has a reputation for being one of the most spacious, friendly and uncrowded ski hills in the country. It receives 400 cm of powder per year, with no need for snow-makers. 9 lifts service 677 ha of skiable terrain, which breaks up into 35% beginner, 35% intermediate and 30% expert. The top elevation is 2601 m, with a vertical drop of 914 m and a longest run of 5.6 km. $56 lift ticket.

Cross-country There's 20 km of groomed trails at **Maligne Lake**. The Bald Hills up above offer plenty of space for telemarking and touring, but the 480 m elevation gain over 5.5 km makes it hard work getting there. The 5 km **Beaver/Summit Lake Trail**, Km 27 on Maligne Lake Rd, gives easy access to the backcountry. There are 1- to 30-km trails at **Pyramid Bench** and around **Patricia Lake**. **Jasper Park Lodge** also has a network of groomed loops from 5-10 km. The 4.5-km **Whistlers Campground** loop is flat, easy and lit up at night. **Moab Lake** is a nice, easy 18-km trail with great views, 20 km south on Hwy 93A.

Edge Control Ski & Outdoor Store, 626 Connaught Dr. Ski and snowboard equipment rentals.

Tour operators

Air Jasper, booked through Sundog Tours (see above). 1 hr flightseeing tours in a Cessna, $175 including shuttle to Hinton airport.

Beyond the Beaten Path, T780-8525650. Maligne Canyon icewalks, plus snowshoe and cross-country ski tours. Also wildlife safaris and van tours with interpretive talks and/or hikes in Maligne Canyon, Icefields Parkway and Mt Edith Cavell.

Brewster Gray Line, T1877-7915500, www.brewster.ca. Bus tours to Banff, Lake Louise, Maligne Lake, Columbia Icefield, and around town. The Snocoach tours can take you right up onto the glacier.

Cold Fire Creek,T780-9686808. 3-4 hr tours and overnight dog-sledding trips.

Currie's Guiding & Tackle, T780-8525650, www.curriesguiding.com. Also runs sightseeing van tours and wildlife searching. Remember that you need a $7/day permit to fish in the park.

Jasper Adventure Centre, T780-8525595, www.jasperadventure centre.com. Rafting, horse riding, ice-walks, snowshoeing, dog sledding, van tours, walking tours, 2-hr 'voyageur' canoe trips, and more. They represent many of the companies below.

Jasper Carriage Co, T780-8527433. Horse-drawn carriage tours in town.

Jasper Source for Sports, 406 Patricia St, T780-8523654. Bike, canoe and ice-skate rental.

On-Line Sport, 600 Patricia St, T780-8523630. The best first stop for most sports equipment, rentals and tours. They rent bikes, snowshoes, fishing gear, canoes and boats, and backpacking gear. Moonlit ski and snowshoe trips.

Overlander Trekking and Tours, T780-8524056, www.overlandertrekking.com. All kinds of hikes in and around the park. Ski and snowshoe guided tours. Maligne Canyon Icewalks.

Pyramid Riding Stables, T780-8527106, www.pyramidridingstables.com. 1-hr to 1-day horse rides above town on Pyramid Bench with views of the Athabasca Valley, and sleigh rides in the winter (T780-8527433).

Sun Dog Tours, T780-8524056, www.sun dogtours.com. These guys can book anything you need in summer or winter: cat skiing, snowshoeing, heli-skiing, flight tours, wildlife tours, hiking, rafting etc.

Skyline Trail Rides, T780-8524215, www.skylinetrail.com. 1 hr, full-day or multi-day pack horse riding trips to their **Shovel Pass Lodge**, $550 for 3 days/2 nights including food and lodging.

Tonquin Valley Pack Trips, T780-8521188, www.tonquinadventures.com. Horse riding trips up Tonquin Valley to the lodge (see Sleeping, p313).

Walks and Talks Jasper, 626 Connaught Dr, T780-8524994, www.walks ntalks.com. Interpretive guided hikes focusing on wildlife or glaciers. Also guided ski and snowshoe tours.

Mt Robson Provincial Park p316
Headwaters Outfiffing, T250-5664718, www.davehenry.com. Backcountry skiing and hiking in Mount Robson.

Mount Robson Whitewater Rafting, T250-5664879, www.mountrobson whitewater.com. Whitewater trips on the Fraser River.

Snow Farmers, T250-5669161, www.snowfarmers.com. Skiing and horseback riding.

⊖ Transport

Jasper Townsite p313, map p314
Bus and train
Local Most of Jasper's important trails are far removed from the town, and for those without their own transport the choices are to hitchhike or use one of the expensive shuttle services: **Jasper Adventure Centre**, T780-8525595; **Walks and Talks Jasper**, T780-8524945. From May-Oct the **Maligne Lake Shuttle**, T780-8523370, connects Jasper with Maligne Lake, leaving every 3 hrs starting 0830 from Jasper, ending 1800 from the

lake. One way is $16, or $10.70 to Maligne Canyon. From 627 Patricia St or Jasper Park Lodge. They will drop you off at trailheads.

Long distance Greyhound, T250-8523926, www.greyhound.ca, runs 4 daily buses to **Edmonton** ($57, 5 hrs), 2 to **Vancouver** ($116, 11 hrs) via **Kamloops** ($61, 5.5 hrs), and 1 to **Prince George** ($55, 5 hrs). **VIA Rail** operates 3 trains per week to **Edmonton** ($127, 5 hrs) and **Vancouver** ($177, 16.5 hrs) or to **Prince Rupert** ($194, 31 hrs) via **Prince George** ($93, 7.5 hrs). The Rocky Mountaineer train, T604-6067245, 2 nights and 3 days to **Vancouver**, starting at $740 including accommodation. A beautiful journey. Sun Dog Tours, T1888-7863641/T780-8534056, www.sundogtours.com, runs a shuttle to Banff ($59) and Calgary ($105) Dec-April only, leaving Jasper at 0800. The same company also operates **Canadian Rockies Hostel Shuttle** in summer, stopping at all hostels between Jasper and Banff ($51). Extra charge for bikes.

Taxi
Jasper Taxi, T780-8523600.

Mt Robson Provincial Park p316
Greyhound buses will drop you off at the visitor centre. 4 daily to Jasper ($24), 1 daily to Prince George, ($46), and 3 from Kamloops ($53).

⊖ Directory

Jasper Townsite p313, map p314
Internet Library. Soft Rock Internet Café, 622 Connaught Dr. **Canada Post** 502 Patricia St. **Laundry** Coin Clean Laundry, Patricia Av. Also coin-op showers. **Library** Jasper Municipal Library, Elm Av/Robson St. **Medical services** Seton Hospital, 518 Robson St, T780-8523344. Cottage Medical Clinic, 507 Turret St, T780-8524885.

Yoho National Park

Yoho is a Cree exclamation of awe and wonder, something like 'Wow!' The scenery in this park is indeed astounding, with many waterfalls, and 28 peaks over 3000 m. Banff may be the most famous of the parks, and Jasper the biggest, but get any Rocky Mountain aficionado talking and they'll soon start waxing passionate about Yoho. Comparatively small, it contains the greatest concentration of quality hikes in the range, mostly clustered in two major areas and one minor. Lake O'Hara has proved

⊘ Getting there Car, bus, shuttle.
⊖ Getting around Car, shuttle.
⊖ Time required 3 days/1 week.
⊛ Weather Changeable.
⊜ Sleeping Camping, hostels, guesthouses.
⊘ Eating Limited.
▲ Activities and tours Hiking, biking.
★ Don't miss... Takakkaw Falls and the Iceline Hike ›› *pp326-327*.

so popular that a complete traffic ban has been imposed, and visitor numbers are strictly limited. A good second choice, if that's too much hassle, Yoho Valley has the park's only hostel, and a fabulous campground. Emerald Lake is a pretty destination and offers one very good hike. The pleasant little village of Field makes a good base for those not camping.

Ins and outs

Getting there and around
Field is on the Trans Canada Highway, receiving three **Greyhound**, www.greyhound.ca, buses from Vancouver, Calgary and all points in between, including Banff and Lake Louise. **Sky Shuttle**, T250-7625200, www.rockymountainskyshuttle.com, runs a shuttle from Calgary to Emerald Lake, stopping at Banff and Lake Louise. ›› ⊖ *p329*.

Tourist information
Unless you know specifically what you want to do, a sensible first port of call is to the village of Field which is close to all of Yoho's sights, and contains the excellent **Visitor Centre/Parks Office** ⓘ *T250-3436783, www.field.ca, summer 0900-1900, rest of the year 0900-1700*. They can help organize accommodation and camping arrangements, give sound advice on what hikes to choose, and issue the very useful backcountry guide, as well as maps. They also take backcountry camping reservations (T250-3436433, $12) up to three months ahead, a must for Lake O'Hara.

Field ⊜⊘▲ ›› *pp328-329*.

Field is a remarkably attractive one-horse town of 300 people built on the side of a mountain and makes a delightful base for day-hikes around the park. There are no sights as such, but Field Mountain, visible across the valley, is the site of the **Burgess Shale**, an ancient sea-bed that has yielded a host of 515 million-year-old fossils. Remains of more than 120 species of soft-bodied marine animals have been found, some so well preserved that scientists can tell what they ate just before they died. This is one of only three places in the world where such fossils are found. An excellent exhibit recreating the sea and explaining its inhabitants is one of the highlights of the Royal Tyrell Museum in Drumheller, Alberta (see p 278). There are also displays at the Field and Lake Louise visitor centres. Long and strenuous guided hikes to the fossil beds are run between July and mid-September by the **Yoho Burgess Shale Foundation**, T1800-3433006. Numbers are limited to 15 per hike.

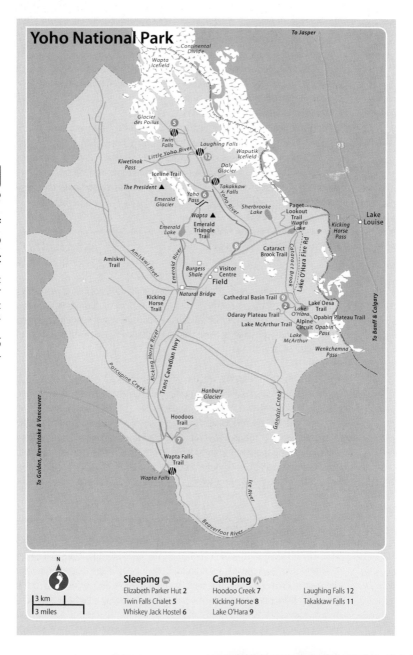

Yoho National Park

N

3 km
3 miles

Sleeping	**Camping**	
Elizabeth Parker Hut **2**	Hoodoo Creek **7**	Laughing Falls **12**
Twin Falls Chalet **5**	Kicking Horse **8**	Takakkaw Falls **11**
Whiskey Jack Hostel **6**	Lake O'Hara **9**	

Fly fishing at Lake O'Hara.

Lake O'Hara 🖥 ▸▸ *pp328-329.*

▸▸ *pp328-329.*

Ins and outs

A shuttle bus runs to Lake O'Hara between 17 June and 4 October (in 2006) from the Lake O'Hara Fire Road parking lot. Turn onto Highway 1A 3 km south of the Continental Divide sign or 1.6 km north of the lodge at Wapta Lake, cross the tracks, turn right and proceed 800 m. Buses leave at 0830, 1030, 1530 and 1730, departing from Lake O'Hara Lodge at 0930, 1130, 1430, 1630 and 1830. To get a place on the bus it is essential to reserve at T250-3436433 as early as 19 March. The fare is $15 return, with $12 reservation fee. Once up there a place on the return bus is first-come, first-served, but practically guaranteed at 1630 or 1830. Bus seats can sometimes be booked at the Field Visitor Centre, but priority goes to those who have reserved accommodation.

To reserve a site in Lake O'Hara Campground, which is essential, call the Field Visitor Centre, T250-3436783, with precise details of dates and numbers as early as possible, or try at www.pccamping.ca. Between 3-5 sites per day are available on a first-come, first-served basis, but to get one of these you need to be lining up at the Field Visitor Centre the day before at 0700. Even those with a reservation also need a Wilderness Pass, or they will lose their space. The only other real choice is the Alpine Club of Canada's **A Elizabeth Parker Hut**, T250-6783200, www.alpineclubofcanada.ca. The hut sleeps 24, is open year-round, and is so heavily booked that they have started a lottery for allotment of spaces.

The Lake

Exquisitely framed by the two lofty mountains, Victoria and Lefroy, that tower over Lake Louise on the other side of the Continental Divide, Lake O'Hara is a rare jewel even in the overflowing treasure chest of the Rockies. When it was first discovered by Canada's hiking community, news of its extraordinary natural beauty and network of quality day-hikes spread like wildfire, and soon the area was too popular for its own good. Parks Canada have taken measures to protect it, so visiting can be difficult unless you book ahead. No traffic is allowed into the region, not even bikes.

Hiking in the Lake O'Hara region is among the most popular and rewarding in the Rockies. On the Continental Divide between here and Lake Louise are a number of the highest and most awe-inspiring peaks in the range. Within a relatively small area are 25 named lakes and an extensive, well-maintained network of trails that radiate out from Lake O'Hara like the spokes of a wheel. There are five main sub-regions that can be combined in any number of ways.

▲▲ **Lake Oesa** ⓘ *5.8-km loop, 240 m elevation gain.* This is a short and easy hike to a stunning turquoise lake set in a rugged cirque. Towering above are the Continental Divide summits of Mounts Lefroy and Victoria, the other side of the stunning massif that towers so dramatically over Lake Louise.

▲▲ **Opabin Plateau** ⓘ *7.2-km loop, 250 m elevation gain.* Set in a beautiful hanging valley, this easy hike offers many temptations for casual exploration among small flower-filled tundra meadows. The loop follows the east and west sides of the same valley. A 0.6-km side-trail leads from the west side to outstanding views from Opabin Prospect. From the east side, a detour leads along Yukness Ledge, a possible highline traverse to Lake Oesa.

▲▲ **Lake McArthur** ⓘ *7 km return, 315 m elevation gain.* This half-day hike is one of the area's finest. The 1.5-km-long lake is the biggest in the area, and an exquisite, deep blue colour due to its 65-m depth. Sheer cliffs rising straight up, more than 600 m above the water, make for a dramatic location.

▲▲ **Odaray Plateau** ⓘ *7-10-km loops, 290-655 m elevation gain.* This is one of the most spectacular routes in the park, but is often closed, or visitor numbers are limited due to grizzly bears. The trail climbs quickly and steeply. Odaray Prospect offers a 180° panorama centred on Lake O'Hara, backed by the wall of high peaks that comprise the Great Divide. Further along, the trail branches off to Odaray Grandview, the only spot in the park from which all of its major lakes can be seen simultaneously. To achieve this prize you have to face a difficult 1.1-km scramble that requires endurance and some experience. At Km 4.5 a junction at McArthur Pass leads back to the start making a 6.5-km loop, or on to Lake McArthur as part of a 9.5-km loop.

▲▲ **Cathedral Basin** ⓘ *13-15 km return, 300 m elevation gain.* This is one of the longest and least crowded day-hikes in the area, but is also one of the lowest and least dramatic. However, after skirting the pretty Linda and Cathedral Lakes, the trail starts to climb towards the mouth of the Cathedral Basin. The wonderful views all along this stretch peak at Cathedral Prospect, which offers one of the most complete overviews of the whole Lake O'Hara region. The climb to the Prospect is fairly steep on a poor, rocky surface.

▲▲ **Alpine Circuit** ⓘ *9.8-12.4 km, 495 m elevation gain.* The classic way to combine some of the area's sights, this is one of the highlights of the Lake O'Hara region, but it's a fairly tough circuit, more route than trail, following cairns and paint-marks across scree slopes and along exposed ledges. Those scared of heights, worried about getting lost, or not in tip-top condition should probably choose another hike. Use a good trail description and carry a good map. Starting the circuit with the toughest section, the ascent to Wiwaxy Gap, is a good idea. Views from the gap are exceptional. The loop can be extended or shortened in a couple of places. The short detour to Opabin Prospect is worth the effort, while the ascent to All Souls' Prospect is an excellent conclusion to the hike.

Yoho Valley ⬤ ▸▸ *pp328-329.*

Logistically easier than Lake O'Hara, and almost equally wonderful, is the Yoho Valley, which is lined with waterfalls, including the dramatic **Twin Falls** and the 380-m **Takakkaw Falls**, one of Canada's highest, whose name comes from a Stoney Indian word meaning 'magnificent'. This is also one of the most exceptional areas for glaciers: the enormous Wapta and Waputik Icefields are both easily visible, as is the beautiful Emerald Glacier. The valley is ringed with monster peaks. To get there, drive 3.7 km northeast of Field, or 12.5 km southwest of the Continental Divide, turn north on Yoho Valley Road and drive about 13 km up a very steep, winding road, not suitable for RVs or trailers.

Hikes in the Yoho Valley

▲ **Iceline** ⓘ *12.8-21.3 km, 690 m elevation gain. Trailhead: Whiskey Jack Hostel.* The steep ascent of this popular hike takes you up to the Emerald Glacier, on a level with truly extraordinary scenery that includes the Daly Glacier and Takakkaw Falls opposite, and the vast Wapta Icefield to the north. Once at the top, the hiking is high, easy and scenically uplifting. A return journey to the highpoint is 12.8 km. Circuits can be made by continuing to the Yoho Valley and possibly the Little Yoho Valley as well, though neither option adds anything that compares to the views from the top. A two-day backpack trip would entail a night at Little Yoho campground or the nearby Stanley Mitchell hut (book with the Alpine Club, T403-6783200), a possible diversion to Kiwetinok Pass, and a return via the stupendous vantage point of the Whaleback.

▲ **Yoho Valley** ⓘ *16.4 km, 290 m elevation gain.* This flat trail through the trees leads to a few waterfalls, ending at the dramatic Twin Falls. It is a nice enough stroll and good for a rainy day, but otherwise there seems no point if you're capable of doing the spectacular Iceline trail, which offers so much more.

Emerald Lake.

Canadian Rockies Yoho National Park

Emerald Lake ⊜❶▲▲ ↦ *pp328-329.*

This is a pretty spot, whose name is accurate if lacking in imagination. To get here, drive 2.6 km southwest of Field, then 8 km on Emerald Lake Road, passing on the way the Natural Bridge, a giant rock that has been carved by the powerful Kicking Horse River. In addition to those listed below, a number of longer trails are better suited to mountain biking. The **Amiskwi Trail**, 35 km one way, follows a river, starting at Emerald Lake Road. The 19.5-km **Kicking Horse Trail** starts at the same point or at the now-closed Chancellor Peak campground.

▲▲ **Emerald Triangle** ① *19.7 km, 880 m elevation gain.* The clear-cut choice for a day-hike. A satisfying loop, the climb is gentle (more gentle in a clockwise direction), but the descent at the end is rapid. As well as the lake, views are of the glaciated ramparts of The President, the sheer cliffs of Wapta Mountain, the Kicking Horse Valley, and the fossil-fields of the Burgess Shale.

Hikes (and biking) from the TransCanada Highway

▲▲ **Paget Lookout** ① *7.4 km return, 520 m elevation gain. Trailhead: Wapta Lake Picnic Area, 5.5 km southwest of BC/Alberta border.* This short but steep climb leads to astounding views that include the mountains encircling Lake O'Hara and the Kicking Horse Valley. Scramblers can ascend a further 430 m to Paget Peak for even better views.

▲▲ **Hoodoos** ① *3.2 km, 455 m elevation gain. Trailhead: 22.7 km southwest of Field, right before campground entrance, 1.5 km to parking area.* A short but very steep hike leads to these fascinating, elongated-mushroom-shaped rock formations. Follow the trail above them for the best views. This can be enjoyed whatever the weather, and combines nicely with **Wapta Falls** ① *4.8 km, 45 m elevation gain. Trailhead: 25 km southwest of Field, 1.8 km down Wapta Falls access road,* a powerful waterfall in a raw setting. The short, level hike is good for spring or autumn, a rainy day, or just a leg-stretch to see the cascade.

⊜ Sleeping

Field *p323*
Almost every residence in Field functions as an informal guesthouse, offering self-catering suites with kitchen for about $100. Contact the visitor centre which has a full, up-to-date list, or check www.field.ca.

A **Alpine Guesthouse**, 2nd Av, T250-3436878, www.alpineguesthouse.ca. A magnificent, spacious 2-bedroom suite with private entrance and kitchen in a lovely wood house with incredible views.

A **Kicking Horse Lodge**, end of Kicking Horse/Stephen Av, T250-3436303, www.kickinghorselodge.net. The only hotel in town, with large rooms, kitchenettes for an extra $14, a nice restaurant and patio, and laundry facilities.

B **Canadian Rockies Inn**, T250-3436046, www.bbcanada.com/7896. 3 nice suites, all with private bathroom and living room, 1 with kitchen.

C **Alpenglow B&B**, T250-3436356. Nice rooms with shared bath and no kitchen.

C **Mt Burgess Guesthouse**, T250-3436480, www.mtburgessguesthouse.ca. 2 rooms with kitchens, private bath and TV.

C **Mt Stephen Guesthouse**, T250-3436441, www.mountstephen.com. 2 en suite rooms with kitchen.

Camping
Kicking Horse Campground, 3.7 km northeast at the Yoho Valley turn-off. 86 very nice private sites, and good showers.

Lake O'Hara *p325*
See also Lake O'Hara Ins and outs, p325.
A **Elizabeth Parker Hut**, T250-6783200, www.alpineclubofcanada.ca. Run by the Alpine Club, the hut sleeps 24 and is open year-round. It tends to be heavily booked.

Camping
The campground, where most people stay, doesn't cater for RVs.

Yoho Valley *p326*

D **Twin Falls Chalet**, at the far end of the valley, a 10-km hike, T403-2287079. Jul-Aug only. A real backcountry experience, with no electricity or running hot water, but wonderful meals included in the price.
E **Whiskey Jack Hostel**, on the way to the campground, T403-2836503, mid-Jun to mid-Oct. The park's only hostel, one of the best in the Rockies. 27 beds in 3 dorms. Kitchen, common room, great views.

Camping
Laughing Falls Backcountry Campground, halfway to Twin Falls. Basic but private, with just 8 sites.
Takakkaw Falls Campground. Beyond the hostel, a group of car parks signals the end of the road. The campground is a 500-m walk from here, and suitable for tents only. It combines the excitement of the backcountry with much of the convenience of less remote camping because there are wagons on which you can cart in as much food and equipment as you wish. The sites are fairly private and very beautifully located close to the falls, with a view of the Wapta Icefield. Some excellent hikes also begin here.

Hikes from the TransCanada *p328*
Camping
Hoodoo Creek. A basic campground with 30 sites and no showers.

🍴 Eating

Field *p323*
🍴 **The Truffle Pigs Café and Bistro**, Kicking Horse/Stephen Av, T250-3436462. Just about the only store in town, with a small but excellent and quite expensive restaurant. The food is fresh, they do gourmet dinner specials, very good coffee, and there's outdoor seating.
🍴 **The Roundhouse Pub and Grill**, in the Kicking Horse Lodge (see Sleeping, above). Good food at modest prices.

Emerald Lake *p328*
🍴 **Cilantro On the Lake Restaurant**, next door to the Emerald Lake Lodge, T1800-3433006. Set in an impressive wood building right on the water, this is a perfect spot for a splurge, or at least a drink. The menu, inspired by Californian, West Coast and First Nations cuisine, incorporates lots of wild game and fish from the area. The atmosphere is that of a casual but upmarket bistro.

🔺 Activities and tours

Field *p323*
There are plenty of trails for cross-country skiing right from Field. The 12 km **Tally Ho Trail** winds its way round Mt Burgess to Emerald Lake. The Info Centre has maps.

There are some world class ice-climbing routes in the Field and Yoho Valleys, but you'll have to look elsewhere (Jasper or Banff) for tour operators.

A few old fire trails and longer hikes make for good mountain biking, but the closest rentals are in Lake Louise.
Alpine Rafting, T1888-5995299, www.alpinerafting.com. Whitewater rafting on the Kicking Horse River, which goes right past Field. All levels

Emerald Lake *p328*
The **Emerald Lake Loop** is a popular, groomed 5-km hiking trail. Fishing is good in Emerald Lake. A portion of the lake is cleared in the winter for ice skating.
Emerald Sports and Gifts, T250-3436000. Canoes can be hired here, also cross country skis, snowshoes and all necessary gear.

🚍 Transport

There are 3 **Greyhound** buses daily from the visitor centre running in both directions: east to **Lake Louise** ($14), **Banff** and **Calgary**; west to **Golden** ($13), **Revelstoke**, **Kamloops** and **Vancouver**.

Kootenay National Park

Situated on the other side of the Continental Divide from Banff, and bounded to the north by Yoho, it would be wrong to expect anything but spectacular scenery from Kootenay National Park, yet this is far and away the least visited of the big four. Besides the relative tranquillity, this park has two major assets: the Rockwall, which is one of the top five backpacking trips in the range; and a large number of short walks right from the highway, ideal for the less athletic, leading to diverse destinations including a forest fire burn and the Paint Pots, a series of multi-coloured mineral pools. A much more comprehensive overview of the Rockies can be gained by taking our suggested loop from Lake Louise through Yoho to Golden, down Highway 93, then through Kootenay Park arriving back near Banff. Entering from this direction, you'll be greeted by the dramatic red walls of Sinclair Canyon.

⦿ **Getting there** Car.
⦿ **Getting around** Car.
⦿ **Time required** 1-2 days.
⦿ **Weather** Changeable.
⦿ **Sleeping** Campgrounds.
⦿ **Eating** Very limited.
⦿ **Activities and tours** Hiking.
★ **Don't miss...** Hikes such as the Paint Pots and the Rockwall.
➽ *p332.*

Ins and outs

There is no public transport to or within the park. The only **Visitor Centre** ⓘ *summer 1000-1800, spring and autumn 1100-1800,* in the park is a privately-run concern at Vermilion Crossing. They hand out the *Backcountry Guide,* whose map and trail descriptions are all you need, and issue backcountry passes ($9 per person per night). There is another, more helpful but less convenient **Visitor Centre** ⓘ *7556 Main St East, T250-3479505, www.radiumhotsprings.com, Jun 0900- 1700, Jul-Aug 0900-1900,* in the village of Radium Hot Springs.

Sights ⦿⦿ ➽ *p333.*

Radium Hot Springs

Kootenay National Park's boundaries neatly parallel the winding course of the Banff-Windermere Parkway (Highway 93) as it makes its way from Castle Junction on Highway 1 to Radium Hot Springs in the East Kootenays. This rather brash and unpleasant town is little more than a string of cheesy motels, which tend to be full throughout the summer. The only thing to see is the **Thousand Faces Sculpture Gallery** ⓘ *Hwy 93/Madsen Rd, $1,* a collection of chainsaw carvings with legends and stories built into them. The artist himself is a curiosity.

Those entering from the south are treated to a fine introduction to the park, as the road snakes its way through the steep and narrow Sinclair Canyon, its cliffs a rich red due to the high iron content. Just to the north are **Radium Hot Springs Pools** ⓘ *T250-3472100, $6.50, $5.50 child, May-Oct 0900-2300, Oct-Apr 1200-2100 (Fri-Sat till 2200),* with a hot pool (40°C) and a cool pool (29°C) surrounded by rugged rocky scenery. These are packed in summer with up to 4000 people a day but since the ticket price includes the admission charge to the park, there seems little reason not to stop. Note that the park is on Mountain Time, an hour ahead of most of BC. The park's other attractions are all reached via hikes, described below.

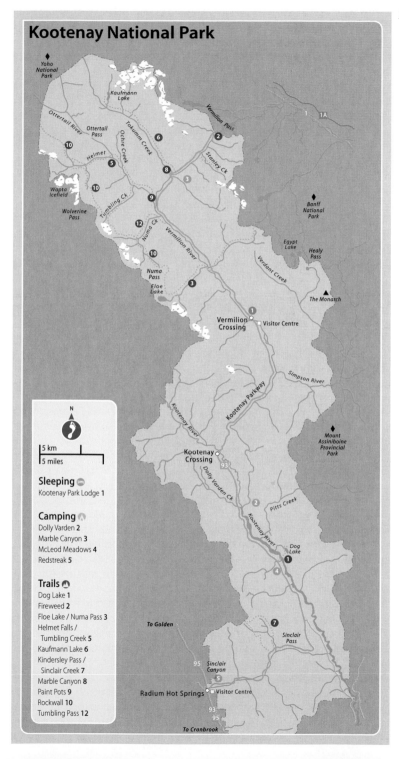

Kootenay National Park

Yoho National Park

Kaufmann Lake

Vermilion Pass

Ottertail River

Ottertail Pass

Tokumm Creek

Ochre Creek

Helmet

Wapta Icefield

Tumbling Ck

Wolverine Pass

Numa Ck

Numa Pass

Floe Lake

Stanley Ck

Vermilion River

Banff National Park

Egypt Lake

Healy Pass

Verdant Creek

The Monarch

Vermilion Crossing

Visitor Centre

Simpson River

Kootenay River

Kootenay Parkway

Mount Assiniboine Provincial Park

Kootenay Crossing

Dolly Varden Ck

Pitts Creek

Dog Lake

Sinclair Pass

To Golden

Sinclair Canyon

Radium Hot Springs

Visitor Centre

To Cranbrook

N

5 km
5 miles

Sleeping
Kootenay Park Lodge 1

Camping
Dolly Varden 2
Marble Canyon 3
McLeod Meadows 4
Redstreak 5

Trails
Dog Lake 1
Fireweed 2
Floe Lake / Numa Pass 3
Helmet Falls /
  Tumbling Creek 5
Kaufmann Lake 6
Kindersley Pass /
  Sinclair Creek 7
Marble Canyon 8
Paint Pots 9
Rockwall 10
Tumbling Pass 12

Canadian Rockies Kootenay National Park

Hikes in Kootenay National Park ⬤🌼 ▸ p333.

Short hikes from north to south

▲▲ **Fireweed Trail** ⓘ *1 km, Trailhead: just south of park boundary*. In 1968 a forest fire started by a single lightning bolt laid waste to a 24 sq km area just south of Vermilion Pass (1651 m). This short trail talks you through the regeneration process and reveals how such fires are an integral part of the forest's natural cycle, to the point that lodgepole pine cones actually require the heat of a forest fire in order to open and spread their seeds.

▲▲ **Marble Canyon** ⓘ *800 m or more. Trailhead: 7 km south of park boundary*. An easy trail takes you to this lovely 600-m-long, 37-m-deep canyon which Tokumm Creek has carved out of the white dolomite limestone that was once mistaken for marble. The highlight is a striking view of a powerful waterfall where the creek forces its way through a narrow opening. In winter, the whole canyon turns into a magical palace of blue and green ice.

▲▲ **The Paint Pots** ⓘ *3 km return. Trailhead: 9.5 km south of park boundary*. This trail leads to a series of fascinating pools where iron-laden mineral springs push through clay sediments to create shades of red, orange and yellow. Native Americans came from far and wide to collect these coloured clays, which were then baked, ground into powder, and added to fat or oil to make paint, which was then used in a number of creative and ceremonial ways.

▲▲ **Dog Lake** ⓘ *5.2 km return. Trailhead: 500 m south of Mcleod Meadows campground*. About the best of the short hikes in the southern half of the park. This shallow, marsh-edged lake sits in one of the Rockies' most temperate valleys, making it a good spot for wildlife. Orchids also abound in early summer.

Longer hikes

▲▲ **The Rockwall** ⓘ *54.8 km, 1490 m elevation gain. Trailhead: 22.5 km south of park boundary*. The Rockwall is the name of the Vermillion Mountains' eastern escarpment, a solid sheet of grey limestone whose sheer cliffs run for 35 km along the Great Divide. Instead of running along a ridge like some highline trails, this one goes up and down like a rollercoaster, crossing three alpine passes then plunging down into valleys, passing on the way a number of hanging glaciers, flower-strewn meadows, gorgeous lakes, and stunning waterfalls. It is one of the most demanding but rewarding hikes in the Rockies, and is comfortably done in four days. Four trails lead to the Rockwall, along Floe, Numa, Tumbling and Helmet Creeks. The optimum approach is to hike up Floe Creek, spending night one at Floe Lake campground (10.5 km), night two at Tumbling Falls (27.9 km), and night three at Helmet Falls (39.7 km). A few shorter hikes take in sections of the Rockwall, although the greatest reward is hiking the whole thing.

▲▲ **Floe Lake/Numa Pass** ⓘ *21-26.4 km, 715-1030 m elevation gain. Trailhead: 22.5 km south of park boundary*. This is the best of the Rockwall day-hikes. Floe Lake is one of the most majestic sights in the Rockies: sheer cliffs rise 1000 m straight up from the azure blue waters, their ice floes mirrored on its crystal surface. The ascent is long, quite steep and mostly through forest, making this more suited to an overnighter than a day-hike. Views from Numa Pass, 2.7 km (one hour) further, are even more striking, another reason to spend an extra day. It's the best place to take in the lake and the rockwall that towers above it. From here, it is possible to descend to the highway via **Numa Creek**, making a total loop of 27.3 km, though it means hitching 8 km back to the trailhead.

▲▲ **Tumbling Pass** ⓘ *24.4-km loop, 800 m elevation gain, 840 m loss. Trailhead: 9.5 km south of park boundary*. As a day-hike, this is extremely long and tough. It starts pleasantly enough by passing by the Paint Pots, but soon sets into a steady ascent with little reward until you reach Tumbling Falls at 9.4 km, where there is a nice campground. The pass is a tough 3.6 km further, but worth it for the awesome sight of the Rockwall and Tumbling Glacier. A 6-km detour to **Wolverine Pass** is also worth the effort, but as a day-hike there's no time. From the pass, return to the trailhead along Numa Creek, a steep but pleasant descent.

▲▲ **Helmet Falls/Tumbling Creek** ⓘ *37-km loop. Trailhead: 9.5 km south of park boundary.* As a two-day trip, it is worth hiking up Ochre/Helmet Creeks to Helmet Falls at the north end of the Rockwall. This impressive cascade is one of the highest in Canada. It is possible to stay at the campground here then ascend through Rockwall Pass and exit to the trailhead along Tumbling Creek, though this is a tough second day.

▲▲ **Kindersley Pass/Sinclair Creek** ⓘ *16.5-20.5-km loop, 1055 m elevation gain. Trailhead: across the highway from the parking area 9.5 km from the west gate at Radium.* This is one of the park's most scenic and most strenuous hikes. The trail ascends steadily for 8.4 km with little reward. From Kindersley Pass, views start to appear northward of the countless peaks of the Brisco Range. For the next 1.4 km to Kindersley Summit vistas of this ocean of summits keep getting better. From here the indistinct trail along Sinclair Creek makes for a convenient loop back to the Highway, though it leaves you 1.2 km northeast of your vehicle.

◉ Sleeping

Kootenay National Park *p330*
Apart from camping, most of the accommodation is in Radium Hot Springs, which admittedly has a lot of choices.

B **Chalet Europe**, 5063 Madsen Rd, T250-3479305 www.chaleteurope.com. On a hill adjacent to the park entrance and a healthy distance from town, with wonderful views. Very attractive suites with private balconies and telescopes to make the most of the incredible views. Sauna, jacuzzi and continental breakfast.

B **Village Country Inn**, 7557 Canyon Av, Radium Hot Springs, T250-3479392, www.villagecountryinn.bc.ca. The nicest of many places to stay in town. Very comfortable rooms with big beds and TVs.

C **Kootenay Park Lodge**, Vermilion Crossing, T250-7629196, www.kootenay parklodge.com. Very small, basic cabins, poor value at this price. The only place to stay in the park itself.

C **Rocky Mountain Springs Lodge**, 5067 Madsen Rd, T250-2859743, www.million dollarview.ca. Up on the hill above town by the park entrance. Plain but decent sized rooms with balcony, and breakfast included. Also serves the best food.

C-D **Pinewood**, 4870 Stanley St, Radium Hot Springs, T250-3479529. The nicest of the motels, an attractive building nestled in spruce trees. Spacious rooms, some with kitchenettes.

D-E **Misty River B&B and HI Hostel**, Hwy 93, by the park entrance, T250-3479912, www.radiumhostel.bc.ca. A small, friendly hostel with 11 dorm beds, 2 private rooms, and 2 family rooms, plus a lounge, kitchen, and bike/canoe rental.

Camping
There are 8 campgrounds, mostly on the **Rockwall** and **Kaufmann Lake** trails.

Marble Canyon. Newly repaired, the only campground in the more interesting upper part of the park, with 61 sites.

McLeod Meadows, 25 km north of Radium. 98 basic sites on the river, open Jun-Sep. Just to the north, and only open in winter, is the tiny (free) **Dolly Varden**.

Redstreak, just north of Sinclair Canyon, T1877-7373783, www.pccamping.ca. May-Oct. The park's biggest campground, with 242 sites, showers, and full hook-ups.

◉ Eating

Kootenay National Park *p330*
▮▮▮ **Old Salzburg**, Hwy 93, 2 km west of the park gates, T250-3476553. Traditional Austrian food such as schnitzel and spaetzle, plus seafood, steak, and yummy desserts.

▮▮ **Citadella Restaurant**, Rocky Mountain Springs Lodge. Wonderful Hungarian food in a winning location.

▮▮ **Horsethief Creek Pub and Eatery**, 7538 Main St, T250-3476400. Good pub grub.

Waterton Lakes National Park

Despite its modest size – a mere 525 sq km – the most southerly of Canada's Rocky Mountain parks delivers landscapes and hiking to rival almost anything further north, but without the crowds. The scenery has a unique flavour of its own, a strange juxtaposition of prairies and mountain. The park's remarkable diversity of geographic zones – prairie, wetlands, aspen parkland, montane forest – has also led to a far greater variety of flora and fauna than any of Western Canada's other parks, with about 1200 plant species, including 55% of Alberta's wild flowers. In 1932, the park combined with Glacier National Park in Montana to become the world's first International Peace Park, and was recognized as a Biosphere Reserve in 1979 and UNESCO World Heritage Site in 1995.

⊘ **Getting there** Car.
⊖ **Getting around** Car, hiking.
⊖ **Time required** 1-3 days.
⊚ **Weather** Rainy and windy.
⊜ **Sleeping** The full range.
⊘ **Eating** Limited.
▲ **Activities and tours** Hiking, boat trips.
★ **Don't miss...** Hiking the Crypt Lake Trail »» *p336*.

Ins and outs

Getting there and around

The closest **Greyhound** station is at 1018 Waterton Avenue, Pincher Creek, 51 km to the north, T403-6272716, which receives daily buses from Vancouver via Highway 3, and from Calgary. The nearest US border crossing is at Chief Mountain on the park's eastern edge, open June to August 0700-2200, and late May and September 0900-1800. At other times, the closest border crossing is east on Highway 2 at Carway, Alberta/Peigan, Montana, year-round daily 0700-2300.

A **Hiker Shuttle Service** from Tamarack Village Square, T403-8592378, will take you to Cameron Lake, Red Rock Canyon and other trailheads. **Crypt Lake Water Shuttle Service** at the marina, T403-8592362, delivers hikers to Crypt Lake Trailhead and points such as Rainbow Falls and Francis Lake.

Best time to visit

The park is open from the long weekend in May until Labour Day weekend in September, though many of the hikes are still under snow until well into June. Prairie flowers bloom in the spring and early summer, while higher elevation wild flowers arrive in late summer/autumn, which is also the best time to see animals such as bears and elk. Waterton receives Alberta's highest average annual precipitation levels, and is one of the province's windiest places.

Tourist information

The **Parks Visitor Centre** ⓘ *Entrance Rd, T403-8592445, Jun-Aug 0800-2100, May and Sep 0900-1700*, is on the way into town. The rest of the year information is available at the **Parks Administration Office** ⓘ *215 Mt View Rd, T403-8592477, Mon-Fri 0800-1600*. A useful website is www.trailofthegreatbear.com. Also useful is the **Waterton Natural History Association** ⓘ *117 Waterton Av, T403-8592624*, which has exhibits, an art gallery, a museum, and sells park-related books and maps. Hikers can buy a 1:50,000 map here or at the visitor centre, though for most people the free map will suffice. A park permit costs $6 per person per day.

Waterton Townsite ⬛🅿🏍❄🛶🏕▲⛰ ⤳ *p338-339.*

As a tribute to the herds that once roamed freely on this land, a Bison Paddock is maintained just north of the park entrance off Highway 6. As you approach the core of the park, the first thing you'll see is the magnificently grandiose **Prince of Wales Hotel**, a fascinating building with a steeply sloping gabled roof, myriad balconies, and extraordinary post and beam lobby. Its location could hardly be more photogenic: high on a bluff overlooking broad expanses of crystal aquamarine surrounded by towering snowy peaks. Be sure to go in and explore.

Waterton Townsite cannot hope to live up to this opening gambit, but it's a pleasant enough spot that gains much from the lake setting. More resort than genuine village, it still feels rather quaint, with mule deer and bighorn sheep wandering freely over the lawns, and Cameron Falls just on the edge of town. Hiking is the main activity around here. Wonderful views are easily attained and a few of the many day-hikes lead right from the townsite. Thanks to the strong local winds, windsurfing is very popular on **Cameron Bay**, as are fishing (with a licence), canoeing and scuba diving.

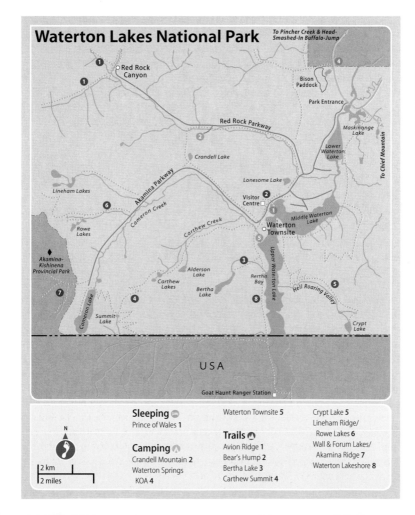

Canadian Rockies Waterton Lakes National Park

Waterton Lakes National Park

To Pincher Creek & Head-Smashed-In Buffalo-Jump

Red Rock Canyon

Bison Paddock

Park Entrance

Red Rock Parkway

Maskinonge Lake

Crandell Lake

To Chief Mountain

Lower Waterton Lake

Lonesome Lake

Lineham Lakes

Visitor Centre

Akamina Parkway

Cameron Creek

Carthew Creek

Middle Waterton Lake

Waterton Townsite

Rowe Lakes

Akamina-Kishinena Provincial Park

Alderson Lake

Carthew Lakes

Bertha Lake

Bertha Bay

Upper Waterton Lake

Hell Roaring Valley

Cameron Lake

Summit Lake

Crypt Lake

U S A

Goat Haunt Ranger Station

N

2 km
2 miles

Sleeping ⬛
Prince of Wales 1

Camping 🏕
Crandell Mountain 2
Waterton Springs
KOA 4

Waterton Townsite 5

Trails ⛰
Avion Ridge 1
Bear's Hump 2
Bertha Lake 3
Carthew Summit 4

Crypt Lake 5
Lineham Ridge/
Rowe Lakes 6
Wall & Forum Lakes/
Akamina Ridge 7
Waterton Lakeshore 8

Hikes in Waterton Lakes National Park

There are over 200 km of trails in the park. A hiker shuttle service to Cameron Lake, Red Rock Canyon and other trailheads is operated by **Waterton Outdoor Adventures**, Tamarack Village Square, T403-8592378, www.watertonvisitorservices.com. **Crypt Lake Water Shuttle Service**, at the marina, T403-8592362, delivers hikers to Crypt Lake trailhead ($14 return). There are nine designated wilderness campgrounds in the park. Limited spaces have resulted in a quota system, with reservations possible 90 days in advance, T403-8595133, which must be booked by credit card. Passes are issued at the visitor centre where a fee is charged per person. After returning from a hike in spring and early summer, we recommend checking for ticks.

From town

▲▲ **Crypt Lake** ⓘ *17.2 km return, 685 m elevation gain. Trailhead: by boat.* This is one of the most popular and exciting trips in the park, with a bit of everything thrown in. You start with a boat trip across the lake, hike an undulating trail through **Hell Roaring Valley**, pass four waterfalls including the stunning **Crypt Falls**, stoop through a dark 20-m tunnel, then ascend a mountainside using a safety cable. The views are fine throughout, and the emerald lake itself sits in a steep and dramatic cirque. You can expect to have plenty of company. There is a backcountry campground at Km 8.

▲▲ **Bear's Hump** ⓘ *1.4 km, 200 m elevation gain. Trailhead: above Information Centre.* Short but steep, leading to great views of mountains, lake and townsite. Snow-free from late May.

▲▲ **Bertha Lake** ⓘ *11 km return, 460 m elevation gain. Trailhead: car park opposite the town campground.* The popularity of this hike is due mainly to its being easy and conveniently located. The trail's highlight arrives at just Km 1.5, with views of the lake and distant prairie. A fork here leads right to Bertha Lake. The left fork descends to the Waterton Lakeshore Trail. This leads to the decent beach at **Bertha Bay**, and beyond to Goat Haunt (15 km in total), where you can catch a boat back. This is only really recommended as a spring or autumn hike, as it's usually snow-free from April to October.

From the Akamina Parkway

▲▲ **Lineham Ridge/Rowe Lakes** ⓘ *17-20 km return, 920-1,060 m elevation gain. Trailhead: Km 10.5 on the parkway.* This trail follows a creek up gentle slopes with valley views and through mature forest before cutting up bare, rocky slopes to the ridge. The pretty Row Lakes are a worthwhile side-trip best saved for the return leg if time and energy allow, because the highlight is Lineham Ridge, which offers excellent views of many of the jagged peaks in Waterton and Glacier Parks.

▲▲ **Wall and Forum lakes/Akamina Ridge** ⓘ *10-20 km return, 915 m elevation gain. Trailhead: at Km 14.6 on the parkway.* There are three possible hikes in Akamina-Kishinena Provincial Park, adjacent to Waterton in British Columbia. Forum and Wall Lakes are distinct, easy hikes to pretty lakes at the base of sheer rock walls. Between the two is Akamina Ridge, the real prize for those not averse to a bit of scrambling, with great views into Waterton and Glacier Parks. The Forum-Ridge-Wall circuit is best done in this order. Be sure to get full details before attempting it, and be ready for strong winds on the ridge.

▲▲ **Carthew Summit** ⓘ *20 km one-way, 700 m elevation gain. Trailhead: at Km 15.7, the end of the road.* This is a one-way hike from Cameron Lake to Cameron Falls on the edge of Waterton Townsite, so is best done using a shuttle to the trailhead. The highlight is the view from Carthew Summit itself, with the steep peaks of Glacier National Park to the south and the curious sight of endless Alberta prairies stretching off to the northeast horizon. From here it's all downhill, in every respect.

Waterton Lakes National Park.

From Red Rock Parkway

▲ **Avion Ridge** ⓘ *22.9-km loop, 944 m elevation gain. Trailhead: canyon car park at road's end*. This long, high, narrow ridge has few truly inspiring viewpoints, but offers panoramas whose very size makes an impression. The loop is best done clockwise, past Snowshoe Campground, over the ridge and down past Goat Lake. Otherwise, take the worthwhile 7-km detour from Snowshoe to Twin Lakes, whose campground is much nicer.

Head-Smashed-In-Buffalo-Jump 🖥️✻ ▸▸ *p338-339.*

Native Americans had thousands of years to refine their techniques for the large-scale slaughter of bison, their ultimate method being the ruthlessly efficient 'buffalo jump'. Situated 18 km northwest of Fort Macleod on Highway 785, Head-Smashed-In-Buffalo-Jump was named a UNESCO World Heritage Site because it is one of the oldest and best preserved of its kind. Over 11 m of bone deposits at the base of the cliff bear witness to at least 5500 years of continual use.

A masterpiece of invention that blends into the sandstone cliff over which the herds were driven, the four-storey **Interpretive Centre** ⓘ *T1800-6611222, www.head-smashed-in.com, mid-May to mid-Sep 0900-1800, otherwise 1000-1700, $9, $5 child; no public transport, taxis from Fort Macleod cost about $25*, uses archaeological evidence and the verbal records of the local Blackfoot to explain the functioning and history of the jump.

The process of the buffalo hunt includes: pre-hunt ceremonies; the **Gathering Basin** – a 40 sq km grazing area of plentiful grass and water to attract the herds; the network of **Drive Lanes**, consisting of stone cairns that helped hunters to funnel the bison towards the cliff; the **Kill Site**, which is just north of the centre, with another visible 1 km north; and the **Processing Area**, where the meat was sliced into thin strips and hung on racks to dry, much of it pounded with grease, marrow and berries to make pemmican. Displays also cover the lifestyle of prehistoric Plains people, their techniques of food gathering, social life and ceremonies; and the geography, climate, flora and fauna of the northwest plains.

Trails at the lower and upper level allow you to explore the site and have a good look at the Drive Lanes and cliff. Tours are conducted by Blackfoot guides. In late July is the three-day Buffalo Days Pow Wow and Tipi Village, featuring native dancers from across North America.

⊜ Sleeping

Waterton Townsite *p335*

Accommodation in Waterton is expensive but embraces a few budget options. Call the Central Reservations Office for package deals, T1800-2152395.
AL Prince of Wales Hotel, T403-2363400, www.princeofwaleswaterton.com. A must for those who can afford it, this beautiful timber-frame building is brimming over with character and a sense of history, and the views are to die for. Ask for a lake view. There's also a dining room, tea room, lounge and gift shop.
A Kilmorey Lodge, Mountain View Rd, T403-8592334, www.kilmoreylodge.com. Old-fashioned but comfortable rooms with big windows in an attractive building. Common room and restaurant.
A-B Aspen Village Inn, Windflower Av, T403-8592255, www.aspenvillage inn.com. Small but decent motel-style rooms with balcony, or more attractive cottages, plus use of hot tub.
A-B Crandell Mountain Lodge, Mountain View Rd, T403-8592288, www.crandellmountainlodge.com. A beautiful old-fashioned country cottage with pleasant rooms, and some suites with kitchenette and fireplace.
A-B Northland Lodge, 408 Evergreen Av, T403-8592353, www.northlandlodge canada.com. 8 pretty and distinctive rooms in a country-style home, with a large living room and a stone fireplace.
C Bear Mountain Motel, 208 Mount View Rd, T403-8592366, www.bearmountain motel.com. Plain rooms with 1-3 beds.
D HI Waterton Alpine Centre, 101 Clematis Av, T403-8592150, www.hi hostels.ca. 21 beds in dorms or private rooms. Shared baths, kitchen and lounge.

Camping

Crandell Mountain Campground, 8 km west on Red Rock Canyon Rd. The nearest to town. 129 sites, fire pits and a kitchen.

Waterton Townsite Campground. An ugly parking lot with 238 sites.
Waterton Springs KOA, 3 km north of gate on Hwy 6, T403-8592247. There are several walk-in sites and some private campgrounds north on Hwy 6 and east on Hwy 5. This one has the best facilities, with 190 sites, showers, laundry and a swimming pool.

Head-Smashed-In-Buffalo-Jump *p337*

A Head-Smashed-In-Buffalo-Jump, T403- 5532731, www.head-smashed-in.com. May-Aug. Their 'rustic tipi camping package' involves staying in a rather luxurious tipi, and includes entrance to the site. For $285 per family, their tipi package includes accommodation, food, activities, guides tours and entrance.

Camping

Buffalo Plains RV Park and Campground, 3 km east of town, T403-5532592, www.buffaloplains.com. 30 pleasant sites with views and laundry but no showers.

⊙ Eating

Waterton Townsite *p335*

Lamp Post, in the Kilmorey Lodge (see Sleeping), T403-8592342. The better choices for food in Waterton are all hotel dining rooms. This one exudes historic charm and has the best menu, which includes some exotic options like ostrich, caribou and elk, and is also the best bet for breakfast.
Royal Stewart Dining Room, in the Prince of Wales (see Sleeping). European and Canadian dishes, decent enough but nothing exceptional. The surroundings and views are superb, however.
Glacier Café, Bayshore Inn (see Sleeping). Good for breakfast, pizza and pasta.
Pizza of Waterton, Fountain Av. The most appealing choice for good value food in attractive surroundings, including an outdoor patio. The pizzas are good, and there's a decent selection of beers.

🍷 Bars and clubs

Waterton Townsite *p335*
Gazebo Café, next to **Kilmorey Lodge**. An outdoor café with some food, a good wine list and cocktails.
Ram's Head Lounge, Kilmorey Lodge. The nicest spot for a quiet drink.
Windsor Lounge, Prince of Wales Hotel. Soak up the atmosphere of the house on the hill by sipping a beer or glass of wine in the sophisticated lounge.

🎭 Entertainment

Waterton Townsite *p335*
Gust Gallery, 112A Waterton Av, T403-8592535. Representing 3 local artists.

🎉 Festivals and events

Waterton Townsite *p335*
Jun The **Waterton Wild Flower-Fest**, www.watertonwildflowers.com. 10 days of events and guided excursions to see photograph, paint and behold the park's local plants.

Head-Smashed-In-Buffalo-Jump *p337*
Jul In late Jul, the 3-day **Buffalo Days Pow Wow and Tipi Village**, features native dancers from across North America.

🛍 Shopping

Waterton Townsite *p335*
Waterton Outdoor Adventures, T403-8592378, Tamarack Village Sq. Outdoor clothing and supplies, plus trail maps.
Trail of the Great Bear, 114 Waterton Av, T403-8592663. Books, maps, information.

🚶 Activities and tours

Waterton Townsite *p335*
Tour operators
Alpine Stables, T403-8592462, www.alpine stables.com. Horse riding and pack trips.

Cameron Lake Boat Rentals, Cameron Lake, 17 km west. Canoes and row boats.
Jammer Tours, T403-8592231. Transport into Glacier Park in a touring bus.
Kimball River Sports, just south of Cardston, T1800-9366474, www.raft alberta.ca. Whitewater rafting, canoeing, kayaking and fishing tours.
Mountain Meadow Trail Rides, Mountain View, halfway to Cardston, T403-6532413, www.mountainmead owtrailrides.com. Horseback adventures and overnight pack trips.
Pat's, Mountview Rd, T403-8592266. Bike and scooter rentals, sales and service.
Trail of the Great Bear, 114 Waterton Av, T403-8592663, www.trailofthegreat bear.com. Arranges hiking trips and will hook you up with other tour companies.
Waterton Lakes Golf Course, T403-8592114, www.watertonpark.com. Surely one of the most scenic in the country.
Waterton Outdoor Adventures, Tamarack Village Sq, T403-8592378, www.watertonvisitorservices.com. Guided hikes. Also runs the hiker shuttle service to most of the trailheads.
Waterton Shoreline Cruises, T403-8592362, www.watertoncruise.com. Interpretive tours of the lake. Also runs the all-important Crypt Lake Water Shuttle Service ($14 round trip).
White Mountain Adventures, T1800-4080005, www.whitemountainadven tures.com. Half- or full-day guided hikes, sightseeing tours, and wildlife watching.

ℹ️ Directory

Waterton Townsite *p335*
Banks Exchange and ATM in Tamarack Village Sq. ATM in **Rocky Mountain Food** on Windflower Av. **Canada Post** Corner Fountain Av/Windflower Av. **Laundry** 301 Windflower Av. **Medical services** Ambulance: T403-8592636. Closest hospitals are in Cardston, T403-6534931, and Pincher Creek, T403-6273333. **Police** T403-8592244.

The Yukon

Dempster Highway

ALASKA
USA

ALBERTA
Calgary

Rocky Mountains

Prince Rupert

Vancouver
USA

ALASKA
USA

NORTHWEST
TERRITORIES
Dawson City
Whitehorse
YUKON
BRITISH
COLUMBIA
Prince George

N

50 km
50 miles

Beaufort Sea

Komakuk Beach
Herschel Is
Herschel

Ivvavik
National Park

Shingle Point
Richard Is
Tununuk

Tuktoyaktuk
Kittigazuit

Mackenzie
Delta
Aklavik
Inuvik

British Mountains

Old Crow Flats

Old Crow

Whitefish
Lake

Crow

Eagle

Coal

Richardson Mountains

Fort
McPherson

Arctic Red River

Mackenzie

Dempster Highway

Eagle
Plains

Eagle Plains

Caribou

Peel

Wind

Bonnet Plume

Noisy

Snake

NORTHWEST
TERRITORIES

Corcoral Range

Nor

Clinton Creek
(abandoned)

Ogilvie Mountains

5

Peel Wilderness

Mackenzie Mountains

Backbone Range

Heritage Trail

Top of the World Highway

9
Sixty Mile
Dawson City
Rock Creek

4

Bear Creek

Granville
(abandoned)

Stewart River
(abandoned)

McQuesten
(abandoned)

White

Yukon

Stewart
Crossing

Fort Selkirk

McQuesten
Lake
Elsa
Keno
Silver
Trail
Mayo
Mayo
Lake

Selwyn Mountains

Hess
Mountains

Tok

Tetlin Junction

Beaver Creek

Snag

Koidern

Dawson Range

Pelly
Crossing

Minto

YUKON

Pelly

Burwash
Landing

Kluane
National Park

Mt Logan
(5959m)

St Elias Mountains

Sheep Mountain

Aishihik

Carmacks

Glenlyon Pk

Little Salmon
Lake

Little Salmon

Mt Sheldon

Ross

Faro

Ross River

Robert
Campbell
Highway

4

p344

p364

Kluane
Mountains

Yukon Plateau

Destruction
Bay
Aishihik
Lake

Haines
Junction

Champagne

Canyon
(abandoned)

Klondike Highway

Big Salmon

Canol Rd

Pelly
Mountains

McPherson
Lake

South
Nahanni

Alsek

Dezadeash

Klukshu

Kusawa
Lake

Robinson

Takhini
Hot Springs

Livingston
(abandoned)

2

Whitehorse

6

Finlayson
Highway

Nat
Natio

Tatshenshini-Alsek
Wilderness Park

3

Haines
Highway

Tatshenshini River

Carcross
Watson

Klukwan

Bennett

Fraser

Skagway

Haines

p357

Klondike Highway

Tagish

Jake's
Corner

Johnson's
Crossing

Teslin

Liard

Tutchitua

Atlin
Lake

1

Atlin

Surprise

Teslin
Lake

Alaska
Highway

Rancheria

Cassiar Mountains

Upper
Liard
Watson Lake

ALASKA
USA

Inklin

Nakina

Tulsequah

Nahilin

Cassiar
(abandoned)

Good Hope
Lake

Lower Post

Fireside

Smith River

Coal River

Don't miss...

★ Atlin, BC ▶▶ p349.

★ Hiking in Kluane National Park ▶▶ p358.

★ Rafting the Tatshenshini ▶▶ p359.

★ Dawson City ▶▶ p365.

★ Dempster Highway ▶▶ p371.

Hyland Post

Introduction

The Yukon's landscapes are wide, magnificent and utterly unspoilt. Canada's highest mountains, most extensive non-polar ice fields and greatest concentration of grizzly bears are protected by Kluane National Park, famed for wonderful, uncrowded hiking trails and sensational whitewater rafting. The territory, whose name means 'great river' in the native Loucheux language, is criss-crossed with rivers made for canoeing, while numerous circuits on backcountry roads lead through pristine wilderness to sleepy villages like the unfeasibly picturesque Atlin. The Dempster Highway, Canada's ultimate frontier road, passes desolate mountain ranges on its way to the frozen north. The laid-back capital, Whitehorse, is the place to plan excursions and relax afterwards.

The greatest Gold Rush of all time led thousands of treasure seekers to the goldfields of the Klondike. You can retrace their steps by hiking the Chilkoot Pass, panning for gold and visiting the renovated but still-living Wild West town of Dawson City, where clapboard houses, boardwalks and saloons line the dirt streets. Thriving First Nations culture and extensive wildlife are two more trump cards, but what keeps visitors coming back is the character and overwhelming friendliness of the Yukon people.

Ratings
Culture
★★★
Landscape
★★★★
Wildlife
★★★★
Activities
★★★
Relaxation
★★★★
Costs
$$

Whitehorse and the south

Although it's the provincial capital, Whitehorse is a very small, friendly town unlikely to evoke any strong reactions. Its riverside location is pleasant enough, but there's nothing like the atmosphere and excitement of Dawson City to the north. It's the best place to organize excursions and pick up supplies, however, and offers a welcome dose of civilization after time in the bush. The canoe trip from here to Dawson City is the most popular in the Yukon and suitable for all levels. Most of Whitehorse's sights are inspired by its river and history, and there's a lot of very good art, much of it by local First Nations. On the way up from BC, Teslin is worth a stop and Carcross gives access to the famous Chilkat Trail hike. The ultimate diversion, however, is south to Atlin, BC, possibly the most beautifully located town in Western Canada.

⊘ **Getting there** Car, bus, plane.
⊖ **Getting around** Car.
⊖ **Time required** 2-4 days
⋙ **Weather** Unpredictable.
⊜ **Sleeping** Reasonable range.
⦿ **Eating** A few nice options.
▲ **Activities and tours** Canoe trips, skiing, hiking.
★ **Don't miss...** The arty, frontier-style village of Atlin ⤷ p349.

Ins and outs

Getting there and around

Most visitors to the Yukon have their own vehicles, as public transport is almost non-existent. Buses follow the Alaska Highway (Highway 1) as far as Whitehorse but distances are vast and it is cheaper and quicker to fly. **Whitehorse Airport** (YXY), www.gov. yk.ca/yxy, is between Downtown and the Alaska Highway; there are regular buses to Downtown. **Air North**, T867-6682228, flies regularly from Vancouver, Calgary and Edmonton; fares start at $195 one-way. The **Greyhound** station is on 2nd Avenue, T867-6672223, www.greyhound.ca, a short walk north of Downtown, with daily buses from Dawson Creek via Watson Lake. Whitehorse is small enough to explore on foot. Most local buses leave from the corner of Ogilvie and 3rd avenues, running through town on 4th and 2nd avenues. Drivers can check road conditions at T1877-4567623, www.gov.yk.ca/roadreport. ⊖ ⤷ p356.

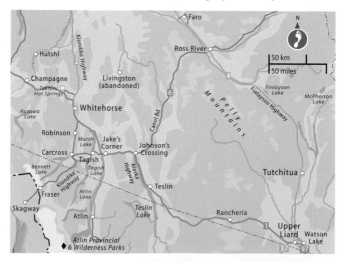

Background

White horses and wild rapids

The first Hudson Bay traders arrived in the area in 1843, followed 40 years later by men toting gold pans. After a lucky strike on Bonanza Creek sparked the Gold Rush of 1898, a stampede of hopefuls travelled upriver in makeshift boats and, for the next 50 years, until the building of the Alaska Highway in 1942 and the Klondike Highway in the 1950s, the Yukon River remained the foremost means of transportation in the province.

The city of Whitehorse was named after a set of fierce rapids, whose thrashing waters resembled the manes of galloping horses. This treacherous stretch of river, which claimed the lives of many men and vessels, began 7 km above today's city at Miles Canyon. Those wary of facing the rapids hauled their belongings around the obstruction on horse-drawn tramways. Makeshift tent settlements quickly developed at either end of the rapids, the one above was named Canyon City, the one below named Whitehorse.

Best time to visit

Being so far north, temperatures and daylight hours vary considerably throughout the year. In January the average temperature is -19° C with six hours of daylight; in July it's 19° C with 19 hours of daylight. Winter is the best time to experience the northern lights and the incredible resilience and friendliness of the Yukon people, but June is the best month for festivals.

Tourist information

The **Visitor Information Centre** ① *2nd Av and Hanson, T867-6673084, www.visitwhitehorse.com, www.touryukon.com, May-Sep 0800-2000*, is very helpful and professional, with information on the whole province. Drivers should ask for a three-day complimentary parking pass. Be sure to pick up the useful *Yukon Vacation Planner*. **Yukon First Nations Tourism Association** ① *1109 1st Av, T867-6677698, www.yfnta.org*, publishes its own impressive brochure.

Whitehorse ⬤🚹🛈🍴✳️🌙⛰️🏨🛏️ ⇥ *pp351-356.*

Yukon River

Approaching Whitehorse from the south, 3 km before town, Miles Canyon Road leads down to the site of the rapids, which were removed by the damming of the Yukon River in 1958. The diversion is still worthwhile, as **Miles Canyon** is now lined with fantastic basalt walls. Across the footbridge are a number of trails that are popular mountain biking and skiing.

Entering town on Robert Service Way, you can't miss the **SS Klondike** ① *T867- 6674511, May-Sep 0900-1900, tours every half hour, $5*, the largest of the sternwheelers that played a vital role in the Yukon's early life. These shallow-bottomed vessels proved invaluable for transporting men, supplies and gold over the treacherous rock-strewn waters. As many as 250 such boats once plied the Yukon River; local forests were cut down to provide fuel.

Across the river from here, Lewes Boulevard leads to Nisutlin Drive and access to the dam. About 1 km below this is the 'intake', a tiny remainder of whitewater, popular with kayakers and canoeists. **Whitehorse Fishway** ① *95 Nisutlin Dr, T867-6335965, Jun-early Sep, by donation*, is the longest wooden fish ladder in the world. You can tour the fishway and watch salmon through underwater viewing windows.

Whitehorse

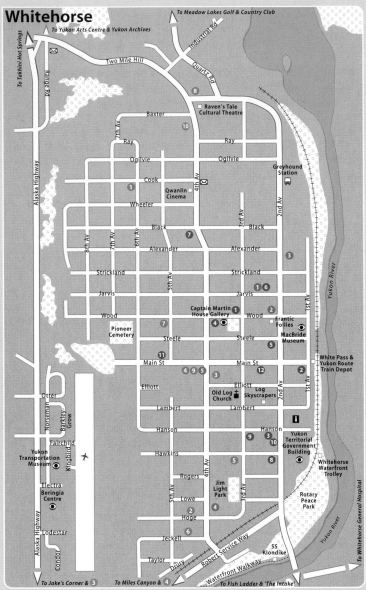

300 metres
300 yards

Sleeping
Beez Kneez Hostel **2**
Hawkins House **5**
Historical House **7**
Hostel Hide On Jeckell **6**
Midnight Sun B&B **1**
Town & Mountain **9**
Yukon Inn **10**

Camping
MacKenzie's RV Park **3**
Robert Service **4**

Eating
Blackstone Café **1**
Cathy & Diana's **12**
Cellar Steakhouse & Winebar **2**
Giorgio's Cuccina **6**
Java Connection **4**
Klondike Rib & Salmon BBQ **5**
Midnight Sun Coffee Roasters **7**
North Dragon **8**
Sam & Andy's **11**
Sanchez Mexican Deli **9**
Talisman Café **10**
The Deli **3**

Bars & clubs
2-0-2 Motor Inn **1**
Backwater Lounge **2**
Lizards Lounge **5**
Roadhouse Inn Saloon **3**
Yukon Mining Co **4**

Downtown

The sights of Downtown Whitehorse are mostly historical. **MacBride Museum** ① *1124 1st Av, T867-6672709, www.macbridemuseum.com, summer daily 0900-1800, winter Tue-Sat 1200-1700, $6, $3.50 child*, housed in a group of log cabins, reveals the stories of the Yukon's First Nations, the Gold Rush, the North West Mounted Police and early pioneers. Highlights include a replica of a 910 cm Tlingit canoe and a carving shed where demonstrations are given. The **Yukon Archives** ① *500 College Dr, T867-6675321*, contain a wealth of material relating to Yukon's First Nations history and culture, including films, photos and interviews with elders. You can even do genealogy research to find out if any of your relatives took part in the Gold Rush.

Many Klondike enthusiasts travel to Skagway (see p350) on the **White Pass and Yukon Route Train** ① *T867-6335710, www.whitepassrailroad.com, US$95 one-way*. Tickets are available from the old depot on the waterfront at the bottom of Main Street. For a cheaper step back in time, the **Whitehorse Waterfront Trolley** runs along the riverfront from behind the Visitor Centre ($3). One of the town's oldest buildings is the **Old Log Church** ① *303 Elliott St, T867-6682555, Jun-Sep 0900-1800, $2.50*, constructed in 1900. It contains Inuvialuits artefacts and photos documenting the impact of the white man's arrival on the native people.

Whitehorse is a good place for art-lovers. The best venue is the **Yukon Arts Centre and Gallery** ① *Yukon college, north of town on Range Rd, www.yukonartscentre.org, Tue-Fri 1200-1800, Sat-Sun 1200-1700, by donation*, which hosts works by national and international artists. The **Yukon Territorial Government Building**, opposite the Visitor Centre, has a rotating exhibit from the permanent Yukon art collection and some nice tapestries and murals. **Captain Martin House Gallery** ① *305 Wood St, T867-6674080*, is home of the Yukon Art Society, and represents 150 provincial artists. A free *Art Walk* brochure is available from the Visitor Centre.

On the Alaska Highway

There are a couple of sights near the airport on the Alaska Highway. During the last ice age, when glaciation caused sea levels to drop dramatically, Siberia was joined to Alaska by a great corridor of land that today is again submerged beneath the Bering Sea. This land bridge bcame a last refuge for thousands of species of plant and animal. Among these were the giant woolly mammoth, scimitar cat and, of course, man. The Yukon **Beringia Interpretive Centre** ① *T867-6678855, www.beringia.com, summer 0830-1900 daily, winter Sun only 1300-1700, $6, $4 child*, uses dioramas, murals and life-sized reproductions of long-extinct wildlife to paint a picture of that frozen land and the people who managed to survive on it.

Just up the road, beside the airport, the **Yukon Transportation Museum** ① *T867-6684792, May-Sep 1000-1800, tours 1130 and 1600, $4.25, $2 child, combo pass with Beringia Centre $9*, documents provincial methods of movement, from moose-skin boats to modern aircraft. Enthusiasts could spend all day watching videos about the White Pass Railway, Alaska Highway, Sternwheelers and the Yukon Dog Sled Race. For most, the highlight is a scale model of the White Pass and Yukon Railway.

Takhini Hot Springs

About 10 km north of Whitehorse, the highway veers west towards Haines Junction and Kluane National Park, while the Klondike Highway continues north to Dawson City. Almost 10 km beyond the junction, a road heads 10 km west to **Takhini Hot Springs** ① *T867-6332706, www.takhinihotsprings.yk.ca, summer 0800-2200, winter 1000-2200, $7, $5.25 child*. The waters of this commercial operation are odourless and range from 47° C at one end to 30° C at the other. There's a campground, restaurant and trail rides. Two kilometres before the Hot Springs is **Yukon Wildlife Preserve** ① *T867-6332922, www.yukonwildlife.ca, May-Sep, $20, $10 child, phone ahead to book tour*, where one-hour guided tours by vehicle offer the chance to observe caribou, moose, elk, musk ox, mountain goats and dall sheep in their natural habitat.

Watson Lake to Whitehorse ⊜🚲❄️🏕️⊝ ➤➤ *pp351-356.*

Watson Lake

The Cassiar Highway (Highway 37) joints the Alaska Highway 22 km west of Watson Lake, where there is a useful gas station. This is a relatively dull little town that fails to justify the 44-km diversion, unless you can make it in mid-July for the Watson Lake Rodeo. One reason to visit, however, is the extremely useful **Visitor Information Centre** ① *T867-5367469, www.yukon info.com/watson, May-Sep 0800-2000*, which can provide guides and maps. There are also displays and a slideshow about the Yukon and the construction of the Alaska Highway.

Before 30,000 US Army personnel arrived in 1942 to work on the highway, Watson Lake was just a tiny airport, part of the Northwest Staging Route Programme that tried to create a Great Circle Route connecting Alaska, Siberia and China. One homesick soldier put up a sign showing the distance and direction to his home town and, unwittingly, began a collection that now includes 53,000 such signs. This 'world famous' **Sign Post Forest**, next to the Information Centre, is the town's number one attraction. Across the highway is the only other attraction, the **Northern Lights Space and Science Centre** ① *T867-5367827, www.northernlightscentre.ca, $10, $6 child*, which shows 50-minute films that present the myths and reality of the aurora borealis, and animal photos set to music.

Teslin

After a brief, barely noticeable foray back into BC, the Alaska Highway joins the attractive shores of **Teslin Lake**, at the town of the same name. Teslin is home to a thriving community of native Tlingit, originally of coastal origin, who moved permanently to their inland summer home in the early 1900s, prompted by the quest for furs. The arts and crafts of their West Coast heritage migrated with them and provide a couple of good reasons to stop.

The largest collection of artefacts is found at the small but splendid **George Johnston Museum** ① *off the Highway north side of town, T867-3902550, www.gjmuseum.yk.net, May-Sep 0900-1800, $5, $2.50 child*. This successful Tlingit trapper and entrepreneur opened the first aboriginal-owned store in town and bought its first car – a 1928 Chevrolet – exhibited in the museum. Of far greater interest is Johnston's collection of black and white prints that candidly document 50 years of Teslin's history.

The best place to witness the work of talented local mask and totem carvers is further north on the highway at the striking **Teslin Tlingit Heritage Centre** ① *T866-8546438, May-Sep 0900-2100, $5*. Interpretive, audiovisual and art displays introduce the history and culture of the Tlinget, and you can watch them at work in an outdoor carving shed.

Teslin Lake is noted for its fishing. Chinook salmon run late July to mid-August while spring and autumn are best for whitefish, trout, northern pike, Arctic grayling and inconnu. The **Nisutlin Delta National Wildlife Area** at the north end of the lake is a major waterfowl staging post, visited in autumn by thousands of ducks, swans and geese, and predators like peregrine falcon, fox, coyote and wolf. Canoeing is also popular. 🏕️ ➤➤ *p355.*

Johnson's Crossing and Canol Road

As well as a popular put-in spot for canoeing the Teslin River to access the Yukon, Johnson's Crossing is the junction with the **Canol Road** (Highway 6). The controversial Canol (Canadian Oil) Pipeline was built by the US in 1942 to pump oil from Norman Wells NWT to a refinery in Whitehorse. It was dismantled after just one year of use. Today its southern section provides a chance to sample some of the Yukon's remote backcountry. The surface can be pretty rough, but the effort is well rewarded by the last stunning stretch before **Ross River**, when the road skirts close to picturesque Pass Peak, then winds its way through the Lapie River Canyon. On

A ramshackle yet charming house in the friendly village of Atlin.

the way are three small campgrounds. From Ross River, Highway 4 heads northwest through Faro to connect with the Klondike Highway near **Carmacks**, a very worthwhile alternative route to or from Dawson City, bypassing Whitehorse. The brand new **Dena Cho Trail**, T867-9692278, is an 80-km hike from Ross River to Faro, with campsites and cabins along the way.

Jake's Corner and around

There is little more of note on the highway to Whitehorse, but at **Jake's Corner** two possible diversions present themselves. Easily the more worthwhile follows Highway 7 south for 95 km to Atlin, BC (see below). The other provides a loop on Highways 8 and 2, which takes in **Carcross**, a dull town but the gateway to the Chilkoot Trail and Skagway, Alaska (see p350). Beyond Jake's Corner, the northern end of **Marsh Lake**, known as **McClintock Bay**, is a critical habitat for migrating waterfowl in April and May. The arrival of thousands of Tundra and Trumpeter swans is heralded annually by the **Celebration of Swans Festival**. There is a viewing deck, the **Swan Haven Interpretive Centre**, and a campground.

Atlin, BC

Highway 7 to Atlin is a rough dirt road that hugs the shore of BC's largest natural lake, also the headwater of the Yukon River. A few campgrounds line the road and Km 6 is the trailhead for the **Mount White Trail**, one of the Yukon's most rewarding day hikes. The path starts on the left at the back of a gravel pit and climbs to a plateau that offers fabulous views.

Atlin itself is a ramshackle little frontier-style village of funky houses, full of friendly, arty and eccentric characters. **Atlin Visitors Association** ⓘ *3rd St, T867-6517522, www.atlin.net*, is in the historical museum. Almost devoid of 'sights' and entertainment, Atlin enjoys a setting of unparalleled magnificence, in an unimaginably vast and timeless wilderness landscape. Rearing up behind broad Atlin Lake is a string of giant glaciated mountains belonging to the Coast Range. The one closest to town is actually on enormous **Teresa Island**, a bear sanctuary. Beyond, and accessible only by boat, are **Atlin Provincial** and **Wilderness** parks. A third of the latter is covered in glaciers, including the massive **Llewellen Glacier**, best seen from the top of **Monarch Mountain**. This stiff 12-km return hike starts 5 km down Warm Bay Road, a rough gravel road which follows the lake to the south, giving access to several campgrounds, beaches and, at Km 24, the **Warm Springs**, a pretty clear pool surrounded by watercress.

The Yukon Railway as it heads through White Pass.

Carcross and around

Atlin is part of a region touted as the **Southern Lakes**, www.southernlakesyukon.com, which contains more than 600 linear kilometres of thin lakes within an area of some 100 sq km. Canoeing, boating and fishing are major local activities, and the winds are often strong enough for windsurfing. A loop on Highways 8 and 2 from Jake's Corner leads to the heart of this area, adding just 38 km to the journey to Whitehorse. Despite a lack of real attractions, many visitors make the diversion thanks to the important role the area played in the Klondike Gold Rush. Skookum Jim Mason, who first sparked the stampede with his discovery of gold on what became known as Bonanza Creek, was a member of the Tagish First Nation, but there is little reason to stop in **Tagish**.

The hub of the region is **Carcross**, whose name was shortened from the more evocative Caribou Crossing. It sits at the north end of Bennett Lake, which has some large sandy beaches and is a favourite with windsurfers. Prospectors who made it over the Chilkoot Pass travelled up the lake to here. The town has clearly remained virtually unchanged since those heady days, and is of interest mainly for its many historical buildings and general run-down frontier town atmosphere. Visitors can also retrace the steps of the many hopefuls on the **Chilkoot Trail**. The **Visitor Centre** ⓘ *T867-8214431, May-Sep 0800-2000*, is in the restored train station.

The train played its own part in transporting prospectors, a role celebrated today by the **White Pass and Yukon Railway** ⓘ *T907-9832217, www.whitepassrailroad.com, US$95 if bought in advance*, which carries tourists along the historic route to **Skagway**, a six-hour train ride. Non-Americans must clear customs in advance, or get off at Fraser. Buses also continue to Skagway, from where there is a scenic trip to Kluane Country via Haines, Alaska (see p361).

Appropriately known as the **Klondike Highway**, Highway 2 follows the Gold Rush Trail north from Carcross through Whitehorse to Dawson City. The southern leg soon passes **Carcross Desert**, really a dried out lake bottom, very small and not especially impressive. A little further are the pretty **Emerald** and **Spirit** lakes, where there is a very primitive private campsite. Annie Lake Road branches west at the Robinson Roadhouse historic site and winds its way up the scenic Wheaton River Valley. There are lots of opportunities for hiking and mountain biking along here, such as the **Red Ridge** and **Two Horse Creek** trails, and experienced paddlers can canoe down the Wheaton or Watson Rivers to Bennett Lake.

◉ Sleeping

The *Yukon Vacation Planner* contains good listings, pick up a copy at an visitor centre, see also www.yukonbandb.com.

Whitehorse *p345, map p346*
Whitehorse has 2 excellent hostels, both 15 mins' walk from the bus station, see below.

B Fox Creek Wilderness B&B, 50 km north on Hwy 2, T867-3333120, www.foxcreekwild.com. If you're heading north, this is a beautiful place to stop. A big gorgeous log house on a hill with views of Lake Laberge and surrounding mountains, and a panorama of the Northern Lights. The rooms are bright, very stylish and comfortable, plus there's a living room, sundeck and garden.

B Hawkins House, 303 Hawkins St, T867-6687638, www.hawkinshouse.yk.ca. 5 beautifully decorated rooms in a lovely Victorian home with hardwood floors, stained-glass windows and balconies.

B Midnight Sun B&B, 6188 6th Av, T867-6672255, www.midnightsunbb.com. 4 nice theme rooms in a large, central house with a big common room, very hospitable hosts, and great breakfasts.

C Historical House, 5128 5th Av, T867-6683907, www.yukongold.com. 2 rooms and a suite in a wooden home with lots of character, 2 blocks from centre. Kitchen available and a stocked fridge to make your own breakfast.

C Town and Mountain Hotel, 401 Main St, T867-6687644, www.townmountain.com. A central hotel with comfortable, spacious rooms and a bright, Mediterranean look. Restaurant and pub downstairs.

C Yukon Inn, 4220 4th Av, T867-6672527, www.yukoninn.com. Fairly plain but decent rooms in a central but quiet hotel.

E Beez Kneez Hostel, 408 Hoge St, T867-4562333, www.bzkneez.com. Relaxed, homey atmosphere, with a kitchen, common room, patio, garden, laundry, free internet and bikes.

E Hostel Hide On Jeckell, 410 Jeckell, T867-6334933, www.hide-on-jeckell.com. Very well organized. Each of the 4 dorms and 2 private rooms represents a different continent. Plenty of books and a library/ book swap. There's a nice kitchen, games in the living room, free internet, coffee and bike use, lockable drawers, a garden, small deck and BBQ.

Camping
Robert Service Campground, 2 mins' drive east, or 20 mins' walk on Robert Service Way, T867-6672846. Tents only, with a nice atmosphere, showers, specialty coffees and baked goods.

MacKenzie's RV Park, 18 Azure Rd, T867-6332337. There are plenty of grim RV parks on the highway south of town, all resembling gravel parking lots. This is the best of a bad bunch.

Watson Lake *p348*
All of the motels are on the highway.

C Belvedere Motor Hotel, T867-5367712, www.watsonlakehotels.com. Recently renovated rooms and the town's most appealing restaurant.

C Gateway Motor Inn, T867-5367744. Acceptable rooms, a pizza restaurant, and a bar that's full of Yukon character.

D Big Horn Hotel, T867-5362020. The best rooms in town at very reasonable rates.

D Cozy Nest Hideaway B&B, 1175 Campbell Hwy, T867-5362204, www.yukonalaska.com/cozynest. 2 rooms and a small cabin right on the lake, with a nice common room and a lovely stone terrace. Close to cross-country skiing.

Camping
Campground Services, just east of town, T867-5367448. Not great, but it has showers and laundry, and is much nicer than the RV parking lot in town.

Watson Lake Campground, just west of town, then 1.5 km on an access road. A nicer ground with 67 sites on the lake, including some pull-throughs.

Teslin *p348*

C Yukon Motel, on the highway, T867-3902575. Tidy rooms in a log building.

Camping
Teslin Lake Campground, 10 km north. 27 fairly nice sites on the lake.

Johnson's Crossing and Canol Road *p348*
AL-A Inn on the River, northeast of Johnson's Landing, T867-6605253, www.innriver.com. A stunning log building right on the lake and surrounded by trees. 4 very tasteful, luxurious jacuzzi suites, with balconies/decks facing the river, and 2 simpler cabin suites. Price includes breakfast and hire of bikes, canoes and kayaks. Delicious but expensive dinner is prepared for guests by arrangement.
D Johnson's Crossing Motel and Campground, just west of Teslin River Bridge and Canol Rd Junction, T867-3902607. Small but pleasant rooms, and campsites.

Camping
Squanga Campground, 22 km further north, with 20 sites.

Atlin *p349*
B Win's Place, T867-6517550. An entire cottage on the lake, charming and spacious. Lower rent for longer stays.
C Atlin Inn, Lake St, T867-6517546. The most likely place to have vacancies. Small but attractive and comfortable rooms, and some slightly cheaper but rather shabby cabins close to the water. Restaurant with burgers, steak, fish and great views, plus pub, and coffee shop.
C Brewery Bay Chalet, McBride Blvd, on the lake, T867-6510040, www.atlin.net. 8 nice 2-bedrooms suites with kitchenette.
C Quilts & Comforts B&B, Pillman Rd, T867-6510007. 3 very small and twee rooms, and a beautiful perennial garden with deck and views. Good breakfast.

D Glacier View Cabins, 12 km on Warm Bay Rd, T867-6517691. 2 simple but lovely log cabins with bedroom, living room/kitchen and decks with the best views of Llewellyn Glacier.

Camping
There are a couple of campgrounds north of town, but the best bet is along Warm Bay Rd to the south.
Pine Creek, at 5 km. Handy, but not as nice as the forestry sites further on, like **Como Lake**, **Surprise Lake** and **Warm Bay**. There's a particularly nice spot right on the lake at Km 24.

● Eating

Whitehorse *p345, map p346*
♥♥♥ **Cellar Steakhouse & Wine Bar**, 101 Main St, T867-6672572, www.edge waterhotel.yk.ca. The town's finest restaurant, serving tapas, as well as steak and seafood dishes. Low lighting, soft music and cocktails make for a romantic atmosphere.
♥♥ **Giorgio's Cuccina**, 206 Jarvis St, T867-6684050. One of the most popular choices with locals, with a menu of comfort food including pastas, pizza, and fish dishes. The decor has an exuberant Classical Rome theme.
♥♥ **Klondike Rib and Salmon BBQ**, 2nd Av/Steele St, T867-6677554. Huge portions of halibut and chips or ribs, with no pretensions. The best bet for a true taste of the Yukon.
♥♥ **North Dragon Restaurant**, 2058 2nd Av. Best of the many Chinese restaurants.
♥♥ **Sam & Andy's**, 506 Main St, T867-6686994. Mexican food, best enjoyed on the outdoor patio.
♥♥ **Sanchez Mexican Deli**, 211 Hanson St, T867-6685858. Authentic Mexican dishes, such as *pollo con mole*, in a nice, colourful setting.
♥♥ **Talisman Café**, 2112 2nd Av. Large portions of international vegetarian food.
♥ **Blackstone Café**, 302 Wood St. Good coffee and breakfast; a nice place to relax.

Y Cathy and Diana's, 211 Main St. Asian foods for lunch, including sushi, mango avocado salad and dim sum.
Y The Deli, 203 Hanson St. Great sandwiches with sausages made from buffalo, caribou, reindeer, etc.
Y Midnight Sun Coffee Roasters, 4168 4th Av/Black St. A local institution.

Watson Lake *p348*
YY Belvedere Motor Hotel, T867-5367712. The best of the motel restaurants.
YY Wolf It Down Restaurant, 26 km west. Good coffee, fresh baking, buffalo steak.

Teslin *p348*
YY Mukluk Annie's, 13 km north of town, T867-3902600. Salmon bake, made with delicious wild sockeye, is their speciality, and is served with all-you-can-eat salad and tasty baked beans, a real bargain at the price. What's more, it comes with a free houseboat cruise on Teslin Lake at 2000. All-you-can-eat breakfast until 1100. Free overnight parking for anyone, or very primitive cabins to rent. Showers and laundry available.

Jake's Corner and around *p349*
Y Jake's Corner Bakery. Famous for its cinnamon buns, but also selling fast food like chicken and ribs by the kg.

Atlin *p349*
When in Atlin, be sure to try the local smoked salmon.
YY Lakeshore Restaurant in the Atlin Inn, Lake St, T867-6517546. The best bet for food, with great views.
YY Pine Tree Café, Discovery Av. Home cooking in a diner-style clapboard house.
Y Kershaws Coffee and Espresso Bar, Pearl Av/1st St. Good coffee, baked goodies and sandwiches.

🜚 Bars and clubs

Whitehorse *p345, map p346*
Every hotel in Downtown Whitehorse has its own bar, but many are sleazy or sterile.

202 Motor Inn, 206 Jarvis St. Live country music and line dancing on weekends.
Backwater Lounge, 102 Wood St. A decent, low-key place, with Yukon beer on tap and regular live music.
Lizards Lounge, 401 Main St. A trendy lounge scene with live music and dancing.
Roadhouse Inn Saloon, 2nd Av/ Strickland. The locals' pub, full of character and characters, tapping their toes to the country and western music.
Yukon Mining Co, High Country Inn, 4051 4th Av. The nicest spot for a drink and very popular. Excellent, locally made Yukon Brewing Co beers on tap. Heated patio seating and pricey pub-style food.

🜚 Entertainment

Whitehorse *p345, map p346*
The daily *Whitehorse Star* has listings.
Frantic Follies, Westmark Whitehorse Hotel, 27 2nd Av, www.franticfollies.com. One of Whitehorse's highlights is this old-time musical revue, a tribute to the gold-rush era that's aimed squarely at tourists, but is well-executed and good fun. Nightly May-Sep. $20, $10 child.
Yukon Arts Centre, College Dr, www.yukonartscentre.org. The Yukon's main arts and entertainment facility has a large art gallery with changing exhibits, a sculpture garden and a theatre that plays host to major visiting acts of all kinds.

🜚 Festivals and events

Whitehorse *p345, map p346*
Many of Whitehorse's festivals take place in Rotary Park on the Yukon River.
Feb The Frostbite Music Festival, T867-6684921, www.frostbitefest.ca, features 3 nights of cold entertainment, music and dance. **Yukon Quest International Sled Dog Race**, T867-6687411, www.yukonquest.com, is a 1600-km race along trap lines ending in Fairbanks, Alaska. Later that month is the **Sourdough Rendezvous Festival**, T867-3934467, www.yukonrendezvous.com.

Winter sports, games and entertainment: a huge party Yukon-style.

Apr Celebration of Swans, T867-6678291, marks the arrival of thousands of swans on the spring migration.

Jun-Aug Yukon International Storytelling Festival, T867-6337550, www.storytelling.yk.net. Storytelling is an important part of native culture and a favourite pastime of the Yukon people. This is probably the highlight of the year, closely followed by the **Gathering of Traditions Potlatch**, T867-6686647, a couple of weeks later, a 1-day celebration of aboriginal culture, featuring storytelling, games, songs, music, and arts and crafts. At the end of Jun is the **Yukon River Quest Canoe and Kayak Race**, T867- 3335628, www.yukonriverquest.com. From Whitehorse to Dawson City, this is the world's longest canoe and kayak race.

Aug The **Yukon River Bathtub Race**, T867-3934467, www.yukonrendez vous.com, is apparently the longest and toughest bathtub race in the world, 776 km from Whitehorse to Dawson.

Watson Lake *p348*
May Watson Lake Music Festival, T867-5362246. A small, grassroots community event held in late May, showcasing local talent.

Atlin *p349*
Jul Atlin Arts and Music Festival, T250-6512181, www.atlinfestival.ca. 3 days in early Jul, celebrating northern culture, with music and performing arts, visual and fine arts, crafts, workshops and children's activities.

○ Shopping

Whitehorse *p345, map p346*
3 Beans Natural Foods, 308 Wood St. Bulk foods, fresh juice, organic produce.
Canadian Tire, 4201 4th Av. Camping and sports gear.
Coast Mountain Sports, Main St. Camping and sports gear.

Mac's Fireweed Books, 203 Main St. Maps and travel books, with a large selection about the north, open till 2400 in summer.
Well-Read Books, 4194 4th Av. Used books.
Wharf On Fourth, 4040 4th Av. Fresh fish.

First Nations arts and crafts
Captain Martin House, 305 Wood St. Run by the Yukon Art Society, with local art/craft and a revolving exhibition space.
Indian Craft Shop Ltd, 504 Main St. The best of many retailers of aboriginal art.
Trappers Association, 4194 4th Av. Fur goods and moccasins.
Yukon Gallery, 2093 2nd Av.

▲ Activities and tours

Whitehorse *p345, map p346*
Tour operators
Many of the following companies offer a broad range of activities throughout the Yukon, and also rent out equipment.
Adventure-Tours Yukon Wild Ltd, T867-6685511, www.yukon-wild.com. Canoeing, hiking, horse riding, snow shoeing, dog sledding.
Cathers Wilderness Adventures, T867-3332186, www.cathersadventures.com. Dog-sledding trips.
Equinox Outdoor Learning Centre, T867-6336956, www.equinoxyukon.com. Rock climbing at Golden or Spirit Canyon.
Gray Line Yukon, T867-6683225. Bus tours of the city and surroundings.
Meadow Lakes Golf and Country Club, 121 Copper Rd, T867-6684653.
Muktuk Kennels, T867-3931799, www.muktuk.com. Year-round tours dog-sledding tours.
MV Schwatka River Cruise, T867-6685944. Boat tours to Miles Canyon, daily in summer at 1800. $25, $12.50 child.
Spirit of the North Guides, T867-4564339, www.spiritnorth.yk.ca. Guided sports fishing.
Tatshenshini Expediting, T867-6332742, www.tatshenshiniyukon.com. 1- or multi-day whitewater raft trips on the Tatshenshini or Tutshi rivers.

Up North Adventures, 103 Strickland St, T867-6677035, www.upnorth.yk.ca. Canoeing, kayaking, boating, biking and skiing.

Yukon Adventure Company, T1866-4177365, www.yukonadventure company.com. Dog sledding, aurora borealis chasing, snowshoeing, hiking in Kluane National Park and the Tombstone Mountains, canoeing, biking, fishing.

Yukon Brewing Company, 102 Copper Rd. Free tours and samples.

Yukon Historical and Museums Society, T867-6674704. Daily heritage walks of the town led by guides in period costumes, $2.

Yukon Horsepacking Adventures, T867-3931947, www.yukonhorsepacking.com. 1- or multi-day horse-riding trips around Fox Lake or Lake Laberge.

Yukon Wings Ltd, T867-6684716, www.yukon-wings.com. Flightseeing tours, charged per mile.

Canoeing and river trips

Canoeing is the major activity in the Yukon. On top of the 2-week trip to Dawson City, a number of short canoe excursions can be made to or from town. It is 40 km, or 1 day, to **Marsh Lake**, to the south, via **Miles Canyon**. Another 1- or 2-day trip could be made to **Lake Laberge** to the north. **Carmacks** is 320 km, or 5-6 days. Most of the canoe operators are around 2nd/1st Av and Strickland, by the river. Some rent by the trip and some by the day ($25-35). They sell maps and all gear/supplies, and offer a shuttle/pick-up service (about $1/km). Some can arrange air transport to remote put-ins. The following are recommended:

Kanoe People, T867-6684899, www.kanoepeople.com. Canoe/kayak rental. Guided trips on the Yukon and Tesla Rivers. Also rents out wilderness cabins.

Nahanni River Adventures, T867-6683180, www.nahanni.com. Trips on the Tatshenshini, Nahanni, Firth and more.

Nature Tours of Yukon, T867-6674868, www.naturetoursyukon.com. Canoe trips on the Liard, Yukon and McQuesten rivers.

Hiking

There are plenty of short hikes around Whitehorse. You can drive to **Grey Mountain** then follow a ridge trail with views of the city. Pick up a copy of the trail map from **Mac's Fireweed Bookstore** (see Shopping). For walks closer to town, the visitor centre has a pamphlet, *Whitehorse Trails*. A useful book is *Hikes and bikes: Whitehorse and area*.

Due North Journeys, T867-3932244, www.duenorthjourneys.com. Backpacking into Kluane, Tombstone and the Arctic.

Yukon Conservation Society, T867-6685678. Free guided 2- or 4-hr hikes.

Skiing

There are plenty of cross-country trails around, including **Miles Canyon** and **Chadburn Lake Recreation Area**.

Mount Sima, T867-6684557, www.mount sima.com, is a tiny ski hill nearby, with 1 lift, a tow rope, snowshoeing trails and rental.

Watson Lake *p348*

There are 80 km of hiking and skiing trails nearby. Ask at the information centre.

Ceasar Lake Outfitters, T867-5362174, www.ceaserlake.com. Wilderness trips with hunting, fishing or horse riding.

Greenways Greens, 10 km west. One of the Yukon's 5 golf courses,

---

Teslin *p359*

Canoeing takes place on **Nisutlin River** or the lake. A fairly easy 4- to 5-day whitewater canoe/kayak trip on the Lower Nisutlin River starts 69 km up the South Canol Rd and ends in Teslin.

Nisutlin Outfitting, T867-3902123, www.nisutlinoutfitting.bigstep.com. Canoe rentals ($25/day), guided tours and shuttle ($1/mile). Guided fishing tours, and boat rentals ($100/day).

Atlin *p349*

www.atlin.net is a useful resource.

Atlin's Happy Trails, T867-6512211, on the lake, McBride Blvd. Rents bikes, sells topographical maps, fishing tackle and basic camping gear, arranges all kinds of tour, and generally knows everything you might want to know about Atlin.

Atlin Lake Houseboat Tours, T867-6510030, www.atlinlakehouseboat tours.com. Tours from the central dock to Teresa Island, or you choose, $90/hr.

Atlin Quest, T867-6517659, www.atlin quest.com. Boat tours, glacier walks, guided hikes, canoeing and art retreats.

Klondike Heliskiing, T1800-8214429, www.atlinheliski.com. Heli-skiing in an untouched area of 5000 sq km.

Monkeyflower Adventures, T867-6512460. Nature walks and snow-shoeing tours. Good for families.

Sidka Tours, T867-6517691, www.sidka tours.com. Rents canoes ($25/day, $150/week) and kayaks ($35/day, $210/week). Also runs a shuttle to Whitehorse, Surprise Lake and Palmer Lake.

Taku Adventures, T867-6512244, www.takuadventures.com. Guided cross-country hikes to Telegraph Creek on a bushwhacking, 362-km, 25-day trail, plus 1- to 3-day hikes and canoe trips.

⊝ Transport

Whitehorse *p345, map p346*
Air
Air North, T867-6682228, www.flyair north.com, has daily flights to **Vancouver** (2½ hrs) and regular flights to **Calgary** (3 hrs) and **Edmonton** (1½ hrs). All start at around $195 one-way. Air North also flies to **Dawson City** (1½ hrs, $140), and indirectly to **Inuvik** (5½ hrs, $230). **Air Canada Tango**, www.aircanada.com, has up to 4 flights daily to **Vancouver** (2½ hrs, $230). **Air Condor**, www5.condor.com, has occasional direct flights from **Frankfurt**, Germany (€500).

Bus
Local For local transit information call T867-6687433, www.whitehorse.ca. Extensive service covering the whole city ($2). There is no service on Sun.

Long distance The Greyhound station is on 2nd Av, a short walk north of Downtown, with daily buses from **Dawson Creek** (20 hrs, $186) via **Watson Lake** (5 hrs, $61). There are no buses to Yukon destinations besides those between Whitehorse and Watson Lake. **Alaskon Express**, run by Gray Line Yukon, T867-6683225, has a daily summer service to **Skagway**, departing Westmark Hotel at 1330. For details of the **Atlin Express**, see below.

Taxis
Global Taxi, T867-6335300. **Yellow Cab**, T867-6684811.

Vehicle rental
For RVs try **Canadream**, 110 Copper Rd, T867-6683610, www.canadream.com. All sizes of unit. 1-way rentals available to Vancouver and Calgary.

Atlin *p349*
The **Atlin Express**, T867-6517617, leaves Mon, Wed and Fri, from the Greyhound Station in **Whitehorse** at 1200, and leaves Atlin from the Atlin Inn on the same days at 0615. $56 return.

With your own transport you could explore the mining roads that cross the area. Otherwise you'll have to rely on tours or rent a canoe. Hitching might entail a long wait.

ⓘ Directory

Whitehorse *p345, map p346*
Canada Post Main office with General Delivery is at the top of Two Mile Hill. Otherwise, **Shoppers Drug Mart**, 211 Main St. **Internet** free at the library. **Laundry** Norgetown Laundry, 4213 4th Av. **Library** Whitehorse Public Library, Govt Building, 2nd Av. **Medical** services Whitehorse General Hospital, Hospital Rd, south side of river. **Money exchange** Thomas Cook, 2101A 2nd Av, T867-6682867.

Kluane Country

Everything in Kluane National Park (pronounced Kloo-ah-nee) is of an exaggerated scale. Forming part of the largest protected area on Earth, Kluane encompasses both the world's second highest set of coastal mountains, the Saint Elias Range, which contains North America's highest peaks, and the largest non-polar ice fields on the planet. Together with the surprisingly lush lower valleys of the front ranges, these dramatic landscapes contain

⦿ **Getting there** Car.
⦿ **Getting around** Car.
⦿ **Time required** 2-4 days.
⦿ **Weather** Extreme.
⦿ **Sleeping** Limited.
⦿ **Eating** Limited.
⦿ **Activities and tours** Hiking and rafting.
★ **Don't miss...** Rafting the Tatshenshini ▶ p359 and 363.

the greatest diversity of flora and fauna in northern Canada, including the world's greatest concentration of grizzly bears. The heart of the park is most easily experienced on a rafting trip down the Tatshenshini River, whereas the front ranges are ideal for hiking. In a land of awe-inspiring landscapes, the drive south to Haines, Alaska, is particularly scenic, while the Top of the World Highway is the most interesting route north to Dawson City.

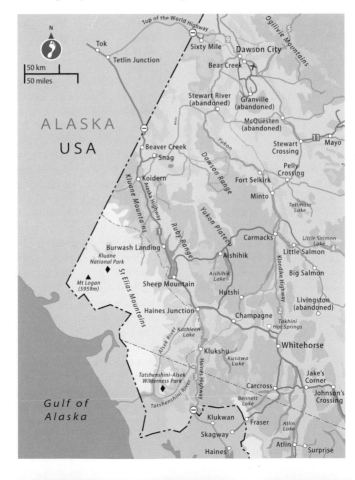

The Yukon Kluane Country

358

West of Whitehorse ⊟🍴❁🏔 ›› *pp363.*

Some 10 km outside Whitehorse, the Klondike Highway continues north towards Dawson City, while the Alaska Highway veers west. After 70 km, a good dirt road heads 20 km south to **Kusawa Lake**, a local favourite for hiking, fishing and canoeing. There is a small campground at Km 14.5, and a bigger one on the lake at Km 22.5. The latter is the start of popular Upper Tatshenshini canoe trip (see p363), ideal for beginners/intermediates. **Kwaday Dan Kenji** (Long Ago People's Place) ⓘ *T867-6676375, tours $10*, 23 km further on, is a traditional First Nations camp with displays on the history and culture of the Southern Tutchone people, and a campground. Another 26 km along the highway, then 42 km on a dirt road, leads to the quiet and remote **Aishihik Lake**, a local fishing hole with a small campground. **Otter Falls**, on the way at Km 30, is home to a small herd of bison and some good mountain bike trails.

Haines Junction

Haines Junction, 92 km further on, is an ugly little town, but a vital stop for organizing excursions into **Kluane National Park**. The **Parks Office** ⓘ *T867-6347207, summer daily 0900-1900, winter Mon-Fri 1300-1600*, provides maps and information on trails and backcountry routes, and takes the essential registrations. **Yukon Tourism** ⓘ *T867-6342345, www.hainesjunctionyukon.com, May-Sep 0800-2000*, deals with provincial enquiries. The junction itself, marked by what looks like a giant cupcake with cement animals crawling out of the icing, is an important one: Whitehorse is 158 km east; Kluane Lake some 60 km northwest, and Haines, Alaska, is 241 km south via one of the region's most stunning roads.

Kluane National Park 🏔 ›› *pp363.*

This extraordinary park is just part of a vast UNESCO World Heritage Site. The Saint Elias Range contains North America's highest peak, **Mount McKinley** (6193 m), in Alaska; and Canada's highest, **Mount Logan** (5959 m). The ice fields here bear sheets of ice over 1.5 km thick, with glaciers extending up to 112 km. As well as harbouring healthy populations of mountain goats, moose, rare silver-blue glacier bears, wolves and dall sheep, this may well be the only protected area in North America large enough to ensure the long-term survival of the grizzly, and the chances of stumbling upon one here are far greater than in the more famous parks.

Ins and outs

Access to most of the park is virtually impossible except by air. Only its eastern boundary is bordered by roads: the southern part, reached from the Haines Highway, tends to be greener and more lush; the northern part, accessed from the Alaska Highway, has the greater concentration of trails and is more arid. Stunning as the views may be, the really big mountains of the St Elias Range are almost perpetually hidden by the lower front ranges, with only the occasional glimpse offering the motorist a hint of what is being missed. Helicopter tours, rafting trips and overnight hikes are the only real ways to get closer. Mountain biking, cross-country skiing and mountaineering are other prime activities. 🏔 ›› *p363.*

The park's main **Visitor Centre** is in Haines Junction (see above) but there's an office 71 km northwest, right in the park at **Sheep Mountain**, open mid-May to September 0800-2000. *Kluane National Park Hiking Guide* by Vivien Lougheed can be picked up at either location. Hikers should be aware that most routes in the park involve difficult creek crossings with no bridges and extremely cold, fast-flowing water; take a pair of creek-crossing shoes, such as old sneakers. Registration for backcountry hiking is obligatory. A fee of $5 per person per night is charged for camping, which is allowed anywhere, except on the Cottonwood Trail, which has designated sites. The normal no-trace ethical rules apply (see box, p17).

The Yukon Kluane Country

Top tips

Tatshenshini and Alsek rivers

Two of the most beautiful, pristine rivers in North America, the Tatshenshini and Alsek, both run through BC's Wilderness Reserve into Alaska. Their forested valleys provide the only corridors through the towering icy realm of the St Elias Mountains, a remote world few people ever get to see. A rafting tour of the Tatshenshini is one of the most highly recommended experiences in Western Canada and suitable for all levels of experience. See Activities and tours, p363.

The Yukon Kluane Country

Day hikes from the Haines Highway

▲▲ **King's Throne** ⓘ *10 km return, 4 hrs, 1220 m elevation gain. Trailhead: Kathleen Lake day use area, 26 km south of Haines Junction.* A well-defined trail switchbacks fairly steeply to a saddle at Km 5, offering expansive views. The hike can be continued along a ridge, with ever-greater views. A possible 10-hour hike in all, and one of the park's most popular.

▲▲ **Rock Glacier** ⓘ *1.5 km, 30 mins. Trailhead: 44 km south of Haines Junction.* Short and easy hike on a former glacier, leading to good views.

▲▲ **St Elias Lake** ⓘ *7.6 km, 3 hrs, 120 m elevation gain. Trailhead: 60 km south of Haines Junction.* A fairly easy but rewarding hike, with the chance of scrambling to better views.

Day hikes from Sheep Mountain

▲▲ **Sheep Creek** ⓘ *10 km, 4-5 hrs, 430 m elevation gain. Trailhead: Visitor Centre.* Exceptional views for such short a hike.

▲▲ **Sheep-Bullion Plateau** ⓘ *24 km, 7-8 hrs, 880 m elevation gain. Trailhead: Visitor Centre.* A beautiful area with diverse plant life as well as views of the valley, a glacier toe and the striking Red Castle Ridge. Home to bear families, so potentially dangerous. Could be treated as a two-day trip.

▲▲ **Soldiers Summit** ⓘ *1 km, 30-40 mins, 90 m elevation gain. Trailhead: 1 km north of the Visitor Centre.* Easily the best very short hike.

▲▲ **Sheep Mountain Ridge** ⓘ *11-km loop, 6-10 hrs, 1310 m elevation gain. Trailhead: 2 km north of Visitor Centre.* Wonderful views of the lake, Slims River Valley, mountains and glaciers, and the chance to see up to 200 sheep.

Hiking in Tatshenshini Alsek Wilderness Park.

Overnight hikes (from south to north)

▲▲ **Cottonwood** ⓘ *83-km loop, up to six days, 520 m elevation gain. Trailhead: 27 or 55 km south of Haines Junction.* A well-marked trail through more lush surroundings giving great views of towering mountains. Lots of creek crossings.

▲▲ **Alsek** ⓘ *52 km, 2-3 days, 90 m elevation gain. Trailhead: 10 km north of Haines Junction on Alaska Hwy.* Long but fairly easy trek down a spectacular valley. Good introduction for the inexperienced hiker.

▲▲ **Slims East** ⓘ *46 km, 2-4 days, 910 m elevation gain. Trailhead: 3 km south of the Visitor Centre.* Not quite as spectacular as the Slims West, but a better trail and certainly recommended. Also has lots of grizzlies.

▲▲ **Slims West** ⓘ *60 km, 3-5 days, 1340 m elevation gain. Trailhead: Sheep Mountain Visitor Centre.* The most popular overnight hike in the park, leading to Observation Peak and offering probably the best views of glaciers and mountains to be had without a guide or backcountry expertise. High concentration of grizzlies causes frequent closures.

▲▲ **Donjek Glacier** ⓘ *96-km loop, 6-10 days. Trailhead: Duke River, 9 km north of Burwash Landing.* A long, demanding hike, very popular with experienced hikers, many of whom come to Kluane just to do it.

Heading south 🚌🚶▲▲🏕 ▸▸ *pp363.*

Haines Highway

Highway 3, the Haines Highway, heads south through glorious alpine terrain that slowly builds over a distance of 144 km to the crescendo of Chilkat Pass. At Km 26 is **Kathleen Lake**, the start of a number of hikes, whose facilities include the only campground within the park. At Km 62 is **Klukshu**, meaning 'coho place' in Tlingit (coho being a kind of salmon). Klukshu is a traditional First Nations salmon-fishing village that welcomes visitors with a small museum, a craft shop, smokehouses and signs detailing the people's traditional way of life. Slightly more authentic is **Dalton Post** (Shäwshe), 22 km further on then 5 km down a dirt road. Situated on the Tatshenshini River, this is a key site for rafts and kayaks (see p363). In BC, the road follows the eastern boundary of **Tatshenshini-Alsek Wilderness Park**, which is almost inaccessible except on a guided rafting trip. The US Customs post at Km 170 is open from 0800 to 2400.

Just south of Klukwan on the Chilkat River is the **Chilkat Bald Eagle Reserve**. The waters here remain unfrozen in October and November, and are full of spawned-out salmon at a time when food is scarce, attracting thousands of bald eagles from as far away as Washington State. From here, the road clings to the river, the massive Tsirku Glacier just 10 km away. It's a breathtaking introduction to Haines, which is cradled within the Y-shaped end of America's longest fjord. Friendly and uncrowded, Haines is ideal for aimless wandering, taking a tour or hiking to Mount Ripinsky or Seduction Point. The main sight is **Sheldon Museum and Cultural Centre** ① *11 Main St, T907-7662368, www.sheldonmuseum.org, summer Mon-Fri 1000-1700, Sat-Sun 1400- 1700; Winter Mon-Fri 1300-1600, $3*, with a collection of dioramas, Tlingit artefacts and exhibits on the town's pioneer history. To find out more about the area visit the **Visitor Information Centre** ① *2nd Av S near Willard St, T907-7662234, www.haines.ak.us, Mon-Fri 0800-1800, Sat-Sun 1000-1600.*

Heading north ⊜ ▸▸ *pp362-363.*

Alaska Highway

Interpretive panels are dotted along this highway, but few are of real interest except to hard-core history enthusiasts. Driving northwest from Haines Junction, the first reason to stop is the **Kluane Lake** viewpoint at Km 60, with winning views over the Yukon's largest lake. Anglers should note that Kluane is a Southern Tutchone word meaning 'lake with many fish'. Another 11 km brings you to the visitor centre at **Sheep Mountain**, which is often dotted with the herd of Dall sheep after which it is named, though they are most easily seen from September to early June when there are no people around to bother them. Nearby on the lake, the **Arctic Institute** has an interpretive room with details on expeditions and research in the St Elias icefields.

North to Dawson City via Alaska

The best reason to continue northwest is to make a loop through Alaska to Dawson City. **Burwash Landing**, *72 km past Sheep Mountain*, is an old community of 100 people, home to the **Kluane Museum of Natural History** ① *T867-8415561, mid-May to mid-Sep, by donation*. As well as fossils and minerals from the area, there is a decent collection of First Nations artefacts and a number of wildlife dioramas. The **Icefield Ranges** viewpoint, 57 km further on, is one of the best places to stop for views of St Elias Mountains, as well as the dramatic Donjek River Valley.

   Just before the border with Alaska is the tiny and grim village of **Beaver Creek**. The coldest temperature ever recorded in Canada was measured close to here at a place called **Snag**: it was minus 62.8°C. There is a **Visitor Centre** ① *T867-8627321, daily 0800-2000, summer only*. The 24-hour border crossing up the road charges a US$6 visa fee, even for those heading straight back into Canada. Unless you want to sample the limited charms of Tok, bear north at **Tetlin Junction** onto Taylor Highway 5, a windy dirt road through a narrow valley, where gold panners can still be seen at work. The drive is unexceptional until you cross back into the Yukon at **Little Gold Creek**. The border here is only open 0900-2100, with the US side one hour behind. From here, the aptly named **Top of the World Highway** affords unspeakably gorgeous views, with bare, multicoloured hills in the foreground and mountain peaks lining up on the horizon. This is the ultimate way to enter Dawson City, 105 km away.

● Sleeping

Haines Junction *p358*
A-B Raven Hotel and Gourmet Dining, T867-6342500, www.yukonweb.com/tourism/raven. The nicest place to stay, with new rooms, a large sundeck and restaurant. Breakfast included.
D Cozy Corner Motel, Alaska Hwy, north end of town, T867-6342119. The best of many standard motels, with a restaurant.

Camping
Pine Lake Campground, 7 km east of town. A lovely spot.

Haines Highway *p360*
C The Cabin B&B, just south of Kathleen Lake, 27 km from Haines Junction, T867-6342626. 5 very nice cabins nestled in the woods, with kitchenettes, decks and sauna.

Camping
Kathleen Lake, Km 26. The only campground actually in the park, with 39 sites.
Million Dollar Falls, Km 79. 35 sites including 8 for tents-only.

Haines, Alaska *p361*
C A Sheltered Harbour, T616-5272732, www.geocities.com/asheltered. 5 very nice, spacious rooms in an interesting building with a large deck in the historic Fort Seward part of town.
C Summer Inn B&B, 117 2nd Av, www.summerinnbnb.com. Plain but decent rooms in a nice house in the centre of town, with a deck and living room.
D-E Bear Creek Cabins, T907-7662259, www.bearcreekcabinsalaska.com. Bunks or rustic cabins. Short walk from town.

Camping
Chilkoot Lake State Recreation Site, 16 km north of Haines off Lutak Rd. 32 sites in a very scenic location.
Portage Cove State Recreation Site, 1.5 km south on Beach Rd. Another very attractive spot, for tents only.

Heading north *p361*
B Westmark Hotel, Beaver Creek, T867-8627501, www.westmarkhotels.com. The best place to stay. Small but pleasant room, with a bar, recreation room, and restaurant with theatre in the evening.
C Burwash Landing Resort, off the highway on the lake, T403-8414441. Well situated close to Sheep Mountain. Standard rooms with old beds and a restaurant with a reasonable menu.
C Kluane B&B, south end of Kluane Lake, T867-8414250, www.kluanecabins.com. Cute but basic A-frame cabins with showers and kitchen facilities, breakfast included.
D-F Kluane Base Camp, T867-8412135, www.kluanebasecamp.com. A nice wood lodge close to the lake, with small, rustic cabins, bunk dorms, and campsites. Shared kitchen/common room, and washrooms.

Camping
Congdon Creek, 17 km west of Sheep Mountain with 81 sites.
Lake Creek, 131 km north of Sheep Mountain, with 27 sites.
Snag Junction, 59 km further, 15 sites.

● Eating

Haines Junction *p358*
¶¶¶ Raven Hotel and Gourmet Dining, T867-6342500. European-style fine dining, named the best restaurant in the Yukon.
¶ Village Bakery and Deli, opposite the Visitor Centre. Good bread, muffins, pizza, quiche, espresso and smoked salmon.

Haines, Alaska *p361*
¶¶¶ The Commander's Room, in Hotel Halsingland, T1800-5426363, www.hotelhalsingland.com.. Sophisticated fine dining in a genteel dining room, lots of seafood.
¶¶ Bamboo Room, 2nd Av, near Main St, T907-7662800. Relaxed, central and friendly. Famous for halibut and chips.
¶¶ Fog Cutter Bar, Main St between 1st and 2nd Avs, T907-7662555. Lively with pool tables, a dance floor and light food.

☸ Festivals and events

Haines Junction *p358*
Jun The **Alsek Music Festival** in early Jun is a 3-day outdoor event featuring music from the Yukon. Later in Jun, the **Kluane Chilkat International Bike Rally** is a 238-km relay race from HJ to Haines.

⛰ Activities and tours

Haines Junction *p358*
Tour operators
Kluane Ecotours, Haines Rd, T867-6342626, www.kluaneco.com. 2- to 10-day hiking/kayaking trips with a naturalist.
Paddle/Wheel Adventures, opposite the visitor centre, T867-6342683, www.paddle wheeladventures.com. Rents bikes and canoes, runs shuttles to trailheads, and can book you onto all kinds of tours.
Trans North Helicopters, T867-6682177, www.tntaheli.com. Glacier tours, flight-seeing and the best way to get into the most striking landscapes for activities.
Yukon Trail Riding, T867-6342386. Horse-riding excursions.

Kluane National Park *p358*
Biking and mountaineering
There are some excellent mountain-bike routes in the park. **Mush Lake Rd** and the **Alsek Trail** are recommended. **Mt Logan**, **Mt St Elias**, and **Mt Steele** are magnets for world-class mountaineering.

Cross-country skiing
This is first class, especially on the **Cotton-wood** and **Dezadeash trails**, or around the Chilkat Pass, where you can ski as late as Jun. The 15-km **Auriol Trail**, 7 km south of Haines Junction is good for its ski trails.

Rafting
Both the Tatshenshini and Alsek rivers provide adrenaline feasts for kayakers and canoeists, but experience is essential. **Tatshenshini River** (215 km, 10-14 days, class III-IV. Dalton Post to Dry Bay, near

Yakutat, Alaska). **Upper Tatshenshini** (40 km, 1-2 days, class III-IV. 110 km south of Haines Junction to Dalton Post), this is the Yukon's most popular day trip, and can be reached via **Blanchard River** (26 km, including 15 km on the Tatshenshini day trip, class II-III. 105 km south on the Haines Hwy to Dalton Post). **Alsek River** (290 km, 10-14 days, with class IV rapids. Dezadeash River, Haines Junction to Dry Bay, near Yakutat, Alaska), a tough trip for experienced kayakers.
Tatshenshini Expediting, Whitehorse, T867-6332742, www.tatshenshini yukon.com. 1- to 11-day trips through incredible scenery on a river that has the best reputation for whitewater rafting in the Yukon. $125 for 1 day.

Haines, Alaska *p361*
Tour operators
Alaska Kayak Supply, 425 Beach Road, T1800-5529257, www.seakayaks.com. Guided kayak trips, rentals and instruction.
Alaska Mountain Guides, Fort Seward, T1800-7663396, www.alaskamountain guides.com. Mountaineering courses, ice climbing, hiking, sea kayaking and rentals.
Alaska Nature Tours, T907-7662876, www.kcd.com/aknature. Hikes, bird-watching, wildlife photography in and around the Chilkat Bald Eagle Preserve.
Chilkat Guides, T907-7662491, www.raftalaska.com. Daily rafting trips through the Chilkat Bald Eagle Preserve
Sockeye Cycle Co, 24 Portage St, Fort Seward. T907-7662869, www.cycle alaska.com. Guided/self guided bike tours.

⊖ Transport

Haines, Alaska *p361*
Regular ferries up the Taiya Inlet to **Skagway** with **Chilkat Cruises and Tours**, T1888-7662103, www.chilkatcruises.com. US$25 one-way, $115 with **White Pass Train**, and **Alaska's Marine Highway**, T1800-6420066, www.dot.state.ak.us/amhs. The 1-hr crossing costs roughly US$30 one-way, $15 child, $30 car.

Dawson City and the north

The unavoidable Gold Rush paraphernalia that can be found in every Yukon village reaches its apotheosis in Dawson City, the ultimate boomtown, site of the biggest stampede to the most productive gold fields of all time. Canadian history doesn't get any more exciting than this. In 1959, the gold all but exhausted, Dawson was declared a National Historic Site, and saved from otherwise inevitable disintegration. Today the perfectly restored buildings – with the help of costumed interpreters, boardwalks, dirt streets and a wealth of interesting sights – present the visitor with a unique slice of living Wild West history, half real town, half museum. There are a number of interesting diversions on the way up from Whitehorse, but nothing to compare to the Dempster Highway, a genuine frontier road, which heads 740 km north to Inuvik, deep in the Arctic, from where a handful of excursions lead still further into the remote frozen realm.

◉ **Getting there** Plane, car.
◉ **Getting around** Car.
◉ **Time required** 3-10 days.
◉ **Weather** Extreme.
◉ **Sleeping** Surprisingly good.
◉ **Eating** Fairly limited.
▲▲ **Activities and tours** Hiking, rafting, gold rush tours.
★ **Don't miss...** Travelling the Dempster Highway as far as Tombstone Mountains. ▶▶ *p371.*

Ins and outs

Getting there and around

Dawson City Airport (YDA) is 19 km southeast of town on the Klondike Highway. **Gold City Tours**, T867-9935175, runs a shuttlebus to Downtown ($10), meeting all scheduled flights. **Dawson Courier Taxi**, T867-9936688, charges $23. **Air North**, T867-6682228, www.fly airnorth.com, has regular flights from Whitehorse (1½ hrs, $140) and Fairbanks in Alaska (1½ hrs, $140). **Alaska Shuttles**, T1800-7707275, www.alaskashuttle.com, runs a regular service from several Alaskan towns including Fairbanks ($160) and Anchorage ($239).

Most people arrive in Dawson in their own vehicle. Entering from the Klondike Highway gives an idea of the extent to which the land has been plundered. For almost 10 km you pass through desolate wasteland, littered with huge boulders and abandoned mining equipment. A free ferry runs 24-hours daily from late May to mid-October across the Yukon River to connect the town with the Top of the World highway, the best campground and a hostel.▸▸ ⊙ *p378*.

Best time to visit

Dawson City hibernates in winter, when average temperatures drop to -30° C. Most sights are only open mid-May to mid-September. The hottest months are July and August, when average temperatures rise to 15° C and the sun shines almost around the clock. However, at this time, the streets throng with tourists, many of them stopping en route from the US to Alaska. June is a good compromise, with the bonus of an excellent festival (see p376). By September the crowds begin to dwindle and the scenery takes on the magnificent colours of autumn.

Tourist information

The **Visitor Reception Centre** ⓘ *Front and King Sts, T867-9935566, www.dawsoncity.ca, www.tourdawsoncity.com, mid-May to mid-Sep 0800-2000*, is by the river. Jointly operated by **Tourism Yukon** and **Parks Canada**, T867- 9937200, this first-class facility has a wealth of information and photos on the town's historical buildings. A popular 90-minute walking tour of town, conducted by guides in period costume, runs daily at 0930, 1100 and 1300. Across the road is the **Northwest Territories Visitor Centre** ⓘ *T867-9936456, summer daily 0900 2000*, a key stop for anyone planning on travelling up the Dempster Highway.

Dawson City ⊖⊘⊕⊙⊛⊙▲⊖⊙ ▸▸ *pp374-378*.

Coming to the Yukon and not visiting Dawson City is like going to Agra and failing to see the Taj Mahal. At the heart of summer, when the atmosphere is more that of theme-park than museum, you may feel that Dawson has been saved at the expense of its character and soul. To get the most out of a visit you have to enter into the spirit of the place. Submerging yourself in the history is essential, maybe by reading a work like Pierre Berton's bestseller *Klondike* (1958), the short stories of Jack London, or poetry by Robert Service. More importantly, Dawson's soul remains that of a party town, so go gambling at Diamond Tooth Gertie's, catch the Gaslight Follies show at the Palace, have a few drinks in the saloon, and dream of gold.

Heritage buildings

Most of the town's century-old buildings are still in use as hotels and saloons. The first to be renovated (in 1960) was the wonderful **Palace Grand Theatre** on King Street. It was originally built by Gold Rush legend Arizona Charlie Meadows from the hulks of two beached paddle-steamers. Every night in summer it hosts the **Gaslight Follies** ⓘ *T867-9936217, $7.50, tours $6.50*, a two-hour Vaudeville musical comedy aimed squarely at tourists, but good fun.

The Yukon Dawson City & the north

The grandest building in town is the **Commissioner's Residence** ⓘ *daily 1500-1700, free, tours daily Jun to mid-Sep at 1400, $6*, at the east end of Front Street. This elegant former home of the Queen's representative to the Yukon has been renovated to reflect the 1912-1916 era. Many of the best structures are on 3rd Avenue, such as the **1901 Post Office** at 3rd Avenue and King Street, which is still in operation. **Harrington's Store**, nearby at 3rd Avenue and Princess Street, displays a collection of rare original photos and journal excerpts from the Gold Rush era entitled 'Dawson as they saw it'. Also worth seeing is the **Firefighters Museum** ⓘ *summer Mon-Sat 1230-1730, by donation*, at 5th Avenue and King Street. The town's cemeteries make an interesting tour: ask for a free *Walking Tour* booklet at the Visitor Reception Centre.

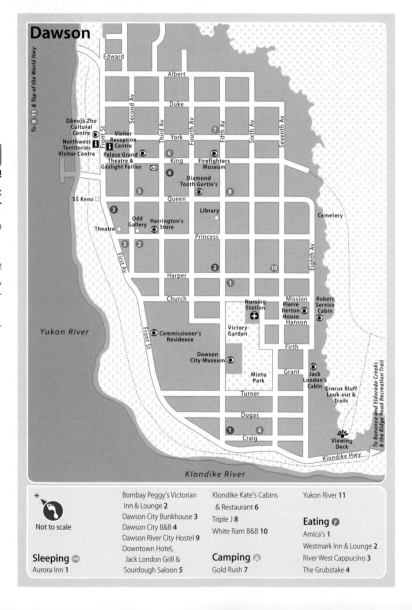

Dawson

Not to scale

Sleeping ⊖
Aurora Inn **1**

Bombay Peggy's Victorian
Inn & Lounge **2**
Dawson City Bunkhouse **3**
Dawson City B&B **4**
Dawson River City Hostel **9**
Downtown Hotel,
Jack London Grill &
Sourdough Saloon **5**

Klondike Kate's Cabins
& Restaurant **6**
Triple J **8**
White Ram B&B **10**

Camping ⋀
Gold Rush **7**

Yukon River **11**

Eating ⓸
Amica's **1**
Westmark Inn & Lounge **2**
River West Cappucino **3**
The Grubstake **4**

Robert Service Cabin.

Dawson City Museum

ⓘ *5th Av/Church St, T867-9935291, late May-late Sep 0900-1800, $6, $3 child.*
Housed in the old territorial administration building, the town museum is an essential stop for soaking up some history. It's packed full of artefacts and photos, First Nations items, diaries and newspaper cuttings. One key highlight is the 27-minute *City of Gold*, a black and white documentary made by Pierre Berton (see p368), which underlines the town's sad demise and helped spur the federal government to action. Tours of the museum building (daily at 1100, 1300 and 1700) take in the old court chambers, the archives and the visible storage area, where a fifth of the museum's 30,000 artefacts are displayed.

Diamond Tooth Gertie's Gambling Hall

ⓘ *4th Av /Queen St, T867-9935575, 1900-0200, $6 for 3 shows.*
An absolute must is a visit to Canada's first legal casino, housed in the old Arctic Brotherhood Hall, which was built in 1899. The atmosphere is wonderful, with three can-can shows every night. The midnight performance is a little more risqué. There are Yukon beers on tap; happy hour starts at midnight. Gambling proceeds go to the continued development of the town.

Dänojà Zho Cultural Centre (Long Time Ago House)

ⓘ *Front St, 1867-9936768, www.trondek.com, May-Sep 1400-1700, slideshow at 1500, $5.*
Guided tours are given daily of the Hammerstone Gallery, where audiovisual displays, photos, dioramas, artefacts, arts and crafts, theatre, dance and slide shows bring alive the history and culture of the Native Tr'ondëk Hwëch'in people. You can arrange to stay at a wilderness camp on the river, or take a tour to Moosehide Island on a restored paddlewheeler.

Authors' Avenue

On Eighth Avenue are the former homes of three famous writers. The **Robert Service Cabin** ⓘ *daily 1300-1500, free,* is a renovated version of the poet's abode, from the time when he worked here as a bank clerk in 1908. Born in Preston, England, Robert Service (1874-1958) became one of the most successful poets of his day, writing verses that romanticized the north but immortalized much of its mystique, charm and eccentricity. Ironically, most of his Gold Rush verse was written before he even set foot in the Yukon. A recital of verses like *The*

→ From rags to riches

When the gold prospectors arrived in Dawson City, the population swelled to 30,000, making this the biggest city north of Seattle. There were casinos and cabarets, show-girls and saloons, brothels and rag-time tunes. Fancy hotels, running water and electricity were all available for those who could pay. Prices ran amok, with gold dust used as currency; it was not unknown for barkeepers who sifted the saloon floor sawdust to find up to $300 worth.

For most, the reality was a harsh squalor. Prospectors had to build fires to thaw the frozen ground, then spend weeks searching through the icy, rocky mud. The Native Americans became strangers in their own land, their culture almost completely destroyed.

Less than a year after the masses arrived, all the accessible gold had been extracted. Dawson City sank into a terminal decline until Parks Canada began to intervene in the 1960s. They named the town a National Historic Site and set about restoring its century-old buildings. Today the whole place is like one big living museum, a fossilized remnant of the Wild West, complete with false-fronted wooden houses, boardwalks, saloons and dirt streets.

Cremation of Sam McGee and *The Shooting of Dan McGrew* takes place in a **theatre** ⓘ *Front St/Princess, daily 1500 and 2000, $8*. Service's poems are very effective when read aloud.

Across the road from the cabin is the home of local author **Pierre Berton**, whose best-seller *Klondike* is the most compelling introduction to the era. Further down, **Jack London's Cabin** was built using 'a few' logs from the original in which the writer lived. Jack London fell in love with the north and made it over the Chilkoot Pass during the stampede. Ultimately finding Dawson too expensive, he left penniless after just a year, having gathered enough inspiration to win fame and acclaim with stories like *Call of the Wild* and *White Fang*. His version of the Yukon is tougher and more realistic than that of Service. **Parks Canada** runs a tour of Author's Avenue daily at 1000 and 1530.

Goldfields

An integral part of the Dawson City experience is to witness **Bonanza** and **Eldorado creeks**, where most of the gold was mined. The action begins at Km 4 on the Klondike Highway, the start of Bonanza Creek Road. Near the turning is **Bear Creek**, a 25-ha site that supported the dredge teams until 1966. Tours take in the shops and the gold room where the dust was processed. On Bonanza Creek Road is the fascinating **Dredge No 4**, the largest bucket-line, wooden-hulled dredge in North America. Monsters like this one scooped up copious quantities of mud and rock, and passed the material through their insides, where it was sifted for gold. Operated by just four men, it extracted a remarkable 25 kg of gold per day between 1913 and 1966. At Km 12 on this road is the cairn marking **Discovery Claim**, where the original lucky strike occurred. Every 150-m claim on this stretch went on to yield around 3500 kg of gold, worth about $25 million at 1900 prices.

The road forks here, the east spur leading along Eldorado Creek, which proved even more bountiful than Bonanza. The other branch runs up to the summit of **King Soloman Dome**. From here you can see the network of trails and roads, all of them littered with ramshackle buildings and the rusting remains of mining equipment. Hunker Road runs back from the summit to the highway. Enthusiasts could spend hours exploring these desolate landscapes.

To take a tour of a mine on Hunker Road, contact **Gold Bottom Mine Tours** (see p377). Or you could try your hand at gold-panning. At about Km 15 on Bonanza Creek Road is **Claim No 6**, where you can usually pan for free. Ask at the Visitor Reception Centre, or call T867-9935575. Pans can be rented at several places in town.

Hikes around Dawson City

Midnight Dome, the hill that rises behind Dawson City, is so named because it's a great place to watch the sun drop to the horizon then rise again at midnight on 21 June, an occasion for much drinking and festivity. A stiff 8-km return hike to the summit is rewarded with superb views of the city, goldfields, Yukon River and rows of mountains. Ask at the Visitor Reception Centre for directions. **Gold City Tours** (see p377) runs regular trips up here in the day and evening. The **Crocus Bluff Lookout Trail** is a short walk leading to good views of the town. Follow King Street southeast above town to the trailhead. The 32-km **Ridge Road Recreation Trail** starts in Upper Bonanza Creek and follows the ridge tops back to the Klondike Valley, with views all the way. It's a three-day hike with two campsites along the way.

Klondike Highway to Dawson City ⊖🛈🏵▲ ▶ pp374-378

By Yukon standards, the Klondike Highway north of Whitehorse is a pretty dull drive. The minor towns of Carmacks and Pelly Crossing offer little reason to stop. A worthwhile side-trip off the beaten track is down the **Silver Trail** (Highway 11) to the tiny, quaint, artist-dominated village of **Keno**. Just south of the turning, a dirt road leads to Ethel Lake, a beautiful camping and fishing spot for those seeking tranquility. Remainders of very large forest fires along the highway offer the chance of hunting for morel mushrooms.

Carmacks and around

The Yukon River crosses the Klondike Highway at **Carmacks**, making this a useful provisions stop for canoeists. The town's main sight is the **Tage Cho Hudan Interpretive Centre** ⓘ *T867-8635830, free*, which has displays on First Nations culture and history, an interpretive trail and local handicrafts. This is also the best place to ask about the 2-km boardwalk, which runs along the river, and about local trails to areas good for seeking agates and other semi-precious stones.

Just north of Carmacks is a viewpoint looking down on **Five Fingers Rapids**, one of the most treacherous spots on the Yukon River. A 1-km boardwalk leads to an observation deck. At **Pelly Crossing** is Big Jonathan House, T867-5373331, which contains displays of native artefacts, arts and crafts. It's a replica of a building still standing in **Fort Selkirk**, due west at the confluence of the Yukon and Pelly rivers, accessible only by water.

Robert Campbell Highway

The region east of Carmacks is named Campbell after **Robert Campbell**, a Hudson's Bay Company employee who was sent here in the 1840s to open up new fur trading routes. Following trails used by the Native Kaska Dena people, Campbell built a chain of trading posts culminating in Fort Selkirk. The highway that also bears his name (Highway 4) heads east just north of Carmacks, passing **Little Salmon Lake**, a fishing spot with two tiny picturesque campgrounds, on the way to **Faro**. This tiny town of 360 is situated on the remarkably broad **Tintina Trench**, an important wildlife corridor that attracts millions of migrating birds and has

Yukon landscape.

one of the highest concentrations of moose and wolves in the province. A breed of sheep unique to the region, the fannin, can be seen at **Mount Mye Sheep Centre**, a 10-km hike from the 1.5-km Van Gorder Falls Trail, or a 7.5-km drive. Ask at the summer-only **Campbell Region Interpretive Centre** ⓘ *T867-9942728, www.faroyukon.ca.*

The Robert Campbell Highway can be used in conjunction with the South Canol Road, which it meets at Ross River, as a scenic route that bypasses Whitehorse and Carmacks. As a further refinement, the Tatchun/Frenchman Road cuts the corner between Highway 4 and the Klondike Highway, offering a remote diversion lined with small lakes and several lovely campgrounds. The 67 km **Dena Cho Trail**, T867-9692278, follows a historic gold prospector route between Faro and Ross River. It's a fantastic with four cabins along the way. Register at the Interpretive Centre; maps can be picked up there or downloaded from their website.

Silver Trail
The Yukon's first small gold rush occurred on the Stewart River in 1883, but ultimately the area proved more successful with its high-grade lead-silver ore. Better known as the Silver Trail, Highway 11 from **Stewart Crossing** is one of the Yukon's more worthwhile side-tracks, leading past abandoned homesteads and mining equipment to the sleepy, ramshackle communities of **Mayo** (Km 53), **Elsa** (Km 96) and **Keno** (Km 112). Watch for moose on the first 15 km of the Silver Trail, as this is a calving habitat.

The road is paved as far as Mayo, whose Interpretive Centre, T867-9962317, is housed in historic Binet House, which also has a collection of historic photos and displays on local natural history, flora and fauna. There's a viewing deck overlooking the river. Minto Lake Road is a good place for genuine gold panning; ask the **Mayo Mining Recorder**, T867-9962256, which streams are open. **Elsa** is essentially a ghost town, though its United Keno Mine continued to operate until 1989. The dirt road deteriorates towards **Keno**, but this funky little village is the highlight of the trip. A small cluster of log cabins mainly populated by artists, miners and eccentrics, Keno's authentic character remains quirky and uncompromised. Housed in a boom-time dance hall, **Keno City Mining Museum** ⓘ *T867-9952792, Jun-Aug 1000-1800*, has an extensive collection of old photographs, mining artefacts and local alpine butterflies. A large number of butterflies congregate at Keno Hill, attracted by the many wild flowers. A network of hiking trails criss-crosses the surrounding area. Ask in Mayo, or visit www.kenocity.info.

Background

→ Flora and fauna in the north

The wildlife of the north includes old favourites like grizzly bears and dall sheep, and species such as musk oxen, polar bears, Arctic foxes and barren ground caribou. Each year, a herd of 120,000 porcupine caribou migrates from central Yukon to calving grounds on the Beaufort Coast, returning south in the autumn. Their migration path crosses the Dempster Highway and it can take hours for the whole herd to cross the road.

Plants have a particularly hard life up here. The average temperature is so low that the ground never thaws, with only a thin top layer melting enough to sustain vegetation. Moreover, Arctic precipitation is so low that it is technically classified as desert. Yet a surprising amount of vegetation survives, such as sedges and dwarf birch, and goes absolutely crazy every summer. The growing season may be short, but it's rendered particularly intense by the constant sunshine. Millions of birds are drawn north to feed on this nutrient-rich vegetation, such as long-tailed jaeger, Arctic tern and snowy owls.

The Silver Trail provides the easiest access to the **Peel Wilderness**, one of the most remote areas on earth. Local paddlers know that some of the Yukon's very best canoeing is down the pristine rivers of the Peel watershed, particularly the Wind, the Snake and the Bonnet Plume. The sanctity of these waters, which flow through the **Mackenzie Mountains** and harbour large animal populations, has been preserved by their very remoteness. Access is by floatplane.

Back on the Klondike Highway, 121 km north of Stewart Crossing, is the **Tintina Trench viewpoint**, with vistas of the Klondike River and a valley so big that it stands out clearly on satellite photos. The product of the largest geological fault in North America, the trench apparently provides visible proof of the concept of plate tectonics. The Dempster Highway branches off 20 km later (see below) and, 39 km beyond, you roll into the ultimate apotheosis of Gold Rush memorabilia, Dawson City.

Dempster Highway ▶ pp374-378.

The 740-km Dempster Highway is Canada's only year-round public road to cross the Arctic Circle. Construction of a highway across the tundra was a great challenge, eventually solved by using a raised gravel pad to insulate the permafrost and keep it from melting. Driving the length of this rough frontier road is also a challenge and an adventure, not to be entered into without adequate preparation (see Ins and outs, below). The effort is amply rewarded by ever-changing, wide-open views. Three very different mountain ranges are crossed, and the continuous freeze and thaw adds a host of unusual features to the landscapes, with names like hummocks, tussocks, frost boils, ground slumping and polygons. In summer, perpetual sunshine causes the vegetation to burst into a riot of colour. Mid-August ushers in the autumn, the most beautiful time of all, when the scenery is filled to the horizon with vivid shades of red, orange, gold, purple and brown, and hosts of berries are ready to pick.

First stop at the **NWT Visitor Centre** in Dawson City, T867-4567623, which provides details on road conditions, weather and which gas stations are open. Drivers should fill up at **Mackenzie Petroleum** in Callison off the Klondike Highway, which is much cheaper. Gas stations are scarce on the highway, so drivers must fill up every time they get the chance. Those with a small tank should take a jerry can and keep it filled. Make sure your tyres are good and take at least two spares, preferably six-ply. Do any routine maintenance before heading out. Gas and tyre repairs are usually only available at **Eagle Plains** (369 km), **Fort McPherson** (542 km) and **Inuvik** (740 km). There is no drinking water available until Fort McPherson. For maps, road reports, and info visit www.yukoninfo.com/dempster.

Tombstone Mountains

You don't have to go far to get the most out of the Dempster Highway. In fact its most beautiful and well-paved section is the first 100 km. A perfect destination is the **Tombstone Mountain Campground** at Km 72, a lovely spot and home to the **Dempster Highway Interpretive Centre** (mid-June to early September). They can give you all the information you need on local wildlife, geology, First Nations culture and some of the most rewarding hikes in the west. The spectacular **Tombstone Mountain Range**, well known for its jagged black granite peaks and idyllic alpine lakes, is a long day's hike away but plenty of shorter trails lead to gorgeous views, and there's a good chance of spotting dall sheep, grizzlies and the hart caribou herd. A useful publication is *Yukon's Tombstone Range and Blackstone Uplands: A Traveller's Guide*.

▲▲ **Goldensides** ⓘ *2½ hrs, 610 m elevation gain. Trailhead: 3 km north of the Interpretive Centre, turn right and drive to the radio tower*. From the top are views of the Klondike River Valley and Tombstone Mountains.

▲▲ **Angelcomb Mountain** ⓘ *10 km return, 3 hrs, 580 m. Trailhead: 9.5 km north of the Centre, park at the gravel pit on the east side of the highway.* A fairly easy and gradual ascent to the first peak, with wonderful views and a fair number of dall sheep and caribou.

▲▲ **Grizzly Valley** ⓘ *8 km round trip, 2-4 hrs, 640 m elevation gain. Trailhead: 12.5 km north of the Centre on the west side.* This is the fastest route into the Tombstone Range and leads to a lookout with great views. To go all the way in is at least a 58.5-km return hike, with possible additional diversions to Divide Lake, Talus Lake or Tombstone Mountain itself (2192 m). A first-class adventure.

North to Inuvik

By the West Blackstone River at Km 115, look upstream: the two low, cone-shaped mounds about 8 km away are not volcanoes but pingoes, strange phenomena caused by mass movements of frost. These ones are thought to be more than 5000 years old. Further on, the highway eventually leads through the **Ogilvie Mountains**, whose peaks are markedly different from the scenic Tombstones. These bare, grey-black piles of shale make for bizarre, landscapes. Beyond, you enter the broad flat horizons of the **Eagle Plains**, arriving eventually at a service centre (Km 371), where you can get gas, tyre repairs and a bed for the night.

Just north, at Km 402, a set of quite interesting interpretive panels marks the 66°33' latitude line of the Arctic Circle. With the best of the scenery gone, this makes a good point to turn back. Should you be here between September and May, however, note that the stretch of road from Km 408 to the Richardson Mountains is part of the porcupine caribou herd's winter range. **Wright Pass**, at Km 465, marks the Continental Divide and the border with the Northwest Territories. The **Richardson Mountains** are softer and rounder than those further south. A moderate hike up to the obvious summit via the ridge on its south side offers a chance to admire their gentle contours. On the other side, the road sweeps down to the Peel River Valley. Near the top, a viewing platform provides equally outstanding vistas.

Igloo Church, Inuvik.

At Km 542 a free ferry crosses the river on demand 0900-0100 from June to mid-October. **Nitainlaii Visitor Information Centre** ⓘ *9 km before Fort McPherson, T867-7773652, 0900-2100 daily Jun-mid Sep to mid Sep*, has interpretive displays focusing on the life of the Gwich'in Dene people. The small native village of **Fort McPherson**, has a mechanic, a hotel and usually gas for filling up (but don't depend on it!). From here the road gets even rougher and far less interesting. At Km 608 is the impressively broad **Mackenzie River**, the small village of **Arctic Red River**, and another free ferry which leaves hourly 0900-0100. The end of the road is **Inuvik**, a grim little town best used as a jumping-off point for even more remote northern communities and parks that can only be reached from here and by plane.

Inuvik, NWT

Inuvik is an unattractive town that may come as a disappointment after 740 gruelling kilometres on a rough dirt road. Most visitors who come this far are planning on continuing to one of the Arctic parks and isolated communities that can be reached from here only by plane. The houses, identical but painted bright colours to add some character, are built with steel poles drilled through to the stable layer of permafrost so that they don't buckle in spring frost heaves.

Almost everything of interest is within four blocks on Mackenzie Road, including the striking **Igloo Church**, which can only be visited on tours in the summer, T867-7772236. On the way into town is the **Western Arctic Visitor Centre** ⓘ *T867-7774727, www.inuvik.ca, www.explorenwt.com, mid-May to Sep 0900-2000*, which has displays on First Nations cultures and a collection of interesting videos; if flying out on an excursion, it's worth watching the video first. You also have to register at the **Parks Canada Office** ⓘ *187 MacKenzie Av, above the post office, T867-7778800, inuvik.info@pc.qc.ca, year-round Mon-Fri 0830-1700*.

A number of small communities and large parks are accessible only by air from Inuvik. These are places where the 'true North' can still be experienced: rugged landscapes, people who still live off the land and exotic animals such as musk oxen. It's possible to get there alone but much easier, and often cheaper, to go with a tour company. When making plans, remember that flights are at the mercy of the changeable weather. Keep your schedule flexible and be prepared to wait.

🛏 Sleeping

Dawson City *p365, map p366*

There is a good list of lodgings with prices and photos in the visitor centre.

A Bombay Peggy's Victorian Inn, 2nd Av/Princess St, T867-9936969, www.bombaypeggys.com. Hands down the nicest place to stay in town: a handful of elegant, classy rooms in a house brimming with historic character.

B Aurora Inn, 5th Av/HarperSt, T867-9936860, www.aurorainn.ca. 20 bright, spacious and very comfortable en suite rooms, with big beds, in a large pine-finished house that also has a great leisure area for guests.

B Klondike Kate's, 3rd Av/King St, T867-9936527, www.klondikekates.ca. 15 pretty log cabins, newly renovated and understandably popular.

C Dawson City B&B, 451 Craig St, T867-9935649, www.dawsonbb.com. 7 rooms with shared bath in an attractive home overlooking the Yukon and Klondike rivers. Great hospitality.

C Downtown Hotel, 2nd Av/Queen St, T867- 9935346, www.downtownhotel.ca. Acceptable rooms in a building with lots of Wild West character in the thick of the action. Those across the road from the office open out on to a plant-filled courtyard with hot tub.

C Triple J Hotel, 5th Av/Queen St, T867-9935323, www.triplejhotel.com. Cabins with kitchenettes, plain motel rooms, and nice, spacious hotel rooms.

C White Ram B&B, 8th Av/Harper St, T867- 9935772. 10 small but tasteful rooms in a nice house with a good atmosphere. Guest kitchen and lounges, large patio with jacuzzi and sauna, hot tub, laundry, internet and bikes.

D Dawson City Bunkhouse, Front St/Princess St, T867-9936164, www.dawson citybunkhouse.com. Simple but cute rooms with shared bath in a nice building.

E Dawson River City Hostel, across the river (on ferry), T867-9936823, www.yukonhostels.com. HI-affiliated. Rustic accommodation in dorms or private rooms, with a large common cabin, cooking facilities, a deck with good views of town, saunas and lockers. Free bike use. Also has some ugly tent sites.

Camping

Gold Rush Campground, right in town on 5th Av/York St, T867-9935247. The only place for RVs, but utterly devoid of charm. Coin-op showers.

Yukon River Campground, across the ferry, walking distance from town. The nicest campground, with sites by the river. Fills up, so arrive in the morning.

Klondike River Campground, 15 km east of town. Not as nice as the Yukon River site, but still a decent and quiet spot.

Klondike Highway *p369*
Camping

The following are Yukon government sites, non-reservable and in gorgeous locations. **Lake Laberge**, 36 km north of Klondike/Alaska junction, has 29 sites. **Fox Lake**, Km 59, has 33 sites. **Twin Lakes**, Km 119, is pretty with 26 sites.

Carmacks *p369*

C Carmacks Hotel, T867-8635221. About the only place to stay, with standard rooms, cabins, RV sites and a restaurant.

Camping

There are 3 lovely government camp-grounds on Tatchun/Frenchman Rd to the west. **Tatchun Creek**, 26 km north of Carmacks at the junction with that road, has 12 very nice sites.

Robert Campbell Highway *p369*

D Faro Studio Hotel, T867-9943003, Dawson Dr, Faro. 16 suites with kitchen facilities, plus a restaurant and lounge.

D Nature Friends B&B, 440 Campbell St, Faro, T867-9942106. A more intimate choice. 5 nice rooms, 1 with en suite, plus a deck and garden, kitchen and laundry. Owners run an adventure tour company.

Camping
On the way are **Little Salmon Lake** and **Drury Creek** campgrounds. 3.5 km towards Faro from Hwy 4 is **Johnson Lake**. At Ross River is **Lapie Canyon**.

Silver Trail *p370*
C **Keno Cabins**, Keno, T867-9952892, www.kenocity.info/cabins. 2 very nice, cosy units.
D **Bedrock Motel**, Mayo, T867-9962290. 12 spacious rooms with continental breakfast included. Licensed lounge.
D **North Star Motel**, Mayo, T867-9962231. 9 rooms with kitchenettes and showers.

Camping
Five Mile Lake Campground, 7 km northeast of Mayo. If you have a tent, head for this government-run ground, with 23 sites, swimming, fishing and a trail around the lake.
Keno City Campground, T867-9952892. 7 sites on Lightning Creek.
Moose Creek, 25 km beyond, to the north of Stewart Crossing. 36 sites, 6 tent-only.
Whispering Willows, Mayo, T867-9962800. In town and catering to RVs.

Dempster Highway *p371*
There are just 2 settlements for beds, food and even fuel on the Dempster Hwy.
A **Peel River Inn**, Fort McPherson, T867-9522417, www.peelriverinn.com. 8 plain rooms with private bathroom. Also a guest lounge, restaurant and fuel.
B **Eagle Plains Hotel**, Eagle Plains, T867-9932453. Standard rooms, plus a reasonably priced restaurant and a basic campground.

Camping
Campgrounds on the highway are as follows: **Tombstone Mountain** at Km 71, 36 sites; **Engineer Creek**, at Km 193, 15 sites; **Rock River**, at Km 446, 20 sites, 3 tent-only; **Nitainlaii Territorial Park**, at Km 541, 5 km from the Peel River ferry; **Vadzaih Van Tshik Campground** at Km 714, big and brand new.

Inuvik *p372*
Beds are overpriced, because the 3 main hotels are owned by the same company.
B **Arctic Chalet**, just before town on the highway, T867-7773535, www.arcticchalet.com. The best choice. Cosy little rooms in log cabins or in the splendid wood lodge. Most have en suite baths and kitchenettes. The owners offer dog-sled tours, and rent kayaks and cars.
B-C **Finto Motor Inn**, 289 Mackenzie Rd, at the south entrance to town, T867-7772647, www.inuvikhotels.com. The quietest location, just outside town. The best rooms have a kitchenette.
C **Mackenzie Hotel**, 185 Mackenzie Rd, T867-7772861, www.inuvikhotels.com. Spacious rooms right in town.
C **Polar B&B**, 75 Mackenzie Rd, T867-7772554. 4 rooms that share a kitchen, bathroom and laundry.

Camping
Happy Valley, northwest end of town on Franklin Rd, T867-7773652. Showers, views of surroundings, nice sites.
Jak Park, south of town on the highway. Quieter, nicer in many ways, and high enough to give good views. Coin-op showers. Both have drinking water.

🍴 Eating

Dawson City *p365, map p366*
🍴 **Amica's**, east end of 5th Av, T867-9936800. Authentic Italian cuisine, a bit on the pricey side, but highly regarded.
🍴 **Jack London Grill**, Downtown Hotel, 2nd Av/Queen St, T867-9935346. A broad menu featuring burgers, steak, fish, and good cheesecake. Also has a heated patio.
🍴 **Klondike Kate's**, 3rd Av/King St, T867-9936527. An authentic 1904 heritage building with a heated patio, always pretty busy. The reasonably priced menu features pasta and fish dishes.
🍴 **Westmark Inn**, 5th Av and Harper, T867-9935542. One of the better restaurants, with a nice deck.

¶ **The Grubstake**, 1054 2nd Av. Subs and pizza. Internet access.

¶ **River West Cappucino Restaurant & Coffee Bar**, Front St across from the *SS Keno*, T867-9936339. Organic fair trade coffee, homemade soups and wraps. Good atmosphere, with outdoor seating.

Silver Trail *p370*
¶¶ **Keno City Snack Bar**, Keno. Pizza and light meals. Summer-only.

Inuvik *p372*
Fish lovers should be try the delicious Arctic char. Each hotel has a restaurant.
¶¶¶ **Peppermill Restaurant**, Finto Motor Inn, T867-7772647. The best ambience with specialities like Arctic char and caribou.
¶¶ **To Go's**, 71 Mackenzie Rd. Musk ox and caribou burgers.
¶¶ **The Roost**, opposite To Go's, serving the same kind of thing.
¶¶ **The Sunrise Café**, Mackenzie Hotel. Basic food, good for breakfast.
¶ **Café Gallery**, Mackenzie Rd. Nice spot for coffee and baked treats.

🎵 Bars and clubs

Dawson City *p365, map p366*
Bombay Peggy's Lounge, 2nd Av/ Princess St. A beautiful, relaxed place for a pint, also boasting a good Martini list. Some light food and a summer patio.
Diamond Tooth Gertie's Gambling Hall, see p367. Beer on tap and a fun atmosphere. Open till 0200.
Sourdough Saloon, Downtown Hotel, see p374. An atmospheric, smoky and authentic place. Watch out for the strange, esoteric ritual of drinking a 'Sourtoe Cocktail', involving a real petrified human toe. You'll see.
Westmark Inn, 5th Av/Harper St, T867-9935542. Nice lounge with a deck. Martinis.

Inuvik *p372*
Cabin Lounge, Finto Motor Inn, see p375. Good for a drink. Sometimes has live music.

The Mad Trapper, Mackenzie Rd. A reasonable pub with a pool table and occasional live music.

🎭 Entertainment

Dawson City *p365, map p366*
See **Diamond Tooth Gertie's** p367 and **Palace Grand Theatre**, p365.
Odd Gallery, 2nd Av/Princess St, www.kiac.org. Dawson's primary location for visual arts, always Canadian and usually very good.

🎉 Festivals and events

Dawson City *p365, map p366*
Mar Dawson International Short Film Festival, T867-9935838, www.dawson arts.com, runs for 3 days in late Mar.
Jun Yukon River Quest canoe and Kayak Race, T867-3335628, www.yukon riverquest.com, is the longest such race in the world and ends here.
Jul The year's biggest event, and rated as one of the best in the west, is the **Dawson City Music Festival**, T867- 9935584, www.dcmf.com, in late Jul. Thousands of come to enjoy 3 days of music. The best up-and-coming Canadian talent is featured. Extra camping is laid on and the atmosphere is fantastic.
Aug The annual **Yukon Riverside Arts Festival**, T867-9935005, in mid-Aug is a weekend of arts, crafts, music, dancing and theatre on the banks of the river, just part of the **Discovery Days Festival**, T867-9932351, a week of games, races and other fun events.

Robert Campbell Highway *p369*
Aug Faro is home to the jamboree bag of the **Fireweed Festival**, T867-9942375.

Inuvik *p372*
Jul Great Northern Arts Festival, T867- 7773536, www.greatart.nt.ca, is a 10-day bonanza in mid-Jul, featuring over 100 artists from north of the Arctic Circle.

● Shopping

Dawson City *p365, map p366*
Bonanza Market, 2nd Av/Princess St.
Groceries, deli, bakery.
Dawson City General Store, Front St.
Bakery, groceries, film, newspapers.
Dawson Trading Post, Front St. Camping
and fishing gear.
Klondike Nugget & Ivory, Front St/
Queen St. Jewellery made from gold
nuggets or mammoth ivory.
Riverwest Cappucino Bar, Front St.
Some health food items.

Inuvik *p372*
Boreal Books, 181 Mackenzie Rd. Maps
and books about the north.
Inuvik Sports, 75 Mackenzie Rd. Sporting
goods, film developing.
Northern Images, 115 Mackenzie Rd.
Inuit sculpture, sealskin slippers, prints.
Northern Store, 160 Mackenzie Rd.
One-stop department store. Groceries,
clothing, tacky souvenirs, pharmacy.

▲▲ Activities and tours

Dawson City *p365, map p366*
Tour operators
Ancient Voices Wilderness Camp, T867-
9935605. First Nations camp with cabins
and tents, offering cultural day trips and
longer excursions along the Yukon or
Pelly rivers with First Nations Guides.
Gold City Tours, Front St, T867-9935175,
www.goldcitytours.info. Tours include
sightseeing in the town, the goldfields,
Midnight Dome and gold-panning. They
can also arrange transport tickets.
Gold Bottom Mine Tours, T867-
9935023, www.goldbottom.com. Tours
of a still-operating placer mine on Hunker
Creek Rd, 1100-1900, $20.
Ruby Range Adventure, T867-6672209,
www.rubyrange.com. Canoe trips on any
of the rivers. They also rent out canoes
and have a shuttle service.

Taiga River Tours, T867-9935539,
www.taigarivertours.com. 1- or multi-day
tours of the Yukon river in a riverboat.
Top of the World Golf Course, T867-
9935888. Offers the rare opportunity to
tee off in the middle of the night and play
a round beneath the midnight sun.
9 holes. Rentals available.
Trans North Helicopters, T867-9935494,
www.tntaheli.com. Flightseeing tours of
the goldfields or Tombstone Mountains.
Yukon Queen II, T867-9935599. Cruises
on the Yukon River from Dawson City to
Eagle, Alaska. Booking office at the
Westmark Inn.

Robert Campbell Highway *p369*
Nature Friends Outdoor Adventures,
440 Campbell St, Faro, T867-9942106,
www.nfyukon.com. Guided hikes and
canoe trips from 1-15 days in and around
Faro. 4-day hike on the Dena Cho Trail. Bike
and canoe rental, free trail information.

Silver Trail *p370*
Mount Joy Wilderness Adventures,
T403-9977111, www.mountjoy
wilderness.com. Boat trips on the Stewart
River and winter dog sled trips. An
authentic experience with a trapper.

Canoe
Canoe trips into the **Peel Wilderness**,
lasting about 2 weeks, with class II-III
waters, are organized by a couple of
well-respected operators.
Big Bear Adventures, T867-6335642,
www.bear.yk.net. A reliable outfit
arranging all kinds of trips on these
rivers, $300 per day all in.

Hiking and biking
There is great hiking and mountain biking
off the Silver Trail, with many mining
roads to explore. A trail map is available
at the Mayo Visitor Centre. For the best
views, hike the **Mount Haldane Trail**,
6 hrs return, from Halfway Lakes between
Mayo and Keno.

The Yukon Dawson City & the north Listings

Dempster Highway *p371*

Bensen Creek Wilderness Adventure, T867-9935468, www.bensencreek.com. Guided hiking trips in the Tombstone Mountains, or canoe trips on the Klondike River. Also has 1 B&B room and a cabin (both **B**) in a fantastic lodge.

Inuvik *p372*

Arctic Nature Tours, T867-7773300, www.arcticnaturetours.com. Tours to Tuktoyaktuk are $275 for 3-4 hrs. Herschel Island $400 for 5-6 hrs. Mackenzie Delta eco-tours by boat, from $65 per person for 2-4 hrs. Babbage River on the edge of Ivvavik National Park, $400 for 6 hrs. **Hyak Wilderness Adventures**, T1800-6637238, www.hyak.com. 11-day rafting trips on the Firth River which takes in Herschel Island along the way. **Mack Travel**, 151 Mackenzie Rd, T867-7772941, www.macktravel.ca. Travel agent. **Western Arctic Adventure and Equipment**, T867-7772594, www.inuvik. net/canoeenwt. Canoe and kayak outfitters. If you're planning a trip up here, this is definitely the man to talk to first. **White Husky Outfitters**, T1800-6859417, www.whitehuskies.com. Dog-sled tours, at about $100 for 1 hr of driving yourself.

● Transport

Dawson City *p365, map p366*
Air
Dawson City's airport is 19 km southeast of town on the Klondike Hwy. **Gold City Tours**, T867-9935175, runs a shuttlebus to Downtown, meeting all scheduled flights. A **Dawson Courier** taxi, T867-9936688, costs $23 from the airport. **Air North**, T867-6682228, www.flyairnorth.com, flies to **Whitehorse**, **Fairbanks** and **Inuvik**.

Bus
Dawson Courier, T867-9936688, www.dawsonbus.ca, formerly ran a bus to **Whitehorse**, but has gone AWOL. Ask at the visitor centre if any company has filled

the void. **Alaska Shuttles**, T1800- 7707275, www.alaskashuttle.com, runs a regular service from several Alaska towns such as **Fairbanks** ($160) and **Anchorage** ($239).

Car hire
Budget, 451 Craig St, T867-9935644.

Inuvik *p372*
Air
Air North, T1800- 6610407, www.flyair north.com has flights from **Dawson City** (4 hrs, $140) and, indirectly, from **Whitehorse** (5½ hrs, $230).

Bus
MGM, T867-7774295, www.mgmbus services.ca. Chartered van journeys with 8 passengers to **Dawson City**, $173 one way, and **Whitehorse**, $234 one way.

Car hire
Norcan Rentals, 60 Franklin Rd, T867-7772346, www.norcan.yk.ca.

● Directory

Dawson City *p365, map p366*
Banks CIBC, Queen St between Front St/ 2nd Av. 24-hr ATM. **Internet** At the library, or **Grubstake**, 2nd Av. **Canada Post** Across from the library on 5th St; 3rd Av/King St. **Laundry** The Wash House, 2nd Av/ Queen St and Princess St. **Library** 5th Av/Queen St and Princess St. **Medical services** Ambulance: T867-9934444. **Nursing Station**, behind the museum on Mission St, T867-9935744. **Police** T867-9935555.

Inuvik *p372*
Banks CIBC, Mackenzie Rd. 24-hr ATM; Bank of Montreal, in the post office. **Internet** Free at the library. **Canada Post** Mackenzie Rd. **Laundry** Happy Valley Campground. **Library** Inuvik Centennial Library, 100 Mackenzie Rd, T867-7772749. **Medical services** Regional Hospital, Inuvik Access Rd, on the way into town, T867-9792955.

Index

Red numbers refer to maps

Credits

Footprint credits

Editor: Nicola Jones
Map editor and proofreader: Sarah Sorensen
Picture editor: Robert Lunn

Publisher: Patrick Dawson
Editorial: Sophie Blacksell, Alan Murphy,
Felicity Laughton, Lyndall Henning
Cartography: Robert Lunn, Claire Benison
Sales and marketing: Andy Riddle,
Daniella Cambouroglou
Advertising: Debbie Wylde
Finance and administration:
Elizabeth Taylor

Photography credits

Front cover: Alamy (Lake Louise)
Inside: Alamy, Matthew Gardner, Alison Bigg,
Andy Bell www.ticket2ride.com,
Al Harvey www.slidefarm.com
Back cover: Matthew Gardner (totem pole)

Print

Manufactured in Italy by EuroGrafica
Pulp from sustainable forests

Footprint feedback

We try as hard as we can to make each Footprint
guide as up to date as possible but, of course,
things always change. If you want to let us know
about your experiences – good, bad or ugly –
then don't delay, go to www.footprintbooks.com
and send in your comments.

Matthew would like to thank all the visitor
information centres for their feedback; Carla
for emergency babysitting; Nicola, for being
so patient, positive and easy to work with;
and Alan for being such a straight-shooter.

Publishing information

Footprint Western Canada
1st edition
© Footprint Handbooks Ltd
June 2006
ISBN 1 904777 82 1
CIP DATA: A catalogue record for this book
is available from the British Library
® Footprint Handbooks and the Footprint
mark are a registered trademark of
Footprint Handbooks Ltd

Published by Footprint

6 Riverside Court
Lower Bristol Road
Bath BA2 3DZ, UK
T +44 (0)1225 469141
F +44 (0)1225 469461
discover@footprintbooks.com
www.footprintbooks.com

Distributed in the USA by

Publishers Group West